Vedic Beliefs and Practices Through Arthavāda

The Udumbara tree (*Ficus Glomerata*)
pp. 153-158

[Photograph by Mr. Manoj Musale &
Designing by Mrs. Vidya Joshi, Lecturer in Art,
J. J. School of Art, Mumbai.]

Vedic Beliefs and Practices Through Arthavāda

Dr. (Mrs.) Sindhu S. Dange
Ex-R.G. Bhandarkar Professor and
Head, Dept. of Sanskrit,
Mumbai University

VOLUME I

Aryan Books International
New Delhi

Vedic Beliefs and Practices Through Arthavāda

ISBN-81-7305- 284-0 (Vol. I)
ISBN-81-7305-286-7 (Set)

First Published in **2005** by :
ARYAN BOOKS INTERNATIONAL
Pooja Apartments, 4B, Ansari Road, Darya Ganj
New Delhi-110 002 (India)
Tel.: 23287589, 23255799; Fax: 91-11-23270385
E-mail: aryanbooks@vsnl.com

Computer Typeset at ABI Prints & Publishing Co., New Delhi
Printed at B.B.N. Printers, New Delhi

To
the loving memory
of
my husband
(late) Dr. Sadashiv Ambadas Dange,
who being my teacher,
made the 'lamp'
know the magic
of its own 'light'.

Preface

There have been studies of Vedic texts from the cultural point of view. These studies concern in great measure the Saṁhitā-texts and many times the Brāhmaṇa-texts, but their complex rites and rituals are left to the background. However, the *arthavāda*-portions which occur in the Brāhmaṇa-texts as eulogising the *vidhi*-s (injunctions laying down rites and rituals), are helpful in presenting a picture of that age. Efforts though not many have been made in this direction. To name some of these. *Studies in Brāhmaṇas* by A.C. Banerjee (Delhi, 1963); *Kauṣitaki-brāhmaṇa-paryālocana* (Banaras, 1961) and *Aitareya-brāhmaṇa-paryālocana* (Banaras, 1962) by Mangaldev Shastri; and *Cultural Gleanings from the Brāhmaṇa Literature* (Yaska Pubns., New Delhi, 1990) by (Mrs.) Sunanda K. Tilak. (Mrs.) Tilak has collected various *arthavāda*-passages from the Brāhmaṇa-literature and has classified them under different heads to present a picture of the civilization and culture in the Brāhmaṇa-s.

Arthavāda-s in the Brāhmaṇa-texts, initially from the 'sacred' tradition of the rites and rituals, bringing directly or indirectly with them the beliefs and practices prevalent in the then society, thus bearing their relation to the 'secular' tradition, have been a topic of my interest for the past some years and I was working on it. With so much material gathered on this topic, my study opened a window for me to have a peep in the Vedic society of the hoary past, some of the traces of which can be marked even in the present day Indian society.

It is my pleasant duty to put on record my thanks to the University Grants Commission for its aid to the project under the scheme of 'Support for Major Research Project' (1991-94). The title of the project aided in that scheme was "Arthavāda—A Study in Vedic Ritual Reasoning", Taking into account the results arrived at the completion of my project, the title is now changed suitably, as the work is being presented to the world of scholars. The *arthavāda*-s about Speech (the goddess Vāc) in all its aspects, formed a basis of my earlier book—*Aspects of Speech in Vedic Ritual* (Aryan Books International, New Delhi, 1996).

My student, Miss Alka Pamdi (now Mrs. Alka Kulkarni), who was the then Research Assistant of the Sanskrit Department helped me in collecting information. She did her work with sincerity and devotion, though her stay in the Department was only for one year.

My sense of gratitude for the scholars whose works (including translations) were of great help to me, though I have differed from them at several places.

I entrusted the work of publication of this project to Shri Vikas Arya (Aryan Books International, New Delhi), who has been publishing our books (mine and those of my husband [late] Dr. Sadashiv A. Dange) since 1994, with a sense of belonging. He has brought out this work also with the same feeling. I am thankful to him.

My son-in-law Sanjay R. Shirgaonkar, Principal, Pillai's College of Architecture, New Panvel, Navi Mumbai, has prepared the cover-design. My thanks for his timely help as well as that of my little grandson Yash B. Jahagirdar, who helped me in arranging the Index-cards of these two volumes.

I shall feel happy if this endeavour of mine can be, to some extent, an aid to know the cultural history of the Indian society of the Vedic times.

Mumbai **(Mrs.) Sindhu S. Dange**
19th May, 2004

Contents

Abbreviations

AV	=	*Atharvaveda*
Ait. Ār	=	*Aitareya Āraṇyaka*
Ait. Br.	=	*Aitareya Brāhmaṇa*
Āp. Dh. S.	=	*Āpastamba Dharmasūtra*
Āp. G.S.	=	*Āpastamba Gṛhyasūtra*
Āp. Ś.S.	=	*Āpastamba Śrautasūtra*
Āśv. G.S.	=	*Āśvalāyana Gṛhyasūtra*
Āśv. Ś.S.	=	*Āśvalāyana Śrautasūtra*
Baudh. Dh. S.	=	*Baudhāyana Dharmasūtra*
Baudh. Ś.S.	=	*Baudhāyana Śrautasūtra*
Bh. G.	=	*Bhagavadgītā*
Bhāg. P.	=	*Bhāgavata Purāṇa*
Bhār. Ś.S.	=	*Bhāradvāja Śrautasūtra*
Bṛhad. Up.	=	*Bṛhadāraṇyaka Upaniṣad*
Chān. Up.	=	*Chāndogya Upaniṣad*
Gau./Gaut. Dh.S.	=	*Gautama Dharmasūtra*
Gobh. G.S.	=	*Gobhila Gṛhyasūtra*
Gop. Br.	=	*Gopatha Brāhmaṇa*
Jaim. Br.	=	*Jaiminīya Brāhmaṇa*
Jaim. Up. Br.	=	*Jaiminīya-upaniṣad-brāhmaṇa*
Kaṭha Up.	=	*Kaṭha Upaniṣad*
Kāṭh. G.S.	=	*Kāṭhaka Gṛhyasūtra*
Kāṭh. Sam.	=	*Kāṭhaka Saṁhitā*
Kāty. Ś.S.	=	*Kātyāyana Śrautasūtra*

Kauṣ. Br.	=	*Kauṣīkaki Brāhmaṇa*
Kau. Sū	=	*Kauśikasūtra*
Khā. G.S.	=	*Khādira Gṛhyasūtra*
Mait. Sam.	=	*Maitrāyaṇī Saṁhitā*
Manu Sm.	=	*Manusmṛti*
Mārk. P.	=	*Mārkaṇḍeya Purāṇa*
Mbh.	=	*Mahābhārata*
Nir.	=	*Nirukta*
P.	=	*Purāṇa*
Pañc. Br.	=	*Pañcaviṁśa Brāhmaṇa*
Pār. G.S.	=	*Pāraskara Gṛhyasūtra*
Rām.	=	*Rāmāyaṇa*
RV	=	*Ṛgveda*
Ṣaḍ Br.	=	*Ṣaḍviṁśa Brāhmaṇa*
Śāṅkh. G.S.	=	*Śāṅkhāyana Gṛhyasūtra*
Śāṅkh. Ś.S.	=	*Śāṅkhāyana Śrautasūtra*
Śat. Br.	=	*Śatapatha Brāhmaṇa*
Sk. P.	=	*Skanda Purāṇa*
Tait. Ār.	=	*Taittirīya Āraṇyaka*
Tait. Br.	=	*Taittirīya Brāhmaṇa*
Tait. Sam.	=	*Taittirīya Saṁhitā*
Vāj. Sam.	=	*Vājasaneyi Saṁhitā*
Vām. P.	=	*Vāmana Purāṇa*
Var. P.	=	*Varāha Purāṇa*
Vas. Dh. S.	=	*Vasiṣṭha Dharmasūtra*
Viṣṇu Dh. S.	=	*Viṣṇu Dharmasūtra*
Vi./Viṣṇu P.	=	*Viṣṇu Purāṇa*
Yāj. Sm.	=	*Yājñavalkyasmṛti*

ABBREVIATIONS OF MODERN TITLES

Bib. Ind.	=	Bibliotheca Indica
BORI	=	Bhandarkar Oriental Research Institute
CASS	=	Centre of Advanced Study in Sanskrit

Ency. of P.B. & P.	=	*Encyclopedia of Puranic Beliefs and Practices*
Ency. of Rel. and Eth.	=	*Encyclopaedia of Religion and Ethics*
Hist. of Dh. S.	=	*History of Dharmaśāstra*
HOS	=	*Harvard Oriental Series*
JAOS	=	*Journal of the American Oriental Society*
SBE	=	Sacred Books of the East Series
VVBIS & IS	=	Vishveshvaranand Vishva Bandhu Institute of Sanskrit and Indological Studies

Introduction

The Veda as is well-known comprises *mantra*-s and *brāhmaṇa*-s. The *mantra*-s help to make the performer remember several topics or subjects (*artha*-s), which are invariably associated with the performance of any ritual.[1] According to Jaimini, besides the *mantra*-s, the remaining bulk of the Vedic literature is called *brāhmaṇa*.[2] The *Āp. Ś.S.* explains the nature of the *brāhmaṇa*-portions by saying that the *brāhmaṇa*-s are injunctions for performing the (sacrificial) actions, i.e., rites.[3] The *Mīmāṁsāparibhāṣā* explains that *brāhmaṇa* is a statement enjoining a particular act, i.e., *vidhi*.[4] The instruction of such *vidhi*-s cannot be acquired from any other source except the *brāhmaṇa*.[5] The last part of the *brāhmaṇa*-portion is termed *arthavāda*.[6] *Arthavāda* is defined as a statement containing either praise (*prāśastya*) of the enjoined or condemnation (*nindā*) of the prohibited.[7] Āpastamba states *arthavāda* as having four types and so lays down with praise and condemnation, two more types of *arthavāda viz. parakṛti* and *purākalpa*.[8] The author of the *vārttika* points out that *parakṛti* states what has been done in the past by a single person, while in the *purākalpa* occurs what has been done in the past by two or more persons.[9] As these two types of *arthavāda* stem from the sphere of sacrifice, it is obvious that the accounts which occur in them are also from that context. *Parakṛti* contains the accounts of the sacrificial performances of the celebrated ritualists and also of the gifts made by the kings to their priests. Here we have the accounts of success, achieved by the sacrificers through their sacrifices and gifts. *Purākalpa* signifies the olden accounts of sacrificial rituals, performed in former times by gods as well as men of antiquity. *Parakṛti* and *purākalpa,* having a thin line of demarcation, are practically same. As these two verge either on praise or condemnation, *arthavāda* is taken to have two broad types, i.e. *prāśastya* (praise) and *nindā* (condemnation).

Śabarasvāmin has added eight more types of *arthavāda,* under the *sūtra* (II. 1.33), thus totalling twelve. These twelve types stated by him are as follows—

1. Abounding in the particle *iti* (*karaṇabahulaṁ*);
2. having the expression — 'so they say' (*āpohanibaddham*);
3. legendary in character (*ākhyāyikāsvarūpam*);
4. stating a reason (*hetu*);
5. explaining through the means of etymology (*nirvacana*);
6. eulogising (*praśaṁsā*);
7. condemning (*nindā*);
8. expressing a doubt (*śaṁśayaḥ*);
9. injunctive (*vidhi*);
10. stating exploits of others (*parakṛti*);
11. stating olden accounts (*purākalpa*) and
12. transpositional (*vyavadhāraṇakalpanā*).

Śabarasvāmin has stated these types with examples.[10]

Śabarasvāmin's classification of *arthavāda*-s is a detailed one. But there is another way in which the *arthavāda*-s are classified broadly under three types, *viz.* Guṇavāda, Anuvāda and Bhūtārthavāda.[11] *Arthavāda* of the Guṇavāda type is one, which is contrary to our means of perception, such as direct perception. The example is, *ādityo, yūpaḥ,* in which *yūpa* is praised. 'The sacrificial post is the sun' — this statement is contrary to our direct perception and is nullified by it. Hence it is to be understood by indication (*lakṣaṇā*). As both the sacrificial post and the sun are lustrous in appearance they are identified. Here the indication is based on the quality (*guṇa*) of lustre. It is thus the Guṇavāda type of *arthavāda*. *Arthavāda* of the Anuvāda type is one which simply confirms our knowledge, acquired by the means such as direct perception. The example is *agnirhimasya bheṣajam* - 'Agni is a remedy against cold'. Here the deity Agni is praised. The quality of Agni namely opposition to cold is understood by us from direct perception. The statement under consideration simply confirms this and so it is Anuvāda type of *arthavāda*. *Arthavāda* of Bhūtārthavāda type is one, which conveys a matter free from contradiction with other means of knowledge (direct perception, etc.). This other means of knowledge neither supports the matter under consideration nor contradicts it. This type simply embodies a statement of the real state of affairs. The example is *indro vṛtrāya vadham udayacchat* - 'Indra raised the weapon (i.e. thunderbolt) for striking Vṛtra.' This type of *arthavāda* describes an accomplished fact, by past event.

The *arthavāda*-portions in the Vedic ritual texts are not taken as expressing their meanings for their own sake. If taken so, it may lead to an occasion of undersirable contingency of having irrelevant portions in the Veda, which has ritual alone in view. Whatever is not connected with any ritual, will stand as irrelevant.[12] And as the Vedic study (*svādhyāya*) is to be recited daily, all the Vedic portions have to be not only meaningful but also relevant. And so the *arthavāda*-s are regarded as meaningful and relevant.

The meaning of an *arthavāda* (statement) is not to be taken by *abhidhā* (power of expression) but by *lakṣaṇā* (power of indication). This becomes all the more patent when we take into account the Guṇavāda type of *arthavāda*. As noted earlier, in this type of *arthavāda*, two entities are brought together by a common quality, giving rise to a metaphor. The Vedic ritual texts are replete with such metaphors.[13]

Even the Anuvāda type of *arthavāda* can at times present such metaphors - *agnirhimasya bheṣajam,* being one of them. In the Bhūtārthavāda type of *arthavāda,* there occur several mythical accounts, hardly leaving any scope to the power of indication (*lakṣaṇā*), for such accounts are to be understood by the power of expression (*abhidhā*) of the words or statements contained therein.

To come to the point of relevance and usefulness of the *arthavāda*-s to their respective *vidhi*-s (i.e. *vidhi-vākyas*—statements of injunction). This has been discussed by the Mīmāṁsakas at a great length. Sāyaṇa says that Jaimini has taken great pains to establish the authoritativeness of the *arthavāda*-s.[14] The *prima facie* view states that as *arthavāda*-s are not injunctive, they cannot have any meaning, i.e. relevance (in the knowledge of *dharma*), for the Vedic texts are mainly injunctive in character. Thus the *arthavāda*-s stand *anitya* (non-eternal, i.e. irrelevant, and thus not having any authority regarding the knowledge of dharma).[15] The Siddhāntin states that though the *arthavāda*-s are not injunctive, they are related in some way to the other part which is directly injunctive, laying down something to be done. After construing together the two parts, it is seen that the *arthavāda* part serves the purpose of eulogising and commending what is laid down in the injunctive part (*vidhi*). Thus in the animal-sacrifice, the *vidhi* (injunction) is laid down *viz.* 'One desirous of prosperity should sacrifice a white (goat) to Vāyu'. The *arthavāda* related to this is — 'Vāyu is the swiftest deity. He runs near Vāyu by his (Vāyu's) own share and he (Vāyu) makes him (i.e. sacrificer) acquire prosperity' (*Tait. Sam.* II. 1.1.1). The *arthavāda* here by eulogising Vāyu, serves to commend the act of sacrificing to the deity Vāyu, which is enjoined by the *vidhi* in the Kāmyapaśukāṇḍa.

The propriety and status of the *arthavāda*-portions of the Veda have been a point of discussion in the Mīmāṁsā philosophy.[16] The doctrine of *ekavākyatā* (syntactical connection) propounded by the Mīmāṁsakas has to be taken into account here, when the exact status of *arthavāda*-portions is to be decided. As pointed out by Navathe,[17] the doctrine of *ekavākyatā,* i.e. syntactical unity, originally introduced in the topic of the *mantra*-s (*yajus-mantra*-s) by Jaimini, has been very effectively used by the Mīmāṁsakas, in respect of the following occasions:

1. There is syntactical connection between the injunctions (*vidhi*-s) of the subsidiaries (*aṅga*-s) and those of the principal (*pradhāna*) *vidhi;* and
2. There is syntactical unity between the *arthavāda*-s and their corresponding injunctions (*vidhi*-s).

The doctrine of syntactical connection (*ekavākyatā*) is taken by the older Mīmāṁsakas with a view to denote *padaikavākyatā,* which takes place through a single word (*pada*) *viz. praśasta* - 'commended'. Thus instead of the verbal knowledge of the usual type, *viz. vāyavyaśvetālambhanena bhūtim bhāvayet,* the verbal knowledge acquired by the *padaikavākyatā* can be expressed as *praśastena vāyavyaśvetālambhanena bhūtim bhāvayet.*[18] This view is strongly rejected by Mādhavācārya, who favours the *vākyaikavākyatā* of the *arthavāda*-s. The statement of injunction (*vidhivākya*) expects commending of the act enjoined by it, for such commending impels a person to undertake the act enjoined. On the other hand, the statement of *arthavāda* expects some act, i.e. object of human pursuit, enjoined by the *vidhi.* The statement of *arthavāda,* indicating by way of *lakṣaṇā*, the excellence (*prāśastya*) expected of by the statement of *vidhi*, has *vākyaikavākyatā* with the latter. The instance seen above from the context of animal-sacrifice, thus, means—'As Vāyu, the deity of this animal (here the animal is 'goat'), due to his swift-going nature is the giver of fruit swiftly, therefore one should sacrifice an excellent animal (i.e. goat) to Vāyu.' In this way, the two sentences could be related. *Arthavāda*-s thus are proved to be an authority in *dharma,* the word *dharma* here meaning sacrificial rites and rituals, which are enjoined.[19] By commending the *vidhi*-s, *arthavāda*-s are syntactically connected with the latter and stand as their part.[20]

While considering the statements of *vidhi* and those of *arthavāda*, it can easily be noticed that the statements of *vidhi* are direct and in most cases very pithy, while the statements of *arthavāda* are elaborate as they are declamatory in nature. These Vedic ritual reasonings, coming by way of *arthavāda* comprise etymologies (at times coming through tradition but in many cases, composers of Brāhmaṇa-texts coining their own etymologies), beliefs, practices prevalent in those times and *gāthā*-s, *śloka*-s, legendary accounts, etc., which originated in secular tradition.

And here we come to an important point and it is of the help rendered by the profane or secular tradition to the sacred Vedic ritualistic tradition. To take the example of *gāthā*-s. As Horsch has very rightly pointed out, the anonymous stanzas (*gāthā*-s) originated mostly in secular and popular circles. The *gāthā*-literature was derived from the non-hieratic or unorthodox sphere such as the *kṣatriya* milieu or the Vrātya community.[21] The *yajñagāthā*-s (most of them occurring in the *Ait. Br.*) were framed on the basis of the popular *gāthā*-s, that had a secular or popular origin. They are termed *yajñagāthā*-s obviously because they extol some sacrificial ritual or practice. As Sāyaṇa explains the terms *yajñagāthā*, "It is one which is sung by all the ritualists having in view a sacrifice."[22] Recitation of the *gāthā*-s in particular rituals and more so of the *yajñagāthā*-s enjoined in the rituals, shows beyond doubt that the priestly class of those times, was ever ready to amalgamate the popular traditions to win over new avenues to extend its influence and to popularise the complex sacrificial ritual by giving support to it by these means. The *yajñagāthā*-s were specifically composed by the priestly class on the pattern of the *gāthā*-s, many of which were already prevalent. Falling in line with the *yajñagāthā*-s are the *śloka*-s, which occur at several places in the Brāhmaṇa-texts. Even the legendary and traditional accounts from the Itihāsa (which really means—'iti-ha-āsa'), i.e. 'This happened so' or 'This was so') and Purāṇa, falling under the types *parakṛti* and *purākalpa* types of *arthavāda,* also originate from the secular tradition or the profane level, though they are deftly given in the setting of rituals. Under the types *parakṛti* and *purākalpa,* we have several mythical accounts as also proto-myths or pseudo-myths. Some of these might be from the profane or secular plane in the origin, but some others are purposefully carved and coined likewise on the same lines. All these go under the name *arthavāda,* which is skilfully contrived to support the *vidhi.* Thus the sacred tradition many times—nay every time, had to take the help of the secular tradition or at least had to come to the profane level, while extolling the *vidhi* or condemning the opposite of that *vidhi.*

Efforts have been made to seek the source of such narrations, traditional or legendary accounts (though in the Brāhmaṇa-texts, most of the accounts mythical in nature, are given succinctly and are primarily 'made to order' to serve the need of the ritualists) and compositions like *gāthā*-s, that do not exactly tally with the Vedic ritual tradition but have been so assimilated with it as to have almost formed part of it. We have mentioned the opinion of Horsch, who has suggested the origin of the *gāthā*-verses to be in the non-ritualistic sphere or even the a-ritualistic sphere. While dealing in details with the Pāriplava, which figures in the Horse-sacrifice, Chakraborti has propounded that while some *ākhyāna*-s originated from the theologians, popular *ākhyāna*-s developed in all probability on the periphery of the sacred literature itself, being included in the Svādhyāya.[23] Hariappa believes that the practice of preserving the narrations of various events was prevalent in the period of the *Ṛgveda* or even earlier.[24] Dandekar has proposed that right from the beginning, there have been two traditions—that of the *mantra*-s and the other preserved by the *sūta*-s.[25] It is very right to see the tradition of the *sūta*-s as the source of the secular compositions and narratives.[26]

This tradition not only preserved this type of literature but also set a norm for composing such type of literature. The accounts in the Brāhmaṇa-texts coming under the *parakṛti* and *purākalpa* types of *arthavāda,* mythical tales of the gods and *asura*-s, *gāthā*-s especially the *yajñagāthā*-s, *śloka*-s, etc. forwarded for the praise (*prāśastya*) or condemnation (*nindā*) of the ritual, are no doubt from the sphere of ritual and are from the ritualists who were steeped in the sacred ritualistic tradition. But while wading through simple or several times complex rituals, these *arthavāda*-portions always catch the finger of the secular mode, come to the profane level, never losing sight of the ritual or rituals, for which they are forwarded. The picture in the Brāhmaṇa-texts is of perfect assimilation of the sacred and the profane.

That the sacred has to take the help of the profane can be seen from a parallel from the western world, when we take into account the origin and history of dramatic art there. The chronicles of Greek village communities have the earliest records of dramatic acting. When a festival of any one of their numerous gods was to be celebrated, the Greek villagers used to gather in a group and act as if they were the old gods. There was not much action but probably much dialogue and recitation. These primitive imitations of the life of a deity were called "mimes" (giving rise to the word "mimic"). Out of this practice arose a crude kind of comedy which entertained the citizens of the old Athenian State. This went on till the rise of the Roman Empire. After the withdrawal of the Roman control from the western Europe, there were the 'Dark Ages,' when there was inactivity and decay in all forms of art. From the Middle Ages, England and France had groups of tavelling entertainers, which were known to the French as *jongleurs.* The performances of these wandering groups attracted the attention of the Church, which started arranging sacred or religious plays drawn from the Bible, at first on the occasions as Christmas or Easter,[27] suiting to those occasions. Gradually other events from the Bible were shown in dramatic form inside the

Church. This shows how the Church took notice of the dramatic activities of the travelling commoners and started having such an activity as a counter attraction, with that great storehouse—the Bible—at hand.

To turn to the Vedic world again. We take the example of the Mahāvrata, which is the penultimate (i.e. last but one) day in the Gavām-ayana *sattra* (extending over 12 months of 30 days each). This day has the name 'Mahāvrata' because it is specially meant for Prajāpati who is '*mahān*' and 'mahāvrata' means '*anna*' (food.).[28] Here are some of the popular features of the Mahāvrata day. That the Mahāvrata is a fertility-rite is made clear from such details as a mock-fight between an *ārya* and a *śūdra* for a white circular skin that symbolises the sun, the fight culminating in favour of the *ārya;* a sexual abusive dialogue between a harlot and a *brahmacārin* on the northern side of the altar; a sexual union between a man and a woman in a screened shed to the south of the Mārjālīya shed; and a *kṣatriya* prince in full armour, armed with a bow and three arrows, discharging those arrows at a hide. At all corners of the altar are placed the drums, which they beat and they strike the earth-drum (*bhūmi-dundubhi*).[29] When the priests chant, the wives of the performers act as choristers to the singing priests and play on several instruments. Eight servants and maids or slaves and slave-girls, placing water-jars on their heads dance thrice round the Mārjālīya (Agni) seat, striking the ground with their right foot and singing popular songs (*gāthā*-s) in which cows are lauded as mothers of 'ghee' and which contain words like 'this is sweet'.[30] Kane has rightly pointed out that the features of the Mahāvrata show that it was some folk festival in the hoary past.[31] But in the light of what we propose further, we cannot agree with him when he says that this festival "was welded on the solemn Vedic sacrifices as a relaxation after the weary days and months of sacrifices."[32] That the Mahāvrata day is specially meant for Prajāpati is already noted by us. The popular features definitely came from the folk-tradition from some festival. These features from the secular tradition or profane level could have their entry in the Vedic ritual or the sacred Vedic plane due to the note of 'fertility' inlaid in them. The *gāthā*-s to be sung at this festival praising the cows as mothers of 'ghee' and having the words 'this is honey' (*idam madhu*) are definite pointers to the rain-phenomenon, the cows standing as the rain-showers and 'ghee' and 'honey' meaning the 'rains'.[33] Hence the inclusion of these popular features, which may be deemed as 'kitsch', are not simply for 'relaxation, after weary days and months of sacrifices' as Kane says, but they are the rain-spells, on the basis of sympathetic magic, especially when the *gātha*-s are sung by the servants and maids or slaves and slave girls placing water-jars on their heads.

The Mahāvrata forms a part of the Gavām-ayana *sattra,* which itself is an elaborate sacrifice. But there are several other rites and rituals in which through the *arthavāda*-passages are reflected the beliefs and practices, prevalent in the then society. At times the sacred matters are spoken of having allusion to worldly phenomena. This also forms part of the *arthavāda.* We are taking here some examples of these to show how the sacred ritualistic level has to take the help of the secular matters and has to come to profane level in order to be convincing.

As Varuṇa the Ṛgvedic god is famous for his nooses, with which he would bind the sinners, anything having knots is thought of as belonging to him. Again the black colour which is not regarded to be good or auspicious, except in rain-rituals where it symbolises the black watery cloud, is associated with Varuṇa in some rituals. In the Rājasūya sacrifice, in the Triṣaṁyukta offerings, a black cloth is a *dakṣiṇā* to be given to the priest when an oblation to Varuṇa is prescribed. Such a cloth with its knots is said to belong to Varuṇa, for the knot is sacred to Varuṇa (*Śat. Br.* V.2.5.17). In the context of the sacrifices (*iṣṭi*-s) to be offered to the deities presiding over the Yama-constellations, the *Tait. Br.*

prescribes that a sacrificial cake of black rice-grains is to be offered to Varuṇa, the presiding deity of the Śatabhiṣaj constellation (*Tait. Br.* III. 1.5.9).

Demons in mythology though strong, are generally regarded as dull-witted and can easily be duped by the hero, who ultimately is victorious in the scuffle. This belief is at the basis of a *vidhi* in the Agniṣṭoma sacrifice, when two cups are drawn for Śaṇḍa and Marka, but are offered to deities. The mythical account coming as *arthavāda* states that the gods drove away the *asura-rakṣas*-es but could not drive away the two demons — Śaṇḍa and Marka. These two used to disturb the sacrificial work of the gods and quickly used to flee away. The gods then thought of a trick to seize these two. They drew two cups of Soma for them and the moment the two demons came down, having seized them, the gods drove them away (*Śat. Br.* IV. 2.1.5,6).

The beliefs about the quarters were firmly fixed in the then society, as we shall see in the chapter on "Quarters." But here is an interesting detail. In the 'three day' (Trirātra) sacrifice he gives thousand cows as the *dakṣiṇā*-s. On each of the three days, he gives three hundred and thirty-three cows. Now remains one, i.e. (the *sāhasrī*—one thousandth). This cow is used for divination. When released by them, if not urged by any man, she goes eastwards, it would mean that the sacrificer has won the happy world. If she goes northwards, the sacrificer would be more glorious in this world. If she goes westwards, he will be rich in dependants and crops. If she goes southwards, the sacrificer will quickly depart from this world. These are the ways of knowing (*etāni vijñānāni*), says the *Śat. Br.* (IV. 5. 8. 11).

Though beliefs about trees will be dealt with in the chapter on "Trees. . .", some details are to be seen about the Arka tree. In the Agnicayana rite (i.e. the rite of building the Great Fire-altar), the fire on the Great Fire-altar is said to be Rudra. The moment he is born, he wants his share of offerings. Hence the Śatarudriya offerings to him. Here for offering the goat's milk, the Arka-leaf is mentioned. The *arthavāda* states that the Aṅgiras-es going to the world of heaven spilled the Gharma, i.e. milk (in the Mahāvīra pot carrying the boiling milk) on the female goat. She tormented by the burning heat, in pain dropped a cluster of her hair, which became the Arka. Hence the name Arka. He offers the goat's milk with an Arka-leaf to unite the Arka-leaf with its birth place, i.e. fire. The idea seems to be - hot milk = Agni, i.e. heat, on the hair of the female goat > Arka leaf. So oblation with Arka-leaf in Agni. As female goat is connected with Agni, so her milk is used here and not the wild sesame and *gavīdhuka* (*Tait. Sam.* V.4.3.1-3). The *Śat.Br.* equates Arka with Puruṣa, who is Agni, and speaks of the leaves, flowers, etc. of the Arka as the ears, eyes, etc. of the Puruṣa (*Śat. Br.* X. 3.4.3 ff). This shows the greatest honour given to the Arka tree. It has to be pointed out here that Arka is not a big tree but a small tree, not exactly a shrub, but in no way a plant, though taken by Keith or Eggeling as a 'plant'.[34]

As Arka is associated with Agni, so is barley (*yava*)—in fact more closely—to Varuṇa. The *arthavāda* is—(in the context of the Agniṣṭoma sacrifice, while offering the Śukra and Manthin cups)—Varuṇa once struck King Soma right in the eye and it swelled. From there arose a horse. Hence the name *aśva* (fr. the root √*śvi* - 'to swell'). A tear of his fell down and therefrom was sprung barley (*yava*). So they say that barley belongs to Varuṇa (*ibid.* IV. 2.1.11). In the four-monthly (i.e. Seasonal) sacrifices, there is the Varuṇapraghāsa *iṣṭi.* The *Kauṣ. Br.* notes (in the *arthavāda*) that by means of the Vaiśvedeva sacrifice, Prajāpati created offspring. As they (the offspring) ate the barely of Varuṇa, Varuṇa grasped them with his nooses. Prajāpati saw the sacrificial rite—'Varuṇapraghāsāḥ'- and sacrificed with it, which pleased Varuṇa, who freed the offspring from his nooses (*Kauṣ. Br.* V. 3). It is significant to note that in this rite which is for Varuṇa, the pots of *karambha* made from the parched grains of barley are offered to Varuṇa (*Kāt. Ś.S.* V.3.2 - *pūrvedyur dakṣiṇāgnau nistuṣa bhṛṣṭayavānām karambhapātrakaraṇam*). The *Śat. Br.* also states practically the same *arthavāda* (*Śat. Br.* II.5.2.1-3). In the context of the Rājasūya sacrifice also, a pap (*caru*) of barley flour is the offering enjoined for being offered to Varuṇa (*ibid.* V.2.5.16; V. 3.3.9).

The Nīvāra plants and the grains of Nīvāra (i.e. the rice-grains, which are not cultivated) are associated with the god Bṛhaspati. When the gods ran the race for plants, it was Bṛhaspati who won the race and separated the Nīvāra-plants from other plants. Hence the name Nīvāra (fr. *nir* + √*vṛ* - 'to differentiate, to separate'). The Nīvāra-grains are the best food of the gods and a pap (*caru*) made of Nīvāra-grains is offered to Bṛhaspati (*Tait. Br.* I.3.6.7,8 f). This is prescribed in the Vājapeya sacrifice. But in the Rājasūya sacrifice also, such a pap of wild rice (*naivāra caru*) is offered to Bṛhaspati (*Śat. Br.* V.3.3.5).

In fact, there are some more types of rice-grains prescribed in the *vidhi*-s, followed by the *arthavāda* in each case. For Savitṛ Satyaprasava (of true impulse), a cake of fast-grown (Plāśuka) rice-grains is offered in the Rājasūya sacrifice by the sacrificer-king with a thought that he also should be quickly impelled (*ibid.* V. 3. 3. 2). Sāyaṇa on this passage says that this is the rice, which springs up again and ripens very quickly. For Agni Gṛhapati a cake from the Āśu rice (ripening quickly in the rainy season) is to be offered by the sacrificer-king with a thought that he also should be quickly led (*ibid.* 3). To Soma Vanaspati (the forest-lord), a pap (*caru*) of Śyāmāka millet is to be offered by the sacrificer-king, for the Śyāmākas among plants undoubtedly are most manifestly Soma's own (*ibid.* 4). For Indra Jyeṣṭha (the supreme one) a pap (*caru*) of red rice-grains (Hāyana) is to be offered by the sacrificer-king with the thought that Indra the Jyeṣṭha will lead him to overlordship. As Indra is outstanding, so are the red rice-plants (*ibid.* 6). We have already noted the pap (*caru*) of wild rice-grains offered to Bṛhaspati (*ibid.* 5).

A pap (*caru*) of Nāmba seeds is offered to Mitra, for these plants belong to him, as those plants which grow in ploughed ground belong to Varuṇa (*ibid.* 8).

To turn to a blade of grass, which is believed to have certain power. In the rite called Sammarśana, after their selection (by the sacrificer), the Hotṛ and the Adhvaryu priests come to the Hotṛṣadana, which is at the side of the Hotṛvedi in between the Gārhapatya and Āhavaṇīya fires. Here a blade of grass (*ekam tṛṇam*) is cut and thrown away and it is believed that Parāvasu the Hotṛ priest of the *asura*-s is defeated. Arvāvasu is the Hotṛ priest of the gods (*ibid.* I.5.1.23, 24; cf. *Kauṣ Br.* VI. 13 for the mention of Arvāvasu, the Hotṛ of the gods). This shows that even a simple blade of grass, accompanied with some desire (or curse), if thrown at a certain person, is believed to work as a weapon or a missile. The belief seems to have percolated in the Puranic period also. In the *Bhāg. P.* we have the account that the sages were performing a sacrificial session in the Naimiṣa forest, and they appointed the *sūta* Romaharṣaṇa as the narrator by giving him the seat of Vyāsa (the compiler of the Purāṇas). When Balarāma came to attend the session, Romaharṣaṇa did not rise from his seat, nor did he fold his hands, in order to show respect to Balarāma. Balarāma flew into rage at his insult and more so on seeing the honour bestowed on a simple (!) *sūta* and shot a pointed blade of grass at Romaharṣaṇa, which killed him. The sages declared Balarāma to have committed the killing of a *brāhmaṇa* and hence the expiation for Balarāma prescribed (*Bhāg. P.* X. 78. 20-40; also *ibid.* chap. 79 for Balarāma's wandering for one year visiting the holy places). Here the blade of grass is full of potent power. May be it is accompanied with a certain *mantra.* If so, we turn to the power of Speech in its various aspects.[35] Not only is Speech (with all its aspects *viz.* metres, *sāman*-s, *śastra*-s, *stoma*-s, etc.) important and indispensable in any sacrifice, but it has its sway even on the cosmic level. In the Gavām-ayana sacrifice, which goes on for the whole year, thus based on the course of the sun, the *stoma*-s and the *sāman*-s are enjoined for being chanted in order to support the sun from above as well as from below. The gods were afraid of his falling from the heaven. So they supported him with the highest worlds of heaven. These highest worlds of heaven are the *stoma*-s (*Ait. Br.* IV. 18 = 18.4).

The ancient world, the Vedic India being no exception, seems to be having some kind of over-protective attitude about the sun. In fact, the whole edifice of the Agnihotra rite is conceptually built up on the basic idea of honouring (and strengthening) the sun by offering oblations in fire in the evening as well as in the morning, fire (Agni) being the womb of the sun, where the sun goes in the evening and from where he comes out in the morning. This anxiety coupled with the apprehension for the sun's safe return on the next morning is marked in the Egyptian as well as the Japanese mythology as we shall see in the chapter on "Sun, Moon and Constellations". The Puranic concept of the Mandeha demons trying to devour the sun at sunset every day, also springs from this very anxiety, which gets nullified when the water at the *sandhyā*-ritual consecrated by the Gāyatrī *mantra* is thrown at the demons resulting into their getting burnt.

In the chapter on "Animals and Birds" we shall see the beliefs about the animals and also their sacrifice in the ritual practices. It is worthy of consideration that even the hair of an animal is used in some rituals, the hair standing for the very animal, on the principle of sympathetic magic, when 'a part stands for the whole'. In the Agniṣṭoma sacrifice, while leading forward the Āhavanīya fire to the Uttaravedi, with other things (*viz.* enclosing sticks of pine-wood, bdellium, i.e. '*gulgulu*' and the fragrant reed-grass), a hair-tuft of a wether, i.e., 'a castrated ram', is placed on the Uttaravedi. The *arthavāda* states that Agni dwelt once for one night between the two horns of a wether. Now whatever Agni's nature is inherent in the wether (here wether's hair-tuft), it is placed on the Uttaravedi (*Śat. Br.* III. 5.2.18). In the Sautrāmaṇī sacrifice, hairs of wild beasts are put into the cups of wine (*surā*), from which the libations of *surā* are made.[36] With the hairs of wolf, he secures vigour (*ojaḥ*), the impetuous rush of wild beasts (*jūtim āraṇyānām*); with the hairs of tiger, courage (*manyum*) as also the sway over the wild beasts (*rājyam' āraṇyānām*) and with the hairs of lion, might (*sahaḥ*) as the rule of wild beasts (*īśām' āraṇyānām*), states the *arthavāda*, obviously based on the belief about a hair standing for the very entity to which it belongs (*ibid.* XII. 7.2.8).

That the creation of several things and beings comes into existence from the body-parts of the great Being is an idea as old as the *RV* and is to be traced to the Puruṣasūkta (*RV*. X. 90). The ritual texts also speak of the creation of some trees, seasons, etc. from the body-parts or body-fluids of Prajāpati as we shall note in the chapter on "Trees, Plants and Varieties of Grass" as also in other chapters. Interesting is a long list of animals and plants which came into existence from the various body-parts of Prajāpati. To see some of these - from his forehead lion; from breast tiger; from belly elephant..., from body-hair Dūrvā plants... (*Jaim. Br.* II. 267).

The ritual belief that 'the *vedi* is as great as the earth' (*Tait. Sam.* II. 6.4.1) could be very well compared to a statement which occurs in the *Pañc. Br.* in the context of a sacrificial session at the river Dṛṣadvatī. The mythical account by way of *arthavāda* runs as follows. Indra and Ruśamā made a wager that whosoever of them should first run round the earth, would be the winner. While Indra ran round the earth, Ruśamā ran around Kurukṣetra only. As they could not come to a decision, they went to the gods, who said "Kurukṣetra is as great as the *vedi of Prajāpati*" and neither of them (two) won the wager (though each of them was correct in his own way) (*Pañc. Br.* XXV. 13.3). The mythical account is important for knowing the high status enjoyed by the Kurukṣetra region in ancient India. Manu, as we come to the Smṛti period, says that the region between the rivers Sarasvatī and Dṛṣadvatī is created by the gods and is called the Brahmāvarta (*Manu Sm.* II. 17). Kurukṣetra together with Matsya, Pañcāla and Śūrasenaka countries is called the Brahmarṣi region and from a *brāhmaṇa* born in this region, all the people on this earth would learn their respective code of conduct (*ibid.* 19, 20). These references show, when tallied with the mythical account from the *Pañc. Br.* noted above, that Kurukṣetra was one of the important spots in the belt of sacrificial religion.

The firm conviction about a person performing a sacrifice or a person chosen for the office of priest, as seen from the ritual texts, is that he becomes non-human, i.e. divine (*Śāt. Br.* I.1.1.6; I.9.1.29). One who is consecrated for sacrifice turns to the gods and becomes one of them (*ibid.* III. 1.1.8). The whole sacrificial ritual is to be done by the divine agency, for man is unsteady (*an-ṛta*—'not eternally true') says the *Śat. Br.* (*ibid.* I. 1.2.17). Hence such *vidhi*-statements that he should cut only a moderate quantity of oblation in the New-moon and Full-moon sacrifices. If he were to cut off a large quantity, he would make it human and what is human is inauspicious at the sacrifice (*ibid.* I.7.2.9). And about the sacrificial cake also. He should not make it too broad, for that would be 'human' (i.e. common cake) and such a 'common' cake is unlucky (or inauspicious) in the sacrifice. Some say that he should make it of the size of a horse's hoof. But, nobody knows the size of a horse's hoof. So he should make it of such a size that it would not be too broad (*ibid.* I.2.2.9,10). In the same context of the New-moon and Full-moon sacrifices, it is said (when five prayers for blessings are to be recited) that he should not offer more than these, for the 'excess' (in any respect?) at the sacrifice would result into the benefit of his spiteful enemy (*ibid.* I.9.1.18). When King Soma arrives in the assembly, some pour out a vessel of water beside him as a mark of hospitality shown to King Soma. The *Śat. Br.* says that the sacrificer should not do this, for they thereby do at the sacrifice what is human and inauspicious for the sacrifice (*ibid.* III.3.4.31). This shows that the rites and rituals in the sacrifice, though performed on the terrestrial level, are taken to have divine layer. Hence nothing having human or terrestrial touch should be done in the sacrifice.

These are some of the beliefs which are reflected in the *arthavāda*-portions, that occur as supporting the *vidhi*-statements. Here are some practices that are seen through the *arthavāda*-passages.

It is said that the sacrificer-king who has performed the Rājasūya sacrifice (in which he is sprinkled with waters brought from various sources) does not shave his hair, for if he shaves his hair, he would cause the vigour or glory (brought by the waters, which reach his head first) fall off from him. He should not shave his hair for a year, for the observance of a vow is for a year (*ibid.* V. 5.3.2).

A worldly practice of making a child sleep by singing a lullaby is made use of for glorifying the Tvāṣṭrī sāman. The *Pañc. Br.* states that Indra was suffering from a disease of eyes. The other beings could not cause him to sleep, but Tvaṣṭr's daughters made him sleep with this melody, i.e. the Tvāṣṭrī *sāman.* This is a wish-granting *sāman*, for such had been their wish at that moment (*Pañc. Br.* XII. 5.19-20).

A couple of practices regarding the behaviour of animals could be noted here. In the context of optional and occasional offerings, it is prescribed, in the rite of offering a barren goat, that he offers with the sound '*Kikkiṭa*'. The *arthavāda* points out that at the sound '*Kikkiṭa*', the domestic animals stop, but the wild run away. His offering with the sound '*Kikkiṭa*' serves to support the domestic animals (*Tait. Sam.* III. 4.3.5). Apart from the importance of the sound '*Kikkiṭa*', which figures in the *vidhi* of offering, the behaviour of the animals is to be marked, which is pointed out by the *arthavāda.* The *arthavāda* regarding the waving of a *prastara* (bunch of grass) is based on daily observation. The *arthavāda* states that the *prastara* is the sacrificer and the Adhvaryu by this way takes the sacrificer to the heavenly world (*Pañc. Br.* VI. 7.17). The mythical account occurring here is — The sacrifice becoming a horse went away from the gods, but the latter brought it to a standstill by a *prastara* (bunch of grass). Hence it is that a horse likes to be wiped with a bunch of grass. The Adhvaryu priest by bearing the bunch of grass soothes the sacrifice (*ibid.* 18).

The *arthavāda* adds one more detail of worldly observation regarding the behaviour of animals, through a mythical account. When Prajāpati created the domestic animals, they becoming hungry, left him. In order to bring them back to himself, Prajāpati presented them a bunch of grass as food and they turned towards him. So the Adhvaryu also must slightly wave the bunch of grass, for the animals turn to a stalk of grass that is waved before them (*ibid:* 19).

In the rite of Agnicayana, having built the Gārhapatya hearth, they pile the three 'Nairṛti' bricks. The *arthavāda* is significant in pointing out the characteristics of the goddess Nirṛti. When the gods built the Gārhapatya hearth, they ascended it (the Gārhapatya being this world) and saw nothing but only darkness. Then they saw the Nairṛti bricks and piling them, they dispelled Nirṛti-darkness, evil (*Śat. Br.* VII. 2.1.1-3). These (Nairṛti) bricks are baked by rice-husks. The husks belong to Nirṛti. These bricks are black, for black was that darkness and black is Nirṛti (*ibid.* 7). Here the principle of sympathetic magic works, black bricks standing for the black Nirṛti and also dispelling the 'evil' Nirṛti.

In the context of the four Seasonal sacrifices, in the Sākamedha rite, it is said that the sacrificer offers to the gods, while standing with his face towards the east, the ritual reasoning (*arthavāda*) being that the gods come from the east to proceed westwards to men (*ibid.* II. 6. 1.11).

It is interesting to mark the different types of butter prescribed in the rituals meant for gods, etc. In the Soma-sacrifice, in the rite of consecration of the sacrificer, they anoint him with fresh butter, for he is in that stage an embryo. It is said that the melted butter (*ājya*) is for the gods, the accumulated butter (*ghṛta*) for the men, half-melted or slightly melted butter (*āyuta*) for the *pitṛ*-s and the fresh butter for the embryos (*Ait. Br.* I.3).

Regarding the offerings of a sacrificial victim, to be given in the fire, the *vidhi*-statement is that he should not make cuttings of the head, the shoulders, the neck and the hind-parts. The *arthavāda* points out that the *asura*-s in the beginning seized a victim. The gods from fear did not go near it. The Earth then said to the gods that she herself would be an eye-witness to what the *asura*-s would do. She told the gods that having offered one oblation, the *asura*-s had left over these same portions. The gods then offered the Tryaṅga oblations (*tri-aṅga*—three parts of the body *viz.* upper part of the right fore-foot, part of the left thigh and part of the intestines) to Agni Sviṣṭakṛt. The *asura*-s then made portions of the head, the shoulders, the neck and the hind-thighs (obviously for offering). So the sacrificer or the priest should not make the cuttings (portions) of these limbs for offering to the gods. Moreover Tvaṣṭṛ spat upon the neck of the animal. So he should not make a cutting of the neck (*Śat. Br.* III. 8.3.27-29). Here the *arthavāda* strengthens the *vidhi* of not offering certain parts of the sacrificial victim's body as oblations. So is the practice of not offering blood of the victim in the sacrifice, for that is regarded as the share of the *rakṣas*-es. The elaborate *arthavāda* runs as follows — The gods and *asura*-s, both of them sprung from Prajāpati were contending about their sacrifice. The gods obtained possession of the whole of the sacrifice and dispossessed those *asura*-s of it, by giving them the worst part of the sacrifice. With the blood of the sacrificial victim, they denied them the possession of the animal-sacrifice and with the refuse of the rice, the possession of the *haviryajña*. The *arthavāda* is quick enough to point out that whosoever obtains a worthless share (in the property) is as good as the one, who is denied any share. But still that person has a hope and says he, 'What share is given to me?'. The gods set apart that (worthless) share for the *asura*-s. The same share the sacrificer (or the priest) gives to the *asura*-s, in that he pours the refuse of the rice right under the black antelope skin. This is casting that share (of the *asura*-s) into blind darkness, where there is no sacrificial fire. Again he casts the blood of the victim into blind darkness, where there is no fire, with a thought that, that is the share of the *rakṣas*-es (*ibid.* I.9.2.34, 35).

The practice of barter as well as of bargain is marked in the rite of buying Soma. The Adhvaryu priest first bargains for King Soma with a cow (which is called the Somakrayaṇī cow in this process of barter). He tells the Soma-seller the ten things coming from the cow (*ibid.* III. 3.3.1-2), thus praising her. Then he speaks of gold, cloth, goat, milch cow, a pair of kine (*mithunau gāvau*) and three other cows as belonging to the Soma-seller (if he sells Soma). The *Śat. Br.* noting the practice of bargain in the *arthavāda,* says that people first bargain and afterwards come to terms. This is true in the case of anything and everything that is for sale here (*ibid.* 4).

The practice of using substitute or substitutes for the materials of worship is seen in the case of Soma (-shoots), in the absence of which Pūtika-plants are used and in their absence, the Arjuna plants (acc. to Sāyaṇa - *śyāmalāni tṛṇāni*). The origin of the Pūtika-plants is tucked to the myth of Gāyatrī bringing Soma, in the *arthavāda* which follows the *vidhi*-statement prescribing substitutes. When Gāyatrī carried away Soma, a Soma-guard shot an arrow at her and cut off a feather of her. (In that confusion) the shoot of Soma which fell down became the Pūtika-plant. In that the gods found help (*ūti* fr. √*av* - 'to protect') hence the name '*pūtika*' (bearing some similarity with the word '*ūti*') (*Pañc. Br.* IX. 5.3, 4).

The worldly practice of driving away a dog with a bow or a staff, is made use of in the *arthavāda* which is stated in the occasional (*naimittika*) sacrifice, if the moon is seen in the west, when the fast is observed on the New-moon day. It is said that the moon is a heavenly dog, who watches the sacrificer's cattle to catch hold of them. After giving oblations for Agni Pathikṛt (the path-maker), Indra Vṛtrahan (the killer of Vṛtra) and Agni Vaiśvānara, he gives a bow with three arrows as *dakṣiṇā,* for with the bow is driven away a dog (here the moon is the dog) and also a staff, with which the dog is driven away (*Śat. Br.* XI. 1.5.1, 10, 11).

The worldly practice of going to an animal from behind is stated in the *arthavāda,* in the context of the Agnicayana rite (i.e. the rite of building the Great Fire-altar), The fire is an animal. An animal destroys (or harms) a person, who moves to it face to face. Hence he should go up to the animal from behind, when the animal is looking forward (or towards the front), in order to prevent injury to himself (*Tait. Sam.* V. 7.6.1).

The practice of observing perfect decency in dress code is reflected in an *arthavāda,* in the context of the New-moon and Full-moon sacrifices. The *vidhi* is of strewing the sacrificial grass all round the fire. The *arthavāda* states that the sacrifice itself was afraid of nakedness and asked to strew the sacrificial grass all round it (*Śat. Br.* I.7.3.28). Earlier in the same context it is said that the sacrificial altar (*'vedi'* Fem.) is a woman and the gods and the priests, who have studied and teach the revealed lore (*śuśruvāṁsaḥ anūcānāḥ brāhmaṇāḥ*) sit around her. In order to cover her (and thus save her from nudity) the sacrificer (or the priest) spreads the *barhis* (sacrificial grass) around her (*ibid.* I.3.3.8). Even the sacrificial cake (*puroḍāśa*) is covered over (with hot ashes), so that the evil spirits and the *rakṣas*-es should not catch sight of it (and pounce on it). Moreover when ready, it should not lie as though naked and robbed of. So the covering of hot ashes on it (*ibid.* I.2.2.16).

Colloquialism noted in the ritual texts forms part of the practices—here practice of speaking in a particular manner with particular words. The (modern-day) colloquial expression 'to set the foot down' or 'to bring something under one's foot' is surprisingly found in the *Sat. Br.* in the context of the Agnicayana rite, when the bricks of Nirṛti, i.e. dedicated to Nirṛti, are laid down. The mythical account figuring as *arthavāda* in this connection runs thus. The gods having created the world, saw nothing but darkness. After meditation, they saw the Nairṛti bricks, piled them up and dispelled darkness by them (*ibid.* VII. 2.1.1,3). These bricks measure a foot (square). The *Śat. Br.* says that he thereby treads evil or corruption under foot (*ibid.* 7).

In the context of the Agniṣṭoma sacrifice, a practical observation couched in a proverbial form occurs in a mythical account, which is stated as *arthavāda* (*Jaim. Br.* I 125-27). The gods and the *asura*-s were contending and both the parties used same measures against each other. The Triśīrṣa *gandharva* alone knew as to which party would be victorious. Triśīrṣa's residence was a floating town (island). Indra knew it and also that Triśīrṣa alone knew about victory. Indra came there and asked Triśīrṣa's wife to know from her husband as to who would win the battle, and himself stayed on the boat in the form of a leech or a blade of grass. Accordingly she asked her husband (the *gandharva* Triśīrṣa) about it, to which he was quick to advise her not to speak loudly, for even the earth was having ears (and so the secret news would be divulged). The mythical account continues that Indra having heard the secret, becoming a parrot flew and the *gandharva* told his wife that to whichever side that green-coloured one (parrot) would descend, they would win. The important detail from our point of view is the Vedic colloquial expression— '*karṇinī vai bhūmiḥ*' ('The Earth has ears'), which tends to be a universal fact and experience, for many a time secrets are divulged, but nobody knows how.

Now we take into account some such *arthavāda*-s, which speak of some universal fact or common experience. In the context of the New-moon and Full-moon sacrifices, it is said that there are only two principles and no third (in the universe) *viz.* moist and dry. That which is dry belongs to Agni and the moist to Soma (*Śat. Br.* I.6.3.23). In the context of the Agnicayana rite (which is to provide for Prajāpati five bodily parts by building five layers of the Great Fire-altar), it is said in the *arthavāda* that after having created creatures, Prajāpati, having run the whole race, became exhausted (lit. 'disjointed' '*vyasraṁsata*'). Even now he who runs the whole race becomes indeed exhausted (*ibid.* VI. 1.2.12). Here a common experience of the profane level figures in the sacred setting of the Agnicayana rite. To continue the above *arthavāda*. Prajāpati said to (his son) Agni - 'Restore me (by providing for me the joints)'. Agni asked something in lieu of that. And Prajāpati said that people would call him after Agni. Here the *arthavāda* comes to the profane level by stating that whichever of the sons succeeds in life, after him they recognise the father, grandfather, son and grandson. Hence even while being Prajāpati, they call him Agni (*ibid.* 13).

The importance of sacrifice is brought out with a ritual metaphor based on worldly phenomenon. In the context of Agnihotra rite it is said that the Agnihotra (rite) is a ship sailing heavenwards. The Āhavanīya and the Gārhapatya are the two sides of that same ship and the milk-offerer (i.e. the sacrificer, who offers the milk-offerings) is the steersman (*ibid.* II. 3.3.15). The Ukthya-rite—'Viśvajyotiḥ' (the third one-day rite of a thousand *dakṣiṇā*-s) sacrifice is said to be yoked with two bullocks. These two bullocks are two *stoma*-s which are chanted at the three pressings of Soma (for each of the pressings, two different *stoma*-s) (*Pañc. Br.* XVI. 10.4, 5). The same metaphor occurs in the context of the Jyotiṣṭoma sacrifice. In the morning-pressing of Soma, are chanted the Trivṛt (nine-versed) and Pañcadaśa (fifteen-versed) *stoma*-s; in the midday-pressing, the Pañcadaśa and the Saptadaśa (seventeen-versed) *stoma*-s; and in the third pressing, the Saptadaśa and the Ekaviṁśa (twenty-one-versed) *stoma*-s (*ibid.* XVI. 1.6).

So are the metaphors about *dakṣiṇā*-s. The *dakṣiṇā*-s are said to be the internal fastenings of sacrifice, which is regarded as a chariot. By a chariot provided with fastenings, one is sure to reach one's destination. And so attains a sacrificer his desired object, with a sacrifice provided with *dakṣiṇā*-s. *Dakṣiṇā*-s are said to be the ornaments of sacrifice. With *dakṣiṇā*-s, he brings beauty into the sacrifice (*ibid.* XVI. 1. 13, 14). More of the *dakṣiṇā*-s can be dealt with in the specific topic on "Dakṣiṇā".

At the Viśvajit sacrifice, as *dakṣiṇā*-s are given all the possessions by the sacrificer, except the earth (i.e. ground) and the inhabitants.[37] Giving away all the property invited bad consequences for the sacrificer of the Viśvajit sacrifice. So the several prescriptions laid down for the sacrificer. As an upper garment he should wear a (cow-)hide and that too of red colour. Red is the colour most common to cattle. By this he will not be separated from his cattle; in fact, he would obtain them in bodily form (*ibid.* XVI. 6.1,2), as he has given them as *dakṣiṇā*-s. The belief clearly springs from the principle of sympathetic magic. After the performance of the Viśvajit sacrifice, the sacrificer has to observe a code of conduct prescribed, for twelve days. 'Twelve' days symbolically amount to a year, which consists of 'twelve' months. These rules (of the code of conduct) speak of the practices followed, each of it reflecting some belief or the other. During the first three days and nights, he dwells in the forest, by which he obtains the food of the forest (*ibid.* 3). The next three days he has to dwell amongst Niṣāda-s, who are given over to the earth (i.e. who subsist by the earth-products by digging the roots, etc.). By this he obtains the food that is found on the earth (*ibid.* 7). This detail is very significant, for it shows the cultural assimilation of the Vedic people with the other tribes such as the Niṣāda-s mentioned here. The next three days the sacrificer has to dwell amongst the people, who are from the neighbouring country, by which he obtains the food of those people (*ibid.* 8). Last three days he stays amongst his own people, by which he obtains the food of his own people (*ibid.* 9). The *arthavāda*, pointing out the reason for his stay amongst each particular group of people, speaks of the belief based on which the practice was followed by the sacrificer-king.

The *arthavāda* stated in the context of the Soma-sacrifice by the *Tait. Sam.* has to be noted for a reference to tiger. The sacrificer consecrated for sacrifice is said to be a foetus, the sacrificial-shed being the womb, from which he has not to come out, lest the foetus should fall out of the womb. The *arthavāda* has one more ritual metaphor here. It is said that the (sacrificial) fire is a tiger, guarding the house (*vyāghraḥ kulagopaḥ yadagniḥ*). If the sacrificer, who is consecrated were to leave the shed, he would be likely to spring up and slay him. Hence the consecrated sacrificer should not leave the sacrificial-shed so that he can protect himself (*Tait. Sam.* VI.2.5.5).

Even the posture of standing prescribed for the sacrificer (or the priest on his behalf) for certain *vidhi*-s, is convincingly supported by the *arthavāda* at the respective places, coming to the profane level. In the rite of Agnicayana, the sacrificer hangs a gold plate round his neck, by wearing it. The gold plate has twenty-one knobs (*Śat. Br.* VI. 7.1.1,2). It is said to be round, for the sun is round. He wears it with the knobs outside, for the knobs are the sun's rays and they are outside (*ibid.* 2). The sun is said to be the twenty-first (*ibid.* I. 3.5.11—12 months + 5 seasons + 3 worlds + that one burning yonder). It is said that the sacrificer puts on that gold plate round his neck while standing. The gold plate is the yonder sun and the sun stands as it were. Again one is stronger, while standing (*ibid.* VI. 7.2.1). In the New-moon and Full-moon sacrifices, while kindling the fire, he recites the invitatory prayer (Anuvākyā), while standing, since it is the yonder sky (addressing) which he thereby recites (*ibid:* I.4.2.18). The *arthavāda* in the *Kauṣ. Br.* becomes more eloquent and convincing, while praising the posture of standing. In the context of the Soma-sacrifice, when the recitations of the Hotrakas at the morning pressing are mentioned, it is said that the Maitrāvaruṇa priest alone gives directions to all.[38] He gives directions standing (thinking) —'While standing one is the strongest and while standing also, one is most easily heard (*Kauṣ. Br.* XXVIII.1). We have noted above that the invitatory prayer is to be recited while standing. Now the offering prayer (Yājyā) or prayers are pronounced by the Hotṛ priest, while sitting, for the Yājyā represents this earth (for the oblation is offered in the sacrificial fire seated in the hearth), and this offering of oblation is done simultaneously with or immediately after the utterance of the sound Vaṣaṭ[39] (*Śat. Br.* I.4.2.19). The explanation of the postures of standing and sitting is given based on belief and in a manner which is simple but convincing.

The information about the *sāman*-s—Bṛhat and Rathantara—falls in the same line. When Prajāpati wanted to be 'many', the Bṛhat *sāman* arose in his mind (in the form of a thought). So it had the embryonic form (and not the full form). When Prajāpati released his speech, it (i.e. the words) became the *sāman* Rathantara.[40] After the Rathantara came out the Bṛhat *sāman* (which was up to that time in the form of an embryo, but with the passage of time becoming big, hence 'Bṛhat', fr. √*bṛh* or √*bṛṁh* - 'to grow, increase' but really it was the older of the two in the process of issuing forth from Prajāpati). Hence just as an eldest son is to a father, Bṛhat (*sāman*) is to Prajāpati (*Pañc. Br.* VII. 6. 1-6). This is an allusion to a worldly experience. The more of it we see when it is said that the *nidhana*-s (finales) of these two *sāman*-s must not be put together, but kept separate, for these two *sāman*-s are the two big trees, which if come together have a collision and then there lies on the ground a great shattering and a great breaking down of branches (*ibid.* 15, 16). The *arthavāda* here has noted a common worldly experience, especially when there is a fierce gale followed by torrential rains. Another such observation is of the Mahāvrata day in the Gavām-ayana *sattra* (long sacrificial session). The atmosphere on this day is of the 'Eat-Drink-and Make Merry' note. The *Tait. Sam.* says that as men being freed from bonds cry aloud, so the sacrificers freed from the bonds of the gods cry aloud by placing food and strength in themselves (*Tait. Sam.* VII. 5.9.2). One more such observation is in the rite of Punarādheya (re-establishment of fires), when the fires are enjoined to be established or set up in the rainy season (*varṣāsu*), for the rains are indeed all the seasons. From the year (*varṣa*) is named, the rainy season (*varṣāḥ*) (*Śat. Br.* II. 2.3.7).

A worldly observation is made use of by the *Ṣaḍ. Br.* in the *arthavāda,* when it is enjoined that the Hotrāśaṁsin-s praise with a *śastra* having five *ṛc*-s or with a *śastra* having many *ṛc*-s. The *arthavāda* cites the illustration of waters which at some places become fordable (and thus are shallow), while at some places, deep (*gambhīrāḥ*), in short the waters have uneven level. They are *uccāvacāḥ*—uneven (*Ṣaḍ. Br.* II. 4.6).

The worldly experience that 'Might' prevails, in other words, 'Law of sea' or 'Law of jungle', is made use of in a couple of *arthavāda*-s, in the rite of New-moon and Full-moon sacrifices. The mythical account states that when Indra killed the three-headed and six-eyed son of Tvaṣṭṛ, the latter (Tvaṣṭṛ) becoming furious brought Soma, from which Indra was excluded. But Indra, even though not invited, consumed the pure Soma-juice of Tvaṣṭṛ. The *Śat. Br.* at this juncture states Indra's action to be that of a stronger person consuming the food of a weaker one, obviously overpowering him (*Śat. Br.* I. 6.3.1-7). The same observation is noted in the well-known mythical account of Manu and the fish — or the Indian 'Flood-legend' — when a small fish, which comes in Manu's hands tells Manu to rear it, for as long as the fish are small, there is great destruction for them as fish devours fish (*ibid.* I.8.1.3). The account runs further stating how Manu takes care of the fish, placing it in the reservoirs, suiting to the growing size of the fish and the fish saves Manu on the days of the great flood (*ibid.* I.8.1.1ff.).

A universal experience is noted in the *arthavāda,* which occurs in the context of the Atirātra sacrifice. The gods took refuge of the day, while the *asura*-s resorted to the night-time. As the *asura*-s were equal in strength, they could not be discriminated. Indra asked as to who would accompany him to attack the *asura*-s through night. But he found no one among the gods, they being afraid of darkness, which is the night and which is the very death. The metres followed Indra. (Hence it is that in the Atirātra sacrifice, the metres are used even in the night-time, which is rather unusual). The *arthavāda* reflects the belief, which is percolated even in our own times, that when a person has gone away at a distance, he is afraid, for the night is darkness as it were, death as it were (*Ait. Br.* IV. 5. = 16.5).

The most commonly seen is the relationship between man and woman - in most cases husband and wife relationship. While eulogising the sacred utterances (Vyāhṛti-s), the *Jaim. Br.* gives a mythical account as *arthavāda.* The gods prevailed over the *asura*-s and *rakṣas*-es with their toil, austerity and celibacy. The *asura*-s knowing this, assumed the form of beautiful women and came in the sight of the gods. The gods moved (or rushed) to them. The *Jaim. Br.* has a universal fact to tell that the women are never disliked by anybody, i.e. they are always liked by any person. The account runs further that the gods sprinkled in them (by uniting with them!) their own lustre, power and vigour earned by them with toils. The *asura*-s ran away taking all these with them. The gods thought themselves as emptied out of all these and desired for a way to get back all these. They saw the Vyāhṛti-s (*Jaim. Br.* III. 352). It is clear that according to the *Jaim. Br.*, every person (man!) has a weakness for a woman. So the trick played by the *asura*-s. In spite of the polygamy prevalent in the then society, the husband-wife relationship seems to be of love and respect, on the part of the wives. The *Jaim. Br.* in the context of the Gavām-ayana, speaks of the six quarters (four main and the upper and the lower) looking at the consecrated sacrificer (*dīkṣita*) without winking their eyes, as would the wives look at their husband. The etymology of the word *dīkṣita* is - *digbhiḥ īkṣitaḥ tasmād dīkṣitaḥ* - 'looked at by the quarters — so *dīkṣita*' (*Jaim. Br.* II. 52). No other parallel could have fit in here except of the wives. The exact six quarters are mentioned by the *Bṛhad. Up.* as Prācī (east), Dakṣiṇā (south), Pratīcī (west), Udīcī (north), Ūrdhvā (upper direction) and Avācī (lower direction) (IV. 2.4).

In the rite of Agnicayana, a live tortoise is placed in the lowest layer of the Great Fire-altar. It is to be placed on the right (south, i.e. *dakṣiṇa*) side of the Aṣāḍhā brick. The tortoise (*kūrma* Mas.) is a male and the Aṣāḍhā is a female. The male lies on the right side of the female at a cubit's distance and so is the tortoise placed at a cubit's distance (on the right side of the Aṣāḍhā) The Aṣāḍhā (being the chief of the bricks) is the consecrated queen (*mahiṣī*) of all the bricks. Being on the right side of this brick, the tortoise is on the right side of all the bricks (*Śat. Br.* VII. 5.1.1, 6). The *arthavāda* is significant, informing us about the normal postures of the husband and wife, striking a note of polygamy at the end.

The whole edifice of sacrifice is based on the concept of 'give-and-take' between the gods and the men. The *arthavāda* in the *Śat. Br.* in the context of the Agniṣṭoma sacrifice states this clearly. The *vidhi* is of reciting the *mantra*-s (verses) to the drops (of melted butter) addressed to Agni. When the Pratiprasthātṛ priest roasts the omentum of the sacrificial victim, the Adhvaryu priest having taken the melted butter with the dipping-spoon, pours it upon the omentum (*vapā*) with a prayer to Agni, with the sound Svāhā. Those drops of melted butter thus reach the fire after becoming cooked offerings with the sound Svāhā ('Hail'). Then on the words of the Adhvaryu priest, the Maitrāvaruṇa priest recites to the drops (of melted butter) verses addressed to Agni. The *arthavāda* is — Rain originates from gifts made from this earth, for from here it is that Agni obtains the rain. By means of the drops (of melted butter falling from the omentum), he obtains those rain drops and those drops rain down (*ibid.* III. 8.2.20-22). This is clearly based on the principle of sympathetic magic—'Like produces like' — drops of melted butter bringing in drops of rain. The note of magic (though in the setting of sacrificial religion) is so patent that these verses recited to the drops addressed to Agni could very well serve as a rain-charm.

The *Śat. Br.* warns the sacrificers that the wilds and ravines of sacrifice take hundreds upon hundreds of days carriage-drives. Any venture into them without knowledge would lead to hunger and thirst, evil-doers and fiends harassing them. But if those who know take upon any venture, they would pass from one stream into another, from one safe place to another and obtain well-being and the world of heaven (*ibid.* XII. 2.3.12). And here we come to the importance of the *brāhmaṇa*-s—the priestly class—who knew the secrets of the science of sacrifice. However the Brāhmaṇa-texts do make a difference between the *brāhmaṇa*-s on the basis of their knowledge of the sacred texts and their capability to impart it to others, '*śuśruvāṁsaḥ*' and '*anūcānāḥ*' being the epithets of the real *brāhmaṇa*-s, who could be regarded as the gods on the earth. This thought could be traced to the *RV*, which states that 'Friends (the word *sakhāyaḥ* applied to the priests), having similar eyes and similar ears, were unequal in the speed of their minds. Some are like tanks, which reach up to the mouth (Sāy. '*madhyamaprajña*' — of medium intellect); some are like tanks, reaching up to the arm-pit (Sāy. '*alpaprajña*' - of low intellect); some are like tanks reaching up to the head (Sāy. '*mahāprajña*' of extraordinary intellect). These i.e. the last type of tanks (priests), are suitable for taking bath, while others (i.e. the first two types of tanks—priests) are meant to be seen only (*RV* X. 71.7). The *Nir.* (I.9) also deals with this *ṛc* and explains it.

The propriety of the *arthavāda*-portions in the Brāhmaṇa-texts has to be judged taking into account the relation between the 'sacred' and 'profane' or 'secular'. The Brāhmaṇa-texts display a detailed but early form of Vedic ritual, which is not codified as we see in the Śrautasūtras. Dealing with the same subject-matter, i.e. Vedic ritual, the pattern of the Brāhmaṇa-texts and that of the Śrautasūtras differ from each other. While the Śrautasūtras do not need any supportive matter in the form of praise or condemnation, as the ritual laid down by them is fixed and codified, the Brāmaṇa-texts at every step seek explanation and forward ritual reasoning or even reasonings (even for a single rite), in the form of *arthavāda*. As we have noted earlier, these *arthavāda*-s deal with traditional accounts (the oft-repeated being, of contending or strife between gods and *asura*-s), beliefs, practices, etc. prevalent in those times. These all can be said to be from the profane or secular level, to which the sacred level of ritual has to come, while explaining the ritual. And here we come to the 'loan' of the secular or profane tradition to the sacred ritual tradition. Several *arthavāda*-s reveal the fact that the ritual thinkers always have to catch the finger of secular matters and have to come to the profane level in order to be convincing. But for the secular tradition, there seems no need to take the help of the sacred tradition, for with its beliefs and practices, the secular tradition has remained undated, independent by itself unlike the ritualistic tradition.

We have already noted the doctrine of *ekavākyatā* (syntactical relation) propounded by the Mīmaṁsakas, working in two ways. Undoubtedly the *vidhi* and *arthavāda* are interdependent, vouchsafed even by the doctrine of the Mīmāṁsakas, which also indicates equal importance of both. The relation between the ritual (*vidhi*) and its glorificatory explanation (*arthavāda*) coming to the a-ritual level, is complementary to each other and stands unique. But taking into account the undated hoary past of the secular tradition, we feel that more weightage has to be given to the secular or profane tradition, for it has provided much matter to the sacred tradition. However we have to say that this secular tradition of the hoary past has come down to us, only by its being incorporated in the ritualistic tradition, in the form of *arthavāda*-s, in the absence of which, these records of beliefs and practices would have remained in the form of floating mass of literature, having only the mouth-to-mouth circulation, with the impending calamity of extinction any day.

The endeavour in the pages to follow is to study the *arthavāda*-s in the Brāhmaṇa-texts from a specific point of view. It has to be pointed out that each and every *arthavāda* in each and every case of injunction (*vidhi*) is not thought to be necessary for being included here, for such a detailed cataloguing at times may not lead us any further. At times, some *arthavāda*-s, when they are viewed in different perspectives and are included under different headings, have to be repeated at the respective places. This inevitable repetition has proved useful in showing the multi-faceted nature of these *arthavāda*-s. The *arthavāda*-s chosen and taken up for this study are supposed to throw light on the then prevalent man's convictions, beliefs and practices in relation to his own world 'within himself' as well as the world 'beyond himself'. However it is necessary not to lose sight of the *vidhi*-s in the context of which the *arthavāda*-s occur. Study of the *arthavāda*-portions in the setting of their respective *vidhi*-s proves most beneficial and serves as an 'Open Sesame' to a vista of the Vedic India.

NOTES AND REFERENCES

1. *Arthasaṅgraha,* ed. by Paranjape, S.M., Bombay, 1927, p. 251 - *prayogasamavetārthasmārakā mantrāḥ;* also *ibid.* p. 51, the statement from the *Mīmāṁsāparibhāṣā...tatra prayogakālīnārthasmaraṇahetutayā mantrāṇāmupayogaḥ/*
2. *Pūrvamīmāṁsāsūtra* II.1.33.
3. *Āp. Ś.S.* XXIV. 1.32.
4. *Arthasaṅgraha,* p. 51, the statement q. from the *Mīmāṁsāparibhāṣā - vidhāyakam vākyam brāhmaṇam/*
5. *Arthasaṅgraha,* p. 51 - *tatrājñātārthajñāpako vedabhāgo vidhiḥ/;* also *Tantravārttika* I.2.4a *vidhiratyantamaprāptau.*
6. *Arthasaṅgraha,* p. 51, the statement q. from the *Mīmāṁsāparibhāṣā - brāhmaṇaśeṣaścārthavādaḥ/;* also *Āp. Ś.S.* XXIV. 1.33 - *brāhmaṇaśeṣo' rthavādaḥ/*

7. *Arthasaṅgraha*, p. 353. — *prāśastyanindānyataraparam vākyamarthavādaḥ/*
8. *Āp. Ś.S.* XXIV. 1.33.
9. *Mīmāṁsābālaprakāśa*, p. 51.
10. Some of these types with examples can be seen—
    (*i*) Stating a reason (*hetu*) - *śūrpeṇa juhoti tena hyannam kriyate/*
    (*ii*) Expressing doubt (*saṁśaya*) - *hotavyam gārhapatye na hotavyam/*
    (*iii*) Transpositional (*vyavadhāraṇakalpanā*)— *yāvato' śvān pratigṛhṇīyāt* i.e. one should perform as many sacrifices, as the horses he receives.
11. *Arthasaṅgraha*, p. 361.
12. *Pūrvamīmāṁsāsūtra* I.2.1; also *Mīmaṁsānyāyaprakāśa* of Āpadeva, ed. by Abhyankar, Vasudevashastri, Government Oriental Series, BORI, Poona, 1937, pp. 14-16.
13. *Metaphors in Vedic Literature* (*Proceedings* of the National Seminar, ÇASS), University of Pune, pub. Class E, No.14, Pune, 1998.
14. Sāyaṇa's Introduction (*bhūmikā*) to his comm. on the *Ṛgveda*, see *RV*, I *maṇḍala*, pub. by the Vaidika Samshodhana Mandala, Pune, 1933, p. 10—*arthavādabhāgasya prāmāṇyam mahatā prayatnena jaiminiḥ samarthayāmāsa*
15. *Pūrvamīmāṁsāsūtra* I.2.1.
16. *Ibid.* I.2.1-18.
17. Navathe, P.D., "On the Mīmāṁsā Doctrine of Ekavākyatā", *Proceedings* of the Winter Institute on Ancient Indian Theories on Sentence-Meaning, University of Poona, Pune, 1980, p. 190.
18. *Ibid.*, p. 192.
19. *Jaiminīya-nyāyamālā* I.2.1.1-3.
20. *Pūrvamīmāṁsāsūtra* I.2.7; I.2.22.
21. Horsch, Paul, *Die vedische Gāthā-und Śloka Literatur*, Francke Verlag, Bern, 1966, III part of the book, chapters on Origin and Development of the *gāthā*-s.
22. See Sāyaṇa on *Ait. Br.* III.43=14.5; V.31=25.6; VII.9=32.8; VIII.21=39.7.
23. Chakrabarti, Samiran Chandra, "A Study of the Pāriplava", *Indo-Iranian Journal*, 32, Kluwer Academic Publishers (printed in the Netherlands), 1982, p. 262.

24. Hariappa, H.L., *Ṛgvedic Legends through the Ages,* Deccan College, Poona, 1953, p. 132.
25. Dandekar, R.N., "The Mahābhārata: Origin and Growth", *University of Ceylon Review,* 12, 1954, p. 65.
26. (Mrs.) Dange, S.S. "Sūta—The Paurāṇika", *Purāṇa,* All India Kashiraj Trust, Varanasi, Vol. XL, No. 2, July 1998, pp. 83-91.
27. See Intrn. to *Hamlet* by Turner, W., The Educational Publishing Company, Bombay, June 1959, p. if.
28. *Pañc. Br.* IV. 10.2; *Śat.Br.* IV.6.4.2. According to *Ait. Ār.* I.1.1, Indra having killed Vṛtra, becomes '*mahān*' and the rite for him is the Mahāvrata.
29. The earth-drum (*bhūmi-dundubhi,* as it is called) is, in fact, a bull-hide spread over a hole dug in the earth to the west of the Āgnīdhrīya shed, which is half inside the altar (*vedi*) and half outside, Beating of the earth-drum is actually striking this bull-hide. vide Kane, P.V., *Hist of Dh. S.,* Vol. II, pt. II, 2nd ed., BORI, Poona, 1974, p. 1244.
30. *Ibid.,* p. 1244 f.
31. *Ibid.,* p. 1245.
32. *Ibid.*
33. For 'ghee' (*ghṛta*) as rain, see Dange, Sadashiv A., *Pastoral Symbolism from the Ṛgveda,* University of Poona, Poona, 1970, pp. 36, 49. For 'honey' (*madhu*) as rain, see Dange, Sadashiv A., *Images from Vedic Hymns and Rituals,* Aryan Books International, New Delhi, 2000, p. 39.
34. See Keith, A.B., *The Veda of the Black Yajuṣ School entitled Taittiriya Sanhita,* pt. 2, HOS, Vol. XIX, 2nd issue, Motilal Banarsidass, Delhi, 1967 (1914), p. 430, tr. of *Tait. Sam.* V.4.3.3; also p. 409, note 2; also Eggeling, J., *The Śatapatha Brāhmaṇa,* pt. IV, SBE, Vol. 43, Motilal Banarsidass, Delhi, 1978 (1885), p. 334, note 4 - "Arka Plant." Elsewhere he says "Arka-tree', see *ibid.* p. 157 his tr. of *Śat.Br.* IX.1.1.4. This shows that Keith and Eggeling are not correct. Macdonell and Keith in the *Vedic Index of Names and Subjects* under the title "Arka" say that it is a 'tree'.
35. For detailed treatment of this, see (Mrs.) Dange, S.S., *Aspects of Speech in Vedic Ritual,* Aryan Books International, New Delhi, 1996.

36. See Eggeling, J., *op. cit,* Vol. V, SBE, Vol. 44, Motilal Banarsidass, Delhi, 1978 (1900), p. 218, note 3.
37. Caland, W., *Pañcaviṃśa Brāhmaṇa,* Sri Satguru Pubns., 2nd ed., Delhi, 1982 (Calcutta, 1931), p. 437, note 1 on *Pañc. Br.* XVI. 6.1
38. *Kauṣ. Br.* XXVIII.1 —The mythical account occurring here is — The deities ran a race regarding the Praiṣa-s (Praiṣa' is an impelling word, e.g. *'yaja',* i.e. 'Perform sacrifice', uttered by the Adhvaryu priest to the Hotṛ priest, so that the sacrificial procedure starts moving). Mitra and Varuṇa won the race. Therefore Maitrāvaruṇa priest (representing these two deities) alone gives directions to all.
39. For Vaṣaṭ, see (Mrs.) Dange, S.S., *Aspects of Speech in Vedic Ritual,* pp. 146-63.
40. The name Rathantara is explained by the *Pañc. Br.* (VII. 6.4) as - 'Indeed, the chariot (*ratham*), it has swiftly reached (*atārīt*)', and so the name 'Ratham-tara' i.e. Rathantara. The *Jaim. Br.* (I. 135) takes Rathas as nine nineties *asura*-s and *rakṣas*-es, having crossed (i.e. overcome fr. √*tṛ* - 'to cross over') over whom, by the chanting of the Rathantara *sāman* (this *sāman* serving as a vehicle), the gods went to the world of heaven. So the name Rathantara.

CHAPTER 1

Etymologies

Etymologies occurring in the Brāhmaṇa-texts have been a topic of separate study and efforts have been made in this direction.[1] The method of giving etymology of a word is inherited by these texts from the ancient works such as *RV* and *AV*. Some examples from these works could be seen in this connection. The etymology of the word *mātariśvan* is stated from the root √*mā* -'to measure', in *RV* (III. 29.11 — *mātariśvā yad amimīta mātari).* It is said that 'as he measured in the mother, he is called Mātariśvan'. Here Vāyu is spoken of as being measured in the mid-region, which is as though his mother. Here the effort for etymology on the part of the seer is patent. However, in many cases, when two similar words are brought together or near, etymology is only indicated. In a prayer to Uṣas, it is said — 'Which ancient one (i.e. Dawn) of them (i.e. Dawns) (was it) at which they (the gods) shaped *(vidadhuḥ)* the works *(vidhānā)* of the Ṛbhus?' (*RV* IV. 51.6 ab). Here the words *vidadhuḥ* and *vidhānā* are brought together. It is said at *RV* (IV. 55. 5 cd) - 'May the lord (*patiḥ* lit. 'protector', here the god is Varuṇa) protect (*pāt*) us from the sin of the people and may the god Mitra (*mitraḥ)* protect us with his friendly outlook (*mitriyāt)'*. The words to be noted here are *patiḥ* and *pāt* (fr. *pā* - 'to protect'), and *mitraḥ* and *mitriyāt* (from the word *mitra* meaning a 'friend'). The etymology of the word *puruṣa,* which occurs in several later works,[2] even the Brāhmaṇa-texts,[3] is seen in the *AV*. It is said - 'He who knows the *brahman's* town (*puram brahmaṇaḥ* acc. to Whitney, *puram* - 'stronghold'),[4] from which man (*puruṣaḥ*) is so called (*AV* X. 2.28 cd, 30 cd). Even a couple of such examples as we have noted above, can amply bring out that the seers of the Saṁhitās knew the importance of the method of etymology for making clear certain words or concepts. The composers of the Brāhmaṇa-texts toed the line by having recourse to the tool of etymology, while stating their ritual reasoning in the form of *arthavāda*-s. This is how etymology figures as an important aspect of *arthavāda*-s in the Brāhmaṇa-texts. Yāska, the first exponent of a systematised school of etymology flourished later, though the etymological thought as such preceded him, as can be seen from the names of thinkers in this line mentioned by him in his *Nirukta*.[5] But the principle propounded by him while giving (any) etymology *viz.* 'One should give etymology on the basis of similarity between letters or even syllables (of words)',[6] is already envisaged by the Brāhmaṇa-texts and also followed, while giving etymologies in the *arthavāda*-portions. And with the doctrine that 'Gods love what is abstruse and they dislike what is direct or open' (*parokṣapriyā vai devāḥ pratyakṣadviṣaḥ*), the composers of the Brāhmaṇa-texts could forward any etymology in any way, having only the required word (i.e. term) to be explained in view in the context of ritual.

The *arthavāda*-portions of the Brāhmaṇa-texts are replete with several etymologies, which at times reflect the beliefs or practices of the society in those times. Some examples which can stand as representative, are taken up here for discussion.

1. Abhiplava (Name of a Rite)

While laying down the Abhiplava Ṣaḍaha rite in the Soma-sacrifice, the *Kauṣ. Br.* states the etymology of the word *abhiplava* (*Kauṣ. Br.* XX. 1). It is said that by this rite, the sacrificers as though mount (fr. *abhi* + √*plu* > *plav*) on the year and in the Year, they obtain this sixfold excellent food *viz.* wild animals, domesticated animals, plants, trees, that which goes in the waters and that which swims. The *arthavāda* indicates how the sacrifice is regarded as a means of procuring the desired things.

2. *Adhvara* (Sacrifice)

The etymology stated by the *Śat. Br.* is from the context of the Full-moon sacrifice. When he recites the last *sāmidhenī mantra* (i.e. the *mantra,* which is recited while kindling the fire) — a *tric* (tristich) - containing the word '*adhvara*' - the following mythical account occurs in the *Śat. Br.* by way of an *arthavāda.* When the gods were engaged in performing a sacrifice, the *asura*-s being their rivals, desired to injure (*dhūrvitum)* them. But they were unable to do so. The sacrifice hence is called '*adhvara'*, i.e. 'not injured' (*Śat. Br.* I. 4. 1.40). The belief reflected in the *arthavāda* through this etymology is - as sacrifice itself is not damaged and is free from injury, it ensures safety from any injury to the sacrificer.

That the sacrifice occupied the highest position in the life of the then Vedic Indians is reflected in the etymology of the word '*adhvara'* given in the *Tait. Sam.* This occurs in an *arthavāda* in the context of the Soma-sacrifice, when the three pressings (*savana*-s*)* are laid down. It is said that the *asura*-s tried to imitate what the gods did at the sacrifice. Howsoever they tried, they could not follow the sacrifice of the gods. They said, 'These gods have become unsurpassable (*adhvartavyāḥ).* The sacrifice (*adhvara)* is unsurpassable.' The gods did prosper and defeated were the *asura*-s (*Tait. Sam.* III. 2.2.3). That the sacrifice did not involve any real injury is a later idea, when the issue of injury to the animal came forward.[7]

3. *Āhuti* (Offering)

The etymology of this word occurs in the context of New-moon and Full-moon sacrifices. It is said that the offering given by the sacrificer becomes his body in the yonder world. When he departs from this world, that offering, being behind him, calls out to him, 'Come here; I am here your body'. As the offering thus calls out (*āhvayati* fr. *ā* + √*hvā* or √*hve* - 'to call out, invoke'), it is called *āhuti* (*Śat. Br.* XI. 2.2.6). It is a pithy account, striking an eschatological note. The *arthavāda*-portion here, based on the etymology of the word *āhuti* speaks of the belief, based on the *karman*-doctrine, the idea being that the offerings given by the sacrificer in the sacrifice, follow him to the other world and become his body, with which he can enjoy in that world. It is this belief that paved a way for the concept of *apūrva* or *adṛṣṭa,* which is a gift from the *Pūrvamīmāṁsā* system to Indian philosophy. *Apūrva* or *adṛṣṭa* is what is stored to the credit of the sacrificer in the other world, when he performs a sacrifice, and offers to the gods.

Another etymology of the word *āhuti* occurs in the context of the rite for building the Great Fire-altar (Agnicayana rite). It is said that whatever they offer in Agni, those (*āhuti*-s) are assigned to him. They are *āhiti*-s (*āhitayaḥ* fr. *ā* + √*dhā* - 'to place, to assign'), mystically called *āhuti*-s, for the gods love the abstruse (*Śat. Br.* X. 6.2.2). The *arthavāda,* through etymology, indicates the aspect of Agni as a messenger-god, for the offerings given in the fire solely belong to him, to be carried to different deities.

Yet another etymology occurs in the *Ait. Br.,* which states that with these (offerings) the sacrificer calls, i.e. invokes (*hvayati* fr. √*hvā* or √*hve*) the gods; so they are called *āhuti*-s. They are also called *ūti*-s (*ūtayaḥ* fr *ā* + √*i* - 'to come'), by which the gods come to the call of the sacrificer (*Ait. Br.* I. 2). Keith takes the word *ūtayaḥ* as 'ways'.[8]

4. Aṅgiras (Name of a Sage)

The etymology of this word occurs in some ritual texts.[9] Here the etymology from the *Gop. Br.* is taken for consideration.

The etymology occurs in the *Gop. Br.* in the cosmogonic account, coming as an *arthavāda*. As Brahmā heats the waters, they are divided into two, the saline waters forming the sea and the sweet waters (*Gop. Br.* I. 1.3). From the sweet waters came the sage Bhṛgu and then Atharvan (*ibid.* 3,4). From the saline waters by successive cosmogonic acts came into being the ocean (*samudra*), Varuṇa, Mṛtyu (=Mucyu, for he was released from the ocean, fr. √*muc* - 'to release, make free') and from the sap (*rasa*) extracted from the limbs (*aṅgebhyaḥ*) of Mṛtyu came Aṅgiras (*ibid.* 7). The etymology (fr. *aṅga* + *rasa* = *aṅgarasa* > *aṅgiras*) is obviously to give status to Aṅgiras, the great ancestor of the later generation of Aṅgiras-es, by whom were 'seen' the *mantra*-s of the Āṅgirasa-Veda. According to Bloomfield, the origin of Aṅgiras from the bitter waters of the ocean, next from Varuṇa and finally from Mṛtyu is intended to turn forth the terrible side of the Āṅgirasa-Veda in contrast with the auspicious Atharvan and Ātharvaṇa-Veda, derived through Bhṛgu.[10] The etymology here of the word Aṅgiras (fr. *aṅga-rasa*) is based on the belief that creation comes from the body-fluids or limbs of a great personality. The myth speaking of creation from the various limbs of the Puruṣa when he is sacrificed (*RV* X. 90) is a precursor of this belief,[11] which is seen in the Brāhmaṇa-texts in the case of Prajāpati[12] and still later in the Purāṇas in the case of Brahmā.[13]

5. Āprī (-Hymns)

The etymology of the word Āprī is stated from *ā* + √*prī* — 'to propitiate, please'. The *Śat. Br.* says that in the animal-sacrifice, the animal when (ritually killed), swelled. By means of the Āprī-hymns, he appeased that animal. So the name Āprī (*Śat. Br.* XI. 8.3.5). Elsewhere the *Śat. Br.* takes the word Āprī from *ā* + √*pyai* - 'to fill up, increase' (*ibid.* III. 8.1.2). The point to be noted here is that the Āprī-s are the prayers, i.e. (*mantra* or) *mantra*-s, which form an indispensable part of any ritual and which combined with ritual are believed to bring in the desired effect.[14] The etymologies of the word Āprī only echo this belief.[15]

6. Aptoryāma (Name of a Sacrifice)

The etymology of the word Aptoryāma stated to glorify the Aptoryāma sacrifice is self-eloquent. The *arthavāda* in the *Tait. Br.* runs as follows. When after creating cattle, Prajāpati could not get them back, he, having tried several sacrifices, ultimately performed the Aptoryāma sacrifice and obtained (*āpnot*) them. So the name of the sacrifice as Aptoryāma, fr. √*āp* — 'to get, obtain' (*Tait. Br.* II. 7.14.2). The *Pañc. Br.* states that the rite is so called because by its performance, one secures whatever object one desires fr. the root √*āp* (*Pañc. Br.* XX. 3.4-5). In tune with these accounts, the *Āśv. Ś.S.* enjoins that he whose cattle do not live or who desires to secure cattle of good breed, should perform the Aptoryāma sacrifice (*Āśv. Ś.S.* IX. 11.1). In this sacrifice, the Aptoryāma *stoma,*[16] composed of thirty-three *stotra*-s is to be recited, as Sāyaṇa states in his commentary on the *Tait. Br.* (II. 7. 14. 2), where occurs the name of the sacrifice, as is noted above. The etymology of the name Aptoryāma is so apt as to give rise to a doubt that the etymology from the root √*āp* might have stood as a basis for the very name.

7. Ariṣṭa *Sāman*

In order to glorify the Ariṣṭa *sāman,* which is to be recited at the end of the Ārbhava- pavamāna laud,[17] the *Pañc. Br.* states a mythical account. The gods and the *asura*-s were contesting. Whomsoever of the gods the *asura*-s slew, that one did not come to life again. On the other hand, whomsoever of the *asura*-s the gods slew, that one came to life again. Having performed austerities, the gods saw the Ariṣṭa *sāman.* With this, whomsoever of the gods the *asura*-s slew, that one came to life again and whomsoever of the *asura*-s the gods slew, that one did not come to life again.

The gods thought that with that *sāman*, they came out unharmed (*nāriṣāma*, i.e. *na ariṣāma)*. Hence the name Ariṣṭa, fr. √*riṣ* — 'to harm'; — *ariṣṭa* — 'free from harm' (*Pañc. Br.* XII. 5. 22, 23).

The conflict between the gods and the *asura*-s is a constantly recurring phenomenon in Vedic mythology. It spreads over to the epic and Puranic tradition, also to the classical Sanskrit *mahākāvya*-s and the plays, where help of a human king is sought by gods, more often by Indra, for vanquishing the demons. The myth of the contending gods and *asura*-s precedes the name of the *sāman*. The *arthavāda* based on the etymology of the word *ariṣṭa* is obviously for stressing the importance of the *sāman*, the singing of which brings about the desired effect,[18] and can stand as a representative of all such etymologies, explaining the names of *sāman*-s.

8. Aṣāḍhā (Name of a Brick)

In the context of the Agnicayana rite, the *Śat. Br.* enjoins placing of the Aṣāḍhā brick in the first layer of the Great Fire-altar and explains the name Aṣāḍhā by giving its etymology through a mythical account. The gods and *asura*-s, sprung from Prajāpati, strove together. The gods noticed this particular brick and placed it on the altar. With the result, the gods conquered and drove away the *asura*-s from this universe. As the gods conquered (*asahanta)* with this brick, the brick is named Aṣāḍhā fr. √*sah* — 'to conquer, overpower' (*Śat. Br.* VII. 4.2.32,33). The etymology here is a mere play on the word *aṣāḍhā*, but it takes us to the firm conviction of the Vedic ritualists that the bricks used in the construction of the Great Fire-altar have importance due to specific purposes. There are many such bricks, Aṣāḍhā being one of them. Here the etymology of only one name, i.e. Aṣāḍhā, is taken into account and it can speak for other such names of the bricks.[19]

9. *Aśva* (Horse)

The etymology of the word *aśva* is stated variously.[20] But the two *arthavāda*-s which derive the word *aśva* from the root √*śvi* —'to swell, expand', are interesting. In the context of the Agniṣṭoma sacrifice, when the Śukra and Manthin cups are being made ready, the *Śat. Br.* states that he (priest or sacrificer) mixes the Manthin cup with barley and the *arthavāda* in this context is as follows. Varuṇa once struck king Soma directly in the eye and it swelled (*aśvayat*) to give rise to a horse. As the horse sprung from swelling, therefore it is called *aśva* fr. √*śvi* 'to swell' (*Śat. Br.* IV. 2.1.11). Another *arthavāda* occurs in the context of the Horse- sacrifice (Aśvamedha). Prajāpati's eye once swelled and fell out. From that was produced the horse. So the name *aśva*, as the eye had swelled fr. √*śvi* - 'to swell' (*ibid.* XIII. 3.1.1). The *arthavāda* ends here in saying that when a horse is offered in the Horse-sacrifice, the sacrificer restores the eye of Prajāpati and makes him complete in body. The same etymology occurs in the *Tait. Sam.* (V. 3.12.1) and (*Tait. Br.* I.1.5.4).

These two *arthavāda*-s, based on the etymology of the word *aśva* serve the specific purpose of glorifying the horse and also display the belief of the ritual-thinkers that as horse has directly come from a deity, it is fit to be sacrificed. As we have already noted, this belief in creation of things and beings from a Great Being, especially from his body-parts or body-liquids, is deep-rooted in the Vedic tradition right from the Puruṣa-sūkta (*RV* X.90), having parallels from other mythologies. The same belief is seen in the Brāhmaṇa-text in the case of Prajāpati and still much later in the Purāṇas in the case of Brahmā.

10. *Avadāna* (Sacrificial Portion Offered)

While dealing with the chief offerings in the context of the New-moon sacrifice, the etymology of the word *avadāna* is stated. It is said that a person who is born owes a debt to the gods. So he satisfies them (*avadayate* fr. *ava* + √*day*) for that debt by making offerings in the fire. Hence the sacrificial portion offered in the fire is called *avadāna* (*Śat. Br.* I.7.2.6). The *arthavāda* passage in this regard is important, for the *Śat. Br.* has here dwelt upon the concept of debts to be paid by a man. It is said that a man is born as owing a debt to the gods, to the seers, to the Fathers and to men. The debt to the seers can be paid off by the study of the Veda, that to the fathers by having offspring and that to the men by giving hospitality to them, when they arrive as guests (*Ibid.* I. 7.2.1-5). The debt to the gods can be paid off by offerings to them in the sacrificial fire, as noted above. Though the etymology of the word *avadāna* in the *arthavāda* passage is stated to glorify the sacrificial portion to be offered to the gods, it has enabled the composer of the Brāhmaṇa-text to speak about the belief in his times.

Kane directs our attention to the idea of debts, developed in India right from the Ṛgvedic times.[21] A prayer in *AV* expresses a wish to be free from the obligations (*anṛṇaḥ* lit. being free from debts) of this world, the next world and the third world (*AV* VI. 117.3; also *Tait. Br.* III. 7.9. 8). The *Tait. Sam.* states the details of these debts. A *brāhmaṇa* as soon as born, has a threefold debt *viz.* of studentship to the seers (*ṛṣi*-s); of sacrifice to the gods and of offspring to the manes (*pitṛ*-s). A person who has a son, is himself a sacrificer and has lived (in the past) as a pupil (in the preceptor's hermitage), is freed from his debt (*Tait. Sam.* VI. 3.10.5).[22] It is the *Sat. Br.* which has added to this list one more debt and that is the debt to men, as we have taken a note of. The *Mbh.* has pursued this idea. It states that men owe four debts *viz.* to the Fathers, gods, *ṛṣi*-s and to men in general. This debt to men is paid back by goodness (*ānṛśaṁsyena)* to all (*Mbh.* Ādi. 120. 17-20). The *Mbh.* at another place speaks of five debts *viz.* the three as noted above, the fourth to the *brāhmaṇa*-s and the fifth to the guests[23] (*ibid.* Anuśāsana 37.17). Kane rightly points out that this theory of spiritual debts being already in the air, the same sanctity came gradually to be transferred to one's promises to repay monetary debts and carry out other secular engagements.[24]

The *arthavāda* passage, explaining the word *avadāna* is hence important, for the belief it reflects in debts and there too the debt to men, which is the addition made by the *Śat. Br.* to the original list of three.

11. *Chandāṁsi* (Metres)

The etymology of the word *chandas* (Sing. No.) is stated from the root √*chad* - 'to cover' or 'to please'. The *arthavāda*-s occurring in the *Tait. Sam* and the *Jaim. Br.* take the word *chandas* from the root √*chad* - 'to cover'. The *Tait. Sam.* states that the gods, getting frightened at the fire-altar, built by Prajāpati, covered themselves with metres and then approached it. So the metres have the name *chandas* (*Tait. Sam.* V.6.6.1). The *Jaim. Br.* states that Prajāpati created gods and thereafter Death. Prajāpati advised the gods to cover themselves with metres by entering in them and thus protect themselves from Death (*Jaim. Br.* I. 283, 284). At both these *arthavāda*-s, the word *chandāṁsi* is traced to the root √*chad* - 'to cover'. The *Śat. Br.* gives the etymology of this word from the root √*chad* - 'to please'. The *arthavāda* here is as follows: 'Prajāpati having freed himself from Death, asked for food. The gods gave him food in the form of bricks, relating to metres (the name of the bricks - 'Chandasyā').' These bricks are put while building the Great Fire-altar in the Agnicayana rite. This Great Fire-altar having five layers is the body of Prajāpati with its five parts (hair, skin, flesh, bone and marrow), which is restored to him, as he became disjointed due to the great exertion of creating creatures.[25] To turn to the *arthavāda* again—'Metres are cattle and cattle are food. The metres (= cattle = food) pleased (*acchadayan* fr. √*chad* - 'to please') Prajāpati and so the name *Chandāṁsi*' (*Śat. Br.* VIII. 5.2.1).

These *arthavāda*-s, based on the etymology of the word *chandāṁsi*, no doubt bring out the importance of the metres.

As *mantra*-s are regarded to give full form (*rūpasamṛddha*) to the sacrifice and as they are composed to metres, metres occupy an indispensable position in the sacrifice.[26]

12. *Dakṣiṇā*-s (Gifts)

The etymology of the word *dakṣiṇā* occurs in the context of giving gifts (*dakṣiṇā*-s) to the priests in a sacrifice. The *arthavāda* is as follows. In a sacrifice, when priests press King Soma, they slay him. When they 'quiet' the victim (i.e. they kill him, but this killing is by smothering the sacrificial victim) they slay it. Again when they pound the offering (*havis*) with mortar and pestle and grind it with upper and lower grinding stones, they slay it. The sacrifice, when slain in this way, was without any vigour. By means of giving gifts (*dakṣiṇā*-s) to the priests, the gods invigorated (*adakṣayan*) the sacrifice. So the name *dakṣiṇā* fr. the root √*dakṣ* - 'to invigorate' (*Śat. Br.* IV. 3.4.1, 2).

The *arthavāda* here regarding *dakṣiṇā* based on the etymology of that word is obviously to stress the necessity and importance of giving gifts to the officiating priests, who had attained a status of gods among humans. The learned *brāhmaṇa*-s are said to be the human gods (*ibid.* II. 2.2.6; IV. 3.4.4; *Gop. Br.* II. 1.6).

The *arthavāda* echoes a belief of averting sin by giving gifts, especially when an incident of death or danger takes place. This practice is prevalent even in modern times and is seen when there is an eclipse of the sun and the moon, who are supposed to be in the clutches of the demon Rāhu (-Ketu). Here it is worthy of taking a note of the gifts given at the Prajātīrtha-muhūrta. It signifies the time of the childbirth when the navel-cord is yet to be cut. This means that the child is yet to be severed or separated from its mother and is not yet out of danger. Hence the gifts to secure longevity for the child and its safety at this critical moment.[27]

13. *Deva*-s (Gods)

Etymologies of the names of some gods:

This forms an important feature of the *arthavāda*-portions. To turn to the etymology of the word *deva.* As Prajāpati is the deity of sacrifice, he is regarded to have created gods from his mouth (Eggeling, J. - 'by the breath of his mouth).[28] The gods (*devāḥ*) were created by him while advancing towards the heaven (*div).* After creating the gods, there was as it were day-light (*divā*) for him (*Śat. Br.* XI. 1. 6.7). The etymology of the word *deva* is from the word *div* (heaven) as also from *divā* (day-light) indicating the shining lustre of the gods (*deva*-s), as heaven (*div)* and day-light (*divā)* have the same shining characteristic, the heaven being associated with the celestial luminaries (like the sun, moon and even stars) and the day-light having its very origin from the sun.

To turn to the etymologies stated to explain the names of individual gods —

In fact, the names and even epithets of Vedic gods etymologically derived by the Brāhmaṇa-texts and many centuries later by Yāska are to be viewed, taking into account the concept of 'name' and its history right from ancient times. As Gonda points out, a name is for primitive and archaic man no abstraction but an essential part of the bearer's personality and there is an intimate connection between this 'part' and his corporal appearance and physical faculties.[29] The ancient Egyptians even went so far as to regard the gods' names as their limbs.[30] Knowing the god's name or epithet, especially knowing the hidden meaning in it is thought to be the right key to have special power (over the god and through it) prosperity. The ritual-thinkers and later on Yāska took a recourse to etymology or etymological explanation with this very motif. Yāska says that without etymology, it is not possible to know the meaning of the *mantra*-s, and also to know the exact deity of the sacrifice or of the ritual (*Nir.* I.15, 18). The etymologies of gods' names stated by the Brāhmaṇa-texts form part of their *arthavāda*-portions but the exact purpose of these etymologies is to know a particular god in his particular aspect. Of the same name, the etymology can be one or more than one, depending upon the particular aspect of that god, which is to be given attention to. The etymologies of the names of gods, at times appearing far-fetched but supported with the explanation that 'The gods love what is abstruse', are therefore important.

(*a*) Agni — The *arthavāda*-account occurring in the context of the Agnicayana rite says that Prajāpati desiring to be 'many' and hence to procreate, entered the waters. There arose an egg. The embryo which was inside was created as the first (i.e. foremost, 'agram'). As it is called '*agri*' (being the first or the foremost), it is Agni (*Śat Br.* IV. 1.1.10, 11). This etymology later on served as a basis for the etymology stated by Yāska[31] and speaks of the foremost position occupied by Agni in the sacrificial context.

In the context of the rite of Agnicayana, a *mantra* from *RV* (VII. 8. 4a) and *Vāj. Sam.* (XII. 34a) speaks of Agni as that of Bharata (tribe)... *agnirbharatasya*....The *Śat. Br.* keeping to the tune of sacrifice says that here *bharata* is Prajāpati, for Prajāpati sustains (√*bhṛ* - 'to hold, sustain') the entire universe. Sāyaṇa on *RV* (VII. 8.4a) takes *bharata* to mean the sacrificer (*bharatasya yajamānasya)*. The *Śat. Br.*, through etymology of the word *bharata* brings in the concept of Prajāpati, who is the deity of sacrifice, i.e. Agni himself.

(*b*) Āditya-s — The etymology of this word occurs in the context of the sacrifice, performed by Janaka of Videha. It is said that the twelve months of a year are the Āditya-s, for they go (pass), while laying hand on everything here or taking (*ādadānāḥ* fr. *ā* + √*dā* - 'to take') everything from here (*Śat. Br.* XI. 6.3.8).

(*c*) Bṛhaspati and Brahmaṇaspati —In the case of the word Bṛhaspati, it is said that *Vāc* (Speech) is *bṛhatī* (fr. *bṛhat*

- 'great') and as the lord of Speech, the god is named Bṛhaspati (*Śat. Br.* XIV. 4.1.22; or *Bṛhad. Up.* I. 3.20).

While explaining the word Brahmaṇaspati, it is said that Vāc (Speech) is *brahman* and being the lord of Speech, the god is called Brahmaṇaspati (*ibid.* XIV. 4.1.23; or *Bṛhad. Up.* I. 3.21).

Bṛhaspati or Brahmaṇaspati is mainly a deity of prayers and is regarded as their lord. The etymology throws light on this aspect of the word.

(*d*) Candramas — In the context of Soma-sacrifice, the *Tait. Br.* dwells upon the etymologies of some deities. Prajāpati, as the mythical account tells us, created Indra. Indra asked for Prajāpati's lustre. Then he desired to have the moon and asked for it (*sa candram ma'āhareti prālapat)*. Here from the words *candram* and *me* ('*me*' dative of the pronoun *asmat),* the word *candramas* (meaning 'moon' fr. *candra* + *asmat)* is explained (*Tait. Br.* II. 2.10.3). As can be clearly seen, the word *'asmat'* does not exactly tally with the word *candramas,* though for the word *candra* there is no difficulty. But the principle seems to be that a person should give etymology on the basis of similarity between letter or syllables. This principle was laid down by Yāska after many centuries but as it seems, it was envisaged several centuries earlier than him by the composers of the Brāhmaṇa-texts.

(*e*) Indra — Nobody could counteract against the power (*indriyam)* of this lord (i.e. Indra). So the name Indra from the word *indriya* (*Tait. Br.* II. 2.10.4). Another etymology occurs in the *Śat. Br.* in a mythical account in the context of the Agnicayana rite. It is said that in the beginning, there existed the vital breaths. The vital breath in the midst was Indra. He by his power (*indriya)* kindled those vital airs. As he kindled (*indha* fr. √*indh* - 'to kindle') he is *indha* (kindler). Him they call 'Indra' mystically, for the gods love what is abstruse (*Śat. Br.* VI. 1.1.1,2).

At some places, some of the epithets of Indra are also explained with the help of etymology, as follows:

(*i*) Parameṣṭhin — As Indra became the foremost (*paramaḥ),* he is 'Parameṣṭhin', fr. *parama* + √*sthā* - 'to stay at the highest position', as Sāyaṇa rightly explains in his commentary on this passage (*Tait. Br.* II. 2.10.5).

(*ii*) Mahendra — In the context of one-day Soma-sacrifice, it is said that after killing Vṛtra, Indra became Mahendra (*mahat* + *indra* = *mahendra,* 'great Indra'). The *Jaim. Br.* here says that this is in line with the worldly way of calling a king (*rājan)*, 'a great king (mahārājaḥ) (Jaim. Br. II. 234).

(*iii*) Maghavat — The context is the Pravargya ritual. When Viṣṇu's head fell off and his body lay stretched out, Indra among the gods was the first to reach him. He encompassed Viṣṇu and became possessed of the latter's glory. He became Makhavat (*makha* = Viṣṇu = sacrifice). Makhavat is Maghavat, for the gods love abstruse (*Śat. Br.* XIV. 1.1. 9-13).

(*f*) Ka — Prajāpati created Indra as the youngest and lowest in status among the gods. But Indra wanted to be foremost among the gods. When he approached Prajāpati and asked for latter's lustre, Prajāpati reacted as to who would he himself be (*ko'ham syām),* after parting with his own lustre. Prajāpati hence is named Ka (*Tait. Br.* II.2.10.1,2).

(*g*) Rudra — The etymology is from the root √*rud* - 'to cry' = roar'; causal 'to cause to cry or yell'. The mythical account occurring as *arthavāda* states that the boy (*kumāra)* born of Prajāpati cried, for he was not given any name. So Prajāpati said that as the boy cried (*arodīt fr.* √*rud*), he be named Rudra (*Śat. Br.* VI. 1.3. 9,10). This *arthavāda* occurs in the context of Agnicayana, when the creation-account is stated. In the same context, when the Śatarudriya offering is enjoined, the *arthavāda*-portion states a similar etymology. When Prajāpati became disjointed, the deities except Manyu left him. As Prajāpati cried, his tears settled on Manyu. He became the hundred-headed, thousand-eyed, hundred-quivered Rudra. The other tear-drops that fell down, spread over these worlds in countless numbers by thousands. As they originated from crying (fr. √*rud* — 'to cry, yell, shout'), they were called Rudra-s (*ibid.* IX.1.1.6). The etymology stated here of the word Rudra or Rudra-s, aptly throws light on the fierce nature of Rudra, who is the great roarer and is known for his howling or yelling.

The ten vital breaths and the spirit (i.e. self) of a man are said to be Rudra-s, for when they depart from this mortal body, they cause wailing— *rodayanti* fr. √*rud* (causal) - 'to cause to cry or wail' (*ibid.* XI. 6.3.7).

(*h*) Soma — Soma is praised in the morning Soma-pressing in an *arthavāda*-passage based on etymology. It is said that Soma decided not to make available his whole self to the gods, as he was their sacrificial food (in the form of Soma-juice). Hence he kept his most pleasing form aside. But the gods ordered him to draw that form of his unto himself. He drew it saying that form was 'my own' (*svā me).* Hence the name Soma (*Śat. Br.* III. 9.4.22). The etymology not warranted by grammar, is important for the belief underlying it. Soma has two forms — one in the form of the 'divine drop' (*indu* or *drapsa)*, which has the potentiality to give heavenly life of immortality and the other in the form of Soma-juice, offered to the gods in the sacrifice.[32]

(*i*) Sūrya — Seeing Indra possessed of power and lustre, the gods said to one another that Indra being powerful would protect them. The word here is *suvīrya* for 'powerful'. The word *sūrya* is derived from the word *suvīrya* (*Tait. Br.* II. 2.10.4). This occurs in the context of

Soma-sacrifice, when the mythical account deals with the world of gods and the creation of Indra by Prajāpati.

(*j*) Vasu-s — The etymology of the word *vasavaḥ* occurs in the context of the sacrifice, performed by Janaka of Videha, when he intended to give a gift (*dakṣiṇā*) of thousand cows to the most learned *brāhmaṇa*. While giving an answer to the question asked by Śākalya (to test Yājñavalkya's knowledge), Yājñavalkya states the etymology of the word *vasavaḥ*. He says that Agni, Earth, Vāyu (Wind), Mid-region (*antarikṣa*), Āditya (Sun), Heaven, Moon and the stars are the *vasavaḥ* (Vasu-s), for they cause all this universe to exist fr. √*vas* (causal) - 'to cause to stay, exist' (*Śat. Br.* XI. 6.3.6). The etymology brings out that these are the very foundations of the universe.

14. *Hiraṇya* (Gold)

This etymology occurs in the *arthavāda* passage in the context of the Agnicayana rite, while enjoining the placing of a golden replica of man in the lowest layer of the altar. It is said that after creating the universe, when Prajāpati was disjointed (being terribly exhausted), his pleasing form went out. The gods then placed that pleasing form into Prajāpati and thus restored him. The gods were pleased (*aramanta fr.* √*ram*) with his pleasing form (*ramyāyām tanvām*). So it is called *hiramya* and *hiramya* is abstrusely called *hiraṇya* for the gods love what is abstruse (*Śat. Br.* VII.4. 1.16). The *Śat. Br.* equates gold with light (*jyotiḥ*) and also with immortality (*amṛtam*) in the same context (*ibid.* VII. 4.1.15). The *arthavāda* based on the etymology of the word *hiraṇya* states the importance of gold used in rituals. Gold is connected to Agni-Prajāpati as also to the sun due to its shining yellow colour.[33]

15. *Iṣṭakāḥ* (Bricks)

The etymology of this word is stated by the *Śat. Br.* in the context of the Agnicayana rite. A long mythical account precedes this etymology, which describes the sacrifice performed by Prajāpati of five animals *viz. puruṣa* (man), horse, bull, ram and he-goat. The heads of these animals were put on the altar and their trunks were floated on the water. Having gathered the clay that had settled, from this water, Prajāpati made bricks and baked them by fire (*Śat. Br.* VI. 2.1.4-9). Prajāpati saw these bricks (*iṣṭakāḥ)* after offering (*iṣṭvā* fr. √*yaj* - 'to offer in sacrifice, to perform a sacrifice') the animal. If the bricks are made before or without an animal-sacrifice, they are *an-iṣṭakāḥ,* i.e. not the bricks worth the name (*ibid.* VI. 2.1.10). The *Śat Br.* enjoins here that in the Agnicayana rite, one must make bricks only after performing an animal-sacrifice. The *arthavāda* here based on the etymology of the word *iṣṭakāḥ* is important, for it throws light on the practice followed in the Agnicayana rite in those times.

16. *Kūrma* (Tortoise)

The etymology of the word *kūrma* occurs in the context of the Agnicayana rite, when a live tortoise is to be put in the lowest layer of the Great Fire-altar to be built. It is said that Prajāpati having assumed the form of a tortoise created the beings. As he created, he made (*akarot* fr. √*kṛ* - 'to do, make'). So he is called *kūrma* (*Śat. Br.* VII. 5.1.5).

The etymology serves to connect Prajāpati to *kūrma* (tortoise), the latter regarded as the form of the former. The incarnation of Viṣṇu as tortoise, which is seen, in the *Mbh.* and the Purāṇa-s, can be traced to the *Śat. Br.,* as we have noted above. Tortoise is said to be the same as the yonder sun, which he puts on the altar (*ibid.* VII. 5.1.6). The concept initially based on the circular size of the tortoise (with its feet and head giving the idea of rays), gets connected to the worldwide belief regarding tortoise as a solar animal.[34] The etymology of the word *kūrma* and the identification of the *kūrma* (tortoise) with the yonder sun (Prajāpati = tortoise and tortoise = the yonder sun) make Prajāpati — Agni-Prajāpati—the deity of sacrifice — on par with the yonder sun. This is in tune with the thought in the Brāhmaṇa-texts that Agni is the form of the sun. In fact, the whole edifice of the Agnihotra-rite is based on this.[35] The firm belief has been that when the sun sets, it enters Agni which is its womb and from this womb the sun comes out in the morning. The *Śat. Br.* states that when the sun sets, then Agni is the light and when the sun rises, then Sūrya is the light (*Śat. Br.* II. 3.1.36).

The etymology stated in the *Śat. Br.* of the word *kūrma* is significant and takes us to the well-known belief—nay the firm conviction—of the Brāhmaṇa-texts.

17. Mahāvrata (Name of a Rite)

In the context of the Mahāvrata rite ('festival', as seen from the popular elements incorporated in it), which is the last day but one in the Gavām-ayana *sattra* (extending over 12 months of 30 days each), occurs the etymology of the word *mahāvrata* (*Pañc. Br.* IV. 10.1; *Śat. Br.* IV. 6.4.2). The *Pañc. Br.* says that Prajāpati created the creatures, which were obviously in his own body and being emptied out, fell down. The gods thought of bringing him mighty *(mahat)* food or food fit for the ritual *(vratam),* which would restore him. They brought to him food which ripens during a year. This food, partaken by him, restored him. Hence the name Mahāvrata fr. *mahat* - 'great' or 'mighty' and *vratam* - 'food'. The *Pañc. Br.* here gives another etymology (IV. 10.2) by saying that Prajāpati himself is great *(mahat)* and this food is this rite *(vrata).* According to the *Ait. Ār.* (I. 1.1), Indra having killed Vṛtra became great *(mahān)* and the rite *(vrata)* for him is the Mahāvrata.

These etymologies are significant for they point out that the name of the rite Mahāvrata could invite more than one etymologies to commend it. In the Mahāvrata rite, there are some details which may be traced to the secular tradition. The name Mahāvrata seems to be somewhat arbitrary, nevertheless proper, as the rite proper has blended several details in it, which might have crept in it at a later stage to make it *mahat* ('extensive', as to spread it over the whole day).

18. *Makha* (Sacrifice)

The etymology occurs in the *arthavāda* passage of the *Gop. Br.*, while eulogising the sacrifice (*Gop. Br.* II. 2.5). It is said that in the word *makha,* the letter *ma* means *mā* (*mā iti pratiṣedhaḥ),* which is a prohibitory indeclinable and the letter *kha* means a 'hole' (*chidram),* i.e. defect or shortcoming of sacrifice, indicating the prohibition of such a defect in the sacrifice. The occasions and factors making a sacrifice defective are enumerated by the *Gop. Br.* in prose portion, which is followed by five verses bringing out the same thought (*ibid.).* The etymology stated here of the word *makha* clearly brings out the firm conviction of the ritualists regarding the perfection to be achieved at every stage while performing a sacrifice, sacrifice being viewed as the very foundation of the whole existence.

19. Om (Sacred Utterance)

The etymology of the sacred utterance Om occurs in the *Ait. Br.* in the context of Agnihotra (rite of offering in fire at the morning as well as after the sunset), when expiation is to be prescribed. It is said that Prajāpati practised austerity. He created the three worlds *viz.* earth, mid-region and heaven. From these in turn came Agni, Vāyu and Āditya, from which came the three Veda-s *viz. RV, YV* and *SV*. From *RV* came the sacred utterance Bhūḥ, from *YV* came Bhuvaḥ and from *SV* came Svar. From these three Vyāhṛti-s (i.e. Bhūḥ, Bhuvaḥ and Svar), came the three letters *viz. a, u* and *m.* These three letters combined gave rise to the sacred syllable Om. The syllable Om is uttered every time before uttering the three Vyāhṛti-s. Om is said to be the heavenly world as also the One, who shines (*Ait. Br.* V. 32 = 25.7). The mythical account coming by way of *arthavāda* noted above traces the origin of the syllable Om, thus bestowing divine status on the syllable, which has to precede the three Vyāhṛti-s.

The *Gop. Br.* derives the syllable Om from the root √*āp* - 'to obtain' (*sarvam āpnoti).* It refers to the opinion of some, who derive this syllable from the root √*av* - 'to protect.' The *Gop. Br.* remarks that the derivation of Om from √*av* bears a phonetic affinity; but, the derivation from *āp* comes close to the meaning, which is more important *(Gop. Br.* I.1.26).

It has to be pointed out that the etymology of the word Om attempted here is to glorify the said syllable, which does not normally convey any specific meaning, but carries a mystic significance with it. This sacred syllable is identified with the highest principle. It is true that Om is the only syllable, which represents all the letters of the alphabet. It starts from the letter *a,* which comes from the glottis and ends with the letter *m,* which is labial. The syllable Om, in this way, houses all the letters of the alphabet, which are uttered right from the opening of the mouth, till it is closed. In this sense, the etymology of the syllable Om from the root √*āp*, stands to reason, as pointed out by the *Gop. Br.* (I.1.26), which we have noted above.

In the Upaniṣadic literature, Om came to be identified with Speech (*Jaim. Up.* I.1.6), as also the quintessence of the three Veda-s (*Chān. Up.* I.9) and pervading the whole creation (*Māṇḍ. Up.* I.1).

It has to be accepted that the syllable Om in itself has no specific meaning, though efforts have been there to attach highest philosophical meaning to this syllable by sectarian thinkers with a doctrinal viewpoint. It is believed that the syllable Om through its three letters, represents the three functions of Brahman *viz.* creation, preservation and destruction and therefore in later times, Om came to mean the Trinity *viz.* Brahmā, Viṣṇu and Śiva through its three letters *a, u* and *m.*[36]

The syllable or the sound Om itself without any meaning, seems to be in imitation of the sound of thunder, which is regarded as the first sound in the universe, when the celestial cow, shedding (rain-) waters, bellowed — *gaurīrmimāya salilāni takṣatī* (*RV* I. 164.41a). This cow is the Vāc, i.e. mid-region Speech.[37]

20. Pragātha (A Combined Metre)

An interesting etymology of the word *pragātha* occurs in the *Jaim. Br.* A Pragātha is a combination of two verses either in Bṛhatī and Satobṛhatī metres or in Kakubh and Satobṛhatī metres. Of these two verses, there are made three verses by repetition. With the Bṛhatī verse preceding, the Pragātha is called a Bārhata Pragātha and with the Kakubh verse preceding, it is named a Kākubha Pragātha.[38] On these Pragātha-s are based the *sāman*-s such as Bṛhat, Rathantara, Kāleya and on most of the Pragātha-s, the Brahmasāman-s.[39]

An *arthavāda*-passage occurs in the *Jaim. Br.* pointing out the etymology of the name Pragātha. It is said that whatever the gods performed in sacrifice, the *asura*-s imitated. The gods knowing this said that they would make the threefold Veda mixed with a *gāthā.* The *asura*-s exclaimed that such never happened. So they left off the threefold Veda. From that threefold Veda, the gods made the essence (*rasa*) swell for the *gāthā.* That became the Pragātha. As the essence *(rasa)* swelled (*prāvṛhanta* fr. *pra* + √*vṛh*) for the *gāthā*, that is the very nature of the Pragātha (*pra* fr. *prāvṛhanta* and *gātha* fr. *gāthā,* making the word Pragātha). In the same passage, the *Jaim. Br.* states another *arthavāda* that in the beginning, *ṛc* and *gāthā* were alike. They entered a wager (*āji*). The *ṛc* made the essence (*rasa)* swell for the *gāthā.* That became the Pragātha (*Jaim. Br.* III. 41).

The etymology of the word Pragātha fr. *pra* + √*vṛh* - 'to swell', with the mention of the word *gāthā* is important, as it shows the status, which the *gāthā* had achieved by the time of the *Jaim. Br.* Here the *gāthā* is believed to be full of the essence of the threefold Veda or of the *ṛc.* It has to be noted that in the Brāhmaṇa-texts following the tradition of *RV* as also Black *YV*, the *gāthā*-s did not enjoy such a position. The *Ait. Br.* differentiates between *ṛc* and *gāthā*, calling the first *daiva* (divine) and the latter *mānuṣa*, i.e. human (*Ait. Br.* VII. 18 = 33.6), but incorporates in its accounts several *gāthā*-s and also *yajñagāthā*-s. This shows the flexible attitude of the *Ait. Br.*, which is of the *RV*-tradition.[40] The *Tait. Br.* certainly undermines the status of the *gāthā* through an old account, which states that once the gods separated the dirty part from the Divine Speech as also from the food. The dirty part from the Divine Speech became the *gāthā*-s and the *nārāśaṁsī*-s, while that of the food became wine (*Tait. Br.* I.3.2.6). The *Tait Br.* belongs to the *Tait. Sam.* of the Black *YV*, which deals with ritualistic matters and leaves very little or practically no scope for any other matter to be included in it. On this background, the status bestowed on the *gāthā* by the *Jaim. Br.* belonging to *SV*, while stating the etymology of the word Pragātha stands unique as it equates the *gāthā* with the threefold Veda or *ṛc*. The reason for this lies in the very nature of *SV* comprising the *sāman*-s to be sung and also some chants which are given the name Grāmageyagāna and Āraṇyagāna. This shows the readiness of *SV* to accept some secular melodies or chants, which probably did not originate in the ritualistic circles.[41] And about the *Jaim. Br.* where actually the etymology of the word Pragātha occurs. This Brāhmaṇa-text of *SV* includes much secular matter[42] as supporting the ritual at hand and so the importance of *gāthā* while stating the etymology of the word Pragātha.

21. Pravargya (Rite); also Gharma (The Pot Used in the Rite)

In the context of the Pravargya ritual, the *Śat. Br.* states interesting etymologies of the words *gharma* and *pravargya*, through a mythical account (*Śat. Br.* XIV. 1.1.4-10). It is said that Viṣṇu became the most excellent of the gods. However, he could not control his pride. Once when he was resting his head on the end of his bow (which was stretched), the ants on the words of the gods, gnawed his bowstring. With the result, the ends of the bow, springing asunder cut off Viṣṇu's head. Viṣṇu's head fell making the sound *ghṛṅ* (the sound here speaks of the velocity of the action of falling). On falling, Viṣṇu's head became the yonder sun. In the Pravargya ritual, the pot used for boiling milk (Mahāvīra-pātra, which is of a particular shape) is called Gharma and the etymology of this word is stated from the word *ghṛṅ* (*Śat. Br.* XIV. 1.1.10). When Viṣṇu's head fell off, the rest of his body lay stretched (*prāvṛjyata*). The name Pravargya of the ritual is explained from *pra* + √*vṛj*- 'to stretch out.' This *arthavāda*-account of Viṣṇu's head being cut off is stated to show that the very sacrifice (Viṣṇu = sacrifice) has lost its head and this head is replaced by the Pravargya ritual. The *Śat. Br.* says that the Pravargya (ritual) is the head of sacrifice (III. 4.4.1 —*yajñasya...śiraḥ pravargyaḥ).* The point can be probed further, ultimately to come to the head of the very sacrificial beast (identified with sacrifice), which is never offered as an oblation in fire and in fact is never seen after being cut off.[43]

22. *Ṛṣi*-s

A somewhat different etymology of the word *ṛṣi* is met in the *Śat. Br.*, when prior to the exposition of the Agnicayana rite, the (*Śat.*) Brāhmaṇa-text touches the point of creation of the universe. There was in the beginning the non-existence (*a-sat)* and it was in the form of vital breaths, which are called *ṛṣi*-s. Sāyaṇa rightly explains in his commentary on this passage that the *asat* at the beginning of the universe was in the form of the subtle body only, i.e. vital breaths (*kevalaliṅgaśarīramevāsīdityarthaḥ).* The *Śat. Br.* explains the epithet *ṛṣi* attributed here to the vital breaths (*prāṇa*-s), by saying that the vital breaths wore themselves out (√*riṣ*) [44] or were active (acc. to Sāyaṇa, who takes the word from the root √*ṛṣ* - 'to go' — *ṛṣī gatau)* with their toil and austerity (*Śat. Br.* VI. 1.1.1).

The *arthavāda* stated here through etymology tries to solve the problem of creation, tracing the beginning of creation to non-existence (*asat*). But this non-existence seems to be existence, but without any distinguishing marks and so in the form of subtle body, i.e. the vital breaths. The *arthavāda* points out how even bound by the set-up of rites and rituals, the ritualists could lay their hands on mythological problem.

23. Śakvarī (Name of Metre also that of Verses)

The *arthavāda*-s occurring in this connection praise the potential strength of these verses. The *Ait. Br.* enjoins the singing of Mahānāmnī verses (*ṛc*-s)[45] on the Śākvara *sāman*. These Mahānāmnī verses actually are in the Anuṣṭubh metre (having four feet). In order to justify their having the nature of the Śakvarī metre (having seven feet) and their being sung on the Śākvara *sāman*, the *Ait. Br.* takes the help of *arthavāda* based on the etymology of the word *śakvarī* and bestows the nature of Śakvarī on these verses. It says that Prajāpati with the help of these Mahānāmnī verses (*ṛc*-s) was able (*aśaknot*, fr √*śak*- 'to be able to') to create everything, after creating all these worlds. These Mahānāmnī *ṛc*-s thus became Śakvarī-s (fr. √*śak*), i.e. having the nature of Śakvarī-s (*Ait. Br.* V.7 = 22.2). The *Kauṣ. Br.* while stating the *arthavāda* in the same context, i.e. the Mahānāmnī *ṛc*-s (which are employed in the Pṛṣṭhya Ṣaḍaha),[46] says that by these *ṛc*-s Indra had strength to slay Vṛtra; therefore they are the strong ones (*śakvaryaḥ* fr. √*śak*)— powers *śaktayaḥ* (*Kauṣ. Br.* XXIII. 2). Yāska while giving the etymology of the word '*śakvaryaḥ*' refers to the same myth of Indra slaying Vṛtra and derives the word in the same way from the root √*śak* (*Nir.* I.8). The *Pañc. Br.* in the context of the Pṛṣṭha-lauds of the fifth day in the Soma-sacrifice, has an interesting mythical account as *arthavāda* in this connection. Indra wishing to slay Vṛtra, approached Prajāpati for help. Prajāpati took valour and strength out of the metres and gave those to Indra saying: 'Be able (*śaknuhi;* fr. √*śak*) by means of this (to kill Vṛtra).' The Śakvarī-verses have their name from this (*Pañc. Br.* XIII. 4.1). These etymologies of the name Śakvarī based on the root √*śak* - 'to be able to', speak of the potentiality of these *ṛc*-s when used as *mantra*-s.

24. Saṁvatsara (Year)

The etymology occurs in the context of New-moon and Full-moon sacrifices. As the sacrifices are enjoined to be performed for all the year round, the year is attributed a special place. Prajāpati says that he has created a counterpart of himself in the form of year, for both the words *saṁvatsara* (year) and Prajāpati consist of four syllables (*Śat. Br.* XI. 1.6.13). Here is stated the etymology of the word *saṁvatsara.* Prajāpati, who created the gods, thinks to himself that everything (*sarva)* he has obtained by stealth (*tsar*). This is *sarvatsara,* for *sarvatsara* is the same as *saṁvatsara* (Year). A person who knows this, is not overcome by any evil, which steals upon (*tsar)* him by magic art and he also overcomes him on whomsoever he practises magic art *(ibid.* XI. 1.6.12).

Even from the non-ritualistic and day-to-day point of view, this etymology of the word *saṁvatsara* appeals, striking a philosophical note, Is it not the year which steals the life of man slowly and lessens his stay in the world? 'Yes', as suggested by the *Śat. Br.*!

25. Sautrāmaṇī (A kind of Sacrifice)

The *Śat. Br.* glorifies the Sautrāmaṇī sacrifice with an *arthavāda,* which explains the name Sautrāmaṇī through etymology. The mythical account stated as *arthavāda* runs as follows. Tvaṣṭṛ had a three-headed (thus having three mouths) and six-eyed son, named Viśvarūpa. Indra cut off these heads of Viśvarūpa. Tvaṣṭṛ becoming furious at the slaying of his son, brought Soma-juice and excluded Indra from having it. Indra, even though not invited, consumed what Soma there was in the tub. But Soma hurt him and flowed in all directions from the openings of his body except the mouth. Being thus purged by Soma Indra walked about tottering. The Aśvins cured him by the offering in the sacrifice. With this (sacrifice) he was supplied with everything, for Soma is everything. The gods were joyous that the two Aśvins saved Indra, who then became the 'well-saved' (*sutrāta).* So the sacrifice, in which this offering was given, is named Sautrāmaṇī (*Śat. Br.* V. 5.4. 2-12).

Here the word Sautrāmaṇī is derived from the root √*trai* - 'to protect, save', with the prefix *su.* The same etymological explanation occurs in the *Śat. Br.* at another place. But here the reference is to the story of Indra and Namuci. It is said that when Indra slew Tvaṣṭṛ's son Viśvarūpa, Tvaṣṭṛ brought Soma-juice, for carrying out witchcraft against Indra. Indra drank that Soma-juice, which was a prohibited one being for the sacrifice by Tvaṣṭṛ. With the result, Indra's vital power flowed away from his every limb. The *asura* Namuci having sought this opportunity seized upon Indra's vital power, his Soma-drink, his food. The gods approached the two Aśvins and the goddess Sarasvatī, who then restored to Indra his vital power and saved him from evil. Indra became '*sutrāta*' (well-protected). Hence the name Sautrāmaṇī (*ibid.* XII. 7.1.1-14). Here also the *arthavāda* is based on the etymology from √*trai* with *su (ibid.* XII. 7.1.14).

26. *Sikatā* (Sand)

In the rite of Agnicayana, when the Gārhapatya altar is to be established, the sacrificer or the priest pours sand into the fire-pan (*ukhā).* Here the sand (*sikatā)* is said to be the seed of Agni Vaiśvānara, which he sprinkles (fr. √*sci* — 'to sprinkle') into the fire-pan, i.e. *ukhā,*[47] which is called the 'womb' or the birthplace of Agni (*Śat. Br.* VII. 1.1.41).

The etymology of the word *sikatā* from √*sci* — 'to sprinkle', warranted by grammar reflects one of the sexual images or symbols, with which the Vedic ritual texts are replete.[48]

27. *Śiras* (Head)

The etymology of this word occurs in the context of Agnicayana rite. The *Śat. Br.* by way of *arthavāda* states the following mythical account. In the beginning, there was non-existent (*asat)* in the form of vital breaths. Indra in the form of vital breath kindled the other vital breaths and they in turn created seven separate persons (*puruṣa*-s*)*. The vital breaths then made one person out of those seven persons. They concentrated the life-essence (*rasa)* of those seven persons and that became the head of that one Person (*Śat. Br.* VI. 1.1.1-3). The *Śat. Br.* here states two etymologies of the word *śiras* (head). It is said that as the vital breaths concentrated the excellence (*śrī)* in the head, therefore the name *śiras.* As the vital breaths resorted to (√*śri* - 'to resort') the head, therefore the name *śiras* (*ibid.* VI. 1.1.4). As the *Śat. Br.* further states, this head is the head of Prajāpati and it is in the form of fire deposited on the built up altar. On this same head, all the gods are dependent (*śrita* fr. √*śri* — 'to depend'), for on it the offering is made for all the gods. Hence also it is called *śiras* (*ibid.* VI. 1.1.7). It is obvious that the etymologies here eulogise the head (*śiras),* which is said to be *uttamāṅga* (the best limb of the body) of a person. The *arthavāda* passage here based on the etymologies, glorifies the fire deposited on the altar, the context being of the Agnicayana rite.

28. *Śmaśāna* (Burial-place)

An interesting etymology of the word *śmaśāna* occurs in the *Śat. Br.* It is said that when a person dies, he is a corpse (*śava)* and for that corpse, food (*anna)* is prepared. This food for the corpse (*śavānna)* is mythically called *śmaśāna.*

Another etymology occurs here only of the same word. It is said that *śmaśāḥ* are the eaters amongst the Fathers (*pitṛ*-s). In the yonder world, these *śmaśa*-s (eaters) destroy the good deeds of a person, who has had no burial-place prepared for him. It is for them, that he prepares food (*anna)* when any person (in the family) dies. This *śmaśānna* (food for the *śmaśa*-s) is mystically called *śmaśāna* (*Śat. Br.* XIII. 8.1.1). The etymologies here are not a mere play on words though they may appear to be so. They reflect a belief of the society in preparing a burial-place for the dead, which practice has been indispensable in the Hindu society even in modern times. A reference to the eaters amongst the Fathers makes the burial-ground have a mystic air about it and so it is believed to be a resort of evil spirits, which is an idea commonly attached to all burial-grounds. The *arthavāda* based on etymology, while praising the *vidhi* of preparing a burial-place helps us to know the social belief of those times.

29. ***Svapna*** **(Dream)**

The etymology coming by way of *arthavāda* occurs in the context of the *vidhi*-statement of laying down two Lokampṛṇā bricks in the Agnicayana rite. Such Lokampṛṇā (lit. space-filling) bricks are laid down each time as they set up the layer (*Śat. Br.* X. 5.2.8). To glorify the pair of the Lokampṛṇā bricks, the *Śat. Br.* turns to the pair of eyes as a parallel. The person in the right eye is said to be the same as Indra and the person in the left eye is the same as Indrāṇī. These two descend to the cavity of heart for union with each other. When they reach the end of union, the man sleeps (*ibid.* X. 5.2.9, 11). The *Śat. Br.* here lays down that one should not therefore forcibly awaken a man who sleeps, for then he would disturb these two, i.e. Indra and Indrāṇī in the two eyes, while they are enjoying union (*ibid.* X. 5.2.12). The man in the eye is the breath (*prāṇa),* for it is he that leads forward (*praṇayati)* all these creatures. The vital breaths (*prāṇa*-s*)* are his own (*svāḥ).* When he sleeps, the vital breaths take possession of him as his own (*svā apiyanti)*. Therefore the word is *svāpyaya,* which they abstrusely call '*svapna*' (sleep), for the gods love the abstruse (*ibid.* X. 5. 2.14). This *arthavāda* passage based on the etymology of the word '*svapna*' points out the belief of the people at that time regarding sleep, which maintains that when a man sleeps, all his vital breaths are concentrated in his chief breath *(prāṇa)* which is the person in the eye. This appears to be rather simple, when compared to the metaphysical concept of 'self' elucidated in the *Bṛhad. Up.*, which is the Upaniṣad of the same tradition, i.e. the white *YV* (*Vājasaneyi-Saṁhitā*). The *Bṛhad. Up.* states that there are two stages - that of this world and that of the other world, and in between is the stage of dream (*svapnasthānam).* A person (i.e. the self) when stationed in this stage (which can be said to be a 'joining' one — *sandhye sthāne tiṣṭhan*) can see both the worlds. He, i.e. Self, being himself awake, can 'see' all the *bhāva*-s, inner and outward, i.e. enjoys all the inward feelings as well as the outward pleasures in the dream (*Bṛhad. Up.* IV. 3.9-13). Thus the original concept of the man in the eye occurring in the *Śat. Br.* in its *arthavāda* portion, has paved the way for the later metaphysical concept about dream.[49]

30. *Ukhā* (Fire-pan)

The etymology of the word *ukhā* occurs in the context of Agnicayana rite, when the sacrificer is said to carry Agni in the fire-pan (*ukhā).* The fire-pan is said to be these worlds. In ancient times, the gods carried Agni by means of these worlds and now the sacrificer carries him with the fire-pan. In those times, the gods dug out these worlds by means of the performance of sacrifice. As they dug out (*udakhanan* fr. *ud* + √*khan* - 'to dig out') these worlds, the fire-pan representing the worlds is called *utkhā.* But they call it *ukhā,* for the gods love what is abstruse (*Śat. Br.* IV. 7.1.22, 23). The *arthavāda* here based on etymology is no doubt stated to commend the fire-pan, which is regarded as the 'womb' or the mother of the fire-god (Agni).[50]

31. Upavasatha (Day of Fast)

The day preceding the rite of Agnyādheya (the rite of establishing the three fires *viz.* Gārhapatya, Āhavanīya and Dakṣiṇa) as stated in the *Śat. Br.* (*Śat. Br.* II. 1.4.1), as also the day preceding the Agniṣṭoma (the principal or model Soma-sacrifice), as stated by the same text (*ibid.* III. 9.2.7), is called the Upavasatha day. On this day, certain rules are to be followed by the sacrificer (as also by his wife), one of them being, taking food in the daytime only and not at the night-time (*ibid.* II. 1.4.1).

In order to glorify the Upavasatha day, the *Śat. Br.* states the etymology of the word *'upavasatha'*, which throws light on the belief prevalent in the ritualists' circle. It is said that as the gods know the mind of man, they can guess that the sacrifice is to take place the next day. So all gods come and stay with the sacrificer in his house on the earlier day, so that they can get their respective shares the other day. So the earlier day is called the Upavasatha day (fr. *upa* + √*vas*—'to stay near'). On this day, the sacrificer is advised to take food only in the daytime, observing fast at the night-time (*ibid.* II. 1.4.1,2).

It is important to note that in the later tradition, the same day came to be recognised as the day of fast for the sacrificer.[51]

The *Śat. Br.* states two viewpoints—one of Āṣāḍha Sāvayasa, who opines that as the gods are staying with the sacrificer on the Upavasatha day without taking any food, so he also should not eat anything and thus observe total fast (*ibid.* I.1.1.7, 8). The other opinion is of Yājñavalkya, who maintains that in the absence of eating anything, the sacrificer would as though become one, who sacrifices for the manes (i.e. performs *pitṛkarman),* and if he eats, that would mean eating before the gods. Therefore he should eat that, which would not be counted as eaten. He should eat only what grows in the forest—may be forest-plants or fruit of trees (*ibid.* I.1.1.9, 10).

The *arthavāda* stating the etymology of the word *upavasatha* is important, for it explains the basic idea of fast observed by the sacrificer. It provides a logical explanation also for the fast observed in India by people, as a part of vow followed by them. As seen above, the idea in the Upavasatha is of the gods coming and staying together with the sacrificer in one and the same abode. This same idea was followed in the ritual named Uposatha in the *saṅgha* of the Buddhist monks, when the monks used to gather at one place once in fifteen days on the Full-moon and the New-moon days. However, this coming together was for giving confession by the guilty monk to the senior-most monk, of the transgression of rules, which were laid down for the monks. At this gathering, there also used to be the recitation of the rules of Vinaya (or the *śikṣāpada*-s) laid down for the monks. The point to be noted is that the idea of coming together in the Uposatha in Buddhism is a loan from the Vedic ritual.[52]

32. Vaṣaṭ (Sacred Utterance)

The sound Vaṣaṭ is to be uttered immediately after the offering prayer (Yājyā) (i.e. at the end of that prayer) but prior to the actual offering of oblation to the deity.[53] The *Ait. Br.* (III. 5 = 11.5) calls the Vaṣat a vessel of gods. The *Śat. Br.* calls the utterance Vaṣaṭ a vessel of gods *(devapātram)* and gives an analogical instance from the worldly life saying that just as men offer food to others keeping it in a vessel, similarly while offering oblations to a deity, after the offering verse (Yājyā), the word Vaṣaṭ is uttered and following it, the actual offering is made. If one makes oblation prior to the utterance of Vasaṭ, the oblation would be as good as dropped on the ground (and thus would go waste), says the *Śat. Br.* (I.7.2.13).

The etymological explanations of the sound Vaṣaṭ are interesting and help us to know the exact nature as well as the probable origin of the term Vaṣaṭ. The *Kauṣ. Br.* having the expression *ṣaṭ* in view, of the utterance Vaṣaṭ, says that by the utterance of Vaṣaṭ, he pleases the seasons, which are (*ṣaṭ)* in number (*Kauṣ. Br.* III. 5). According to the *Ait. Br.*, the sound Vaṣaṭ is to be uttered as Vauṣaṭ (Vau + Ṣaṭ). Sāyaṇa in his commentary on this passage of the *Ait. Br.*, says that 'Vau' meaning 'yonder' signifies the 'sun' and Ṣaṭ, i.e. 'six' signifies the seasons. Thus the priest places the sun in the seasons and establishes the sacrificer in the seasons (*Ait. Br.* III.6 = 11.6 and Sāy.'s comm. on it). The *Ait. Br.* here quotes the view of Hiraṇyadat Baida,[54] for another explanation of the term *ṣaṭ*. The *Śat. Br.* takes the call Vaṣaṭ as Vauṣaṭ and says that the two words here are *vaug* and *ṣaṭ*. Sāyaṇa in his comm. on this passage explains that Vaug is really Vāg. Speech (Vaug = Vāg i.e. Vāk) is said to be the semen and this semen is sprinkled in the seasons, which thereby procreate all the subjects (*Śat. Br.* I.7.2.21). The *Śat. Br.* states the same etymology at another place (*ibid.* I.5.5.21). At some other places, the *Śat. Br.* says that he places the fire in the fire-pan on the newly built fire-altar in the Agnicayana rite with the sound Vaṣaṭ, for Vauk is Agni and Ṣaṭ is the six-layered or sixfold food (*ibid.* X. 4.1.3, 14, 20). Eggeling and Weber try to derive the form Vaṣaṭ from a verb.[55]

The etymological explanations such as Vau + Ṣaṭ or Vaug + Ṣaṭ show that they are arbitrary explanations in the setting of *arthavāda* and only prove that Vaṣaṭ is a unit of phonemes, not having any morphological basis. With its force and strength being identified with the thunderbolt, Vaṣaṭ can be compared with certain utterances, which occur at the end of some Tantric formulas (*mantra*-s). The etymologies of the word Vaṣaṭ lead us to the conclusion that Vaṣaṭ could be one of the oldest, symbolic, non-meaningful yet powerful Tantric utterances.[56]

33. Vighana (A Special One-day Sacrifice)

The *arthavāda,* stating the etymology of this word, runs as follows. Formerly when Indra was ruling, the Maruts who formed his subjects did not honour him. In order to punish them, Indra thought of this one-day sacrifice and set at naught (fr. *vi* + √*han*) the adverse behaviour of the Maruts towards him. Hence this one-day sacrifice is named Vighana, fr. *vi* + √*han* - 'to kill completely' (*Tait. Br.* II. 7. 18.1).

The etymology of the word and also the *arthavāda* are important from the mythological point of view. Maruts are regarded as the helpmates of Indra, so much so that the epithet Marutvat is practically attributed to Indra alone (*RV* V. 42.6; IX. 65.10). However in *RV* itself, a note of discord between Indra and the Maruts occurs at a couple of places (*ibid.* I. 170. 2; cf. 171.6). The *arthavāda* from the *Tait. Br.*, taking the help of etymology supports this rare detail from *RV* and hence is important.

34. *Yajña* (Sacrifice)

The etymology of the word occurs in the context of the morning Soma-pressing. It is said that the pressing of Soma (Soma-shoots) amounts to the death of Soma, as he is slain being pressed. When they spread him in sacrifice, they produce him or cause him to be born. As Soma is born (*jāyate* fr. √*jan* - 'to be born'), being spread (*tāyamānaḥ* fr. √*tan*- 'to spread') also moving (*yan* fr. √*i*—'to go, move'), we have the name *yañja,* which is the same as *yajña* (*Śat. Br.* III. 9.4.23).

The *arthavāda* here, giving the etymology of the word *yajña,* actually commends the *vidhi* of the morning Soma-pressing and Soma. Here the material (*dravya)* Soma-juice from the triad - *dravya* (material), *devatā* (deity) and *tyāga* (the ritual of offering) constituting the sacrifice, is identified with the very sacrifice (*yajña).* The image of Soma has made possible the etymology of the word *yajña.* The etymology here unfolds the very idea, that lies at the basis of performing a sacrifice. It is not only a rebirth of Soma as stated here or of the sacrificer or rejuvenation of Agni-Prajāpati in the Agnicayana rite, but it is the rebirth and thus the procreation of everything that is sought to be achieved by the performance of sacrifice. The etymology of the word *yajña* thus goes a long way in explaining the firm conviction of the Vedic ritualists.

The etymologies discussed above can ably speak for many such etymologies, which occur in the ritual-texts. These are not a mere play on words but they reflect the beliefs, convictions and practices of the then society in the Vedic age. At times we may not be sure about the exact root at the basis of a form, say the word *āhuti*[57] and there may not be the help of the Brāhmaṇa-text in that direction, but the etymology can give a philosophical thought, as we have noted in the context of the word "Āhuti" Again the name of a god, when explained etymologially, can be a mirror to show different aspects of that god.[58] To understand the exact nature and qualities of a particular god in order to have power over him, so that he may favour the sacrificer, was not an easy task. We notice in the *Chān. Up.*, Uṣasti Cākrāyaṇa admonishing the various priests for their ignorance about the deities praised by them (*Chān. Up.* I. 10). This shows that even at the times of the Upaniṣads, ignorance to some extent, about the exact nature or identity of the deities had set in among the sacrificial circles. Visualising such a condition, the Brāhmaṇa-texts might have provided some etymologies. On the whole, etymologies form a part of the mega-plan of the Brāhmaṇa-texts of commending the rituals, through *arthavāda*-s.

The composers of the Purāṇa-s in later times treaded on the same path, by stating the etymologies of names of gods and goddesses, demons, sages, beings and things in the world. These etymologies given in simple language, at times standing as a mirror to the beliefs of those times, speak of the efforts of the Purāṇa-s to reach the common masses, which was their aim.[59]

NOTES AND REFERENCES

1. One such work is by Fatah Singh, *The Vedic Etymology,* The Sanskriti Sadan, Kota, 1952. The work does not strictly restrict itself to the etymologies from the Brāhmaṇa-texts.

2. *Nir.* I.13 - *puruṣam puriśaya ityācakṣīran* |
3. *Śat. Br.* XIII. 6.2.1..... *ime vai lokā pūḥ* |
ayameva puruṣaḥ | *yo'yam pavate* | *so' syām puri śete* | *tasmāt puruṣaḥ* |
4. Whitney, W.D., *Atharva-Veda-Saṁhitā* (tr. with comm.), Vol. II, HOS Vol. 8, Reprint 1984 (1905), Delhi, p. 571. *AV* X.2.28 cd, 30 cd.
5. On Yāska's own authority, there were at least 16 predecessors before him, as he mentions them in course of discussion. But he made all of them recede to the background.
6. *Nir.* II. 1
7. *Ibid.* I.9 — *adhvara iti yajñanāma/ dhvaratirhiṁsākarmā tatpratiṣedhaḥ* |.
also the commonly occurring statement - *yajñiyā hiṁsā dharmasādhanam* |
8. Keith taking into account the expression here -
ye vai panthāno yā srutayastā vā ūtayaḥ-
'paths and passages are *ūti*-s', translates further statement as - 'verily thus are they the roads to heaven of the sacrificer', thus taking the word *ūtayaḥ* as 'ways'. Keith, A.B., *Rigveda Brahmanas* (tr.), HOS Vol. 25, 2nd Reprint, Delhi, 1981 (1920), p. 108.
9. *Ait. Br.* III. 34 = 13.10; *Jaim. Up. Br.* II. 4.2.8; *Gop. Br.* I.1.7; *Bṛhad. Up.* I. 3.19.
10. Bloomfield, M., *The Atharvaveda,* Starassburg, 1899, p. 107.
11. (Mrs.) Dange, S.S., "Ṛgvedic Accounts", *Myths of Creation,* ed. by (Mrs.) Dange, S.S., Bombay University Pubn., Bombay, 1987, pp. 7-11.
12. *ibid.,* pp. 12-17, for later Vedic and Brahmanical accounts.
13. *ibid.,* pp. 22-27, for Epic and Puranic accounts.
14. (Mrs.) Dange, S.S., "Speech and its Aspects", *Aspects of Speech in Vedic Ritual,* Aryan Books International, New Delhi, 1996, pp. 1-35.
15. *Nir.* VIII. 6 — *āpriyaḥ kasmāt / āpnoteḥ prīṇātervā* / fr. √*āp* - 'to get, obtain' and √*prī* - 'to please'; and the etymologies from the Brāhmaṇa-texts noted by us.
16. For the terms *śastra, stotra, stoma* and *stobha* employed in the context of *sāman*-s, see Kane, P.V., *Hist of Dh.S.,* Vol. II., pt. II, BORI, Poona , 2nd reprint, 1974, pp. 1181-82.

Stoma means a group of verses (usually three) which are increased to 15, 17, 21, etc. by repetition in various patterns, which are called Viṣṭuti. These patterns differ in the order and number of repetitions. *Ibid.,* p. 1182.

17. For the metres and the chants of the Ārbhava-pavamāna laud, see *Pañc. Br.* XIII. 4&5.
18. (Mrs.) Dange, S.S., *Aspects of Speech in Vedic Ritual,* pp. 190-200.
19. Dūrvā brick - the name derived from the root √*dhūrv* - 'to undo'; the name Dhūrvā mystically called Dūrvā (*Śat. Br.* VII. 4.2.12).

    Svayam-ātṛṇṇā brick - the word is self-eloquent as it signifies the naturally-perforated brick (*ibid.,* III. 4.2.1 ff.).

    Two Retaḥsic bricks - 'seed-shedding bricks' (*ibid.,* VII. 4.2.22).

    Viśvajyotis brick — 'all-light bricks (*ibid.,* VII. 4.2.25). Apasyā bricks — water-bricks (*ibid.* VII.5.2, 40, 41), obviously from the word *'apas'* meaning 'water'. Muhūrtā bricks—from the word *muhūrta* (*ibid.* X. 4.2.18, 27). These bricks straightway (*muhu*) save (√*trai*); they are called *muhūrtāḥ* (*ibid.* X. 4.2.18).

    Lokampṛṇā bricks — Even being small, they fill (*āpūrayanti* - the root in the word is √*pṛ* - *pṛṇāti*) these worlds or spaces (*loka*) (*ibid.* X. 4.2.18).

    These are some of the names of the bricks (totalling 10,800), to give an idea.
20. *Śat. Br.* XIII. 1.2.7; *Tait. Br.* III. 8.7.2; III. 8.13.2; *Ait. Br.* V.1 = 21.1. Here the etymologies are stated from the root √*aś* - 'to pervade'.
21. Kane, P.V., *op. cit.,* Vol. III, 2nd ed., Poona, 1973, pp. 414 ff.
22. The context here is of animal-sacrifice. The word in the passage of *Tait. Sam.* (VI.3.10.5) as also in that of *Śat. Br.* (I.7.2.6) is *avadayate*, to explain the word *avadānam.* Keith translates the word *avadayate* as he 'performs', vide, Keith, A.B., *The Veda of the Black Yajus School entitled Taittiriya Sanhita,* pt. 2, HOS Vol. 19, p. 526. He says — "This (debt) he performs (*avadayate*) by these cuttings off, and that is why the cuttings-off (*avadāna*) have their name" (*Tait. Sam.* VI. 3.10.5). Eggeling translates the word *avadayate* as he 'satisfies', though in the note he says that the word is really derived form *ava-dā* (*do*), 'to cut off', vide Eggeling, J. *The*

Śatapatha Brāhmaṇa, pt. I, SBE Vol. 12, Delhi, 1988 (1882), p. 191, note 1. Whitney states the root √*day*—'to share', and says that is a secondary form of the root √*dā*—'to divide', from which it is hardly worth separating. See Whitney, W.D., *The Roots, Verb-Forms and Primary Derivatives of the Sanskrit Language*, American Oriental Society, Connecticut, 1945 (Leipzig, 1885), p. 70.

23. The *Mbh.* through the myth of Oghavatī and the guest strikes a note of sexual hospitality to be given to a guest (Anuśāsana *parvan* 2.37 ff.). This myth is to be interpreted as pointed out by Dange, on the basis of Kaimutika *nyāya* (rule of explanation), meaning 'what if... when, even. So, even when a wife can be given to a guest, what if one gives other precious things?' See Dange, Sadashiv A., *Myths from the Mahābhārata*, Vol. 2, Aryan Books International, New Delhi, 2001, pp. 94-104 for the detailed myth and p. 103 for his statement quoted above.
24. Kane, P.V. *op. cit.,* Vol. III., p. 416.
25. *Śat. Br.* VI. 1.2.12-17.
26. (Mrs.) Dange, S.S., "Metres and their Magic", *Aspects of Speech in Vedic Ritual*, pp. 36-112.
27. (Mrs.) Dange, S.S., *The Bhāgavatā Purāṇa — Mytho-Social Study*, Ajanta Pubns., Delhi, 1984, p. 139 note 55, where quotations are given from Jaimini, Vyāsa and *Viṣṇudharmottara P. Viṣṇudharmottara P.* says — *acchinnanāḍyām yad dattam putre jāte....| saṁskāreṣu ca putrasya tadakṣayyam...||*: also see *Pār. G.S.* I. 16.2-3, ed. by Pt. G. Nene, Benares, 1925.
28. Eggeling, J., *op. cit.,* pt. V, SBE Vol. 44, Motilal Banarsidass, Delhi, 1978 (1900), p. 13 tr. of *Śat. Br.* XI. 1.6.7.
29. Gonda, J., *Epithets in the Ṛgveda,* The Hague, The Netherlands, 1959, Intrn. pp. 32-33.
30. Leeuw, G. Van der, *Religion in Essence and Manifestation,* London, 1938, p. 148.
31. *Nir.* VII. 15 - *agniḥ kasmāt, agraṇīrbhavati - agram yajñeṣu praṇīyate |*
32. For detailed discussion, see Dange, Sadashiv A., "The Advent of Soma," *Images from Vedic Hymns and Rituals,* Aryan Books International, New Delhi, 2000, pp. 115-25.
33. (Mrs.) Dange, S.S., "Symbolism of Gold", *Hindu Domestic Rituals — A Critical Glance,* Ajanta Pubns., New Delhi, 1985, p. 27 f.

34. (Mrs.) Dange, S.S., *The Bhāgavata-Purāṇa—Mytho-Social Study*, pp. 238-40.
35. *Kauṣ. Br.* XXV.5; *Śat. Br.* II. 3.1.3ff; *Jaim. Br.* I.4, 5 & 7; also *Ait. Br.* V. 29-31 = 25.4-6 for an interesting discussion about the exact time when the offerings in the Agnihotra are to be given—whether before the rise of the sun or after it.
36. Fatah Singh, *op. cit.*, pp. 115-16.
37. (Mrs.) Dange, S.S., *Aspects of Speech in Vedic Ritual*, Intrn., p. xvii.
38. Caland, W., *Pañcaviṁśa Brāhmaṇa*, 2nd ed., Delhi, 1982 (1931), p. 50, note 1 on *Pañc. Br.* IV. 4.1.
39. *ibid.*, p. 50, note 2 on *Pañc.* Br. IV. 4.1.
40. In the *Ait. Br.* occur several *gāthā*-s. The story of Śunaḥśepa is said to have hundred *gāthā*-s (*Ait. Br.* VII. 18 = 33.6), though only ten *gāthā*-s figure here, the remaining being the prose-portion (*ibid.* VII. 13-18 = 33.1-6). The *yajñagāthā*-s found in the *Ait. Br.* are - *ibid.* V. 30 = 25.5; V. 31 = 25.6; VII. 9 = 32.8; VIII. 21 = 39.7, etc.

    It is in this Brāhmaṇa-text that we find the chants of the Sarpa-seer mixed by the gods with their *ṛc*-s. This was done by the gods to remove the poison in the chants of the Serpent - seer (*Ait. Br.* VI.1 = 26.1). For more details see (Mrs.) S.S. Dange, "Some Non-Vedic Rituals in the Vedic Tradition", *Proceedings* of the All-India Oriental Conference, XXXII Session (Ahmedabad 1985), p. 166 f.
41. The *Āp. Dh. S.* (I. 3.10.19) includes singing of a *sāman* in the sounds forbidden (for being heard) at the time of the daily *(svādhyāya)* recitation of the *mantra*-s, the other sounds being barking of a dog, yelling of a fox or wolf, sound of an owl, roar of a tiger and crying. The *sāman* referred to above must be of a secular origin - definitely non-ritualistic origin. So its prohibition.

    The *Sāmavidhāna Br.* in its second part is associated with songs, concerning magical rites.
42. The second and third *kāṇḍa*-s of *Jaim. Br.* are important from the legendary and geographical points of view.
43. For details, (Mrs.) Dange, S.S., "The Severed Head in Myth and Ritual", *Annals*, BORI, Amṛtamahotsava Vol., Vols. LXXII & LXXIII (1991 & 1992), Poona, 1993, pp. 487-96; for the head of the sacrificial beast, pp. 493-94.

44. See Eggeling, J., *op. cit.,* pt. III, SBE Vol. 41, Motilal Banarsidass, Delhi, 1989 (1894), p. 143. tr. of *Śat. Br.* VI. 1.1.1
45. For Mahānāmnī verses, see Sāyaṇa on *Ait Br.* V. 7 = 22.2.
46. Pṛṣṭhya Ṣaḍaha (a period of six Soma days) forms part of the Daśarātra (ten nights' or days' period), the latter forming part of the Dvādaśāha or twelve days' performance. For more details about Pṛṣṭhya Ṣaḍaha, see Eggeling, J., *op. cit.,* pt. II, SBE Vol. 26, Motilal Banarsidass, Delhi, 1988 (1885), p. 402 f, notes 2 and 4.
47. *Ukhā* (fire-pan) is said to be the mother of the fire-god ad is prepared out of clay in such a manner as to show teats. *Śat. Br.* VI.5.2.16-18.
48. For more information on this point, see Dange, Sadashiv A., "Sex-coupling in Sacrifice", *Sexual Symbolism from the Vedic Ritual,* New Delhi, 1979, p. 63.
49. For more about 'Dream' in the Vedic-Hindu context, see Dange, Sadashiv A., "Dream (Svapna) in the Vedic Concept", *Vishveshvaranand Indological Journal,* VVBIS & IS, Panjab University, Hoshiarpur, Vol. XXX, pts. i-ii, June-Dec. 1992 (pub. in 1997), pp. 1-6, and also by the same author, "Dream, Myth and the Hindu Context", *Annals* of BORI, Vol. LXXIX (1998), Pune, 1999, pp. 61-82 (being the R.G. Bhandarkar Anniversary Address delivered at BORI, Pune, on Sunday, 7th Sep. 1997).
50. See note 47 *supra.*
51. *Śaṅkh. Ś.S.* XII. 32; *Manu S.* XI. 190; *Yāj. S.* I. 175; III. 190; also Eggeling, J., *op. cit.,* pt. I, SBE Vol. 12, Delhi, 1988 (1882), p. 5, note 1.
52. (Mrs.) Dange, S.S., *Bauddha Dharma āṇi Tattvajñāna,* Continental Pubn., Poona, 1980, pp. 65-68.
53. A sacrificial oblation consists of four factors *viz.* (i) the invitatory prayer (Anuvākyā); (ii) the offering prayer (Yājyā); (iii) the Vaṣaṭ call; and (iv) the deity for which the sacrificial oblation is destined (*Śat. Br.* I.7.2.7).
54. *Ait. Br.* III. 6 = 11.6. According to Hiraṇyadat Baida, the six (*ṣaṭ)* which are established are *viz.* (i) established on the atmosphere; (ii) atmosphere on the earth; (iii) earth on the waters; (iv) waters on truth (*satya);* (v) truth on the holy power (*brahman*); and (vi) holy power on fervour (*tapas).*
55. Eggeling, J. tries to derive the word Vaṣaṭ (or Vauṣaṭ) from the root √*vah* - 'to bear, carry', taking it as a *seṭ* - subjunctive

form, while Weber proposes to derive it from the root √*vakṣ* - 'to grow, increase.' For this, see Eggeling, J., *op. cit.*, pt. I, SBE Vol. 12, Motilal Banarsidass, Delhi, 1988 (1882), p. 88, note 2.

56. For the full exposition of the concept of Vaṣaṭ, see (Mrs.) Dange, S.S., "Mystic Utterances in the Vedic rituals", *Aspects of Speech in Vedic Ritual,* pp. 146-63.
57. The word *āhuti* in *Śat. Br.* XI.2.2.6. The root for the form *āhvayati* can be *ā* + √*hvā* or √*hve*. According to Whitney, it is √*hvā*. See Whitney, W.D., *The Roots, Verb-Forms and Primary Derivatives of the Sanskrit Language,* Lithoprint, Michigan, 1950 (1885), p. 206, while for this form, the root is stated to be √*hve* by Sir Monier Monier-Williams in his *A Sanskrit-English Dictionary.*
58. See Bhattachary, Dipak, "Indian Etymologists and their Etymologies", Lectures delivered under the Wilson Philological Lectureship Endowment, University of Bombay (Mumbai), 1987, pub. by the School of Vedic Studies, Rabindra Bharati University, Kolkata, 2002, pp. 42-44.
59. See (Mrs.) Dange, S.S., *Puranic Etymologies and Flexible Forms* (*Some Glimpses*), Viveka Pubns., Aligarh, 1989, pp. 7-121.

CHAPTER 2

Sun, Moon and Constellations

The sun has unique importance as is seen in the Vedic ritual texts. Though only one, when the sun rises, every person thinks that the sun has come up (i.e. arisen) towards him only (*Tait. Sam.* VI. 5.4.2; also *Kāṭh. Sam.* XXVIII. 2). In the New-moon and Full-moon sacrifices, in the concluding rites, there is enjoined looking towards the east, for the east is the region of the gods (*Śat. Br.* I.9.3.13, 14). He then looks up to the sun, for the sun is the final goal (*gatiḥ*) and the safe resort (*pratiṣṭhā*) (*ibid.* 15). To that final goal the sacrificer thereby goes.

The *Tait. Br.* lays down that the rite of Odanasava[1] should be undertaken on the constellation Rohiṇī but that also at the rise of the sun. This is obviously because all the creatures become delighted at the sunrise (*Tait. Br.* II. 7.9.4).

In the context of setting up of Agni-s (Fires) in the rite of Agnyādheya, the *Śat. Br.* states that one can take the sun for one's constellation (*nakṣatra*) and set up fires. The *arthavāda* points out that there were so many different powers (*kṣatra*-s). But as soon as the sun arose, he took away ($\bar{a} + \sqrt{d\bar{a}}$) from them their energy and their power, rendering them powerless. So is the sun called Āditya (*Śat. Br.* II. 1.2.18, 19). The *Jaim. Br.* states together with the power (*kṣatra*) of the constellations, various other items got by the sun from several entities. This supports the etymology of the word *āditya* from the root ($\bar{a} + \sqrt{d\bar{a}}$) - 'to get, obtain' (*Jaim.*

Br. III. 358). The *Jaim. Br.* points out that they mention the sun by the word *ādita* as he gets or obtains (fr. *ā* + √*dā*) several things and that is the nature of being *āditya* (*ibid.* III. 356). The *Jaim. Br.* explains the word '*sūrya*' as '*so'ryaḥ*' which leads to the word '*sorya*' and the same is known as Sūrya, for the gods love what is abstruse. The *Jaim. Br.* says that the devotees praise him (i.e. the sun) as 'you are our *arya;* you are our sustainer—'*bhartā*' (*ibid.* III. 357).

The relation between the sun and the moon is explained in an *arthavāda*-passage, which occurs in the context of the New-moon and Full-moon sacrifices. The *arthavāda* explains the purpose of offering *sānnāyya*[2] in these sacrifices, to Indra as the Vṛtra-slayer. It is said that the sun (one who shines yonder) is Indra and the moon is no other than Vṛtra. The former is of a nature hostile to the latter and so though the moon (i.e. Vṛtra) previously rises at a great distance from the sun (i.e. Indra), he on the New-moon night glides towards him and enters into his open mouth (*Śat. Br.* I.6.4.18).[3] The *arthavāda* is significant as it brings out the mythical fight of Indra and Vṛtra, as based on the cosmic drama of the two important luminaries *viz.* the sun and the moon. Elsewhere the moon and the sun are called father and son respectively. The moon is situated yonder (*paraḥ),* while the sun is nearer (*aparaḥ).* Both the luminaries have attained the place of importance among the gods (*Jaim. Br.* III. 368).

In the context of the Gavām-ayana sacrifice, while speaking about the Viṣuvat day (the middle-most day of the Gavām-ayana *sattra*) a mythical account occurs in the *Jaim. Br.* which runs as follows. In the beginning, the sun was here in the *cātvāla.*[4] He excessively shone on everything. The gods being afraid of his extreme heat apprehended that he would burn everything. Hence they decided to carry him high to the upper region (i.e. heaven). They carried him up together with the six seasons and placed him in the Viṣuvat day, where he shines brightly. He is Viṣuvat (i.e. Viṣuvān). As the spokes of a chariot-wheel are to the axle of the chariot, so are all the worlds connected with him, i.e. the sun (*ibid.* II. 5).

A mythical account dealing with the sun occurs in the context of the Agniṣṭoma sacrifice, in which at one stage, the Bahiṣpavamāna laud (*stotra)* is to be chanted. It is to be chanted in an expiatory oblation for the sin incurred due to the drops of Soma-juice split during the pressing. The oblation hence is called *viprḍ-homa* (i.e. *viprṣām homaḥ).* The laud noted above is to be chanted near the *cāṭvāla.* The mythical account in this regard states that in the beginning (prior to rising) the yonder sun was at the *cātvāla.* The seasons embraced him and ascended from here to the heavenly world, where the sun burns firmly established in the seasons. The priests by chanting the Bahiṣpavamāna laud as though embrace the sacrificer and ascend from here to the heavenly world obviously with him (*Śat. Br.* IV. 2.5.9). The *Pañc. Br.* also speaks in the same way. By chanting the Bahiṣpavamāna laud, the gods bore the sun from the *cātvāla* (where he was earlier) to the world of heaven. When the priests chant the Bahiṣpavamāna laud while looking at the *cātvāla* they bear the sacrificer to the world of heaven (*Pañc. Br.* VI. 7.24).

This *arthavāda* is important for several points—

(*i*) It speaks of the power of *mantra* (here the Bahiṣpavamāna laud), which is a common feature of many such *arthavāda*-s in the Brāhmaṇa-texts.[5]

(*ii*) When speaking about the *cātvāla* (where the sun was placed earlier), it indicates a search for the nocturnal sojourn of the sun, after its setting in the west and later on its rising in the east. The *cātvāla* is situated outside the altar in the north-east corner. The journey of the sun could be from west→north→north-east→east.

(*iii*) It shows the inseparable connection between the sun and seasons, the sun being the maker of the latter.

(*iv*) It shows the ultimate goal *viz.* heaven, of the sacrificer while performing a sacrifice.

(*v*) Lastly it speaks of the help rendered by the priests to the sacrificer, in his achieving his ultimate goal.

The *arthavāda*-s in the context of the Agnihotra rite clearly point out the close association of the sun and Agni.

When the sun sets and goes down, Agni (fire) is the light. When the sun rises, Sūrya is the light . Hence in the evening, while offering libation, the *mantra* is, 'Agni is the light, the light is Agni, Svāhā!' In the morning, the *mantra* accompanying the offering rite is, 'Sūrya (the sun) is the light, the light is 'Sūrya, Svāhā!' (*Vāj. Sam.* III. 9, 10) so says the *Śat. Br.* (II. 3.1.30, 36). That Agni and the sun are the aspects of one and the same principle of cosmic fire and light is also brought out by the *Jaim. Br.*, when it says that this world is endowed with light due to Agni and that one (i.e. the other world—heaven) with the sun (*Jaim. Br.* I. 232). The *Jaim. Br.* makes this point clear in the context of the Agnihotra rite by saying that whatever sin is committed by him during daytime, that the sun makes him to do and the sin committed by him in night, that Agni wants him to do (*ibid.* I. 9). Sūrya and Agni, both being important, each of them decides to offer his own self to the other. When the sun sets, he offers himself to Agni. Agni follows the sun when the latter rises. Thereby Agni offers himself to the sun (*ibid.*).

The *Tait. Br.* states that as oblations were offered for Agni, the sun desired to have such oblations. So both Agni and the sun coming to agreement decided that the evening offering would be for Agni and the morning one for the sun (*Tait. Br.* II. 1.2.6). If one offers prior to sunrise in the morning and has already offered at the previous evening to Agni, both these offerings virtually belong to Agni. So the morning offering to the sun should be after sunrise (*ibid.* 7). The *Ait. Br.* takes up for discussion this point of Agnihotra and states decisively taking by way of *arthavāda* the instance of two wheels of a chariot. Day and night are the two wheels of the Year-chariot. A person who offers in the morning prior to the rise of the sun, travels with only a one-wheeled chariot. To gain both the wheels (for the chariot), the evening offering should be in the night (when after the sunset, darkness sets in), while the morning offering should be after the sun is actually seen, i.e. has arisen (*Ait. Br.* V. 31 = 25.6).

The *Tait. Sam.* has an interesting passage of *arthavāda*, which states that once the sun went from this world to the yonder world. But he thought of this world and came back but was afraid of Death. So he praised Agni, who made him go to the heavenly world (*Tait. Sam.* I.5.9.4, 5).

As has been noted above, the whole edifice of the Agnihotra rite is conceptually built up[6] on the basic idea that when the sun sets, he enters Agni, which is his womb and from this womb the sun comes out in the morning.[7]

The curiosity to know about the sojourn of the sun when he sets and the anxiety mixed with apprehension for his return on the next morning is not unique to our land. In Egyptian mythology, the idea is that the sun-god Ra goes on a night voyage by boat every evening and reappears in the morning. In the Japanese mythology, the sun-goddess Amaterasu hides herself in a cave and the gods ponder over a device, in which they become successful, to take her out from that cave to save the whole universe from darkness. A folk-ritual regarding Lāl Thakur ('Red Lord') represented by a small decorated earthen doll to be sailed every year in a small dummy boat to cultivate and rule over the island property, is worth noting in this connection. To this Lāl Thakur his devotees bid farewell by saying —

'O Lāl ! Sail to-day but return tomorrow
Every year thy boat repeat to row!'

Here the 'Red Lord' is none other than the sun, who sets on journey in a boat.[8]

The same anxiety about the rising of the sun continues in the Purāṇa-s, which believe that the demons named Mandeha try to devour the sun at sunset every day (*Brahmāṇḍa P.* I. 2.21.110 ff; *Skanda P.* I.2.38.17-19) and also try to eat him as he rises (*Garuḍa P.* I. 205. 61-62). Only when the water consecrated at the *sandhyā*-ritual by the Gāyatrī *mantra* is thrown at them, they get burned.[9]

The thought that the sun is a dispeller of evil, is marked in an *arthavāda*-passage in the *Śat. Br.*, in the context of the Agnyādheya rite (the rite of establishing sacred fires). For setting up the fires, the *Śat. Br.* lays down spring season for a *brāhmaṇa,* as spring is a symbol of priesthood; summer season for a *kṣatriya,* for summer is a symbol of nobility; and rainy season for a *vaiśya,* for rainy season is a symbol of common people (*Śat. Br.* II. 1.3.5). The *Śat. Br.* states that these three seasons *viz.* spring (Vasanta), summer (Grīṣma) and rains (Varṣā) represent the gods and autumn (Śarad), winter (Hemanta) and dewy season (Śiśira) represent the Fathers (*ibid.* II. 1.3.1). The *Śat. Br.* says that both these classes of seasons have the evil dispelled from them by the sun as soon as he rises, for he is the dispeller of evil. Hence the sacrificer should set up his fires at any time, when he feels called upon to sacrifice (obviously because the sun is the protector from evil). He should not postpone it from one day to the morrow, for who knows the morrow of man? (*ibid.* II. 1.3.9). The *arthavāda* passage here is significant, for it speaks of the eternal truth of the momentariness of life (*ibid.—ko hi manuṣyasya śvo veda).*

Some significant ritual metaphors leading to the beliefs about the sun occur in the *arthavāda*-passages in the context of the rite of Agnicayana. In this rite, the sacrificer has to carry fire in the fire-pan (Ukhya Agni, the fire-pan being called *ukhā)* during the period of consecration. He also wears a gold plate (*rukma)* round his neck. This gold plate (*rukma)* is said to be the truth, which is able to sustain the fire in the fire-pan (*ibid.* VI. 7.1.1). The next *arthavāda*-passage speaks of several beliefs about the sun. As gold plate is the truth, the truth is the same as the yonder sun. The plate is of gold. Gold is light and so is the sun, light (*jyotiḥ)*; gold is immortality and so is the sun, immortality (*amṛtam).* The gold plate is round, for the sun is round (*parimaṇḍalaḥ).* The gold plate has twenty-one studs (*ekaviṁśatinirbādhaḥ)* and so is the sun twenty-first (*ekaviṁśaḥ).*[10] The twenty-one studs of the gold plate are outside, for the studs are the sun's rays, which are always outside (*ibid.* VI. 7.1.2).

The sacrificer, as already noted above, hangs the gold plate round his neck. Together with it, there is Ukhya Agni in the fire-pan, by means of a netting.[11] The *arthavāda* occurring in the *Śat. Br.* in this connection runs as follows. The gods were afraid that the *rakṣas*-es would destroy their Agni. They made the yonder sun to be Agni's protector, standing by his side. The sacrificer, following this act of the gods, makes that plate to be Agni's protector by his side (*ibid.* VI. 7.1.5). The firm conviction at the basis of this *vidhi* is that the sun and Agni (here sacrificial Ukhya Agni) are closely related. The *Jaim. Br.* metaphorically calls the Trivṛt *stoma* to be chanted earlier (in the day) in the Atirātra sacrifice (the sacrifice performed in the day and extended over to the whole night) to the Bahiṣpavamāna melody as Agni, and at twilight the Trivṛt *stoma* (appropriately making Sandhistotra - *sandhi* meaning 'joint' here 'twilight') to be chanted to the Rathantara melody as Āditya.[12] By Agni this (terrestrial) world is full of light and by Āditya (i.e. the sun) the yonder world (*Jaim. Br.* I. 232). In the *arthavāda*- passage from the *Śat. Br.* (VI. 7.1.5), which is already noted above, there is no direct mention of the sun. The mention of the gold plate serves the purpose, for gold stands as a symbol of the sun in ritual.[13] The belief in the equation 'sun = Agni = gold' has undoubtedly brought the gold plate in the *vidhi,* which figures in the Agnicayana rite.

In the context of the New-moon and Full-moon sacrifices, it is enjoined that after uttering the invitatory verse (i.e. *mantra)* in the Gāyatrī metre and the offering verse in the Triṣṭubh metre, he should offer after the sound Vaṣaṭ has been uttered. The sound Vaṣaṭ is said to be the yonder shining sun and the sun is said to be the same as Death (*Śat. Br.* XI. 2.2.5). It is said that whatever is there on this side of the sun, all that is held by Death and he who builds (the Great Fire-altar in the Agnicayana rite) on this side is as though held by Death (*ibid.* X. 5. 1.4) and he surrenders his own self unto Death. But he who builds it there above conquers the recurring Death (*ibid).* The same thought is expressed by the *Jaim. Br.* when it says that the sun verily is Death, the one who injures. He pacifies the sun with oblations, when he offers Agnihotra. By this he attains nearness with the sun — to be at a place where the sun is and also to become one with the sun (*Jaim. Br.* I. 27).

In the context of the Gavām-ayana *sattra,* the *Jaim. Br.* speaks of the sun, at length, as a consecrated sacrificer. The downward and upward rays of the sun are mentioned as his beard and hair respectively and the day and night created by him are said to be the black antelope hide, which he carries. The day is said to be the white portion of the antelope hide and the night is the black portion of it. The orb of the sun stands for the waters and the food therein as the nectar. The quarters are his wives. The three quarters (excepting the south) transgress him. But the southern quarter follows him. Hence even if he rises from the northern side, to the south only he turns. Hence the dear wife of the sacrificer should be made to sit near him in the southern direction. The man in the orb (of the sun) is full of lustre and endowed with metres (i.e. having the power of *mantra*-s). He is the vital breath, Indra, Prajāpati and he is the one consecrated (*Jaim. Br.* II. 62). At another place, also, the *Jaim. Br.* speaks of the sun as a sacrificer consecrated for a sacrifice and describes him in the same way, though not so elaborately. It is said that the wife of this Sun-sacrificer is the goddess Dawn and Soma is his draught (*ibid.* III. 359). The sun is said to be *dīkṣita* as he has made his stay (*kṣayam)* in the heaven *divi* fr. *dyu* (*ibid.* III. 358). Here the etymology of the word *dīkṣita* is from the word *dyu* (heaven) and the root √*kṣi* - 'to stay, reside'. The *Jaim. Br.* adds that he who performs a sacrifice attains a stay in the heaven (*ibid.).* And as the sun (the heavenly *dīkṣita)* is accompanied by his wife, one should be accompanied by one's wife while sacrificing (*ibid.* III. 359). This brings out the importance of the sacrificer's wife in the sacrificial ritual.

As the context noted above is of the Gavām-ayana sacrifice, it will be proper to get some idea about that sacrifice and see the *arthavāda*-passages connected with it. The *Pañc. Br.* states a mythical account by way of *arthavāda* and tries to explain the name of the sacrifice. Once upon a time, the cows held a sacrificial session (of the Gavām-ayana). In the course of ten months they got horns. Some of them decided to continue the session during the remaining two months also (i.e. total twelve months). The horns of these cows got curved in the course of twelve months. However, they obtained all food (*Pañc. Br.* IV. 1.1,2). The *arthavāda* is stated obviously to explain the word Gavām-ayana. But as the word *go* also denotes the rays of the sun, the rite is related to the course of the sun.

Gavām-ayana is a series of Soma-sacrifices lasting a year of 360 days.[14] The *Pañc. Br.* gives the precise scheme of this sacrificial session (XXIV. 20.1). *Ayana* means 'going' (fr. √*i* - 'to go') and speaks of the moving of the sun to the north and south of the equator, the Viṣuvān. The middle-most day of the Gavām-ayana is termed Viṣuvān (or Divākīrtya). The wings of the Gavām-ayana comprising six months each are joined with Viṣuvān day, like two sloping rafters of the roof of a house to the central beam (*Tait. Br.* I.2.3.1,2). The *Pañc. Br.* says that the Viṣuvān (original word, i.e. *prātipadika*, being '*viṣuvat*') day is the body (i.e. trunk) of the year and on both sides of it, i.e. before and after, are the two halves of the year (*Pañc. Br.* IV.7.1). The *arthavāda* regarding the Viṣuvān day aptly brings out the precise position of that day in the scheme of the Gavām-ayana sacrifice and sheds light on its importance as the middle-most day.

As the sun is the source of light and lustre, the lustre of the sun is sought for being brought in the Vasatīvarī waters, which are collected on the previous day of the sacrifice.[15] Therefore it is laid down that the sacrificer or priest should take the Vasatīvarī waters by daytime, for he thereby takes him who burns yonder. He also takes thereby

All Gods (Viśve Devāḥ) for they are the rays of him, i.e. the sun (*Śat. Br.* III. 9.2.6). If the sun has set and the Vasatīvarī waters are not collected, let the Adhvaryu priest take them from his tank, if he has performed a Soma-sacrifice before this, for those (Vasatīvarī) waters of his, have been (formerly) taken by day (*ibid.* 8). If he is unable to obtain either kind of waters, let him take a firebrand to the flowing waters and collect those flowing waters, while holding that firebrand close above them or let him take those (waters) while holding a piece of gold close above them. Thus the waters are made (to have lustre) like the yonder burning sun (*ibid. 9).* Here it is clear that fire (Agni) and gold stand for the sun.

Though the three Soma-pressings at three times in a day are in honour of Vasu-s, Rudra-s and Āditya-s respectively, the *Kauṣ. Br.* interestingly at one place states that all the three pressings are connected with the sun. The context here is of Soma-sacrifice and it is about the final bath *(avabhṛtha).* The *Kauṣ. Br.* says that by the three pressings they seek the sun, who yonder gives heat. By the morning pressing they seek to obtain the sun in his rising, by the mid-day pressing, him in the middle of his course and by the third pressing him in his setting. The sun enters the waters and becomes Varuṇa. So a cake on one potsherd is offered to Varuṇa for prosperity (*Kauṣ. Br.* XVIII. 9).

The moving of the sun towards northwards and southwards has specific importance in the ritual. This is seen in the *arthavāda* which occurs in the context of Agnyādhāna (setting up of the sacred fires). When the sacrificer establishes his fires, as the sun moves northwards, he dispels the evil from himself (i.e. from the sacrificer). When the sun moves northwards, the sun stays among the gods and protects them. By him, the gods have evil dispelled from them and so is of the sacrificer as noted above. The gods are immortal by the sun and so is the sacrificer. The *Śat. Br.* is quick enough to add that though there is no prospect of immortality for the sacrificer (he being mortal), he attains the full measure of life (*Śat. Br.* II. 1.3.4) - *na'amṛtatvasya' āśā' asti / sarvamāyureti).*

When the sacrificer sets up his fires as the sun moves southwards, the sacrificer does not dispel the evil from himself. At this time, the sun is among the Fathers. But the Fathers have not the evil dispelled from them by the sun. The Fathers are (once) mortals. Hence if the sacrificer sets up his fires, when the sun moves southwards, he dies, before he has attained the full measure of life (*ibid.*).

An *arthavāda*-passage in the context of a special sacrifice laid down for having a cure for eyesight, is significant for a couple of points. It is told that Rajana Kauṇeya went to Kratujit Jānaki for a cure for eyesight. The latter performed a sacrifice for the sake of the former and a cake on eight potsherds was offered to Agni and an oblation to Sūrya. It is said that men see by the eye of Agni and the gods by the eye of the sun. When he offers to these two deities with their shares, they bestow good eyesight on him (*Tait. Sam.* II. 3.8.1, 2).

It is quite obvious that the light in the eye and the search for the cure of (bad) eyesight bring the two shining deities *viz.* Agni and the sun, in this context. In fact, Agni and the sun are the aspects of one deity *viz.* that of fire or heat. Moreover the sun is said to be the eye of Mitra and Varuṇa (*RV* I.115.1; VI.51.1; VII.61.1; 63.1; X.37.1). The eye with which Varuṇa is said to observe mankind is undoubtedly the sun (*ibid.* I.50.6). Together with Aryaman, Mitra and Varuṇa are called sun-eyed (*ibid.* VII. 66.10), which is a term applied to other gods also. The sun is the eye of Agni as well (*ibid.* I. 115.1). The goddess Dawn is said to bring the eye of the gods, i.e. the sun (*ibid.* VII. 77.3). The sun is the 'lord of eyes' (*AV* V. 24.9) and is the 'one eye' of the created beings (*ibid.* XIII. 1.45). And to him ultimately the eye of the dead man is said to go (*RV* X. 16.3). The ritual of offering to the two shining deities *viz.* Agni and the sun, which are the deities of light and lustre, to get back the light and lustre of the eyes, is based on the principle of sympathetic magic *viz.* 'like produces like'. The belief in offering to the sun or Agni, for getting good eyesight percolates even up to the Puranic times.[16]

An interesting *vidhi* together with its *arthavāda* occurs in the context of the rite of Agnicayana. When all the five layers of the Great Fire-altar are completed, the firebrand[17] is carried forward to the Great Fire-altar, where it would now be designated as Āhavanīya and established as such on the Great Fire-altar so built. To the south of the Āgnīdhra's fire-shed the Adhvaryu priest lays down a small round variegated stone on the northern part of the Great Fire-altar. The *arthavāda* states that this round stone is the yonder sun, which is established. Its being variegated stands for the disk of the sun, which is variegated due to the rays.[18] The stone is set up between the Āhavanīya and the Gārhapatya fire-places, which stand for the heavenly world and the terrestrial worlds respectively. The sun shines between the two worlds (*Śat. Br.* IX. 2.3.14).[19] The stone (as seen above) is placed near the Āgnīdhra's fire-shed, the latter standing for the air. The sun also has his stay in the air (*ibid.* 15).

In the context of the Pravargya rite, the mythical account occurring by way of *arthavāda* states that the gods were performing a headless sacrifice. With the result whatever desire they entertained in the sacrifice, they could not obtain, for the head of the sacrifice was cut off. This cut off head of the sacrifice is this very Āditya—the sun (*Jaim. Br.* III. 126). The *Śat. Br.* clearly states that the pot or vessel (Gharma, also called Mahāvīra, in which milk is boiled) stands for him, who burns or dazzles yonder (*Śat. Br.* XIV. 1.1.31). The Pravargya rite, in which the Mahāvīra pot symbolises the sun, stands for the head of the sacrifice. The *Śat. Br.* has woven a mythical account of Cyavana, who imparts the knowledge of the (lost) head of sacrifice to the Aśvins. The account figures in the context of Agniṣṭoma sacrifice, while explaining the Soma-cup (*graha)* to be offered to the Aśvins (*ibid.* IV. 1.5.1 ff). But the 'severed and (then) lost head' itself is a matter, which invites discussion.[20]

The lost 'head' of the sacrifice is none other than the sun and the performance of the Pravargya rite is for getting back this head of the sacrifice, i.e. the Sun. The several prohibitory rules laid down reflect this firm belief of the ritualists. The rules are — The sacrificer, while performing the Pravargya rite should not cover himself with a garment, lest he should be concealed from the sun. He should not spit while the sun shines, lest he should spit upon the sun. Let him not pass urine while the sun shines, lest he pass it upon him. Even while taking food at night, he should strike a light. Thereby he makes it a form of him, who shines yonder (*ibid.* XIV. 1.1.33).

The myth of the demon Svarbhānu and the sun occurs at many a place in the ritual texts and requires consideration to some extent.

To stress the importance of reciting the Divākīrtya *sāman*-s on the Viṣuvat day, the *Pañc. Br.* notes a mythical account in the *arthavāda.* It is said that once the demon Svarbhānu struck the sun with darkness, but the gods drove away that darkness by singing the Divākīrtya *sāman*-s. The Divākīrtya *sāman*-s metaphorically are said to be the rays of the sun, by which they take hold of the sun (*Pañc. Br.* IV. 6.12, 13). The mythical account can be traced back to the *RV,* where Atri is said to have found, with the *mantra* (*turīyeṇa brahmaṇā* - 'with the fourth *mantra'*) the sun, concealed by the demon Svarbhānu (*RV.* V. 40.6) and to have placed him in the sky (*ibid.* 8). Several other ritual texts mention this myth.[21] In the context of the Dvādaśāha (twelve-day) sacrifice, the *Pañc. Br.* (XIV. 11, 12, 14) while laying down the *sāman*-s of the Ārbhavapavamāna laud of the eighth day, states the importance of the Bhāsa *sāman*, through the etymology of the word *bhāsa* (he who praises with it, shines — *bhāsam bhavati bhāti tuṣṭuvānaḥ, ibid.* 12). The mythical account occurring in this connection reflects a belief, which has percolated even to this day. It is said that when the demon Svarbhānu struck the sun with darkness, by singing the Bhāsa *sāman*, Atri repelled the darkness, and the sun shone again (*ibid.* 14). The belief here is in the efficacy of chanting a *mantra* in the form of the *sāman.*[22] In the Gavām-ayana *sattra,* three days in the first half of the year preceding the middle-most day, i.e. the Viṣuvat day, and three days in the second half of the year, following the Viṣuvat day, are called the Svarasāman-days, for on these days, the *sāman*-s named Svara are chanted. In connection with these *sāman*-s also, the same mythical account about the demon Svarbhānu occurs. Here the sun is released by the gods with the chanting of the Svara *sāman*-s (*ibid.* IV. 5.1, 2).[23]

The mythical account in the Brāhmaṇa-texts and the references from the *RV* and *AV* are a clear indication of a solar eclipse, which had taken place in the hoary past. Most probably it was a 'total' eclipse of the sun, which was an event to be remembered and hence to be recorded in the Saṁhitā-s and the Brāhmaṇa-s and the more of it we shall see in the chap. "Arthavāda-s on Varied Topics (Miscellanea)" under "Eclipse". The pseudo-myth of the demon (Svarbhānu) taking the sun in his clutches, got developed in the *Mbh.* and the Purāṇa-s, in a full-fledged myth of the demon Rāhu (-Ketu) swallowing the sun and the moon.[24]

To turn to another celestial luminary — the moon—

Like the sun, the moon is said to be linked to the year by means of seasons (*Śat. Br.* VI. 7. 1. 19). The *Jaim. Br.* in the context of Agniṣṭoma sacrifice points out in the *arthavāda* that there are four excellent lights of the gods *viz.* Agni on the earth; the sun in the heaven; the moon among the constellations; and lightning in the waters (of the rain-clouds). One who sacrifices with the Agniṣṭoma ritual conquers the lustrous worlds of these excellent lights (*Jaim. Br.* II. 333).

The moon is visible in the western sky.[25] The reason of this is stated in an *arthavāda,* which occurs in the context of the New-moon and Full-moon sacrifices. At both these sacrifices, the *sānnāyya* offering[26] to be given is prepared. Having collected that Soma or moon from the waters and the plants, the sacrificer (or priest) causes the moon to be born out of the oblations and so the moon becomes visible in the western sky (*Śat. Br.* II. 4.4.20). That the *mantra*-s and offerings give strength to the deities is a firm conviction of the ritualists.[27] Right from the Ṛgvedic times, it is believed that worship of the gods with sacrifices, obeisances, offerings and prayers strengthens them.[28] In the same vein, the thought here is that the very birth of the moon is from the oblations.

The *arthavāda* in the *Śat. Br.* in the context of the Agniṣṭoma sacrifice, traces the birth of the moon to the pairing (*mithuna)* of Soma the male and waters the female, in the Havirdhāna shed.[29] Thereby food (i.e. moon) is produced from food (i.e. Soma and waters). The moon is the food of the sun — the one who shines yonder (*ibid.* IV. 6.7. 12). Such passages from the Brāhmaṇa-texts bear testimony to the identification of the Soma and the moon.[30] The *Śat. Br.* says that King Soma, the food of the gods is none other than the moon (*ibid.* I.6.4.5).[31] The *Kauṣ. Br.* points out that the yonder moon is the King Soma and the former enters into the latter, when the latter is purchased (*Kauṣ. Br.* VII. 10). The *Jaim. Br.* has the same thought to give, though couched in different words. Retasyā, the first verse of the Bahiṣpavamāna laud is said to be the moon and the moon is said to be the other form (*pratirūpaḥ*) of King Soma, the draught of gods (*Jaim. Br.* I. 316).[32]

On the New-moon day, the moon is neither seen in the east nor in the west. He comes to this world and enters the waters and the plants. As he dwells here together with the waters and the plants (*amā* - 'together' or 'at the house' and √*vas* - 'to stay, dwell'), the New-moon night is called *amāvasyā* (*Śat. Br.* I.6.4.5), The *arthavāda,* stating the etymology of the word *amāvasyā*[33] occurs in the context of the New-moon and Full-moon sacrifices, and aptly concurs the belief about Soma or the moon coming from the waters and the plants as noted above (*ibid.* II. 4.4.20).

At one place, the *Śat. Br.* states the moon to be one of Agni's forms. While making the clay for the fire-pan (*ukhā*), the water is to be boiled by means of the resin of the Palāśa tree for giving the fire-pan firmness. The Palāśa tree is Soma[34] and Soma is the moon, and moon is one of Agni's forms (*ibid.* VI. 5.1.1).

The moon is said to be Prajāpati (*Jaim. Br.* II. 6; *Śat. Br.* VI.1.3.16). The *Jaim. Br.* quotes the opinion of Śāṭyāyani that this moon is the Year, Prajāpati as well as the month. The moon makes the month, for he waxes for fifteen nights and wanes for fifteen nights. He becomes food by the contact with the terrestrial world and enters the waters and the plants (*Jaim. Br.* II. 3).

A metaphor coming by way of *arthavāda* points out the importance of the New-moon day and incidentally that of the moon. The *Śat. Br.* in the context of the New-moon and Full-moon sacrifices, states that Prajāpati — the Sacrifice - is the Year. The New-moon day night is its gate and the moon is the bolt of the gate. On the New-moon day, when he establishes the two fires (in the rite of Agnyādhāna), it is as though entering a stronghold by the gate, when the gate is open and this leads him to the heavenly world (*Śat. Br.* XI. 1.1.1; also for the same idea *ibid.* XI. 1.1.7).

An interesting *arthavāda* occurs in the *Śat. Br.* in the context of the New-moon and Full-moon sacrifices (*ibid.* XI. 1. 5.1-3). The sacrificer observes fast and then the moon is seen in the west. The *arthavāda* states that the moon is the heavenly dog, watching the sacrificer's cattle to seize them and that would not be good to the cattle, if some offerings are not given.[35] The sacrificer and the priests go to the shade. So much is the fear of (any) dog that people call any burning pain *śvalucita,* i.e. dog's clutch (*ibid.* XI. 1.5.1). The image of moon regarded here as a dog invites the *dakṣiṇā* also of that sort, which can drive away the dog (here the 'moon-dog'). The *dakṣiṇā* mentioned here is — a bow with three arrows, also a staff, for with a bow a dog is driven away (i.e. by shooting an arrow) and also with a staff.[36] The *arthavāda* noted above takes for its basis the fear of moonless night, which is dark. Hence the fear of the theft of cattle. So the *dakṣiṇā* of bow and arrows and a staff!

The *arthavāda* noted above then shifts from the image of dog to the image of hare on the moon (*ibid.* XI. 1.5.3). While pointing out the importance of the rite of Agnihotra, the *Jaim. Br.* says that there is a hare in the moon and he rules over everything (*Jaim. Br.* I. 28). There is Yama in the moon, who controls (*yamiti* fr. √*yam* - 'to control') everything here. He is Death. The sacrificer who offers *agnihotra* daily, pacifies him (Yama) with offerings and stays in the region of the god Yama and becomes one with him (*ibid.*).

The black spot on the moon, known by the name hare, deer, etc.[37] is mentioned in a mythical account of the symbolic marriage of Heaven and Earth (*Ait.* Br. IV. 27 = 19.5; also *Jaim. Br.* I. 145). It runs as follows. Heaven and Earth, which were together in the beginning, later on got separated. As it did not rain and the five classes of the people suffered,[38] the gods thought of bringing the two worlds together, by marriage. This mythical account, coming as *arthavāda* is obviously brought in to stress the importance of the *sāman*-s. The *Ait. Br.* states that the Earth is wedded to the Heaven in the form of the Rathantara *sāman* and the Heaven is wedded to the Earth in the form of the Bṛhat *sāman;* again, the Earth is wedded to the Heaven in the form of the Naudhasa *sāman* and the Heaven is wedded to the Earth in the form of the Śyaita *sāman* (*Ait. Br.* IV. 27 = 19.5). In the *Jaim. Br.* we note that the Bṛhat and the Rathantara *sāman*-s decide to perform this marriage of Heaven and Earth, with their (i.e. *sāmans')* bodies, the Śyaita *sāman* being the dear body of the Rathantara and Naudhasa that of the Bṛhat (*Jaim. Br.* I. 145).

The *Jaim. Br.* interestingly mentions the 'give-and-take' of gift between the two worlds (bridegroom and the bride). Heaven sent the saline earth to the Earth as *śulka*[39] in the marriage. She sent smoke of the sacrifice to the Heaven. He gave rain as *śulka* to her and she gave *devayajana* (sacrificial ground) to him (*ibid.* I. 145). This *devayajana* is the black spot on the moon (*Ait. Br.* IV. 27 = 19.5).

The *Śat. Br.* also mentions in the context of the New-moon and Full-moon sacrifices, the sacred sacrificial ground (*devayajana)* and the black spot on the moon, without referring in any way to the marriage of the Heaven and Earth. The Āgnīdhra priest makes the altar smooth by stroking along it. The mythical account occurs in the *arthavāda*-portion. The gods in order to save their imperishable place of worship on the earth, from the *asura*-s, removed it to the moon. The same is seen in the form of the black spot in the moon (*Śat. Br.* I.2.5.18). The *arthavāda* here is important for another point also. It sheds light on the basic concept of sacrifice that the sacrifice performed on the terrestrial level is to be taken basically as performed on the cosmic level.

The main trait of the moon — this unique celestial luminary — is that even after 'dying' he is born again. The moon is not seen on the New-moon day (*Kauṣ. Br.* III. 6). No study-session is to be held on this day. The *Ṣaḍ. Br.* gives an elaborate explanation for this in its *arthavāda* passage. It is said that the gods get consecrated for sacrifice in the first half of the month and they partake of Soma (Soma-juice) in the next half through three *pātra*-s (here 'cups', though the meaning of *pātra*-s is 'vessels' or 'pots') *viz.* the earth, mid-region and heaven. In this half of the month, the Āditya-s partake of the first five *kalā*-s (parts) of the moon by the divine cup, i.e. heaven, up to the fifth day; the Rudra-s, the next five *kalā*-s up to the tenth day with the mid-region-cup and the Vasu-s, the next five *kalā*-s by the fifteenth day with the earth-cup. Only the sixteenth part of the moon remains. Hence it is that the moon is endowed with sixteen parts. He enters the herbs, plants, cows, beasts, the sun, *brahman* and also the *brāhmaṇa*-s. On the New-moon day, the moon becomes very feeble due to only one part (i.e. the sixteenth one) remaining with him. Hence the gods — both Soma-drinking as well as not drinking Soma — with Indra as their senior god sit by the moon's side on that whole night (i.e. fifteenth night), as do the relatives (Sāy. - 'son etc.'), being apprehensive of the death of father, grandfather, great-grandfather or any old man in the family, when he is suffering from serious illness (*Ṣaḍ. Br.* V. 6.2). The New-moon (Amāvasyā) day being associated with such inauspicious colour, is enjoined to be avoided for any study-session.

But the moon is born again — nay again and again. This thought figures in the Brahmodya (theological discussion) between the Hotṛ and the Brahman priests in the Aśvamedha sacrifice (*Śat. Br.* XIII. 2.6.11, where the *mantra*-s from the *Vāj. Sam.* XIII. 9, 10 figure). This cosmic drama of the moon's Birth, Death and Rebirth has given this celestial luminary its own importance even in comparison with the sun. The *mantra*-s in the Saṁhitā-s hence declare in unequivocal terms that the moon stretches out (i.e. extends) long life (i.e. the length of life).[40]

To turn to constellations—

The knowledge about constellations forms an integral part of the sacrificial lore, for the constellations are mentioned in connection with various rituals.[41] The *RV* mentions the word *nakṣatra* (I. 50.2; III. 54.9; VII. 86.1) and the ritual texts refer to them. The constellations consist of one, two, three, four stars but Kṛttikā-s are many stars (*Śat. Br.* II. 1.2.2). The *arthavāda* passages occurring in these texts in this connection reflect the beliefs about the constellations prevalent in the Vedic times.

The association of the constellations with the sky is explained by the *Tait. Sam.* in an *arthavāda* in the context of New-moon and Full-moon sacrifices. Based on the cosmic drama of waxing and waning of the moon, it is said that on the Full-moon day, Vṛtra the demon is slain but on the New-moon day he rises again. Therefore the *mantra*-s uttered at the Full-moon and New-moon refer to these recurring events. It is said that when Indra taking his thunderbolt went against Vṛtra, Heaven and Earth (Dyāvāpṛthivī) entreated upon Indra not to hurl the thunderbolt at them and chose a boon that Heaven (the sky) should be adorned with constellations and the Earth with variegated things (*Tait. Sam.* II. 5.2.5).

The word *nakṣatra* as pointed out by Kane[42] is used in three senses: (i) a star in general; (ii) 27 equal parts of the zodiac; and (iii) asterism in the zodiacal belt (which may each consist of one or more stars). When the word *nakṣatra* means a star in general, this star (*nakṣatra)* obviously is the sun. In the context of establishing the fires (Agnyādhāna rite), the *Śat. Br.* lays down that if the sacrificer is desirous of having a *nakṣatra* for setting up of his fires, then certainly the sun is a faultless (*anaparāddham) nakṣatra* and through that auspicious day (marked by the rising and setting of the sun) he should try to obtain the benefits of whichever of those constellations he may desire (*Śat Br.* II. 1.2.19). The reasoning here is supported by the etymology of the two words *viz. āditya* and *nakṣatra.* The *Śat. Br.* states that the moment the sun arose, he took (*ādatta* fr. *ā* + √*dā* - 'to take') from the *nakṣatra*-s their energy (*vīrya)* and their power (*kṣatra).* So the sun is called Āditya (*ibid.* II. 1.2.18). And so the powerlessness (*na-kṣatratvam*) of the *nakṣatra*-s (*ibid.* 19).[43]

In the Agnicayana rite, the *nakṣatra*-s are interestingly spoken of as born from Prajāpati's hair-pits. When Prajāpati was creating living beings, Death overpowered him. He practised austerities for a thousand years, striving to leave evil behind him. While he was practising austerities, light went upwards from his hair-pits (*loma-gartebhyaḥ).* Those lights are the stars (*nakṣatrāṇi)* (*ibid*. X. 4. 4. 1, 2). The general belief regarding the constellations is that they are the light of those righteous men (*jana),* who go to the celestial world (*ibid.* VI. 5.4.8). This belief occurs in the context of the Agnicayana rite, when the fire-pan made of clay is to be baked and so the prayer here is to Dhiṣaṇā-s, connected here to *dhiṣṇyā*-s (five-hearths), for baking the fire-altar. The Dhiṣaṇā-s metaphorically are said to be the constellations. It is as though with the stars that he bakes the fire-pan (*ibid.)*. This is for getting the divine light and lustre. The *Tait. Br.* also voices the same thought. There was (cosmic) water in the mid-region. The constellations (*tārakā*) crossed over (*ataran)* it. So, their power of crossing. One who performs sacrifice here (terrestrial region) resorts to this world (i.e. the upper one, where the stars are).[44] Constellations are indeed the houses of gods (*Tait. Br.* I.5.2.6).

The *Tait. Br.* speaks of the constellations as forming the body of Prajāpati as — Hasta is the hand (i.e. two hands), Citrā is the head; Niṣṭyā (Svātī) is the heart; Viśākhā-s (two stars) are the thighs; and Anūrādhā-s are the feet. This is the Nakṣatriya Prajāpati (*ibid.* I.5.2.2). In later times the Purāṇa-s elaborate this concept and speak of constellations as a whole forming the body of Viṣṇu (*Vām. P.* 54 the whole chap.), Janārdana Viṣṇu (*Bhaviṣya P.* Uttarakhaṇḍa 108. 16 ff.) or even Śiva (*Vām. P.* 5.38 ff), taking these gods to be the Nakṣatra-Puruṣa.[45]

In the Agnicayana rite, the Great Fire-altar is said to be the constellations, for the number seven hundred and twenty of the bricks is calculated from the twenty-seven constellations, each constellation having twenty-seven secondary stars accompanying it (*Śat. Br.* X. 5.4.5). The correct calculation comes to 729, but as pointed out by Eggeling, the Fire-altar being identical with the Year, the 729 bricks taken as 720 bricks represent the days and nights of the Year.[46] The information from the *Tait. Sam.* helps us to know more in this respect. In the Agnicayana rite, the *Tait. Sam.* while laying down the placing of bricks representing constellations (*nakṣatra-iṣṭakāḥ)* says that these are the lights of the heaven, which he wins and constellations are the lights of the persons who have performed good deeds (*Tait. Sam.* V. 4.1.3).

The *Tait. Br.* mentions two types of constellations *viz.* Devanakṣatra and Yamanakṣatra. The list of the

Devanakṣatra-s starts with Kṛttikā-s and ends with Viśākhā-s and that of the Yamanakṣatra-s begins with Anūrādhā-s and ends with Apabharaṇī-s (*Tait. Br.* I.5.2.6,7). The constellations are mentioned here for laying down that a ritual-act is to be performed under the particular constellation meant for it. The exact location of that constellation[47] (for it will move from east to west) at the time of that ritual also is to be decided beforehand at the day-break itself, for after the rise of the sun, the constellation will not be visible. Hence till the time the sun has not traversed the sky and not reached that location of the constellation, the ritual act is to be carried out.[48] This way alone the person can be said to perform the ritual on an auspicious day. The *Tait. Br.* here quotes the examples of Yajñeṣu and Satyadyumna who obtained their desired aims, for the priest Mātsya made them perform sacrifice at the auspicious hour (*ibid.* I.5.2.1). The *Tait. Br.* explains the names of the Yamanakṣatra-s by giving their etymology. In the fight with the *asura*-s, at the Anūrādhā-s (constellation) the gods became prosperous (fr. √*rai* - 'to give'). At the Jyeṣṭhaghnī (commonly known as Jyeṣṭhā) the gods killed a towering personality (*jyeṣṭha*) among the *asura*-s. At the Mūlabarhaṇī the gods shattered the original place of residence (*mūlam nivāsasthānam*) of the *asura*-s. A hymn from the *AV* (*AV* VI. 110) which is for 'a child born at the unlucky time', mentions three constellations *viz.* Jyeṣṭhaghnī ('One that slays the oldest'), Vicṛtau and Mūla, which are all the constellations in the 'Scorpio' (asterism). The *Kauśika Sūtra* also says that the *AV* hymn (VI. 110) is to be used for a child born under a *pāpanakṣatra* (*Kauśika Sūtra* XLVI.25). At the Āṣāḍhā-s the *asura*-s were not able to bear (*yanna asahanta*) the disaster caused by the gods. At the Śroṇā (Sāy. — 'a collection' *saṅgha*) the *asura*-s had many attacks from the gods. At the Śraviṣṭhā-s (commonly known as Dhaniṣṭhā) the *asura*-s bore (i.e. heard) wordy attacks from the gods. At the Śatabhiṣak the gods thought about the attack from the *asura*-s or counter-attacked them (Sāy. —

abhiṣajyata). At the Proṣṭhapadā-s the gods became ready with their weapons against the *asura*-s. At the Revatī the gods uttered terrible words *(aravanta)* to frighten the *asura*-s. At the Aśvayuj-s *(aśvayujoḥ)* the gods harnessed the horses to the chariot. At the Apabharaṇī-s the *asura*-s had to lose *(apāvahan)* the lives of great warriors in the battle (*Tait. Br.* I.5.2.8,9). Sāyaṇa in his commentary on this passage states that these constellations are known as Yamanakṣatra-s, for they like Yama became the cause of *asura*-s' death *(yamavad asurāṇām maraṇahetutvāt yamanakṣatrāṇi).* We have already noted the details about the Devanakṣatra-s. The *Tait. Br.* says that one should perform rituals when the Devanakṣatra-s are there. By that he will be performing the ritual on an auspicious day (*ibid.* 9).[49] The *Kauṣ Br.* enjoins that he should perform sacrifice under the constellation of his choice (IV. 12). This has in view a particular thing desired by the sacrificer and its relation with a particular constellation, obviously based on the belief about that constellation.

Belief about the efficacy of constellations was so deep-rooted in the mind of the Vedic ritualists that the *Tait. Br.* states that villages, towns, etc. on this earth are like constellations helping the human beings. Therefore the place which is *aślīla* (*aśrīra* - without any glory) and thus not of any good use, should be avoided for residence as well as for performing sacrifice (*Tait. Br.* I.5.2.6). A *brāhmaṇa* (obviously a priest here) together with the twenty-seven constellations is counted as the twenty-eighth. As the ritual is dependent on the appropriate constellation, so it is on the appropriate instruction of a *brāhmaṇa* (*ibid.* I.5.3.4 and Sāyaṇa on it).

The concept of constellations reaches also to that of day and year. The five divisions of day such as *prātaḥ* (morning), *saṅgava,*[50] *mādhyandina* (mid-day), *aparāhṇa* (afternoon) and *sāyam* (evening) are said to be five auspicious constellations and the four joint-periods of these five parts are *aślīla* constellations (without any glory left with them), for with them (i.e. with their glory) the sacrifices such as Agniṣṭoma, Ukthya, Ṣoḍaśin and Atirātra are made. These nine, the *pradoṣa-kāla* (the advent of night) and the *uṣas-kāla* (the dawn) make the number eleven and the twelfth is the *brāhmaṇa* (priest). This number twelve makes a year and a person preforming a ritual daily obtains fruit which could be obtained by performing it for a full year (*ibid.* I.5.3.1-4).[51]

An interesting *arthavāda* occurs in the *Tait. Saṃ.* in the context of an *iṣṭi.* This *iṣṭi* is laid down for a person, caught hold of by *yakṣman* (ailment of consumption) and in this *iṣṭi* offerings are given to the sun (*āditya)* on the New-moon day.[52] The mythical account stated as *arthavāda* runs as follows. Prajāpati gave his thirty-three daughters to King Soma, i.e. moon. The thirty-three daughters here are the thirty-three constellations.[53] As King Soma, being enamoured of Rohiṇī, was partial to her, the other daughters of Prajāpati (i.e. wives of Soma) became angry and approached their father Prajāpati. Prajāpati made King Soma take an oath, the word of which was not abided by the latter. Hence every month *yakṣman* (consumption) seizes King Soma (*Tait. Sam.* II. 3.5.1-3; also *Kāṭh. Sam.* XI. 3). This *arthavāda* tries to explain the lunar nature of the constellations and the waning and waxing of the moon.

To turn to some constellations, the *arthavāda*-s in the context of which, reflect the beliefs about these constellations —

Abhijit

The constellation Abhijit from its very name indicates victory over one's adversary, attacking him from the front side. The *arthavāda* in the *Tait. Br.* points out how in the fight against the *asura*-s, the god scored victory over them under this very constellation. Hence the constellation Abhijit well deserves its name — fr. *abhi* + √*ji* - 'to conquer'; this is, while advancing from the front side - *abhi* (*Tait. Br.* I.5.2.3,4).

Ārdrā

The constellation Ārdrā is associated with Rudra. The *arthavāda* in the *Tait. Br.* relates that once Rudra longed for cattle (he is already known as 'Paśupati'). So he offered to Rudra (obviously the deity imagined of former times) in waters a *praiyaṅgava* (of Priyaṅgu fruit) *caru* on the constellation Ārdrā. Therefore he obtained cattle (*Tait. Br.* III. 1.4.4).

Citrā

The *Śat. Br.* lays down setting up of fires under the Citrā constellation. The mythical account occurring here as *arthavāda* runs as follows. Gods and *asura*-s, both sprung from Prajāpati, were contending for superiority and were desirous of rising to the heavenly world. The *asura*-s constructed the fire-altar Rauhiṇa with the thought of ascending (*samārokṣyāma* - fr. *sam* + *ā* + √*ruh*) to the other world. Indra became apprehensive that if they become successful in constructing the fire-altar, they would prevail over the gods. Hence having secured a brick, he approached the *asura*-s, disguised as a *brāhmaṇa* and also calling himself *so* and expressed a wish to put his brick there, to which they agreed. He placed his brick there and when the fire-altar was very near to completion, he wanted to have his brick back. He pulled it out and down came the fire-altar, with the *asura*-s. Indra converted the bricks of the fire-altar into thunderbolts and clove the necks of the *asura*-s. The gods expressed surprise and joy — "Wonderful it has been with us that we have slain so many enemies". So the wonderful nature (*citrātvam)* of the constellation Citrā. Wonderful it becomes with him, who sets up his fires under the Citrā, for he thereby slays his rivals and his spiteful enemy (*Śat. Br.* II.1.2.13-17).[54] The *Mait. Sam.* relates the same mythical account, where the brick of Indra is called Citrā and the setting up of fire on the Citrā is laid down for a person, whose rival and enemy is slain thereby (*Mait. Sam.*

I.6.9). The *arthavāda* noted above also figures in the *Kāṭh. Sam.* but here the brick of Indra is not called Citrā, while the constellation Citrā is said to belong to Indra (*aindram nakṣatram).* It is said that if a person wants to take away the enemy's strength and valour, he should set up fire under the Citrā (*Kāṭh. Sam.* VIII.1).

The *Tait. Br.* taking into account the meaning of the word '*citra*' as 'variegated', lays down an *iṣṭi* in which an eight-potsherd cake is to be offered to both Tvaṣṭṛ and the constellation Citrā, if a person desires to have offspring of variegated nature (as Sāyaṇa explains for the next sentence — *citram nānāvidhatvam.. putrapautraduhitṛdauhitrarūpeṇa nānāvidhatvam,* i.e. consisting of sons, grand-sons, daughters and sons of daughters). The *arthavāda* here is that the god Tvaṣṭṛ desired to have variegated progeny. He (not Tvaṣṭṛ as such but some individual of olden times yet to be known as Tvaṣṭṛ, on the lines of Sāyaṇa's explanation on the *Tait. Br.* III. 1.4.1, which would be seen in the context of the constellation Kṛttikā) offered an eight-potsherd cake to both Tvaṣṭṛ and the constellation Citrā (*Tait. Br.* III. 1.4.12).; The *Tait. Br.* seems to be carried away by the meaning of the word '*citra*' (also '*citra*' as 'variegated') and so lays down this constellation for the Horse-sacrifice, supporting it by an *arthavāda* passage that the Horse-sacrifice, due to many rituals of varied nature to be performed in it, is indeed 'variegated' in nature (*citram vā etal kurma).* Hence the constellation Citrā enjoined for the Horse-sacrifice for getting prosperity (*ibid.* III. 8.1.1. Does this indicate that prosperity would be many-faceted?)

Hasta

About the constellation Hasta, it is stated that whosoever desires that presents (or gifts) should be offered to him, should set up his fires under this constellation, for whatever is offered with the hand *(hasta)* that indeed is given to him (*Śat. Br.* II. 1.2.12). Here again the *arthavāda* has taken the help of etymology (the name Hasta fr. the noun '*hasta'*).

Kṛttikā-s

Of all the constellations which find mention in the ritual context, the important ones are the Kṛttikā-s comprising seven stars. While laying down *iṣṭi*-s on the Devanakṣatra-s, the *Tait. Br.* speaks of the oblations offered to these stars individually and mentions them by name. The seven stars are — Ambā, Dulā, Nitatni, Abhrayantī, Meghayantī, Varṣayantī and Cupuṇikā (*Tait. Br.* III. 1.4.1).[55] The Kṛttikā constellation is particularly that of Agni. A mythical account occurring in the *Tait. Br.* states that when Agni desired to take food for the gods, the sacrificer offered eight-potsherd cake to Agni on the Kṛttikā constellation. Thus the sacrificer became a giver of food to the gods through Agni with the help of the Kṛttikā constellation (*ibid.)*. In the Agnicayana rite, while laying down the bricks named Sayuj, the *Tait. Sam.* says that by Agni (Fire) the gods went to the heavenly world and became the yonder Kṛttikā-s. He for whom these are placed goes to the world of heaven, attains brilliance and becomes resplendent (*Tait. Sam.* V.3.9.1). The belief seen here is that the constellations are the righteous persons who have gone to the heavenly world. The ritual-texts enjoin establishing of Agni or Agni-s (Agnyādheya rite) on the constellation Kṛttikā-s.[56] The main reason, most probably a true observation based on the astronomical data available at the time of the *Śat. Br.* is that all other constellations move away from the east, while the Kṛttikā-s do not. (*Śat. Br.* II. 1.2.3; and also II. 1.2.4... 'The group of stars called Saptarṣi rises in the north but the Kṛttikā-s do rise in the east'). The Kṛttikā-s thus sticking to the east, which is the quarter of the rising sun, are regarded as the most appropriate constellation for establishing the fires — Gārhapatya and especially the Āhavanīya (*ibid.* II. 1.2.1). The basic concept here is that the sun and Agni are the two aspects of the same source of light and lustre.[57] The Āhavanīya fire-altar is always to the east. The ritual-texts put forth many *arthavāda*-s, while laying down the establishing of Agni or

Agni-s under the constellation Kṛttikā. The *Śat. Br.* says that by this he would establish rapport between his fires and the constellation. The other lunar constellations consist of one, two, three or four stars but the Kṛttikā-s are the most numerous of them. The sacrificer thereby obtains abundance. Again the Kṛttikā-s do not move away from the eastern quarter, while the other constellations do (*ibid.* II. 1.2.1-3). Another opinion stated by the *Śat. Br.* is that a person should not set up the fires under this constellation, for originally the Kṛttikā-s (the seven stars of this constellation) were the wives of the sages called Ṛkṣa-s (the stars in the Great Bear). But as the Ṛkṣa-s rise in the north and the Kṛttikā-s in the east, the latter faced hindrance in having union with their husbands (the Ṛkṣa-s). A person establishing his fires under the Kṛttikā-s may face the same fate (*ibid.* 4). The *Śat. Br.* however presses forth its final word that he should establish his fires under the Kṛttikā-s for Agni is their mate, with whom they can have union (*ibid.* 5). In the *Kāṭh. Sam.* occurs a mythical account that the gods could not know the quarters. Then the Kṛttikā-s illuminated the eastern quarter for Agni. When he establishes the fire under the Kṛttikā-s, he indeed establishes it in the east. This constellation belongs to Agni. The Kṛttikā-s are said to be the head of Agni (-Prajāpati). When he establishes the fire on the Kṛttikā-s, he becomes prominent in the world to be placed at the head. The Kṛttikā-s are seven and seven are the vital breaths in the head. By establishing his fire under the Kṛttikā-s, he obtains control over all the sense-organs and vital breaths, nourishment of his offspring and cattle (*Kāṭh. Sam.* VIII. 1).

The *Mait. Sam.* restricts the establishing of fires of a *brāhmaṇa* under the Kṛttikā-s, for a *brāhmaṇa* belongs to Agni and the Kṛttikā-s also to Agni. The Kṛttikā-s are the head of Prajāpati and Agni is the mouth. By the head (here 'mouth') food is eaten and so he obtains proper food, when he establishes the fire on the Kṛttikā-s. The seven Kṛttikā-s are the seven vital breaths in the head, which are placed in him

(*Mait. Sam.* I.6.9). The *Tait Br.* echoes the words of the Saṁhitā-s (*Tait. Br.* I.1.2.1; I.5.1.1). The Kṛttikā-s are the mouth (*mukha)* of the constellations. He who establishes fire under the Kṛttikā-s becomes the chief (*ibid.* I.1.2.1... '*mukhya*' fr. '*mukha*').

However right from the beginning there was some apprehension about this constellation. We have noted above the unfavourable opinion from the *Śat. Br.* Here is another one from the *Tait. Br.* It points out that as this constellation belongs to Agni, which burns (i.e. Agni can burn) houses, hence it is to be avoided (*Tait. Br.* I.1.2.1).

Mṛgaśīrṣa

A person can establish his fires on this constellation. The *arthavāda* account occurring in the *Tait. Br.* brings out the importance of this constellation. Once Soma desired to rule over the kingdom of plants. He gave away a *caru* of unhusked rice-grains to Soma (obviously the deity Soma of former times!), to acquire the kingdom of plants for him. From the *mantra*-s it appears that actual offerings were given in the name of the constellation also—*somāya svāhā mṛgaśīrṣāya svāhā invakābhyaḥ*[58] *svāhā* (*Tait. Br.* III. 1.4.3).

The *Śat. Br.* maintains that the constellation Mṛgaśīrṣa is the head of Prajāpati and head means excellence. So he should establish his fires under the constellation Mṛgaśīrṣa (*Śat. Br.* II. 1.2.8). The *Śat. Br.* here states another opinion that as the constellation Mṛgaśīrṣa is the body of Prajāpati and body is unholy, sapless and a mere dwelling (*vāstu)*, he should not set up his fires under that constellation (*ibid.* 9). However the final viewpoint is to establish the fires under this very same constellation (*ibid.* 10). The *arthavāda* occurring in the *Śat. Br.* earlier at another place explains the connection of Prajāpati with this constellation. The *Śat. Br.* alludes to the myth of Prajāpati having a passion for his own daughter (either the Sky or the Dawn) and uniting with her; Rudra, on the insistence of other gods, shooting a three-knotted arrow at Prajāpati and injuring him (*ibid.* I.7.4.1 ff.).[59]

Phalgunī-s

This constellation has two stars *viz.* Pūrvā and Uttarā. The *RV* mentions the constellation Phalgunī-s by the name Arjunī-s (*RV* X.85.13). This constellation is said to belong to the god Bhaga or at times to the god Aryaman. The *Kāṭh. Sam.* lays down setting up of fire under the constellation Pūrvā Phalgunī-s by a person desiring good fortune, for this constellation belongs to god Bhaga (god of bounty). One who desires that his offspring should be generous (having a desire to give) should set up fire under the constellation Uttarā Phalgunī-s, for this constellation belongs to god Aryaman—the god who always gives (*Kāṭh. Sam.* VIII. 1).[60] The *Mait. Sam.* also ascribes the Pūrvā and Uttarā Phalgunī-s to the same gods as seen above (*Mait. Sam.* I. 6.9).

Interestingly the *Tait. Br.* states that he should not set up fire under the Pūrvā Phalgunī-s, for that is the last night of the year. A person setting up fire under this constellation as though sets up fire at the back of the year and so becomes sinful (*pāpīyān*). He should set up fire under the constellation Uttarā Phalgunī-s, for that is the first night of the year. He as though sets up fire at the mouth of the year and becomes prosperous. Sāyaṇa enlightens us on this passage by saying that for the setting up of fire with some desire in mind (*kāmya ādhāna*), both Pūrvā and Uttarā Phalgunī-s are important, but for regular setting up of fire (*nitya ādhāna*), the Uttarā Phalgunī-s are recommended but not the Pūrvā Phalgunī-s (Sāy. on *Tait. Br.* I.1.2.8). The *Śat. Br.* does not make any distinction between these two and in clear terms lays down setting up of fire under the Phalgunī-s. Under the Pūrvā Phalgunī-s the advancing (*purastāt*) sacrifice accrues to him and under the Uttarā Phalgunī-s a progressive (*uttarāvat*) well-being accrues to him (*Śat. Br.* II. 1.2.11). The *Śat. Br.* says that the Phalgunī-s are Indra's constellation and correspond to him in name. The mystic name of Indra is Arjuna and so are the Phalgunī-s called Arjunī-s. And as nobody can dare to utter the mystic name ('Arjuna') of the god Indra,[61] even the constellation Phalgunī-s are not called by their name Arjunī-s. Hence their name 'Phalgunī' (*ibid.*). The *arthavāda* here reflects the belief that the name stands for the very person, one of whose names is kept secret. A person can be overpowered and can fall prey to black magic if his name is known to all. Hence the real name is kept secret and the other for communication.[62]

Punarvasu

If the original or the first setting up of fires proves unsuccessful (i.e. in case the sacrificer does not become prosperous or at times even sustains losses), there is laid down the repetition of the *ādheya* rite, i.e. the setting up of the fires.[63] The Saṁhitā-s and the Brāhmaṇa-s prescribe the Punarādheya rite specifically under the Punarvasu constellation.[64] The *arthavāda* which occurs in the *Tait. Br.* in this regard explains the name Punarvasu taking the help of etymology. The gods being affluent desired to establish Agni. Due to their being proud of wealth, Agni was not properly established by them. With the result, their choicest wealth left them. They established Agni again under the Punarvasu constellation. And their choicest wealth returned to them. If a rich person (by any stroke of fate) becomes wretched in condition, he should establish fire under the Punarvasu constellation and then comes back to him his choicest wealth (*Tait. Br.* I. 1.2.2, 3). Sāyaṇa explains the name Punarvasu in his commentary on the passage from the *Śat. Br.* (II. 1.2.10) as — *nakṣatram caitat naṣṭasya vasunaḥ punaḥ prāptihetutvāt punarvasvākhyam* - 'The constellation is named Punarvasu because it enables a person to get back his lost wealth'. Here the belief clearly stems from the principle of sympathetic magic, based here on the words '*punar*' ('again') and '*vasu*' ('wealth').[65]

Revatī

The constellation Revatī is associated with the increase of cattle. The *arthavāda* in the *Tait. Br.* states that when Prajāpati created the cattle, they resorted to one constellation after the other, only to remain the same in number without any addition. However when they resorted to the constellation Revatī, they multiplied. Hence whatever offering is to be given in the sacrifice, it should be on this constellation (*Tait. Br.* I.5.2.4).[66] It has to be noted that this constellation figures in the list of the Yamanakṣatra-s (*ibid.* 8, 9) and the etymological explanation of the word is that on this constellation the gods uttered such sounds (*revatyām aravanta,* fr √*ru* - 'to make a sound,' actually 'to roar'), which frightened the *asura*-s.

Rohiṇī

The *Kāṭh. Sam.* lays down establishing of fires (in the Agnyādhāna rite) under the constellation Rohiṇī and supports it by the *arthavāda* which points out that the gods as well as Prajāpati established their respective fires on the constellation Rohiṇī (*Kāṭh. Sam.* VII. 1). The *Tait. Br.* also enjoins the constellation Rohiṇī for the rite of Agnyādhāna and the *arthavāda* here states that Prajāpati created Agni on the constellation Rohiṇī and the same Agni was established by the gods under the same constellation. Thereby the gods ascended all the heights (of glory and gain). This is the *rohiṇītva* (nature of ascendance) of the constellation Rohiṇī (fr. √*ruh* - 'to ascend'). One who establishes Agni on the Rohiṇī prospers and ascends all heights (*Tait. Br.* I.1.2.2). It is interesting to note that Sāyaṇa in his commentary on this passage introduces the constellation Rohiṇī as one without any defect (*nirdoṣam nakṣatram).* This may be in comparison with the blame attached to the Kṛttikā-s (*ibid.* I.1.2.1), which we have noted already. The *Tait. Br.* prescribes the constellation Rohiṇī for the rite of Odanasava,[67] for this constellation with other seven ones is *'brāhmaṇa'*.[68] Sāyaṇa makes this clear by saying that this constellation is praiseworthy like a *brāhmaṇa.* The priest by performing the Odanasava takes the sacrificer to the towering position among the equals. This rite is to be performed at the time of the rising sun, as all beings become joyous at the rising sun (*ibid.* II. 7.9.3,4). Though not pointed out by Sāyaṇa, the mention of the constellation Rohiṇī in this rite, which is to be performed at the hour of the rising sun, is very appropriate because the rising sun is the one who is '*rohan*' ('ascending' fr. √*ruh* - 'to grow, ascend').

It is interesting to see that the same tool of etymology has brought cattle in connection with the constellation Rohiṇī. The *Śat. Br.* while laying down the constellation Rohiṇī in the rite of Agnyādhāna, has the *arthavāda* that Prajāpati set up his fires under the Rohiṇī and obtained creatures thereby, which remained with him unchanged and constant, like the red cows (*rohiṇī*-s). So the nature of the Rohiṇī (*Śat. Br.* II. 1.2.6). Here the etymology is based on the word '*rohiṇī*', meaning a 'red cow' and also the constellation 'Rohiṇī.' The *Śat. Br.* mentions (even) the cattle setting up their fires (?) for the Agnyādhāna, thinking that they might attain (*rohema)* the desire of men and they obtained it (*ibid.* 7). Here the etymology is the usual one from √*ruh* - 'to ascend", here 'to attain.' These etymologies reflect on the thought-process of the Vedic ritualists. The *Mait. Sam.* lays down setting up of fire under the constellation Rohiṇī by a person desirous of cattle, for the plants grow under this constellation, multiplying the cattle thereby (*Mait. Sam.* I.6.9). The *Tait. Br.* prescribes an *iṣṭi* (sacrifice) in which *caru* (rice boiled in milk) is to be offered to the god Prajāpatī as also to the constellation Rohiṇī. The *arthavāda* here runs as follows. When Prajāpati created creatures, the latter fled away from him. He desiring their return, meditated on the constellation Roḥinī and offered *caru* to the Prajāpati of yore (Sāy. - *atītakalpagatāya prajāpataye*) and the Rohiṇī. So whatever 'dear' has left a person, that returns to him, who offers this oblation and performs this *iṣṭi* (*Tait. Br.* III. 1.4.2). Rohiṇī is regarded as the constellation of Prajāpati (*ibid.* I.5.1.1).[69]

Of a person, who establishes his fires after coming back from journey, the metre Virāj of the *mantra*-s is said to ascend upwards and become the constellation Rohiṇī, under which he establishes his fires. He prospers thereby. Here both the metre (i.e. Speech) and constellation are taken help of in the ritual (*ibid.* I.1.10.6).

Svātī also called Niṣṭyā

It is said that whosoever desires that his daughter should be dear to her husband, should give her in marriage on the constellation Niṣṭyā. She becomes dear to him and does not return to her father's place, being repudiated by her husband (*ibid.* I.5.2.3).

Though performed on the terrestrial plane, the Vedic sacrifice extended far beyond it, taking into its gamut the entire concept of the very existence, as a result of which even the celestial luminaries like the sun and the moon and the celestial bodies like constellations could figure in the *vidhi*-s and the *arthavāda*-s, the latter eloquent about the practices and beliefs of this 'celestial' world. And this celestial world is the world of light - 'light', which is regarded as the first of the gifts of life and in which alone, the religion can fulfil the duties of life.[70]

NOTES AND REFERENCES

1. Odanasava is a rite, which is to be performed by a person desirous of excellent food. At the rise of the sun, on the constellation Rohiṇī, four oblations are to be offered of the cooked rice *(odana)* accompanied by four *mantra*-s addressed to the goddess of lustre *(tviṣiḥ),* who gave birth to Indra, endowed with highest glory (*Tait. Br.* II. 7.7.1, 2 and the comm. of Sāyaṇa at the beginning of II. 7.7).
2. Curds are dropped into warm milk to prepare *sānnāyya* with the *mantra - somena tvā - ātanacmi — indrāya dadhi* (*Tait. Sam.* I.1.3.1, 2). Here curds are believed to be Soma, the favourite drink of Indra.

3. Also see *Śat. Br.* I.6.4.21, where it is stated that *sānnāyya* according to some is to be offered to Mahendra - the Great Indra - for after slaying Vṛtra he became Mahendra. The *Śat. Br.* however states that it is to be offered to Indra.
4. The *cātvāla* is situated outside the altar in the north-east corner. Vide Kane, P.V., *Hist.* of *Dh. S.*, Vol. II, pt. II, diagram opposite p. 1133.
5. See (Mrs.) Dange, S.S., "Speech and its Aspects", *Aspects of Speech in Vedic Ritual*, pp. 1-35.
6. *Kauṣ. Br.* XXV. 5; *Śat. Br.* II. 3.1.3 ff.; *Jaim. Br.* I.4, 5&7; also *Ait. Br.* V. 29-31 = 25.4-6.
7. A practice in India from centuries bygone, of lighting a lamp at the evening time — a practice followed religiously, the lamp being placed near the idols of the gods — is for indicating that the sun has left his lustre in Agni, i.e. fire, thus lighted.
8. Kamat, Vidya, *Ancient Indian Myths and Symbols in Pictorial Expression (As seen from Sanskrit and Allied Literature),* Thesis, University of Mumbai, 1999, p. 228.
9. For details, see Dange, Sadashiv A., *Ency. of P. B. & P.*, Vol. II, Navrang, New Delhi, 1987, p. 412.
10. *Ait. Br.* IV. 18 = 18.4. The sun is identified with the Ekaviṁśa or Viṣuvat day, the central day of the year, by which the gods raised the sun up to the heaven.

    Jaim. Br. II. 344 points out that the sun is the Viṣuvat (day) and is the twenty-first — the twelve months of the year, five seasons and three worlds making twenty.
11. Eggeling, J., *op. cit.*, pt. III, SBE Vol. 41, p. 268, note 3. Apparently a round netted mat, on which the fire-pan is to be placed and which is fastened to a cord by means of six strings, thus somewhat resembling the scale of a balance.
12. See Kane, P.V., *op. cit.*, Vol. II, pt. II, p. 1205; also *Ait. Br.* IV. 6 = 16.6; also Eggeling, J., *op. cit.*, pt. III, SBE Vol. 41, Intrn., pp. xviii - xix.
13. See chap. on "Waters", note 12 *infra.*
14. One of the types of the Gavām-ayana extends over ten months only, the other extending over twelve months. Another based on *nakṣatra-māsa* extends over 325 days including Viṣuvan day, since *nakṣatra* -month consists of 27 days.

See, Dharmadhikari, T.N., "Gavām-ayanam," in *Sacrifice in India - Concept & Evolution,* ed. by (Mrs.) Dange, S.S., Viveka Pubns., Aligarh, 1987, p. 32.

15. The etymology of the word Vasatīvarī is stated in more than one ways:
    (*i*) As the gods come to stay in the sacrificer's house on the Upavasatha day (i.e. preparation-day or the day when the gods 'stay' √*vas*, 'near' - *upa,* the sacrificer), they stay (actually) in the Vasatīvarī water, brought by the sacrificer on that day. Hence the name Vasatīvarī fr. √*vas* - 'to stay *Śat Br.* III. 9.2.7.
    (*ii*) The Vasatīvarī waters are beneficial (*vara)* to the dwellers (*vasat)* of the (sacrificer's) house. So the name. *ibid.* III. 9. 2.16.
    (*iii*) The gods divided the sacrifice on Āgnīdhra's shed (which is half-inside half-outside the altar Mahāvedi). About what was left over, they said, 'Let it stay here'. So the name Vasatīvarī (fr. √*vas* - 'to stay'). In the morning also, the gods could not arrange to divide the sacrifice, which was remaining. They placed that part of the sacrifice in waters, which are known as Vasatīvarī (again fr. √*vas*). *Tait. Sam.* VI. 4.2.1
16. *Brahma P.* 29.35 cd; 36 — One who worships the sun with a lamp, containing ghee or sesame-oil does not become blind. *Ibid.* 27.36 ab — The giver of a lamp gets faultless eye-sight. Cf. *Agni P.* 200.3a, also *Varāha P.* 207.53 cd — People obtain lustre by giving a gift of lamp.
17. This firebrand is taken from the Gārhapatya fire. The Gārhapatya fire in this context is none other than the Ukhya Agni, which is carried about by the sacrificer in the fire-pan (*ukhā),* during the period of his consecration. See note 11 *supra.*
18. Light dispersion, through the process of refraction (as seen in prism, rain-drops, natural or artificial crystals, etc.) or diffraction (when light encounters sharp edges, boundaries of materials, glass or reflecting surface, etc.) helps in segregation of its constituent colours, which are seven (VIBGYOR).
19. Cf. *RV* I. 160. 1 cd — where the divine bright Sūrya (the sun) is said to move between the two divine bowls, i.e.

Dyāvāpṛthivī — Heaven and Earth. For the variegated stone standing for the sun and also the beliefs about the stone, see (Mrs.) Dange, S.S., "Aśman in Vedic Ritual and Belief", *Śrījagannāthajyotiḥ*, Jagannath Sanskrit Uni. Journal of Indology, Vol. 8, 2003, pp. 14-20.

20. See (Mrs.) Dange, S.S., "The Severed Head in Myth and Ritual", *Amṛtamahotsava Vol. Annals* of the Bhandarkar Oriental Research Institute, Vols. LXXII & LXXIII (1991 & 1992), Pune (pub. in 1993), pp. 487-96.
21. *AV*. XIII. 24.12, 36 — Atri finding out and placing the sun in the sky.

    Śat. Br. IV. 3.4.21 — The priest Atri dispelling the darkness; also *ibid.* V. 3.2.2. *Tait. Sam.* II. 1.22.1; *Pañc. Br.* IV. 5.2; VI. 8.1; *Kauṣ Br.* XXIV.3; *Jaim. Br.* I. 80.
22. See (Mrs.) Dange, S.S., "Sāman-s and Lauds", *Aspects of Speech in Vedic Ritual,* pp. 182-205.
23. The Svara (*sāman*-s) are also called Spara (*Pañc. Br.* IV. 5.2) and Para (*ibid.* 3), because the gods delivered (*asprṇvan)* the sun from darkness (*ibid.* 2) and also they carried (*apārayan)* the sun to the heavenly world (*ibid. 3*), with the chanting of these *sāman*-s.
24. *Mbh.* Ādi 14.5-9 (southern version); Ādi 17.4-8 (Crit. Ed.); Ādi 19.4-9 (northern version).

    Padma P. Brahmakhaṇḍa 10.21; also *Agni P.* 3.14-16; *Brahma P.* 106. 24-31. For more details, see Dange, Sadashiv A., *Ency. of P.B.&P.,* Vol. IV, Navrang, New Delhi, 1989, p. 1115 f. under "Planets".
25. The *Ṣaḍ. Br.* (II. 4.3) notes that the moon comes from the south.
26. Eggeling, J. *op. cit.,* pt. I, SBE Vol. 12, p. 381, note 2. He states the view of Dākṣāyaṇa that at the New-moon day sacrifice, *sānnāyya* or *payasyā* offered to Mitra and Varuṇa is prepared in the usual way, i.e. by fresh milk being added to the sour milk of the preceding night's milking. At the Full-moon day offering, the sour and sweet milk remain separate and constitute two different *havi*-s to Indra.
27. Cf. Tylor, E.B., *Primitive Culture,* Vol. II, London, 1891, p. 375. Tylor points out that both prayer and sacrifice go hand in hand. As prayer is a request made to a deity as if it was human, so sacrifice is a gift made to a deity as if to a human.
28. Ex. given - *RV* VII. 33.4.

29. At the Agniṣṭoma sacrifice, in the Mahāvedi, among other structures, the Havirdhāna shed is an important structure. It holds the two small carts, containing the shoots of Soma — the two carts thereby called *havirdhāna-śakaṭe*. For more details, see Dange, Sadashiv A., *Vedic Sacrifices — Early Nature*, Vol. I, Aryan Books International, New Delhi, 2000, pp. 211 ff. (the chap. "The Havirdhāna and Other Sheds").
30. See Eggeling, J., *op. cit.,* pt. I, SBE Vol. 12, p. 176, note 3. He says that the identification of the Soma (plant and juice) with the moon already occurs in some of the hymns of the *RV*, all of which, however, probably belong to the later ones. According to *St. Petersburg Dictionary*, the identification was probably suggested from the *indu*—'drop', 'spark', which applies both to the Soma and the moon; also see Dange, Sadashiv A., *Images from Vedic Hymns and Rituals,* Aryan Books International, New Delhi, 2000, chap. "The Advent of Soma," pp. 115-25.
31. For the same idea, *Śat. Br.* II. 4.4.15; XI. 1.4.4.
32. *Jaim. Br.* I. 246 — Moon - the excellent food of the gods.
33. The etymology of the word *amāvasyā* is stated in yet another way by the *Sat. Br.* (I. 6.4.3). The mythical account states that Indra hurled the thunderbolt at Vṛtra but thinking that he had not slain the latter, concealed himself. Agni having discovered Indra, stayed with him as a guest that day and night. The gods said that as their '*vasu*' (treasure', Indra being the towering personage amongst them) was dwelling together with Agni (*amā* - near √*vas* - 'to stay') on that day (the New-moon day being hence called the *amāvasyā* day), a sacrificial cake on twelve potsherds should be offered to Indra and Agni on the New-moon day.
34. *Śat. Br.* I.7.1.1 - When the metre Gāyatrī was bringing Soma from the heaven, a footless archer severed one of the feathers (*parṇa*) either of the Gāyatrī or of Soma. The same feather (*parṇa)* falling down became a Parṇa (Palāśa) tree. Hence the Parṇa, i.e. Palāśa tree is said to be Soma.
35. *Ibid.* XI. 1.5.5 — Three chief oblations laid down in connection with this are — a cake on eight potsherds for Agni Pathikṛt (the path-maker), one on eleven potsherds for Indra Vṛtrahan (the slayer of Vṛtra) and a cake on twelve potsherds for Agni Vaiśvānara.

36. Here the pseudo-myth of the moon regarded as a dog becomes a functional myth, for the rite of giving *dakṣiṇā* of a particular sort comes in following this myth.
37. See Sāyaṇa on *Ait. Br.* IV. 27 = 19.5.
38. The *Jaim. Br.* makes clear the motif of this marriage. It says that the gods and men were dying of hunger due to want of rain. The gods live on the offerings sent from here and the men on gifts from there, i.e. in the form of rain from the heavens (*Jaim. Br.* I. 145).
39. *Śulka* is that, taking which the girl is given away in marriage, loosely tr. as 'bride-price.'
40. The *mantra* is *pra candramā tirate dīrgham āyuḥ* (*AV* has 'tirase' for 'tirate'). See *RV* X. 85. 19d; *AV* VII. 81. 2d; XIV. 1. 24 d; *Tait. Sam.* II.4.14.1d; *Mait. Sam,* IV. 12.38d; *Kāṭh. Sam.* X. 12 d, also *Nir.* XI. 6 d.
41. For detailed information about the constellations, see Macdonell, A.A. and Keith, A.B., *Vedic Index of Names and Subjects,* Vol. I, under the title "Nakṣatra"; Kane, P.V., *Hist. of Dh. S.,* Vol. V, pt. I, 2nd ed., Poona, 1974, pp. 495 ff.; Pandit, Vasant Kumar R., "Origin and Growth of the Jyotiṣa-śāstra", *Jnl. of the University of Bombay,* Vol. XXVI (New Series), Part 2, Arts No., Sept. 1957, pp. 83-90; also (Mrs.) Dange, S.S., "Constellations", *Hindu Domestic Rituals — A Critical Glance,* Ajanta Pubns., Delhi, 1985, pp. 1-9.
42. Kane, P.V., *op. cit.,* Vol. V, pt. I, p. 495.
43. Aufrecht and Weber state the etymology of the word '*nakṣatra*' from *nakta-tra* meaning 'protector of night' (√*trai* - 'to protect), while Macdonell and Keith, *op. cit.,* give it from *nak-kṣatra* - 'ruling over night'.
44. *Nir. III.* 20 gives the etymology of the word *nakṣatra* fr. √*nakṣ* - 'to get, obtain'.
45. See Dange, Sadashiv A., *Ency. of P.B.&P.,* Vol. I, Navrang Pubn., New Delhi, 1986, p. 306.
46. Eggeling, J., *op. cit.,* part IV, SBE Vol. 43, p. 383, notes 1&2.
47. The *Tait. Sam.* (V. 4.1.4) states that the constellations move both towards west and east. The *Śat. Br.* (II. 1.2.3) however says that all constellations except the Kṛttikā-s move away from the east. It says that a group of stars called Saptarṣi, rises in the north, but the Kṛttikā-s rise in the east (*ibid.* II. 1.2.4).

48. Sāyaṇa on *Tait. Br.* (I.5.2.1)... *tacca nakṣatram yāvat prācyam udayam prāpya paścimābhimukham gacchati/*

For the passage, *Tait. Br.* (I.5.2.7, 8) - *yāni devanakṣatrāṇi tāni dakṣiṇena pariyanti/*
yāni yamanakṣatrāṇi (7) *tānyuttareṇa iti/*

Sāyaṇa here takes the suffix 'enap' (in the words '*dakṣiṇena*' and '*uttareṇa*') in the sense of 'vicinity' (*adūrārthavācitvāt)* and says that the Kṛttikā-s, etc. move to the southern side near the Devaloka and Anūrādhā etc. on the northern side near the Yamaloka.

49. The *Tait. Br.* further states the Puronuvākyā (invoking) and Yājyā (offering) *mantra*-s of each of the Devanakṣatra-s and the Yamanakṣatra-s (III. 1. sections 1&2 on the rituals).
50. The word *saṅgava* is derived from *sam-go* — the time when grazing cows are collected for milking or when they are together with their calves (3 *muhūrta*-s after the *prātaḥ,* i.e. morning).
51. The *Tait. Br.* puts forth here another idea, replacing the *pradoṣa-kāla* and the *uṣaḥ-kāla,* by night (*āgneyī rātriḥ)* and by day (*aindram ahaḥ)* and the *brāhmaṇa* by the sun (*ādityaḥ),* making again the number twelve to represent the year (I.5.3.4) and the daily ritual to be equal to the ritual performed for the whole year.
52. This is obviously because on the New-moon day, the moon comes so close to the sun that it is 'eaten' up by the latter. So to release the moon, offerings are given to the sun.
53. Twenty-six constellations and the seven stars of the Kṛttikā constellation make for the number thirty-three.
54. Also *Tait. Br.* I.1.2.4-6.
55. Also *Kāṭh Sam.* (XL.4) for these names; *Tait Sam.* (IV. 4.5.1) while laying down the bricks on the Great Fire-altar in the names of constellations, mentions these names when the constellation-bricks in the name of the Kṛttikā-s are laid down.
56. *Kāṭh. Sam.* VIII. 1; *Mait. Sam.* I.6.9; *Tait. Br.* I.1.2.1; 5.1.1; *Śat. Br.* II. 1.2.1.
57. *Śat. Br.* II. 3.1.36 — When the sun sets, then Agni is the light and when the sun rises, Sūrya is the light.
58. The constellation Mṛgaśirṣa is also named 'Invakāḥ' (Fem. plural), as it indicates a group of stars.

59. In the *Ait. Br.*, the myth of Prajāpati and his daughter becomes a star-myth. Prajāpati transforms himself into a roe-buck (*ṛśya)* and approaches his own daughter, who assumes the form of a deer, here 'doe' (*rohita).* Prajāpati is pierced by the arrow of Bhūtavat (i.e. Rudra) who is created by the gods out of their most fearful forms. Prajāpati is bounded up to the sky, where he becomes the constellation called Mṛga (i.e. Mṛgaśīrṣa) and his daughter becomes the constellation Rohiṇī (*Ait. Br.* III.33=13.9).
60. *Tait. Br.* mentions these two constellations but reverses the presiding gods in that the two stars of Pūrva Phalgunī (*pūrve phalgunī*) are governed by Aryaman and the two stars of Uttara Phalgunī (*uttare phalgunī)* by Bhaga (I.1.2.3,4).
61. The great Mahābhārata personality Arjuna is said to be the son of Indra. Is it a reflection of the name 'Arjuna' given to Indra in the ritual tradition? In the ritual tradition, both the names (Indra and Arjuna) are of the same god (i.e. one person), while in the *Mbh.* the two names denote two separate personalities.

    It is enjoined that after seeing a rainbow, a *snātaka* (i.e. a student, who has taken a final bath as a mark of completion of his studies at the preceptor's hermitage and is to enter the stage of a householder) should not directly utter the word '*indradhanuḥ*' but should say the word '*maṇidhanuḥ*' (*Pār. G.S.* II. 7.13). This is obviously to avoid the anger of the god Indra.

    It is interesting to note that the twin-trees, to which child Kṛṣṇa was tied (giving him further the epithet 'Dāmodara') and which were uprooted by him, were the Arjuna trees. Does the name of the trees indicate Kṛṣṇa's clash with Indra, as we see in the Govardhana-episode? For more details, see (Mrs.) Dange, S.S., *The Bhāgavata Purāṇa — Mytho-Social Study,* pp. 166-70, 187-89.
62. The belief occurs in the *RV* where the god Apām Napāt is said to have a secret name (*RV* II. 3.11 ab) and Varuṇa is said to know the secret names of the 'cows' (*ibid.* VIII. 87.4). For the information from the Gṛhyasūtra-s, see (Mrs.) Dange, S.S., "Naming of the Child (Nāmakaraṇa)", *Hindu Domestic Rituals — A Critical Glance,* pp. 21-24.
63. Eggeling, J., *op. cit.*, pt. I, SBE Vol. 12, p. 285, note 2.
64. *Tait. Sam.* 1.5.1.4; *Kāth. Sam.* VIII. 15; *Mait. Sam.* I.7.2; *Śat. Br.* II. 1.2.10; *Kauṣ Br.* I.3.

65. Sāyaṇa explains this with the help of a term in Mīmāṁsā namely 'Liṅga', on which principle, one can join the two concepts *viz.* that of the constellation Punarvasu and the rite of Punarādheya (Sāy. on *Śat. Br.* II. 1.2.10).

    'Liṅga' is the power of word (*śabdasāmarthyam liṅgam)* and this power is convention itself (*sāmarthyam rūḍhireva).* See *Arthasaṅgraha* of Laugākṣibhāskara, ed. by Paranjape, S.M., Nirnaysagar, Mumbai, 1927, p. 108.

    In the words 'Punarvasu' and 'Punarādheya', the word '*punar'* is important, which has brought the two concepts together.
66. Sāyaṇa in his commentary on this passage remarks that the offering of cattle enjoined by such expressions as *vāyavyam śvetam ālabheta,* etc. prior to the Soma-sacrifice, should be undertaken under the Revatī constellation.
67. For Odanasava, see *Tait. Br.* II. 7.7; the Kalpa tradition as quoted by Sāyaṇa on this passage. Also see note 1 *supra.*
68. See Sāyaṇa on *Tait. Br.* II. 7.9.4, where he quotes from the tradition of the Jyotiḥśāstra.
69. See note 62 *supra.*
70. Hastings, J., *Ency of Rel. and Eth.*, Vol. XII. 457 a.

CHAPTER 3

Quarters

Quarters mentioned in Vedic rituals are not mere 'directions' (fr. √*diś* - 'to point'), but are regarded as conducive to some miraculous effect and hence have a definite place in the sacrificial set-up.

Quarters are believed to have divine origin. A mythical account as *arthavāda* occurs in the *Śat. Br.* that when Prajāpati united with the sky (*divam, - 'dyu'* Fem.) by means of the sun, there arose an egg. The juice sticking to the shell (of the egg) gave rise to intermediate quarters, and the principal quarters came out of the shell itself (*Śat. Br.* VI. 1.2.4). It is by the quarters that these worlds are firmly joined together with the sun. This belief is echoed in the context of building the Great Fire-altar in the rite of Agnicayana. The sacrificer has to carry the fire in an earthen fire-pan by means of netting (*śikya).* He, thereby, is said to sustain the whole world with Agni, Agni being the form of the sun.[1] The strings of the netting holding the fire-pan and thus bearing Agni are likened to the quarters as the latter firmly join the worlds with the sun (*ibid.* VI. 7. 1.16). The strings of the netting are six and so are there six quarters (*ibid.).* In the same rite, in the ritual of making the fire-pan (*ukhā),* the deity of Sound, i.e. Speech, and the deities *viz.* Quarters, are joined together. When the sacrificer or the priest has to dig the earth for a lump of clay for making the fire-pan, he takes the spade with four formulas (*mantra*-s*).* Here number four stands for four quarters and the formulas in turn for Speech, for they are one of the aspects of Speech.[2] While·taking the clay from the ground, as noted above, these four formulas and the four metres in which these formulas (*mantra*-s) are, make for the number eight, which number stands for the four main quarters and the four intermediate quarters, thus enabling the sacrificer or the priest to lay Speech in all quarters (*ibid*,. VI. 3.1.44). The idea of joining any two or more entities on the basis of 'number' is a common feature noticed in the ritual texts.[3] In the same rite (i.e. Agnicayana), the quarters are given special importance in that five bricks in the name of quarters (the bricks are called 'Diśyā', fr. *diś* - 'quarter') are enjoined to be laid down in the third layer of the Great Fire-altar. This is for bestowing quarters (and their support) in the layer of the altar. The *Śat. Br.* here associates the quarters with different metres *viz.* east with Gāyatrī, south with Triṣṭubh, west with Jagatī, north with Anuṣṭubh and the upper region with Paṅkti (*ibid.* VIII. 3.1.11, 12), which (i.e. metres) are also an aspect of Speech.

Quarters are said to be four or eight. At some places, they are said to be five—four principal quarters and the upper quarter. In the Rājasūya sacrifice, the king is made to ascend the five regions (situated at) — east, south, west, north and the upper one. The *Śat. Br.* states that ascending the quarters amounts to ascending the seasons as also the year, symbolically making the king stand high above everything. Here the east is associated with spring, south with summer, west with rainy season, north with autumn and the upper quarter with winter. This ascending on the part of the king is symbolic of the king's victory over all regions lying in different quarters as well as over seasons, the latter again making up a year, which is also acquired by the king (*ibid.* V. 4.1.3-8). Occasionally the quarters are said to be seven or nine or ten — seven, when a hymn of seven verses is enjoined for being recited (*ibid.* IX. 5.2.8); nine, when eight *mantra*-s addressed to Savitṛ (in the Gāyatrī metre) and the sound 'Hail' (Svāhā) making a total of nine, are laid down; ten, when together with the nine, as mentioned above, the libation is also taken into account (*ibid.*).

The importance of quarters is brought out even with respect to a small ritual. In the Agnicayana rite, while taking a lump of clay from the earth for preparing the fire-pan, a hole is caused in the earth, which action as though hurts the earth. For healing the earth, pouring of water in the hole and fanning air into the hole with the hand are enjoined. Together with these, healing the earth by means of quarters is also laid down.[4] This is done by pushing some of the loose soil into the hole in a particular way. The *Kāty. Ś.S.* (XVI. 3.4) says that the sun-wise movement is obtained by the hand moving from east (along the south) to west, and then from south (along the west) to north. The *Śat. Br.* says that whatever is injured and torn in this earth, that is healed by the quarters (*Śat. Br.* VI. 4.3.5).

The quarters are believed to be the abode of all gods. In the Pravargya ceremony, if the Gharma (Mahāvīra) pot breaks, in the expiatory rite which is laid down, he offers with the *mantra* from the *Vāj. Sam.* (XXXIX. 2) to the quarters, having first offered to vital breaths (*prāṇa*-s), Earth, Agni, Mid-region, Air, Sky, Sūrya, Moon, Constellations, etc. With this offering to the quarters, which are said to be the abode of all gods, he heals whatever has been unsuccessful in sacrifice (*Śat. Br.* XIV. 3.2.10). The later concept of the quarter-gods (*lokapāla*-s) guarding the regions of the quarters, occurring prominently in the Purāṇa-s can be traced to the Vedic ritual tradition. The *Varāha P.* states that on the words of the four main quarters, Brahmā gave them their controllers (in the form of the guards). Even the guards of the four intermediary quarters were created by him. These quarter-gods are — Indra, Agni, Yama, Nirṛti, Varuṇa, Vāyu, Kubera and Īśāna. Brahmā himself controlled the Ūrdhvā (upper quarter) and gave the Adharā (nether quarter) to the serpent Śeṣa.[5]

The main function of the quarters according to the ritual tradition seems to be to make the worlds firm on all sides.

This belief is reflected while making a fire-pan in the rite of Agnicayana. When the fire-pan made of clay is ready, he silently draws four verticle lines on the fire-pan *(ukhā)*. The *arthavāda* here states that the gods having made the fire-pan, made these worlds firm on all sides by means of quarters. The sacrificer follows the gods in this respect and makes the worlds firm on all sides by means of quarters, which are indicated by the four verticle lines drawn on the fire-pan (*Śat. Br.* VI. 5.2.14). The same belief is seen in later times as can be seen in the *Var. P.* Brahmā having created the creatures thought as to who would support them. As he thought, there came forth from his ten ears (because he had five heads) ten very brilliant girls. They became the six main quarters *viz.* East, South, West, North, Upper One (Ūrdhvā) and the Lower One (Adharā) and the four intermediary quarters (*Var. P.* 29.3 ff). This shows that Brahmā created the quarters (as per this account, they could be taken as his daughters) to support the creatures (i.e. the worlds). The idea that the world has to be supported as resting on something is marked in ancient Egyptian mythology also, where we have an idea that the world is supported on firm pillars.[6]

That the quarters are beneficiary to the living beings is stated in the context of the rite of Agnicayana. While laying down the Spṛta bricks, which are for freeing (fr. √*spṛ*), it is said that by means of the chant of praise consisting of four *stoma*-s[7] (Catuṣṭoma), he freed for the sake of living brings, all the four quarters from evil as also from death (*Śat. Br.* VIII. 4.2.10).

The importance of the main quarters can be traced to the *RV*, where the earth is said to be four-angled (*RV* X. 58.3 *bhūmim caturbhṛṣṭim)*. The *Śat. Br.* at times associates the four main quarters with the four main priests. In the Sarvamedha sacrifice, which goes on for ten days, the Viśvajit Atirātra sacrifice with all the Pṛṣṭha-*sāman*-s is performed on the tenth day. While prescribing the *dakṣiṇā*-s for this sacrifice, it is said that whatever there is in the middle of the kingdom other than the property of the *brāhmaṇa,* but (that middle part of the kingdom) including land and men, of that, the eastern quarter (region) belongs to the Hotṛ priest, the southern quarter (region) to the Brahman priest, the western quarter (region) to the Adhvaryu priest and the northern quarter (region) to the Udgātṛ priest and the Hotṛka-s share this along with them (*Śat. Br.* XIII. 7.1.13). However, the *Śat. Br.* is quick enough to add a *śloka* here, which is said to be spoken by the earth and which states that no mortal whosoever can give her to anybody.[8] This is obviously the folk-belief, which is further recorded by the *Jai. Sū* (VI. 7.3) and Śabarasvāmin commenting on it.

The quarters viewed individually are associated with certain beliefs. Prior to taking up that point, it will be interesting to see a couple of details from the ritual texts. To take the first. In the 'Garga three-day' sacrifice, thousand cows are given as *dakṣiṇā*-s. On each of the three days, 333 cows are to be given and the remaining 1,000th cow, which is a red and spotted one and has not been approached by any bull, remains as standing for Speech of unimpared vigour. This cow is to be released and while not being urged by any person would go in any direction, indicating thereby, as per the beliefs of the Vedic ritualists, the fruit to be achieved by the sacrificer, of the 'Garga three-day' sacrifice. The going of the cow eastwards indicates the sacrificer's winning the happy world; going northwards, the sacrificer's becoming more glorious in this world; going westwards, his becoming rich in dependents *(ibhyatilvila)* and the crops *(dhānyatilvila);* and going southwards, the sacrificer's quickly departing from this world (*Śat. Br.* IV.5. 8. 1-3, also 11). The other detail is regarding the Agnihotra rite, in which milk is to be heated for the offering. The vessel of milk is an earthen one and not prepared by the potter's wheel. (obviously then by the hand). The milk is to be heated to a certain degree (not getting into bubbles and boiling).[9] Then the vessel is to be dragged (from the fire) to the north, the line of ashes being visible. This is said to be for continuation. The *Tait. Br.* says that if it (i.e. the vessel) is placed to the east, it would cause anguish to the sacrificer; if to the west, it would torment the sacrificer's wife; if to the south, it (i.e. the offering) would belong to the *pitṛ*-s. As there is no danger either from gods or from men in the northern quarter, it is a peaceful quarter. So the vessel of milk should be placed to the northern side (of the Āhavanīya fire-place). (*Tait. Br.* II. 1.3.4, 5). Even the *Kāṭh. Sam.* has already stated this (*Kāṭh. Sam.* VI. 4). The quarters are mentioned in the rite of the great anointing of Indra. Whatever kings there are of the eastern peoples, they are anointed for overlordship in the eastern quarter. Whatever kings there are of the Satvants, they are anointed for paramount rule in the southern quarter. Whatever kings there are of the southern and western peoples, they are anointed for self-rule in the western quarter. In the northern quarter, the kings of the land of the Uttara Kurus and Uttara Madras, beyond the Himavat are anointed for sovereignty. In the established central quarter, whatever kings there are, they are established for kingship (*Ait. Br.* VIII. 13-14 = 38.2-3).

These references from the ritual texts make clear that the ritualists had fixed notions and beliefs about the quarters. However, it has to be pointed out that the Vedic ritualists do not hold the same fixed beliefs regarding individual quarters at all places. Even then, we may be able to mark some generalisations regarding certain quarters, which got percolated even in the Puranic age.

The most auspicious of the quarters is the east, as it is the quarter of the rising sun and in the sacrifice, of Agni. The *Kauṣ Br.* states that the gods having reached the heavenly world by means of the introductory sacrifice (Prāyaṇīya *iṣṭi)* could not discern the quarters. To Agni, they offered a libation of butter as per his wish and Agni discerned for them the eastern quarter. Therefore, in the sacrifice, they lead Agni forward (Agnipraṇayana) to the east and the sacrifice is extended eastwards (*Kauṣ. Br.* VII.

6).[10] The mythical account stated in the context of Agnipraṇayana, of Agni's falling out from the mouth of Māthava Videgha on hearing the word *'ghṛta'* in the word *'ghṛtasno'* (Vocative Singular, addressed to Agni, *RV* V. 26.2a), uttered by the priest Gotama Rāhūgaṇa and his (i.e. Agni's) marching towards the east up to the river Sadānīrā, is to be noted in this context (*Śat. Br.* I.4.1.10-14). Initially, this mythical account indicates the eastward spread of the sacrificial religion of the Aryans, by the time of the *Śat. Br.* It is interesting to note that this historical detail is enshrined in the myth, as noted above, the latter serving as a 'charter' for the rite of Agnipraṇayana (to the east). In the rite of Agnicayana, the priests and the sacrificer, for taking a lump of clay for making a fire-pan, proceed eastwards, for the east is Agni's region (*ibid.* VI. 3.3.2). Again while carrying the fire kept in the fire-pan, the sacrificer is to drive first to the east, it being the region of Agni (*ibid.* VI 8.1.8).

It is obvious that the east being the quarter of the rising sun and Agni being regarded as the form of the sun, the east came to be associated with Agni. The *Tait Sam.* in the rite of Agnicayana enjoins ten bricks named Prāṇabhṛt (lit. 'supporters of breaths') to be placed in the east. Number ten is connected to the metre Virāj, having ten syllables in one foot. *Virāj* (fr. *vi* + √*rāj* - 'to shine excessively') is the light of metres. By placing the Prāṇabhṛt bricks in the east, he places *virāj*, i.e. light (sun) in the east (*Tait. Sam.* V. 3.2.2, 3). In the Prāyaṇīya *iṣṭi* one who desires brilliance (*tejas)* and splendour (*brahmavarcas)* should turn towards the east with the libations of fore-offering (*prayāja-āhutis).* Eastern quarter is brilliance and splendour (*Ait. Br.* I.8 = 2.2). A similar idea is reflected in the *Śiva P.*, when it is said that while muttering *(japa),* if one faces the east, that is conducive for gaining control (*Śiva. P.* VII. 2.14.46).

East being the repository of solar (light) is naturally connected with the world of heaven and is also spoken of as the abode of gods. In the New-moon and Full-moon sacrifices, he puts forward the bunch (*prastara)*[11] with its points to the east. By this he makes the sacrificer go to the world of heaven (*Tait. Sam.* II. 6.5.4). The *Śat. Br.* often states that the east is the quarter of the gods (*Śat. Br.* I.7.1.12; 8.3.18; 9.3.13). The altar in the New-moon and the Full-moon sacrifices should be sloping towards the east as it is the quarter of the gods (*ibid.* I.2.5.17). This belief is echoed by the *Vām. P.* in later times, when it says that to the east stay the gods such as Nārāyaṇa, Nara, Brahmā, Śiva along with Indra (*Vām. P.* 21.21 f). Even a tree, which is to be felled for making a sacrificial post in the animal-sacrifice (for Agni and Soma), is enjoined to be so cut as to fall towards the east, for the east is the quarter of the gods (*Śat. Br.* III. 6.4.12). With this same belief, the sacrificial hall (*śālā*) is to be erected with its top-beams running from west to east and even while offering to gods one has to stand with his face towards the east (*ibid.* III. 1.1.6).[12] Hence it is that one should not sleep with his head towards the west for, in that case he would sleep stretching his legs towards the east, i.e. the gods. The Śrautasūtra-s also lay down several injunctions having the importance of east in view,[13] though they do not explicitly state the reasoning behind these, as there is no scope for it in such type of literature, which is meant for codification of matters. In later times, Purāṇa-s contain significant details which speak of the importance of east.[14]

The highest importance given to the eastern quarter is obviously due to its association with the rising sun, which is the very foundation of all existence. This is very well reflected in the ritual-practice of placing the enclosing-sticks (*paridhi*-s), for the Āhavanīya fire (in which the oblations to the gods are to be offered), on its three sides *viz.* southern, northern and western only, and not on the eastern side because the sun signifies the east[15] and serves as the enclosing stick on the eastern side.[16] The enclosing-sticks are for protecting Agni, as he was afraid of the sound Vaṣaṭ, so goes the mythical account.[17] As the sun is the best protector, he serves as the enclosing-stick on the eastern side.

Next to the east in importance comes the north. As the eastern quarter is associated with the gods, the northern quarter is with men (i.e. human beings.) This is stated on several occasions in the rituals. In the New-moon and the Full-moon sacrifices, the bunch of the sacred grass (*prastara)* is to be thrown into the fire, either to the east or to the north (*Śat. Br.* I.8.3.18). In the same sacrifices, he has to put the strainer on the pot in such a way that the top is turned eastwards or northwards (*ibid.* I.7.1.12). In these sacrifices, the altar should be sloping towards the north, it being the quarter of men (*ibid.* I.2.5.17). The tree out of which the sacrificial stake is to be made, should be cut in such a way as to fall towards the east or towards the north (*ibid.* III. 6.4.12). In the Agniṣṭoma sacrifice, the tie-beams of the *sadas* (shed) should run from the south to the north, because north is the quarter of men (*ibid.* III. 6.1.23). A mythical account occurring in the context of purchasing Soma also points out the same belief regarding the northern quarter. The Somakrayaṇī cow figures in this ritual as a symbol of Speech (Vāk). In this mythical account, which comes by way of *arthavāda* we find that the gods sent Vāk to the *gandharva*-s, but she returned to the gods together with Soma (which the *gandharva*-s had taken away from the gods earlier), when the gods wooed her. In the actual ritual of purchasing Soma, the sacrificer also wooes the Somakrayaṇī cow and she turns to him. They lead this cow northwards round, for the north is the quarter of men and so of the sacrificer (*ibid.* III. 2.4.22). It has to be noted that the *Ait. Br.* states Soma the king to be in the north. It is laid down in the Prāyaṇīya *iṣṭi* that one desirous of drinking Soma should turn to the north with the libations of fore-offerings, i.e. *prayāja-āhuti*s (*Ait. Br.* I.8 =2.2). In later tradition, i.e. of the Śrautasūtras, the *Baudh. Ś.S.* says that the Somakrayaṇī cow is brought from the north (VI. 12). Even the Agnihotra cow (the cow of which the milk-offerings are offered in the Agnihotra-rite) is made to stand facing the north when a *brāhmaṇa* wants to milk her.[18] Having first tasted the milk with a finger, he should turn towards the north and consume the milk with the ladle so that the handle of the ladle is turned towards the east. The water used for cleaning the ladle is to be thrown to the north. This amounts to propitiating the Saptarṣi-s.[19]

That the northern region was famous for its cultured speech-habits, could be seen from a mythical account stated as *arthavāda* in the *Kauṣ. Br.* When the gods reached the heavenly world by means of the Prāyaṇīya *iṣṭi,* they could not discern the quarters. To the deity Pathyā Svasti they offered one libation on her word and she discerned the northern quarter for them. Pathyā Svasti (though originally the deity of paths)[20] is Speech. The *Kauṣ, Br.* states here that in the northern quarter, speech is uttered with more discernment and men go northwards to learn speech. They hearken a person who has come from the north (*Kauṣ. Br.* VII. 6).[21]

While the gods in general are associated with the eastern quarter, it is Rudra alone who is said to be having north as his quarter. While dealing with the Agnihotra-offerings, the *Kauṣ. Br.* enjoins holding twice the offering-ladle to the north, thereby pleasing Rudra in his own quarter. It is said that one should not stand to the north of the offering as it is made. By this, one would not be in the vicinity of this dreadful god (*Kauṣ. Br.* II. 2). In the Tryambaka offerings, which form the last part of the Sākamedha *parvan,* rice-cakes—as many as there are descendants exceeded by one — are offered to Rudra. While taking out the rice for these cakes and threshing it, the sacrificer has to face the north. The two mill-stones are to be so placed on the black antelope skin as to incline towards the north and the potsherds, on the north side of the Gārhapatya altar. Here the quarter spoken of is north, for it is the quarter of god Rudra (*Śat. Br.* II. 6.2.5). The mythical account occurring as *arthavāda* to praise the hymns composed by Nābhānediṣṭha (*RV* X. 61, 62), which are to be recited on the sixth day of the Pṛṣṭha Ṣaḍaha (as forming part of the Soma-sacrifice) is to be noted in this regard. When Nābhānediṣṭha was gathering the thousand *dakṣiṇā*-s (cows) together, a man in black garments, coming from the north insisted on having the *vāstuha,* i.e. what was left on the place of sacrifice (*Ait. Br.* V. 14 = 22.9). Practically the same account though differing in some details but not referring to the northern quarter, clearly states the name of the god as Rudra, who at that time came to the place of sacrifice (*yajñavāstu)* and said that whatever was left at the place of sacrifice belonged to him (*Tait. Sam.* III. 1.9.4-6). These two accounts when considered together point out north to be the quarter of the god Rudra.[22]

South is the quarter associated with the Fathers as also Death. Hence a place of worship should be one somewhat raised up towards the south, for if it is inclined towards the south, the sacrificer would quickly depart from this world to the yonder world (*Śat. Br.* III. 1.1.2).[23] For making a sacrificial post in the animal-sacrifice (to Agni and Soma), care has to be taken to keep the tree from falling towards the southern quarter, as it is the quarter of the Fathers (*ibid.* III. 6.4.12). South being associated with the Fathers (*pitṛ*-s*),* it is but natural that this quarter is mentioned in the Mahāpitṛyajña in the Sākamedha *parvan* of the Four-monthly sacrifices (Cāturmāsya *iṣṭi*-s*).* For this sacrifice, he raises a square altar south of the Dakṣiṇa fire. He takes out rice for the cake of six potsherds, himself seated behind the Gārhapatya altar and looking towards south. The two mill-stones are to be so placed on the black antelope skin as to be inclined towards the south and the six potsherds are to be put on the south part of the Gārhapatya altar. The *Śat. Br.* states that the quarter mentioned here is south, for it is the quarter of the Fathers (*ibid.* II. 6.1.8, 9).[24]

This quarter is said to be associated with food also. An *arthavāda* passage in the *Ait. Br.,* occurring in the context of the *iṣṭi,* points out how in order to enable the gods discern the sacrifice, Aditi made the gods know the quarters, thus through herself (viewed as Pathyā Svasti) the east, through Agni the south, through Soma the west and through Savitṛ the north-west. While eulogising the south, it is said that from south the plants come first ripened, for the plants are connected with Agni (*Ait. Br.* I.7=2.1). It is said further that he who desires proper food (*annādya)*, should turn in the Prāyaṇīya *iṣṭi* towards south with the libations of fore-offerings (*ibid.* I.8 = 2.2).

West is the quarter associated with the setting sun. In the evening Agnihotra rite, he rubs the remnant of milk from the offering-ladle on the north side as it points west, thereby making the sun set (*Kauṣ. Br.* II. 2). When the gods having reached the world of heaven by means of the introductory sacrifice (Prāyaṇīya *iṣṭi)* could not discern the quarters, they offered for Savitṛ on his word one libation and he discerned for them the western quarter. So men see the god Savitṛ going to the west (*ibid.* VII. 6).[25]

Being the quarter of the setting sun, the west came to be associated with the evil spirits, as the latter have their sway only when the sun sets and the darkness ushers in. In the Agnicayana rite, in the ritual of ploughing the sacrificial ground, if he loses the animals to the west, the *rakṣas*-es are said to destroy them (*Tait. Sam.* V. 2.5.3). The *Śat. Br.,* while laying down the erection of a sacrificial hall or shed (*śālā*) in the sacrifice, with the top-beams running from west to east, says that east is the quarter of the gods and west that of the snakes (*Śat. Br.* III. 1.1.7).

As east is the quarter of gods and north as that of men, the intermediary quarter north-east is believed to have a special importance in the Vedic ritual tradition. The other name for this quarter is *aparājitā* 'unconquered.' A mythical account occurs by way of *arthavāda* in the context of purchasing Soma, bringing it to the sacrificial pendal and taking down Soma from the east facing the north-eastern quarter. It is said that in every quarter, the *asura*-s conquered the gods, except in the north-eastern quarter. In this quarter one should strive or cause striving, because one has power to dispose of debts in this quarter (*Ait. Br.* I. 14 = 3.3). The *Kauṣ. Br.,* in the context of purchase of Soma in the Soma-sacrifice, has a different account to state. It states that in this quarter, the *asura*-s hindered the gods. But this being the north-east quarter, the gods anointed Soma in kingship and with him as the king, pushed away the *asura*-s from these worlds (*Kauṣ. Br.* VII. 10). In the rite of Agnicayana, while placing the fire-pan on the fire, he has to stand with his face towards the north-east, for it is the quarter of both gods and men. Again this quarter is regarded as a gate to the heavenly world. Therefore standing with his face in this quarter, one should offer libations and lead up to the *dakṣiṇā*-s (i.e. carry the *dakṣiṇā*-s). The priest thereby makes the sacrificer enter the world of heaven by the gate in the form of the north-east quarter (*Śat. Br.* VI. 6.2.2-4).

The importance of the north-east quarter is maintained even in later times also, as can be seen from the Puranic tradition. The *Matsya P.* says that the Kuṇḍa type of altar should be prepared at the north-eastern quarter of the pendal (*Matsya P.* 92. 87 cd) and the band (*mekhalā)* should dangle on the north-eastern quarter (*ibid.* 89 cd). It is said that in the dwelling, the apartment for the gods and also the 'peace-apartment' (for the ritual of purification if needed) should be to the north-east side (*ibid.* 255.33).

The south-western quarter is ascribed to Nirṛti, which is the deity of death and evil. In the rite of Agnicayana at the piling of the Gārhapatya fire, he places three bricks, which are dried up (or baked) by the chaff-fire (*tuṣapakvāḥ).* Here the chaff (when burnt, of black colour) indicates the form of Nirṛti and the sacrificer, priest, etc. go to the south-west to propitiate Nirṛti (*Tait. Sam.* V. 2.4.2, 3). The *Śat. Br.* also mentions this detail and names the three bricks 'Nairṛti'. With these bricks they proceed towards the south-western quarter, because that is the quarter of Nirṛti (*Śat. Br.* VII. 2.1.3, 7, 8). The same belief percolates in later times and the *Agni P.* states that in sorcery, blood and flesh are to be offered to the goddess Nirṛti in the south-west quarter (*Agni P.* 185.12).

Together with these quarters, sometimes there occurs mention of the upward quarter. In the Agnihotra rite, in the morning he rubs the offering-ladle on the south side as it points upwards. He thereby leads the sun upwards (*Kauṣ. Br.* II. 2).

From the details noted above, it seems that in the belief of the Vedic ritualists, the auspicious quarters were — east, north and north-east—while south and south-west were not so, south being allotted to the Fathers (*pitṛ*-s) and south-west to Nirṛti. Practically the same beliefs are attached to the quarters in the Puranic age[26] and are seen even in the modern-day Hindu India.

NOTES AND REFERENCES

1. *Śat. Br.* VI. 3.3.16; VI. 4.1.11.
2. This point has been elucidated in details. See (Mrs.) Dange, S.S., *Aspects of Speech in Vedic Ritual.*
3. See *Vāj. Sam.* IX. 31-34; also *Śat. Br.* V. 2.2.17; also see the chap. on "Complementary Numbers".
4. *Śat. Br.* VI. 4.3.1-5 and also see Eggeling, J., *The Śatapatha Brāhmaṇa,* pt. III, SBE Vol. 41, Motilal Banarsidass, Delhi, 1989 (1894), p. 221, note 2, where he explains the concept of healing by means of quarters.
5. *Var. P.* 29. 3-15; also see Dange, Sadashiv A., *Ency. P. B. & P.* Vol. IV, Navrang, 1989, p. 1145 f.
6. Rundle Clark, R.T., *Myth and Symbol in Ancient Egypt,* Thames and Hudson, London, 1959, p. 236.
7. *Stoma* etymologically means 'praise' or 'laud' (fr. √*stu* - 'to praise'). It is a group of verses (usually three), which are increased to 15, 17, 21, etc. by repetition in various patterns (which are called Viṣṭuti). These patterns differ in the order and number of repetitions. See Kane, P.V., *Hist. of Dh. S.,* Vol. II, pt. II, BORI, Poona, 1974, p. 1182, also (Mrs.) Dange, S.S., *Aspects of Speech in Vedic Ritual,* p. 200 f, for the terms *śastra, stotra, stoma* and *stobha.*
8. The *śloka* in the *Śat. Br.* occurs at XIII. 7. 1.15, and is placed in the mouth of the earth. When Viśvakarmā, the son of Bhuvana performed the Sarvamedha (sacrifice), he

promised his priest Kaśyapa the whole earth as a sacrificial gift. The earth says that Bhauvana Viśvakarmā is slow to know that no mortal whosoever can give her to anybody. If he tries to do it, she would plunge in waters and Viśvakarmā's promise to Kaśyapa would prove to be false. The same legendary story occurs with the same verse with slight variations in the *Ait. Br.* (VIII. 21 = 39.7), where Sāyaṇa calls the verse a *gāthā*. The context in the *Ait. Br.* is of Aindra Mahābhiṣeka.

9. Dange, Sadashiv A., *Vedic Sacrifices — Early Nature*, Vol. I, p. 67 f.
10. For the same thought, *Śat. Br.* III. 2.3.16 — They take Agni to the east from the Gārhapatya to the Āhavanīya fire, for to Agni belongs the eastern quarter.
11. For *prastara* a bunch of Aśvavāla-grass (Saccharum Spontaneum) — *Śat. Br.* III. 4.1.17; as of reed-grass *ibid.* I.3.3.5.

    Kane, in the context of *Barhirāharaṇa* (bringing in the bundles of sacred Kuśa grass in use) in the Darśa-Pūrnamāsa sacrifices, notes that the first handful of blades of grass that are cut is called *prastara.* See Kane, P.V., *Hist. of Dh. S.*, Vol. II, Pt. II, p. 1013.
12. *Śat. Br.* II. 6.1.11 for the same thought.
13. The sacrificer should sleep with his head towards the east, see *Śrautakośa,* Kashikar, C.G. and Dandekar, R.N., Vol. I., pt. ii, Vaidika Samshodhana Mandala, Poona, 1958, p. 664. The fire for cooking the Brahmaudana should be to the east of the central beam of the pendal. *ibid.* p. 23. The rites of the Vaiśvadeva-*parvan* of the Four-monthly (Seasonal) sacrifices commence on a piece of ground slightly sloping to the east, *ibid.* p. 662.
14. *Vām. P.* lays down resorting to or worshipping the eastern quarter (21. 21-23). *Agni P.* states that one should give a gift facing the east and the person should accept it facing the north. By this the donor gets a longer life and that of the person accepting it does not diminish (209. 21). When a cow is to be donated, she is made to stand facing the east, her feet to the north (*ibid.* 210.15ab).
15. *Śrautakośa,* Vol. I, pt. i, p. 316.
16. *Ibid.*, p. 321.
17. *Śat. Br.* I. 3.3.13, 14; *Mait. Sam.* III. 8.6 — Three Agni-s left the gods one after the other being afraid of the Vaṣaṭ call. Hence

the fourth Agni asked the gods to enclose him by those three Agni-s in the form of enclosing-sticks. The gods agreed and placed the three-enclosing-sticks on the three sides, except the east.

18. *Śrautakośa,* Vol. I, pt. i, p. 42.
19. *Ibid.,* p. 42 f.
20. See (Mrs.) Dange, S.S., "Pathyā Svasti — The Vedic Deity of Paths", *Vishveshvaranand Indological Journal*, Panjab Univ., Hoshiarpur, Vols. XXXIII-XXXVIII, June-Dec. 1999-2000 (pub. in 2002), pp. 1-5.
21. Keith, A.B., *Rigveda Brahmanas* tr., HOS Vol. 25, Motilal Banarsidass, Delhi, 1981 (London 1920), p. 387, note 2. Keith points out that Weber and Muir cite this passage in connection with the northern region of the Aryans and it is clearly an evidence of speech cultivation in the north.
22. However, at one place, Rudra is connected to both east and north (*Kauṣ. Br.* II. 2). Out of the three readings here, Keith (*op. cit.* p. 353, note 5) prefers the reading, which according to him is with 'the general view of the north-east as Rudra's quarter'.
23. For the same idea, also see *Śat. Br.* I. 2.5.17.
24. *Kauṣ. Br.* II. 2 — In the context of Agnihotra rite it is said that when in the evening, he rubs the remnant of milk from the offering ladle the second time, he lays down his outstretched hand to the south of the mat; thereby he delights the Fathers.

    This shows how even a small action in the southern direction connects it to the Fathers (*pitṛ*-s).
25. For the same thought, *ibid.* III. 2.3.18.
26. See Dange, Sadashiv A., *Ency. of P.B. & P.*, Vol. IV, Navrang Pubn., New Delhi, 1989, pp. 1145-1149 (under the title "Quarters").

CHAPTER 4

Time and its Units

The ritual texts elucidate the concept of Time through that of day and night, months, seasons and year. These units of Time are mentioned in ritual-texts. The *arthavāda*-s concerning these speak at times, of the beliefs prevalent among the people of those times.

'Day and night', even though a small unit, carries importance. It is said that the seasons and months are established on day and night (*Śat. Br.* XII. 8.2.35). It is said that in a Soma-sacrifice, two chips (here metal-chips) — '*kuśī*-s' — one each of gold and silver, are placed near the *cātvāla* (pit).[1] The gods cast off these two *kuśī*-s. The golden one became the day and the silver one became the night. When the sun rises, he follows the golden *kuśī* and when he sets, he enters this very same silver *kuśī* (*Tait. Br.* I.5.10.7).[2] White is the form of the day and dark (i.e. black) of night (*Mait. Sam.* II. 5.7). Even the (spotted) black antelope skin gives us the idea of the day and the night. The white spots on the black antelope skin stand for the colour of day, while the black colour of the antelope skin speaks of the colour of night (*Tait. Sam.* VI. 1.3.2). The *arthavāda* in the *Kauṣ. Br.* speaks of the belief that the white and black colours stand as the symbols of day and night. Hence in the animal-sacrifice, which forms a part of the Soma-sacrifice, the animal to be offered to Soma has to be of two colours. Agni and Soma are day and night.[3] In the context of the

New-moon and Full-moon sacrifices, the *Śat. Br.* states the origin of day and night through a mythical account. It is said that Prajāpati made the day from the light, which was there with him on creating the gods and from the darkness which was with him, after creating the *asura*-s, he made the night (*Śat. Br.* XI. 1.6.11). The Great Fire- altar, when fully constructed stands for Prajāpati, who thereafter became relaxed. When he relaxed, his joints became days and nights (*ibid.* X. 1.1.3). Day and night make the entire Prajāpati (*Jaim. Br.* II. 358). Interesting *arthavāda*-s regarding day and night occur in the *Jaim. Br.*, in which are noticed certain beliefs of those times. The gods said that the sun did not take away (*na hārṣīt*) (any lustre). The same became the day (*ahar;* the etymology - fr. *a* - √*hṛ* - 'to take away; to carry away, *a* here signifying 'negation'). To him was given (*rātam*) (offering) and he became the night (*rātriḥ*, etymology from √*rā* - 'to give'). This is the origin of day and night. One who knows this can rule over the day and night and the two do not transgress his order. Everything here does have a limit. The day and night do not have any. The two are limitless (*Jaim. Br.* III. 357). The same belief is seen in the context of building the Great Fire-altar. It is said that he throws sand on the Uttaravedi, by day and night (*Śat. Br.* VII. 3.1.27). The *arthavāda* here points out that endless is the sand and endless are the days and nights (*ibid.* VII. 3.1.38). It is very clear that the endless and eternal nature of the principle of Time is spoken of through such *arthavāda*-s.

The *Jaim. Br.* in the context of the Atirātra sacrifice (day-followed by-night-sacrifice) speaks of how closely are connected the day and night. The day is not without night and night not without day. Day and night form this whole (Universe), these worlds. They are the ones who create the concept of past and future times - *bhūtam bhavyam prajanayataḥ* (*Jaim. Br.* I. 207). The *Jaim. Br.* points out that night has more speed than the day (*ibid.* I. 189). This obviously is based on the fact of daily observation, for the night passes very easily of a person due to sleep on his part, while the day appears to be a long one but with slow speed as there are several activities to be performed at the daytime.

In the context of Agnihotra rite, while indicating that the *agnihotra* offerings should be offered at both times — morning as well as evening, at the advent of night—, the *Jaim. Br.* compares, through a metaphor, day and night with two seas, which cannot be pervaded, i.e. crossed (*ibid.* I.5). The metaphor except for the word '*acaryau*' (fr. √*car* - 'to move', here 'to prevade, cross over') follows the one stated in the *Tait. Sam.* (III. 2.2.1 where the word is '*ajūryau*'— 'which cannot become old' meaning that the two are 'unaging'). The *Jaim. Br.* says that those sacrificers, who offer *agnihotra* (in the fire) at the rise of the sun, enter the sea *viz.* the day and those who offer the same at the night time (i.e. at the twilight after the sun-set) enter the sea *viz.* the night (*ibid.* I.5). The *Jaim. Br.* gives a word-picture of the day and night by calling the day 'dappled' (*śabala)* and the night 'dark' (*śyāma)* in colour. Those who offer at the night-time, enter the 'dark', i.e. night. Those who offer when the sun has arisen, enter the 'dappled', i.e. the day (*ibid.* I. 6).

The *Kauṣ. Br.*, in the context of Agnihotra, has several striking metaphors to give for 'day' and 'night'. Day and night are the flood (*samudra)*,[4] that takes all. The two twilights are the two unfathomable or deep (*agādha)*[5] crossings of it. Day and night are the missile of the god that goes on its way eager to kill. The two twilights (morning and evening) are the two wings (*pakṣau)*.[6] As a journey is swiftly completed with wing, so is it of the two twilights, when the offerings are given. Day and night are the encircling arms of death. A man about to grasp with encircling arms may be evaded between the arms. Similarly he evades death by offering at the twilights (*Kauṣ. Br.* II. 9). The *Kauṣ. Br.* points out that the time of these two twilights is the time of going to the gods, grasping which he reaches safely the world of gods. If he offers at another time, the dark one (i.e. night) and the dappled one (i.e. day) tear apart his *agnihotra*-offerings (*ibid.*).

The concept of day and night being all-pervading has entered even small rituals. In the context of the Agnicayana rite it is said that he takes hold of Ukhyāgni (Agni in the fire-pan) by means of two pads of straw (*iṇḍve*). The *arthavāda* states that Agni is the yonder sun and the two pads are day and night. He takes hold of the yonder sun by means of the day and the night (*Śat. Br.* VI. 7.1.25). In the same context it is said that he worships (or propitiates) Prajāpati with the Vātsapra-rite[7] and the Viṣṇu-strides.[8] The Viṣṇu-strides are the day and the Vātsapra-rite the night. When Prajāpati created this universe, he enclosed it on both sides by day and night. Similarly the sacrificer, when he has generated this universe (here the Great Fire-altar, the body of Prajāpati - the creator), encloses it on both sides by day and night (*ibid.* VI. 7. 4.12).

Night being dark and giving less scope to persons for movement, is connected in belief with evil-minded rivals. The gods overpowered (transgressed) the night. He who knows this overpowers the world of rivals (*Jaim. Br.* I. 198). The *Ait. Br.* in the context of the Atirātra sacrifice relates a mythical account, which reflects the belief regarding night. It is said that the gods took refuge in the day and the *asura*-s, in the night. As they were of equal strength, Indra sought the help of the gods to attack and drive (away) the *asura*-s through the night. But he found no one among the gods, as they were afraid of night, the darkness, death. Therefore even now if one has gone away in the night, any distance whatever, he is afraid, for the night is darkness as it were, (even) death as it were (*Ait. Br.* IV.5 = 16.5). The main feature of the night is that at that time nothing is visible (*Jaim. Br.* I. 341).

As compared to night, day enjoys praise. An idea, reflecting a belief, worthy of note, is that it is the day that gives the concept of year, for the whole year is just 'day after day'. The understanding of the 'year' as 'day after day' is the mystic import of the year (*Śat. Br.* XII. 2.2.23).

Day and night are taken to be the symbols of Time. This belief can be noted in the rite of Agnicayana in the process of heating the fire-pan made of clay. The *Śat. Br.* states that the divine protectresses *viz.* the days and nights, have already heated the clay fire-pan in the lap of the earth and now he heats it by them. By days and nights everything is covered here (*ibid.* VI. 5.4.6). Though very simple, the *arthavāda* here indicates a subtle concept that the fire-pan (made of clay) was lying in the interior of the earth in the form of mere clay from an undated time. And this principle of Time is indicated by 'days and nights'.

The *Śat. Br.* speaks highly of 'day and night', though the praise cannot be taken as a direct one. The context is of the Horse-sacrifice and the belief recorded is that distinction and royal sway depart from him, who (i.e. king) performs the Horse-sacrifice. The practice was to call the lute-players to sing and play on lute, for when a man attains to distinction, the lute is played to him. The *Śat. Br.* states that one of the lute-players is a *brāhmaṇa* and the other a *rājanya* (*kṣatriya).* By this the royal glory (*śrīḥ)* is guarded on either side by the priesthood and the nobility. The *brāhmaṇa* sings by day, for the day is a form of the priestly dignity.[9] The *rājanya* sings at night, for the night is a form of the nobility[10] (*ibid.* XIII. 1.5. 1-5).

Together with the days and nights, fortnights, months and seasons are established in the year (*ibid.* XII. 8.3.14). A year generally consisting of twelve months, has sometimes an intercalary month—a thirteenth month. The year (consisting of twelve months) is said to be a bull and the thirteenth month is said to be the hump of that bull (*ibid.* XIII. 1.2.2). It is interesting to note the belief regarding the thirteenth month, which as noted above, is not a regular feature of every year. Soma (to be used in the sacrifice) was to be purchased in the year, which had thirteen months and particularly in the thirteenth month of that year. The *Ait. Br.* tries to identify the thirteenth month with the Soma-seller (*somavikrayī*), from whom Soma is purchased. It says that as the thirteenth month is non-existent (as the regular months are twelve in number), so is the Soma-seller non-existent. Soma-seller is 'evil' (and so is the thirteenth month?) (*Ait. Br.* I. 12=3.1). The *Śat. Br.* states how the Soma-seller does not get either the Somakrayaṇī cow or the gold (in compensation for the cow).[11] Thus both the thirteenth month and the Soma-seller are regarded as the same in status. Dange says that it is difficult to know the significance of the thirteenth month; but probably this is to indicate that Soma is not usual: that it is mysterious — like the *indu-drapsa!*[12]

The *Pañc. Br.* regards the Phālguna month as the mouth of the year (*Pañc. Br.* V. 9.8), and the observation of the *Jaim. Br.* regarding the sun is of its being the hottest in the Jyeṣṭha month, which has also the name Nidāgha (*Jaim. Br.* II. 342).

It is interesting to note that the months pertaining to each season are mentioned, with their significant names, in the context of the ritual of drawing the Soma-cups for the seasons. The Adhvaryu priest draws the first cup and the Pratiprasthātṛ priest draws the second. The *arthavāda* states that these two cups stand for the months of the spring season. In spring, plants sprout and trees are brought to ripeness. Therefore these two months are known as Madhu ('sweet') and Mādhava (*Śat.* Br. IV. 3.1.14). The third cup is drawn by the Adhvaryu priest and the fourth one by the Pratiprasthātṛ. These two cups stand for the months of the summer, for during them it burns utmost. Hence these two are called Śukra (clear) and Śuci (bright) (*ibid.* 15). The fifth and the sixth cups are drawn for the months of the rainy season. As (in these months) it rains from the sky, these two are called Nabhas and Nabhasya — both concerning the meaning 'sky' (*ibid.* 16). The seventh and the eight cups are drawn for the months in the autumn, for in the autumn, food (*ūrj*) and juice (*rasa*), i.e. plants signifying strength ripen.

So the names of the months Iṣa and Ūrja (*ibid.* 17). The ninth and tenth cups are drawn for the months in the winter. The winter season by force (*sahas*) brings these creatures into his power. So the names of the months — Sahas and Sahasya (*ibid.* 18). The eleventh and the twelfth cups are drawn for the months of the dewy season (Śiśira), for during these months it freezes most severely. So these months are Tapas and Tapasya (*ibid.* 19). The concept of month is joined with that of the year, for the month revolving again and again forms the year (*Jaim. Br.* II. 335). Even the half-months are joined with the year. It is said that he presses the Soma-shoots for twenty-four times. The twenty-four half-months are joined with the year, which is Prajāpati, which again is the very sacrifice (*Śat. Br.* IV. 1.1.15).

Seasons are regarded as having great importance in the ritual tradition. Soma-cups are drawn for the seasons, as can be seen in the context of the Agniṣṭoma sacrifice (*ibid.* IV. 3.3.12). A mythical account by way of *arthavāda* occurs in the *Śat. Br.* in the context of New-moon and Full-moon sacrifices, which brings out the importance of the seasons in the ritual tradition. It is said that the seasons were desirous of having a share (of offerings) in the sacrifice of the gods. Even when entreated upon not to exclude them from the sacrifice, the gods did not approve of the seasons. Consequently the seasons went to the *asura*-s, who (with the help of the seasons) throve in a stupendous manner, so much so that even without tilling, the plants ripened forthwith for them. This obviously caused anxiety to the gods and they decided to invite the seasons by offering prayer to them first of all at the sacrifice. They asked Agni to approach the seasons on their behalf. Agni went to the seasons and told them that he had obtained for them a share in the sacrifice among the gods. The seasons said to Agni that they would let the latter share along with them in the sacrifice, for he had obtained for them a share in the sacrifice among the gods (*ibid.* I.6.1.1-8). The *Śat. Br.* points out that whosoever knows that Agni is thus allowed to share in the sacrifice along with the seasons, for him, being possessed of Agni, the seasons themselves possessed of Agni, ripen the plants and everything here (*ibid.* I. 6.1.8). This *arthavāda* is important in more than one ways. It brings out the importance of the seasons. It speaks of the offering-prayer to the seasons, along with Agni. The significant point is that it indicates how the principle of heat (here 'Agni' is mentioned) - obviously heat of the sun—gives rise to different seasons. Depending on this principle of heat, the seasons differ. It is said that the same year has different forms because the seasons differ (*Kāṭh. Sam.* XX. 10; XXI. 3). The seasons come again and again but they do not wither away (*ibid.* XX. 10; *Tait. Sam.* V. 3.1.2).

The number of seasons is said to be six. But at times they are said to be five, for the seasons Hemanta and Śiśira are taken together. They are said to be in pairs on account of their similar character (*Tait. Śam.* V. 4.2.1). Hence broadly they are taken to be three (*Śat. Br.* III. 4.4.17). These three are—summer, rainy season and winter. It is interesting to see the beliefs attached to the spring, summer, rainy season and autumn. The spring is said to be the priesthood. Whosoever (*brāhmaṇa*) desires to become endowed with the holy power, should set up his fires in the spring. The summer is the nobility. A *kṣatriya* desiring to become a power (*kṣatra)* in prosperity and renown, should set up his fires in summer. The rainy season is taken to be (associated with) common people, and the people means food. A *vaiśya* desiring to be rich in progeny and cattle, should set up his fires in the rainy season (*ibid.* II. 1.3.5-8). Even the *Tait. Br.* says that the spring is the season of a *brāhmaṇa* and the summer that of a *kṣatriya.* However it differs with respect to the season associated with a *vaiśya.* Instead of the rainy season, the season spoken of is the autumn, for autumn is the season of a *vaiśya.* A *brāhmaṇa* setting up his fires in the spring becomes endowed with spiritual lustre. A *kṣatriya* setting up his fires in the summer becomes endowed with power and a *vaiśya* having his fires set up in the autumn, possesses cattle (*Tait. Br.* I.1.2.6, 7). The association of the three *varṇa*-s with the respective seasons is on a logical basis. The plants withered away in the winter, sprout up again in the spring (*Kāṭh. Sam.* XXIV.4), spring thus becoming conducive to the gain of spiritual lustre. So it is the season of a *bṛāhmaṇa.* Summer (*Grīṣma*) the hot season is rightly said to belong to the *kṣatriya.* Rainy season in which the agricultural activities such as ploughing, etc. are undertaken or the autumn when the crops are ready, has to belong to a *vaiśya.*

The *Jaim. Br.* has to give a mythical account by way of *arthavāda,* regarding the creation of the seasons. Prajāpati toiled and (with this first toiling-heat), he created summer; so it is very hot in summer. When he toiled for the second time, there was created the rainy season. In the rainy season, it rains and it is also hot. When he toiled for the third time, he created the season Hemanta, which is very cold. He then created spring from summer, autumn from rainy season and Śiśra from Hemanta. The seasons in this way are created as if being in juxtaposition (*Jaim. Br.* III. 1). Elsewhere the *Jaim. Br.* states the names of the six seasons in order *viz.* spring (Vasanta), summer (Grīṣma), rainy season (Varṣā), autumn (Śarad), and the two seasons of winter *viz.* Hemanta and Śiśira (*ibid.* II. 356).

The two seasons of winter, though differ actually in degree of coldness though not in the kind of coldness, are taken together. Hence at times the seasons are said to be five and not six, as noted above, while taking into account the number of seasons. Both the months of winter stand for cold - extreme cold. As winter comes at the end of the seasons, it is as if at the other side of spring (*Śat. Br.* I.5.3.13). Hemanta is said to be the Svāhākāra (i.e. the utterance 'Svāhā', which comes at the offering of oblations of gods). This metaphor (a ritual metaphor) is as though explained by the facts of observation. Hemanta subjects all creatures to its will, in that, the plants wither away; the leaves fall of the trees; the birds retire (i.e. come to their nests) more and more and fly lower and lower and the hair of a wicked person as though fall off (*ibid.* I.5.4.5). The *Ṣaḍ. Br.* also points out that in this season, people remain still without any movement (*Ṣaḍ. Br.* III. 4.24). Śiśira, the second month of the winter, makes the plants wither away (*Kāṭh. Sam.* XXV. 4). It is the irritating (*aśānta)* season (*Mait. Sam.* I.8.2) and the most cruel one (*Kāṭh. Sam.* VI. 2). We are here reminded of the etymologies stated by Yāska in later times of the word *Śiśira.*[13]

In the context of seasons, two ritual metaphors coming as *arthavāda* are worthy of consideration. The *Ṣaḍ. Br.* calls *saṁvatsara* ('Year') a *sāman* (chant or melody), constituted of six elements *viz.* spring as Hiṅkāra, summer as Prastāva, rainy season as Udgītha, autumn as Pratihāra and winter (Hemanta) as Nidhana (*Ṣaḍ. Br.* III. 4.23). Hence it is that in the Hemanta (winter season), as we have noted above, the people's activities come to standstill (*ibid.* III. 4.24), as Hemanta is Nidhana ('finale' of the *sāman).* Another ritual metaphor occurs in the *Śat. Br.* in the context of the New-moon and Full-moon sacrifices. The sacrificer is the Year and the various priests are said to be the seasons, who officiate for him. The Āgnīdhra priest is spring (Vasanta). When the forest-fires take place in spring, that is a form of Agni. The Adhvaryu priest is summer (Grīṣma), for summer is as it were, scorched. The Adhvaryu priest (who is the offering priest, sitting near the fire) comes forth like something scorched. The Udgātṛ priest (singing the *sāman-*s*)* is the rainy season, for when it rains heavily, a sound like that of a chant (*sāman)* is produced. The Brahman priest is the autumn (Śarad), for when (in the autumn) the corn ripens, they say, 'The creatures are rich in growth (*brahmaṇvatyaḥ).*[14] The Hotṛ priest is the winter (Hemanta), for in the winter, the cattle waste away (or are a standstill), with (as though) the Vaṣaṭ call uttered over them. These (seasons) are the divinities that officiate for the sacrifice, as priests (*Śat. Br.* XI. 2.7.32).[15]

The *Jaim. Br.*, in the context of the Gavām-ayana sacrifice, explains the concept of seasons on both - the microcosmic and macrocosmic levels. It states that formerly seasons were of two types *viz.* seasons in the form of vital breaths and seasons in the form of deities. The breath *(prāṇa)* was the spring; speech, the summer; eye, the rainy season, for as the eye has moisture, so is the rainy season full of moisture; ear as the autumn; mind as the Hemanta (the first month of the winter) and whatever waters are there in a man, the Śiśira (the second month of the winter). These are the *prāṇa-ṛtavaḥ* (seasons in the form of vital breaths). To turn to the *deva-ṛtavaḥ* (seasons in the form of deities) - Vāyu (wind) as the spring; Agni as the summer; Parjanya (as a deity) the rainy season; the Sun (Āditya) as the autumn; the moon as the Hemanta and whatever divine waters are there, the Śiśira (*Jaim. Br.* II. 51). The *arthavāda* is important as it brings out the all-encompassing concept of seasons.

The more of this concept (regarding the seasons) is seen in the rite of Agnicayana, in which the Great Fire-altar is built, in five layers, with bricks. In each layer, the bricks named Ṛtavyā (in the name of seasons) are placed. As Agni is Prajāpati and Prajāpati is the Year, the Ṛtavyā bricks are to be placed while building the Fire-altar, which stands for the body of Prajāpati. This is for providing him (Agni-Prajāpati = Year) the seasons (*Śat.* Br. VIII.2. 1.16). As there are six seasons each having two months, the total Ṛtavyā bricks are twelve in number, spread out in five layers. The details are interesting to be noted. The first two Ṛtavyā bricks are Madhu and Mādhava, named after the two months of the spring season and they are placed in the first layer of the Great Fire-altar (*ibid.* VII. 4.2. 29-31). In the second layer are placed the Ṛtavyā bricks Śukra and Śuci, standing for the two months of the summer season (*ibid.* VIII. 2.1.16-18). The first layer stands as the foundation of Agni-Prajāpati's body, as is the spring season, coming first—the foundation - among the seasons (*ibid.* VII. 4.2.31), while the second layer stands for that part of Prajāpati's body which is above the feet and below the waist and that same part of his is the summer season (*ibid.* VIII. 2.1.18). In the third layer are placed four Ṛtavyā bricks *viz.* Nabha and Nabhasya standing for the two months of the rainy season and Iṣa and Ūrja for the two months of the autumnal season. The ritual reasonings forwarded for placing four bricks (instead of two as seen above) in the third layer, are interesting (*ibid.* VIII. 3.2. 7-12). As the third layer is the middle-most layer (out of the five layers of the Great Fire-altar), by placing four bricks standing for the middle-part of the year (rainy season and the autumn being the middle part), he restores the middle part of the body of Agni-Prajāpati (*ibid.* VIII. 3.2.8). The *arthavāda*-s here are based on the concept of number 'four' and they can be considered when we take a note of the *arthavāda*-s dealing with 'Numbers'. In the fourth layer are placed two Ṛtavyā bricks named after the two months of the winter season *viz.* Saha and Sahasya. These are for resting that part of Agni-Prajāpati's body, which is above the waist and below the head (*ibid.* VIII. 4.2.14,16). In the fifth layer (which is the last one) are placed the two Ṛtavyā bricks Tapa and Tapasya named after the two months of the Śiśira. These two Ṛtavyā bricks are for restoring the head of Agni-Prajāpati, for the Śiśira season (coming last) is the year's head (*ibid.* VIII. 7.1.5, 8). The concept regarding the Ṛtavyā bricks does not stop with that of restoring the body of Agni- Prajāpati as if in its physical form. In fact, it becomes a part of the wider and bigger concept of the 'cosmic' body-form of that deity. Thus Madhu and Mādhava, the two Ṛtavyā bricks of spring, being of the first layer, stand for the foundation (*ibid.* VII. 4.2.31). Śukra and Śuci, the two Ṛtavyā bricks of Grīṣma (summer), of the second layer, stand for the region above the earth but below the atmosphere (*ibid.* VIII. 2.1.17). In the third layer, Nabha and Nabhasya, the two Ṛtavyā bricks of the rainy season and Iṣa and Ūrja, the two ones of the Śarad (autumn), stand for the air-world (i.e. *antarikṣa* region *ibid.* VIII. 3.2.7). Saha and Sahasya, the two Ṛtavyā bricks of the Hemanta stand in the fourth layer for the region above the air but below the sky (*ibid.* VIII. 4.2.15). And lastly, Tapa and Tapasya, the two Ṛtavyā bricks of the Śiśira, in the fifth layer stand for the sky (*ibid.* VIII. 7.1.7). In this way, the seasons, the bricks obviously representing them in the rite of Agnicayana, build up Agni-Prajāpati's cosmic form *viz.* the Year. However there are other bricks also, representing metres, water, etc., which are placed in the five layers and they are also eulogised in the *arthavāda*-passages in the context of the Agnicayana rite, mentioning, at times indicating, the beliefs about them. In the present context, the importance of the seasons as joined with the concept of the Year is to be noted.[16]

All the units of time are established in the Year. They are the days, nights, fortnights, months and seasons (*ibid.* XII. 8.3.14). The *Ṣaḍ. Br.* takes the *saṁvatsara* (year) to be a *sāman* and states that the days and nights are its Hiṅkāra; the fortnights are Prastāva; the months are Ādi; the seasons are Udgītha; the full-moon nights are Pratihāra; the Aṣṭakā-s are Upadrava and the new-moon nights are Nidhana (*Ṣaḍ. Br.* III. 4.22).[17] The concept of eternal Time is seen in the year, which revolves without end (*Śat. Br.* IV. 3.1.7) and which is without cessation (*ibid.*).

The oft-repeated identification of the Year to be noted is with Prajāpati or Agni (the deity of sacrifice). We read in the context of New-moon and Full-moon sacrifices that Prajāpati created a counterpart of himself and that is in the form of *saṁvatsara* (Year). The *arthavāda* further runs that the word *saṁvatsara* has four syllables and so has the word *prajāpati* four syllables. Year thus is a counterpart of Prajāpati (*ibid.* XI. 1.6.13). That Prajāpati or Agni or Sacrifice is the Year occurs many a time in the Brāhmaṇa-texts (*ibid.* VII. 4.2.30; X. 4.1.16; X.5.4.10; XI.1.1.1; *Jaim. Br.* III. 326; III. 375).

Interesting *arthavāda*-s occur in the *Pañc. Br.* in this connection. It is said that Sacrifice is (as though) the Year transposed. In the third pressing of Soma (which is attributed to the Ṛbhus, hence known as Ārbhava), there are five metres and seven *sāman*-s. These make twelve (5 + 7 = 12). Year consists of twelve months. In the midday pressing of Soma are employed five *sāman*-s. Thus in the Ārbhava pressing, there are obtained the seasons as well as the months and in the midday pressing, the seasons. This gives us the Sacrifice as a transposed Year (*Jaim. Br.* I. 166). We have already noted that the seasons though six in number, are sometimes mentioned as five, when the winter-months (Hemanta and Śiśira) are taken to be one.

Elsewhere in the *Jaim. Br.*, the Year is said to be Prajāpati. For each six months, it lifts up either of the feet (Year being imagined as a Being *viz.* Prajāpati). When he lifts up the hot one, it is hot above but cool, down. This being the phenomenon in the summer (Grīṣma) season, in that season the wells carry cool waters (though it is hot above). When the Year lifts up the cool foot, it is cool above but hot, down. This is seen in the winter (Hemanta) season. Hence in the winter season, the wells carry lukewarm (*uṣṇāḥ*) waters (though it is cool or even cold above). In this way, the Year taken to be Prajāpati sustains the creatures (*ibid.* I. 167).

In the context of the Gavam-ayana sacrifice, the *Śat. Br.* speaks of the Year (for the Gavām-ayana *sattra* goes on for a year.)[18] as Man (Puruṣa) and various Soma-sacrifices performed in this *sattra*, on various days as the various parts or limbs of that Man (*Śat. Br.* XII 1.2.1-3; XII.2.4. 1-16). In the same context it is said that the Year is a great eagle. The six months which they perform prior to the Viṣuvat (middle-most day) are the one wing and those which they perform subsequent to, are the other wing and the Viṣuvat day is the body (*ibid.* XII. 2.3.7).

The *arthavāda* stated in the *Jaim. Br.* shows how *saṁvatsara* is joined with days and nights, fortnights, months and seasons. It is said that he obtains *stoma*-s with metres; with *stoma*-s the Bṛhat and Rathantara (*sāman*-s); with the Bṛhat and Rathantara, the day and night; with day and night the fortnight; with the fortnight the month; with the month the season and with the season, the Year (*Jaim. Br.* II. 60). The *arthavāda* here from the ritual context glides into the realm of metaphysics and says that he (i.e. the sacrificer) should know that he is the Year. Here the Year signifies the principle of eternal Time.

The *Jaim. Br.* then says that the Year is the Sun (*āditya).* To Āditya, all glory, all success, all gods resort. Whatever of the Āditya (i.e. the orb of the sun) appears to us that is *saṁvat* and the black circle in the orb is *sara.* Thus forms the Saṁvatsara (Year). This is the thought about the Year from the 'deity' point of view (*adhidevatam).* The concept of the Year concerning the body (*adhyātmam*) is that Saṁvatsara is the man in the eye. Whatever white part is there of him, that is *saṁvat* and the dark circle in the middle is the *sara.* Again Āditya is the *saṁvat* and the moon is the *sara.* To him (i.e. the sun), the moon follows and reaches on the full-moon day. Again they say that vital breath is *saṁvat* and speech is *sara.* He obtains (pervades) with these two. The *sāman*-s employed in the Agniṣṭoma sacrifice, of the Saṁvatsara, form a path leading to the gods—*devayānaḥ panthāḥ* (*ibid.*).

It seems that among the units of time, Saṁvatsara (Year) is set as a limit. In the context of the Pravargya ceremony, it is said that the knowledge of Pravargya is to be imparted to one, who dwells with him as a pupil for one year. Year (Saṁvatsara) is that which shines yonder and Pravargya is that sun. By the Pravargya ceremony, he gratifies the sun. Hence the knowledge of the Pravargya to be given for a year to the disciple, who dwells with him for one full year (without any break ?) (*Śat. Br.* XIV. 1.1.27). In the context of expiations it is said that they should perform a sacrifice for the bones of the deceased, after a year. The year is the allayment of all (*saṁvatsaro vai sarvasya śāntiḥ*) (*Pañc. Br.* IX. 8.13). Sāyaṇa here points out in his comm. that this is in the case of the death of consecrated sacrificer.

In the context of kindling the fires (Agnyādheya), the units of time are woven with the concept of gods and fathers.

The seasons *viz.* spring, summer and the rainy season represent the gods and the autumn, Hemanta and Śiśira (the two seasons of winter) represent the Fathers. The fortnight which increases represents the gods and the one which decreases represents the Fathers. The day represents the gods and the night, the Fathers. The first part of the day (forenoon) represents the gods and the latter part of the day (afternoon), the Fathers (*Śat. Br.* II. 1.3.1). Those seasons then are the gods and the Fathers. With his invocation of the gods, the gods respond and with that of the Fathers, the Fathers comply. This favour from the gods and the Fathers he gets, when he invokes the seasons as the gods and the Fathers (*ibid.* II. 1.3.2).

In the context of the Gavām-ayana sacrifice, the 'ten' days (two Atirātra days, Ārambhaṇīya and Mahāvrata days, Pṛṣṭhya and Abhiplava days, Viśvajit and Abhijit days, Svara-sāman days—taken as one unit and the Viṣuvat day) are first equalled with the metre Virāj, having ten syllables in a foot. From another point of view, they are taken to be nine—then eight—then seven, etc. and on the basis of 'number' are equalled with several entities of that number. When the days are viewed as six, they are equalled with six seasons, which make up a year, and the year verily the sacrifice. When taken as two, they are the day and night—the two—equalled with the two worlds (the terrestrial and the upper), the two vital breaths *viz.* Prāṇa and Apāna and the two-footed man. When the days are viewed as one (unit), that is the day—the unit of time. (Though the smallest unit), the day is the foundation of Year. It is the 'day' which gives the concept of 'past' and 'future'. In fact, 'past' only (passing through 'present'!) becomes 'future'. Agni, Vāyu, the Sun, Indra and the moon - the age-old deities - rule over the 'past' and the 'future' (*Jaim. Br.* II. 431). This passage from the *Jaim. Br.*, though from the context of the Gavām-ayana *sattra*, is important for knowing the belief about the Father Time.[19] The Vedic belief reflected here comes very close to the thought of Plato that God wished the created world to resemble the intelligible one as far as possible. It was not possible for the world to be eternal and the nearest analogue to eternity which he could provide was to make 'a moving image of eternity'. This is 'Time'. The image (of eternity) has a motion according to number (i.e. divisions of time). 'Past' and 'Future' are created species of time, which we wrongly transfer to the eternal essence; strictly 'was' and 'will be' are to be asserted only of generation in time, for they are motions.[20]

It is important to note that in the din and bustle of the ritual atmosphere, the *Śat Br.*, unreservedly speaks of the belief about Year that it is the same as Death (*mṛtyuḥ),* for it is he (Father Time Prajapati),[21] who by means of day and night, destroys the life of mortal beings. He (Year) indeed is one who brings about the end (*antakaḥ),* by day and night, of the mortals. But he who knows Year to be Death as also Antaka (one who brings about the end) does not reach the end of his life, before old age and attains full extent of life (*Śat. Br.* X. 4.3.1,2). This thought occurs in the context of the Agnicayana rite. In order to lay down the importance of this rite, a mythical account occurs by way of *arthavāda.* The gods were afraid of Prajāpati (= Year = Death = Antaka). In order to attain immortality (and avoid the end of their life), the gods performed several sacrifices *viz.,* the Agnihotra, the New-moon and Full-moon sacrifices, the Cāturmāsya *iṣṭi*-s, the Animal-sacrifice and the Soma-sacrifice; and also built a fire-altar. But they did not attain immortality. Then Prajāpati told them the entire procedure of building the Great Fire-altar (i.e. the rite of Agnicayana). The gods followed it and became immortal. Death afraid of his share being deprived of, if all men following the gods would become immortal, expressed his anxiety. The gods consoled him by saying that thenceforward no one would become immortal with the body. When Death would take away the body as his share, the men would become immortal only through knowledge or through holy work. And in the ritual context, this knowledge is of building the Great Fire-altar and the holy work is actually building the Great Fire-altar. Those who do not know this become the food of Death time after time. When he builds the Great Fire-altar, he gains Agni Prajāpati, Year, Death, Antaka (*ibid.* X. 4. 3.1 - 11). Here the hard truth of life, about Death, through the concept of Year is brought home. Elsewhere (i.e. in the context of the New-moon and Full-moon sacrifices) Saṁvatsara (Year) is said to be '*sarvatsara*' which steals everything (*sarva* - 'all'; √*tsar* - 'to steal, to approach stealthily'). One who has the knowledge of Saṁvatsara, is not overcome by any evil (*ibid.* XI. 1.6.12). The belief in Year, composed of several units like day and night, fortnights, etc. thus points to the stark reality of life ending in death—but with an assurance of immortality through knowledge and holy work.

NOTES AND REFERENCES

1. *Tait. Br.* I.5.10.1,2. Sāyaṇa explains *kuśī* as a small wooden stick or peg, which is placed on the ground by the *sāma*-chanters. This is for counting the components of a *stotra,* when they are making that *stotra.* As they (the priest and/the sacrificer) make the *cātvāla* on the earth (Aditi), it is called 'Āditya' and being (as though) caught hold of by the two *kuśī*-s, it is called 'Kauśika' (*ibid.* I.5.10.2).
2. See note 1 *supra.* Sāyaṇa while commenting on *Tait. Br.* I.5.10.1,2, points out that the *vidhi* of *kuśī*-s is for counting the *stotriya*-s and later on, to be removed.
3. *Kauṣ. Br.* X. 3. Here the animal is said to be of white and red colours, which are the symbols of Agni and Soma. However the belief in this passage of the *Kauṣ. Br.* (X. 3), regarding the white and black colours has to be noted.
4. *Kauṣ. Br.* II.9. Keith translates the word *samudraḥ* as 'flood'. See Keith, A.B., *Rigveda Brahmanas* (tr.), p. 356. This is proper, for the *samudra* is said to take all (*sarvaṁharaḥ).* This obviously should refer to a 'flood'.
5. Keith translates the word *agādhe* (in *agādhe tīrthe)* as 'fordable', which word in fact means 'difficult to cross, unfathomable, deep'. for Keith, *op. cit.,* p. 356. Keith might have taken the meaning of the word *agādhe* as 'fordable', taking into account the *agnihotra*-rite prescribed at the two

twilights. Offerings given at the two twilights in the *agnihotra*-rite speak of the importance of the two twilights.

6. Keith, A.B., *op. cit.,* p. 356, note 3, suggests by the word *pakṣau* - 'two side horses', though he himself translates the word in the text as 'wings'.
7. See Eggeling, J. *The Śatapatha Brāhmaṇa,* pt. III, SBE Vol. 41, p . 283, note 1. In this rite, there is a recitation of *Vāj. Sam.* XII. 18-28 or 29 (*RV* X. 45) ascribed to the seer Vatsaprī Bhālandana.
8. Viṣṇu-strides (three) are taken by the sacrificer, in imitation of Viṣṇu, the god known for his three steps right from the *RV*. This is in view of the identification of the sacrificer with Viṣṇu, the very sacrifice. For a couple of references to sacrificer's taking the Viṣṇu-strides *Śat. Br.* I.9.3.8 ff.; XI. 7.2.1.
9. See Eggeling, J., *op. cit.,* pt. V, SBE Vol . 44, p. 286, note 1. This singing by day on the part of the *brāhmaṇa* lute-player is at the fore-offerings of the three cake-offerings (*iṣṭi*-s) to Savitṛ, whilst staying in the south part of the sacrificial ground.
10. *Ibid.,* p. 286, note 2. The singing by night on the part of the *rājanya* is during the performance of the Dhṛtis (i.e. Dhṛti-offerings) after sunset.
11. *Śat. Br.* III. 3.3.7; also see Eggeling, J., *op. cit.,* pt. II, SBE Vol. 26, p. 71, note 1, where he quotes the texts which point out the unkind treatment given to the Soma-seller. But he rightly points out that 'the whole transaction was a feigned purchase, symbolising the acquisition of the Soma by the gods from the Gandharvas'.
12. See Dange, Sadashiv A., *Images from Vedic Hymns and Rituals,* p. 103.
13. *Nir.* I. 10 - *śiśiram śṛṇāteḥ śamnātervā,* The first etymology is from √*śṝ* - 'to crush', and the second one is from √*śam* — 'to end'. Both the etymologies point out the fierce nature of the biting cold winter season.
14. Here the etymology is from √*bṛh* - *bṛṁh* - 'to grow'; the same root is in the word Brahman (priest).
15. *Śat. Br.* XI. 2.7.32 says that even if Aiṣāvīra-s officiate for the sacrificer, he should meditate upon the seasons (-deities). Sāyaṇa in his comm. says that Eṣāvīra is a condemned specific *brāhmaṇa* (sub-caste), and the priests belonging to

this are Aiṣāvīra-s.

The point is, even if the priests, in reality, are of such condemned status, the sacrificer should think of the season-deities, as the latter actually officiate as priests for him.

16. Also see *Śat. Br.* IV. 3.1.3, 4 — The Adhvaryu proceeds with the libations of the seasons, when the Acchāvāka is seated. The Acchāvāka belongs to Indra and Agni, the latter representing a productive pair. From this same productive pair, he produces the seasons, the year, which are everything.
17. Here the different parts of the *sāman* are mentioned. Sāyaṇa explains in his comm. the words Ādi and Upadrava of this ritual metaphor.
18. See Dharmadhikari, T.N., "Gavām-ayanam", *Sacrifice in India - Concept and Evolution,* ed. by (Mrs.) Dange, S.S., Viveka Pubns., Aligarh, 1987, p. 32. One of the types of Gavām-ayana extends over ten months only, the other extending over twelve months. The Gavām-ayana is a series of Soma-sacrifice consisting of Agniṣṭoma, Ukthya, Ṣoḍaśī and Atirātra performed separately or as parts of Pṛṣṭhya-Ṣaḍaha, Abhiplava-Ṣaḍaha, Navāha or Daśarātra, etc.
19. For the expression 'Father Time', see Eggeling J., *op. cit.,* pt. V, SBE Vol. 44, Intrn., p. xiv.
20. See *Ency. of Rel. and Eth.* ed. by Hastings, James, Vol. XII, p. 343 b.
21. See Eggeling, J., *op. cit.,* pt. IV, SBE Vol. 43, p. 356, note 1.

CHAPTER 5

Water

Being one of the requisites of Vedic sacrifice, water is glorified as having several qualities. Some of these qualities speak of the facts about water, while some spring from the beliefs of people about it and yet others could be traced to priestly psyche and the reasoning thereof.

The actual observation of water cleansing a person of any dirt has made the ritualists speak of water as a purifying agent. In the New-moon and Full-moon sacrifices while preparing the altar, when he washes his hands, the *arthavāda* states that thereby he removes whatever there was bloody or injured on the altar (*Śat. Br.* I.2.5.23). As a concluding part of the Sākamedha *iṣṭi* in the Cāturmāsya *iṣṭi*-s (four-monthly Seasonal sacrifices), there are offered oblations to Rudra. After this offering relating to Rudra is over, they touch water because water is a means of purification (*ibid.* II. 6.2.18... . *śāntirāpaḥ...).* This is specially in view of a rite related to Rudra, the fierce god. In the New-moon and Full-moon sacrifices, when he sips water, it is said clearly that water is a means of purification (*ibid.* I. 7.4.17). In these sacrifices, in a series of rites, water is used with the sole idea of purifying the entities. The Adhvaryu (priest) has to sprinkle water on the firewood with a mantra (*Vāj. Sam.* II. 1) says the *Śat. Br.* (I.3.3.1). Thereafter the altar is to be sprinkled with water (*ibid.* I.3.3.2). This is for making it sacrificially pure for grass covering. Water is sprinkled on the sacrificial grass,[1] which has been placed on the altar with the knot turned to the east with the *mantra* (*Vāj. Sam.* II. 1), for making that grass sacrificially pure for the spoons (*Śat. Br.* I. 3.3.3). Water is sprinkled on the oblations meant for the deities, the idea being to purify sacrificially these oblations (*ibid.* I.1.3.10,11). On the sacrificial vessels water is sprinkled with a *mantra* (*Vāj. Sam.* I.13) with the same idea. Here the *Śat. Br.* raises an apprehension that may be a carpenter or some other impure person has on this occasion desecrated the sacrificial vessels by touching them and so is their purification with water (*Śat. Br.* I.1.3.12). Earlier in the *Tait. Sam.* occurs the same belief about water as a purifying agent, in the context of the New-moon and Full-moon sacrifices. Water is enjoined to be sprinkled on the kindling wood and sacrificial strew to make them pure. It is said that the altar which is rough, hairless and impure, he makes pure by sprinkling it with water (*Tait. Sam.* II. 6.5.1).

The two *arthavāda*-s, presented by the *Śat. Br.*, are of interest to note. In the Agniṣṭoma sacrifice, it is enjoined that the sacrificial beast is to be sprinkled with water. This is to make it sacrificially pure. The *arthavāda* traces the origin of the beast to water, i.e. rains. From rains are produced plants. By eating plants and by drinking water, there originates sap (*rasaḥ*). From the sap comes seed (*retaḥ*) and the seed generates beasts. Beast thus is generated from rains, i.e. water. So it is made sacrificially pure by sprinkling it with water (*Śat. Br.* III. 7.4.4). The *arthavāda* indicates that the beast is as though taken to its birthplace, i.e. water, when water is sprinkled on it. Another *arthavāda* figures when water is enjoined to be sprinkled on the (three) lines, which the Adhvaryu draws with the wooden sword on the Gārhapatya fire-place.[2] Here water is said to be food, for when water (i.e. rains) comes to this world, food is produced here. When the Gārhapatya fire-place (i.e. lines on it) is sprinkled with water, he supplies food to the fire (*ibid.* II. 1.1.3).

Arthavāda-s about water at times speak of man's purification from the spiritual point of view. In the context of the Soma-sacrifice, the *Tait. Sam.* states that when the consecrated sacrificer sips water, he becomes internally pure (*Tait. Sam.* VI. 1.1.3). While being consecrated for the Agniṣṭoma-sacrifice, when the sacrificer takes bath, it is said that water makes him internally pure, for man indeed is impure and is dirty within as he speaks untruth. So the pure and purifying water to make him pure (*Śat. Br.* III. 1.2.10). The same thought is expressed, when in the New-moon and Full-moon sacrifices, the sacrificer is about to enter the vow and standing between the Āhavanīya and Gārhapatya fires with his face towards the east, touches water. By his touching the water, his internal purification is brought into effect, for man (generally) speaks untruth and so is impure for the purpose of sacrifice (*ibid.* I.1.1.1).

Together with the idea of purification, water is glorified as having a healing effect. When he digs for the site of an altar, he as though acts cruelly with the ground. So he pours down water, for healing the ground which is dug up (*Tait. Sam.* II. 6.5.2). In the rite of Agnicayana, when a lump of clay for making the fire-pan is taken out from the earth, a hole is created in the earth. He pours water into that hole, to join and heal by water whatever is injured or torn in this earth (*Śat. Br.* VI. 4.3.1). Similarly in the Agniṣṭoma sacrifice, while fixing the Audumbarī (a post made of the Udumbara tree),[3] he undertakes digging and then pours water in that pit. The *arthavāda* states that water is poured to give soothing effect to the earth as there is caused injury to the earth in the process of digging (*ibid.* III. 6. 1.19). These *arthavāda*-s will not appear far-fetched if we take into account the principle of animism. The belief in 'animism' made the ancient mind think that the world in general especially trees, plants and even inanimate entities like earth, etc. are animate and have souls and so have the various feelings. This belief of unknown times is seen percolated in the *arthavāda*-s noted above, where water is said to give healing or soothing effect, when the earth is dug up for the rite. Even the very *vidhi* of pouring water into the hole made in the earth has sprung up from this very belief. The earlier part of the *vidhi* or the earlier *vidhi* is simply of digging the earth for the site of altar or for the lump of clay for fixing the Audumbarī post. The *vidhi* of pouring water on the dug up portion of the earth does not seem to be that way necessary. But the belief in animism (here with respect to the earth) makes the *vidhi* and *arthavāda* figure here.

The healing and soothing qualities of water are spoken of in the *arthavāda*-s stated in the context of certain *vidhi*-s. In the Agniṣṭoma sacrifice, even though they 'quiet'[4] and later on cut up the animal-victim, they wound this victim. So the soothing and healing of the victim by means of water (*ibid.* III. 8.2.30). In the rite of purchasing Soma, the Somakrayaṇī cow is made to take seven steps, with the result there are seven foot-prints of hers (i.e. of her right fore-foot). He follows the cow stepping into her footprints, and taking a wooden sword (*sphya)* draws lines around the seventh footprint. Scratching all over the footprint, taking out the loose dust, he throws it into the fire-pan. In this as they injure the earth and knock off anything from her, water is poured at the seventh footprint for healing the earth (*ibid.* III. 3.1.5-7). In the rite of Agnyādhāna (establishing the three fires) they dig up the earth at the site of the fire-altars and take away the impure part. The injury caused to the earth is healed up with water (*Tait. Br.* I.1.3.1).

In the Agniṣṭoma sacrifice, when the Uttaravedi is prepared, he sprinkles it with water. This is to appease Vāc, who had become a lioness and had roamed about unappeased, water being a means of appeasement (*Śat. Br.* III 5.1.35). It has to be noted that as the Uttaravedi (high altar) and Vāc are conceptually identified, the mythical account of Vāc becoming a lioness is extended to the actual high altar and then the ritual acts such as pouring of ghee[5] (while the fire is held over the high altar) and sprinkling of water are glorified.

The *Tait. Sam.* in the context of the Soma-sacrifice lays down the *vidhi* (injunction) of sprinkling water on the high altar. By this the sacrificer repels his enemies from the quarters. It is said that it was on the right side of the high altar that Indra gave the *yati*-s (ascetics) to the wolves (*sālāvṛka*-s) which ate them.[6] Whatever cruel is there on the right side of the high altar, that is appeased by the water, which is sprinkled over (*Tait. Sam.* VI. 2.7.5).

The *Kauṣ. Br.* in the context of the New-moon and Full-moon sacrifices says that at the end he sacrifices to Agni Sviṣṭakṛt. At this time, after uttering the sound Vaṣaṭ, he touches water. The *arthavāda* stating the belief in the healing and medicinal qualities of water, assures that healing and medicine are produced at the end in the sacrifice (*Kauṣ. Br.* III. 6). The *Śat. Br.* glorifies the appeasing effect of water in the concluding ceremonies of the New-moon and Full-moon sacrifices. There is a rite of pouring the Praṇītā water on the altar. The *arthavāda* points out that when he spreads the sacrifice, he yokes it. But when completed, the sacrifice being unyoked would injure the sacrificer. So the Praṇītā waters are poured out (*Śat. Br.* I.9.2.32). The belief which suggests itself from this is interesting to note. Here sacrifice is viewed with awe, may be because of the magical effect it brings about and the enormous power it has to bring about this magical effect. So the Praṇītā waters to appease it. The same appeasing effect of water is spoken of, when he sprinkles water on the Mahāvīra-pot (in which milk is boiled) in the Pravargya ceremony (*ibid.* XIV. 3. 1.25). The Fire-altar in the Agnicayana rite is sprinkled with water for appeasing Agni-Rudra, though the latter is first appeased by Śatarudriya offering, as the gods had done in the former times (*ibid.* IX. 1.2.2, 3). Simply touching the vessels filled with water leads to soothing. In the Agniṣṭoma sacrifice, the ten *camasin*-s touch their respective *camasa* cups, filled with water.[7] The *arthavāda* states that when a yoked animal hurts by rubbing or scratches itself, water is a means of soothing. Similarly when the priests fret or scratch themselves, they soothe by means of water (*ibid.* IV. 4.3.13).

In the concluding rite of the New-moon and Full-moon sacrifices, it is enjoined that the Adhvaryu priest should walk round the fire to the south and pour out a vessel of water towards north. The *arthavāda* states that water is used for cooling the path, by which the sacrificer desires to go after his sacrifice is complete (*ibid.* I.9.3.1).

It is interesting to note that a vessel full of water has a particular significance in the Vedic ritual. For the Vedic sacrifice, it was necessary to first keep a jar of water ready alongside of the sacrificial fire. The water to be placed in this jar was collected on the previous day. This water is called Vasatīvarī, more about which we shall see later. We have already noted that in the concluding rite of the New-moon and Full-moon sacrifices, the Adhvaryu priest should pour out a vessel full of water towards north. The full vessel of water indicates that he thereby lustrates that path with all.[8] He pours it out continuously, uninterruptedly, lustrating the path in a continuous uninterrupted manner (*ibid.* I.9. 3. 1-3). If in sacrifice anything is done in a wrong way, there they wound the sacrifice. So he heals that with waters (*ibid.* I.9.3.4).

At some rituals, the idea is of expiating by the sacrificer by means of water. In the New-moon and Full-moon sacrifices, he touches the sacrificial cake over with water, either once or three times. This he does, for in the process of preparing the sacrificial cake, when they thresh or grind the rice-grains, they either injure or tear asunder the rice-grains. Water being a means of expiation, he thereby expiates with water (*ibid.* I.2.2.11). If any of the three unclean animals *viz.* a vicious boar, a vicious ram and a dog, runs about in between the Gārhapatya and Āhavanīya fires, while the Agnihotra-offering is put on the fire, he should pour water out of a bowl of water, from the ground in front of the Gārhapatya upto the Āhavanīya fire-altar, for whatever is injured or unpropitiated in the sacrifice, for all that the means of propitiation or expiation is water (*ibid.* XII. 4.1.5). If the earthen milk-vessel in the Agnihotra-rite breaks, he should pour out a bowlful or potful of water, as the water is the means of propitiation in such a case of something injured or unpropitiated (*ibid.* XII. 4.1.8).

We have already noted an *arthavāda* from the *Kauṣ. Br.* (III. 6), which speaks of water as having medicinal qualities. The *Tait. Sam.* has already stated it in the context of the Soma-sacrifice. It is said that the life and breath of a person, who draws the Soma-shoots, depart. So he should touch waters for the waters are medicine (*Tait. Sam.* III. 3.4.3....*bheṣajam vā'āpaḥ...).*

In the Rājasūya sacrifice, various kinds of water are collected for the purpose of sprinkling the king with them. It is said that as water is vigour (*vīryam vā'āpaḥ)* by collecting all types of water, he collects vigour (*Śat. Br.* V.3.4.1).

The thought that water is an elixir of immortality (*amṛtam vā' āpaḥ*) occurs in the *Śat. Br.*,[9] in the context of the Agniṣṭoma sacrifice, when the priests touch their respective cups (*camasa*-s*)* filled with water and also touch their faces with water (*ibid.* IV. 4.3.15). Immortal nature of waters is spoken of, when there is enjoined anointing with water in the great coronation of the kings (*Ait. Br.* VIII. 20 = 39.6). The *arthavāda* in the context of the morning prayer and preparatory ceremonies for the Soma-sacrifice, speaks of the imperishable nature of the waters, the *vidhi* being of drawing (Ekadhanā) water in vessels and pitchers for washing feet. It is said that in spite of so much food and drink being consumed, the waters are not diminished (*Śat. Br.* III. 9.3.27). The *Tait. Sam.* enjoins sprinkling the Fire-altar with water, stating that waters are ambrosia. It is said that with this thought they sprinkle with water him who faints (*Tait. Sam.* V. 6. 2.1, 2). When in the Soma-sacrifice, a libation is offered with a *ṛc* from the Aponaptrīya hymn (*RV* X. 30.10), which is a hymn invoking the deity Apām Napāt, i.e. "Son of Waters", the waters are glorified as strength and sap and also immortality. In this context, there occurs a mythical account in the *Kauṣ. Br.*, which is as follows. The *rakṣas*-es who wanted to destroy the sacrifice, used to watch the waters at the fords. Whosoever came to the waters, they killed him. Kavaṣa 'saw' the Aponaptrīya hymn (*RV.* X. 30), by reciting which he smote the *rakṣas*-es from the fords. With the invocation of the deity of waters, they could return in safety and uninjured from the sacrifice (*Kaus. Br.* XII. 1). The thought that water bestows immortality is marked when it is enjoined for the sacrificer's wife to cleanse the openings of the sacrificial beast with water. It is said that when they 'quiet' and then cut off that victim, they actually kill it. But the food of the immortal gods in the form of the victim has to be immortal. As the waters stand for vital breaths, the wife cleansing the openings of the victim, puts those vital breaths in the victim. With the result, this food of the gods becomes a live one and also an immortal one (*Śat. Br.* III. 8.2.4). The initiate is asked to sip water, for waters are ambrosia (*ibid.* XI. 5.4.5... *amṛtam vā āpaḥ).*

Water is glorified as Truth at several places in the Vedic ritual contexts. In the rite of Agnicayana, while building the first layer, the *sāman* named Satya,[10] signifying 'Truth' is sung (*ibid.* VII. 4.1.3-5). This *sāman* is said to be Agni's mouth, obviously because it is sung first. Now waters are said to be 'Truth'. These waters are the flowing ones and due to them everything which exists is said to have been produced here (*ibid.* VII. 4.1.6.... *āpo hi vai satyam...).* In the context of daily Agnihotra offerings, water is said to stand for both — consecration (Dīkṣā) for sacrifice as also for the final bath (*avabhṛtha*) — as he has to touch water prior to the Agnihotra offering as well as at the end of these offerings. Here waters are glorified as 'Truth' (*satyam vā āpaḥ),* by the *Jaim. Br.* (I. 4).

The Vasatīvarī waters (which are collected on the previous day of sacrifice), enjoined to be used in sacrifice, are to be brought from the flowing (current of) waters. The statements of *arthavāda* in this connection, bring forth several beliefs, regarding the flowing waters. It is said that when the head of the sacrifice was struck off, its sap entered the flowing waters. The flowing waters contain this sap, which he could gather and put it into sacrifice (*Śat. Br.* III. 9.2. 1-4). The flowing waters are praised as the only ones which never take rest on this earth. Everything on this earth, including the wind, takes rest while the flowing waters do not. So they are collected for protection (*ibid.* III. 9.2.5). These waters are carried round for the sake of protection and they repel the evil spirits (*ibid.* III. 9.2.16). The Vasatīvarī waters are to be collected by daytime,[11] the reason in the *arthavāda* being, the sun shines yonder in the day and all the gods coming in his house, for whom he takes the waters, are the rays of the sun's light. He makes the gods on this day of preparation (Upvasatha day) enter (*saṁveśayati)* those waters. Hence the name Vasatīvarī (*ibid.* III. 9.2.6,7).[12] Just as Vasatīvarī waters are to be collected in the daytime, obviously for catching the sun's lustre in them, with the same thought the waters of rain to be collected, when the sun is shining, are used for sprinkling and lustrating the king in the Rājasūya sacrifice. The *arthavāda* is that such rain-waters in sunshine are brilliance and splendour, which are conferred on the king (*Ait. Br.* VIII.8 = 37.4).

The *Tait. Sam.* states that the Vasatīvarī waters are to be taken with radiance or light in them (i.e. in day-time), or having deposited gold (in a jar) they are taken if the sun sets or they are to be taken from the Vasatīvarī waters kept in a jar (*kumbhyānām)*.,[13] of a *brāhmaṇa,* who performs many sacrifices (*bahuyājī)* and thus has collected the Vasatīvarī waters (*gṛhītavasatīvarīkaḥ) (Tait. Sam.* VI. 4.2.2). It is worthy of note that the Vasatīvarī waters are connected either with the sun or Agni or gold or a *brāhmaṇa,* all of them having lustre (in the case of a *brāhmaṇa,* the lustre of *brahman).*

The ritual-texts particularly stress the importance of the flowing waters through the *arthavāda*-s. The *Tait. Sam.* states a mythical account that Indra slew Vṛtra, who then died on the waters. The pure part of the waters, which was fit for sacrifice and thus divine, was set free (*Tait. Sam.* V. 4.2.3). The account indicates that this divine part is the flowing waters. The same text specifically states further that he should not take stagnant waters. Here the reasoning through *arthavāda* is that the stagnant waters are seized by Varuṇa. If he takes of stagnant waters, he would cause Varuṇa to seize his sacrifice (*ibid.* VI. 4.2.4). The *Śat. Br.* echoes the same thought when it speaks of the final bath (*avabhṛtha*) to be taken by the sacrificer in a standing pool of flowing water (*syandamānānām sthāvaro hradaḥ).* The *arthavāda* here states that the parts of flowing water, that do not flow and thus are saturated at one place are held by Varuṇa. The final bath belongs to Varuṇa and it is for freeing himself from Varuṇa (*Śat. Br.* IV.4.5.10). The idea is that for freeing himself from Varuṇa, the sacrificer has to be away from Varuṇa, i.e. the stagnant waters, at the same time entering the flowing waters with a *mantra* to Varuṇa, to cut off from himself the snares or nooses of Varuṇa (*ibid.* IV. 4.5.11). In spite of Varuṇa being regarded as having a sway over all waters,[14] this particular injunction regarding the final bath (*avabhṛtha*) shows that according to the ritualistic belief the snares of Varuṇa are more acute at the places of stagnant waters, while they could be cut off (at least with the recitation of a *mantra* to Varuṇa) at the flowing waters. The thought that Varuṇa takes hold of a person, who dies in water (*ibid.* XIII. 3.8.5) reflects the natural fear that the dead, i.e. stagnant waters, may take a person away.

The same trend of giving importance to the flowing waters could be felt when the *Jaim. Br.* glorifies the waters (the flowing ones) as a thunderbolt killing and carrying away the sacrificer's sin. The context is of the Gavām-ayana sacrifice and the occasion is of entering waters for the Avabhṛtha rite. It is said that as the waters would flow and he would plunge in every flowing wave (for taking bath), he should desire that they should carry away his sin (*Jaim. Br.* II. 67). The standing waters make the evil of the persons taking bath stop (or stay), the flowing waters carry away their evil (*Śat. Br.* XIII. 8.4.6). The *Śat. Br.* glorifies the final bath (*avabhṛtha*) in the context of the Soma-sacrifice, that the pressed Soma-plants (i.e. Soma husks) are taken down to the waters, as the latter are the essence (*raso vā āpaḥ).* Thereby Soma is produced (i.e. the plants become juicy again) and so is the sacrificer produced (i.e. his spirit is restored) after the final bath (*ibid.* IV. 4.5.1; also cf. *ibid.* IV. 4.5.20). The sacrificer and his wife, having taken the final bath wrap themselves in fresh garments.[15] It is said that after this final bath, as a snake casts its skin, the sacrificer casts away all his sins (*ibid.* IV. 4.5.23).

With these qualities of purifying, cooling and healing, waters are said to possess the power of slaying and are regarded as thunderbolt. While preparing the altar in the New-moon and Full-moon sacrifices and also digging for it, the *Tait. Sam.* lays down pouring down waters on the earth. It is said that waters are *rakṣas*-slaying and by pouring waters, he slays the evil spirits (*Tait. Sam.* II. 6.4.4).

The sacrificer consecrated for the Agniṣṭoma sacrifice, has to shave (the hair of) his head, beard and cut his nails. Now for cutting the right whisker, he moistens it first with water. It is said that waters are a thunderbolt, for wherever the waters flow, they make a hollow and destroy whatever they come near. The same thunderbolt in the form of waters he appeases with the *mantra viz. 'imā āpaḥ śamu me santu devīḥ'*, while moistening the right whisker (*Śat. Br.* III. 1.2.6).

In the context of the New-moon and Full-moon sacrifices, the *vidhi* is of bringing forward water and placing it near the Gārhapatya fire-altar, thus spreading the sacrifice. The mythical account tells that in the fight between the gods and *asura-rakṣas*-es, the gods saw a thunderbolt in the form of waters. It is in the safe and foeless shelter of this thunderbolt, i.e. waters, that the Adhvaryu priest spreads the sacrifice (*ibid.* I.1.1.17). In the same context, when the waters to be sprinkled are strained through two strainers (*ibid.* I. 1.3.3) and also when the sacrificer or Adhvaryu takes them with a ladle and makes them spirt upwards with his right hand (*ibid.* I.1.3.7), the mythical account of Indra slaying Vṛtra is stated to show the importance of waters. It is said that Vṛtra when slain by Indra flowed forth towards the waters as ocean lies in every direction. It is thought that Indra killed Vṛtra with the help of waters (*ibid.* I.1.1.8,9). The same account of Vṛtra being killed with waters is mentioned as *arthavāda,* when Nigrābhyā waters are enjoined to be poured on Soma (Soma-shoots) in the morning pressing (*ibid.* III. 9.4.14).

The effects of the flowing waters are the same as that of a thunderbolt which strikes. The gods took up this thunderbolt (i.e. waters) and in its safe shelter they performed the sacrifice. The Adhvaryu bringing forward the Praṇītā waters, spreads the sacrifice in its safe shelter, devoid of enemies (*ibid.* I. 1.1.17). The importance of the Praṇītā waters is explained by the *Śat. Br.* through *arthavāda* in the context of the Sautrāmaṇī sacrifice. It is said that the Sautrāmaṇī sacrifice (here imagined as an animate being) was with the *asura*-s. But he (i.e. the Sautrāmaṇī sacrifice) went to the gods. He came to the waters, which welcomed him. He spoke to the waters of his fear from the *asura*-s. The waters then led him forward (*pra-anayan)* and in this move of theirs, they themselves are 'led forward' in the sacrifice, getting the name Praṇītāḥ (fr. *pra* + √*nī* (*ibid.* XII. 9.3.8).

The *Śat. Br.* in the context of the New-moon and Full-moon sacrifices enjoins that the coagulated milk when prepared is to be covered over by a vessel with the hollow part upwards containing water. As waters are a thunderbolt, he drives away from the vessel, the evil spirits as well as the *rakṣas*-es (*ibid.* I.7.1.20). In the context of the Sautrāmaṇī sacrifice, the *Śat. Br.* states that when he takes waters in his cupped hands, he makes a covenant (*mitradheyam)* with the thunderbolt, i.e. waters. He should sprinkle water in whatever direction he who hates may be and thereby should vanquish him (*ibid.* XII. 9.2.6.)[16] The same thought is expressed in the context of the Pitṛmedha-*karman.* When the funeral ceremonies are over, they bathe at any place where there is water. Taking water in his cupped hands, he throws it in the direction of his hateful enemy and vanquishes him. (*ibid.* XIII. 8.4.5).

Waters as thunderbolt can separate the living world from the world of spirits. While building the fire-altar, three bricks in the name of goddess Nirṛti (Nairṛti-s) are to be placed and on the space between the sacrificer and the bricks, he has to pour out a jarful of water. The *Śat. Br.* says that as water is a thunderbolt, he separates from himself, evil (*pāpmānam)* and Nirṛti (the deity of evil) with water (*ibid.* VII.2.1.17). The belief indicated here in the *arthavāda* can be marked even in our own times, when it is believed that ghosts and evil spirits cannot cross a water-pond or even the lines drawn with water.

For the lustration of king in the Rājasūya sacrifice, waters from various places are brought, the common idea being of waters standing for vigour (*ibid.* V. 3.4.1....*vīryam vā āpaḥ).* It will be of interest to note these and especially the reasoning (*arthavāda)* stated in respect of each of them, for such a reasoning reflects the ritual-belief.

The waters taken first are from the river Sarasvatī. The *arthavāda* is that Sarasvatī is the goddess of Speech and he thereby sprinkles the king with Speech (*ibid.* V. 3.4.3). Thereafter the two waves of water, which flow in different directions (i.e. one rising up in front of him and the other, rising up behind him) are taken for sprinkling the king. The *arthavāda* states that when a beast or man plunges into the water, the water that rises is actually the vigour of the water (*ibid.* V. 3.4.4-6). The king then is sprinkled with the flowing waters, for the waters flow with vigour (*ibid.* V.3.4.7). The waters taken next are those which flow against the current, as they have vigour for flowing in such a manner (*ibid.* V. 3.4.8). The Adhvaryu then takes waters that flow off the main current, for sprinkling the king. The *arthavāda* stated here indicates the political insight of the ritualists. It is said that as the flow of waters, separating from the main current comes back to it, so a person belonging to another kingdom but staying in the country of the king is absorbed by the king in his own kingdom (*ibid.* V.3.4.9). Thereafter waters taken are from the sea, which is the lord of rivers, for making the king lord of people (*ibid.* V. 3.4.10). The waters then figure are from a whirlpool. The *arthavāda* here refers to the phenomenon of childbirth, stating that as waters enclose the offspring (embryo), the Adhvaryu by sprinkling the king with these waters, makes him the offspring of people (*ibid.* V. 3.4.11). The king is sprinkled with waters taken from a pool of flowing waters, at a place exposed to sunlight, thereby making the king endowed with solar lustre. It is said that even being a part of flowing waters, the pool has steady waters and these according to belief belong to Varuṇa. The Rājasūya rite being the Varuṇasava, i.e. impelling of Varuṇa (fr. √*sū* - 'to generate, impel'), the waters from such a pool are taken (*ibid.* V.3.4.12). Then the Adhvaryu takes for sprinkling, waters which are of rains, while the sun is shining. The *arthavāda* in this regard is that by these waters Adhvaryu makes the king lustrous like the sun (as these waters have caught the solar lustre). Moreover he makes the king pure with these waters, for such waters are pure as he catches them prior to their reaching the earth (*ibid.* V. 3.4.13). The Adhvaryu takes waters from a pond, for sprinkling the king, thereby making the people in the kingdom steady and faithful to the king (*ibid.* V. 3.4.14). The waters from a well are drawn for sprinkling. By this, some of the waters even beyond this earth (i.e. the underneath waters) are brought and thus waters employed in this ritual become complete (*ibid.* V. 3.4.15). Dew-drops are collected to sprinkle the king with. The *arthavāda* states that the yonder sun, even at the rising hour, burns the plants. The dew-drops (at the early morning) coming down quench the heat on the earth. In the absence of dew-drops, there would not be any food left on the earth. The Adhvaryu sprinkles the king with food, when he makes the use of the dew-drops (*ibid.* V. 3.4.16). The Adhvaryu takes honey to sprinkle the king with. Honey stands as the essence of waters and plants, with which the king is sprinkled (*ibid.* V. 3.4.17). The embryonic waters of a cow, which is about to deliver a calf are taken for sprinkling, the Adhvaryu thereby consecrating the king with cattle (*ibid.* V. 3.4.18). He then sprinkles with milk as well as with clarified butter. These waters stand for cattle, for milk and clarified butter are the products of cow (i.e. cattle), thereby making the king possess the cattle (*ibid.* V. 3.4.19,20). The Adhvaryu catches light sun-rays with his cupped hands and mixes them (with other types of waters). The *arthavāda* points out that these light sun-rays are self-ruling waters, because without yielding to one another's superiority, these waters flow. With the use of these, the self-ruling powers are bestowed on the king (*ibid.* V.3.4.21). The waters used in this lustration ritual are of seventeen kinds. As Prajāpati, identified with the very sacrifice is seventeenfold, the Adhvaryu makes the sacrificer-king, Prajāpati, i.e. the very Sacrifice (*ibid.* V. 3.4.22,23).

In the Sautrāmaṇī sacrifice, when the sacrificer is consecrated by sprinkling him with the fat of the sacrificial animals, each time the residue is poured into a bowl made of reed. The *arthavāda* states that the reed has its birth in the waters, which stand for all the deities (*ibid.* XII. 8.3.12, 15). This *arthavāda* could be traced to the creation-hymn in *RV*, where primeval waters are spoken of as existing prior to creation or at the time of creation. In *RV* (X. 129), the deep, unfathomable waters are said to exist in the beginning (*ibid.* X. 129. 3b), and the gods came afterwards (*ibid.* 6c). In one hymn, the gods are said to dance in the primeval waters (*RV*. X. 72.6), the latter existing prior to the gods.

The concept that water stands for female principle in the scheme of creation, is clearly stated in the *arthavāda* occurring in the context of the rite of Agnyādhāna. When he brings waters, it is said that waters are female (*yoṣā vā āpaḥ*) and fire (Agni) is male. He thus provides for Agni, a productive mate in the form of waters (*Śat. Br.* II.1.1.4). In the context of building the Fire-altar in the Agnicayana rite, a mythical account occurs as *arthavāda*. It is said that

Prajāpati desired to create the universe from the primeval waters. So he entered the waters with the three Veda-s. Then was created the golden egg, the first expression of creation. Agni (-Prajāpati) is the male principle and the waters stand for the female principle (*ibid.* VI. 1.1.10). Elsewhere the creation is said to come into existence from the waters alone, which has to be regarded as the female principle (*ibid.* XI. 1.6.1). Such an account is thought of from the fact of life, when the actual birth of a child is seen from a female only, in the process of childbirth. Though waters are said to be 'seed' *(reto vā āpaḥ)* in the rite of consecration, when the sacrificer is sprinkled over with waters prior to the anointing with butter (*Ait. Br.* I.3 = 1.3), it is the potentiality of the waters in the process of creation, that is spoken of here, for by sprinkling with waters, the sacrificer is made an embryo, when he is consecrated. Waters are mainly regarded as the female principle in the creation-scheme. The *arthavāda* states that they are the wives of Agni; everything here is created from waters. In the context of Agnicayana rite, referring to a similar practice by the gods, it is enjoined that the ashes removed from the fire-pan (*ukhā)* are to be taken to the waters, with a thought that Agni, now in the form of ashes, can be reborn from them, they being the wives of Agni, as seen in the *arthavāda* noted above (*Śat. Br.* VI. 8.2.3). The idea that the waters would bear Agni, as the mother bears the son (-husband) is sublime. The concept of husband becoming son reaches back to *RV*, where the god Apām Napāt is said to be the 'seeder'- bull, generating the foetus in waters and becoming their newborn son sucking them, they in turn licking him (*RV* II. 35.13), and the god Sarasvat (the male deity of the river Sarasvatī), who grew strong among the females (i.e. waters) and who is the 'seeding' bull (*vṛṣabhaḥ)* and the 'child-son' — *vṛṣā śiśuḥ* (*ibid.* VII. 95.3).

Together with this place of prime importance of being regarded as a significant factor, sometimes the only factor, in the creation of the universe, waters have unique importance of being the foundation of everything (*Śat. Br.* VI.8.2.2... *āpo vā asya sarvasya pratiṣṭhā).* In the context of the Agnicayaṇa rite, it is said that waters are Agni's foundation, for on the waters these worlds are founded (*ibid.* VI. 7.1.17). For making a fire-pan, the sacrificer has to dig and collect clay. A horse is led to the ground for that purpose. When the horse steps forth, the sacrificer or the Adhvaryu priest on his behalf pours down water. The *arthavāda* here speaks of the actual facts in the world, while praising this pouring down of water. It is said that where there are waters, there are seen plants. The springing up of plants brings cattle. The sacrifice finds support in cattle; the sacrificer in sacrifice and offspring in the sacrificer. So the pouring of water is for support (*Tait. Sam.* V. 1.3.1).

The all-pervasiveness of waters is spoken of in some *arthavāda*-statements. In the context of the Agnicayana rite it is said that when he sprinkles the Fire-altar on every side with waters, he encompasses the worlds by ocean, for the Fire-altar stands for the worlds and the waters for the ocean (*Śat. Br.* IX.1.2.3). In the context of the New-moon and Full-moon sacrifices, a mythical account dealing with the creation-myth occurs, which states that Parameṣṭhin, the son of Prajāpati desired to become everything here and he became waters. The *Śat. Br.* says that waters are everything here, for he who digs here on earth, finds water. The waters abide in the furthest place (*ibid.* XI. 1.6.16). In the same sacrifices (noted above), waters are enjoined to be brought forward (Praṇītā waters), for putting them down to the north of the Gārhapatya fire, subsequently to be carried to the north of the Āhavanīya fire. It is said that all this universe is pervaded by waters (*ibid.* I.1.1.14.....*adbhirvā idam sarvam āptam).*

Waters are regarded as completing that which has remained incomplete. This can be marked in the context of the Vājapeya sacrifice, when the horses to be yoked for running a race are sprinkled with water. It is said that when the horse in the beginning was produced from waters, it was produced incomplete. It could not stand on all its feet. The *Śat. Br.* says that whatever was left behind it in the waters, with them the sacrificer or the Adhvaryu now completes it and the horse is made whole (*ibid.* V. 1.4.5). In the context of the New-moon and Full-moon sacrifices, it is said that whatever here (in these sacrifices), the Hotṛ or the Adhvaryu or the Brahman or the Agnīdhra or the sacrificer himself cannot accomplish, all that is obtained by waters (*ibid.* I.1.1.15).[17]

The etymology of the words *āpaḥ* and *vāḥ* meaning 'water' amply bring out the nature of waters. In the context of Agnicayana rite, in the ritual of making a fire-pan, a mythical account occurs which states that Prajāpati created waters out of Vāc (Speech). As they pervaded or acquired (fr. √*āp* - 'to acquire') everything here, they are called *āpaḥ* and as the waters covered (fr. √*vṛ* - 'to close, cover'), they are called *vāḥ,* i.e. *vār* (*ibid.* VI. 1.1.9).

When the waters are brought forward (*āpaḥ praṇayanti)* in the sacrifice, the *Tait. Br.* speaks of the importance of waters by stating ritual-metaphors. It is said that 'Waters are faith' (*śraddhā vā āpaḥ);* 'Waters are sacrifice' (*yajño vā āpaḥ).* They are said to be thunderbolt, as also the killers of evil spirits (*rakṣoghnīḥ).* Waters are all deities (*āpo vai sarvā devatāḥ).* The sacrificer has to cross over after having touched them (i.e. waters), lest they should burn him and the Adhvaryu (*Tait. Br.* III. 2.4.1-4). Such metaphors occur even in the *Śat. Br.* Waters are not only all gods, but all creatures as well as all desires (*Śat. Br.* X. 5.4.14, 15; also *ibid.* XII. 8.3.15). Waters are ocean; waters are seed (*ibid.* III. 8.4.11). Waters are heaven; waters are the lotus-leaf (*ibid.* VI. 4.1.9). Waters are food; waters are ambrosia, waters are a beautiful object (*ibid.* XIII. 8.1.9,13). All these ritual-metaphors are the examples of *gauṇī sāropā lakṣaṇā* based on a specific quality of waters (which is the *upameya,* i.e. that which is to be compared) common with that of the various *upamāna*-s (i.e. standards of comparison) such as ocean, heaven, lotus-leaf, food, etc., with the superimposition of the latter on waters.

The importance of waters in the sacrifice is brought out in the metaphor - 'Waters are sacrifice' (*ibid.* I.1.1.12; III. 1.4.15). The *Ṣaḍ. Br.* says that the sacrificial ground has three lustres *viz.* fire, waters and the sun, bringing waters on par with Agni and the sun (*Ṣaḍ. Br.* III. 3.17......*agnirāpa ādityastaddevayajanam tattriśukriyam).* This is the highest tribute paid to waters in the sacrificial tradition.[18]

NOTES AND REFERENCES

1. See Eggeling, J., *The Śatapatha Brāhmaṇa,* pt. I, SBE Vol. 12, Delhi, 1988 (1882), p. 84, note 2 .
2. See Eggeling, J., *op. cit.,* pt. I, p. 276 tr. of *Śat. Br.* II. 1.1.2; and also pp. 276-77, note 2.
3. See Dange, Sadashiv A., *Vedic Sacrifices—Early Nature,* Vol. II, Aryan Books International, New Delhi, 2000, Appendix C on "Audumbarī - In Puranic Myths", p. 486 f.
4. The animal-victim is said to be 'quieted', as its killing in the ritual is by smothering it, *Śat. Br.* (III. 8.1.15). Śamitṛ (fr. the root √*śam* - causal - 'to make quiet) is the one, who makes the animal-victim 'quiet', i.e. kills it by smothering it.
5. The mythical account in this connection is as follows. In the Soma-sacrifice named Sadyaḥkrī, the Aṅgiras-es acted as officiating priests for the Āditya-s. The Āditya-s brought Vāc as sacrificial fee for the Aṅgiras-es. But the latter did not accept it. So the Āditya-s brought Sūrya (Sun) to the Aṅgiras-es, which they accepted. Speech becoming angry as the Aṅgiras-es did not accept her, went away and becoming lioness went on seizing upon everything of both the parties — the gods and the *asura*-s. Both of them wooed her. She ultimately was willing to go over to the gods, on the condition that the offering should reach her even before it reached Agni. When he pours ghee on the high altar that offering reaches Vāc even before Agni (*Śat. Br.* III. 5. 1. 13-23).
6. See Dange, Sadashiv A., "Wolves that Devoured the Ascetics", *Towards Understanding Hindu Myths,* Aryan Books International, New Delhi, 1996, pp. 223-41, where he deals fully with this mythical account.

7. For details, see Eggeling, J., *op. cit.,* pt. II, SBE Vol. 26, Delhi, 1988 (1885). p. 373, note 5.
8. 'The filled jar' (*pūrṇa-kumbha)* has special importance in the Hindu tradition as reflected in the Purāṇas. It was auspicious to see or to glance at such a jar, while going out for the daily business (*Skanda P.* II.2.11.56). It is enjoined that a householder should touch a jar of water (i.e. jar full of water) as he goes out for any work, so that the work should get success and it is believed to be so (*Vām. P.* 14.36). For more about jar, see Dange, Sadashiv A., "The Jar in Symbolic Rites", *Puanic Myth and Culture*, Ajanta Pubns., Delhi, 1987, pp. 49-58.
9. For water as ambrosia, see also *Śat. Br.* I.9.3.7.
10. Eggeling, J., *op. cit.,* pt. III, SBE, Vol. 41, Delhi, 1989 (1894), p. 363, note 1.
11. It is interesting to see that if the waters are required to be collected after the sunset, he has to hold a firebrand or a piece of gold close above the waters. This is for having the effect of the yonder burning sun (*Śat. Br.* III.9. 2.9) on waters, for both fire and gold are shining by nature. Fire is regarded as the other form of the sun and gold is said to be the seed of Agni.

    When Agni united with waters, his seed became gold (*Śat. Br.* II. 1.1.5).
12. The etymology of the word Vasatīvarī is stated in yet another way. It is said that these waters are agreeable (*varam)* to the dwellers (*vasatām).* Hence the name Vasatīvarī (*Śat. Br.* III.9.2.16).
13. Keith, A.B., on *Tait. Sam.* VI. 4.2.2 takes the word *kumbhyānām* to mean 'from thc tank'. Vide, *The Veda of the Black Yajus School entitled Taittiriya Sanhita,* pt. 2, p. 529. This is not convincing. The word *kumbhī* denotes a 'jar' and with the suffix *yat,* the word *kumbhyā* would mean 'water in a jar' and *kumbhyānām* thus would be *kumbhyānām apām,* i.e. 'of the waters from a jar'.
14. See Macdonell, A.A., *Vedic Mythology,* Motilal Banarsidass, Delhi, Reprint 1995 (1898), p. 25 f.
15. For details, see Eggeling, J., *op. cit.,* pt. III, SBE Vol. 41, p. 385, note 1.
16. The Puranic detail of king Saudāsa intending to throw the potent water accompanied with the muttering of a curse on

Vasiṣṭha can be taken note of here. Due to the intervention of his considerate wife Madayantī, who pacifies him, the king drops that water on his own feet that are turned black. Hence he is called 'Kalmāṣapāda'. See *Bhāg.* P. IX. 9.23-25; *Vi. P.* IV. 4. 56-57; *Sk. P.* Brahmottarakhaṇḍa 3.3.2.

17. See *Śat. Br.* IV. 5.7.7 — If anything (according to *Kāty. Ś.S.* XXV. 2.9 — 'Soma') is spilt in the sacrifice, he has to pour water on it, because everything here is pervaded or obtained by water.
18. In fact, water figures prominently in the magico-religious cults all the world over. This is because water being the first need of man in a primitive state of culture was regarded as possessed of *'mana'* (a mysterious power associated with persons and things). See Hastings, J., *Ency. of Rel. and Eth.*, Vol. XII, p. 704a-704b.

Chapter 6

Trees, Plants and Varieties of Grass

Trees, plants and several varieties of grass have unique importance in the Vedic ritual. Kindling-sticks as well as sacrificial utensils are of wood. Lord of forest (Vanaspati) figures as a separate deity, to which offering is given. The offering verse in this ritual can be traced from the *Śaṅkh. Ś.S.*[1] Due to this offering to Vanaspati, the sacrificer's oblation (i.e. the sacrificial animal) goes to the gods with life (i.e. being fully alive), for the lord of forest stands for the breaths of the sacrificial animal (*Ait. Br.* II.10 = 6.10). The *Kauṣ. Br.* echoes this thought. It states in the *arthavāda* that in the absence of a reference to the lord of forest in the inviting prayer, the sacrificial victim would be without any breath, which should not happen. So is the invitatory prayer to the lord of forest (*Kauṣ. Br.* XII. 7). The deity of forest (Vanaspati), which is in the form of huge trees and Araṇyānī which in reality is the whole forest deified, can be traced to *RV*,[2] bringing out the importance of forest-world in the life of the Vedic Aryans.

The kindling-sticks to be placed in the fire could vary in kind as well as size, as the *mantra* - 'whatever logs we place in thee' (*yadagne yāni kāni ca)* points out. But from the *arthavāda* a practice in those times could be marked. The *arthavāda* refers to a certain seer Prayoga by name, who made Agni accept what was not cut by the axe. In former times, Agni would not burn what was not cut by the axe

(*Tait. Sam.* V. 1.10.1). This shows that in later times, sticks for kindling, cut by means even other than the axe, could be used for being placed on fire.

The tree struck by lightning was thought to be of special importance. The *Tait. Br.* enjoins *sambhāra* (seven items from the earth and six items from particular trees, to be scattered at the site of the Gārhapatya fire)[3] from a tree struck by lightning. The *arthavāda,* while glorifying this *vidhi,* states that the Maruts once terribly troubled Agni with waters and grabbed his heart. It became the lightning (*Tait. Br.* I.1.3.12). The *sambhāra* here of a sacrificial stick from a lightning-struck tree, stands for the heart of Agni, who is to be established with his very heart.

Several trees have been reckoned as the sacrificial trees. A detail common about them according to *Śat. Br.* is of their being green and thus fresh, for that is what constitutes their living element, by which they are vigorous and possessed of strength (*Śat. Br.* I.3.4.1). The *Śat. Br.* mentions Palāśa (Butea Frondosa), Vikaṅkata (Flacourtia Sapida), Kārṣmarya (Gmelina Arborea), Bilva (Aegle Marmelos), Khadira (Acacia Catechu) and Udumbara (Ficus Glomerata) as the sacrificial (*yajñīya)* trees and mentions enclosing sticks from them (*ibid.* I.3.3.19, 20). The *Śat. Br.* notes that there are two kinds of objects coming from the trees *viz.* the wheels of chariots and wagons. As Soma is the lord of woods (Vanaspati) with an offering to Soma, the sacrificer-king in the Rājasūya sacrifice pleases the wooden pieces of the chariot coming from the trees (*ibid.* V. 4.3.16).

The *arthavāda*-s regarding these trees as also certain others reflect beliefs and practices of the Vedic times. To turn to these trees —

1. Arka (Calotropis Gigantea)

In the rite of Agnicayana, when the building of the Great Fire-altar has been completed, Agni is said to be the deity Rudra and the Śaturudriya offering is given to him. In lieu of the ordinary offering-spoon, the Arka-leaf is used for giving the offering.[4] The *arthavāda* states that the Arka-tree is food and thus Agni (-Rudra) is gratified with food (*Śat. Br.* IX. 1.1.4). We have already discussed about the Arka tree in the "Introduction".

2. Aśvattha (Ficus Religiosa)

The fruits from the Aśvattha tree are to be used in the great anointing (Mahābhiṣeka) of the king, the belief being that the Aśvattha tree stands for the overlordship (*sāmrājyam)* of the trees (*Ait. Br.* VIII. 16 = 39.2). Before buying Soma, fruits of Nyagrodha, etc. were to be kept ready. The *arthavāda* states that the Aśvattha tree was born from brilliance (*tejasaḥ)* and stands for the overlordship of the trees. As the sacrificer-king stands for the lordly power, by using the Aśvattha wood, he or the priest places brilliance (*tejaḥ)* and the overlordship (*sāmrājyam)* of the trees in the lordly power- '*kṣatre*' (*ibid.* VII. 32 = 35.6), The kindling sticks from an Aśvattha tree, which, is here called '*citriya*' (fr. √*cit* - 'to know', *citriya* — 'worthy of being known') are enjoined to be placed on the fire (Agni), on which Brahmaudana (rice cooked in ghee) is to be prepared. The *arthavāda* based on etymology states that by this *vidhi* there will be '*citra*', i.e. shining prosperity (*Tait. Br.* I.1.9.5. Sāyaṇa - *vicitram evaiśvaryam bhavati)*. The belief that propitiation of Agni with the kindling sticks of '*citriya*' leads to '*citra*', is obviously based on the principle of sympathetic magic.

While glorifying the *sambhāra* from the Aśvattha tree and the *vraja* (shed) from the wood of the same tree, the *Tait. Br.* relates a mythical account. The *Tait. Br.* says that Prajāpati taking the form of a horse hid from the gods. In that form (i.e. *aśva* - 'horse') of his, Prajāpati took resort in the Aśvattha tree for a year. Therefore the Aśvattha tree is named so ('coming from *aśva*' .... *aśva* + √*sthā* - 'to stand' > *ttha*). With the Aśvattha *vraja* (shed), the priest or the sacrificer establishes Prajāpati in his own birthplace (*ibid.* III. 8.12.2). While laying down the *sambhāra* of the Aśvattha wood, the *Tait,. Br.* relates the same mythical account, but the god, who concealed himself taking the form of a horse is Agni (*ibid.* I.1.3.9). The leaves of Aśvattha are enjoined for packing saline soil (*ūṣāḥ),* such packages being thrown by the common people towards the sacrificer, when he has ascended the sacrificial post together with his wife. This *vidhi* occurs in the Vājapeya sacrifice, which stands for the supreme sovereignty of the sacrificer (*ibid.* I.3.7.6). The *arthavāda* stated by the *Śat. Br.*, in this respect is that Indra on former occasion called upon the Maruts, when they were staying on the Aśvattha tree. Maruts are the peasants or common people (*viśaḥ)* of Indra and in similar relation stand the common people to the sacrificer, who performs the Vājapeya sacrifice (*Śat. Br.* V. 2. 1.17).

3. Bilva (Aegle Marmelos)

The *Ait. Br.* enjoins a sacrificial post of the Bilva wood in the animal-sacrifice. This Bilva tree should be one which gets fruits every year, which is a symbol of proper food. Again this tree should be one, which is covered with branches up to its roots and that is the symbol of prosperity (*Ait. Br.* II. 1 = 6.1).

The *Śat. Br.* enjoins a stake from this tree in the Horse-sacrifice and traces its creation from the *'kuntāpa'* and the marrow of Prajāpati, which burst forth from his ear and became the Bilva tree. The tree is yellowish, for the marrow of Prajāpati is yellowish (*Śat. Br.* XIII. 4.4.8).

4. Karīra (Capparis Aphylla)

The fruits of Karīra tree are enjoined to be offered on the northern altar (Uttaravedi) in the Varuṇapraghāsāḥ - *iṣṭi* (in the Four-monthly Seasonal sacrifices). The *Mait. Sam.* states by way of *arthavāda* a mythical account, which traces the origin of the Karīra trees. It says that formerly mountains had wings and Indra cut them off, for the mountains were creating instability and thus havoc by falling anywhere as per their wish. The (cut-off) wings became clouds, which even now cling to the peaks of mountains. The liquid which first flowed from the bodies of the mountains, became the fruits of the Karīra trees. Hence when he offers Karīra fruits in the Varuṇapraghāsāḥ-*iṣṭi*, it is for getting abundant rains (*Mait. Sam.* I. 10.13). The Karīra fruits are said to be belonging to Soma for they came into being from the Soma-draught, which flew upwards. When this offering belonging to Soma (*saumī āhuti)* in the form of Karīra fruits is offered, it impels the rains for the abundance of food (*ibid.* I. 10.12; cf. *Kāṭh. Sam.* XI. 10; also *Tait. Br.* I.6.4.5). It is worthy of taking note that in the sacrifice named *Kārīrīṣṭi*,[5] along with several black things used for inducing the black rainy clouds to shower rains, on the basis of sympathetic magic, flour of Karīra fruits is also required.

As noted above, the Karīra fruits are related to Soma. The *Kāṭh. Sam.* refers to an interesting practice in those times, stating that the Karīra fruits are not to be given to women and *śūdra*-s, for they are not entitled for drinking Soma (*Kāṭh. Sam.* XI. 10).

5. Kārṣmarya (Gmelina Arborea)

The enclosing-sticks of this tree are mentioned in the Ātithya-*iṣṭi* (guest-offering) performed in honour of King Soma, in which a sacrificial cake is offered to him on nine potsherds. The *arthavāda* glorifying this *vidhi* states that once upon a time, the gods perceived that among all the trees, the Kārṣmarya tree is capable of killing the *rakṣas-es.* The enclosing-sticks used for the Ātithyeṣṭi are of the Kārṣmarya wood with the idea that the evil spirits may not injure this head of sacrifice, i.e. this important rite *viz.* Ātithya-*iṣṭi* (*Tait. Sam.* VI. 2.1.5,6; *Śat. Br.* III. 4.1.16). The two *vapāśrapaṇī*-s (omentum-roasters) are laid down to be of the Kārṣmarya wood.[6] It is said that when the gods seized an animal victim and drew (√*karṣ*) it upwards, its sacrificial essence so flowed downwards as to make a tree spring forth from it. So the name of the tree Kārṣmarya. The two Kārṣmarya-spits are used to give perfection to the animal, which thereby becomes whole (*Śat. Br.* III. 8.2.17).

6. Khadira (Acacia Catechu)

The wood of the Khadira tree was used for making the sacrificial post (*yūpa).* In the context of the animal-sacrifice leading to Soma-sacrifice, the *Ait. Br.* by way of *arthavāda* states that the gods won the heavenly world by a post of Khadira and so wins the sacrificer, the world of heaven, by the Khadira post (*Ait. Br.* II.1 = 6.1). In the Horse-sacrifice, out of the twenty-one stakes, six are of Khadira wood — three on one side and three on the other side. The *arthavāda* states that as the Khadira tree was produced from Prajāpati's bones, it is hard and is of great strength, for bone is hard (*Śat*. Br. XIII. 4.4.9).

While explaining the importance of the Udumbara post (Audumbarī), the *Śat. Br.* states the mythical account of the quarrel between Suparṇī and Kadrū and Suprarṇī's bringing in the metres for carrying away Soma for her redemption from Kadrū's slavery (*ibid.* III. 6.2.2-15). Out of the metres, Gāyatrī could fetch Soma, by taking possession of it (*ā-cakhāda)* with a stick of Khadira wood (*ibid.* III. 6.2.12). The etymology of the word Khadira is given here from the root √*khad* and through this etymology the Khadira tree is associated with the account of Soma, giving the tree a holy touch. The wooden sword (*sphya)* is made of the Khadira wood (*ibid.*). While laying down ladles from different trees, for the offerings to be given in the New-moon and Full-moon sacrifices, the *Tait. Sam.* states the importance of the Khadira ladle through an *arthavāda*-account. It says that when the Vaṣaṭ call (Vaṣaṭkāra) cleft the head of the metre Gāyatrī, the sap of the latter fell away and entered the earth. It became the Khadira tree. Therefore he whose dipping spoon is made of the Khadira wood, whatever he cuts off, that becomes endowed with the sap of metres and his oblations are full of sap (*Tait. Sam.* III. 5.7.1).

7. Kṛmuka

In the rite of Agnicayana, when the consecrated sacrificer has to attend on fire, the *Śat. Br.* enjoins a kindling-stick of Kṛmuka wood to be put on fire. The *arthavāda* stated here is a mythical account of the gods and *asura*-s, both sprung from Prajāpati vying with each other. The gods having placed Agni in front of them went up to the *asura*-s, who cut off the point of that flame, held forward. This portion of the flame settled on earth and became the Kṛmuka tree. This tree is sweet as it is teeming with vital essence and is also red as it is a part of the flame. When the sacrificer or the priest places a Kṛmuka-stick on the fire, it is actually with the portion of fire that the sacrificer imparts growth to the (main) fire, i.e. Agni (*Śat. Br.* VI. 6.2.11). The principle of magic working here is 'Like produces like', the red tree making the fire blaze and thus making it red.

8. Nyagrodha = Nyubja (Ficus Indica)

While enjoining fruits from certain trees, Nyagrodha being one of them, for the great anointing of the king (*Mahābhiṣeka),* it is said that Nyagrodha is the lordly power (*kṣatram)* of the trees (*Ait. Br.* VIII. 16 = 39.2). The *Ait. Br.* lays down that a *kṣatriya* when consecrated for sacrifice, should press together the descending shoots (*avarodhāḥ)* as well as the fruits of the Nyagrodha tree and the fruits of the Udumbara, Aśvattha and Plakṣa trees and partake of them (*ibid.* VII. 30 = 35.4). The importance of the Nyagrodha tree is stated through an *arthavāda* as follows. The gods went to the heavenly world by offering a sacrifice. At that place of sacrifice, the gods tilted over (*nyubjan)* the cups and these cups became the Nyagrodha trees. Even today in Kurukshetra region, people call the Nyagrodha trees by the name Nyubja. The Nyagrodha trees are really Nyagroha (*nyak-roha),* for they grow downwards. But as the gods like what is abstruse, they call them Nyagrodha (*ibid.* VII. 30 = 35.4; also VII.31 = 35.5). It is clear that through the olden account (*purākalpa*) of the gods, the *arthavāda* is based on the etymology (for explaining the word 'Nyagrodha') from *nyak* (downwards) - √*ruh* ('to grow').

9. Palāśa = Parṇa (Butea Frondosa)

The Vedic ritual texts enjoin the use of the Palāśa-wood on quite a number of occasions. The dipping spoon and the sacrificial post (*yūpa*) are made of the Palāśa wood. The kindling sticks as well as the enclosing sticks are of the Palāśa wood. As in the case of other things, here also the Vedic ritual-texts have glorified the Palāśa wood with various *arthavāda*-statements, which reflect the beliefs about the Palāṣa tree.

In the animal-sacrifice, the sacrificial post is made of the Palāśa wood, by a person desirous of brilliance and splendour, for the Palāśa tree stands for these two (*Ait. Br.* II.1 = 6.1). In the Rājasūya sacrifice, when the Four-monthly Seasonal sacrifices are to be performed, if the dipping spoon (*sruvaḥ*) is of the Palāśa wood, he slays the fiends and *rakṣas*-es with Brahman, the Palāśa tree being Brahman (*Śat. Br.* V. 2.4.18). In the rite of Agnicayana, when the kindling-sticks are to be put on fire, leaving some,[7] the remaining ones are of the Palāśa wood. As the Palāśa tree is Brahman, it is with the Brahman that Agni is kindled (*ibid.* VI. 6.3.7).[8] Even a Palāśa leaf is said to be Brahman, for when the sacrificer offers with the leaflet of a Palāśa to Tryambaka in the Sākamedha (Seasonal) sacrifice, he is said to offer with Brahman (*ibid.* II. 6.2.8).[9]

It has to be noted that a reference to Palāśa occurs many a time in the context of Soma-sacrifice, while on some other occasions, with the mention of the Palāśa, Soma is brought into the context. The *Śat. Br.* lays down that in the animal-sacrifice (i.e. Soma-sacrifice), the sacrificer should make the sacrificial post (*yūpa*) from the Palāśa wood. He thereby performs the animal-sacrifice with Soma (*ibid.* XI. 7.2.8). In the Agnicayana rite, the kindling-sticks should be of the Palāśa wood.[10] As the *arthavāda* states, the Palāśa tree is Soma and Soma is the supreme offering. The offering of the kindling-stick of the Palāśa wood in fire is in fact the offering of Soma, by which Agni is gratified (*ibid.* VI. 6.3.7). The *Kauṣ. Br.* also echoes this thought, when it says that the offering of the Palāśa-stick in the Agnihotra rite stands for the first Soma-libation, as the Palāśa stands for Soma (*Kauṣ. Br.* II. 2).

The offering-ladle (*juhū*) in the sacrifice has to be of the Palāśa wood. The *arthavāda* states that Soma was in the third heaven. When the metre Gāyatrī fetched it, a leaf (*parṇa*) of Soma was cut off and it became the Parṇa tree (Palāśa tree is also called Parṇa). When the gods discussed regarding Brahman, the Parṇa (i.e. Palāśa) tree overheard it. Therefore he becomes famous whose ladle is made of the Parṇa-wood (*Tait. Sam.* III. 5.7.2; *Tait. Br.* I.1.3.10; I.2.1.5,6). The mythical account regarding the birth of the Palāśa tree occurs with some more details, when the ritual of taking away calves from the cows with a branch of the Palāśa (Parṇa) tree, is laid down. This occurs in the New-moon and Full-moon sacrifices as well as the rites preliminary to the Soma-sacrifice (*Śat. Br.* I.7.1.1; I.8.2.10; III.3.4.10). The *Śat. Br.* in these accounts mentions a footless archer aiming at the Gāyatrī (metre), when she was carrying off Soma. The archer severed one of her feathers or one of the leaves of King Soma (i.e. of the Soma-plant)[11] and falling down it became the Palāśa tree. It is clear that the frequent use of the Palāśa wood in the Soma-sacrifice has given rise to such an *arthavāda*-account, showing the importance of the Palāśa tree as equal to that of Soma in the thought of the Vedic ritualists. We can agree with the *Tait. Br.* when it states that as the Parṇa tree is born from the *parṇa* (leaf) of Soma (plant), the sacrificer or the priest says that he takes the ladle made of Parṇa-wood for enjoying the draught of Soma (*Tait. Br.* I.1.3.10, 11; I.2.1.5, 6). Out of the twenty-one stakes enjoined for tying twenty-one Agnīṣomīya animal-victims (i.e. victims to be offered to the deities Agni and

Soma), there are six stakes of the Palāśa wood—three on one side and three on the other side. To glorify these stakes of the Palāśa wood (also the Palāśa tree), it is said that the Palāśa tree was produced from Prajāpati's flesh. As flesh is red, so has the tree red juice (*Śat. Br.* XIII. 4.4.10).

10. Pūtudru (Acacia Catechu or Pinus Deodora)

The indispensable part played by the Pūtudru tree in sacrifice in the form of enclosing-sticks (*paridhi*-s) from that tree, is marked in an *arthavāda*-account in the *Tait-Sam.,* which occurs in the context of the Soma-sacrifice. Agni had three brothers. They were also Agnis. They perished one after the other, while carrying the offerings to the gods.[12] So Agni (i.e. the fourth one) being afraid ran away. When the gods found him, the latter agreed to come back asking a boon and it was of having enclosing-sticks around him for his protection. Whatever of the offering fell outside the enclosing-sticks, that was the share of his three elder brothers. Agni thought that his three elder brothers perished because they had bones. With a desire to survive, Agni shattered his bones and they became the Pūtudru tree and the flesh which died on them became bdellium. When the sacrificer or priest brings the sticks of the Pūtudru tree to serve as the enclosing-sticks, it is in fact bringing or making Agni in its full form (*Tait. Sam.* VI. 2.8.4-6). It has to be noted that the enclosing-sticks are to be placed on the three sides of the Āhavanīya fire-altar, i.e., to the north, west and south. The east being the quarter of the rising sun, Agni has no danger to face from that side, as the sun is the protector there and moreover Agni is a form of the sun, which the latter would definitely protect.

11. Pītudāru (Pinus Deodora)

In the Horse-sacrifice, there are twenty-one sacrificial stakes, out of which two are made of the Pītudāru wood. The *Śat. Br.* glorifies the Pītudāru tree by saying that what watery fire (*āpomayam tejaḥ)* and what fragrance there was with Prajāpati, that flowed together and burst forth from the eye of Prajāpati and became the tree Pītudāru. The wood of Pītudāru is sweet-smelling, for it has originated from the fragrance of Prajāpati and it is inflammable, as it has come from fire, i.e. Agni - Prajāpati (*Śat. Br.* XIII. 4.4.7).

12. Plakṣa (Ficus Infectoria)

While laying down the fruits from certain trees for the great anointing (Mahābhiṣeka) of king, the Plakṣa tree is spoken of as standing for self-rule (*svārājyam)* and sovereignty (*vairājyam)* of the trees (*Ait. Br.* VIII.16 = 39.2). It is said that Plakṣa tree was born of glory (*yaśasaḥ),*[13] and the self-rule and control of trees are placed in the royal power (*kṣatre)* when the fruits of the Plakṣa tree are brought for the king (*ibid.* VII.32 = 35.6). In the Soma-sacrifice, when the animal-offering is to be given, a branch of the Plakṣa tree is placed above the strew (*barhis).* The *Tait. Sam.* states the *arthavāda* that by means of the sacrificial animal, the gods went to the world of heaven. With the thought that men would follow them to the heavenly world, the gods cut off the animal's head and made the animal's sap stream forth. The sap became the Plakṣa tree. With the branch of the Plakṣa tree above the strew, he cuts off from the victim when it has its sap (*Tait. Sam.* VI. 3.10.2). The *Śat. Br.* states that the Pratiprasthātṛ priest cuts off the portions of the animal-flesh on the branches of the Plakṣa tree. While commending this *vidhi* concerning the Plakṣa branches, the *arthavāda* stated here takes the help of etymology. It is said that when the gods first seized an animal for offering it in the sacrifice, its sap flowed down, from where a tree sprang up. The gods perceived that tree and as it was visible (*prakhya),* it got the name Plakṣa. When the flesh of the animal is cut into portions on the Plakṣa branches, the animal is made full of the sacrificial sap (*Śat. Br.* III. 8.3.12). The etymology of the word Plakṣa is from *pra* + √*khyā* - 'to see closely' and further on the non-difference between the syllables *'ra'* and *'la'* (*ralayorabhedaḥ).*

13. Rajjudāla = Śleṣmātaka (Cordia Myxa Latifolia)

Among the twenty-one sacrificial stakes enjoined at the Horse-sacrifice, the central one is of the wood of Rajjudāla tree.[14] The *arthavāda* states that the body of Prajāpati began to swell and the phlegm *(śleṣma)* burst forth from inside through the nose to give rise to the Rajjudāla tree. As it has originated from the phlegm, the Rajjudāla tree is viscid and the same quality the Rajjudāla stake has (*Śat. Br.* XIII. 4.4.6).

14. Śamī (Prosopis Spicigera or according to some Mimosa Suma)

Pieces of Śamī wood are enjoined in some rites. The *Tait. Br.* lays down churning of Agni from a stick of Aśvattha tree, the branches of which are intertwined in the interior of the Śamī tree.[15] It is said to be the sacrificial body of Agni (*yajñīyā tanūḥ),* which is said to be produced from this churning (*Tait. Br.* I.1.9.1). A Śamī-stick is used as a *sambhāra.* The *Tait. Br.* states the etymology of the word *śamī* through a mythical account. It is said that Prajāpati created Agni, but was afraid that the latter would burn him. He extinguished it with a branch of the Śamī tree. The *Tait. Br.* here says that the use of Śamī as *sambhāra* is for cooling effect (i.e. *śamitva)* and for freedom from burns (*ibid.* I.1.3.11, 12). The same etymological explanation (fr. √*śam* - 'to appease, pacify') of the word *śamī* (i.e. 'Śamī' tree) figures in the *arthavāda*-s, which occur in the *Śat. Br.* In the rite of Agnicayana, when the Āhavanīya fire is established, the sacrificer gratifies him with food, in the form of pieces of wood and oblations. He first puts on one piece of the Śamī wood. But this is not for giving Agni food but to appease him. The *arthavāda* states that in early times, when the oblation was offered by gods, the enkindled Agni blazed so much as to cause fear in the minds of the gods. The gods saw the Śamī tree and appeased Agni with it. So the name

Śamī given to that tree (*Sat. Br.* IX. 2.3.36,37). In the context of the funeral ceremonies, the *Śat. Br.* says that round the sepulchral mound, they fix pegs, one of which on the left (i.e. north corner) is of the Śamī wood. The idea is that there may be peace for the soul of the dead person (*ibid.* XIII. 8.4.1). A stick of the Śamī-wood is to be placed on the fire in the fire-pan for pacification - '*śāntyai*' (*Tait. Sam.* V. 1.9.6).[16]

It has to be pointed out that these *arthavāda*-s, based on the etymology of the word *śamī* (meaning a Śamī tree) need not be taken simply as a play on word. They point out a belief about the Śamī tree, deeply rooted in tradition. The belief that fire is extinguished with the branch of a Śamī tree or stick of the Śamī-wood, gave rise to a further belief that fire or Agni, when extinguished enters the Śamī tree.[17] In later literature, the Śamī tree is regarded as containing fire or as a resort of fire.

The Śamī tree is also associated in belief with bliss (*śam*). In the rite of Varuṇapraghāsāḥ (one of the Four-monthly, i.e. Cāturmāsya sacrifices), while laying down the scattering of the Śamī leaves upon the two dishes of curds, it is said that with the Śamī leaves, Prajāpati bestowed bliss (*śam*) on the creatures and so does the sacrificer (*Śat. Br.* II.5.2.12).

15. Sīdhraka

In the Horse-sacrifice, a dog is killed and is made to float under the horse's stomach. A pestle made of the Sīdhraka tree is enjoined for killing the dog and is spoken of as accomplishing the ritual act (*Tait. Br.* III. 8.4.1). As Sāyaṇa points out in his commentary here, this tree is possessed of iron-like essence of black or red colour and accomplishes pounding, etc. of the grains as desired by the sacrificer.

16. Udumbara (Ficus Glomerata)

Among all trees, Udumbara occupies a place of prime importance in the Vedic ritual. The oft-repeated *arthavāda* about it is that it stands for strength and food. As Udumbara stands for strength, the sacrificer thereby wins for himself strength (*Tait. Sam.* II. 5.4.3,4). For many *vidhi*-s such as using a mortar made of the Udumbara wood for pounding grains for preparing the sacrificial cake (*ibid.* V. 2.8.7); the kindling-sticks of the Udumbara wood in the rite of Agnicayana (*ibid.* V. 4.6.1); the stick of the Udumbara wood to be placed on the fire in the fire-pan (*ibid.* V.1.10.1), the *arthavāda* at these and many more such places laying down the use of Udumbara has the same note and that is of 'strength'. In the rite following that of sprinkling the king with water (*abhiṣekottara-karman),* he has to hide an Udumbara branch in the wheel-track and touch that branch with the *mantra* - 'Sustenance you are; bestow sustenance on me' (*Śat. Br.* V.4.3.25,26). In the Sautrāmaṇī sacrifice, the seat of the consecrated king is made of the Udumbara wood. The Udumbara stands for strength and so is the sacrificer consecrated for strength (*ibid.* XII. 8.3.5). In the rite of Sattrotthāna (completion of the sacrificial session), they have to sit touching the Udumbara post. He invigorates speech with the Udumbara tree, which stands for strength (*ibid.* IV. 6.9.22). While laying down the *sambhāra* of the Udumbara wood, the *Tait. Br.* relates that when the gods divided strength, the Udumbara tree stood up from that strength (*Tait. Br.* I.1.3.10). When the Adhvaryu priest anoints the sacrificer-king with the rite of Aindra Mahābhiṣeka (the great anointing of Indra), the products ('fruits' as Sāyaṇa says *phalāni)* of the Udumbara tree are brought, as this tree is regarded to bestow on the king paramount rule of the king (*Ait. Br.* VIII. 16 = 39.2).

In the Agnicayana rite, while tending the fire in the fire-pan, he has to offer an Udumbara-stick on fire. A mythical account occurs at this place in the *Śat. Br.* to explain this *vidhi.* The gods and *asura*-s both sprung from Prajāpati vied with each other. All the trees went to the side of the *asura*-s, except the Udumbara, which did not forsake the gods. When the gods conquered the *asura*-s, they took possession of the latter's trees also. The gods favoured the Udumbara tree by placing in it all the pith and essence of all those trees.

Hence it is that the Udumbara tree is always moist, full of milky sap and has fruit equal to that of all the other trees. The Udumbara tree is thus all food, acquired from all trees and Agni is gratified by such food (*Śat. Br.* VI. 6.3.2,3).

It has to be noted that as small fruits cling right to the stem of the Udumbara tree and the stem oozes out milky sap, it could come in line with other such trees that stand as the Mother-goddess trees, because the small fruits clinging to the stem of the tree bear resemblance with the breasts. Some ancient mythologies mention such Mother-goddess trees. The Mexican Mother-goddess of this kind was Mayauel, who was believed to be a woman of four hundred breasts, and the gods on account of her fruitfulness changed her into the plant Maguey. The wine of this plant is called "pulque."[18] The Mother-goddess everywhere figured as seated before or on the Agave (Maguey) plant.[19] The Greek goddess Artemis was believed to have four hundred breasts and was the Fig-(tree)-goddess, the fig fruits regarded as teats in ancient times. The green part of the fig tree including the fruit, distil a white milk-like juice in abundance. As the fruits in the fig tree appear before the leaves, the tree was personified as "goddess of many breasts".[20] The ancient Egyptian goddess Hathor was the sycamore tree in one of her forms. The peculiarity of the sycamore tree is that the fruit all adhere to the stock of the tree and not to the end of the branches.[21]

It has to be pointed out that nowhere the Brāhmaṇa-texts mention the Udumbara tree as a Mother-goddess tree. However when they speak of the Udumbara tree as 'strength and food', it is clear that rather than simply glorifying the tree through a ritual metaphor, they certainly reflect some mythological belief about this tree. The mention of the Udumbara tree or the things made from the Udumbara wood in the Vedic ritual vouchsafes this. The sacrificer offers oblation with a ladle (*sruva)* made of the Udumbara wood (*Tait. Br.* I.3.8.2). The seat of the Udgātṛ priest is made of the Udumbara tree, mounting which the

Udgatṛ sings (*ibid.* I.2.6.5). In the Viśvajit sacrifice, the sacrificer has to dwell in the wood full of the Udumbara trees (*Kauṣ. Br.* XXV. 15). In the rite of Punarabhiṣeka (renewed anointing), the throne of the sacrificer and the goblet are of the Udumbara wood and there is a branch of the Udumbara tree (*Ait. Br.* VIII. 8 = 37.4). The waters brought from different places for sprinkling the king with in the Rājasūya sacrifice are mixed together in an Udumbara vessel (*Śat. Br.* V.3.4.2). In the Vājapeya sacrifice, the drink is kept in a vessel of the Udumbara wood (*ibid.* V. 2.2.2) and the seat of the sacrificer is made of Udumbara wood (*ibid.* V. 2.1.22,23). A staff made of the Udumbara wood is to be handed over by the Adhvaryu to the sacrificer, undergoing the rite of consecration (*ibid.* III. 2.1.32, 33). In the middle of the *sadas,* he places a post of Udumbara wood (*ibid.* III. 6.1.2). In the Agnicayana rite, when Agni is led forward to the altar, he puts on the fire, a stick of the Udumbara wood (*ibid.* IX.2.3.40). The *arthavāda*-portions at all these *vidhi*-s have a common note that the Udumbara stands for strength and best food.

The *Ait. Br.* reasons for Udumbara's standing for sap and strength by a mythical account. On the tenth day in the Soma-sacrifice, the sacrificer and the priests hold together an Udumbara branch with a *mantra,* 'Sap and strength I lay hold of'. The *Ait. Br.* says that when the gods distributed sap and strength, the Udumbara came into being. Hence it ripens thrice in a year (*Ait. Br.* V. 24 = 24.5). In the context of the Rājasūya sacrifice, the *Ait. Br.* points out that the Udumbara tree was born from strength and food and stands for the pre-eminence of the trees (*ibid.* VII. 32 = 35.6). We have noted above that an Udumbara-stick is placed on Agni (i.e. fire) in the Agnicayana rite. The *Śat. Br.* states that the Udumbara tree has forking branches and forking branches (resembling horns?) are cattle. The sacrificer gratifies Agni with cattle, i.e. food (*Śat. Br.* IX. 2.3.40).

A (Soma-) cup made of the Udumbara tree is offered to Prajāpati. It is said that the Udumbara tree belongs to

Prajāpati (*ibid.* IV. 6.1.3). As this tree belongs to Prajāpati (i.e. Agni, the deity of sacrifice), it produces red fruit (*Mait. Sam.* I.8.1.). As the redness of Agni went in the earth and the Udumbara tree was born, its fruit is red (*Kāṭh. Sam.* VI. 1; *Kaṭha Kapiṣṭhala Sam.* III. 12). The *Jaim. Br.* relates that when Prajāpati distributed strength among the beings created by him, Udumbara topped them. Hence Udumbara tree belongs to Prajāpati (*Jaim. Br.* I.70). The *Jaim. Br.* says that the Udgātṛ priest stands for Prajāpati. Therefore the sacrificer chooses other priests but not the Udgātṛ. In the Agniṣṭoma sacrifice, when the Udgātṛ priest takes hold of the staff of the Udumbara wood (Audumbarī), he gets himself chosen for his specific priestly function by his own deity (i.e. Prajāpati). Thus the Udgātṛ priest, Prajāpati and the Udumbara tree are related to one another (*ibid.).* In the same context it is stated by the *Jaim. Br.* that the *sadas*[22] is the belly of Prajāpati and Udumbara is strength. As the Audumbarī is fixed in the *sadas*, behind the *dhiṣṇya*[23] of the Maitrāvaruṇa priest, the priest provides food and strength[24] for the created beings. The created beings become endowed with food and become nourishers (for others). The Udgātṛ priest (standing for Prajāpati as already noted above), fixing the Audumbarī staff provides for gods also, because the *sāman* sung by him is the food of the gods[25] and the Udumbara tree of which the Audumbarī is made stands for strength. The gods thus receive both food and strength (*Jaim. Br.* I.71). The *arthavāda viz.* Udumbara is 'strength' or 'food', echoes the belief entertained by the Vedic ritualists about the Udumbara tree.

The etymology of the word Udumbara, which occurs in the *Śat. Br.* in an *arthavāda* passage, could be taken as indicating the indispensable role of this tree in the Vedic ritual. Prajāpati (the very deity of sacrifice) is said to remark that the Udumbara tree lifted him up (*udabhārṣīt)* from all evil. As it lifted him up, so the tree is called Udumbhara (*ud-* 'up' or 'above' + √*bhṛ* — 'to sustain, bear'). And

Udumbhara, they call Udumbara for the gods love what is abstruse (*Śat. Br.* VII. 5.1.22).

17. Varaṇa (Crataeva Roxburghii)

A peg of the Varaṇa tree is enjoined to be fixed round the sepulchral mound (with a peg each of the Palāśa and the Śamī trees). The *arthavāda* here is based on the etymology of the word *varaṇa.* It is said that by the peg of the Varaṇa tree, he may ward off (fr. √*vṛ* - causal √*vāray* - 'to ward off') sin from the dead person (*Śat. Br.* XIII. 8. 4.1).

18. Vikaṅkata (Flacourtia Sapida)

For the offerings to be given in the New-moon and Full-moon sacrifices, there are mentioned ladles from various trees, one of them being from the Vikaṅkata tree. It is said that when Prajāpati sacrificed, the Vikaṅkata tree sprang from that place, where the oblation found support. Prajāpati created offspring at that place. The sacrificer whose ladle (*dhruvā*) is made of the Vikaṅkata wood finds solace and is propagated in progeny (*Tait. Sam.* III. 5. 7.3.).

In the Soma-sacrifice, the Manthin cup is made of the Vikaṅkata wood, and in it Soma-juice is mixed with barley. In this regard a mythical account occurs in the *Tait. Sam.* It is said that when the eye of Prajāpati swelled, it fell out and entered the Vikaṅkata tree. Subsequently it entered barley and stayed there (*ibid.* VI. 4.10.5). Therefore in the ritual, Vikaṅkata and barley are combined.

In the context of the Agnihotra rite, the *Śat. Br.* states that the Vikaṅkata wood is suitable for sacrifice (*yajñīyaḥ)* and is proper for sacrificial vessels *(yajñapātrīyaḥ).* In the *arthavāda* statement, the *Śat. Br.* speaks of the Vikaṅkata tree to have sprung forth from Prajāpati, when he rubbed his hands (*Śat. Br.* II. 2.4.10). In the Agnicayana rite, it is said that the consecrated sacrificer has to put a Vikaṅkata-stick on fire (as offering). The *arthavāda* traces an old mythical account when Prajāpati performed the first offering and after that cleansed his hands, a Vikaṅkata tree sprung up. The Vikaṅkata-stick thus stands as the first offering (*ibid.* VI. 6.3.1).

The Vikaṅkata tree is associated with radiance. It is said that when Pajāpati created Agni, the lustre of the latter entered the Vikaṅkata tree. The *sambhāra* of the Vikaṅkata wood is for acquiring lustre (*Tait. Br.* I.1.3.12). In the Agnicayana rite, when the sacrificer puts a stick of the Vikaṅkata wood on the fire in the fire-pan, he is said to win radiance (*Tait. Sam.* V.1.9.6)

With these *arthavāda*-s, an *arthavāda* commonly occurring in the case of entities such as water, ghee, etc. is found in the case of the Vikaṅkata tree also. The *Śat. Br.* enjoins a dipping-spoon made of the Vikaṅkata wood in the Four-monthly sacrifices and says that the Vikaṅkata wood is the thunderbolt, with which the sacrificer slays his enemies — the *rakṣas*-es (*Śat. Br.* V. 2.4.18).

There are several plants as also some kinds of grass mentioned in the Vedic texts, about which occur *arthavāda*-s. These *arthavāda*-s indicate the beliefs maintained by the ritual tradition about these plants and the kinds of grass.

1. Ādāra Plants

Ādāra plants are enjoined as a substitute for Soma plants (i.e. Soma shoots), in the context of the Agniṣṭoma sacrifice. The reason stated in the *arthavāda* is that when the head of the sacrifice was cut off, the Ādāra plants sprang from the sap, which spirted from it (*Śat. Br.* IV. 5.10.4). The Ādāra plants are mentioned in the Pravargya rite also. The *arthavāda* states a mythical account that when Indra encompassed Viṣṇu, the vital sap of the latter flowed away, leaving him stinking. As this vital sap burst open (*ā* + √*dṛ* - *dar* - 'to burst open') the Ādāra plants originated (*ibid.* XIV. 1.2.12). It is very clear that the latter *arthavāda* is based on etymology, while both the *arthavāda*-s try to trace the origin of the Ādāra plants to the very Sacrifice, in the first account to the head of the Sacrifice and in the second account to

Viṣṇu, who is said to be the very 'Sacrifice' (*viṣṇur vai yajñaḥ* being an oft-repeated statement).

The *Śat. Br.* says that the Ādāra plants are also called 'Pūtīkāḥ', for Viṣṇu lay there stinking (*pūyan*), when his vital sap flowed away (*ibid.*). Here again, the *arthavāda* lays hands on etymology connecting the Pūtīka plants to Viṣṇu, i.e. Sacrifice.

2. Apāmārga Plants (Achyranthes Aspera)

Prior to the Rājasūya sacrifice (sacrifice for the rejuvenation of king), when the Cāturmāsya *iṣṭi*-s (Four-monthly sacrifices) are performed, there is enjoined the offering of Apāmārga grains in fire, i.e. Apāmārga-homa (*Śat. Br.* V. 2.4.15). The *arthavāda* here is based on etymology. The *Śat. Br.* says that by means of the Apāmārga plants, the gods wiped away (fr. *apa* + √*mṛj* - 'to wipe off') their enemies - the *rakṣas*-es and won the conquest (*ibid.* V. 2.4.14).

The same etymology of the word 'Apāmārga' works in another context. After the funeral rites are over, the persons cleanse themselves with Apāmārga plants. Thereby they wipe away (*apa* + √*mṛj* sin with the *mantra* from the *Vāj. Sam.* (XXXV. 11), says the *Śat. Br.* (XIII. 8.4.4).

3. Avakā Plants (Blyxa Octandra Rich)

In the Agnicayana rite, when the Great Fire-altar is built up, the sacrificer or the priest on his behalf (fastening) a frog, Avakā plant (a mossy plant, generally known as *śaivāla*) and a bamboo-shoot (to a cane) draws (i.e. drags) them over all the parts of the Fire-altar (*Śat. Br.* IX.1.2.20) and thereby places calmness into Agni's own self (*ibid.* 30). The Great Fire-altar stands for the body of Agni (-Prajāpati). While glorifying this *vidhi*, the *Śat. Br.* states the *arthavāda*, in which occurs the etymology of the word *avakā* as also of the word *vetasa* (The latter will be dealt with under "Vetasa"). It is said that the vital breaths (called here *ṛṣi*-s, as they wore themselves out fr. √*ṛṣ* - 'to wear out, get exhausted', with toil and austerity)[26] made Agni and sprinkled water on him. The water dripped off and became frogs. The water said to Prajāpati that their essence (*kā)* had gone down (*avāk).* So they (i.e. waters) came to be known as Avākkā-s. They mythically call waters Avakā-s (mossy plants), for the gods love what is abstruse (*ibid.* IX. 1.2.21, 22 & 24). Mahīdhara on *Vāj. Sam.* (XVII. 4) translates *avakayā* by *śaivalena* (*śaivala* meaning a 'mossy plant'). It has to be noted that Eggeling translated the word *avakā* at every place in this section of the *Śat. Br.* as 'lotus' or 'lotus-flower', which is not correct.[27] However he corrects himself later.[28]

In the Agnicayana rite in the third layer, the two Ṛtavyā bricks (pertaining to the *ṛtu*-s, i.e. seasons) are to be placed on the Avakā plants. These two bricks again are to be covered with the Avakā plants. These plants signify waters (*Śat. Br.* VIII. 3.2.5). The use of the Avakā plants being placed under the Ṛtavyā bricks as well as above them is meant for getting abundant rains in that season. The bricks Nabha and Nabhasya (of the rainy seasons) and the bricks Iṣa and Ūrja (of the autumnal season) are placed *once* only on the Avakā plants, for getting abundant rains in the two months of the rainy season and prior to the autumnal season (*ibid.* 5, 6).

The etymology of the word *avakāḥ* indicating that they are themselves waters (*avāk + ka,* as noted already) is based on the belief about the mossy plants, which grow on water or by the side of water. The use of the Avakā plants in the Agnicayana rite is also based on the belief that they being waters would bring rains (coolness) and the principle of magic working here is 'Like produces like.'

The *Tait. Sam.* speaks of the Avakā-plant as the cream of waters (*Tait. Sam.* V.4.4.1,2... *apām śaro'vakā...).* The *Tait. Sam.* enjoins the placing of the Avakā plant, after the seasonal (Ṛtavyāḥ) bricks are laid down. With the Avakā plant, he piles up the fire with its birthplace (*ibid.* V. 4.2.1). At this level of the Fire-altar, the water and fire are brought together, the former regarded as creating the latter.

It is interesting to note that in the ritual of constructing a house also, before installing pillars in the pits, Avakā plant and Śīpāla plant are to be put in the pits by the householder. It is said that by doing this, Agni would never burn his house (*Āśv. G.S.* II. 8.14).

It is clear that as the Avakā plants are regarded as waters, they like waters are included in the ritual, from two points of view—(i) as mitigating the effect of fire, i.e. Agni and (ii) as the birthplace of Agni i.e. water.

4. Phālguna Plants

In the Agniṣṭoma sacrifice (which is the model of the Soma-sacrifices), if the Soma is carried off by somebody and they do not find it, the substitutes are enjoined by the *Śat. Br.*, giving the *arthavāda*-s regarding them. Out of the two kinds of Phālguna plants *viz.* the red-flowering and the brown-flowering, the *Śat. Br.* enjoins the pressing of the Phālguna plants with brown flowers, the *arthavāda* bringing out that they are akin to the Soma-shoots in colour (*Śat. Br.* IV. 5.10.2). This reflects the belief in the magical effect of invigoration of Soma to be brought in through the sameness of colour.

If such brown-flowering plants are not found, the sacrificer or priest may press the '*śyenahṛta*' plant, i.e. the plant carried away by a hawk or in that case any bird. The mythical account occurring as *arthavāda* states that when the metre Gāyatrī flew up for bringing Soma, after obtaining it, a sprig of Soma fell from her. It became the '*śyenahṛta*'-plant (*ibid.* IV.5.10.3).

5. Priyaṅgu (Panicum Italicum)

The green shoots of Priyaṅgu-s, i.e. panic seeds, are to be brought for the great anointing (Mahābhiṣeka) of king. They stand for the paramount rule (*bhaujyam)* of the plants (*Ait. Br.* VIII. 16 = 39.2).

6. Puṣkara—Lotus or Lotus-leaf (Nelumbium Speciosum or Nymphaea Nelumbo)

Though lotus-plant is not mentioned, its leaf (i.e. lotus-leaf) has special significance in the ritual tradition, for in the Agnicayana rite, a small golden image of Agni (i.e Agni-Prajāpati) is enjoined to be placed on a gold-plate, the latter again to be put on a lotus-leaf. The lotus-leaf is said to be a womb and also a foundation, i.e. the earth. The mythical account states that Indra having smashed Vṛtra felt that he had not really killed the latter. Being afraid, he entered the waters and requested them to make a safe place for him to stay. The waters brought their essence on their surface and made (*akurvan)* a safe place (*pūḥ)* for him (*puṣkara - pūḥ = pūṣ-kara* fr. √*kṛ* — 'to make'). *Pūṣkara* is mystically called *puṣkara* (lotus) for the gods love abstruse (*Śat. Br.* VII. 4.1.11-13). Here *puṣkara-parṇa* (lotus-leaf) is mentioned and it serves as a seat for Agni (-Prajāpati), though the etymology stated is of the word *puṣkara* (lotus). The *vidhi* of putting (a small image of) Agni on a gold plate and that too on a lotus-leaf as mentioned here can be traced to a mythical detail occurring in *RV.* It is said that Atharvan churned out Agni on a lotus (i.e. lotus-leaf—*puṣkarāt adhi),* which stands at the head of the universe (*RV* VI.16.13; also *Tait. Sam.* V.1.4.4). As waters are regarded as an active female principle in the creation of the universe, lotus or lotus-leaf appears to be the first creation in the world, and it is regarded to have a place of importance. The fact of observation is here shrouded with mythical layers and lotus or lotus-leaf comes to have a unique position in the ancient Indian mythology.

7. Soma Plants

Tending to become scarce, the Soma-plants invited several substitutes at the time of the Brāhmaṇa-texts themselves, as we have occasions to note. The unique status of the Soma (plants or shoots) is pointed out by the *Śat. Br.* in an *arthavāda,* which states that Soma stands for nobility and the other plants for the common people. The common people are nobleman's food (*Śat. Br.* III. 3.2.8).

Dange states that from the etymology of the word 'Soma' (fr. √*sū* - ' to press' - Soma is 'the pressed one'), it is seen that the word '*soma*' was applied to the juice primarily and to the plant only secondarily.[29] As he points out, the word generally used for the juice of the Soma-plant is *indu* or *drapsa,* which hints at the original conception of the first oozed out 'drop'. This divine drop is called *andhas* (nourishing food) and is said to descend from heaven upon the earth, naturally in the sacrificial Soma-plant on the mountain-top.[30]

8. Vetasa (Calamus Rotang)

In the Agnicayana rite, when the Great Fire-altar is built up, the sacrificer or the priest drags a frog, Avakā plant and Vetasa-shoot over all the parts of the Fire-altar to give Agni coolness. The *arthavāda* states that in the beginning, Agni was sprinkled over with water. The water when dripped off became frogs. The waters then said to Prajāpati that their essence had gone down. Pointing to the bamboo-shoot, Prajāpati said that he (Vanaspati—the Tree-god residing in every tree or plant, here in the Vetasa-shoot) should know (*vettu saḥ)* and he should taste (*sam vettu).* Hence they mystically call bamboo-shoot ('Vetasa' - from the words *vettusa* and *saṁvettu*, the root being √*vid* - 'to know' (*Śat Br.* IX. 1.2.20, 22). Vetasa is said to be the flower of waters (*Tait. Sam.* V.4.4.1). The offerings to be given of horse's limbs are first kept on a cane(-bamboo)-mat. As both the horse and the cane have waters as their birth-place, he establishes the horse in its birthplace, i.e. waters—here the cane-mat (*Tait. Br.* III. 8.20.4).

9. Vrīhi - Rice (Shoots)

The *Ait. Br.* enjoins bringing together the green shoots (*tokmakṛtāni)* of rice (*vrīhi*-s*)* and also of large rice (*mahāvrīhi*-

s) for the great anointing (Mahābhiṣeka) of king. It is said that the green shoots of rice stand for the lordly power (*kṣatram*) of the plants and those of large rice for the overlordship (*sāmrājyam*) of the plants (*Ait. Br.* VIII. 16 = 39.2).

10. Wheat (Plants)

The head-piece (*caṣāla*) on the sacrificial post (*yūpa*) in the Vājapeya sacrifice is made of wheat flour. Man is nearest to Prajāpati and he is skinless. Among plants, wheat comes nearest to man, for it has no skin (*Śat. Br.* V. 2.1.6).

11. Yava-Plants (Barley-Plants)

For the great anointing (Mahābhiṣeka) of king, the green barley-shoots are brought. These stand for the leadership of the plants (*Ait. Br.* VIII. 16 = 39.2). While enjoining the sprinkling of water containing barley-grains, on the Audumbarī post, the *arthavāda* says that when all the plants went away from the gods to the side of the *asura*-s, the barley-plants alone remained with the gods. When the gods had an upper hand over the *asura*-s, they attracted to themselves all the plants of their enemies by means of the barley-plants. As the barley-plants attracted (*ayuvata* fr. √*yu* - 'to join' — here 'to attract') the other plants, the barley-plants are called 'Yava'. The gods put the sap of all other plants in the barley-plants. Therefore the barley plants thrive lustily when other plants wither. By using the water (for sprinkling) containing the barley-grains, the sacrificer takes possession (*yute,* i.e. 'joins') of the plants of his enemies (*Śat. Br.* III. 6.1.7-10). The *arthavāda* explains the importance given to the barley-grains in the Vedic ritual tradition.

Barley grains, Avakā plant and Darbha grass are mentioned in the funeral rites. The *Śat. Br.* says that having prepared the sepulchral mound, he sows barley grains (*yava*) thinking, "May they ward off (*yavaya fr.* √*yu* - 'to separate'; here 'to ward off') sin from me". He covers that mound with Avakā plants in order that there may be joy (or moisture *ka)* for him; and with Darbha grass (Poa Cynosuroides), he covers it for the sake of softness (*ibid.* XIII. 8.3.13).

To turn to some kinds of grass —

1. Aśvavāla (Saccharum Spontaneum)

In the Soma-sacrifice, there is a rite of guest-offering (Ātithya-*iṣṭi*), in which a sacrificial cake is offered to Soma on nine potsherds (on fire). There is a mention of *prastara* (bunch or strew, obviously to blow off softly the ashes from fire). The *prastara* is of Aśvavāla (*Kāśa)* grass,[31] and in order to keep this *prastara* separate from the sacrificial grass *(barhis)* covering the altar, stalks (*vidhṛti*-s*)* of sugar-cane are placed on the *barhis.* The *Tait. Sam.* while glorifying the ritual of making a *prastara* states here a metaphor. It is said that these shoots of Aśvavāla grass are the eyelashes of Prajāpati and the eyelids are the stalks or pieces of sugar-cane. As these two kinds of shoots are employed in sacrifice for making a *prastara,* it is said that by this he brings together the eye of Prajāpati (*Tait. Sam.* VI. 2.1.5). While mentioning *prastara,* the *Śat. Br.* glorifies the Aśvavāla grass through a mythical account. It is said that once the sacrifice ran away from the gods, taking the form of a horse. The gods chasing it and taking hold of its tail (*vāla),* tore it out and threw it down in a lump. The hair of the horse's tail then grew up as those shoots of Aśvavāla grass. With the guest-offering as the head of the sacrifice and the *prastara* of Aśvavāla grass (standing as the tail as the Aśvavāla grass came from the horse's tail, i.e. hair of the tail) he encompasses the sacrifice on both sides (*Śat. Br.* III. 4.1.17).

2. Barhis (Sacrificial Grass)

In the New-moon and Full-moon sacrifices, he offers the *barhis.* While glorifying the *barhis,* the *Śat. Br.* says that the *barhis* is this world and the *barhis* consists of these plants. By the offering, the plants are safely established in this world (*Śat. Br.* I.9.2.29).

3. Balvaja (Eleusine Indica)

In the Pravargya ceremony, the seat (*āsandī)* made of Udumbara wood, meant for the Pravargya pot to be placed on, is wound all over with cords of Balvaja grass. The *Śat. Br.* says that when the head of sacrifice was cut off, its vital sap flowed out to give rise to Balvaja grass. Thus with the life-sap, the Pravargya rite is completed (*Śat. Br.* XIV. 1.3.11).

4. Darbha (Poa Cynosuroides)

The *Tait. Sam.* prescribes that the sacrificer be purified with bunches of Darbha grass. The *arthavāda* states that when Indra slew Vṛtra, the latter died upon the waters. The pure, divine and sacrifice-worthy part of the waters went out and became Darbha grass. When the priest purifies the sacrificer with the Darbha grass, he purifies him with waters which are pure, divine and fit for sacrifice. He purifies him with two stalks, meaning 'by day and night'; with three stalks, meaning 'with three worlds' (*Tait Sam.* VI. 1.1.7). The *Tait. Br.* prescribes purification of the sacrificer, in the rite of Odanasava, with three bunches of Darbha grass. It says that the Darbha-s are the lustre and vigour of waters. With these of the waters, he purifies the sacrificer.

The three bunches of Darbha stand for three worlds. With the three worlds, he purifies him (*Tait. Br.* II.7.9.5). Apart from the belief related to the Darbha-grass, the numbers 'two' and 'three' mentioned in the *arthavāda*-s noted above, get related to the beliefs, commonly occurring about these numbers in the Vedic ritual texts. While piling the Fire-altar, a blade of Darbha-grass is offered. It is said that the Darbha-s are the nectar and they are the strength of the earth. These he offers on the Fire-altar (*Tait. Sam.* V. 6.4.1,2). In the rite of Agnicayana, while preparing the site of the

Āhavanīya fire-altar, he places a bunch of Darbha grass on the middle of the altar-site. The *arthavāda* states that in times bygone, the gods had placed plants on the altar-site; so does the sacrificer place plants on the altar-site in the form of the Darbha grass. Another *arthavāda* is that as Agni is built up here, he is born here for all kinds of food. The Darbha plants contain both kinds of food, because they are both water and plants. The pure and sacrifice-worthy water, despising Vṛtra, rose up on the dry land forming bushes and became the Darbha grass (fr. √d*rbh*). The Darbha grass stands thus for both water and plants (*Śat. Br.* VII. 2. 3.1,2). The *Tait. Br.* also refers to the mythical account of Indra and Vṛtra and the pure part of the waters becoming Darbha grass, when it speaks of purifying the sacrificer with two bunches of Darbha grass (*Tait. Br.* III. 2.5.1). As the Darbha grass stands for purity, the girdle of the sacrificial horse is made of this grass. The reason given is that the horse (of the Horse-sacrifice) wanders anywhere and goes near impure things. In order to purify the horse, its girdle is of Darbha grass. Thus they sacrifice a pure and holy horse (*ibid.* III. 8.2.3, 4).

5. Dūrvā (Panicum Dactylon)

The Dūrvā grass (shoots) is mentioned in the context of the Vyūḍhadvādaśāha sacrifice. While laying down the Ādāra plants as the substitute of Soma-plants, it is said that if they cannot get the Ādāra plants, the sacrificer or the priest may press down Dūrvā grass as it is akin to the Soma-plants (*Śat. Br.* IV. 5.10.5). The importance of the Dūrvā grass is brought out through the etymology of the word *dūrvā.* In the Agnicayana rite, the Dūrvā brick is placed on the naturally-perforated (*svayam-ātṛṇṇā*) brick. It is said that when Prajāpati having created the universe, became exhausted and was disjointed, his hair were lying on the ground and those became the Dūrvā grass. As the vital breath went out of Prajāpati, he fell down. He said that the vital breath has undone (or harmed) him. Hence the name *dhūrvā* (fr. √*dhūrv* - 'to undo, injure, harm'), which is *dūrvā*, mystically called so, for the gods love what is abstruse. The Dūrvā grass is the *kṣatra* (the ruling power) for it is the vital sap or breath. Laying down of the Dūrvā brick is like laying down of all plants (*ibid.* VII. 4. 2.10-12). The same thought is marked in the *Ait. Br.* (VIII. 8 = 37.4).

6. Gavedhukā (Coix Barbata)

The Gavedhukā grass is enjoined for smoothening the Mahāvīra pot in the Pravargya ceremony. The *arthavāda* explains that when the sacrifice had its head cut off, its vital sap flowed away to give rise to the Gavedhukā plants (grass-tendors). By using the Gavedhukā grass, he supplies to the sacrifice the original vital sap and thus completes the former (*Śat. Br.* XIV. 1.2.19). The Gavedhukā plants sprang forth from the place, where Prajāpati lay disjointed (*ibid.* IX. 1.1.8).

7. Iṣīkā

This grass is mentioned in the context of Horse-sacrifice. In a rite in this sacrifice, the horse (to be sacrificed afterwards) is made to enter water and it is to be goaded to the bank for coming out of the water. The horse is to be goaded with a rod, to which a bunch of Iṣīkā grass is tied. Iṣīkā grass is here said to be the very span of long life (*āyuḥ*) as also nectar. By using the Iṣīkā grass, he puts both these in the sacrificer (*Tait. Br.* III. 8.4.3).

8. Muñja (Saccharum Sara)

The girdle of the sacrificer has to be made of the Muñja grass. Muñja grass is said to be strength, which is bestowed on the sacrificer (*Tait. Br.* III.8.1.1). In the rite of Agnicayana he deposits Muñja grass in the fire-pan (*ukhā*), for this grass is strength and this strength is bestowed upon fire (*Tait.*

Sam. V. 1.9.5). The *Śat. Br.* says that the fire-pan (in the above rite) is covered with a layer of Muñja grass. This is to avoid injury to Agni. Muñja grass is a womb and the womb does not injure the child (*Śat. Br.* VI. 6.1.23).

9. Śara (Saccharum Sara)

The sacrificer's girdle in the Soma-sacrifice is to be made of the Śara grass, as it would give strength to the sacrificer. The *arthavāda*-s occurring here are interesting. According to one *arthavāda,* the Aṅgiras-es going to the other world divided their strength. What was left over became the Śara grass, which is strength. The other *arthavāda* states a mythical account that when Indra hurled his thunderbolt against Vṛtra, it divided into three parts, one-third part becoming the wooden sword (*sphya),* one-third the chariot and one-third the sacrificial post. The internal arrows, which Indra threw at Vṛtra, were split (*aśīryanta fr.* √*śṝ*) became the Śara grass and hence the name Śara given to that grass. It is also said that with the girdle made of the Śara grass, the sacrificer or the priest drives away hunger — the man's enemy—from the middle of the man's body (*Tait. Sam.* VI. 1. 3. 3-5).

10. Śaṣpa and Tokma

In the rite of re-anointing the king (Punarabhiṣeka), there is made use of grass (*śaṣpāṇi)* and sprouts (*tokmāni.* Sāyaṇa-'*aṅkurān*'). The *Ait Br.* says that these are a symbol of refreshment and growth and also of propagation. All these he confers upon the sacrificer-king (*Ait. Br.* VIII. 8 = 37.4).

There are such several kinds of grass mentioned in the context of Vedic rituals.[32] From the details noted above about the trees, plants and kinds of grass, mentioned in the Vedic ritual, we arrive at the following points which are worthy of taking note —

1. These trees, plants and several kinds of grass were important for sacrificial purpose or purposes in the Vedic tradition.
2. About some of them certain beliefs were prevalent in the Vedic tradition. These beliefs led to their entry in the Vedic ritual. Example can be given of the Udumbara tree, which could be taken as the Mother-goddess tree, though it is not specifically mentioned as such. The phenomenon of its fruits clinging to the very stem or trunk of the tree can lead to the idea of the tree having breasts or teats, the prominent trait of the Mother-goddess. The Vedic ritual texts speak only of the 'food, strength and sustenance' aspects of the Udumbara tree.
3. Trees such as Śamī are regarded as joined with or inherent with the fire-principle, and thus related to Agni-Prajāpati—the very deity of sacrifice.
4. Substitutes of Soma are suggested on the basis of brown colour, which is the colour of the plant or juice of Soma.
5. At times, practice of using some of the trees, plants, etc. in the Vedic ritual from bygone times compelled the ritualists to give some kind of glorificatory explanations for their use in the ritual. However it has to be pointed out that these explanations are perfectly based on the principles of sympathetic magic or as Frazer would like to call it 'homeopathic' magic. On the basis of 'A part stands for the whole,' a stick or faggot of a sacrificial (*yajñīya)* tree stands for that tree and so its ritual use. Again based on the principle *viz.* 'Like produces like', there occur statements as - 'Palāśa tree is born from Prajāpati's flesh. As the flesh is red, so the Palāśa tree has red juice.' Avakā plants and Vetasa (bamboo) shoots grow by the side of waters, Avakā plants even on waters. So they are dragged on the Great Fire-altar to give coolness and

calmness to Agni, they being the watery plants. The Aśvavāla grass (called Kāśa) resembling horse-hair is said to be the very hair of the horse's tail, when it was pulled and torn by the gods. As we have noted earlier (under 'Aśvavāla'), this horse was the very sacrifice, which escaped from the gods.

6. Some trees are said to have been born from a limb of Prajāpati or from his bones, flesh, phlegm etc. This could be traced to the universal concept of the splitting up of the body of a Creation-Being, giving rise to several things and beings in this world. Lang notes various trends in the savage myths of creation, one of them being that the world or its various parts, had been formed out of the body of some Supernatural Being, a god or a giant or a member of some mysterious race. On the Indian scene we have the great Cosmic Puruṣa of the famous Puruṣasūkta, from whose body-parts everything in this universe comes into existence.[33]
7. At times the celestial sap or the sap from the head of sacrifice gives rise to a plant, grass, etc. The Gavedhukā grass-tendors are said to be from the sap, which flowed from Sacrifice's head. The belief at the basis of this is of complementary magic. The goal is to make the sacrifice complete by supplementing it with vital sap.

Varied is the world of flora of the Vedic period as seen from the ritual texts and so are the *arthavāda*-s about it, but basically working on the principle of animism seen by them in this world of flora.

NOTES AND REFERENCES

1. Keith, A.B., *Rigveda Brahmanas* (tr.), Motilal Banarsidass, Delhi, 2nd Reprint 1981 (London 1920), p. 142 (tr. of *Ait. Br.* II.10 = 6.10), also note 3.
2. Macdonell, A.A., *Vedic Mythology,* Motilal Banarsidass, Delhi, 1995 (1898), p. 154.

3. Two types of *sambhāra*-s are mentioned prior to the establishment of the fires (Agni-ādhāna). the *sambhāra*-s are the things comprising earth and those from the wood of certain trees. The things from the earth are - sand, saline earth, earth dug up by moles, earth from an ant-hill, clay from a never-drying lake, pebbles and gold. The things relating to wood are — sticks or faggots from the following trees *viz.* Aśvattha, Udumbara, Parṇa, Śamī, Vikaṅkata and a tree struck by lightning. For detailed information, see Dange, Sadashiv A., *Vedic Sacrifices - Early Nature*, Vol. I., Aryan Books International, New Delhi, 2000, pp. 21-26.
4. In this context (i.e. of the Śatarudriya offering) while explaining the *mantra* to Rudra (*Vāj. Sam.* XVI.1), the commentator Mahīdhara states that while making the continual offerings on one of the three enclosing stones (standing for three Agni-s), the priest holds the Arka-leaf in his right hand and a piece of Arka-wood in his left hand.
5. See Upadhyaya, S.A., "Kārīrīṣṭi—A Sacrifice to be performed for securing Rain", *H.D. Velankar Comm. Vol.*, pub. by Prof. H.D. Velankar Comm. Vol. Committee, Bombay, 1965, pp. 161-75.
6. For details, see Eggeling, J., *op. cit.*, pt. II, SBE Vol. 26, p. 194.
7. There is a kindling-stick of the Vikaṅkata-wood, of the Udumbara-wood, that one not cut by an axe, and one that has lain on the ground. Leaving these, the rest are of the Palāśa-wood.
8. Also *Śat. Br.* I.3.3.19.
9. Eggeling, J. translates the word 'Brahman' here (*Śat. Br.* II.6.2.8) by 'priesthood'. See *The Śutapatha Brāhmaṇa*, pt. II, SBE Vol. 26, which is not correct. The word *'brahman'* is generally translated as '*mantra*' or 'prayer'. But as pointed out by Sāyaṇa '*brahman*' being *parivṛdham karma,* at times also means 'rite' or 'ritual' (see Sāyaṇa on *RV* I.105.15; 129.4, etc.). It also stands for the 'result' or the 'miraculous' brought into effect by both the ritual (*vidhi)* and the prayer (*mantra).* Keith, A.B., translates the word *brahman* as 'holy power' vide his tr. of *Tait. Sam.* III. 5.7.2. See his *The Veda of the Black Yajus School Entitled Taittiriya Sanhita*, Part 1, p. 284.
10. These are the remaining kindling-sticks leaving off some. See note 7 *supra.*

11. See Eggeling, J., *op. cit.,* pt. II, p. 78. *Śat. Br.* III. 3.4.10. Here the word '*gāyatryai*' is taken in the sense of the genitive case, i.e. (feather) of Gāyatrī. This shows a doubt on the part of the *Śat. Br.* regarding the exact entity to whom the *parṇa* (taken as 'feather' or 'leaf') belonged. The composer of the *Śat. Br.* is here relating the mythical account available in his times. The older version seems to be of the *Tait. Sam.* (III. 5.7.2) where a leaf of Soma is said to be cut off. The earliest version is of the *RV,* which mentions an archer shooting an arrow at the hawk (*śyena),* when it flew for bringing the Soma. At this occasion, a feather (*parṇa)* of the hawk fell off (*RV.* IV. 27.3,4).
12. According to another account, the sound Vaṣaṭ (Vaṣaṭkāra) killed the three earlier Agnis (the three elder brothers of Agni). *Śat. Br.* I.3.3.13; *Mait. Sam.* III. 8.6. For the significance of Vaṣaṭkāra, See (Mrs.) Dange, S.S., *Aspects of Speech in Vedic Ritual,* pp. 146-63.
13. Keith, A.B. takes *yaśasaḥ* to mean born of 'might', vide *Rigveda Brahmanas,* (tr.), p. 316.
14. Eggeling, J., *op. cit.,* pt. V, SBE Vol. 44, p. 373, note 2.
15. *Tait. Br.* I.1.9.1 — *śamīgarbhādagnim manthati* / and Sāyaṇa on it — *śamīvṛkṣasya garbhagatenāśvatthena niṣpāditamaraṇimavasthāpyāgnim manthet* /
16. Keith, A.B., *The Veda of the Black Yajus School entitled Taittiriya Sanhita*, pt. 2, Delhi, 1967 (1914), p. 400 where Keith takes the word '*śāntyai*' (*Tait. Sam.* V.1.9.6) to mean 'atonement'.
17. Cf. *Mbh.* Śalya parvan 47.14-19. Agni when cursed by Bhṛgu disappeared but was found in the Śamī wood.
18. Mackenzie, Donald, *Myths of Pre-Columbian America,* London, year not given, p. 177. The botanical name of the plant Maguey is "Agava Americana" and "pulque" the name of wine from it, is derived from the language of the natives of Chile.
19. *Ibid.,* p. 180 and also the plate which is given opposite. The plate shows the milk-yielding tree with fruits in the form of teats.
20. *Ibid.,* pp. 182-83.
21. *Ibid.,* p. 183.
22. Eggeling, J., *op. cit.,* pt. II., SBE Vol. 26, pp. 140-41, note 3.
23. *Ibid.,* p. 148, note 4.

24. Cf. *Śat. Br.* III. 6.1.2.
25. *Sāman*-s, *ṛc*-s, *yajus*-es, etc. are regarded to encourage the gods for showering favours on the devotees. *Sāman* is one of the aspects of speech, which in turn is indispensable in any of the Vedic rituals. Vide (Mrs.) Dange, S.S. "Sāman-s and Lauds", *Aspects of Speech in Vedic Ritual*, pp. 182-205.
26. For the account, see *Śat. Br.* VI. 1.1.1-5 and for the etymology from the root √*ṛṣ*, *ibid.* VI.1.1.1.
27. Eggeling, J., *op. cit.*, pt. IV, SBE Vol. 43, Motilal Banarsidass, Delhi, 1978 (1885), pp. 174-76 for his tr. of *Śat. Br.* IX. 1.2.20, 22-25. He obviously follows here Weber, who has given the meaning of Avakā as "lotus-flower". Vide Eggeling, J., *op. cit*, pt. IV, p. 49, note 1, where he quotes Weber, *Indische Studien,* XIII, p. 250.
28. See Eggeling, J., *op cit.*, pt. V, SBE Vol. 44, p. 436, note 2, where he says that in *Śat. Br.* IX. 1.2.22, read 'Avakā-plant' instead of 'lotus-flower'.
29. Dange, Sadashiv A, "The Advent of Soma", *Images from Vedic Hymns and Rituals,* Aryan Books International, New Delhi, 2000, p. 116, p. 123, note 13.
30. *Ibid.*, p. 116 f.
31. For the Aśvavāla grass, see Eggeling, J., *op. cit.,* pt. II, SBE Vol. 26, p. 89, note 3.
32. For a detailed treatment of these kinds of grass, see Gonda, J, *The Ritual Functions and Significance of Grasses in the Religion of the Veda.*
33. (Mrs.) Dange, S.S., "Ṛgvedic Accounts", *Myths of Creation*, University of Bombay Pubn., Bombay, p. 8.

CHAPTER 7

Animals and Birds

The Vedic sacrifice is based on the indispensable triad *viz.* (i) *dravya* (material of offering); (ii) *devatā* (deity, to which offering is made); and (iii) *tyāga* (ritual of offering).[1] The *dravya* or the material which is offered in sacrifice, could be in the form of an animal or a simple corn-offering in the form of a sacrificial cake or a *caru,* etc. Both, the animal and the sacrificial cake, are said to be having five constituents (*pāṅkta).*[2]

In the case of animal-offering, the animal offered is regarded as closely connected with the god, at times through its colour or form. And as the offering of the animal is given in fire (Agni), it could be taken as the very form of Agni or the sacrifice. The *Śat. Br.* in clear terms elucidates this idea through a mythical account. Prajāpati thought of Agni's forms *(agnirūpāṇi).* He searched for Agni, who had entered different forms. And, these were the five different animals *viz.* man *(puruṣa),* horse, bull, ram and he-goat. Prajāpati was convinced of their being Agni (*Śat. Br.* VI. 2.1.5), and killed them to place them in himself, as Agni's forms (*ibid.* VI.2.1.1-6, 18). Hence in the Agnicayana rite, the heads of these five animals are placed in the lowest layer of the Great Fire-altar. The *Śat. Br.* points out Prajāpati to be the first sacrificer to kill these five animals, Śyāparṇa Sāyakāyana the last and in the interval period, several other persons to kill these animals. But in later times, only two animals are sacrificially killed — a hornless dark grey (he-goat) for Prajāpati (*ibid.* VI. 2.2.1-2) and a white, bearded (he-goat) for Vāyu Niyutvat — Wind, driving a team of horses (*ibid.* 6).

This mythical account, though a piece of *arthavāda,* is worthy of note, for it brings out the firm conviction of the ritualists and the reasoning lying at its basis. The very Prajāpati has a desire to have Agni's forms fixed in himself. Hence the sacrificial killing. However it has to be noted that killing of man is a debatable point.[3] The remaining four domestic animals are definitely sacrificed. In this context, the *Tait. Sam.* makes a mention of four heads, that of a man, horse, bull and serpent (*Tait. Sam.* V. 2.9.2-5). Though the *arthavāda* passage, as seen above, mentions only five animals as the forms of Agni, all the animals of which the oblations are offered in fire, can be regarded as standing for the very sacrifice or Agni.

Of all the sacrificial animals, goat (*aja*) is regarded as the most prominent animal. A hornless goat (*tūpara*) is to be offered to Prajāpati to beget offspring and cattle, for such a goat is believed to possess the characteristics of the domesticated animals. The goat possesses beard, characteristic of man; lack of horns, of the horse; having incisors on one side only, that of cattle; having sheep-like hooves, that of sheep; and the goat nature, that of goats (*ibid.* II. 1.1.5; cf. *Śat. Br.* VI. 2.2.15). Sāyaṇa in his commentary on the *Tait. Sam.* (*ibid.* II.1.1) and especially on the statement of injunction (*vidhi)* — 'He should offer a white (beast) to Vāyu' (*ibid.* II.1.1.1), says that wherever there is no specific mention of a particular animal, the 'goat' alone is to be understood as the animal meant, due to the earlier mention of goat (in the *vidhi-* statement) not being refuted. Hence, in the context of special animal-sacrifices, in the *Tait. Sam.* at several places, the statement of injunction (*vidhi-vākya)* has to be taken as referring to a 'goat'. Of interest it is to find that in these statements of *vidhi,* the 'goat' to be offered gets connected to the deity by its colour and form. To take some examples. One should offer (*ā labheta*)[4] to Prajāpati a black-coloured beast (goat) having spots on its body and low (i.e. bent) horns. This black-coloured beast is believed to be the form of rain. Being spotted, it produces lightning and sheds rain. Having low horns, it brings down the rain for the sacrificer (*ibid.* II.1.8.5). It is clear that the black colour mentioned here, signifies the black colour of the rainy cloud and the belief here is — 'Like produces like', working on the line of sympathetic or homeopathic magic. A dwarf beast (goat) is to be offered to Viṣṇu by a sacrificer, who is engaged in a struggle. The sacrificer then becomes Viṣṇu and conquers these worlds (*ibid.* II. 1.3.1). Here the belief that by the dwarf beast, the deity Viṣṇu (in the 'dwarf'-form) will definitely be propitiated, is again based on the principle of sympathetic magic. A beast (goat) with black neck is to be offered to Agni (*ibid.* II. 1.2.4, 6-9), and a brown beast (goat) to Soma, for various purposes.[5] The beast with black neck drives away darkness from the person who offers it and the brown colour of the beast for Soma is believed to place splendour in that person (*ibid.* II.1.2.8). Brown beast also procures food for him, as brown is the colour of food (*ibid.* II. 1.3.3), and also of Soma, thereby bringing prosperity (*ibid.* II. 1.3.4).[6] A dusky-coloured beast with spots on its forehead (*dhūmralalāma*) is enjoined to be offered to Aśvins by a bad *brāhmaṇa* (*durbrāhmaṇa),* who desires to drink Soma-juice. This is obviously at a sacrifice, where normally he cannot be invited (as a priest) due to his bad qualities (may be inefficiency in carrying out the priestly duties!). With the dusky colour of the beast, the sacrificer (here 'the bad *brāhmaṇa*) drives away the darkness (i.e. his bad qualities) from him and the spots on the head of the beast (*lalāma)* are believed to bestow prosperity on that (bad) *brāhmaṇa* sacrificer (*ibid.* II. 1.10.1,2). The importance of Aśvins — the specific deity — to whom the offering is given, though not pointed out by the *Tait. Sam.* is clear. The Aśvins could not drink Soma-juice in the beginning and acquired this privilege at a later stage on the advice of the sage Cyavana. Cyavana told them about the 'lost head' of the sacrifice, which knowledge (of the Pravargya rite) they imparted to the gods and obtained their share in Soma (*Śat. Br.* IV. 1.5.1-16). The Aśvins having this experience of their own, are shown to give the bad *brāhmaṇa* an opportunity of drinking the Soma-juice (*somapītham),* when the offering of dusky beast, with spots on its forehead, is given to them. A black beast with one white foot is to be offered to Varuṇa, when a person is seized by him. The black colour of the beast is believed to wipe off the dark sin of that person and thus make him free from Varuṇa's noose. The white foot (hoof) of the animal signifies a bright future prosperity for him (*Tait. Sam.* II. 1.2.1,2). The belief about the black and white colours is very clear. A beast (goat) of white colour is to be offered to Bṛhaspati for spiritual lustre - *brahmavarcas* — (*ibid.* II. 1.2.4), the white colour itself is eloquent of the purpose.

That the goat is an important sacrificial animal can be seen from a mythical account which occurs in the *Śat. Br.* According to it, the sacrificial essence went out of man, entered subsequently the horse, then the ox, later in the sheep and then the goat, Thereafter it entered the earth to come out in the form of rice and barley, of which is made the sacrificial cake, i.e. *puroḍāśa* (*Śat. Br.* I.2.3.6,7). the *Ait. Br.* states that as the sacrificial essence dwelt for the longest time in goat, goat is the most often employed of all the sacrificial animals (*Ait. Br.* II. 8 = 6.8). The *Jaim. Br.* also speaks highly about goat (II. 371). In the Horse-sacrifice, a goat is led before the horse. Here the goat is said to be the first share offered to the god Pūṣan,[7] and thus declaring the sacrifice to the gods. On the night previous to the rite of Agnyādhāna (rite of kindling and establishing the three fires *viz.* Gārhapatya, Āhavanīya and Dakṣiṇa), a goat having dark spots on its skin is tied towards the north of the place for the Gārhapatya fire, with a *mantra.*[8] In the rite of Agnicayana, while preparing the fire-pan (*ukhā)* of clay, the sacrificer or the Adhvaryu priest mixes the clay with a goat's hair, for the goat is said to be the form of all cattle (*Śat. Br.* VI. 5.1.4), and the female goat is said to be Agni's dear form (*Tait. Sam.* V.1.6.2).[9] Goat is believed to have sprung from Prajāpati's head and Prajāpati is Agni (*Śat. Br.* VI. 5.4.16). In the Sautrāmaṇī sacrifice, the strainer is of goat's hair and sheep's wool (*ibid.*, XII. 8.1.13).

In the context of animal-sacrifices, it is said that the Caraka-s offer a dark-grey (*śyāma),* hornless he-goat to Prajāpati, for Prajāpati is hornless (*ibid.* VI. 2.2.1, 2). The *Tait. Sam.* lays down an offering of a white beast (goat) to Vāyu. As Vāyu is the swiftest deity, he makes the sacrificer swiftly attain prosperity (*Tait. Sam.* II. 1.1.1). The *Śat. Br.* connects this white, bearded goat to Prajāpati, saying that such a goat to be offered to Vāyu Niyutvat (having a team of horses) has come into being from the seed of Prajāpati (*Śāt. Br.* VI. 2.2.6). Having this 'goat-Agni-Prajāpati' close connection in view, the tradition of the Śrautasūtra-s prescribes offering of oblation on the right ear of a she-goat (*Bhār. Ś.S.* IX. 4.5) or according to some, in the absence of a she-goat, on the ear of a he-goat (*Āp. Ś.S.* IX. 9.3). The *Mbh.* mentions Naigameya Agni becoming goat-faced to amuse Skanda (Vana *parvan* 226.29; 228.3&5). The Purāṇa-s speak about the holiness of goat's mouth.[10] Goat standing as a symbol of Fire (-god) is seen even in sculptures.[11]

The same belief prevails while using a goat-skin in rituals. In the Vājapeya sacrifice, the goat-skin is spread, for it is none other than Prajāpati (the deity of sacrifice). The goats bring forth thrice in a year and produce two or three kids at a time.[12] The sacrificer sitting or stepping on a goat-skin is made Prajāpati — the lord of generation (*Śat. Br.* V.2.1.24; cf. *Tait. Br.* I.3.7.7) and also if he is desirous of prosperity, he should be anointed on a goat's skin (*Śat. Br.* IX.3.4.14). The firm conviction of the Vedic ritualists is that the skin or hide of an animal stands for the animal. This is obviously on the principle of magic *viz.* 'A part stands for the whole'. The skin is to be placed in the ritual in such a way that the part of the neck will face a particular direction (which is enjoined) and the hairy portion will be up. This shows that the skin is to be placed in such a way that it resembles the animal, of which the skin is. The whole idea in using the animal-skin is that the person for that time is closely associated with that animal, imbibing its strength in himself.[13] This holds good for that goat-skin, which is prescribed for being used in the rituals, having in view the close connection between goat and Agni or Prajāpati.

A fat ram (*meṣa*) is referred to in *RV* as being cooked, probably for being offered to the gods.[14] This speaks of a detail of the ritual that was lost afterwards.[15] Mini-replicas of ram (*meṣa)* and ewe (*meṣī)* made of barley, are enjoined to be offered to Varuṇa in the rite of Varuṇapraghāsāḥ in the Four-monthly Seasonal (Cāturmāsya) sacrifices. The *Śat. Br.* states here that ram is Varuṇa's victim and by offering it to Varuṇa, the sacrificer releases the creatures from Varuṇa's noose. And so is the pair of ram and ewe offered for the same purpose (*Śat. Br.* II. 5.2.16). It is interesting to note that a ewe with complete teeth (*apannadatī)* is offered to the deity Sarasvatī by a person, who in spite of being a master of speech, cannot speak properly. The importance of the ewe having all teeth is, because of men uttering entire speech with all their teeth (*Tait. Sam.* II. 1.2.6,7). One whole hymn in the *AV* (III. 29) praises the *śitipād avi* (white-footed sheep), which is prescribed to be given before death and is believed to wash away sin (*AV* III.29.1). A strainer for Soma-juice was made of sheep-wool (*RV.* IX. 78.1 cd). In the Sautrāmaṇī sacrifice, they purify Soma with the strainer made of goat's hair and sheep's wool. Such a strainer is regarded as a symbol of goats and sheep (*Śat. Br.* XII. 8.1.13). This is based on the principle of sympathetic magic, which in this case is — 'A part stands for the whole', the goat's hair and the sheep's wool standing for the respective animals, so closely connected with the sacrifice. The *Tait. Sam.* relates a mythical account, which, while trying to explain the different colours of the sheep also displays the belief entertained by the Vedic ritualists. When Svarbhānu the *asura* pierced the sun with darkness, the gods desired an atonement for him. The first darkness struck by them became a black sheep; the second a reddish-coloured one; the third a white one; what they cut from the upper part of the bone became a barren ewe—*avirvaśā* (*Tait. Sam.* II.1.2.2). An interesting detail to be noted is that the female sheep (*avikā)* from the Gandhāra country was famous for having profuse wool (*RV.* I. 127.7 cd).

The sacrifice of a horse is traced to *RV* (I.162; 163). That the horse stands for the sun is clearly brought out, when the goddess Dawn (Uṣas) is said to lead a beautiful white horse (*RV* VII. 77.3b). There is a mention of some mythical horses in *RV.* Dadhikrā or Dadhikrāvan (*ibid.* IV. 38-40; VII. 44) is taken to represent the orb of the sun, as the deity associated with it is Dawn (Uṣas).[16] Tārkṣya is another divine horse, which represents the sun.[17] The horse brought by the Aśvins to Pedu is called Paidva (*ibid.* I. 119.10; VII.71.5, etc.). A myth regarding the horse Etaśa mentions a race between him and the sun, in which Indra helps Etaśa. By this Etaśa gets a point over the sun. However the sun chooses Etaśa as the horse for his chariot.[18] The seven mares of the sun are said to be the daughters of the sun's chariot (*ibid.* I.50.9). All these horses have some divine halo about them and in most cases they are associated with the sun; some stand for the sun. However their sacrifice is not mentioned.

The sacrificial horse is believed to have been created by the gods from the sun (*ibid.* I. 163. 2d; also *Ait. Br.* VI. 35 = 30.9) In the Agnicayana rite, while going to bring clay for making a fire-pan, they carry a horse, donkey, and goat. The horse is said to be the yonder sun, which, acting as a thunderbolt made the gods drive off the *asura*-s (*Śat. Br.* VI. 3.1.29; also *ibid.* VI.3. 3.10; VII. 3.2.10). In the same rite, the horse is made to smell a layer of bricks. The horse is said to be the yonder sun and the bricks are the creatures on the earth or in the worlds (*ibid.* VII. 3.2.12,13). This horse has to be white, for it is the form of the sun, which shines (*tapati* lit. 'burns') yonder (*ibid.* VII. 3.2.16). The mythical accounts coming as *arthavāda* speak of this belief. A white horse is given as *dakṣiṇā* in the Sadyaḥkrī sacrifice. Sadyaḥkrī sacrifice is a one-day (*ekāha)* Soma-sacrifice at which the consecrations, buying and pressing of Soma are compressed into one day.[19] The *Śat. Br.* states that when the Aṅgiras-es officiated as priests for the Āditya-s in the Sadyaḥkrī sacrifice, to them was offered Vāc as *dakṣiṇā,* which they refused to accept. Sūrya (the sun) then was offered to them as *dakṣiṇā.* Hence in the Sadyaḥkrī sacrifice, a white horse stands as the *dakṣiṇa* (*ibid.* III. 5.1.17-20). The *Tait. Br.* has a different account to give, though the parties mentioned are the same. The Āditya-s and Aṅgiras-es ran a race for heaven. The Aṅgiras-es then gave to the Āditya-s, a *dskṣiṇā* (gift) of the sun in the form of a white horse (*Tait. Br.* III.9. 21.1). The white horse in the Agnicayana rite, seen above, has to have a reddish mouth.[20]

It is patent that the 'white' colour of the horse connects it to the sun. A detail from the *Tait. Sam.* supports this. It is said that he who desires splendour, should offer a white cow (*śvetām vaśām)* to Sūrya, for then he has recourse to Āditya. It is said that when Āditya did not shine, the gods offered a white cow to Sūrya and thereby restored the brilliance of Āditya (*Tait. Sam.* II. 1.8.1). Here obviously Āditya and Sūrya are shown as different from each other. The *Tait. Sam.* lays down that a person desirous of the splendour of *brahman* (*brahmavarcaskāmaḥ)* should offer to Bṛhaspati a *vaśā* (cow) with white back (*ibid.* II. 1.7.2). Here the white colour is associated with lustre or splendour. We have already mentioned that a beast with black neck (*kṛṣṇagrīvam)*[21] is to be offered to Agni. This beast (goat) has to be white and is to be offered by a *brāhmaṇa,* who in spite of his study does not win. The beast with its black neck drives away darkness from that *brāhmaṇa* and being white, it bestows brilliance on him (*ibid.* II. 1.2.8,9). In the Śunāsīrīya *parvan* of the Seasonal Sacrifices, oblation is offered to the sun. The *dakṣiṇā* (sacrificial gift) to the priest in this rite is a white horse, in its absence a white bull, whereby it is made of the form of the yonder scorching sun (*Śat. Br.* II. 6.3.9).

In the Rājasūya sacrifice, having offered the oblations at the dwelling-places of the *ratnin*-s ('jewels', i.e. various important personalities of the kingdom), he offers a *caru* to Soma and Rudra. It is cooked in milk from a white cow, which has a white calf. The mythical account points out that when the *asura* Svarbhānu struck the sun with darkness and the latter did not shine, Soma and Rudra were the deities to remove his darkness. In the Rājasūya sacrifice, the king also enters darkness, when he offers oblations at the dwelling-places of some *ratnin*-s (important officials), who are of *śūdra* or low caste. Soma and Rudra remove the king's darkness. The *caru* offered to them, cooked in milk from a white cow having a white calf, indicates thereby the total extinction of (black) darkness of the king, who is to be rejuvenated and also suggests his radiance, after the performance of the Rājasūya sacrifice, like that of the sun (*ibid.* V.3.2.1-2). In the Agnicayana rite, when Agni is about to be laid on the fire-altar, he gives offering to Agni with milk from a black cow, which has a white calf. The black cow is the night and the white calf is the yonder sun (*ibid.* IX. 2.3.30). In a special animal-sacrifice, a cow (*vaśā)* of two forms (Sāy.—'of two colours') is to be offered to Mitra and Varuṇa, by a person desirous of offspring (*Tait. Sam.* II. 1.7.3). The cow seems to be of two colours *viz.* white and black, for it is said that the 'day' ('light' i.e. white colour) stands for Mitra and the 'night' ('darkness' i.e. black colour) stands for Varuṇa (*ibid.* II. 1.7.3,4).

The white colour seems to be of great importance in other countries as well as in some tribes. In Europe the king of snakes is said to be white, which can be compared to the concept of Śeṣa, the great serpent in the Hindu mythology, which is also said to be white in colour. White horses were regarded especially sacred. In Japan white animals have a high importance and great fortune for the house is inferred from their appearance. In Indo-China the cult of the white elephant is well-known.[22] White animals were often preferred as a victim. The Woguls offer a white horse in autumn and the Shans of Annam sacrifice a white buffalo annually. The Battas also select white victims. White animals were thought for being sacrificed for getting sunshine.[23]

Having noted the worldwide belief about the 'white' colour, of which colour the horse has to be in the Vedic rite of Agnicayana, to turn to the beliefs about the horse again. As the sun and Prajāpati (the deity of sacrifice) are believed to be the two forms of the same principle viz. Agni,[24] horse is said to be the form of Prajāpati also. The Vedic ritual texts at every step echo this belief.[25] While giving the etymology of the word *aśva* ('horse') it is said that the eye of Prajāpati swelled and fell away. That eye became a horse. As the eye swelled (*ásvayat* fr. √*śvi*) the *aśva* (horse) has its name.[26] In the rite of Agnyādhāna, when the horse is led from the Gārhapatya fire to the east to the site of the Āhavanīya fire, Agni (who is indeed Prajāpati - *eṣa vai prajāpatiḥ/yadagniḥ)* also follows it, as Prajāpati sees his own eye in the form of the horse (*Tait. Br.* I.1.5.5). In the Agnicayana rite, when they go for bringing clay to make a fire-pan, the sacrificer or the Adhvaryu priest offers two oblations on the footprint of the horse. It is said that the horse is the same as Agni and these two libations come to be offered over Agni (*Śat. Br.* VI. 3.3.22). When the fire-pan is ready, he fumigates it with dried horse-dung to protect it from injury, for the horse is sacred to Prajāpati and Prajāpati is Agni. No one injures one's own self (*ibid.* VI. 5.3.9). The *Tait. Sam.* states that the horse through its dung, in the rite of fumigating the fire-pan, is connected with the place of his birth, i.e. Prajāpati (*Tait. Sam.* V.1.7.1). When the horse is made to sniff the 'naturally perforated' (*svayam-ātṛṇṇā)* brick, it is placing the horse's breath in the Great Fire-altar and as horse is connected with Prajāpati, it is through Prajāpati that he piles the Fire-altar (*ibid.* V.3.7.4).[27] At a couple of places, horse is said to belong to Varuṇa.[28] Barring these references, the horse is primarily believed to be the animal related to Prajāpati and originally to the sun. In the context of the Horse-sacrifice, the *Śat. Br.* says that both gods and men guard the sacrificial horse, without turning (i.e. driving) it back. This is because the horse is the sun, who shines yonder. And who is able to turn the sun back? If they do so, everything here would certainly go backward (i.e. go to ruin) (*Śat. Br.* XIII. 4.2.16).

Skin of a black antelope is mentioned by the Vedic ritual texts in several rites. Unlike that of goat or horse, the actual sacrifice of a black antelope is not mentioned in these texts.[29] Not the black antelope, but the deer is known to the *RV* for its speedy gait.[30] The solar horse coming out of the ocean is said to have wings of hawk and the arms of a deer (*RV.* I. 163.1). The *AV* believes in the medicinal properties curing tuberculosis, being there in the head of deer (*AV* III. 7.1).

That the black antelope was not domesticated is clearly brought out in the *Tait. Sam.* The *Tait. Sam.* prescribes gathering of clay for making a fire-pan, on the hide of a black antelope. This has a specific purpose. If he were to gather the clay with the skin of tame animals, he would afflict them with pain. Hence he gathers it with the black antelope skin. So the wild animals are afflicted with pain (*Tait. Sam.* V.1.4.2,3). Obviously the tame ones are saved. In a one-day Bṛhaspatisava-sacrifice, the sacrificer is sprinkled, while sitting on a black antelope skin, which is the priestly lustre (*Pañc. Br.* XVII. 11.8). The horn of a black antelope is mentioned, but that too as connected with the sacrifice. While laying down the rules for consecration of the sacrificer, a horn of a black antelope is enjoined to be tied to the sacrificer's garment. The *Śat. Br.* at this place relates on elaborate mythical account as *arthavāda* (*Śat. Br.* III. 2.1.18-28). When Indra became an embryo and entered into the union of Yajña and Vāc, he tore off the womb and placed it on the head of Yajña, which was none other than the black antelope. The horn of the black antelope used in the rite of consecration is the same as that womb *(ibid.* III. 2.1.28).[31]

An important point to be taken note of is that the goat and horse (of which we have already noted the details) are not directly identified with (Agni-) Prajāpati but are said to be his form or are closely connected with him. But the black antelope is said to be the very sacrifice (*ibid.* III.2. 1.8, 28; VI.4. 1.6; IX.3. 4.10; XII.8. 3.3) and obviously Prajāpati, he being the deity of sacrifice. The *Tait. Sam.* relates a mythical account that the sacrifice did not resort to Śaṁyu, the son of Bṛhaspati, entered fire and emerged from it in the form of a black antelope (*Tait. Sam.* V.2.6.4,5). The *Śat. Br.* states that once upon a time, the sacrifice escaped the gods and having become a black antelope roamed about. The gods finding it, stripped it of its skin, which they brought about with them (*Śat. Br.* I.1.4.1).

It is interesting to note that even the hair on the black antelope's skin are not missed from the ritualists' eye. These hair are connected with *mantra*-s and are regarded as important. The white and black hair represent the *ṛc*-s and *sāman*-s respectively or even *vice versa.* The brown and yellow hair represent the *yajus*-formulas.[32] A mythical account occurring in the *Tait. Sam.* in the context of the Soma-sacrifice states that the *ṛc* and the *sāman,* unwilling to stay with the gods for sacrifice, departed from them, taking the form of black antelope. The white colour of the black antelope's skin (i.e. of the hair on the skin) is the colour of *ṛc* and also of day and the black colour of it (i.e. of the hair on this hide) is the colour of *sāman* as also of night (*Tait. Sam.* VI. 1.3.1, 2). In the context of the Agniṣṭoma sacrifice, the *Śat. Br.* says that the white hair on the hide are an image (*rūpam)* of the sky, the black ones that of the earth or *vice versa,* and the brown-coloured ones that of the mid-region. Thus the Adhvaryu consecrates the sacrificer seated on this skin, at these three worlds (*Śat. Br.* III.2.1.3).

In the context of building the Great Fire-altar, the *Tait. Sam.* enjoins for the sacrificer, wearing of shoes made of black antelope's skin. The reasoning is that both the metres as well as the black antelope hide stand for holy power. When he puts on these shoes, he clothes himself with the metres and then approaches the fire, to prevent injury to himself. In former times, the gods clothing themselves with the metres, had approached the razor-edged fire, piled by Prajāpati (*Tait.* Sam. V. 4.4.4; V.6.6.1).

The black antelope skin came to be looked upon as the very sacrifice.[33] though the black antelope to which it belonged was not actually sacrificed, as there is no Vedic record to prove it otherwise. The skin of black antelope is prescribed for being used in the rite of Agnicayana, while preparing a fire-pan, as a lump of clay is to be placed on it. This skin is regarded as sacrifice (*Tait. Sam.* V. 1.6.2,3; *Śat. Br.* VI.4.1.9). We have already noted in connection with the goat-skin that on the principle of sympathetic magic, the skin or hide of an animal stands for that animal. The black antelope skin is to be placed in a particular way obviously with its hairy part above. In the rite of Pravargya (in which milk is boiled in a particularly shaped pot called Gharma or Mahāvīra for being offered) the black antelope skin is spread out on the left (north) side, with its neck part to the east, the north signifying the quarter of humans and the east tending towards the gods (*Śat. Br.* XIV.1.2.2); cf. also *ibid.* IX. 3.4.14). In the New-moon and Full-moon sacrifices, while preparing the offerings the black antelope skin is spread on the ground with its neck part turned to the west and the prayer is to Aditi (*ibid.* I.1.4.5).

To turn to the beliefs about the black colour, of which colour the antelope is.

We have already noted that a person desirous of rain should offer to Prajāpati, a black-coloured beast (goat), having spots on its body and bent horns, for the black colour stands for the rain (i.e. black rainy cloud); the spots on the body for lightning and shedding rain (rain-drops); and the bent horns bringing down the rain to the earth (*Tait. Sam.* II. 1.8.5). The image presented by the black beast is clearly of the rain-phenomenon. This becomes all the more patent, when the sacrifice named Kārīriṣṭi is taken into consideration. The materials which are required for this sacrifice are: a black garment, an upper garment with black border, a black horse, a black fetter, skin of a black antelope, black honey, groats of Karīra fruits (Karīra-Capparis Aphylla - a thorny plant growing in deserts and fed upon by camels), a black pitcher which is half-baked, a black cart with three roofs (*gadhā*-s), a black female sheep, a black bunch of Varṣāhū (Boerhavia Procumbens) faggot and reed-plants (*vetasa*). The *dakṣiṇā* to be given in this sacrifice, consists of a black garment, a black horse and a black female sheep.[34] The *mantra*-s and some details of this sacrifice occur in the *YV* Saṁhitā-s (*Tait. Sam.* II.4.7-10; *Kaṭh. Sam.* XI.9; *Mait. Sam.* II.4.7). It is very clear that the black colour of the things used in this sacrifice is for inducing the black rainy clouds to shower rains on the basis of sympathetic magic. Keith explains the meaning of some *mantra*-s,[35] in the *Tait. Sam.* (II. 4. 7-10), concerning this sacrifice.

We have already taken a note of the use of black antelope skin in various rites, apart from the Kārīriṣṭi. Dange rightly points out that the magical importance of the antelope, black or the tawny (as an alternative) in fertility or the gain of rain is clear from the tale of the sage Ṛṣyaśṛṅga, who is said to have on his head the horn of an antelope and who was specially brought by the king Romapāda to cause it to rain, by offering his daughter to the sage.[36] The skin, specially that of an antelope, marks an important stage in ritual-history.[37]

Having in view the black colour of the sacrificial beast serving as a rain-charm, the Wambugwes of East Africa offer a black sheep and a black calf when they want rain and the Garos of Assam, offer a black goat on the top of a very high mountain in times of drought.[38] The *Mait. Sam.* states that a person desirous of rain should offer a spotted (female) beast sacred to Agni and Maruts. Agni eulogises rain from here and the Maruts release it from the sky. This female beast is spotted (*pṛśniḥ*), for the Maruts have Pṛśniḥ (the spotted Sky-cow) as their mother (*Mait. Sam.* II. 5.7). In this connection, it will be interesting to take a note of another female beast, which is black-spotted. Such a black-spotted female beast (*kṛṣṇaśabalīm)* sacred to the Earth (*bhaumīm)* is to be offered by a person desirous of food (*ibid.)*. Here food is obviously corn or rich crop, striking a note of fertility, which could be obtained by offering a female beast. According to Dange (*'bhaumī'* mentioned here), probably is in view of the patches of dark green trees and standing corn-stalk.[39]

We have already noted, while dealing with the details about beasts of white colour, that a black cow stands for night (with its white calf for the yonder sun) and also that a cow of two colours *viz.* white and black, stands for the day and night. Thus apart from being taken as conducive to rains, the black-coloured beast stands for night also. In the rite of Agnicayana, the sacrificer has a white horse on his right side and a black horse on his left side. While putting down the bricks, he should stroke the white horse and when about to put down the mortar, he should stroke the black horse, thus with days and nights he builds the Fire-altar (*Tait. Sam.* V. 7.1.2,3). Again black colour is associated with the goddess (of Death, sin and misfortune) Nirṛti.[40] The dusky colour, which is akin to black colour also indicates inauspiciousness, but the details will be seen while dealing with the animal *viz.* cow.

That the dark (i.e. black) colour is connected with water or rain is seen even in the Sūtra-tradition. The texts in this tradition are much later than the Vedic texts but certain details which occur in them speak of the beliefs and practices of ancient times, though recorded and also codified later. In the Sūtra-tradition, a student observing one of the Veda-vratas (vows) named Mahānāmnī, has to wear clothes of dark (i.e. black) colour and has to partake of dark food (*Gobh. G.S.* III. 2.7-46; *Khā. G.S.* II.5.23ff). Kane has pointed out that the virtue of the Mahānāmnī *vrata* is centred in water.[41] This is seen from the observances prescribed for that student. He is required to bathe thrice a day, not to seek shelter when it is raining and not to cross a river without bathing in it. The Mahānāmnī verses (*Ait. Ār.* IV; *Jaim. Sam.* of the *SV* at II.7), which are to be sung to the student, are all in praise of the god Indra - the god of rain.

Bull and cow, the domesticated animals familiar right from the Ṛgvedic times,[42] are mentioned also in the Vedic rituals. The *RV* mentions a ritual of cooking a spotted bull, with a note that these were the rituals of bygone times (*RV* I. 164. 43 cd). Again we find that *ukṣan-s* ('stud bulls,' kept for procreation fr. √*ukṣ* - 'to sprinkle'), *ṛṣabha*-s (= *vṛṣabha*-s - virile, sprinkler bulls for √*vṛṣ* - *varṣ* - 'to sprinkle') and *vaśā*-s (barren cows) are offered to Agni (*ibid.* VI. 16.47). The word *vṛṣan* or *vṛṣabha* ('a sprinkler bull', as seen above, strictly kept for impregnating cows) becomes an epithet in the case of the gods Rudra (*ibid.* II. 33.6a), Indra (*ibid.* II. 12.12a) and Soma (*ibid.* IX.16.6; 69.4; 96.7). Soma is said to be connected with the waters as is the bull with the cows, which he impregnates (*ibid.* X. 36.8; cf. IX.19.5). Both Apām Napāt and Sarasvān (the male deity of the river Sarasvatī) are said to be *vṛṣan* (the 'sprinkler' bull) as well as *śiśu* (the infant). They sprinkle their seed in the waters and both are born as *śiśu* from the same waters.[43] The sublime concept of husband becoming the child (son) of his wife is noted in the later tradition.[44] The concept of the virile *vṛṣā* or *vṛṣabha* reminds us of the epithet of Indra *viz. gaura avaskandin* ('*gaura*' - male counterpart of *gaurī*, i.e. cow) which occurs in the later Subrahmaṇyā *nigada.* Among the domesticated animals, horse and bull occupied a place of prime importance in the life of the Vedic Aryans. There is no wonder therefore that these two animals could play a role in the beliefs and practices of the Vedic people. As Ghurye has pointed out, like many other ancient people, the Vedic Aryans were the people having the bull-complex and horse-complex.[45]

A definite ritual of sacrificially killing a bull cannot be maintained in the ritual of the Brāhmaṇa-texts. The information about the Śūlagava-rite, in which a bull is sacrificed to Śūla (i.e. one who bears a *śūla*-trident—*śula* + *ac* (suffix) according to *Pāṇ* V. 2.127-*arśa ādibhyo'c),* i.e. Rudra, occurs in the *Aśv. G.S.* (IV. 9.1-40). This tradition is much later than the ritual-tradition of the Brāhmaṇa-texts. However, the bull is often mentioned in the Brāhmaṇa-texts. In the rite of Agnicayana, in the case of not getting white horse or any horse (to lead the procession of the sacrificer and the priests, from the Gārhapatya fire-place to the Āhavanīya one), a bull could be chosen. The *Śat. Br.* enjoins this by saying that the bull is of Agni's nature (*Śat. Br.* VII. 3.2.16 — *āgneyo vā'anaḍvān).* This belief must have worked in several rituals, where the use of red bull hide is enjoined by the Gṛhya and the Śrauta *sūtra*-s,[46] the red colour obviously standing for blazing form of Agni and the hide for the bull. Both signify Agni. That the *vṛṣabha (= ṛṣabha)* 'sprinkler' bull is believed to be a progenitor (*prajanayitā)* is clearly stated by the *Tait. Br.,* while prescribing the use of its hide for a *vaiśya,* desiring for nourishment (i.e. prosperity). The *vaiśya* is to be anointed with curds, seated on the bull's hide, with the neck-part of the hide to the east and the hairy part upwards.[47] In the Rājasūya sacrifice, in the context of *ratninām havīṁṣi* (offerings given at the houses of the *ratnin*-s), the *Śat. Br.* prescribes a pap (*caru)* to be offered to Bṛhaspati at the house of the Purohita, i.e. the king's court chaplain (*Śat. Br.* V.3.1.2). In the Daśapeya offering in the Rājasūya sacrifice, a *caru* is to be offered to Bṛhaspati (*ibid.* V. 5.1.12). On both these occasions, the *dakṣiṇā* (sacrificial gift to the priest) prescribed is a white-backed (*śitipṛṣṭhaḥ)* bullock. To Bṛhaspati, the god, belongs that upper region (*ūrdhvā dik)* and there above the path of Aryaman (i.e. sun - ... 'Aryaman' the sun viewed as a 'goer' fr. √*ṛ* - 'to go'). Here the white-backed bull is connected to Bṛhaspati through its white colour, for Bṛhaspati stands for the spiritual power as he is the lord of the *mantra*-s.

Moreover his region is near that of the sun. A pair of twin bullocks is given as *dakṣiṇā,* when a cake on two potsherds is offered to Aśvins in the house of the Charioteer. This is given by the sacrificer-king in the Rājasīya sacrifice. As Aśvins are the twin-gods, so are the twin bullocks of the same womb. If the sacrificer-king cannot obtain twins, two bullocks produced by successive births of the same cow may also be given as *dakṣiṇā* (*ibid.* V. 3.1.8). In the same context it is stated that a dwarfish bull is the *dakṣiṇā* to the priest when a cake on three potsherds is offered to Viṣṇu (*ibid.* V. 2.5.4). The *Śat. Br.,* in the context of preparation of altar, states a mythical account in the *arthavāda,* in which Viṣṇu figures as a dwarf (*ibid.* I.2.5.1-9). In the Rājasūya sacrifice, at the house of the Chamberlain (*kṣatṛ),* a cake on either twelve or eight potsherds is offered to Savitṛ and the sacrificial gift made is a reddish-white draught-bullock. Reddish-white is the sun (Savitṛ) both in rising and setting (*ibid.* V.3.1.7). In the same context, it is stated that a cake on seven potsherds is offered to the Maruts at the house of the Headman (*Grāmaṇī)* and the sacrificial gift to be given is a spotted bullock, for in such a spotted bullock, there are many colours and so are the Maruts as a group, many (*ibid.* V. 3. 1.6). A brown bull is the gift in the Triṣaṁyukta offering (in the Rājasūya sacrifice), for such a brown bull is of Soma's nature (*ibid.* V. 2.5.12). A cake on eleven potsherds is offered to Indra in the Daśapeya (offering) in the Rājasūya sacrifice and the gift is a bull, for the bull is Indra (*ibid.* V. 5.1.9). Elsewhere also the *Śat Br.* says that a bull is the form of Indra (*ibid.* II. 5.3.18). In the Daśapeya offering (noted above), a *caru* (pap) is offered to Soma and the gift is a brown bull, for the brown bull is sacred to Soma (*ibid.* V. 5.1.9). It is clear that brown is the colour of the Soma juice and so is the bull of that colour. In the Rājasūya sacrifice, when a pap (*caru)* is offered to the Viśve Devāḥ, a piebald bullock is the gift given. As Viśve Devāḥ are clans (*viśaḥ),* they signify abundance and so is the gift of a bullock, which has patches of many colours (*pṛṣan gauḥ)* (*ibid.* V. 5.1.10). In the same sacrifice, when at the house of the Carver 'tax-collector' (Bhāgadugha), a *caru* is offered to Pūṣan, the gift is a dark-grey bullock (*ibid.* V. 3.1.9). The significance of giving such a gift (*i.e.* of such a colour) is explained by the *Śat. Br.* elsewhere (i.e. in the Triṣaṁyukta sacrifice). The dark-grey (*śyāma)* colour presents two forms *viz.* white and black, and thus a productive pair. Pūṣan is cattle (he being a pastoro-agricultural deity) and cattle is productiveness (*ibid.* V.2.5.8). In the Triṣaṁyukta sacrifice, a bull is a gift for the oblation given to Vaiśvānara. Vaiśvānara is the Year and so is Prajāpati the Year. The bull (*ṛṣabhaḥ*) is Prajāpati (*ibid.* V.2.5.17). In the Rājasūya sacrifice, a cake on twelve potsherds is offered to Indra and Agni and the gift to be made to the priest is a bull. By its shoulder, the bull is of Agni's nature and by its testicles, of Indra's nature. By offering this cake the sacrificer becomes possessed of vigour and energy as did Indra become, after slaying Vṛtra, when he gave this offering (*ibid.* V.2.3.8). Interestingly in the Caraka-Sautrāmaṇī sacrifice, a castrated bull is given as a sacrificial gift. This bull is neither female nor male. Or a draught-mare is given as a gift, for as it pulls the cart, it is not a female and being a female, it is not a male *(ibid.* V.5.4.35). No *arthavāda* pointing out the exact motif of this *dakṣiṇā* is stated by the *Śat. Br.* However we can know it taking into account that the Caraka-Sautrāmaṇī sacrifice is to cure a person, purged by Soma when he is emptied out of everything. Can we say that he becomes powerless and so the sacrificial gift is also of that sort? The *Śat. Br.* has stated a lengthy mythical account of Indra cutting off the three heads of Viśvarūpa—the three-headed, six-eyed son of Tvaṣṭṛ—; Tvaṣṭṛ becoming furious, bringing Soma-juice but withholding it from Indra; Indra though uninvited, consuming what pure Soma there was in the tub; Soma hurting him and flowing in all directions from the openings of Indra's vital airs, thus emptying Indra of everything; the Aśvins curing Indra with the Sautrāmaṇī rite, making him *sutrāta* ('well-saved'); so the name Sautrāmaṇī (*ibid.* V. 5.4.2-12).

Another important domesticated animal is cow (*go*), which was useful for various purposes, as could be judged from the various meanings of the word *go*, occurring in the *Nir.*[48] Cow is addressed as the goddess Aditi and hence she is not to be killed.[49] The same belief is seen in the rite of *ratninām havīṁṣi* in the Rājasūya sacrifice, when a pap (*caru*) is offered to Aditi, for Aditi is this Earth and also the wife of the gods. The sacrificial gift on this occasion is a milch cow (*dhenu*), for this Earth is as it were a milch cow, yielding to men all their desires (*ibid.* V. 3. 1.4). The *AV* hails *dhenu* (milch cow) for prosperity (*AV* III.10.2). The deity Apām Napāt — 'Son of Waters' — is said to have a milch cow in his abode (*RV* II. 35. 7a). This could be taken as a clear reference to a river, imagined to be a cow, nay, identified with the latter. And the expression has to be taken in this light, as Apām Napāt primarily is a deity connected with waters, later on identified with Agni. This concept of the river-cow, coming for the first time in *RV* and that way in the Indian literature as such, stands important in the Indian River-mythology. The example is of the river Godāvarī in the Puranic tradition.[50]

That the cow was taken to be of divine nature is marked in the Indraturīya offering in the Four-monthly Seasonal sacrifices of the Rājasūya sacrifice. It is said that the yoke-trained cow (*anaḍuhī vahalā*) is the sacrificial gift for this offering. This cow by her shoulder is of Agni's nature, for her shoulder is, as it were, fire-burnt. Being a female she draws the chariot. But that is improper and hence of her Varuṇic nature. As sour curds (*dadhi*) for Indra comes from her, she is of Indra's nature. As she is a cow, she is of Rudra's nature. The yoke-trained cow is thus related to all (gods) (*Śat. Br.* V. 2.4.13).

We have noted already the beliefs about the black as well as white colours. Here are some related to the cow and also her calf. After the rite of *ratninām havīṁṣi* in the Rājasūya sacrifice, he offers a *caru* to Soma and Rudra. The *arthavāda* states that when Svarbhānu, the *asura*, struck the sun with darkness, the latter could not shine. Soma and Rudra removed that darkness and with evil removed, the sun shines yonder. So a *caru* offered to them. This rice is cooked (for *caru)* in the milk from a white cow, which has a white calf. Even the sacrificial gift for this is a white cow, which has a white calf (*ibid.* V.3.2.1-2). It is clear that the white colour of the cow and the calf stands for light as also the sun. In the rite of Agnicayana, while leading forward Agni to the fire-altar, he makes offering on the firebrand, while it is held above (the naturally perforated brick), of milk from a black cow, which has a white calf. The black cow is the night and her calf is the yonder sun (*ibid.* IX. 2.3.30).

Apart from the white and black colours, the colour mentioned is reddish or tawny. The *AV* speaks of a herb that is reddish or tawny like a cow or bull of similar colour (*AV.* I.22.1 - *go rohitasya varṇena).* We shall take note of these colours of the cow later on.

The belief in the highest sacredness of the cow is marked in the rite of Pravargya, when the milk (also called *'gharma')* of the cow is to be boiled. The sacrificer (or the priest) while stepping behind the Gārhapatya, addresses the cow by the names Iḍā, Aditi and Sarasvatī, for the cow is really Iḍā, Aditi and Sarasvatī (*Śat. Br.* XIV. 2.1.7). Gifts of cows are recorded and extolled in the *śloka*-s, which are stated in the *Ait. Br.* (VIII. 22 = 39.8; VIII. 23 = 39.9).

There is a mention of a *vaśā* cow, which was to be offered in the fire for getting food (*RV* VIII. 43.11). Sāyaṇa takes the word *vaśā* to mean a barren cow.[51] In the *AV*, *vaśā* is deified and is praised in thirty-four *mantra*-s (*AV* X. 10). She is said to be the wife of Parjanya (*ibid.* X. 10. 6c - *vaśā parjanyapatnī)* and is clearly the cloud-cow. The *Tait. Sam.*, in the context of special sacrifices, enjoins offering of several types of *vaśā*-s. It is said that when the sound Vaṣaṭ (Vaṣaṭkāra) cleft the head of the Gāyatrī, the sap thereof fell away. The sap, which fell at first became a *vaśā* (cow) with a white back; the second sap, a *vaśā* of two forms (i.e.

two colours); the third sap, a *vaśā* of many forms. The blood became a fierce red *vaśā*. These four *vaśā*-s (cows) are offered respectively to the deities *viz.* Bṛhaspati for splendour (the white back of the first *vaśā* suggesting that); Mitrā-Varuṇā, a dual deity, for getting rains for day and for night (the white and the black colour of the second *vaśā* suggesting that); Viśve Devāḥ- All Gods, for getting food, obviously of all forms (the *vaśā* of many forms according to Sāyaṇa, i.e. colours, suggesting it); and Rudra, when a person practises witchcraft (the red colour of the *vaśā* suggesting it). This account from the *Tait. Sam.* (II. 1.7.1-7) is important for knowing the beliefs about the colours. *Vaśā* or any such cow is mentioned for quite a number of times.[52] A dusky-coloured cow is chosen for being the Anustaraṇī cow. This cow is called Anustaraṇī (fr. *anu* + √*stṛ* - 'to place on'), for it is immolated sacrificially and its limbs are placed on the limbs of the dead *āhitāgni* (the sacrificer who maintains the three fires) and the omentum on the face of the *āhitāgni.*[53] Such a cow is aged, scurvy and hornless or a dusky one, of two years with shorter fore-legs (*Pañc. Br.* XXI. 1.7). Here the dusky colour, which is the colour of the smoke also inauspiciousness, suits the purpose for which it is employed (i.e. cremation of the *āhitāgni).* The Śrautasūtra-s[54] and the Gṛhysasūtra-s[55] provide all details in this respect.

We have already referred above to the *vaśā* (cow) of red colour to be offered to Rudra, by a person, who practises witchcraft (*Tait. Sam.* II. 1.7.7). We have also noted already that black colour induces rains but in some cases stands for night and also in yet others, for Nirṛti (goddess of death, sin, evil). The Sūryā-hymn in the *RV* speaks of the garment of the bride, which is of black and red colour, and is believed to be haunted by the evil spirit called Kṛtyā. This garment is to be given away, lest the female evil spirit, obtaining feet should enter the body of the bridegroom, i.e. husband (*RV.* X. 85. 28, 29). This garment of the bride is one, she wears on the night of the consummation of marriage. The *AV* also refers to the bride's garment (*AV.* XIV. 1. 25-27). The *Āśv.*

G.S. (I.8.13) and *Āp. G.S.* (III. 9.11) mention the rite of giving away the bride's garment after the marriage ritual, obviously on the day after the night of the consummation of marriage. The same instruction occurs in the *Sk. P.*, where it is said that the *nīlīrakta* garment (i.e. the garment dyed with black or blue colour or is of black-and-red colour, keeping in tune with the Ṛgvedic *nīlalohita* garment) of the bride is to be thrown away at a distance. Such a garment, however, is not inauspicious at the time of love-sports in the bed (*Sk.P.* IV. 40.142). It is probable that the black and red colours were used to attract the attention of the evil spirits, which are later on vanquished by a *mantra*.[56]

A *rohiṇī* (lit. 'red cow') is said to belong to the Vṛtra-killer (*Śat. Br.* III. 3.1.14). In the case of a beast, it is difficult to imagine a purely red colour. Hence the colour should be taken as 'reddish' or 'ruddy.' A reddish cow (*rohiṇī)* with reddish-white eyes (*śyetākṣī)* is said to belong to the *pitṛ*-s (Fathers) and is to be sacrificed to them (*ibid.).* In the case of not getting a Somakrayaṇī cow, a dark red cow (*aruṇā)* can be obtained for being the Somakrayaṇī cow. In the absence of that (i.e. *aruṇā),* the cow to be obtained is the ruddy or reddish one (*rohiṇī),* which is of Indra (the Vṛtra-killer).[57] But he should never have a ruddy cow with reddish-white eyes (*rohiṇī śyetākṣī)* as a Somakrayaṇī cow (*ibid.* III. 3.1.15). We have noted above that such a cow is sacrificed to the Fathers (*pitṛ*-s*).* The Somakrayaṇī cow is said to be of tawny (*babhru)* colour and having red-brown eyes (*piṅgākṣī)* as is stated in the *Śat. Br.* (III. 3.1.13-15) and also *Tait. Sam.* (VI. 1.6.7, 8).

The tawny colour of the Somakrayaṇī cow and also the shade of tawny (or red-brown) colour, of its eyes are akin to the colour of Soma, the principle 'Like produces like' of sympathetic magic working here. The cow here stands for the Vāc (Speech)[58] which was sent by the gods to the *gandharva*-s for bringing back Soma, stolen by the latter. She (Vāc - a 'woman') allured them (*gandharva*-s*),* they being fond of women and she then returned to the gods together with Soma. This mythical account in the *Śat. Br.* relates further that both the *gandharva*-s and the gods tried to woo Vāc, the former reciting the Veda-s to her and the latter creating the lute and playing on it and singing for her, she ultimately turning to the latter (i.e. gods), for women are attracted to him, who dances and sings (*Śat. Br.* III. 2.4.1-6, 10).

Cow being important in the daily life of the Vedic Aryans, its image entered other spheres. As noted above, the cow Somakrayaṇī stood as a symbol of Speech. The thundering cloud-cow is taken to be the symbol of the mid-region Speech, which makes a sound while showering rains.[59] The cow Anustaraṇī (when immolated sacrificially) in the form of her various limbs figures in the last rites of the *āhitāgni* and accompanies him to the other world.[60] In the three-day-rite of Garga, the *Pañc. Br.* states an elaborate *arthavāda* about the Anustaraṇī (XXI. 1.1-8).

The cow-hide is used at rituals right from the Ṛgvedic times. The stones for pressing the Soma-shoots are kept on the hide of a cow.[61] In the Mahāvrata-rite, which falls on the last but one day of the Gavām-ayana *sattra,* a *kṣatriya* is required to shoot three arrows consecutively in such a way that they get stuck into a hide, that is kept stretched between two posts, with such a skill that the arrows just stick in the skin and do not pierce it through.[62] The very nature of the Mahāvrata being symbolic, the hide signified the earth to be 'fructified' by the 'shaft'. Again there is a sham fight (to the west of the Āgnīdhra shed) for a round piece of white hide, between an *ārya* and *śūdra* in which the former emerges victorious.[63] The circular white piece symbolises the sun, for which the gods and the *asura*-s fought laying claim on the sun as their own. When the *ārya* wins (made to win !) in the fight, there is an indication that the *ārya* will get all seasons good and fruitful. Though not mentioned here specifically, these hides used in the Mahāvrata-rite seem to be of a cow and bull respectively. Even a tail-whisk of a cow or a horse is used in the Sautrāmaṇī sacrifice to purify the sacrificer. Such a tail-whisk is regarded as a form of kine and horses (*Śat. Br.* XII. 8.1.14).

The Brāhmaṇa-texts are eloquent of the greatness of cow. In the rite of Agnihotra, in which daily offerings of milk are given in the fire, it is said that cow's milk is Agni's seed, for even while the cow is raw, the milk in her is cooked warm. Moreover even when it is from a black or a red cow, it is always white and shining like fire, it being Agni's seed (*ibid.* II. 2.4.15). In the same context, it is said that truly the cow is sacrifice and without her no sacrifice is performed (*ibid.* II.2.4.13). In the rite of buying Soma, in the barter, a cow is offered to the Soma-seller (Hence her name Somakrayaṇī). The Adhvaryu on this occasion, enumerates the things which come from a cow, thus giving stress on her importance. These (things) are - fresh milk, boiled milk, cream, sour curds, sour cream, curdled milk, butter, ghee, clotted curds and whey (*ibid.* III.3.3.2). Interestingly in the rite of Agnicayana, when making the fire-pan, at the top part of it, he forms four nipples of the udder. The fire-pan is said to be a cow and the cow has four nipples. From the nipples (of the cow, milk and) of the fire-pan, which is also said to be these worlds, the sacrificer gets all his desires fulfilled (*ibid.* VI.5.2.16-18). He should not make nipples fewer or more than those of a cow, for then they would not make the fire-pan like a cow, but like a bitch, or a ewe or a mare (*ibid.* VI. 5.2.19). In the rite of consecration, after taking the bath, the sacrificer puts on a garment for the sake of completeness, for it is his own skin that he puts on himself. An interesting *arthavāda* occurs here referring to cow. The mythical account relates that the gods, in order to enable the cow to endure rain, cold and heat put on her the skin which man had on him formerly. So they flayed the man. Here a daily observation is recorded that wherever (on man's body) a stalk of grass or some other object cuts him, the blood trickles out. Hence they put on that skin, i.e. the garment on him. So one should take care to be properly clad. People like to see even an ugly person properly clad, since he is with his own skin. One should not be naked in the presence of a cow. She knowing that she wears the man's skin, runs away from the naked man with the fear that he would take her skin, but fondly goes near him, who is properly clad (*ibid.* III. 1.2.13-17).

The very epithet *'aghnyā'* ('not to be killed') occurring in *RV* several times[64] brings out the indispensable position of the cow in the life of the Vedic Aryans. Even a barren cow had her own importance. At the Agniṣṭoma sacrifice, after the Udayanīya-*iṣṭi*, there is the Anūbandhyā sacrifice. It is prescribed that a barren cow (*vaśā)* be offered to Mitra and Varuṇa and that too after the sacrifice. The well-offered part of the sacrifice, Mitra takes and again surrenders it to the sacrificer. The ill-offered part of the sacrifice Varuṇa takes and makes it well-offered and gives it back to the sacrificer (*ibid.* IV. 5.1.6-7). The explanation stated here is not convincing, but it supports the practice of offering a barren cow (*vaśā*) to Mitra and Varuṇa.

Though generally the dog was not looked at with favourable attitude, the mythical account in the context of the Abhiplava, of the bitch Saramā helping the gods to get back their cows from the Paṇi-s, with the result her descendants in the Vidarbha region are born strong even to kill a tiger, has to be noted (*Jaim. Br.* II. 440-42). The killing of a four-eyed (two natural eyes and two marks above the eyes) dog is mentioned in the Horse-sacrifice. The *Śat. Br.* says that having killed the dog, it is made to float under the horse's stomach in between the fore and the hind feet of the horse. The dog here stands for the wicked enemy, which the sacrificer stamps down with the horse serving as the thunderbolt (*Śat. Br.* XIII.1.2.9).[65] The same thought occurs in the *Tait. Br.,* when a dog is killed in the Horse-sacrifice (*Tait. Br.* III. 8.4.1). The killing of a dog here cannot be regarded as a sacrificial offering. But the dog was sacrificed, as it is clearly mentioned in the *RV* (IV. 18.13) and *AV* (VII. 5.5).[66] The four-eyed dog mentioned above, reminds us of the two dogs of Yama, which are graphically described both in *RV* (X. 14.10-12) and *AV* (XVIII.2.11-13). These dogs are said to move among people (in the terrestrial world), watching them minutely. The dog mentioned in *Avesta* is said to guard the Cinvat bridge, which the dead has to cross. That some kind of inauspiciousness is attached to a dog is indicated in the *Tait. Sam.*, when it says in the context of additional details in the Soma-sacrifice, that if a dog touches the speckled butter (*pṛṣadājya)* of the sacrificer, his cattle would be likely to die (*Tait. Sam.* III. 2.6.2). Among the three unclean animals, together with a vicious boar and a vicious ram, a dog appears (*Śat. Br.* XII. 4.1.4; *Jaim. Br.* I.51).

A mention of elephant occurs in the *RV* (the words occurring are *ibha, hastin* and *varaṇa)*[67] and the *AV* (III. 22.3a). The *AV* here says that the elephant has come into being with splendour. Interestingly the belief reflected in the *Śat. Br.* about the elephant speaks the other way. In the context of the consecration offering (Dīkṣaṇīya-iṣṭi) in the Soma-sacrifice, it is said that some offer a rice-pap (*caru)* to Āditya-s. The mythical account coming by way of *arthavāda* states that Aditi had eight sons. The gods—the sons of Aditi — were only seven, and the eighth one was Mārtāṇḍa - the unformed one. The gods (sons of Aditi) then thought of fashioning the Mārtāṇḍa and fashioned it as a man is fashioned. The flesh cut off from the Mārtāṇḍa and thrown down in a lump, became the elephant. Hence they say that one must not accept an elephant as a gift, as the elephant has sprung from man (*Śat. Br.* III. 1.3.2-4).

Ass or donkey referred to by the words *gardabha* and *rāsabha,* is mentioned in the *RV.*[68] There is no mention of its sacrifice in the Vedic ritual tradition, though in the Dharmaśāstra tradition, the sacrifice of an ass (*gardabha)* to the deity Nirṛti and wearing of the ass-hide to cover the body while begging alms for one year, are enjoined for an *avakīrṇin,* i.e. a *brahmacārin* who has swerved from the vow of celibacy.[69] This sacrifice, however, has to be on the ordinary fires, which are not to be kindled with any *mantra.*

Though domesticated and used for gathering the earth (i.e. clay) for making a fire-pan, the ass is not looked at with a favourable attitude, in the Vedic ritual texts. The earth is gathered (and carried) by the ass. With grazing, the ass becomes fat beyond other animals (*bhārabhāritamaḥ).* It is said that with the ass, they gather food and light. The ass being of double seed is born as the lowest of animals, for Agni (here of the fire-pan) burns his place of birth (*Tait. Sam.* V. 1.5.5). That the ass has double seed is explained by the *Tait. Sam.* through an *arthavāda.* In the context of the Soma-sacrifice, it is said that by the Agniṣṭoma sacrifice, Prajāpati created and grasped the offspring (of his). When he was grasping them, the mule escaped. Following it, he took its seed and placed it in the ass. Hence the ass has double seed (*ibid.* VII. 1.1.2). The *Śat. Br.* has a different *arthavāda* in this respect in the context of the Agnicayana rite, when a libation to Savitṛ is to be offered. It is said that in former times, when such a libation was offered, Agni went away from the gods. As Agni is regarded as a cattle, the gods thought that if they searched Agni with all cattle, the latter would become used up and would afford no livelihood and if not with all cattle, they would get Agni incomplete. They saw one animal as 'one' substitute for the 'two', i.e. cow and sheep. Hence that 'one' (he-ass), though being one, has a double seed (*Śat. Br.* VI. 3.1.22-23). The he-ass impregnates a she-ass and a mare. But the belief about the ass is that it is a dusty animal. In the concluding rite of the Agniṣṭoma sacrifice, a barren cow (*anūbandhyā*) is offered to Mitra and Varuṇa. The gods caused the seed (that was cast) to spring. From it sprung the burning coals (*aṅgārāḥ),* and from the latter the Aṅgiras-es and after that the other animals. From the dust of the ashes (of those coals) was produced the ass. Hence when it is dusty anywhere, people say that it is the very place of the asses (*ibid.* IV. 5.1.5, 8-9).

In the context of New-moon and Full-moon sacrifices, there is a mention of camel in the list of five animals, whose flesh one should not eat, they being deprived of sacrificial essence (*ibid.* I.2.3.9).

Together with the camel, we have a mention of *kiṁpuruṣa, gavaya* and *śarabha,* whose flesh also is not to be eaten, as their sacrificial essence has left them. They are thus unholy (*ibid.*). *Gavaya* and *śarabha* are wild animals and not domesticated. About *kiṁpuruṣa,* we have to think. Eggeling has discussed this point and has come to the conclusion that 'perhaps one of the species of apes which particularly resembled man, is intended by it' (i.e. by the word *kiṁpuruṣa).*[70] A probe further takes us to a single reference to monkey (*kapi)* in the *RV* and that is to a hairy monkey of huge size *viz.* Vṛṣākapi (*RV* X. 86). According to Dange, the Ṛgvedic hymn speaks of a lost ritual of the sacrifice of a monkey.[71] The work *Ṛgvidhāna,* which deals with the magical effects produced by the recitation of the Ṛgvedic hymns, also has pointed out that this hymn (i.e. *RV.* X. 86) is prescribed by some (teachers), for men, in a rite for regaining virility - *pauruṣe karmaṇi* (*Ṛgvidhāna* III. 127 ab). About the *kiṁpuruṣa* again — Is it probable that such a big monkey or ape (hairy all over) might be raising a doubt in the mind of the persons, seeing it from a distance, whether it is (really) a man (*'kim puruṣaḥ?'*— hence the word *kiṁpuruṣa).*

There is a mention of *mahiṣa*-s killed for Indra (*RV* VIII. 12.8) and their flesh cooked for him (*ibid.* VI. 17.11). *Mahiṣa* may here signify a huge buffalo, but there is no trace of its being sacrificed for Indra. There does not seem any such ritual practice. No milk of she-buffalo, is mentioned. Is it because of she-buffalo's being black in colour?

Lion is mentioned in the *RV* and *AV,* at several places, as a standard of comparison while eulogising the gods.[72] This importance attributed to lion further caused this animal to become a symbol of the earth-spirit. The sacrificial altar (*vedi)* is called *siṁhī* (*Vāj Sam.* V. 10) and the *vedi* is identified with the earth (*Tait. Sam.* I.2.12.2). The Nṛsiṁha (Man-lion) incarnation of Viṣṇu symbolised the overlordship of the earth.[73]

Tiger (*vyāghra)* is not mentioned in the *RV* but in *AV* (IV. 3.1, 3, 4 & 7; VI. 140. 1a). Macdonell and Keith note under "*vyāghra*", that by the time of *AV,* the Vedic Aryans had reached Bengal, since tiger is found in this region even in present times.[74] In the Rājasūya sacrifice (rite for rejuvenation of the king, the king is symbolically 'reborn', after this rite - *rājā anena sūyate),* a piece of lead (or copper) is placed on the skin of a tiger, in front of the hearth (*dhiṣṇya* of the Maitrāvaruṇa priest). On the skin, a hundred-measure piece of gold is placed, hundred to suit man's expected life-years. The king has to step on the skin and toss away the piece of baser metal with his foot. This piece symbolises the head of Namuci.[75]

The symbolic significance of the tiger-skin in this rite of lustration or rejuvenation of the king has to be taken note of. The tiger-skin is first the symbol of Soma, it being addressed "You are the lustre (*tviṣi)* of Soma" (*Tait. Br.* I.7.8.1; *Śat. Br.* V. 4.1.11). When the king steps on the tiger-skin, the lustre of Soma is bestowed on him. The *Śat. Br.* says that when Indra drank the Soma-juice and it flowed through his body, he became a tiger. By this address to the tiger-skin (which stands for tiger) and stepping on it, the king assumes the qualities of Soma and of tiger (*Śat. Br.* V.4.1.11; also *Vāj. Sam.* X.15 for the *mantra*). The *Tait. Br.* has a different thought to give. It states that the colour of tiger is the colour (*varṇaḥ)* of death. To ward off death, a gold-piece is to be placed upon the tiger-skin and under the foot of the king, for gold stands for immortality (*amṛta).* The piece of gold is placed with a *mantra*[76] — 'Save me from death' (*Tait. Br.* I.7.8.1; cf. *Tait Sam.* I.8.14.1). In the rite of Punarabhiṣeka (renewed anointing of the king after the concluding ceremony of the Rājasūya sacrifice), the throne-like wooden seat of the king is covered with a tiger-skin. The tiger (tiger-skin standing for that) is the lordly power of the wild animals and so is the *rājanya* (*kṣatriya),* the lordly power. The lordly power is made to prosper with the lordly power (*Ait. Br.* VIII. 6 = 37.2).

Though having only a couple of references to it, boar is a significant beast in the Vedic rituals. In the rite of Pravargya, for making the Mahāvīra vessels (of clay), together with other things he takes the earth torn up by a boar with the *mantra* from the *Vāj. Sam.* (XXXVII. 5). The *arthavāda* points out that in the beginning the earth was only so large as of the size of a span. A boar called Emūṣa raised her up and he was her lord Prajāpati. So the earth torn up by a boar is used (*Śat. Br* XIV. 1.2.11). Like other skins, the boar-skin stands for the boar. In the Rājasūya sacrifice, the king to be rejuvenated has to put on the shoes of boar's skin. The *arthavāda* states a mythical account that once the gods put on the fire a pot of ghee. From there, a boar was produced. Boar is fat, for it was produced from ghee. So the cows readily take to a boar, for it is indeed their own essence. When the king puts on shoes of boar-skin, he firmly establishes himself in the essence of the cattle (*ibid.* V. 4.3.19). Even the *Tait. Br.* prescribes for the king wearing of boar-skin shoes and says that boar is the *manyu* (mettle) of the animals. That *manyu* he places in himself, by wearing such shoes, in the Rājasūya rite (*Tait. Br.* I.7.9.4).

In the context of the Horse-sacrifice, there occurs a long list of hundreds of animals and birds, in the *Vāj. Sām.* (XXIV). These animals and birds, thirteen in each group, are to be brought and tied to the post, such posts being twenty-one in number and the interval spaces between these posts being twenty, where the animals and birds are to be brought. Kane states that the animals and birds, mentioned from *kapiñjala* onwards (*Vāj. Sam.* XXIV. 20 ff) are let off, after fire is carried or waved round them.[77] Of these animals and birds brought here, each one was meant for a particular deity or the entity which has become a deity. To take some examples — the birds such as *kapiñjala, kalaviṅka, tittiri,* etc. were for different seasons (*ibid.* XXIV. 20); *śiśumāra*-s were for ocean; frogs were for rain; fish for water, etc. (*ibid.* 21). The list seems to be all exhaustive, inviting our attention to identify these animals and birds with the ones found in our own times. As pointed out by Kane, this is the tradition of the Śrautasūtra-s[78] which are of later times as compared to the Brāhmaṇa-texts. Carrying (or waving) fire round the animals and birds obviously signifies their symbolic sacrifice and not the actual one. However as per a mention occurring in the *Śat. Br.*, the practice seems to be of sacrificially immolating a hornless goat, and *gomṛga*,[79] the *paryaṅgya* animals (animals encircling the horse) and other animals, together with the horse (*Śat. Br.* XIII. 2.2.1-19).

In the rite of Agnicayana, a live tortoise is enjoined to be kept at the lowest level (*ibid.* VII. 5.1.1). Though not directly mentioned as sacrificed, the tortoise could be taken so, for it is said to be originally a sacrificial cake, which is offered to the gods. In the context of the New-moon and Full-moon sacrifices, a mythical account occurs in the *Tait. Sam.*, which states that the Aṅgiras-es were the last to go to the world of heaven. When the sages came to the place of sacrifice, they saw the sacrificial cake, creeping about having become a tortoise. When they asked it to be firm at one place, in the name of Indra. Bṛhaspati and All Gods, it did not. On their instruction to be firm for Agni, it became firm (*Tait. Sam.* II. 6.3.2,3). In the rite of Agnicayana, a similar mythical account states further that the sacrificial cake becoming a tortoise crawled after the Aṅgiras-es when they went to the world of heaven. So the live tortoise when placed at the lowest level leads the sacrificer straight to the world of heaven (*ibid.* V.2.8.4,5). In the same context, the *Śat. Br.* while enjoining the placing of a live tortoise, says that Prajāpati having become a tortoise created the beings (*Śat. Br.* VII. 5.1.5). Prajāpati in the shape of a tortoise crept over the three worlds (*ibid.* 9). Tortoise is also said to be the sun (*ibid.* VII.5.1.6). This gets related to the worldwide belief that tortoise is a solar animal. The resemblance of the tortoise with the sun should be marked, the former being circular in form with its head, legs and tail standing for the rays of the sun. The folk-belief that 'a turtle when killed will not die until sundown'[80] possibly echoes the same idea and suggests that the turtle is the representative of the sun.

When the Great Fire-altar, in the rite of Agnicayana, is complete (in its construction), the sacrificer or the priest drags a frog, a Avakā (plant) and a bamboo-shoot (tying them to a cane) across the central part of the altar. We have already noted the belief about the Avakā plant (*śaivāla* — moss) and the bamboo-shoot in the chapter on "Trees and Plants". These two together with the frog are dragged on the central surface of the fire-altar to appease (Agni-) Prajāpati, for the Great Fire-altar stands for the very Prajāpati (i.e. his body, since new body is provided for him, as he is exhausted or worn out after creating the creatures).[81] The *arthavāda* states that in the beginning, when the vital breaths (*ṛṣi*-s) made up that Agni, i.e. fire-altar, to be built,[82] they sprinkled him with water. That water dripped off and became the frogs (*ibid.* IX. 1.2.21). It is very clear that the frogs (also the Avakā plant and the bamboo-shoot) are brought here, for they are connected with water, which gives cooling effect. They are employed as 'waters' themselves.

We have a picturesque description of frogs at the advent of rains (*RV* VII. 103. 1-10; *AV*. IV. 15.13). The hymn in *RV* (VII. 103) is clearly a rain-spell to propitiate frogs, because as found in worldwide beliefs, frogs as many other animals are believed to be in control of rains.[83] In *AV* (IV. 15.14), a female frog (*maṇḍūkī*) is mentioned for rain. In the Horse-sacrifice, among the animals to be offered to various deities, frog figures for the deity Parjanya (*Mait. Sam.* III.14.2). The *Kauś. Sū.* prescribes that to remove the fever of a patient, a frog should be tied to the patient's cot and then the water used to wash the patient obviously would be dropped on the frog (*Kauś. Sū* XXXII. 17). The belief of the Vedic times is that the frog being associated with waters would absorb all heat caused due to fever and would give cooling effect. In fact, the *Tait. Sam.* makes the frog a proxy-victim absorbing all heat, in the rite of Agnicayana, when he drags the frog on the (surface of the) Great Fire-altar. The fire when piled up is liable to burn up the beast that first steps over it. The frog is such an animal, on which no one subsists. It does not have a place among the domesticated as well as the wild beasts. Actually the sacrificer afflicts the frog with pain and thus transfers the pain of the sacrificial victim (i.e. animal) to it (*Tait. Sam.* V.4.4.3).

A reference to mole (*ākhu)* occurs in the context of the *sambhāra*-s. These are the seven from the earth and six from the wood of sacrificial trees, to be scattered at the site of the Gārhapatya fire. The earth from the mole-hill (*ākhu-karīṣa*) is brought as one of the *sambhāra*-s. The *Tait. Br.* relates the *arthavāda* that Agni once concealed himself from the gods and having become a mole, dug himself into the earth. The mole-hills thrown up by him have some of Agni's nature, attached to them. Hence it is that the earth from the mole-hill forms one of the *saṃbhāra*-s (*Tait. Br.* I.1.3.3; also a ref. to it, *ibid.* I.2.1.2). The *Śat. Br.* is more elaborate in the *arthavāda.* It says that the moles certainly know the savour of this earth. By entering deeper and deeper into this earth, they grow very fat, knowing (and enjoying) the savour of this earth. They cast this earth in the form of mole-hills. Hence he supplies the fire with the savour of this earth in the form of mole-hill (*Śat. Br.* II. 1.1.7).

In the ritual-texts, ants (*vamrī*-s and among them also, a special kind *viz. upadīkā*-s) are mentioned. Like the moles mentioned above, these ants (*upadīkā*-s*)* also find a way in the earth by going deep, and bring up the savour of the earth (i.e. collection of the moist earth) to form the ant-hill. The earth from the ant-hill (*valmīkavapā)* forms one of the earth-*sambhāra*-s. This is giving strength (*ūrjameva rasam)* of the earth to fire. Ant-hill is said to be an ear of the earth (*Tait. Br.* I.1.3.4). The *Mait. Sam.* while dealing with the *sambhāra*-s calls the ant-hill the breast of Prajāpati and says that Prajāpati gives his breast (i.e. milk) to fire (*Mait. Sam.* I.6.3). In the Agnicayana rite, for making a fire-pan (*ukhā)* when he fetches a lump of clay, a hollow ant-hill is laid down mid-ways between the lump of clay and the Āhavanīya fire. He looks along it. The ant-hill is this earth, and this earth is these worlds. As the gods searched for Agni part by part, so he searches for Agni part by part in these worlds (*Śat. Br.* VI. 3.3.1-5). Hence the ant-hill is brought in this rite. A mythical account occurs in the Pravargya rite, which is enjoined to replace symbolically the head of Viṣṇu, i.e. sacrifice, which was cut off. Being the excellent of the gods, Viṣṇu felt proud. He stood, resting his head on the end of the bow. Not daring to harm him in any way, all the gods (simply) sat around him. The ants (as though knowing the mind of the gods) got a promise from the gods that they (i.e. the ants) would get constant enjoyment of food and would find water in desert. They then gnawed Viṣṇu's bowstring. When the bowstring was cut, the end of the bow, springing asunder, cut off Viṣṇu's head, which became the yonder sun (*ibid.* XIV.1.1.7-11). In the Pravargya rite, for making the Mahāvīra (clay-) vessels to boil milk (*gharma),* along with other things, a *valmīkavapā* (omentum-like inner lump, i.e. very soft inner portion, of the ant-hill) is brought and placed on the black antelope-skin to be mixed with the clay. It is said that the way in which the head of sacrifice (i.e. Viṣṇu) was cut off (by the ants acting as agent), in the same way it is supplied with those ants (i.e. with the clay from the ant-hill, they have formed) (*ibid.* XIV. 1.2.10). The ants in the Pravargya-rite are called *vamrī*-s or *upadīkā*-s (*ibid.* XIV. 1.1.8). The *vamrī*-s might be a bigger variety of ants. It is said that the son of a woman being eaten up by the *vamrī*-s in the ant-hill, was saved by Indra (*RV* IV. 19.9 ab).

The beliefs about serpents were so deep-rooted as to give rise to accepting that creature as a totem of a tribe and the tribe eventually coming to be known by the name of that totem. Thus is the Sarpa tribe in ancient India. The Sarpa-s, in spite of being outside the Aryan fold in the beginning, gradually came into contact with the Aryans and could have some hymns to their credit (*RV* X 76; 94; 175 &189). The loan of the Sarpa-tribe to the Vedic-brahmanical ritual is manifold *viz.* possibly the very method of pressing Soma-shoots with the *grāvans;* the *mantra*-s to be recited at the midday pressing in praise of the pressing-stones; probably the very office of the Grāvastut priest; the lore Sarpavidyā of Sarpaveda, nullifying the venom of serpents (*Śat. Br.* XIII. 4.3.9); the Vyāhṛti 'Vṛdhat' from the Sarpaveda (*Gop. Br.* I. 1.10); the Sarpa-*sāman*-s, which got entry into the Araṇyageyagāna of *SV* (*Pañc. Br.* XXV. 15.1)*;* the deity Sarparājñī, originally connected in the Sarpa-tribe with serpents but in the Vedic ritual identified with the Earth, as a queen of what creeps (Sāyaṇa on *Ait. Br.* V. 23 = 24.4; *Kauṣ. Br.* XXVII. 4; *Ṛgvidhāna* pointing out that with the recitation of *RV* X. 189, there will not be any fear from the serpents); and the Gṛhya ritual of Sarpabali.[84]

The word *sarpa* (meaning 'serpent') occurs only once in the *RV* (X. 16.6), where it is said to eat the part of the dead body. *AV* in some hymns contains a prayer for protection from the serpents (*AV.* VI. 12; VI. 56 — *sarpebhyaḥ rakṣaṇam). RV* mentions the word *ahi* meaning serpent. Vasiṣṭha expresses a desire that Soma may give away his slanderers to serpent (*RV* VII. 104. 9c). This amounted to giving them a death-punishment. However, in most of the passages, where the word *ahi* occurs, there is a reference to the demon Vṛtra, who is in the form of a serpent, to be killed by Indra (*ibid* I.32.1,5; 186.5; V.31.4d; VIII.96.5b, etc.).

An interesting *arthavāda,* stated in the *Ait. Br.* in a *yajñagāthā,*[85] speaks of a unique variety of serpents — a fact of observation of the Vedic ritualists. In the Agniṣṭoma sacrifice, the beginning (Prāyaṇīya) and ending (Udayanīya) *iṣṭi*-s (rites) have the same deity *viz.* Aditi and the offering also the same *viz. caru.* Hence a person will not be able to know the difference between the two rites. The *yajñagāthā* enjoined to be recited in this connection by the *Ait. Br.*, states the analogy of the gait of a Śākala type of serpent (III.43 = 14.5). This serpent while crawling takes its tail in its mouth.[86] At that time, it is not possible to know as to which is its mouth and which the tail. Likewise it is not possible to know the difference between the beginning and ending rites.

Porcupine is mentioned for its quill, at few places in the Vedic ritual tradition. A porcupine's quill spotted at three places is regarded as important (and not the porcupine itself, though the quill comes from it). In the Seasonal sacrifices (Cāturmāsya-*iṣṭi*-s), when the sacrificer has his shaving, a three-spotted porcupine's quill is used for that. The quill is important for the three spots. Of the gods, prosperous are the sets of three. There are three (important) metres; three Soma-pressings; (these) three worlds. (By using the three-spotted porcupine's quill) he is established in prosperity and vigour in these worlds (*Tait. Br.* I. 5.6.6). In the context of the Vaiśvadeva *parvan* of the Seasonal sacrifices, the *Śat. Br.* prescribes that in the shaving of the sacrificer, a porcupine's quill spotted at three places and a copper razor be used. Such a quill (of the porcupine) with three spots, resembles the threefold science (the three Veda-s) and the copper razor resembles the Brahman, for the Brahman is fire and fire is of reddish *(lohita)* colour. When with these, the sacrificer's head is shaved around, the Adhvaryu (as though) encompasses him with the Brahman and the threefold science (*Śat. Br.* II. 6.4.5). The same, i.e. the porcupine's quill and the copper razor, are to be used in the Varuṇapraghāsāḥ and the Sākamedha *parvan*-s of the Seasonal sacrifices and the *arthavāda* also is the same as stated above (*ibid.* 6-7).

A reference to hare occurs, when sacrifice is said to be like a hare. If some rite in the sacrifice is left over, a hole (i.e. defect) is caused in the sacrifice. The *Jaim. Br.* while explaining this point says that if one desires to get a hare, which is let loose, one would not get it. If one desires to get a hare which is not let loose (i.e. is steady at one place), one will catch it (*Jaim. Br.* II. 395). Here the *Jaim. Br.* has made a good use of the natural tendency of the hare of speedily running away.

Even a bee (*saraghā)* is pressed into service in an *arthavāda*-account. In the three-day-rite in the Horse-sacrifice, the *arthavāda* occurs that a bee tore out a piece of thigh of the horse (to be sacrificed). This the gods restored by means of the Catuṣṭoma. That is the Catuṣṭoma-day which is for making the horse whole (*Pañc. Br.* XXI. 4.4). In the three-day-rite, the Catuṣṭoma-agniṣṭoma is the first day (*ibid.* XXI. 4.1).

The motif of offering the animals to various gods is clearly mentioned in the context of the Sautrāmaṇī sacrifice. The passages in the *Śat. Br.* are significant in this regard. The grey-coloured he-goat is sacrificed for the Aśvins. The two Aśvins are the eyesight and by offering a victim sacred to the Aśvins, eyesight is bestowed on the sacrificer. Even ear (i.e. hearing ability) is also bestowed on him (*Śat. Br.* XII. 7.2.4). By offering a ram to Sarasvatī, breath (one of the vital powers) is bestowed on the sacrificer (*ibid.* 5). By offering a bull to Indra, speech and strength are bestowed on the sacrificer (*ibid.* 6). When the sacrificer offers he-goats to Aśvins, ewes to Sarasvatī and cows and bulls to Indra, by the propitiation of those deities, he gains those very same animals. This is clearly a 'Give- and-take' dealing between the humans and the gods.

As the hides or skins of the animals stand for the respective animals, so do the hair of the animals. In the Caraka-Sautrāmaṇī sacrifice, the hair of a lion, those of a wolf and those of a tiger are put into the fermented liquor, from which libations are made (*ibid.* V. 5.4. 18-19). In the Sautrāmaṇī sacrifice also, hair of wild beasts are put into the cups of spirituous liquor for the purpose of securing the wild beasts; hair of wolf for obtaining vigour of wild beasts and also the impetuous rush (of them); hair of tiger for having the courage and sway of wild beasts and hair of lion for getting the might and the rule of wild beasts (*ibid.* XII. 7.2.8). The *Śat. Br.* in the context of Sautrāmaṇī states in a mythical account which comes as *arthavāda* that when Indra though not invited consumed Tvaṣṭṛ's Soma, it hurt him and it flowed in all directions from the openings of his vital airs. From his nose sprang a lion; from what flowed from the ears sprang a wolf and from what flowed from the lower opening, wild beasts sprang, tiger being the foremost among them (*ibid.* V. 5.4.8,10).

The Vedic ritual texts give more importance to the domesticated animals that too cattle and goats. Several ritual metaphors occur regarding the cattle, they sometimes standing as standards of comparison (*upamāna)* and at times as compared ones (*upameya).* Thus *'Iḍā'* (offering) is said to be cattle (*ibid.* I.8.1.12, 20); metres are said to be cattle (*ibid.* I.8.2.8); wealth is cattle (*ibid.* III. 3.1.8); Pūṣan (the god) is cattle (*ibid.* III. 9.1.10); food is cattle (*ibid.* IV. 6.9.1); increase of wealth is cattle (*ibid.* IV.6.9.9); sacrifice is indeed cattle (*ibid.* III. 1.4.9), etc. Here the cattle serve as *upamāna.* And in — cattle are food (*ibid.* V. 2.1.16; VI.8.2.7); cattle are the heavenly subjects (*daivīḥ viśaḥ*) for they approach gods (*ibid.* III. 7.3.9); cattle are indeed a home (*ibid.* I.8.2.14); cattle are glory (*ibid.* I.8.1.36), etc. the cattle serve as *upameya.* Both types of passages ably bring out the importance of cattle in the life of the Vedic Indians.

About the sacrificial victims, the *Śat. Br.* says that it is difficult to obtain beasts with the prescribed perfections. In that case, he may slaughter only goats, for they are easier to cook (*Śat. Br.* V. 5.4.1). Is this the reason why goats are often mentioned as sacrificial victims?

Birds are mentioned in the Vedic ritual texts, but the direct references are scanty. The *Tait. Sam.* echoes a belief that if a black bird touches the speckled butter, the sacrificer's slaves would be likely to die (*Tait. Sam.* III. 2.6.2). A Śyena-yāga (sacrifice) is stated in the *Ṣaḍ. Br.* Just as a hawk pounces on its 'food', so does he take possession of his enemy, when he performs the Śyena-sacrifice. A hawk is the swiftest of all birds (*Ṣaḍ. Br.* IV. 2. 1-3). When King Soma (i.e. Soma-stalks) is made to enter the sacrificial pandal, he is asked to fly after becoming a falcon (*Śat. Br.* III.3.4.15). Agni is said to be a bird. If the sacrificer, who has piled the fire (in the Agnicayana rite) were to eat of a bird, he would be eating the fire and would go to ruin. He should observe the vow for a year (*Tait. Sam.* V.7.6.1; also *Śat. Br.* X.1.4.13).

The shape of the Great Fire-altar to be built in the rite of Agnicayana is that of some large bird — probably an eagle or a falcon — flying towards the east, the gate of heaven.[87] While enjoining the piling of altars of different shapes, depending upon the desire of the sacrificer for particular things, the *Tait. Sam.* says that as hawk (*śyena)* is the best flier among birds, when the sacrificer piles the fire-altar in hawk-shape, he becoming a hawk flies to the world of heaven (*Tait. Sam.* V.4.11.1). The *Śat. Br.* clearly states that the sacrificer fashions Agni (Great Fire-altar) into a beautiful-winged bird (*Śat. Br.* IX. 2.3.34 - *suparṇam garutmantam cinoti ...;* also *ibid.* VI. 7.2.5-8). The *Śat. Br.* repeats this idea at other places (*ibid.* IX. 4.4.4,6) and says that according to some, the Great Fire-altar is built in this shape for a specific reason. By such altar, Agni, having become a bird shall bear the sacrificer to the sky (*ibid.* VI. 1.2.36). This shows that the image of a bird is always present before the Vedic ritualists, for no other creature could be thought of as going directly to the heaven. This image of a bird is not lost sight of by the *Pañc. Br.* when it speaks of the third thirty-three day rite. The *arthavāda* points out that these days are winged. Whatever wish the sacrificers desire to see fulfilled, they reach it by these days, for wherever a bird desires to go, it reaches there (*Pañc. Br.* XXIV. 3.3). Sāyaṇa explains that in this *sattra,* the Viśvajit-atirātra (sacrifice) forms the body of the bird. On its two sides, two 'five-days' units (one on each side) are there as the wings. Being associated with the bird, the nights belonging to the *sattra* are *pakṣiṇī*-s (i.e. having wings). Hence the sacrificers obtain whichever desire they cherish, with these wing-like nights, as a bird reaches that spot, where he wants to reach.

A bird, by the word 'Suparṇa' or 'Śyena', is mentioned in the *RV.* The bird 'Suparṇa' is mentioned at many places (*RV* I.35.7; 164.20; II.42.2; IV.26.4; VIII.100.8, etc.) He is said to be the son of the bird *śyena* (*ibid.* X. 144.2) and is distinct from the latter (*ibid.* II. 42.2). The *AV* refers to Suparṇa's speech (*AV* II. 30.3) and he is said to stay on mountains (*ibid.* V. 4.2). The bird *śyena* is mentioned at various places in *RV (RV* I.32. 14; 33.2; 118.11; 163.1; 165.2). It could pounce upon the lambs (*ibid.* IV. 38.5). *AV* says that *śyena* is *nṛcakṣas,* i.e. keeping an eye on men (*AV* VII. 41.2). This shows that it can soar high into the sky. *Śyena* is said to bring Soma from the heaven, when Kṛśānu, the guardian of Soma, shot an arrow at the *śyena* and the feather of the latter fell down (*RV* IV. 27. 3,4). *Śyena* and Suparṇa became a symbol for bringing the drink of immortality. In the *RV* (IV. 26; also Sāyaṇa on *RV.* IV. 26.4), Vāmadeva (or Indra) is said to take the form of *śyena* and bring Soma for Manu. This *śyena* is called Suparṇa (*ibid.* IV. 26.4), In the same hymn (*RV* IV. 26.5 cd, 6 abc and 7). *śyena* is spoken of, who is referred to earlier as Suparṇa. In the later tradition, teeming with rituals, *śyena* receded and only his epithet Suparṇa became a symbol of bringing the elixir of life, i.e. Soma or later nectar. Thus in the *Tait. Sam.* (VI. 1.6.1-4), the metre Gāyatrī, having Suparṇī (i.e. the yonder heaven) as mother (hence all metres together with Gāyatrī are called 'Sauparṇeya' and in the *Kāṭh. Sam.* XXXIII. 10 and the *Mait. Sam.* III.7.8, called 'Sauparṇa') flew forth and brought Soma.[88] In the *Mbh.* Garuḍa brings nectar from the heaven to release his mother Vinatā from the slavery of her co-wife Kadrū (*Mbh.* Ādi chap. 33; for the whole legend *ibid.* Ādi, chaps. 16-34). Garuḍa is named Suparṇa 'of beautiful wings' (*ibid.* Ādi 33. 22-24). Such a bird is noted in the Middle-Eastern mythology.[89]

The Vedic ritual-texts have mainly sacrificial animals in their view. With the firm belief that animals belong to Agni, they are offered to him. A mythical account of the *Śat. Br.* states that once Agni went away from the gods and they searched for him by different kinds of cattle, with the thought that as Agni himself is (cattle or) an animal, he will become manifest with his own form (*Śat. Br.* VI. 3.1.22). The *Tait. Sam.* says that Agni is an animal (V.7.6.1), and so says the *Śat. Br.* (VI. 3. 1.22); VIII. 1.4.7). The gods deposit all their beasts, both domestic and wild, with Agni (*Śat. Br.* II.3.4.1, 2). The *Ait. Br.* states that the sacrificial victim was not willing to go to gods, as it saw death before it. It asked somebody to go before it. Agni went before. Therefore it is said that every animal is connected with Agni, for it follows Agni and submits to it (*Ait. Br.* II. 6 = 6.6).

A mythical account coming as *arthavāda* in connection with the sacrificial victims, is important, as it tried to give a reasonable explanation (in its own way!) of the practice of not offering certain parts (especially head, and the neck) of the victim, to the god. It occurs in the context of Agniṣṭoma (Soma-sacrifice, in which animal-offering figures). It is said that when the gods, at first, seized an animal for offering it in the sacrifice, Tvaṣṭṛ first spat upon its head, with the thought that the gods (taking the animal to be dirty or impure) would not touch it, for animals belonged to Tvaṣṭṛ. That spittle of Tvaṣṭṛ became the brain in the head and the marrow in the neck bone of the victim. One must not eat that part of the animal, as it was spitten by Tvaṣṭṛ (*Śat. Br.* III. 8.3.11). The *Śat. Br.* further says that as the *asura*-s made portions of the head, the shoulders, the neck and the hind-thighs of the animal for being offered, one must not do so (*ibid.* III. 8.3. 29). The question is — where was the head laid or placed? The practice seems to be to bury the parts of the beast (including the head) not used as offerings, at the Śāmitra-enclosure.[90] But of these parts (head, neck, shoulders and the hind-thighs) of the victim, head is thought to be important, for even in actual life, head stands for the individual (either human being or animal), as it contains power possessed by that individual. In common language the head is called *'uttamāṅga'* ('the best part of the body) and by it only the individual can be recognised. The severed head of the sacrificial beast, not offered (being buried) and thus lost (!) gave rise to the myth of the sacrifice itself losing its head, for the sacrificer, sacrificial beast and the sacrifice are all at many places equated. Though the Vedic ritual texts are cautiously silent about this 'severed' head of the sacrificial beast, they often display an anxiety to replace the head of the sacrifice by laying down the Pravargya rite and the Divākīrtyaḥ verses. The Divākīrtyaḥ verses *(RV* X. 170. 1-3), eulogise the sun, which is contemplated as the head of the sacrifice, due to its circular shape and lustre.[91] The simple *arthavāda*-passage in the *Śat. Br.* (III. 8.3.11) regarding Tvaṣṭṛ breathes an ancient practice of severing the head of the victim, not offering it in the sacrifice and placing it far away deep in the bosom of the earth.

NOTES AND REFERENCES

1. *Kāty. S.S.* I.2.2 — *dravyam devatā tyāgaḥ* and Devayājñikapaddhati on this — *devatoddeśena dravyatyāgo yāgaḥ.*
2. *Śat. Br.* I.2.3.5 — *paśurha vā eṣa ālabhyate yat puroḍāśaḥ;* also *ibid.* I.2.3.8 — *pāṅktaḥ paśuriti.*
3. See Heesterman, J.C., "The Case of the Severed Head", *Wiener Zs für die Kunde S. - und O.* — Asiens 11 (1967), pp. 22-43 (esp. 38-41).
4. The verb *'ā labheta'* means 'should seize' or 'should take hold of'; but as this seizing is for offering or sacrificing, it is translated henceforth as 'should offer'.
5. *Tait. Sam.* II. 1.2.6-9 — The purposes for offering to Agni and Soma are; to have one's long illness cured; to win fame if one does not get it, in spite of one's study; to score victory, when there is a dispute for getting the position of a priest (*purodhāyām spardhāyām).*
6. Keith, A.B., *The Veda of the Black Yajus School entitled Taittiriya Sanhita,* pt. 1, HOS Vol. 18, p. 136, translating the word *'babhṛ'* as 'brown', *Tait. Sam.* II. 1.3.3.4; Eggeling, J., *The Śatapatha Brāhmaṇa,* pt. II, SBE Vol. 26, p. 62, takes the word *'babhṛ'* as 'brown', *Śat. Br.* III. 3.1.14; Macdonell, A.A., *A Vedic Reader for Students,* Oxford Univ. Press, Madras, 14th Impression, 1988 (1917), p. 60, *'babhṛ'* as 'ruddy brown'; Sir Monier Monier-Williams, *Sanskrit-English Dictionary, 'babhṛ'* meaning 'deep brown, reddish brown, tawny'.
7. *RV* I. 162.3 ab, 4 cd. Sāyaṇa takes *pūṣṇaḥ* as *poṣakasya agneḥ,* probably having the later tradition in view. Also *ibid.* I. 163.12.
8. See Kane, P.V., *Hist. of Dh. S.,* Vol. II, pt. II, p. 991; also *Śat. Br.* II. 1.4.3 for this practice.

9. Also see *Tait. Sam.* V. 4.3.2. Milk of a she-goat is offered in the rite of Agnicayana, for the she-goat is connected with Agni. In the Pravargya rite, he takes she-goat's milk, for the goat was produced from the heat, when the sacrifice had its head cut off, for this *Śat. Br.* XIV. 1.2.13. The she-goat is Prajāpati's bodily form of heat (*tapas);* she brings forth three times in a year, hence most excellent of the animals (*ibid.* III. 3. 3.8).
10. *Agni P.* 156.10b — *śuddham aśvājayor mukham;* also *Sk. P.* IV. 40.46 ab - *aśvājayor mukham medhyam.*
11. Agrawal, R.C., "Agni in Early Indian Art", *Journal of Indian History*, Vol. XLIII, pt. I, Apr. 1965, p. 151 ff., fig. on p. 153.
12. *RV* refers to bringing a she-goat (*ajā*) by her ears for suckling the lamb (*RV* VIII. 17.15).
13. See (Mrs.) Dange, S.S., "Animal-Hides", *Hindu Domestic Rituals — A Critical Glance*, pp. 82-87.
14. *RV* X. 27.17a - *pīvānam meṣam-apacanta vīrāḥ.* Sāyaṇa understands by the word *vīrāḥ* Aṅgiras-es, the sons of Prajāpati.
15. Cf. *Rām.*, Ayodhyā 56.19-30. While in exile, Lakṣmaṇa for pacifying the place of residence (*vāstuśamana),* made of leaves, kills a black deer (*aiṇa* or *kṛṣṇamṛga)* on the word of Rāma and throws that whole deer into the fire. The parts of that cooked (i.e. roasted) deer are offered by Rāma to the gods. The fact to be noted is that such a ritual of roasting the whole sacrificial victim (animal) is not referred to or mentioned in any ritual in later times, though the *Mbh.* states it at a couple of places, at one place, as aetiological explanation (*Mbh.*, Śānti, chap. 272 - the sage Satya throwing the whole deer in the sacrificial fire; the account preaching that sacrifice in the real sense does not plead such an injury to animal) and at another place, as a magic-rite (*abhicāra-karma).* This magic-rite is performed by Agastya by offering the omentum of a deer (*ibid.* Ādi. 109.14-15), obviously on the lines of the Vedic sacrificial rite. Also cf. *Old Testament*, "Numbers", chap. 19.1-10. A red cow after being killed with its blood sprinkled at the four quarters of the tent, is burnt in fire by (the priest) Eleazar, for her ashes to be dissolved in water to make it purificatory for being used at rituals. Here again there is a reference to burn the whole animal.

16. See Macdonell, A.A., *Vedic Mythology,* pp. 148-50.
17. For Tārkṣya, *RV* I.89.6; X. 178.1; also *Vedic Mythology,* p. 284.
18. *Ibid.,* p. 285.
19. See Eggeling, J., *op. cit.,* pt. II, SBE Vol. 26, p. 114, note 3.
20. This white horse has, as it were, a scorched mouth (according to Sāyaṇa a reddish mouth). The mythical account relates that when Agni went away from gods and entered the water, Prajāpati becoming a horse went in search of him. When Prajāpati found Agni on a lotus-leaf and eyed him, Agni scorched his mouth. *Śat. Br.* VII. 3.2.14.
21. Here in the case of the white beast, the black colour of the neck signifies smoke and thereby the beast gets related to Agni, who is exclusively given the epithet '*dhūmaketu*' ('having smoke as his banner') in the *RV*. See Macdonell, A.A., *op. cit.,* p. 90.
22. Hastings, J. (Ed.), *Ency. of Rel. and Eth.,* Vol. I, p. 485 a.
23. *Ibid.,* p. 485 b.
24. The principle of Agni (Fire) is believed to be manifest in three different forms at three levels *viz.* Sūrya (sun) in the highest heaven; Vāyu or Indra (indicating the lightning fire) in the mid-region; and Agni (terrestrial fire; also sacrificial fire) on the terrestrial level, cf. *RV* X 158.1; also *Nir.* VII. 5. In the context of sacrifice, the lightning-fire has significance, for the sacrificial sticks to be used, have to be from such a tree which has been struck with lightning (*Tait. Br.* I. 1.3.12). And the sun and (Agni-) Prajāpati (the sacrificial fire imagined as a deity) are regarded as the two forms of Agni.
25. *Tait. Br.* III. 9.8.2 (in the context of Horse-sacrifice) *prājāpatyo vā aśvaḥ;* also *ibid.* II. 7.2.3; *Jaim. Br.* II. 129 - *prajāpater vā etad rūpam yadaśvaḥ; Śat. Br.* VI. 3.3.22 - *agnireṣa yadaśvaḥ; ibid.* VI. 3.1.29 - Horse is the yonder sun; *ibid.* VII. 3.2.18.
26. *Tait. Sam.* V. 3.12.1,2 (in the context of Horse-sacrifice), they cut from the horse on the left side, for it was the left eye of Prajāpati that swelled. Also *Jaim. Br.* II. 68.
27. Cf. *Tait. Sam.* III.2.6.3. The horse is made to sniff the speckled butter used in the Soma-sacrifice and the horse is connected with Prajāpati.
28. *Śat. Br.* V. 3.1.5 — In the context of the Rājasūya sacrifice, while honouring the *sūta* (one of the *'ratnin-*s' - jewels, i.e. chiefs in the town, who are to be honoured by offering *'ratninām havīṁṣī'*), a barley pap is offered to Varuṇa and

the sacrificial gift is a horse, as horse belongs to Varuṇa.

Tait. Br. III. 9.16.1 — In the context of the Horse-sacrifice, while laying down the special offerings at the Avabhṛtha (final bath) ritual, it is said that the horse belongs to Varuṇa, but the same is made to belong to Prajāpati (in the Horse-sacrifice) through Varuṇa. Also see Eggeling, J., *op. cit.,* pt. V, SBE Vol. 44, Intrn. pp. xix-xx.

29. See Dange, Sadashiv A., "The Riddle of the Black Antelope", *Images from Vedic Hymns and Rituals,* pp. 276-83.
30. *RV.* V. 78.2 — The two Aśvins are invoked to come speedily to the Soma (-juice, prepared for them), as two deer rush to the grass.
31. Also *Tait. Sam.* VI. 1.3.7—Indra wrapping the womb in his hand, depositing it among wild beasts, it becoming the horn of a black antelope; *ibid.* 8—the sacrificer casting away the horn of the black antelope in the pit, the latter being the sacrificer's womb and the sacrificer thus throwing womb in womb.
32. *Śat. Br.* I.1.4.2 in the context of the New-moon and Full-moon sacrifices; also *ibid.* VI. 7.1.6,7; XIV. 1.2.2.

    Jaim. Br. states that the black antelope hide is the form of all Vedas, the white hair on it standing as the form of the *sāman*-s, the black ones as that of the *ṛc*-s and the brown-yellow as that of the *yajus*-es (II. 66).
33. *Tait. Sam.* V.1.4.2; V.1.6.3; *Śat. Br.* VI. 7.1.6; IX.3.4.10; XII.8.3.3; XIV.1.2.1, 2, etc.
34. See Upadhyaya, S.A., "Kārīriṣṭi - A Sacrifice to be performed for securing Rain", *H.D. Velankar Comm. Vol.,* pub. by Prof. H.D. Velankar Comm. Vol. Committee, Bombay, 1965, pp. 161-75.
35. See Keith, A.B., *The Veda of the Black Yajus School entitled Taittiriya Sanhita,* p. 180, note 3, where he points out (*Tait. Sam.* II. 4.7) that Kārīriṣṭi is a rain spell. Interestingly, as he points out, the Karīra groats are deposited on the black antelope skin and the ends of the skin are tied together. Also see *ibid.* p. 181, note 3 for further use of the black antelope skin brought for this sacrifice.
36. For the account of Ṛṣyaśṛṅga, see *Mbh.* Vana, chap. 113; also *Bhāg. P.* IX. 23. 8 ff.
37. See Dange, Sadashiv A., "The Riddle of the Black Antelope", *Images from Vedic Hymns and Rituals,* p. 278 f.

38. For black colour, *Ency, of Rel. and Eth.*, Vol. I, p. 485b.
39. See Dange, Sadashiv A., *Divine Hymns and Ancient Thought*, Vol. II (Ritual and the Quest for Truth), Navrang, New Delhi, 1995, p. 207.
40. *Mait. Sam.* II.6.3 - In the Rājasūya sacrifice, while giving offering to the goddess Nirṛti, the *dakṣiṇā* to be given is a black garment torn at the end.
41. Kane, P.V., *op. cit.*, Vol. II, pt. I, Poona, 1974, p. 372.
42. *RV* III. 53.18 ab—Indra invoked to give strength to the bulls; *ibid.* X. 59.10 a—Indra invoked to impel cow and bull; *ibid.* X.85. 10 cd—reference to two lustrous bulls in the context of Sūryā going to the house of her husband.
43. *Ibid.* II.35.13 ab - in the case of Apām Napāt and *ibid.* VII. 95.3 ab - in the case of Sarasvat.
44. *Ait. Br.* VII. 13 = 33.1
    patir jāyām praviśati garbho bhūtvā sa mātaram/
    tasyām punarnavo bhūtvā daśame māsi jāyate //
    Also Manu S. IX.8.
45. Ghurye, G.S., *Vedic India*, Bombay, 1979, pp. 23-63.
46. See (Mrs.) Dange, S.S., "Animal-Hides", *Hindu Domestic Rituals - A Critical Glance,* p. 82 f.
47. *Tait. Br.* II.7.2.2 and Sāyaṇa explaining the Vaiśyasava 'ritual for *vaiśya'*, quoting from one Sūtra.
48. *Nir.* II.1.
49. Macdonell, A.A., *Vedic Mythology,* p. 151.
50. *Brahma P.*, chap. 74; *Śiva P.*, Rudrasaṁhitā 4, chaps. 24 & 25. The cow in Gautama's hermitage, struck with a stick by Gautama, died but was revived with the waters of Gaṅgā brought down by Gautama. The same cow turned into a river, to be named Godāvarī afterwards.

    A folk-tale prevalent in the Andhra province relates that once a calf was carried away by a hawk (*garutmantaḍu*). The cow chased the shadow of the calf. As she could not control the milk oozing out from her udder due to affection for the calf, from the stream of milk, sprang the river Godāvarī. See John Cain, "Native Custom of Godavari," *Indian Antiquary*, Vol. 4, 1875, p. 198.
51. *RV* VI.16.47d — Sāy. - *vaśābhiḥ vandhyābhir gobhiḥ; ibid.* X. 91.14b—Sāy. - *vaśāḥ svabhāvavandhyāḥ.*
52. *Śat. Br.* XIII. 6.2.16 - eleven barren cows (*vaśā*-s) offered to Mitrāvaruṇā, Viśve Devāḥ and Bṛhaspati; *ibid.* XIII. 5.4.25—

twenty-one *vaśā*-s are offered, sacred to the deities mentioned in the context of the Puruṣamedha; *ibid.* III.2.2.9, cow as one of the *'paryaṅgya'* animals (animals encircling the horse) is a sacrificial victim for Indra; *RV* X. 111.2b—Indra's epithet *gārṣṭeya,* as he was the son of *gṛṣṭi* (*ibid.* IV. 18.10b), *gṛṣṭi* being a cow, giving birth to only one calf (Sāy. on *RV* X. 111. 2b); *Śat. Br.* II. 4.4.14; IV. 5.1.5 - a barren cow called Anūbandhyā, enjoined to be offered to Mitra and Varuṇa in the Soma-sacrifice; *ibid.* IV. 5.1.10,11 — a (barren) cow to All-Gods and also such one to Bṛhaspati; *ibid.* V. 1.3.3 - a spotted sterile cow to the Maruts in the Vājapeya sacrifice.

53. *Śrautakośa,* ed. by Dandekar, R.N. and Kashikar, C.G., Eng. Tr., Vol. I-ii, Poona, 1958, p. 1067.
54. *Ibid.,* pp. 1053, 1071.
55. Ram Gopal, *India of Vedic Kalpasutras,* Delhi, 1959, pp. 360-61.
56. (Mrs.) Dange, S.S., "The Garment of the Bride", *Hindu Domestic Rituals - A Critical Glance,* pp. 10-14.
57. See Eggeling, J., *op. cit.,* pt. II, SBE Vol. 26, p. 62, note 2 (on *Śat. Br.* III. 3.1.14). He says that the red cows are compared to the red clouds, which appear after the thunderstorm (after king Indra's battle with Vṛtra).
58. *Śat. Br.* III.2.4.10,15; also *ibid.* III.3.1.16. Such a cow is without any bodily defect, is uniform (*ekarūpā),* for Speech is uniform and perfect.
59. *RV* I, 164.41a - *gaurīr mimāya salilāni takṣatī* and Sāyaṇa—*gaurī garaṇaśīlā mādhyamikā vāk.*
60. There is a mention of the donation of a cow at the time of death to cross the terrible river Vaitaraṇī, by holding the tail of that cow, vide Kane, P.V., *op. cit.,* Vol. IV, 2nd ed., Poona, 1973, p. 183, note 427.

    In normal circumstances (not at the time of death as mentioned above), the donor of an 'Ubhayatomukhī' cow is said to obtain the heavenly world (after death). This cow is said to have two faces — one its own and the other of the calf, while the cow delivers it, cf. *Yāj. S.* I. 206, 207.
61. *RV* X. 94.9b. Sāyaṇa takes the word *gavi* to mean *adhiṣavaṇacarmaṇi.* Yāska also has given the same meaning. *Nir.* II. 2.
62. *Śaṅkh. Ś.S.* XVII. 5; also Ram Gopal, *op. cit.,* p. 170.

63. Kane, P.V., *op. cit.,* Vol. II, pt. II, p. 1244.
64. Macdonell, A.A., *op. cit.,* p. 151.
65. Kane, P.V., *op. cit.,* Vol. II, pt. II, p. 1230.
66. Dange, Sadashiv A., *Sexual Symbolism from the Vedic Ritual,* Ajanta Pubns., Delhi, 1979, pp. 161-76.
67. Agni is invoked to move like a king on elephant. See *RV.* IV.4.1 ab - *yāhi rājevāmavān ibhena.* Sāyaṇa takes *ibha* to mean an 'elephant'. Also *Nir.* IV. 16; also Geldner, vide Geldner, K.F., *Der Rigveda,* I, HOS Vol. 33, 2nd Reprint. Cambridge, 1978, p. 422— on *RV* IV.4.1ab - "König auf dem Elefantan".

    For *RV* I.65.7 — 'Agni is said to burn the forests as a king, the '*ibhya*-s'. Here Ṣāyaṇa takes the word *ibhyān* as *śatrūn* ('enemies'). However, on the basis of the above discussion, we can take it as meaning, 'enemies seated on the elephants.'

    About the word *vāraṇa* — According to Macdonell and Keith, *vāraṇa* means an elephant, while Roth takes it to mean 'a wild animal', The word *vāraṇī* signifies 'a female elephant'. See Macdonell, A.A. and Keith, A.B., *Vedic Index of Names and Subjects* (Hindi tr.), Varanasi, 1962, under the title "*Vāraṇa*", also "*Hastin*".
68. For *gardabha* (a domesticated variety), *RV* I.29.5 and also Sāyaṇa on it—Indra invoked to kill a donkey, i.e. donkey-like enemy, who slanders openly; *ibid.* III. 53.23 — Viśvāmitra pointing out that Vasiṣṭha cannot compete with him, for people never carry a donkey in front of a horse. For *rāsabha, ibid.* I.34.9 cd; VIII. 85.7 *rāsabha*-s are yoked to the chariot of the Aśvins. Though of the same species, *rāsabha* is a bigger animal—a semi-domesticated variety.
69. *Manu S.* XI. 118, 122. Kane, P.V., *op. cit.,* Vol. II, pt. I, p. 374.
70. Eggeling, J., *op. cit.,* pt. I, SBE Vol. 12, p. 51, note 3.
71. See Dange, Sadashiv A., "A Virility-Charm (Ṛgveda X. 86)", *Vedic Concept of "Field" and the Divine Fructification,* Bombay Uni. Pubn., Bombay, 1971, pp. 49-67.
72. *RV.* I.174.3 - Indra like a lion; *ibid.* I.95.5; V. 15. 3d — Agni compared to a lion; *ibid.* V. 83.3 - The thunders of the god Parjanya are said to be the roars of a lion. *AV* V. 20.2a — a drum sounding like a lion.
73. (Mrs.) Dange, S.S., *The Bhāgavata Purāṇa - Mytho-Social Study,* pp. 243-44.
74. Macdonell, A.A. and Keith, A.B., *op. cit.,* under "*Vyāghra*".

75. For information about the baser metal (either lead or copper) used in this rite, from different Vedic texts, see Dange, Sadashiv A., *Vedic Sacrifices — Early Nature,* Vol. II, pp. 330-31.
76. For the variant use of the *mantra, ibid.* p. 332.
77. Vide Kane, P.V., *op. cit.,* Vol. II, pt. II, p. 1234, where he refers to *Kāty. Ś.S.,* XX. 6.9; *Āp. Ś.S.* XX. 17.5.
78. *Ibid.*
79. For *gomṛga,* see Eggeling, J., *op. cit.,* pt. V, SBE Vol. 44, pp. 338-39, note 1.
80. Hyatt, H.M., *Folk-lore of Adams County Illinois,* New York, 1935. See (Mrs.) Dange, S.S., *Bhāgavata Purāṇa—Mytho-Social Study,* pp. 240-41.
81. *Śat. Br.,* VI. 1.2.12-18.
82. *Ibid.,* VI.1.1.1-5.
83. See Mitra, Sharad Chandra, "Frog in the North-Indian Rain-controlling Rites", *Folk-lore and Traditions in India,* Vol. XIV, p. 429 ff.; Waddel, L.A., "Frog-worship in Nepal", *Indian Antiquary,* XXII, p. 293; Bloomfield, M., "The Frog-hymn" *JAOS,* Vol. 17, p. 173 f; Norman Brown, "Some Notes on the Rain Charms", *New Indian Antiquary,* Vol. II-2, May, 1921.
84. See for details (Mrs.) Dange, S.S., "Some Non-Vedic Rituals in the Vedic Tradition", *Proceedings* of the All India Oriental Conference, XXXII Session (Ahmedabad, 1985), p. 166 f; for the Gṛhya ritual of Sarpabali, see (Mrs.) Dange, S.S., "Sarpa-bali", *Hindu Domestic Rituals—A Critical Glance,* pp. 88-94.
85. *Yajñagāthā*-s are formed on the basis of the popular *gāthā*-s, which had a secular origin. They are stated to be recited in the sacrificial context and are termed *yajñagāthā*-s, for they extol some sacrificial ritual or practice. Sāyaṇa explains the term as "*yajñagāthā* is the one which is sung by all the ritualists having in view a sacrifice." (Sāy. on *Ait. Br.* III. 43 = 14.5; V. 31 = 25.6; VII. 9 = 32.8; VIII. 21 = 39.7). For details, see (Mrs.) Dange, S.S., *Aspects of Speech in Vedic Ritual,* pp. 209-12.
86. That such a variety of serpents is still existent is verified from the account narrated by (late) Dr. S.B. Deo, Professor of Archaeology and Ex-Director, Deccan College Post-graduate and Research Institute, Poona, whose team while engaged in excavations saw such a serpent. The serpent

greatly disturbed by their digging, taking its tail in its mouth, forming itself into the shape of a tyre chased their car for a long distance. On this background, Keith's comment that 'Sāyaṇa's explanation of Śākala being a kind of serpent is absurd', is not correct. See Keith, A.B., *Rigveda Brahmanas* (tr.), HOS Vol. 25, 2nd Reprint, Motilal Banarsidass, Delhi, 1981 (London 1920), p. 192, note 1.

87. Eggeling, J., *op. cit.*, pt. IV, SBE Vol. 43, Intrn., p. xxi; also see *Śat. Br.* X.2.1.1, where this shape of the Fire-altar is explained convincingly through an *arthavāda*.
88. For this myth of bringing Soma by Gayatrī, also see *Ait. Br.* III. 25-28 = 13.1-4; *Pañc. Br.* VIII. 4.1; *Śat. Br.* IV. 3.2.7-9.
89. In the Middle-Eastern mythology, in the myth of Gilgamesh, the Zu bird brings the tablets of destiny.
90. The procedure followed in the times of the ritual-texts was of killing the victim by keeping its mouth and nostrils closed. This was the duty of the Śamitṛ, who used to make the victim quiet (fr. √*śam* - causal - 'to make quiet or peaceful'). The place reserved for the Śamitṛ for his work might be a bit away from the actual sacrificial place.
91. For a detailed discussion, see (Mrs.) Dange, S.S., "The Severed Head in Myth and Ritual", *Annals* of the Bhandarkar Oriental Research Institute, Pune, Vols. LXXII and LXXIII (for the years 1991 and 1992), pub. in 1993, Amṛtamahotsava (1917-1992) Vol., pp. 487-96.

CHAPTER 8

Complementary Numbers

Sacrifice being the pivot of the Vedic ritual texts, they have evolved their own methods of complementing the sacrifice. One of them is resorting to a particular 'number'. This is prominently seen in the permutation and combination of metres, depending upon the number of syllables in each foot (line) of a metre or in all feet (lines) of that metre, which is under consideration. Such combinations are mentioned by the expressions *viz. sampad, sampadyate, abhisampadyate,* etc. which indicate a certain result to be achieved (from *sam* + √*pad* or *abhi* + *sam* + √*pad).* And this result is the full or perfect form of the sacrifice in hand.[1]

We, take here a couple of examples of such '*sampad-s*'. While going to fetch the Ekadhanā waters, for pressing the Soma-shoots, twenty verses of the Aponaptrīya hymn (praising the god Apam Napāt) are to be recited. He recites the first verse thrice and the last one thrice. They make up twenty-four, for though originally it is 1 + 18 + 1 = 20, after being rearranged, it is 3 + 18 + 3 = 24. These twenty-four verses are said to accomplish the Gāyatrī-*sampad* (*Kauṣ. Br.* XII.3), for a verse in the Gāyatrī metre has total twenty-four syllables (eight in each of its three feet). The *sampad* noted above indicates that even when the Gāyatrī metre was associated with the morning-pressing (normally), there was another tradition of reciting verses in some other metres in the morning-pressing. Hence the effort to have the *sampad* of the Gāyatrī. *Sampad*-s on similar lines are stated by the *Kauṣ. Br.* (XIX. 4) and the *Tait. Br.* (I. 1.5.3). Such *sampad*-s for getting the Gāyatrī metre are for obtaining Agni—the very sacrifice—for the Gāyatrī is said to be the favourite metre of Agni.

A *sampad* of Anuṣṭubh metre occurs in the context of the Agnicayana rite. A seven-versed hymn, i.e. seven *mantra*-s, from the *Vāj Sam.* (XVIII. 68-74), is to be recited. The mythical account states that Indra saw the seven-versed hymn suitable for making good what was deficient, for reducing what was redundant and for making perfect what was imperfect. Now these verses become equal to the Anuṣṭubh, for the Anuṣṭubh is Speech and it is by speech that he secures for Agni all that which is as yet not secured for him (*Śat. Br.* IX. 5.2.1, 8). The seven verses are as follows—two Gāyatrī-s (24 x 2 = 48 syllables), four Triṣṭubh-s (44 x 4 = 176 syllables, for a verse in Triṣṭubh metre has eleven syllables in one foot and has four feet, thus having 44 syllables), and one Anuṣṭubh (32 syllables, for a verse in Anuṣṭubh metre has four feet, each foot having eight syllables). These come to 256 syllables (48 + 176 + 32 = 256), which would make eight Anuṣṭubh-s (of the seven verses). So this *sampad* is for getting Speech, which secures everything not yet obtained for Agni.

While enjoining an interesting *sampad* of the Anuṣṭubh metre on the tenth day of the Daśarātra (ten-day) sacrifice, the *Kauṣ. Br.* states that he should recite there the Virāj verses. According to the *Kauṣ. Br.* the Virāj and the Anuṣṭubh are the same (though the three-footed i.e. Tripadā, Virāj has thirty-three syllables, each of its feet having eleven syllables, while the Anuṣṭubh has thirty-two syllables), for nor by one syllable is a metre made different nor yet by two (*Kauṣ. Br.* XXVII.1).

Thus the *sampad*-s are not mere arithmetical calculations but are laid down for getting a positive result. However the 'number' of syllables in a metre was of great importance, as we have seen in the *sampad*-s, discussed above.

Apart from the context of metres, the concept of 'number' plays an important role in the sacrificial details and accessories. The belief in and practice of using a particular number of entities or things in a ritual are based on the principle of magic *viz.* 'Like produces like'. Some ritual details having in view 'number' will elucidate this point.

To turn to the number 'Two' —

In the context of the Pravargya ceremony, it is said that the vessels to be used are in pairs (i.e. two every time). The *arthavāda* explains that a pair means strength, for when two units take hold of each other, they put forth strength. Again coming together of two units forms a pair, which is a productive union. With such a productive union he completes the sacrifice (*Śat. Br.* XIV. 1.3.1).[2] Performing something twice is doubly productive. In the Soma-sacrifice (Abhiplava Ṣaḍaha), twice they have the Jyotis (*stoma),* by which they obtain a double portion of proper food, wild animals and domesticated animals. By the Go (*stoma*) twice, they get a double portion of proper food, plants and trees. By the Āyus (*stoma)* twice, they obtain a double portion of proper food, that which goes in the waters and that which swims (*Kauṣ. Br.* XX. 1).

To come to number 'Three' —

In the context of the Vaiśvadeva offerings in the Four-monthly sacrifices (*iṣṭi*-s*),* the *Śat. Br.* enjoins the tying up of *barhis* (sacrificial grass) in three bunches and then again in one bunch. The *Śat. Br.* states in the *arthavāda* that father and mother form a productive pair and what is born, i.e. an issue, forms a third element. Such is the characteristic form of generation (*prajananam)* and, that which is threefold again is reckoned as one (*Śat. Br.* II.5.1.18). In the rite of consecration of the sacrificer, he has to have a girdle - a triple cord made of *śaṇa* grass. It is said that food is three-fold; father, mother and the issue born make three. Hence is the cord threefold (*ibid.* III. 2.1.12). In the context of Odanasava,[3] it is said that he purifies the sacrificer with three bunches of the *darbha*-grass. Here number three stands for three worlds, with which he purifies the sacrificer (*Tait. Br.* II.7.9.4,5). The same *arthavāda* of taking the number three for the three worlds occurs in the context of the Horse-sacrifice, while laying down three times circumambulation of the dead horse (*ibid.* III.9.6.2). The deities in honour of which the morning litany (Prātaranuvāka) is recited are three *viz.* Agni, Uṣas and Aśvins. These three deities signify here the threefold worlds, which the priests serve to conquer (*Ait. Br.* II.17 = 7.7). In the context of the New-moon and Full-moon sacrifices, it is enjoined while reciting the Sāmidhenī verses, that he should recite the first verse and the last one thrice without drawing breath. The *arthavāda* points out that there are three worlds, which he gains. There are three breaths is a man. The recitation without drawing breath causes him to be extended, not cut short by death (*Śat. Br.* I.3.5.13).

It is interesting to see that number three, multiplied by two and multiplied by four, can give the numbers six and twelve respectively; the latter two numbers (i.e. 6 & 12) again are connected to the concept of six seasons and twelve months (the twelve months making a year) respectively. We have referred to circumambulating thrice the dead horse. That is from right to left (in the regular manner). The *Tait. Br.* lays down again, the thrice circumambulation but that is from left to right (in the opposite manner). With the first circumambulation for three times, he shakes (i.e. as though makes it get up) the dead horse from the three worlds, and with the second circumambulation (again for three times), taken with the first one (three times), which make six and six being the seasons, he shakes (i.e. as though makes it walk) the horse with the seasons (*Tait. Br.* III. 9.6.2). From the number three, the *Tait. Sam.* arrives at number twelve as follows. He cleanses (*sam-mārṣṭi*) the enclosing-sticks (*paridhīn*). He cleanses the middle one *thrice.* The breaths are three, which he conquers thereby. He cleanses the southern enclosing-stick *thrice.* The worlds are three, which he conquers. He cleanses the northern enclosing-stick *thrice.* There are three paths leading to gods, which he thereby conquers. He fans the fire (in order to make it ablaze) *thrice.* The worlds of gods are three, which he conquers. These four triads (of each action undertaken *thrice)* make for number twelve. The year has twelve months. He brings the year for him to gain the world of heaven (*Tait. Sam.* II.5.11.5,6).

To come to number 'Four' —

In the context of the Brahmaudana (rice prepared in a special way), it is said that the waters to be used for cooking are *catuṣṭayī* (fourfold), for they are brought from four quarters. The *arthavāda* states that these are called so, because the horse in the Horse-sacrifice, belonging to Prajāpati, has four hooves (*Tait. Br.* III.8.2.1). In the context of the Vājapeya sacrifice, it is enjoined that a *rājanya (kṣatriya)* shoots seventeen arrows' ranges northwards from the edge of the altar. Apart from equating the number seventeen with Prajāpati, who is said to be seventeenfold, the *arthavāda* ventures for some other uncommon explanations. A *rājanya (kṣatriya*—here a king) can be related to Prajāpati (i.e. lord of creatures), for both though 'one' (without anybody's help) rule over many. The other explanation is more important from our point of view, as it is based on number four. The word *prajāpati* (*pra-jā-pa-ti)* has four syllables and the word *rājanya* (*rā-ja-ni-a)*[4] has also the same number of syllables. So the *rājanya* shoots the arrow (*Śat. Br.* V.1.5.14).

To turn to number 'Five' —

In the rite of buying Soma from the Soma-seller, it is said that the priest should bargain five times. The *arthavāda* stated here puts forth a logical reason. It says that the sacrifice is of equal measure with the year, which has five seasons (when the two seasons of the 'winter' are taken together). When he bargains for Soma five times, he obtains

Soma, i.e. sacrifice in five divisions (*ibid.* III. 3.3.5). The equation could be as follows - Soma five times = Year (with five seasons = Sacrifice.

In the rite of Agnicayana, in the making of fire-pan (for placing Agni in it), while kneading the clay, he uses three *mantra*-s, for Agni is threefold. When he mixes two verses with these, that makes five. The *arthavāda* explains the efficacy of the number five that the Great Fire-altar to be built would consist of five layers. There are five seasons in a year and Year is Agni (*ibid.* VI. 5.1.12).

In the context of the Agniṣṭoma sacrifice, it is enjoined that he should press Soma (i.e. Soma-shoots), at each turn, five times, if he is desirous of cattle. The *arthavāda* states that he thereby acquires cattle, for the cattle (sacrificial animals) consist of five parts.[5] The *arthavāda* runs further on the same lines, as in the examples noted above, pointing out to the five seasons in a Year, equating Prajāpati with Year and Sacrifice with Prajāpati. Thus by pressing the Soma-shoots five times, i.e. with the number five, he establishes the sacrifice with its great measure (*ibid.* IV. 1.1.16). To simplify —

Five times pressing Soma-shoots → sacrificial animal having five parts→Year with five seasons = Prajāpati = Sacrifice.

In the rite of Pravargya, the five equipments required for making the Pravargya (i.e. Mahāvīra) pots are five *viz.* lump of clay, inner lump of an ant-hill (*valmīka-vapā* according to the commentary on *Kāt. Ś.S.* XXVI 1.2 is the *'vapā'* - omentum - like inner lump of an ant-hill), earth torn up by a boar, Ādāra-plant and goat's milk. The *arthavāda* having the number five reaches up to the concept of the Year as seen above, but takes Year to be the Sun, which shines above. Moreover the Pravargya ceremony is the Sun, which the sacrificer gratifies thereby (*Śat. Br.* XIV. 1.2.14).

In the Soma–sacrifice, in the Anūbandhyā rite,[6] as a concluding part a cake is offered on five potsherds. The *Kauṣ.*

Br. in its *arthavāda* dwells on number five taking it to the five *pāda*-s (feet) of the metre Paṅkti and finally to the sacrifice, which is fivefold (*Kauṣ Br.* XVIII. 14).

In the Soma sacrifice, after preparing the Uttaravedi, he sprinkles it five times. Here again the *arthavāda* joins the number five to the fivefold Paṅkti metre and also to the fivefold sacrifice, the latter (i.e. sacrifice) gained by through number five (*Tait. Sam.* VI. 2.8.3).

Apart from such *arthavāda*-s, having the fivefold fabric of the Year as also of Sacrifice as their centre, there are some *arthavāda*-statements regarding the number five, apparently pointing to some secular ideas, however ultimately dealing with sacrifice. In the rite of building the Great Fire-altar, while leading forward Agni to the (Āhavanīya) fire-altar,[7] the offering of ghee in five ladlings is enjoined. The *arthavāda* states that when Agni was about to go forward, the gods restored him beforehand with food, i.e. with these oblations of ghee. And so does the sacrificer now, when Agni is about to go forward. The *arthavāda* runs forward that the number five here signifies the fivefold division of the vital air and the places where they reside *viz.* the mind, the speech, the breath, the eye and the ear. The five times offering of ghee (by a ladle) thus amounts to the fivefold divided vital air, which he lays into the head (i.e. flame) of Agni, to make it sharp[8] (*Śat. Br.* IX. 2.2.4,5).

Another *arthavāda* related to number five occurs in connection with the Vṛṣākapi hymn in the context of Śilpa-s[9] to be recited. Having recited the Sukīrti hymn, which stands as a birthplace of the gods and from which the sacrificer is produced, he recites the Vṛṣākapi hymn. The Vṛṣākapi hymn is the body (provided for the sacrificer). It is in the Paṅkti metre, which has five *pāda*-s (feet or lines). A man (i.e. human being) is fivefold *viz.* hair, skin, flesh, bone and marrow. With the Paṅkti metre he makes the sacrificer have the same measure as of man (*Ait. Br.* VI. 29 = 30.3).

To come to number 'Six'—

The *arthavāda*-s connected with number 'six' speaks invariably of six seasons, which make up for Year. Some of the instances can be seen.

We have already seen that three times circumambulation in the regular way and three times *vice versa* come to number six, which number signifies six seasons (*Tait. Br.* III. 9. 6.2). In the rite of building the Great Fire-altar, it is said that he digs the earth with one *mantra;* sets down the fire-pan with one *mantra;* kindles the fire with one *mantra;* heats the fire-pan with one *mantra* and bakes the fire-pan with two *mantra*-s, the two *mantra*-s signifying that in a year food is ripened twice. The total number of *mantra*-s come to six. Six seasons make a year and Agni (= Sacrifice) is the Year. The ritual of making the fire-pan associated with the recitation of six *mantra*-s is of the measure of Agni (*Śat. Br.* VI. 5.4.9).

In the rite of Punarādheya (re-establishment of the sacred fires),[10] while reciting the offering-prayers, six case-forms of the word *'agni'* are employed: for at the fore-offerings (Prayāja-s) and two at the after-offerings (Anuyāja-s).[11] These come to six and seasons are six, where Agni entered by the six case-forms. He produces Agni out of the six seasons (*ibid.* II.2.3.26). The *arthavāda* runs further and deals with numbers twelve and thirteen, which can be taken up for consideration here. The six case-forms of the word *agni* contain twelve or thirteen syllables. There are either twelve or thirteen syllables in a year and Agni has entered the year, the seasons. Out of the seasons he produces Agni (*ibid.* II. 2.3.27). The Ukthya Soma-cup is Indra's special portion and it is accompanied by three *śastra*-s (songs of praise recited) in the morning feast and by three *śastra*-s in the midday feast—making for number six, leading to six seasons, which fulfil all wishes (*ibid.* IV. 2.3.6).

To come to number 'Seven'—

In the Pravargya rite, seven oblations are enjoined to be offered in fire. The *Śat. Br.* says that the vital airs in the head have seven channels and these he bestows on Agni (*ibid.* XIV. 2.2.39). While making a fire-pan (*ukhā)* seven balls of cow-dung are used, accompanied by the recitation of seven *mantra*-s. The *Śat. Br.* here relates the number seven to the sevenfold deities and to the seven vital airs, which are in the head. It is said here that the expression seven times seven (7 × 7 = 49) is also spoken of as seven. Thus by the number seven, he as though puts the vital airs into the head, i.e. Agni (*ibid.* VI. 5.3.11).[12] In the context of the Rājasūya sacrifice, in the ritual, after that of besprinkling the king with several types of water, there is propitiation of chariot, with the *mantra* addressed to the Maruts. With this *mantra,* he pleases the part of the chariot belonging to the Maruts. The horses of the chariot are four, the chariot is the fifth, the warrior sitting in the chariot sixth and the charioteer the seventh. Here the number seven is related to the host of the Maruts, which consists of troop of seven each. The *arthavāda* runs further saying that the Maruts signify the peasants and it is over the peasantry that the kingship of the sacrificer-king is rendered free (*ibid.* V. 4. 3.17). The morning litany (Prātaranuvāka) consists of hymns addressed to deities. He should recite hymns for Agni in seven metres (according to Sāy., these being Gāyatrī, Anuṣṭubh, Triṣṭubh, Bṛhatī, Uṣṇik, Jagatī and Paṅkti). The *arthavāda* relates the concept of seven here to the world of gods. The hymns for Uṣas in seven metres are related to the seven tame (*grāmya)* animals (according to Baudhāyana as quoted by Sāyaṇa there are — she-goat, horse, cow, she-buffalo, pig, elephant and she-mule). The hymns for Aśvins in seven metres are related to the seven ways in which Speech spoke (meaning thereby the seven tunes of Speech such as Ṣaḍja, Ṛṣabha and others). The number seven of the metres is for securing the whole of Speech and thus the entire *brahman,* i.e. holy power (*Ait. Br.* II. 17 = 7.7).

The number seven is at times taken to signify the metre Śakvarī, consisting of seven *pāda*-s (feet). In the context of the rite of Agnicayana, it is said that Indra saw this seven-versed (*saptarcyam)* hymn, for obtaining what is deficient, for reducing what is redundant and for making perfect what is imperfect. It is a hymn of seven verses. The perfecting is of three things - the perfecting of the fire-altar, the perfecting of him who has built it for the sacrificer and the perfecting of the sacrificer, who builds it (*Śat. Br.* IX. 5.2.1,2). In the rite of purchasing Soma, the sacrificer follows the Somakrayaṇī cow stepping into her six foot-prints, and offers on the seventh footprint (*Tait. Sam.* VI. 1.8.1). The *Śat. Br.* says that the sacrificer follows her, stepping into her seven footprints (*Śat. Br.* III. 3.1.1). The *Tait. Sam.* as well as the *Śat. Br.* relate the seven steps of the cow and the sacrificer following her, to the metre Śakvarī having seven feet. These relate to the beasts. There are seven domestic (*grāmyāḥ)* beasts, seven wild beasts and seven metres for obtaining both types of animals (*Tait. Sam.* VI. 1.8.1). In the context of the Agniṣṭoma sacrifice, while stating details about the Vasatīvarī water, the *Śat. Br.* says that seven *mantra*-s are employed, in this connection. With four *mantra*-s he takes the Vasatīvarī water, with one he puts it down behind the Gārhapatya, with one he carries it round, with one he puts it down in the Āgnīdhra (fire-place). All these make seven. The *arthavāda* is significant. It states that when the metres were produced from Speech (Vāc), that one consisting of seven feet, i.e., Śakvarī, came the last (*parārdhyā),* i.e. the highest of them. He brings about that completeness (with number seven) (*Śat. Br.* III. 9.2.17).

The belief about the number seven is primarily of completeness or totality. The fire-god (Agni) is said to have seven tongues of flames or has seven sisters (*RV.* I.71.7; at *RV* I.164.3 we have the seven 'sisters' of the Sun-god). The seven demons in a group are mentioned (*ibid.* X. 120.6). The concept of the seven regions of the earth is of totality (*ibid.* IX.114.3; I.12.16). Taking seven steps together, mentioned in *AV* (V. 11.9) indicative of perfect (i.e. complete) friendship and taking seven steps (by the bride-groom and the bride) together as a symbol of permanent friendship, are to be noted in this connection.[13]

To turn to number 'Eight'—

Not many instances of this number are noted in the Brāhmaṇa-texts, in the *arthavāda-ṣ.* But the belief about this number can be noted even in them. The *Jaim. Br.* says that there were eight followers of gods, eight of Fathers, eight of men and eight of *asura*-s. Indra becomes 'eighth' (*aṣṭamaḥ)* among them due to his power (*māyā),* and desires to kill Vṛtra (*Jaim. Br.* II. 155). In the *RV,* the divine Agni is said to be the 'eighth' *(aṣṭamaḥ)* — Agni in whom the seven *raśmi*-s are spread (*RV.* II. 5.2). By the seven *raśmi*-s are meant the seven priests, and even seven 'reins', with which Agni (as though a horse) is bound. The belief in number eight or eighth seems to be of 'pervading' as pointed out by Yāska (*Nir.* III. 10 from the root √*aś* - 'to pervade'). The pervading one becomes the overpowering one.[14] The cake to Agni is offered on eight potsherds and the metre of Agni is Gāyatrī, having eight syllables in each foot (*Ait. Br.* I.1).

This belief in the 'pervading' and thus the 'obtaining' nature of eight (units) is marked in the context of carrying the Soma-shoots when bought. The *Ait. Br.* states that in these rites, eight verses are recited to win powers and strength. The *arthavāda* has here a mythical account. When Soma was bought and he was going to men, his strength and powers went away to the quarters. These they sought to win by one verse but they could not; with two, with three, with four, with five, with six, with seven, they could not win. With eight (verses) they won, with eight they obtained. 'Eight' (*aṣṭa)* has its name by this (fr. √*aś* - 'to pervade', here 'to obtain') (*Ait. Br.* I.12 = 3.1).

To turn to number 'Nine'—

The *arthavāda*-s in different contexts join number nine to the nine vital airs in a man. In the New-moon and Full-moon sacrifices, in the ritual of kindling Agni, nine *nigada*-s[15] are said to be the nine breaths or vital airs in a man, which (i.e. the vital airs) are put into the sacrificer (*Śat. Br.* I.5.2.5). In the Rājasūya sacrifice, a gold plate perforated with nine holes is enjoined for being placed on the head of the sacrificer-king. The *arthavāda* states that the nine holes signify nine vital airs in a man, which obviously are placed in the king (*ibid.* V. 4.1.13). The same *arthavāda* regarding number nine is expressed in the context of the Carakasautrāmaṇī sacrifice, in which the pitcher used is said to have nine or hundred holes (*ibid.* V. 5.4.27). Nine verses are to be recited for Soma, when bought. By this he confers nine vital airs on the sacrificer, for completeness of life in this world and for immortality in the yonder world (*Kauṣ. Br.* VII. 10).[16] When Soma (in the form of Soma-shoots) arrives in the pendal, guest-reception (*ātithyam)* is offered to him on nine potsherds, the latter connected to nine breaths (*Ait. Br.* I.15 = 3.4). In the last part of the Gavām-ayana rite (i.e. Mahāvrata day), among the details enjoined is that of Adhvaryu singing nine verses. Number nine of the verses is connected to the nine breaths in man, which he places in the sacrificer. As all these verses are addressed to Indra, he places power (*indriya)* in the breaths. He sings these verses (as *sāman)* without the Pratihāra (part).[17] Hence the man can contract all the limbs of the body except the head.

To turn to number 'Ten'—

The *Pañc. Br.* enjoins a ten-day (Daśarātra) sacrifice, which is called Trikakubh.[18] The *arthavāda* has a mythical account. Indra having slain the *asura*-s was afraid that he had done an unheard of deed, i.e. a bad deed. The gods performed this sacrifice for him, by which he was freed from his bad lot (*sa pāpmano nairdaśyamagacchat)*. One who has been wounded by an arrow or a stick is out of danger after the tenth day (*nairdaśyam gacchati) (Pañc. Br.* XXII. 14. 2,3) The *Tait. Sam.* refers to the account of Indra and calls this sacrifice Trikakud (*Tait. Sam.* VII. 2.5.2, 3). *Śaṅkh. Ś.S.* states that what is tenfold, that he reaches by the ten-day rite (*Śaṅkh. Ś.S.* XVI. 29.1). The account from the *Pañc. Br.*, noted above, contains a significant word *viz.* '*nairdaśyam*', meaning 'a state of being more than ten' (applied to days, not to years, as is rightly pointed out by Caland). Caland has also pointed out that for the infant and its mother, the first ten-days-period is dangerous and when it passes away, the state would be of being out of danger. The word *nairdaśyam* is connected to both the concepts.[19] It is very clear that the *arthavāda* here is concerned with number ten. A probe further leads us to a folk-belief in observing pollution for ten days at the time of death as well as at the time of birth. After these ten days of pollution and the final oblations, the danger no longer remains. The period of ten days symbolises in the case of the childbirth the process of completion in the womb—ten days signifying the nine months and a part of the tenth month, while with the dead it may signify the same period prior to his final attainment of the Pitṛloka.[20]

In the rite of Agnicayana, when the Great Fire-altar is completed, Agni is said to be the deity Rudra. The Śatarudriya offering is given to him for appeasing him (*Śat. Br*. IX. 1.1.1, 7). The *mantra*-s in the *Vāj. Sam.* (XVI. 64-66) are to accompany the three oblations to the Rudras in the sky, the air and on earth respectively. The words — 'To them (I stretch) ten (fingers) forwards, ten to the right, ten backwards, ten to the left, ten upwards', are to be added to the *mantra*-s mentioned above (*Śat. Br.* IX. 1.1.35-38). The *arthavāda* connects the number ten here to the metre Virāj and Agni is said to be Virāj (fr. *vi* + √*rāj* — 'to shine brilliantly'). Seasons are ten (five seasons doubled), vital airs also ten. There are ten fingers while folding hands. By saying 'ten' 'ten' he makes reverence to the Rudras in each quarter (by folded hands). The worldly instance is stated (in the *arthavāda)* that he who is frightened places his hands together (i.e. folds his hands) (*ibid.* IX. 1.1. 38, 39). The *arthavāda* regarding the number ten speaks of nine breaths in man and the navel the tenth. These are said to be placed in the sacrificer. Again the metre Virāj is of ten syllables (in each foot). It signifies food and the sacrificer finds support thereby. For this *arthavāda,* the *vidhi* is of offering ten oblations in the Horse-sacrifice (*Tait. Sam.* VII. 5.15.2). The same *arthavāda* of the number ten connecting it to the nine breaths and the navel (being the 'tenth' number) and to the metre Virāj, Virāj signifying light (fr. *vi* + √*rāj*) of metres, occurs in the *Tait. Sam.*, in the context of the Agnicayana rite, when ten 'breath-supporters' (*prāṇabhṛtaḥ*) bricks are placed in the east, in the second layer of the Great Fire-altar (*ibid.* V. 3.2.2,3).

The *Śat. Br.* speaks of the Mitravindā sacrifice, which is for establishing the sacrificer in Virāj, in prosperity and food. Ten offerings are enjoined in this *iṣṭi* and they are - a sacrificial cake on eight potsherds to Agni; a *caru* to Soma; a sacrificial cake on ten potsherds to Varuṇa; a *caru* to Mitra; a sacrificial cake on eleven potsherds to Indra; a *caru* to Bṛhaspati; a sacrificial cake on twelve or eight potsherds to Savitṛ; a *caru* to Pūṣan; a *caru* for Sarasvatī and a cake on ten potsherds for Tvaṣṭṛ. Here the deities are ten, offerings ten, oblations ten, gifts (*dakṣiṇā*-s) ten. Metre Virāj has ten syllables (in one foot). Virāj stands for Śrī (beauty, prosperity) and thus he establishes the sacrificer, in the Virāj, in prosperity and food (*Śat. Br.* XI. 4.3.1-5, 18).

To turn to number 'Eleven'—

An interesting *arthavāda* occurs in the rite of enkindling Agni in the fire-pan, in the context of the Agnicayana rite. He puts on eleven kindling-sticks (some of them brought from certain trees and some of them under certain conditions),[21] in the fire-pan. It is said that these eleven kindling-sticks he puts on for one who is not either a noble, or a *purohita* (domestic priest), for these eleven are incomplete and incomplete is a person, who is not either a noble or domestic priest (*ibid.* VI. 6.3.12).

To come to number 'Twelve'—

As sacrifices are performed the year round and as a year completes a cycle of days, nights, months and seasons, the oft-repeated identifications in the ritual texts are of Agni or Sacrifice as Prajāpati and the latter as Year. Again Sacrifice is said to be Viṣṇu, the Sun, who makes the Year.

The distinguishing mark of the Year is twelve months. Hence the *arthavāda*-s following a *vidhi,* which deals with number twleve, verge finally on the idea of obtaining the Year.

While establishing the fires, *Kauṣ Br.* enjoins to give twelve cows (as *dakṣiṇā*). The *arthavāda* points to the Year, having twelve months, which is to be acquired with these cows (*Kauṣ. Br.* I.1). In the context of the Agnicayana rite, ploughing of the sacrificial ground as well as scattering seeds of diverse kinds are enjoined. It is said that he scatters seeds in twelve furrows. The Year has twelve months and verily with the Year he cooks food for him (*Tait. Sam.* V. 2.5.5). The *Tait. Br.,* while dealing with the auspicious and inauspicious times (in a day) states that there are five auspicious constellations and four inauspicious constellations. They make up nine. Whatever (constellation) is beyond and whatever (constellation) is near make two. The *brāhmaṇa* is the twelfth. One who knows this, follows a yearly vow (of twelve months). The *Tait. Br.* again dwells on this point saying that the nine constellations (noted above), with night as belonging to Agni and day as belonging to Indra, make up eleven. Āditya (the Sun) is the twelfth. This again makes for his yearly vow (*Tait. Br.* I.5.3.4).

To come to number 'Thirteen'—

It is interesting to note that while dealing with the concept of the Year, the intercalary month also is taken into account. Hence any thirteen units are supposed to make up for Year. A couple of examples will bring out the point.

In the ending rite (Udavasānīya *iṣṭi)* of the Rājasūya sacrifice, it is said that there are either twelve or thirteen gifts. These could be the calves of the three milch cows (*Śat. Br.* V. 5.5.17, 19), or optionally the gift counting to the Āgnīdhra[22] (*ibid.* V. 5.5.19). The *arthavāda* here states that this *iṣṭi* has the measure of a year. Hence the gifts are twelve or thirteen in number (*ibid.*). We have already noted that in the rite of establishing the fires, twelve cows are given as *dakṣiṇā,* which make for twelve months of a year, thereby getting the Year. In the same context, the *Kauṣ. Br.* adds that he gives a horse as *dakṣiṇā* as the thirteenth unit, to make up the thirteenth month of the year (*Kauṣ. Br.* I. 1). Thus Year is acquired by this. In the rite of Agnicayana, it is said that the four feet of the seat (on which the sacrificer sits), the four boards or planks (*anūcyāni)* which are on the (four) sides of that seat, the netting, the sling of the gold plate, the pan, the fire and the gold plate make thirteen units. They signify Year and Year is Agni = Sacrifice (*Śat. Br.* VI. 7.1.28).

To come to number 'Fourteen'—

In the rite of Agnicayana, there is ploughing of the sacrificial ground and scattering of seeds of diverse kinds along the furrows, this latter small rite accompanied with the recitation of fourteen *mantra*-s. The *arthavāda* states that this enables them to win the seven (kinds of) domesticated plants and seven (kinds of) wild plants (*Tait. Sam.* V. 2.5.5).

The *Pañc. Br.* states three Fourteen-day rites (XXIII. 3-5). Out of them, the *arthavāda*-statement regarding the first Fourteen-day rite is interesting. This rite is said to be wish-fulfilling. The first ten days are equal to the Virāj; the eleventh is the person who performs the rite; the twelfth is progeny; the thirteenth is cattle; and the fourteenth serves for obtaining the wish (*Pañc. Br.* XXIII. 3.2,3).[23]

To turn to number 'Seventeen'—

The thought oft-repeated about the number seventeen is of Prajāpati, who is said to be seventeenfold. In the Vājapeya sacrifice, all units amount to seventeen, which are for securing the seventeenfold Prajāpati, i.e. Sacrifice (*Pañc. Br.* XVIII. 7.5). A race of seventeen chariots is enjoined (as the distances marked for these are seventeen). A seventeenfold *stotra* is there. The gifts (*dakṣiṇā*-s*)* given away are in the groups of seventeen each. The *Tait. Br.* while enjoining these details says that these are for obtaining the seventeenfold Prajāpati (*Tait. Br.* I.3.6.3, 4).[24] The *Śat. Br.* also in the same context (i.e. Vājapeya sacrifice) enjoins seventeen drums to be put up along the edge of the altar, from the Āgnīdhra backwards (towards the west). This is to win the seventeenfold Prajāpati (*Śat. Br.* V. 1.5.6). If a *rājanya* (*kṣatriya*) performs this sacrifice, he shoots seventeen arrows' ranges,[25] for Prajāpati is seventeenfold (*ibid.* V.1.5.14).[25] For kindling Agni in an *iṣṭi* (sacrifice, which is performed in order to obtain the fulfilment of a special wish, which sacrifice thus is called a *kāmyeṣṭi*), the seventeen Sāmidhenī verses are to be recited. As the *arthavāda* here points out, number seventeen stands for twelve months in a year, together with the five seasons (the seasons Hemanta and Śiśira are taken together), making for the seventeenfold Prajāpati (*ibid.* I.3.5.10). The same *arthavāda* is stated by the *Ait. Br.*, the context being the consecration-rite at the Soma-sacrifice (I.1).

To come to number 'Eighteen'—

Number eighteen is associated with the concept of Year, in the *Tait Br.* The context is of Horse-sacrifice and the *vidhi* is of offering eighteen animals.[26] The mythical account as *arthavāda* relates that the deity of Horse-sacrifice went away from Prajāpati. In order to have that deity back, he offered eighteen animals, spoken of by the *mantra*-s '*rohito dhūmrarohitaḥ...*' The *arthavāda* further says that number eighteen is the image of Year, for twelve months and five seasons (Hemanta and Śiśira taken together) make seventeen and the Year itself is the eighteenth (*Tait. Br.* III. 9.1.1, 2).

To turn to number 'Twenty-one'—

Twenty-one Sāmidhenī verses (for kindling the fire) are to be recited at the New-moon and Full-moon sacrifices. Twelve months, five seasons and three worlds make twenty units and twenty-first is the sun, which shines here. The sun is the ultimate resort. The *arthavāda* states that the sacrificer obtains this resort, when he recites twenty-one verses (*Śat. Br.* I.3.5.11).

Twenty-one kindling verses are enjoined in the animal-sacrifice. The *arthavāda* for this *vidhi* presents two ideas. The first one is the same as seen above but here twelve months, five seasons, three worlds and the yonder sun make the twenty-onefold Prajāpati, who is Agni. The second one states that man is twenty-onefold as there are ten fingers, ten toes and the body (in the case of man). Twenty-onefold man is Prajāpati, who is Agni. The thought expressed here is – the measure of twenty-one verses, by which Agni is enkindled is as great as Agni (= Prajāpati), who himself is twenty-onefold (*ibid.* VI. 2.2.3,4).

To come to number 'Thirty-three'—

It is said that in the Bṛhaspati-sava, eleven gifts (*dakṣiṇā*-s) are taken away at the morning-pressing, eleven at the midday-pressing, and eleven at the third pressing. All these three make up number thirty-three. And the gods are thirty-three in number. These thirty-three gifts are given away for obtaining the help from the gods (*Tait. Br.* II.7.1.3).

To come to number 'Sixty'—

In the context of the Agnicayana rite, while offering a sacrificial victim to Prajāpati, various units are said to make number sixty and the *arthavāda* portions in the *Śat. Br.* explain the efficacy of number sixty. In this animal-offering to Prajāpati, there are twenty-one kindling verses (Sāmidhenī-s), twelve Āprī verses, eleven after-offerings (Anuyāja-s), eleven by-offerings (Upayaj-s), omentum (of the animal), offering of the other parts of the animal (*paśupuroḍāśa),* chief oblation and two libations of ghee—these make number sixty (*Śat. Br.* VI. 2.2.36). For the victim of Vāyu Niyutvat, these are the following — seventeen kindling verses, twelve Āprī verses, eleven after-offerings, eleven by-offerings, omentum, *paśupuroḍāśa,* chief oblation, two libations of ghee, two oblations to Agni Sviṣṭakṛt, the lord of forest (Vanaspati) and the oblation of gravy (Vasāhoma)—these make sixty (*ibid.* VI. 2.2.37). The *arthavāda* in this context explains the importance of number sixty as follows — Number 'sixty' makes a month, for the days and nights in a month are sixty. Through the gain of the month, the season is gained and through the latter, the year. The Year is Agni (= Sacrifice). The wishes which are cherished in the year and what other food than that there is in the year, all is gained by him (*ibid.* VI. 2.2.35, 37). The point of fulfilment of the wishes and the gain of food is not so significant as that of the gain of Sacrifice, through the Year, the latter obtained through number 'Sixty.' The principle of 'Like produces like' no doubt works here. But there is also the motif of complementing the Sacrifice or its procedure through the magic of 'Number.'

To turn to number 'Hundred'—

The *arthavāda*-s while explaining the importance of the number hundred, are practically the same at every place. The wish of the ancient people that a man should live for hundred years, is spoken of in these *arthavāda*-s. Moreover the man should have hundred energies and hundred powers. Here are some rites, speaking of number hundred. In the Caraka-Sautrāmaṇī sacrifice, the pitcher which is enjoined to be used (for pouring liquor in it) has either hundred or nine holes (*ibid.* V. 5.4.27). We have already noted the significance of number nine. In an additional rite concerning the Soma-sacrifice, the gold to be used is of hundred measures (*Tait. Sam.* III. 2.6.3). It is enjoined that the sacrificer should breathe over the gold, which is of hundred *kṛṣṇala*-s in weight (*ibid.* III. 3.4.3). In the Rājasūya sacrifice, the sacrificer-king has to step on the piece of gold of hundred measures (*Tait. Br.* I.7.8.1,2). A gold plate, perforated either with a hundred or with nine holes, is laid upon the head of the sacrificer-king in the Rājasūya sacrifice (*Śat. Br.* V. 4.1. 13, 14). On the Mahāvrata day, which is the last but one day of the Gavām-ayana *sattra*, there is playing on lute, which has a hundred strings (*Tait. Sām* VII. 5.9.2). The *Kauṣ. Br.* enjoins hundred verses to be recited in the morning-litany, i.e. Prātaranuvāka (*Kauṣ. Br.* XI. 7).

The normal term of man's life is thought to be of hundred years. This is in a way immortality which he achieves. The *arthavāda*-s stated to glorify the 'Hundred-day rite' and the 'Hundred years' sacrificial session', strike this note. The gods being afraid of death, resorted to Prajāpati, who gave them through the rite of 'Hundred days', immortality, which is the normal term of life (*Pañc. Br.* XXIV. 19.1,2). Before the time of the present gods, there were Sādhyas. They undertook the 'Hundred years' sacrificial session'. They throve and together with their cattle and their people, went to the heavenly world. This sacrificial session of hundred years is equal in duration to the normal life of man, i.e. hundred years (*ibid.* XXV. 8. 1-3).

To come to number 'Thousand'—

The context is of the Viśvajit sacrifice, which as the year-long session, is composed as an Agniṣṭoma with all the *stoma*-s and all the *pṛṣṭha*-s, or as a one-day rite; or as the middle day of a night session, it would be an Atirātra. About the gifts (*dakṣiṇā*-s) to be given in this sacrifice (i.e. Viśvajit), he should give all, says the *Kauṣ Br.* (XXV. 14). But the *Kauṣ. Br.* also opines that he can offer a thousand (gifts). The thousand is all and so is the Viśvajit sacrifice, all (*ibid.*). The *Pañc. Br.* speaks of thousand-day *sattra* and the thousand sacrificial days are said to be established in the highest Virāj, for the highest Virāj is of a thousand syllables (*Pañc. Br.* XXV. 9.4). As Caland rightly points out, here the word '*virāj*' (fr. *vi* + √*rāj* - 'to shine brilliantly') is the sense of 'splendour'.[27]

It is interesting to note that together with this etymological meaning of the word *virāj* (of the Virāj metre) and the normally occurring ten syllables (in one foot) of this metre, even thirty syllables of the three-footed (Tripadā Virāj) are taken into account to make the number 'Three hundred'. In the Vaiśvadeva rite of the Four-monthly sacrifices, it is said that he offers three hundred Audgrahaṇāni oblations. The *arthavāda* tries to reach the number three hundred through the metre Virāj which has thirty syllables (when the verse in the Virāj metre runs in three lines). The metre Virāj signifies food. Thus by three hundred oblations, the proper food is acquired (*Tait. Br.* III. 8.10.4).

This dealing with a particular number and stating the *arthavāda* about it, is extended by the ritual texts to more numbers, the *arthavāda*-s pointing out the beliefs associated with them. Some instances will clarify this point. The *Pañc. Br.* states that for the Brahma *sāman* at the Pṛṣṭha lauds, they should employ thirty-three Pragātha-s.[28] The gods are thirty-three in number, whose firm support they now have continuously. They apply twenty-four Pragātha-s. Twenty-four half-months are there in a year, the support of which they have continually. Twelve Pragātha-s signify twelve months in a year. Six Pragātha-s signify six seasons in a year; four Pragātha-s four-footed cattle, obtaining a continuous firm support from all these. When they apply two Pragātha-s, it signifies the two-footed sacrificer, who has to walk in the heavenly world, for in walking, man stands firmly now on this, now on that foot (*Pañc. Br.* IV. 4.11). When the sacrificer having shaved his hair and beard and having trimmed his nails, enters the sacrificial chamber named Prācīnavaṁśa (for the beams of it point to the east—hence Prācīnavaṁśa), he is purified with two Darbha (stalks),[29] i.e. with the day and night (these being 'two'); with three Darbha (stalks), i.e. the three worlds; with five Darbha (stalks), for number 'five' signifies the metre Paṅkti (having five feet) and the sacrifice is fivefold; with six, i.e. with the six seasons and with seven, i.e. with the seven metres;[30] with nine (stalks), i.e. nine breaths, with which he is purified and with twenty-one (stalks), by which he is completely purified, for there are ten fingers and ten toes, the twenty-first being the body (*Tait. Sam.* VI. 1.1.7,8).

The *Jaim. Br.* in two passages deals with the *arthavāda*-s regarding the numbers from one to seventeen. The passages have many significant, at times, common details about these numbers, the latter concerning the syllables uttered as chanted interjections in a *sāman*. This *sāman* is the Rathantara *sāman* as can be known from the earlier passage (*Jaim. Br.* I. 130 *eṣa vai devaratho yad rathantaram).* Here though the Rathantara *sāman* is said to be 'the chariot of gods', the *Jaim. Br.* in the earlier passage states sacrifice as the chariot of gods (*ibid.* I. 129). But as the Rathantara *sāman*, chanted in the sacrifice is important and is a matter to be dealt with, it is here said to be the '*devaratha*'. To turn to the number of syllables, as chanted interjections in the *sāman.* The (Udgātṛ) priest utters one syllable as interjection. Hence with (each rotation of) the spoke, the chariot, being firm, moves on. He utters two syllables. The chariot has two flanks. He makes the *devaratha* ('chariot of gods' here the Rathantara *sāman*) established with the flanks (i.e. the two syllables, which are uttered). He utters three syllables. The sacrificer has two feet and his self stands as the third (unit). So it becomes steady in the sacrificer. Again there are these three worlds. It (i.e. the Rathantara *sāman*) obtains those worlds. He utters four syllables. The quarters are four and the beasts have four feet. It establishes itself among the quarters and the beasts. He utters five syllables. Sacrifice is fivefold and beasts are also fivefold. It thereby gets established among the sacrifice as well as the beasts. He utters six syllables. Six are the seasons. It settles among the seasons. Six are the metres.[31] It acquires them. He utters seven syllables. The metre Śakvarī has seven feet and it stands for beasts. It settles down among the beasts as well as the Śakvarī metre. There are seven (principal) metres, the syllables of which go on increasing by four. Again there are seven principal vital airs. It acquires them. He utters eight syllables. Gāyatrī metre is eight-syllabled and stands for lustre, which is spiritual power. By eight syllables, it is established in lustre for getting spiritual power, as well as among beasts having eight hooves (*ibid.* I.131). He utters nine syllables. He thereby cuts off the vital breaths of an envious enemy and places them in his own self. He obtains the *stotra* of the Trivṛt *stoma.* He utters ten syllables. The metre Virāj is ten-syllabled and stands for food. It settles in the Virāj metre and proper food. Again there are ten vital breaths, which he acquires. He utters eleven syllables. Triṣṭubh metre is eleven-syllabled and this metre stands for bodily vigour, which is obtained. He utters twelve syllables. Jagatī metre is twelve-syllabled and stands for cattle. It settles among the cattle and the Jagatī metre. There are twelve months, which are obtained. He utters thirteen syllables, by which he obtains the thirteenth month. He utters fourteen syllables. Saṁvatsara (Year) is the fourteenth (together with the months noted above which are thirteen). He thereby settles in the year. He utters fifteen syllables. There are fifteen nights in a half-month. He obtains Year through (such) half-months. He utters sixteen syllables. The Puruṣa (man) has sixteen phases. These phases (*kalāḥ)* drag the envious sinful enemy downwards and he gets prosperity. It obtains the *stotra* of the Ṣoḍaśin *stobha*. He utters seventeen syllables. Prajāpati is seventeenfold. It settles in Prajāpati (*ibid.* I.132). This passage is important for it brings together practically all significant concepts associated with seventeen numbers, the aim obviously being to obtain the Year or Prajāpati through the process of complementation based on 'number.' The *arthavāda* from the *Kauṣ. Br.* can be taken into account here. The *Kauṣ. Br.* points out that the Ājya *śastra* is recited at the beginning of the Agniṣṭoma sacrifice and the Agnimāruta *śastra* at the end. What has to be recited makes up three hundred and sixty *ṛc* verses. Three hundred and sixty are the days of the year. The recitation thus serves to obtain the Year (*Kauṣ. Br.* XVI. 9).

Though a detailed study of offerings has been made by Gonda,[32] the association of a cake on a particular number of *kapāla*-s, i.e. potsherds (on which the sacrificial cake is placed for baking), with a particular deity, is worthy of consideration, for, in these cases the concept of 'number' plays an important part. We can take some of these into account.

The Tryambaka-offerings are offered to Rudra in the Sākamedha *parvan* (of the Four-monthly Seasonal sacrifices). These belong to one deity (only) and so these offerings in the form of cakes are on one potsherd (*ekakapālāḥ),* so says the *Śat. Br.* (II. 6.2.3). In the same *parvan* (noted above), a cake on one potsherd is offered to Viśvakarman. The *arthavāda* takes the help of etymology here. The gods, having performed the Sākamedha *iṣṭi* and having obtained victory over Vṛtra (the demon), had their all (*viśva)* work (*karman)* complete and all was conquered. The sacrificer performing the Sākamedha *iṣṭi* also has all his work complete and all is conquered by him. Hence a cake on one potsherd for Viśvakarman (*Śat. Br.* II. 5.4.10). The *arthavāda* takes recourse to pun while glorifying the *vidhi* of offering a cake on one potsherd to Ka (i.e. Prajāpati) in the *parvan* Varuṇaprahāsa (actually 'Varuṇapraghāsāḥ', always in plural) in the Seasonal sacrifices. It is said that Prajāpati himself offered one-potsherd cake to Ka (i.e. Prajāpati of yore) and bestowed *ka* (happiness) on the creatures. The sacrificer bestows happiness (*ka)* on the creatures by offering one-potsherd cake to Ka (Prajāpati) (*ibid.* II. 5.2.13). In the Śunāsīrīya *parvan* (of the Seasonal sacrifices), a cake on one potsherd is offered to Sūrya. It is he (Sūrya) that governs all this world (*ibid.* II. 6.3.8). At the *avabhṛtha* (final bath) rite in the Agniṣṭoma (Soma-sacrifice), a cake on one potsherd is offered to Varuṇa. It is this cake that as though puts sap into the Soma-husks, when the juice is taken out from them for offerings. Soma thus produced, produces the sacrificer (*ibid.* IV. 4.5.15). For Heaven and Earth,[33] there is a cake on one potsherd (*ibid.* II., 5.1.17).

In the Rājasūya sacrifice, there is a rite of offering oblations at the houses of the *ratnin*-s (specific persons, who are the recipients of these sacrificial honours) by the sacrificer-king.[34] At the house of the charioteer (*saṅgrahītṛ),* a cake on two potsherds is offered to Aśvins, as these two are from the same womb. So are the warrior and the charioteer (*sārathi,* i.e. driver) from the same chariot (*ibid.* V. 3.1.8). The importance of the two potsherds pointed out by the *arthavāda* is self-explanatory. The *Tait. Br.,* in the context of offerings to be given to Yama-*nakṣatra*-s (Yama-constellations)[35] prescribes a cake on two potsherds for the Aśvins (*Tait. Br.* III. 1.5.13). In the New-moon and Full-moon sacrifices, two butter-portions are offered to Agni and Soma. They stand as the two eyes of the sacrifice (*Śat. Br.* I.6.3.38). There is no reference to potsherd here, but the number ('two') is significant. Similar is the case of Iḍā offering. In the context of the New-moon and Full-moon sacrifices, the Iḍā offering consists of a fivefold cutting. The Iḍā is cattle and cattle consists of five parts (*ibid.* I.8.1.12). Here also there is no reference to 'potsherd' but the number 'five' is connected to cattle having five parts. A cake on six potsherds is associated with the manes (*pitṛ*-s). In the Mahāpitṛyajña, a cake on six potsherds is offered to *pitṛ*-s, who are possessed of Soma or to Soma accompanied by the *pitṛ*-s. It is said that the seasons are six and the Fathers (*pitṛ*-s) are the seasons. So a cake on six potsherds for them (*ibid.* II. 6.1.4). The *Tait. Br.* prescribes such a cake (on six potsherds) to be offered to the constellation Maghā-s. It is said that the Fathers desired to go to the Pitṛloka (the world of manes, which was already existent). They offered a cake on six potsherds to the *pitṛ*-s on the Maghā (plu.) constellation. They prospered there. He should offer to the Maghā-s, to the *pitṛ*-s a cake on six potsherds, by which he prospers in the world of manes (*pitṛ*-s) (*Tait. Br.* III. 1.4.8). In the Vaiśvadeva *parvan* of the Seasonal sacrifices (Cāturmāsya-s), a cake on seven potsherds is offered to Maruts. The *arthavāda* points out that the host of the Maruts is divided into troops of seven each (*Śat. Br.* II. 5.1.12,13). The *RV* speaks of their number as thrice seven (*RV.* I.133.6; also *AV* XIII. 1.13). They are said to be sixty-three in number, divided into nine troops of seven each (*RV* VIII. 96.8). We have already referred to the rite of offering oblations at the houses of the *ratnin*-s, in the Rājasūya sacrifice. At the house of the headman (*grāmaṇī*), the sacrificer-king offers a cake on seven potsherds to the Maruts. The Maruts are the common people (*viśaḥ*) and the headman, a *vaiśya* (the head of that particular locality appointed by the king). So a cake to Maruts (*Śat. Br.* V.3.1.6).

A cake on eight potsherds though is offered to different deities, Agni has the upper hand in getting it. Such a cake is offered to Agni in the Rājasūya sacrifice (*ibid.* in the Vaiśvadeva *parvan* of the four Seasonal sacrifices II.5.4.3; V. 2.4.11; V. 4.5.16; V. 5.1.1; XI. 1.5.5 for the Pathikṛt Agni).

As Vasu-s are believed to be eight, a cake on eight potsherds is offered to them (*Tait. Br.* I.5.11.3; III.1.5.8). Such a cake (on eight potsherds) is offered to the god Tvaṣṭṛ for the Citrā constellation. The god Tvaṣṭṛ offered such a cake to Tvaṣṭṛ of yore and the Citrā constellation. He obtained variegated (*citra*) creatures. So gets the sacrificer also (*ibid.* III. 1.4.12). A cake on eight potsherds or that on twelve potsherds is offered to Savitṛ (*Śat. Br.* V.3.1.7; V.4.5.6; V.5.4.29 the context at these is of the Rājasūya sacrifice). A cake on eleven potsherds is offered to Indra in the Rājasūya sacrifice (*ibid.* V. 4.5.10; V.5.1.1; V. 5.4.29); in the New-moon and Full-moon sacrifices (*ibid.* XI. 1.5.5); while giving offerings to the Jyeṣṭhā constellation, for obtaining the foremost status (*jyaiṣṭhyam*) among his equals (*Tait. Br.* III. 1.5.2). In the midday Soma-pressing, to the Rudra-s is offered eleven-potsherds cake (*ibid.* I.5.11.3).

We now come to the offering of a cake on eleven potsherds, to dual-divinity. In the additional rites in the context of Agnyādhāna (the rite of establishing fires), a cake on eleven potsherds is offered to Indra and Agni, for these two gods have their power never exhausted (*ayātayāmānau*). The sacrificer obtains his power and vigour by this (*ibid.* I.1.6.4). In the context of the offerings given to the Devanakṣatra-s the *Tait. Br.* prescribes a cake on eleven potsherds to Indra and Agni at the two Viśākhā constellations, for obtaining a position of pre-eminence like these two gods (*ibid.* III. 1.4.14). On the Upavasatha day (i.e. the day, prior to the day of offering oblations to the gods), in the Rājasūya sacrifice, he offers a cake on eleven potsherds to Agni and Soma (*Śat. Br.* V. 3.3.1). In the New-moon and Full-moon sacrifices, a cake on eleven potsherds is offered to Agni and Soma. The *Śat. Br.* by way of *arthavāda* here, states an elaborate mythical account. Tvaṣṭṛ had a three-headed, six-eyed son named Viśvarūpa. Indra hated him and cut off his heads. Tvaṣṭṛ was furious. He brought Soma-juice, from which Indra was excluded. Indra, though not invited, consumed what pure Soma there was in the tub. Tvaṣṭṛ again got furious and he let flow in the fire the little Soma remaining in the tub. That (little) Soma developed (whilst on its way to the fire) into Vṛtra, possessed of Agni and Soma. While Indra was moving on in pursuit of Vṛtra (to slay him), he addressed Agni and Soma and requested them to come back to him, for they belonged to him and he to them. Agni and Soma heeded to his request on the condition that a cake on eleven potsherds be offered to them (*ibid.* I.6.3.1-15). A cake on eleven potsherds is offered to Agni and Soma in the Rājasūya sacrifice (*ibid.* V.2.5.9.10). In the same sacrifice, a cake on eleven potsherds is offered to Agni and Pūṣan (*ibid.* V. 2.5.5,6).

It seems that the ritualists had a fixed belief about the cake to be offered to a deity and the potsherds concerned, though such a belief is not clearly expressed in each case. Here is one example, which can clearly explain the point. A cake to Agni and Viṣṇu on eleven potsherds is offered in connection with the consecration of the Soma-sacrifice. The *Ait. Br.* says that the arrangement (*kḷpti)* and the division (*vibhakti)* is — that (cake) of Agni is on eight potsherds, for the metre Gāyatrī has eight syllables (in one foot) and it is the metre of Agni; that (cake) for Viṣṇu is on three potsherds, for Viṣṇu had three strides (*Ait. Br.* I.1). The *Śat. Br.* also enjoins a cake on eleven potsherds for Agni and Viṣṇu in the consecration rite (*Śat. Br.* III. 1.3.1). In the Rājasūya sacrifice, a cake on eight potsherds to Agni and that on three potsherds to Viṣṇu is clearly prescribed (*ibid.* V. 4.5.16).[36] The belief about a cake on twelve potsherds is very patent. It is offered to Viśve Devāḥ in the third Soma-pressing (*Tait. Br.* I.5.11.3); to Savitṛ at the Hasta constellation (*ibid.* III. 1.4.11); to Indra and Agni in the New-moon and Full-moon sacrifices (*Śat. Br.* I.6.4. 1-3). Though no reference to twelve months occurs in the above examples, the *arthavāda* in the following ones is clear, bringing out the efficacy of number 'twelve' based on belief. In the Rājasūya sacrifice, a cake on twelve potsherds is offered to Agni Vaiśvānara.

Vaiśvānara is truly the Year and Prajāpati is the Year. As there are twelve months in the year, so a cake on twelve potsherds to Vaiśvānara (*ibid.* V. 2.5.13-15; also *ibid.* XI.1.5.5—such a cake to Vaiśvānara is prescribed, though explanation is not given). Such a cake (on twelve potsherds) is offered to Indra and Viṣṇu in the Rājasūya sacrifice, and the *arthavāda* mentioning twelve months of the year and the *iṣṭi* (sacrifice) of the measure of the Year (*ibid.* V.5.5.8). The same *arthavāda* of twelve months leading to the Year (Saṁvatsara) and that too to Prajāpati and Prajāpati as Dhātṛ (or Dhātā - Nom. sing.), occurs when a cake on twelve potsherds is prescribed in the Agnicayana rite (*ibid.* IX. 5.1.38). A cake on fifteen potsherds is to be offered to the Moon, i.e. the reflection (*pratīdṛśyāyai)* of the moon (in waters). By this, having obtained day and night, fortnights, months, seasons and lastly Saṁvatsara (Year), the sacrificer goes to the world of the moon and enjoys the vicinity of the moon (*Tait. Br.* III. 1.6.1). Here the number fifteen of the potsherds is significant, for it shows the increasing and decreasing phases of the moon and is thus symbolic.

It is clear that in all these details relating to sacrifice, the 'number' mentioned or prescribed is not arbitrarily brought in, but it breathes of some kind of belief concerning that number. In most cases, the anxiety is of getting to the Year (Saṁvatsara) - the Father Time — which is Prajāpati —the very Sacrifice.

NOTES AND REFERENCES

1. See (Mrs.) Dange, S.S., "Sampad-s of Metres", *Aspects of Speech in Vedic Ritual,* pp. 113-45.
2. See Dange, Sadashiv A., "Sex-Coupling in sacrifice (Mithunīkaraṇa)," with the chart, *Sexual Symbolism from the Vedic Ritual,* Ajanta Pubns., Delhi, 1979, pp. 51-70.
3. Sāyana in his comm. on *Tait. Br.* II.7.7 (at the beginning) explains the rite of Odanasava.
4. For this, see Eggeling, J., *op. cit.,* pt. III, SBE Vol. 41, p. 25, note 2.

5. The *Śat. Br.* points out that hair, skin, flesh, bone and marrow are the five parts of the sacrificial animal and applies these metaphorically to the five stages, while making the *puroḍāśa* (sacrificial cake) ready. *Śat. Br.* I.2.3.8.
6. In the Anūbandhyā rite, a cow is offered to Mitra and Varuṇa, see *Kauṣ. Br.* XVIII. 11, 13.
7. See Eggeling, J., *op. cit.,* pt. IV, SBE Vol. 43, p. 191, note 1, where he clarifies this. A burning piece of wood is taken from the Gārhapatya hearth to serve as the new Āhavanīya on the Great Fire-altar. The Gārhapatya fire, was the Ukhya Agni, carried in the fire-pan (*ukhā*) by the sacrificer during his time of initiation lasting normally for a year. At the end of this period, at the beginning of the opening sacrifice (Prāyaṇīya *iṣṭi*), this Ukhya Agni was transferred from the fire-pan to the newly-built Gārhapatya hearth.
8. This is indicated by the words '*tigmena śociṣā*' contained in the *mantra* from the *Vāj. Sam.* XVII. 16, which is employed at this time.
9. The term 'Śilpa' occurs in the context of the Viśvajit and Atirātra sacrifices as well as in the rites of the sixth day of the Pṛṣṭhya sacrifice. It denotes the skilful compositions employed in reciting the praise-formulas (*śastra*-s*).* The combination of verses in a hymn or certain methods of reciting the verses in a hymn is a striking feature in the Śilpa-s. For this and more information about the Śilpa-s, see (Mrs.) Dange, S.S., *Aspects of Speech in Vedic Ritual,* pp. 103-8.
10. See Eggeling, J., *op. cit.,* pt. I, SBE Vol. 12, p. 313, note 2, for more details.
11. See *Aśv. Ś.S.* II.8.5-7. The cases used are vocative (*agne*), accusative (*agnim),* instrumental (*agninā)* and nominative (*agniḥ).* These are four case-forms at the fore-offerings. Two more stated by the *Śat. Br.* (II. 2.3.25) are *agneḥ* (genitive) and *agnau* (locative—also pronounced as *agna-u),* at the after-offerings. The total comes to six.
12. For practically the same idea, see *Śat. Br.* IX. 3.1.8. In the rite of Agnicayana, the Vaiśvānara oblation is a single one, pointing out to the head (which is also one). The oblations to Maruts, of seven potsherds each, are seven in number, pointing out the seven vital airs in the head. Again for the same idea and for the same context of making a fire-pan (as

in *Śat. Br.* VI. 5.3.11), we have *Tait. Sam.* (V. 1.7.1), where the fire-pan is said to be the head of the sacrifice and the seven verses used for fumigating the fire-pan are said to be the breaths in the head.

13. For more information on this point, see (Mrs.) Dange, S.S., "Symbolism of the Numbers Three and Seven," *Hindu Domestic Rituals — A Critical Glance,* pp. 64-69.
14. For the full explanation of *aṣṭama,* see Dange, Sadashiv A., "Aṣṭama", Vidarbha Samshodhana Mandala, *Annual No.,* Nagpur, 1991 (pub. in 1992), pp. 13-23.
15. *Nigada* is a prose (*yajus) mantra*, which occurs in the *RV*. For the *nigada*-s employed here, see *Āśv. Ś.S.* I.4.10,11. The *nigada*-text starts from *'agnir hotā...' etc.* up to the word *'agnim'*; then a pause, then the words '*hotāram avṛthāḥ*'. The *nigada* text is completed (for uttering) with *'ghṛtavatīm... yajñiyān*' (*Tait. Sam.* II. 5.9.6).
16. Also see number nine connected to nine vital airs, in the context of the Sautrāmaṇī sacrifice. *Śat. Br.* XII. 8.1.12; also *Ait. Br.* I.20=4.3, nine Pāvamānī-verses, in honour of Pavamāna (Soma) deity, connected to nine vital breaths.
17. The five components of a *sāman* are Hiṅkāra, Prastāva, Udgītha, Pratihāra and Nidhana. While singing the nine verses, the Adhvaryu should avoid the Pratihāra part (and sing further). Pratihāra signifies contracting, which is to be avoided when the Adhvaryu priest comes to the climax (in singing the nine verses). The allusion here is to a worldly fact, in that a person can contract all his limbs but not the head (which occupies the highest position in the body-structure).
18. Sāyaṇa says at the beginning of *Pañc. Br.* (XXII. 14) that there are four ten-day sacrifices enjoined. Out of these, the first one is named Trikakud. On *Pañc. Br.* (XXII. 14.7) he says — '*kakudeva kakup*', thus pointing out that *kakud* and *kakup* are the same. Both mean 'eminent', 'foremost'.
19. See Caland, W., *Pañcaviṃśa Brāhmaṇa,* Sri Satguru Pubns., Delhi, 1982 (Calcutta 1931), p. 581, note 1 on *Pañc. Br.* XXII. 14.2.
20. (Mrs.) Dange, S.S., *The Bhāgavata Purāṇa—Mytho-Social Study,* p. 139 f.
21. *Śat. Br.* VI. 6.3.1-7.
22. See Eggeling, J., *op. cit.,* pt. III, SBE Vol. 41, p. 142, note 3.

23. The fourteen days of this rite are — a six-day-rite with the Pṛṣṭha-*sāman*-s; a six-day-rite with the Pṛṣṭha-*sāman*-s; beginning with the thirty-three-versed day and an over-night-rite.

The first Ṣaḍaha is of six days having 9, 15, 17, 21, 27 & 33 verses and the second Ṣaḍaha is of six days having 33, 27, 21, 17, 15 and 9 verses (the order of the verses reversed). See Caland, W. *op. cit.*, p. 587, note 1 on *Pañc. Br.* XXIII. 3.1.

24. The details from the *Āp. Ś.S.* are stated by Kane, which give a thorough idea for knowing the characteristic features of the Vājapeya sacrifice, centring round number seventeen. Kane, P.V., *Hist. of Dh. Ś.*, Vol. II, pt. II, p. 1206.

25. The *rājanya* has to shoot these arrows northwards through the space between the *utkara* and *cātvāla*. See Eggeling, J., *op. cit.*, pt. III, SBE Vol. 41, p. 25, note 1.

The *Śat. Br.* points out that as much as is one arrow's range, so much is Prajāpati crosswise and as much as are seventeen arrows' ranges, so much is Prajāpati lengthwise. *Śat. Br.* V. 1.5.13.

26. There are many other animals from the forest brought for this sacrifice, which are tied to the *yūpa*-s but after carrying Agni round them, these are to be let off. *Tait. Br.* III. 9.1.2-4.

27. See Caland, W., *op. cit.*, p. 634, note 1 on *Pañc. Br.* XXV. 9.4.

28. Pragātha is a kind of stanza, a combination of Bṛhatī or Kakubh (metre) verse with a Satobṛhatī verse, so as to form a triplet.

29. The *Tait. Sam.* at this place states the *arthavāda* glorifying the use of the Darbha grass. The mythical account coming by way of the *arthavāda* says that when Indra slew Vṛtra, the latter died upon the waters. That part of those waters, which was fit for sacrifice, pure and divine, went out of the waters and became Darbha grass. When the priest purifies the sacrificer with bunches of Darbha grass, it is this part of the waters, with which he purifies him. *Tait. Sam.* VI. 1.1.7.

30. Though the seven metres are not specifically named here, generally they are taken to be the ones, which go on increasing by four syllables, when the total number of syllables of each is taken into account. These are—

(*i*) Gāyatri - 24 syllables (8 × 3, i.e.. 8 syllables in each foot and total 3 feet).
(*ii*) Uṣṇih - 28 syllables (8, 8 & 12 syllables) or Kakubh — 28 syllables (8, 12 & 8 syllables).
(*iii*) Anuṣṭubh - 32 syllables (8 × 4, i.e. 8 syllables in each foot and total 4 feet).
(*iv*) Bṛhatī — 36 syllables (8, 8, 8 &12 syllables).
(*v*) Paṅkti - 40 syllables (8 × 5, i.e. 8 syllables in each foot and total 5 feet).
(*vi*) Triṣṭubh - 44 syllables (11 × 4, i.e. 11 syllables in each foot and total 4 feet).
(*vii*) Jagatī - 48 syllables (11 × 4, i.e. 12 syllables in each foot and total 4 feet).

31. Generally in the ritual texts, seven are said to be the principal metres as seen in note 30 *supra.* But here, six are said to be the metres.
32. Gonda, J., *Rice and Barley Offerings in the Veda,* Leiden, 1987.
33. We expect a cake on two potsherds for Heaven and Earth. But in the Vaiśvadeva *parvan* of the Four-monthly sacrifices, both are taken as one single unit. The *arthavāda* states that Prajāpati created the living beings with offerings and enclosed them within heaven and earth. The same, the sacrificer does and so a cake on one potsherd to Heaven and Earth (*Śat. Br.* II. 5.1.17).
34. For the eleven offerings called *ratninām havīṁṣi, Śat. Br.* V. 3.1; also Eggeling, J., *op. cit.*, pt. III, SBE Vol. 41, p. 58, note 2, which gives more information on this.
35. The Yamanakṣatra-s begin with Anūrādhā-s and end with Apabharaṇī-s. See *Tait. Br.* I.5.2.7.
36. After being bought, when Soma is carried to the sacrificial pendal, guest-offering is given to him in the form of a cake on nine potsherds. Nine are the vital breaths. This is for the arrangement and the recognition of vital breaths. The deity here is Viṣṇu, for Viṣṇu is sacrifice (Ait. Br. I.15 = 3.4). Here the number of potsherds for the cake are 'nine' and not three, as we have noted. Does it mean triple 'three', making it nine?

[illegible] Practices
Through Ayurveda

Vedic Beliefs and Practices Through Arthavāda

Dr. (Mrs.) Sindhu S. Dange
Ex-R.G. Bhandarkar Professor and
Head, Dept. of Sanskrit,
Mumbai University

VOLUME II

Aryan Books International
New Delhi

Vedic Beliefs and Practices Through Arthavāda

ISBN-81-7305- 285-9 (Vol. II)
ISBN-81-7305-286-7 (Set)

First Published in **2005** by :
ARYAN BOOKS INTERNATIONAL
Pooja Apartments, 4B, Ansari Road, Darya Ganj
New Delhi-110 002 (India)
Tel.: 23287589, 23255799; Fax: 91-11-23270385
E-mail: aryanbooks@vsnl.com

Computer Typeset at ABI Prints & Publishing Co., New Delhi
Printed at B.B.N. Printers, New Delhi

Contents

Contents

Abbreviations

AV	=	*Atharvaveda*
Ait. Ār	=	*Aitareya Āraṇyaka*
Ait. Br.	=	*Aitareya Brāhmaṇa*
Āp. Dh. S.	=	*Āpastamba Dharmasūtra*
Āp. G.S.	=	*Āpastamba Gṛhyasūtra*
Āp. Ś.S.	=	*Āpastamba Śrautasūtra*
Āśv. G.S.	=	*Āśvalāyana Gṛhyasūtra*
Āśv. Ś.S.	=	*Āśvalāyana Śrautasūtra*
Baudh. Dh. S.	=	*Baudhāyana Dharmasūtra*
Baudh. Ś.S.	=	*Baudhāyana Śrautasūtra*
Bh. G.	=	*Bhagavadgītā*
Bhāg. P.	=	*Bhāgavata Purāṇa*
Bhār. Ś.S.	=	*Bhāradvāja Śrautasūtra*
Bṛhad. Up.	=	*Bṛhadāraṇyaka Upaniṣad*
Chān. Up.	=	*Chāndogya Upaniṣad*
Gau./Gaut. Dh.S.	=	*Gautama Dharmasūtra*
Gobh. G.S.	=	*Gobhila Gṛhyasūtra*
Gop. Br.	=	*Gopatha Brāhmaṇa*
Jaim. Br.	=	*Jaiminīya Brāhmaṇa*
Jaim. Up. Br.	=	*Jaiminīya-upaniṣad-brāhmaṇa*
Kaṭha Up.	=	*Kaṭha Upaniṣad*
Kāṭh. G.S.	=	*Kāṭhaka Gṛhyasūtra*
Kāṭh. Sam.	=	*Kāṭhaka Saṁhitā*
Kāty. Ś.S.	=	*Kātyāyana Śrautasūtra*

Kauṣ. Br.	=	*Kauṣīkaki Brāhmaṇa*
Kau. Sū	=	*Kauśikasūtra*
Khā. G.S.	=	*Khādira Gṛhyasūtra*
Mait. Sam.	=	*Maitrāyaṇī Saṁhitā*
Manu Sm.	=	*Manusmṛti*
Mārk. P.	=	*Mārkaṇḍeya Purāṇa*
Mbh.	=	*Mahābhārata*
Nir.	=	*Nirukta*
P.	=	*Purāṇa*
Pañc. Br.	=	*Pañcaviṁśa Brāhmaṇa*
Pār. G.S.	=	*Pāraskara Gṛhyasūtra*
Rām.	=	*Rāmāyaṇa*
RV	=	*Ṛgveda*
Ṣaḍ Br.	=	*Ṣaḍviṁśa Brāhmaṇa*
Śāṅkh. G.S.	=	*Śāṅkhāyana Gṛhyasūtra*
Śāṅkh. Ś.S.	=	*Śāṅkhāyana Śrautasūtra*
Śat. Br.	=	*Śatapatha Brāhmaṇa*
Sk. P.	=	*Skanda Purāṇa*
Tait. Ār.	=	*Taittirīya Āraṇyaka*
Tait. Br.	=	*Taittirīya Brāhmaṇa*
Tait. Sam.	=	*Taittirīya Saṁhitā*
Vāj. Sam.	=	*Vājasaneyi Saṁhitā*
Vām. P.	=	*Vāmana Purāṇa*
Var. P.	=	*Varāha Purāṇa*
Vas. Dh. S.	=	*Vasiṣṭha Dharmasūtra*
Viṣṇu Dh. S.	=	*Viṣṇu Dharmasūtra*
Vi./Viṣṇu P.	=	*Viṣṇu Purāṇa*
Yāj. Sm.	=	*Yājñavalkyasmṛti*

ABBREVIATIONS OF MODERN TITLES

Bib. Ind.	=	Bibliotheca Indica
BORI	=	Bhandarkar Oriental Research Institute
CASS	=	Centre of Advanced Study in Sanskrit

Ency. of P.B. & P.	=	*Encyclopedia of Puranic Beliefs and Practices*
Ency. of Rel. and Eth.	=	*Encyclopaedia of Religion and Ethics*
Hist. of Dh. S.	=	*History of Dharmaśāstra*
HOS	=	*Harvard Oriental Series*
JAOS	=	*Journal of the American Oriental Society*
SBE	=	Sacred Books of the East Series
VVBIS & IS	=	Vishveshvaranand Vishva Bandhu Institute of Sanskrit and Indological Studies

CHAPTER 9

Sense-Organs and Body-Parts

The Vedic ritualists seem to have a fixed and clear idea of the mortal and the immortal elements of human body. The *arthavāda* occurring in the context of the fifth layer of the Great Fire-altar in the rite of Agnicayana is eloquent in this respect. It is said that Prajāpati created living beings. From his upward breathings he created gods and from his downward breathings, he created mortals and above the mortals, Death as their consumer. One half part of Prajāpati was mortal and other half was immortal. With the mortal part, Prajāpati was afraid of Death and entered the earth, becoming twofold, i.e., in the form of clay and water. When Death enquired after Prajāpati, the gods gathered Prajāpati in the form of clay and water, i.e. brick. The five bodily parts of him which are mortal are—the hair on the mouth (*āsaṁlloma),* the skin, the flesh, the bone and the marrow and the five immortal parts are—the mind, the voice, the vital air, the eye and the ear (*Śat. Br.* X. 1.3. 1-4). Prajāpati is no other than the Great Fire-altar (which is built to reconstruct Prajāpati's body, for he was completely exhausted after creating the universe). The layers of earth stand as the five mortal parts of him and the layers of bricks stand as the five immortal parts of him (*ibid.* 5). This passage from the *Śat. Br.* is important for it clearly speaks of the subtle sense-organs in the human body, according to the Vedic ritualists.

It has to be noted that in the Vaiśeṣika philosophy of Kaṇāda, which flourished about the beginning of the Christian era, the topic where the sense-organs are dealt with, we have the mention of *tvac* (lit. 'skin'), which is the sense-organ of touch and which resides on the entire body (*Tarkasaṅgraha* 13). The sense-organs of perception (*jñānendriya*-s) according to the Vaiśeṣika-s are five *viz.* nose (*ghrāṇa*), tongue (*rasanā*), eye (*cakṣus*), ear (*śrotra*) and skin (*tvac*). In reality, these are super-senses, for they are not the organs which we actually see, but they are the abodes of the imperceptible sense of smell, taste, vision, hearing and touch, respectively. The process of getting the knowledge of a particular being or thing is as follows. The sense-organ (*indriya*) comes into contact with the object of sense (*indriya-viṣaya*) and carries the impressions to the mind (*manas*), which in its turn takes them to the soul (*ātman*), which is thus enabled to have the knowledge required. Mind (*manas*) acts as a sort of clearing office for the various impressions, obtained by the sense-organs. Had there been no *manas* (mind), there would have been simultaneous impressions (of knowledge) through the various sense-organs. But this is not the case and this is verily the distinguishing mark of mind (*manas*).[1] According to some, *manas* is said to be the internal sense-organ.

We have taken note of the passage from the *Śat. Br.* (X. 1.3. 1-4) and shall be considering several other passages from the ritual texts. It has to be noted that the Vedic ritual texts, do not consider anything as a sense-organ of touch (*tvac*). The *Śat. Br.* has an interesting *arthavāda* regarding the skin of a man, which when the man was flayed, went to the cow, for the gods put that skin on the cow. With this skin, she endures rain, cold and heat. But as the man has no skin, if a stalk of grass or some other object cuts him, the blood trickles out from him. The gods then put that skin i.e. the garment, on man. Hence it is that only a man, of all the beings, wears a garment, for it was put on him by the gods as his skin. The *Śat. Br.* here states that one should take care to be properly clad, so that he may be completely endowed with his own skin. A cow knows that she wears the skin of a man and runs away from a naked man with the fear that he may take back his skin from her. Cows come fondly near a person, who is properly clad (*Śat. Br.* III. 1.2.13-17). This *arthavāda* comes in the context of the rite of consecration in the Agniṣṭoma (model Soma-sacrifice), when wearing of a garment is prescribed for the sacrificer. The *Śat. Br.* has several details to tell about this garment of the 'to-be-consecrated' sacrificer (*ibid.* III. 1.2. 13, 18-20). What is important from our point of view is that in the passages from the Vedic ritual context, we do not have any mention of a sense-organ of touch, unlike the one which we find in the scientific study of 'Perception' in the philosophy of the Vaiśeṣika-s, later times.

Again we do not have a mention of tongue as a sense-organ of taste exclusively.[2] An *arthavāda* in the context of the New-moon and Full-moon sacrifices, in the rite of preparing the rice-offering, refers to tongue, while stating a ritual-metaphor. For this offering, he grinds the rice with the two millstones (or the grinding-stones)—the upper mill-stone and the lower millstone. The upper millstone being smaller of the two, is called the daughter of the lower mill-stone. He beats the two millstones with a wedge (*śamyā*).[3] The two millstones are as it were two jaws and the wedge is the tongue. When he beats the two millstones with the wedge, it is with the tongue that he speaks (*ibid.* I. 2.1.17). The mention of tongue here is based on our day-to-day experience of speaking and does not take any note of the sense-organ of taste, concerning the tongue. In the ritual-texts, there is often the mention of *vāc* (speech) and not the tongue. *Vāc* (speech), which in reality is the result of tongue, is placed on par with breath (*prāṇa*), eye (*cakṣus*) and ear (*śrotra*). Mind (*manas*), which is not regarded as a sense-organ and if so regarded, only as the internal sense-organ (*antar-indriya),* in the later philosophy, figures in the Vedic ritual texts as a sense-organ. In the context of the Agnicayana rite, there occurs the dialogue between Dhīra Śātaparṇeya and Mahāśāla Jābāla. The former comes to the latter for knowledge; but the latter, having come to know the former's knowledge about Agni being everything here, steps down and respects him. Here we have the passage— Speech is Agni himself; eye the yonder sun; mind is that moon; ear is the quarters; breath is the wind that blows here (*ibid.* X. 3.3.7,8). In the same context, the various metres are identified with the sense-organs. The Gāyatrī is the breath (*prāṇa)* (of Prajāpati—the Fire-altar); the Uṣṇih is the eye; the Anuṣṭubh is the voice (or speech); the Bṛhatī is the mind; the Paṅkti is the ear; the Triṣṭubh is the generative breath (*prajananaḥ prāṇaḥ*) and the Jagatī is the downward breathing (*avāṅ prāṇaḥ*) (*ibid.* X.3.1.1). The *Śat. Br.* in the context of the Agnicayana rite, relates a mythical account of the creation of the world. Going on the lines of the concept occurring in the Nāsadīya hymn of the *RV* (X. 129.1), by making its specific mention, the *Śat. Br.* says that it was Mind that was really neither the non-existent nor the existent. Mind practised austerity. It created Speech, the latter creating Breath, which in its turn creating Eye. Eye created Ear and Ear created Work (*karma),* obviously connected with sacrifice. Work created Fire (Agni). Thus the five sense-organs—mind, speech, breath, eye and ear are spoken of as agents in the context of Agni, i.e. Fire-altar (*ibid.* X. 5.3.1-11).[4] The *Jaim. Br.* speaks of Agni Vaiśvānara as Puruṣa - the Man. Of him, the enkindling-stick is the speech; the lustre is the eye; the smoke is the vital breath; the sparks of fire are the mind and the burning coals are the ear (*Jaim. Br.* I. 45).

We have noted a couple of ritual metaphors above. The *Jaim. Br.* enlightens us more on this point. At one place, it states that the Gāyatrī (metre) is the vital breath; the Uṣṇih and Kakubh (they being two) are the two eyes; Jagatī is the ear; Anuṣṭubh is the speech; Bṛhatī is the mind; Paṅkti is the soul and Triṣṭubh is the strength (*ibid.* II. 58). Elsewhere the *Jaim. Br.* says that Triṣṭubh metre is the eye (i.e. organ of eyesight) and the Paṅkti metre is the seasons, making Gāyatrī, Jagatī and Anuṣṭubh stand for vital breath, ear and speech respectively as we have noted in the earlier ritual metaphor (*ibid.* I.102; also I. 260).

In the context of the New-moon and Full-moon sacrifices, while kindling fire, the kindling verses (Sāmidhenī *mantra*-s) are prescribed for being recited. By reciting the first Sāmidhenī *mantra,* is kindled the vital breath (*prāṇa);* by the second one, the backward breathing (*apāna);* by the third one, the high-flaming breathing (*udāna);* by the fourth one, the ear (*śrotra);* by the fifth one, the voice or speech (*vāc);* by the sixth one, the mind (*manas);* by the seventh one, the eye (*cakṣus);* by the eighth one, the central breath (*madhyama prāṇa);* by the ninth one, the penis (*śiśna);* by the tenth one, the downward breathing (*avāk prāṇa*); and by the eleventh one, the entire body from the nails and the hair on the body, is enkindled (*Śat. Br.* I.4.3.1-10).

The priestly duties allotted to and to be carried out by the four principal priests are likened to the functions carried out (respectively) by the sense-organs. These metaphorical passages occur in the *Ṣaḍ. Br.* in the context of the midday Soma-pressing as well as the third Soma-pressing. In the midday Soma-pressing, the sacrificer should loudly utter the words, "Speech is my Hotṛ priest"; "Eye is my Adhvaryu priest", "Mind is my Brahman priest"; and "Ear is my Udgātṛ priest" (and he should say each time, "May he permit me or give me consent") (*Ṣaḍ. Br.* II,. 6. 1-2). Permitted by the deities Vāc, etc., the sacrificer, who is the *apāna* (backward breathing) air, eats (*ibid.* II. 6.4-6). In the third Soma-pressing, only the breath with its types is mentioned. The sacrificer should loudly utter the words, "The vital breath (*prāṇa)* is my Hotṛ priest"; "The backward breathing (*apāna)* is my Adhvaryu priest"; "The breathing moving through the whole body (*vyāna)* is my Brahman priest"; and "The breathing situated at the cavity of the navel (*samāna)* is my Udgātṛ priest" (and he should say each time, "May he permit me") (*ibid.* II. 7. 1-2). Permitted by these deities, the sacrificer, who is the *udāna* (upward breathing), eats (*ibid.* II. 7.1-2, 5-6). The *Ṣaḍ. Br.* further says that if the Hotṛ priest, inadvertently, leaves off his priestly duty, speech deserts the sacrificer. In the case of Adhvaryu's failing in duty, eye deserts the sacrificer. And so do mind and ear, when the Brahman priest and the Udgātṛ priest (respectively) fail to perform their duty properly. When these four priests carry out that duty of theirs, speech, eye, mind and ear (respectively) are placed by them in the sacrificer (*ibid.* III. 1.1-4). The relation of these priests with the respective senses is quite clear, for to the Hotṛ priest is allotted the duty of reciting the *mantra*-s (so connected with speech). The Adhvaryu is the officiating (-offering) priest, hence connected with eye, for the eye (i.e. his properly seeing all offerings) is essential for him. The Brahman priest is the overall supervisor, at times also prescribing the expiatory rites in the case of shortcomings or failures in the sacrificial procedure. He has to be always vigilant, thus needing a sound and balanced mind. The Udgātṛ priest has to sing the various *sāman*-s, *stoma*-s, *stobha*-s, etc. For him, ear is the important sense-organ. The *arthavāda* here thus has a perfectly logical basis.

The sacrifice though terrestrial is thought of to have divine and thus supra-terrestrial status, making it a cosmic activity. The *arthavāda*-s concerning the senses, at times, are important from this point of view. The sacrificer after the rite of consecration in the Agniṣṭoma sacrifice, is not to offer the daily milk offering at the Agnihotra (i.e. in the fire), but has to drink the fast-milk himself, this milk being called *vrata* (and the cow from which this milk is taken - '*vratadughā*'). The *arthavāda* states a mythical account that the gods gained supreme authority by means of sacrifice. For making the heavenly world unattainable to men, they sipped the sap of the sacrifice. They drained the sacrifice, scattered it by means of the sacrificial post and disappeared. Having heard this, the seers (*ṛṣi*-s) collected the sacrifice. The consecrated sacrificer becomes the sacrifice, for it is he that carries the sacrifice on. By sipping the fast-milk (*vrata*), he restores again the sucked out and drained sap of the sacrifice. He should not offer that milk in the fire, for that will not do any good to the sacrifice. He should 'think' that he is offering in fire and not otherwise (*juhvadu haiva manyeta nājuhvat*), for the vital airs (*prāṇa*-s) are born of the mind (the sense-organ, which thinks), endowed with mind, of intelligent power. Agni is speech; Mitra and Varuṇa are the in-breathing and the upward-breathing; Āditya is the eye and All-gods are the ear. So when he drinks that milk (*vrata*), he really makes offering to these deities (*Śat. Br.* III. 2.2.11-13). In this *arthavāda*, the sense-organs, speech, etc. are joined with the heavenly deities, showing thereby the macro-microcosmic relationship viewed by the Vedic ritualists. The same relationship is thought of as being there, in the ritual metaphors, which occur in the *Jaim. Br.*, concerning the sense-organs and the seasons as also the sense-organs and the deities. The *Jaim. Br.* says that formerly there were two types of seasons (*ṛtavaḥ*) *viz, prāṇartavaḥ* and *devartavaḥ*. The *prāṇartavaḥ* (sense-organs imagined as seasons) are - *prāṇa* (vital breath) is the spring; speech is summer (Grīṣma); eye is the rainy season; ear is the Śarat; mind is the Hemanta and whatever waters are there in a man, the Śiśira (*Jaim. Br.* II. 51). In the wordy quarrel, later on ending in reconciliation, between Keśin Dārbhya and Yājñasena, the latter makes clear some concepts. He says that when the sacrificer gives his mind to the Brahman priest, it is actually the moon which he gives, meaning thereby that as long as the moon does not perish, his *dakṣinā* (which he has given) does not perish. On similar lines, the further exposition runs on as - speech given to the Hotṛ priest, meaning thereby the fire (Agni) given; the vital air (*prāṇa)* to the Adhvaryu priest, *prāṇa* meaning Vāyu; eye given to the Udgātṛ priest, eye meaning Āditya; the soul (*ātmā)* given to the Sadasya, soul meaning space or the sky (*ākāśa);* the ear given to the Hotraka-s, ear meaning the quarters; the hair on the body, given to the Prasarpaka-s, the hair on the body meaning the plants and herbs. As long as the moon, Agni (fire), Vāyu (wind), Āditya (the sun), the sky, quarters and plants and herbs stay in this world (i.e. they stay permanently), so long the gifts offered by the sacrificer in the sacrifice will stay. This is the (knowledge of) *a-kṣiti,* i.e. eternality, of the sacrificer's *iṣṭāpūtra,* i.e. whatever sacrifices he performs and whatever works of social well-being he carries out (*ibid.* II. 54). This *arthavāda* passage is important on more than one accounts. It shows how the ritualistic or metaphysical discussions might have been there, taking place healthily, without any note of jealousy or enmity from either side. It deals with the 'permanent' nature of the *dakṣiṇā*-s, when given in the sacrifice. And from our present point of view, dealing with 'Perception', it equates the sense-organs with the deities (such as Agni, etc.) and the ear with the quarters. The soul equated with the sky and the hair on the body equated with the plants and herbs are the details, to be taken note of. The soul when equated with the sky, reminds us of the later doctrine propounded by Pravāhaṇa Jaivali that *ākāśa* is the origin of all things and one should meditate upon *ākāśa* (space or the sky) as the highest reality (*Chān. Up.* VII. 12.1,2). About the detail concerning the hair on the body — The *Śat Br.,* in the context of laying down the Dūrvā bricks on the Great Fire-altar, states that Prajāpati after creating the universe, being exhausted, became disjointed. The hair on his body (*lomāni)* which were lying on the ground became the herbs namely Dūrvā (*Śat. Br.* VII. 4.2.11).

To turn to the *arthavāda*-s regarding the sense-organs viewed individually —

Breath; Vital Airs

While establishing the three Agni-s, when on that occasion, they produce fire by churning, the sacrificer breathes upon it. Fire (Agni) is breath. By breathing (i.e. blowing) upon the fire, the sacrificer produces the Agni that is already produced. The sacrificer again draws in, his breath. By this, he esablishes that fire (Agni) in his innermost soul (*ibid.* II. 2.2.15). The *Śat. Br.* has a ritual metaphor to state. The Āhavanīya and the Gārhapatya are said to be *prāṇa* (in-breathing) and *udāna* (upward breathing) respectively, the Anvāhāryapacana fire is the through-breathing (*vyāna*) (*ibid.* II.2.2.18). There is another ritual metaphor in the context of the Agniṣṭoma sacrifice. The Upāṁśu (Soma-cup) is the in-breathing (*prāṇa*) of the Sacrifice, the Upāṁśu-savana (press-stone) is the through-breathing (*vyāna*) and the Antaryāma (Soma-cup) the upward breathing (*udāna*) (*ibid.* IV. 1.1.1).[5]

At many places, the Brāhmaṇa texts eulogise *prāṇa* - breath in general, without referring to any particular type of it. While dealing with the offering of oblations, the *Śat. Br.* says that the Pavamāna (blowing) Agni is *prāṇa* (breath), which is put into the sacrificer, by means of offering. Breath is food and the offering also is food (*ibid.* II. 2.1.6). Beasts have Vāyu (wind) as their leader; Vāyu is breath, for by means of the breath that beasts move about (*ibid.* IV. 4.1.15; cf. *ibid.* X. 3.3.7). Gāyatrī and Triṣṭubh are said to be *praṇa* (*ibid.* X.3.1.2,7). While building the Great Fire-altar, he lays down the bricks named Prāṇabhṛtaḥ ('breath-holders'), in the first layer. These are said to be the vital breaths, which the sacrificer bestows upon Agni (*ibid.* VIII. 1.1.1). In the rite, noted above, of building the Great Fire-altar, when the fire-pan (*ukhā*) is ready, he puts the head of the victims in the fire-pan. The *arthavāda* states that when Prajāpati was alone at first, he desired to be reproduced and fashioned animals from his vital airs - a man from his mind, a horse from his eye, a cow from his breath, a sheep from his ear and a goat from his voice. So people say that animals are vital airs (*ibid.* VII. 5.2.6). Before putting the heads of the animals mentioned above, he thrusts gold chips into each of them. As gold is vital air (*prāṇa)* and as vital airs go out of these animals when slaughtered, he replaces the vital airs into each of the animals by thrusting gold chips (*ibid.* VII. 5.2.8). While dealing with the Agnihotra rite, the *Jaim. Br.* has taken a note of an uncommon situation. The sacrificer having established the fires, proceeds on journey. In what way, his Agnihotra offerings are to be given, is the problem. The *Jaim. Br.* taking a rational view says that in all the worlds, the vital air is always awake. So the oblation (to be offered in Agni) is to be offered (mentally) in the vital air. Hence they say that Agnihotra (rite) is the vital air (*Jaim. Br.* I.20). A proverbial expression from the *Jaim Br.* in the context of *prāṇa* has to be noted, for in simple words it enshrines a great truth. When the seers Jīvala Kārīrādi, Aṣāḍha Sāvayasa and Indradyumna Bhāllaveya approach Āruṇi, he enlightens them on Gāyatrī. Āruṇi says that Gāyatrī (the metre) is the vital air (*prāṇa*) and to everybody the vital air is dear. There is nothing dearer than the vital air (*ibid.* I. 272). The common experience of the survival of body dependent on breath is pointed out in an *arthavāda* from the *Kauṣ. Br.* In the context of Soma-sacrifice (Pṛṣṭhya Ṣaḍaha), it is said that he should not draw in breath between the *pada* and the repeated *pada.* The *pada* is the body and the repeated *pada,* the breaths. If one draws in (his) breath between these two (*pada*-s*),* it would be separating the body from the breath and a person will not live. Thus would be his uttering of the *pada*-s without any life (*Kauṣ. Br.* XXIII. 6). The *Kauṣ. Br.* while prescribing the same priests in the introductory (Prāyaṇīya) and concluding (Udayanīya) rites in the Soma-sacrifice, substantiates its stand by referring to, in the *arthavāda,* the process of breathing, which is everybody's experience. The *Kauṣ. Br.* states that the process of in-breathing (*prāṇa)* and upward breathing (*udāna)* are alike. The two rites mentioned above are like *prāṇa* and *udāna* (*ibid.* VII. 5). The *Kauṣ. Br.* then turns to the metaphor of a chariot. Sacrifice is a chariot of the gods and its two sides are the introductory and concluding sacrifices. Just as one can go on journey to a desired destination, by driving on in a chariot with two sides alike, the sacrificer safely attains the world of heaven with the Prāyaṇīya and Udayanīya sacrifices, which are alike (*ibid.* VII. 7).

In the context of vital air, the words meaning 'breathing' or 'blowing' on something, 'smelling' or 'sniffing' something, occur and they all indicate placing the breath in something, thereby imparting the very life to it. An interesting *vidhi* and the *arthavāda* following it are worthy of consideration here. The *Śat. Br.* deals in details with the Sahasradakṣiṇa Trirātra, i.e. sacrifice of three pressing days, with a thousand cows as the priests' *dakṣiṇā* (*Śat. Br.* IV. 5.8.1-16).[6] On each of the three Soma-pressing days, three hundred and thirty-three cows are given as *dakṣinā* to the priests. And there remains one-thousandth cow. This cow is of particular colour and of unimpared vigour (not been approached by a bull), for she is in reality Vāc (Speech). The *vidhi* (rite) is — the priest or sacrificer makes her 'smell' the trough of Soma-juice (*droṇakalaśa)* at the north of the Havirdhāna shed and south of the Āgnīdhra fire-house. As *droṇakalaśa* is the sacrifice, by making the cow (Speech) smell (involving obviously the process of in-breathing) that (*droṇakalaśa*), he makes her 'see' the sacrifice (*ibid.* IV. 5.8.5). The purpose of this is complementing the sacrifice with Speech (Vāc), through the *prāṇa* (vital air of in-breathing) bestowed on the sacrifice by the cow (= Speech). The *Jaim. Br.* says that Speech and vital air (*prāṇa)* form a divine pair (*Jaim. Br.* I.306), It is clear that the action of 'seeing' the *droṇakalaśa* by the cow cannot be vouchsafed, while her 'smelling' can. Hence the rite of making the cow 'smell' the *droṇakalaśa* is introduced here, which also points out the importance of the process of breathing (here 'in-breathing), which is on par with 'seeing' and that too 'seeing the trough.'

In the rite of Agnicayana, the sniffing of a naturally perforated brick (*svayam-ātṛṇṇā),* by a horse is prescribed by the *Tait. Sam.* The *Tait. Sam.* says that thereby the sacrificer places breath in that brick, which symbolically stands for the yonder sky. As horse stands for Prajāpati, it is by Prajāpati that he piles the fire (*Tait. Sam.* V. 3.7.4).

The same belief of imparting life through sniffing, smelling, etc. works in the *arthavāda,* which glorifies the Śyaita *sāman.* It is said that Prajāpati created the creatures but they languished. He sniffed[7] at them by means of the Śyaita *sāman* with the word *'hummā.'*[8] By that sniffing or breathing upon them with the Śyaita *sāman,* the cattle throve (*Pañc. Br.* VII. 10.12-15). It is said that the Udgātṛ priest makes the sound '*him*' (i.e. '*hum*') by means of the Śyaita *sāman* and thus becomes Prajāpati and sniffs at the young ones, with the result they prosper (*ibid.* VII. 10.16). The passage in the *Pañc. Br.* hardly needs any more explanation.

A reference to smelling occurs in the *arthavāda* in the context of the rite of Tānūnaptra, which is a rite of mutual assurance between sacrificer and officiating priests.[9] It is said that he should smell (*ava jighret)* the butter thrice, saying, "I offer in Prajāpati; in the mind I offer." This gives support to the Tānūnaptra (*Tait. Sam.* III. 1.2.2). As noted already, smelling imparts new life to the substance or person and can be said to provide support to him.

A mythical account coming by way of *arthavāda* occurs in connection with the Āgneya *sāman.* This *sāman* is a midday Pavamāna laud to be sung on the fifth day in the Pṛṣṭhya Ṣaḍaha (six-day period) of the twelve-day rite. The *arthavāda* occurring here points out that Agni though created (i.e. churned out) did not flame. With this *sāman,* Prajāpati blew on it and there upon it flared up. With this *sāman,* he obtains brilliancy and spiritual lustre (*Pañc. Br.* XIII. 3.21,22). The belief here is of imparting life-breath on any entity by blowing on it. The concept goes back to the *RV* (X. 72). It is said that at the beginning of the universe, the Existent (*sat*) came out of Non-Existent (*asat*). However for the actual creation of the universe, it was Brahmaṇaspati, who blew the births of the gods as a blacksmith blows his bellows (*RV*. X. 72.2 ab—*brahmaṇaspatiretā sam karmāra ivādhamat*). In the Śrauta ritual, blowing or breathing on the sacrificial material or the kindled fire is enjoined.[10] The belief is that the sacrificer himself imparts his life-principle to Agni or the sacrificial matter. The tradition of the Gṛhyasūtra-s refers to the rite of smelling the head of the son or daughter by the father, when the latter returns from a journey. Even the Purāṇa-s are replete with references to the smelling of the head of the younger ones, especially the son, by the elders.[11] The rite of smelling the head is closely associated with the principle of imparting the life-breath, with a belief that it would prolong the life of person thus smelt.

Mind

We have already noted that in the later Indian philosophical thought, mind (*manas*) is not the regular sense-organ on par with the other sense-organs, but it is regarded as unique being the internal sense-organ. In the ritual texts, mind occupies a very important status. In the rite of Agnicayana, the sacrificer puts the heads of sacrificial victims in the fire-pan (*ukhā*). In this context, the *Śat. Br.* states a mythical account as *arthavāda* that when Prajāpati was alone, he fashioned animals from his vital airs — a man from his mind, a horse from his eye, a cow from his breath, a sheep from his ear and a goat from his voice. The mind is the first of the vital airs (*prāṇa*-s). All the vital airs are established in the mind (*Śat. Br.* VII. 5.2.6). In the context of the New-moon and Full-moon sacrifices, while explaining the *mantra* from the *Vaj. Sam.* (II. 13) which refers to mind, the *Śat. Br.* eulogises the mind that by it all this (whole universe) is pervaded. The sacrificer also obtains all by the mind (*Śat.*

Br. I.7.4.22). In the Agniṣṭoma sacrifice, the consecrated sacrificer has to drink the fast-milk (which is called *vrata).* He is not to offer it in the fire. When he drinks that milk, he offers it to the deities *viz.* Agni which is Speech; Mitra and Varuṇa the in-breathing and upward breathing; Āditya the eye; and the All-gods the ear. The vital airs mentioned here are all born of the mind, endowed with mind, of intelligent power (*ibid.* III. 2.2.13). The macro-micro-cosmic relationship between the deities such as Agni, etc. and the vital airs such as Speech, etc. is to be marked. The *Śat. Br.* elsewhere says that *manas* (mind) is the overlord of the vital airs (*ibid.* XIV. 3.2.3). The Brāhmaṇa-texts equated mind with Prajāpati or *vice versa* (*ibid.* IV. 1.1.22; *Jaim. Br.* II. 9; 45; 174). The *Śat. Br.* connects mind with one of the elements *viz.* Vāyu (wind) and says that Vāyu, having become the mind, remained in the right side of the body (*Śat. Br.* VIII. 1.1.7) and says that from out of the mind, the summer season (Grīṣma) is fashioned (*ibid.* 8).

In the rite of Tānūnaptra or covenant of Tanūnapāt, a mythical account occurs, which points out how the gods know the thoughts in the mind of men. It is said that having come to know the bad intention of the *asura-rakṣas*-es, the gods come to an agreement keeping the mighty Tanūnapāt — the yonder blowing wind — as the witness, who enters the in-breathing and upward breathing. When the man proposes in his mind, it passes on to the breath, the breath to the wind and the wind tells the gods, what the mind of man is (*ibid.* III. 4.2.1-2. 5-6). The same thought is expressed when the context is of the sacrificer, who is about to set out on a journey. He first approaches the Gārhapatya fire and thereafter the Āhavanīya, prior to his taking up the journey. He (as other householders) approaches the fires with (muttered) prayer, obviously for the well-being of his house, offspring and cattle. He may also approach the fires silently, for the gods certainly know the mind of men (*ibid.* II. 4.1.3-5, 10-11).

Mind and Speech

Now we come to an important point and that is — respective status of mind and speech. At some places, they are spoken of as being on par. Bṛhat *sāman* is said to be Mind, and the Rathantara *sāman* is Speech (*Jaim. Br.* III. 316; I.329). Speech is the truth of the *ṛc*, while Mind is that of the *sāman* (*ibid.* I.326). In the context of the Agniṣṭoma (sacrifice), it is said that they perform the sacrifice with the Mind and with Speech. The *mantra* employed is — 'They harness the mind and they harness the thoughts' (*RV.* V. 81.1; *Vāj. Sam.* V.14). Here by 'thoughts' we have to understand 'Speech', for people following their respective intelligence (*dhī*), while making their living, actually use their speech alone (*Śat. Br.* III. 5.3.11). They spread (i.e. perform) the sacrifice with these two (mind and speech). In the context of the twelve-day sacrifice, the Adhvaryu priest is said to be the Mind and the Hotṛ priest to be Speech (*ibid.* XII. 1.1.5). The *ṛc*-s and *sāman*-s are the Speech, and *yajus*-es are the Mind (*ibid.* IV. 6.7.5,19). Sarasvān (the male aspect of Sarasvatī) is the Mind, while Sarasvatī is Speech (*ibid.* VII. 5.1.31). In the context of the Agnicayana rite, Speech and Mind are said to be the young parents (*ibid.* VIII. 6.3.22). The *Jaim. Br.* says that Mind and Speech are the two yokes. Speech is born from Mind. Speech has Mind as her eye; hence she is *manonetrā* (*Jaim. Br.* I. 320). In the context of the New-moon and Full-moon sacrifices, the full moon is said to be the Mind, for this Mind is as it were the full moon and the new moon is Speech, for the Speech appears as it were (like the new-moon). These two — Mind and Speech — are clearly the full moon and new moon as regards the body (*Śat. Br.* XI. 2.4.7). In the rite of Agnihotra (i.e. daily offering of oblations in fire in the morning and the evening), the Agnihotra cow (i.e. the cow, from which milk for oblations is obtained) is the Speech of the Agnihotra and the calf is its Mind. Mind and Speech, being one and the same are, as it were, distinct from each other. So they tie up the calf and its mother with one and the same rope (*ibid.* XI. 3.1.1). The *Jaim. Br.* also speaks about the Speech and the Mind in the same way. Mind was there formerly in the beginning. Speech followed the Mind, and both Speech and Mind are there due to the vial air (*prāṇa*-breath in general) (*Jaim. Br.* I.19). Mind is fastest in all the worlds (*ibid.* I.20).

In the context of the Soma-sacrifice (animal sacrifice), the Maitrāvaruṇa priest is said to be the Mind of sacrifice, and Hotṛ is the Speech. Speech is set into motion, impelled by the Mind. The Speech which a person speaks with his mind diverted elsewhere, that speech is demoniacal and not acceptable to the gods (*Ait. Br.* II.5=6.5). Mind thus is superior to Speech. This thought is expressed at many places in the ritual tradition. The *Jaim. Br.* states a mythical account that the gods said to the *asura*-s to speak out first. But the *asura*-s replied that the gods should speak first. The gods then spoke of the Mind and the *asura*-s of Speech. Those gods cut off (and thus separated) the speech of the *asura*-s by means of their (i.e. gods') mind. Hence it is that whatever one gets with the mind, that (thought) he speaks with his voice, i.e. speech (*Jaim. Br.* II. 291-92).

The *Śat. Br.* in clear words, states the importance of mind, in the context of Soma-sacrifice. While purchasing Soma from the Soma-seller, a cow is given to the Soma-seller in the bargain (the cow hence is called the Somakrayaṇī cow). The gods in former times had sent Vāc (Speech) to the *asura*-s for bringing from them Soma. In the rite of purchasing Soma, the cow is given as standing for the Vāc (Speech), of former times. While explaining the *mantra* from the *Vāj. Sam.* (IV. 17) in this connection, the *Śat. Br.* speaks of the exact status and importance of both—mind and speech. It says that our speech is indeed upheld by the mind, for the Mind goes before Speech and instructs her, "Speak thus! Do not say this!' were it not for the Mind, Speech would indeed talk incoherently (*Śat. Br.* III. 2.4.10-11). In the same context it is said that Adhvaryu priest goes near the Soma-cow and praises her with a *mantra* (*Vāj. Sam.*

IV. 19) that she (i.e. the Soma-cow) is the thought and she is the Mind. As noted already, the Soma-cow is Speech, and Speech speaks following the thought, following the Mind (*Śat. Br.* III. 2.4.16). The *Jaim. Br.* says that Mind is at the head of Speech (*Jaim. Br.* II. 9). The thought that it is the Mind that created the Speech occurs in the *Śat. Br.* (X. 5.3.4) as also in the *Jaim. Br.* (III. 334).

In the context of the Soma-sacrifice (Agniṣṭoma sacrifice), it is said that the *ṛc*-s and *sāman*-s are Speech and the *yajus*-es are the Mind. Those who perform with the *ṛc* and *sāman* are Speech and those who perform with the *yajus* are the Mind. Hence unless ordered by the Adhvaryu, nothing is done in the sacrifice (for the Adhvaryu is connected with the *yajus*, i.e. the Mind). Those who perform with the *ṛc* or those who perform with the *sāman* perform it, only when the Adhvaryu priest gives them the instruction. This is because, Speech speaks not but what is conceived by the Mind (*Śat. Br.* IV. 6.7.19).

The comparison between the Mind and Speech and the superiority of the former to the latter is brought out by the *Śat. Br.* in an interesting manner. It is said that in the New-moon and Full-moon sacrifices, when the fire is kindled, he makes the first two oblations to Mind and Speech. The libation which he makes for the Mind, he makes sitting and standing that which he makes for Speech. Mind and Speech, when yoked together, convey the sacrifice to the gods. When one of the two yoke-fellows is smaller than the other, they give him a shoulder-piece (*upavaha)*. Speech is indeed smaller than Mind, for Mind is the more unlimited and Speech is the more limited of the two. By standing he gives a shoulder-piece to Speech. And then as well-matched yoke-fellows, Mind and Speech convey the sacrifice to the gods (*ibid.* I.4.4.7).

The mythical account of the quarrel between Mind and Speech as to which of the two was better, also shows that Mind is certainly superior to Speech. When these two approach Prajāpati for his verdict, Prajāpati decides in favour of Mind, saying to Speech that she is only an imitator of the Mind's activities (of thinking) and a follower in its wake and so inferior of the two (*ibid.* I.4.5.8-11).

Eye

Of all the sense-organs, the eye is of utmost importance. Some of the rituals and the *arthavāda*-s following them are to be taken into account in this regard. In the context of the New-moon and Full-moon sacrifices, there is a ritual of looking in the downward direction, at the butter by the Adhvaryu priest or the sacrificer. Now this simple ritual is glorified by the *arthavāda* that the eye (i.e. the act of seeing) is undoubtedly the truth. The *arthavāda* here refers to a worldly conviction regarding the eye or the act of seeing anything directly. If two persons come to dispute over a certain matter, one of them saying, 'I have seen it' and the other 'I have heard it', we should believe him who said, 'I have seen it', and not the other. By directly looking in the downward direction at the butter, he (i.e. the Adhvaryu priest or the sacrificer) causes the butter to increase by means of truth (*ibid.* I.3.1.26-27).[12] The same thought is expressed by the *Tait. Br.*, when it prescribes that the Āhavanīya fire-place should be at twelve *vikrama*-s (*prakraṁa*-s, they being measure of distance) from the Gārhapatya fire-place. Now this distance, according to the *Tait. Br.*, need not be exact by actually measuring it but simply by looking at it. By this he avoids both the measured ground as well as the one not measured. The reason forwarded by the *arthavāda* is — A man speaks (i.e. can speak) false with speech (i.e. with tongue), so does he think of false in his mind. But whatever he sees with the 'eye' is 'truth' — *cakṣur vai satyam* (*Tait. Br.* I. 1.4.1, 2). Sāyaṇa, in his commentary on this passage explains that whenever a person comes from a long distance, they ask him whether he has 'seen' (a particular thing) or 'heard' (about that thing), and when he says that he has 'seen' it, they believe in him. So the measurement of twelve *vikrama*-s of the ground should simply be by taking a glance at it. The *arthavāda* passage in the *Tait. Br.* winds up in stating that the sacrificer, who has established fires, should not speak false and in his house, a *brāhmaṇa* should not stay without food. The sacrificer has to give him food (*ibid.* I.1.4.2).

The eye due to its lustre is many times connected with the sun. In the context of the Agnicayana rite, while constructing the first layer, one of the *mantra*-s from the *Vāj. Sam.* (XIII. 56) speaks of 'This one behind the all-embracer', meaning thereby the yonder sun. The *arthavāda* explains that the sun having become the eye, remained behind and so it is that this form he bestows on Agni, while building the Great Fire-altar (*Śat. Br.* VIII. 1.2.1). The same *mantra* from the *Vāj. Sam.* (XIII. 56) indicates further that the eye is fashioned out of the all-embracer, i.e. the sun and the rains are the offspring of the eye (*Śat. Br.* VIII. 1.2.2). The *Śat. Br.* has obviously eye and tears and the sun and rains in view.

The relation of the eye and the sun has to be traced to the *RV*, where the sun is said to be the eye of the deities Mitra and Varuṇa (*RV.* I. 115.1; VI.51.1; VII.61.1; VII. 63.1; X. 37.2). Uṣas (the goddess of Dawn) is said to bring the eye of the gods (i.e. the sun) (*ibid.* VII. 77.3). The sun is said to store all waters on the earth.[13] That the sun is the reservoir of all waters is also echoed in the expression from the *Tait. Ār.* (I.8.1 — *āpaḥ sūrye samāhitāḥ).*

The sun and eye are closely connected in belief. From the Puruṣa's eye, the sun was born (*RV.* X. 90.13). It is said that the eye of the dead person should go to the sun (*ibid.* X. 16.3). An expiatory offering is prescribed in the context of the Horse-sacrifice. In case an eye-disease befalls the sacrificial horse, a pap (*caru)* should be offered to Sūrya. The *arthavāda* states that the sun is the eye of the creatures, for when the sun rises everything moves here. By means of the eye of the world, he bestows eye upon the sacrificial horse, as the horse is suffering from eye-disease (*Śat. Br.* XIII. 3.8.4). Here the pap (*caru)* itself, which is offered is identified with the sun and is spoken of symbolically as the eye of the world. And with this eye, the eye of the horse is cured. The principle working here is of sympathetic magic. The same is seen while explaining the propriety of offering the *caru*. By means of the eye, this self (*ātman)* moves (*carati) (ibid.)*. Here the *arthavāda* takes the help of etymology, again following the principle of sympathetic magic (*caru* and *carati* joined).

For being endowed with good eyesight, the sacrificer-king in the Rājasūya sacrifice offers mirror as gift (*dakṣiṇā)* to each of the priests *viz.* Adhvaryu and the Pratiprasthātṛ. This gift of the mirror when given, brings good eyesight (according to Sāyaṇa—*dṛṣṭipāṭavam)* to the sacrificer (*Pañc. Br.* XVIII. 9.10). Even in the Gṛhyasūtra tradition, when the child is made to cast the first glance at the moon or look at the sun for the first time, a mirror is prescribed as a gift to be made.[14] Here the idea is of divine light and the gift of the mirror stands as a symbol for the gain of continued light.[15]

An ailment of eyes making a person 'gravel-blind' is mentioned in one *arthavāda* by the *Ṣaḍ. Br.* (I.7.2). The context is of looking at the melted butter (*ājya),* which is added to the *caru (*specially boiled rice) offered to Soma and which has remained in the *pātra* (container) after being offered. The mythical account runs as follows. The Sādhya-s when engaged in a sacrificial session became gravel-blind (*śarkarā akṣasu jajñire).* The gods resorted to Indra and asked him a remedy to remove that eye-trouble. Indra gave them the brown-coloured melted butter (*śyāvam ājyam)* for being put on the *caru* meant for Soma. The Sādhya-s looked at that melted butter and thereafter became able to see properly.

The *Pañc. Br.,* making a reference to the physical structure of the eye-phenomenon, states the *arthavāda* in the context of the Dvādaśāha—Twelve-day sacrifice. The Dvādaśāha-sacrifice is enclosed by an Atirātra (overnight sacrifice) at the beginning and at the end. In the remaining Ten-day-sacrifices' period, there are eight Ukthya days in the middle and two Agniṣṭoma days on both sides.[16] The *Pañc. Br.* says that the two Atirātra sacrifices are the two eyes and the two Agniṣṭoma sacrifices are the pupils of the two eyes. As noted above, the two Agniṣṭoma sacrifices are at the inside of the two Atirātra sacrifices. Hence it is said that the pupil being at the inside (in the middle of the eye) has the advantage of being protected by the outer structure of the eye (*Pañc. Br.* X. 4.2). In the same context occurs the *arthavāda* making a reference to two fangs (*ibid.* X. 4.3.). Here the Dvādaśāha sacrifice is said to be the Year (Saṁvatsara) the concept obviously being based on the number 'twelve', the Year having twelve months. It is said that the two Atirātra sacrifices are the two fangs of the Year. On these two days, one should not sleep, obviously because the sacrifice goes on in the night also, otherwise one may set oneself on the fangs of the Year (*ibid.*). The same two Atirātra sacrifices are said to be the *prāṇa* (in-breathing) and *udāna* (upward breathing) respectively[17] (*ibid.* X. 4.1).

The two eyes figure as a standard of comparison (*upamāna*) in a ritual metaphor in one *arthavāda*. The two butter-portions to Agni and Soma are said to be the eyes, in the context of the New-moon and Full-moon sacrifices. In a very simplistic statement, the *arthavāda* states that he offers these butter-portions in front (of, or before, the offering), for the eyes are in front of the head (*Śat. Br.* I.6.3.38). Even the physical structure of the eye finds mention at this place in the *arthavāda*. Having recited a *ṛc* (-verse) as Anuvākyā (invitatory *mantra*), he recites by way of Yājyā (offering *mantra*), containing the word 'pleased' (*juṣāṇa*). The *arthavāda* states that by these , 'boneless' eyes are set in what is bone (*ibid.* I.6.3.40). If on the other hand, while reciting a *ṛc*-verse as Anuvākyā, if he were to use a *ṛc*-verse as the Yājyā, he would make it bone instead of eye (*ibid.*). The white portion of the eye is related to Agni and the black one to Soma. If someone says the other way, i.e. black to Agni and white to Soma, it would be — what sees is of the nature of Agni, for dry as it were are the eyes of one who looks and what is dry relates to Agni, and what sleeps is of the nature of Soma, for moist as it were are the eyes of one, who is asleep and moist also is Soma. The *arthavāda* here ends on a Puranic style that he who knows the two butter-portions to be eyes, remains endowed with eye-sight till old age in this world and starts in yonder world possessed of eyesight (*ibid.* I.6.3.41).

In the rite of consecration in the Soma-sacrifice, the eyes of the sacrificer are anointed with collyrium. The *Śat. Br.* prescribes that the sacrificer anoints first the right eye. The *arthavāda* states the human practice of anointing the left eye first, while with the gods it is the right eye that is anointed first (*Śat. Br.* III. 1.3.14). The *arthavāda,* apart from bringing out the practice of anointing the left eye first, also speaks of the divine status of the consecrated sacrificer, who has to do things like the gods.

The eye which gives a true picture of a thing or being, can be a carrier of 'evil', which is cooked in the mind of an onlooker and can transfer that 'evil' to the thing or being, coming in its range. This refers to a mythical account which occurs in the *Ait. Br.* (VI.1=26.1). It runs as follows. A sacrificial session of the gods remained unsuccessful due to the evil, as the sacrifice was lacking in a detail. At that time, there came a seer named Arbuda Kādraveya (the son of Kadrū, the mother of serpents) of the Sarpa clan, who advised them to invoke the pressing stones (*grāvan*-s) at the midday pressing and thus wipe off the evil thereby. Arbuda Kādraveya himself invoked the pressing-stones for the sake of the gods. But the gods being apprehensive of the Sarpa-seer looking at Soma and thus putrefying it by his sight, bound his eyes with his head-wear. This *arthavāda* is stated to explain and support the *vidhi* of winding round (the face) a turban (*uṣṇīṣa* = head-wear) and then praising the grinding-stones, at the midday pressing. The mythical account coming by way of *arthavāda* supporting the *vidhi,* has no doubt at its basis the belief regarding the 'evil' power of the eye of an inimical person. Moreover the *arthavāda* has to be taken as pointing out a trend of assimilation of the

Aryans with the Sarpa tribe regarding the midday pressing of Soma. It might be that the practice of winding round (the face) a head-wear (or turban) and then praising the grinding-stones was a loan from the Sarpa tradition.[18]

The same ritual of praising the grinding-stones, while wearing a turban is mentioned by the *Kauṣ. Br.* In the *arthavāda* it is mentioned that Arbuda Kādraveya (of the Sarpa clan) praised wearing a turban, with his eyes tied up. It is said that the 'eye' came; it was a serpent; together with that, poison came to the priests. In order to repel the poison and purify the ritual, the priest used particular verses connected with Soma (*Kauṣ. Br.* XXIX. 1). The *arthavāda* from the *Ait. Br.* (VI.1=26.1) deals with this point in details. It says that when Soma-juice after being drunk was maddening the gods, they thought it to be the effect of the Sarpa-seer's chants while invoking the Soma. Hence the gods mixed his chants with their *ṛc*-s. This again speaks of the assimilation of the Vedic Aryans with the Sarpa-clan regarding the *mantra*-s or chants, to be recited at the midday Soma-pressing at the Agniṣṭoma sacrifice, in which context this mythical account occurs.

The *vidhi* and the *arthavāda* noted from both the Brāhmaṇa-texts, are based on the concept of the evil power of the eye, when that 'eye' is of an inimical person. The same has percolated in our own times, and even in the modern age, means are suggested to alleviate or completely drive away the dangerous effects of the 'evil' eye.

Ear

Ear is one of the five vital airs. We have already noted that Prajāpati created animals from his vital airs—a man from his mind, a horse from his eye, a cow from his breath, a sheep from his ear and a goat from his speech (*vāc,* i.e. voice). So people say that animals are vital airs (*Śat. Br.* VII. 5.2.6). While laying down ten bricks in the first layer, in the rite of Agnicayana, he mentions the quarters as being on the upper (left) side. The *mantra* from the *Vāj. Sam.* (XIII. 57) - 'This, on the upper side heaven', points out that the regions as quarters are in the upper side and are above everything. They are the heavenly world or light. They having become the ear remained above. It is this form that he now bestows on Agni. From out of that form, the regions, he fashioned the ear and from out of the ear, he fashioned the autumn (*Śat. Br.* VIII. 1.2.4-5).

In the context of the Sautrāmaṇī sacrifice, when the victim for the goddess Sarasvatī is offered, an offering is given together to the deities Indra, Sarasvatī and the two Aśvins. Indra is the mind, Sarasvatī is speech and the two Aśvins are the ears. Whatever one thinks in the mind, that, one speaks with one's speech and what one speaks with one's speech, that, one hears with one's ears (*ibid.* XII. 9.1.13).

The *Śat. Br.* says that the vital air is divided fivefold in the head—the mind, speech, the breath, the eye and the ear (*ibid.* IX. 2.2.5). The five vital breaths and the five sense-organs are spoken of as being together in the context of the rite of Agnicayana. When the Prāṇabhṛt bricks are placed in the first layer of the Great Fire-altar, it is said that the bricks laid down in front are the holders of the *prāṇa* (in-breathing); those behind are the eye-holders, the holders of *apāna* (downward air); those on the right side are the mind-holders, the holders of *vyāna* (circulating air); those on the left side are the ear-holders, the holders of *udāna* (upward air) and those in the middle are the speech-holders, the holders of *samāna* (pervading air) (*ibid.* VIII. 1.3.6).

Body-Parts and Limbs

Practically all the limbs and parts of the human body figure in the ritual metaphors, which occur in the context of the Sautrāmaṇī sacrifice. A couple of examples can be stated *viz.* Indra's cake is the man's heart; the cake of Savitṛ his liver; the cake of Varuṇa his lung, etc. (*ibid.* XII. 9.1.2-17). The details in the Sautrāmaṇī rite are spoken of as the limbs and parts of the body metaphorically and from the point of view of beliefs and practices, there is hardly anything which can be discussed.

As sacrifice is enjoined with the aim of having some positive miraculous result in the form of individual gains as well as the well-being of the society at large (the latter, especially when the sacrifice is performed by a king), the concept of 'fertility' naturally predominates in many rites and rituals, which are enjoined. In this regard, the mention of 'Breasts' in some ritual metaphors deserves consideration.

Breasts

In the Dvādaśāha (twelve-day) sacrifice, in the context of the Ārbhava Pavamāna laud of the sixth day, there is chanted a *sāman* with the word *'madhuścut'* as *nidhana* (*finale* at the end of the *sāman)* and also the *sāman* with the word *'ghṛtaścut'*. The *Pañc. Br.* takes recourse to a metaphor and states in the *arthavāda* that Prajāpati is Sacrifice and by means of these two *sāman*-s, which are the breasts of Agni-Prajāpati, the sacrificer or the Adhvaryu priest on his behalf, gets out of Agni-Prajāpati the essence of what is desirable (*Pañc. Br.* XIII. 11.16-18). The *Jaim. Br.* also states that the two *sāman*-s (mentioned above) are the breasts of *yajña* (= Prajāpati), adding that by these two *sāman*-s (= 'breasts' as in this ritual metaphor), Indra milked all his desires out of the sacrifice (*Jaim. Br.* I. 225). Thus Indra obtained all his desires by performing the sacrifice with these two *sāman*-s. In the context of the Agnyādhāna rite (i.e. the rite of establishing the fires), the *Mait. Sam.* states a metaphor (by way of *arthavāda)* that the Full-moon day and the New-moon day are the two breasts of Prajāpati. When the sacrificer establishes the fires on these two days, he milks Prajāpati himself (*Mait. Sam.* I.6.9). Among the fourteen *sambhāra*-s, which are to be placed at the site of the fires,[19] figures the moist earth from the (inside part of the) ant-hill, which is said to be the *valmīkavapā* (soft skin of the ant-hill). The *Mait.*

Sam. says that the ant-hill is the breast of Prajāpati (*Maït. Sam.* I.6.3). The ritual metaphors, noted above, in which breasts (or in the last metaphor 'breast') figure as standards of comparison (*upamāna*-s), can be taken as instances of ritual poetry. But apart from this metaphorical mention in the case of Prajāpati, Prajāpati himself is regarded here as an androgen (i.e. male-female combined in one, or the Great He-She) in the ritual-texts.

In the context of the Vaiśvadeva rite (one of the four Seasonal sacrifices), a mythical narrative coming by way of *arthavāda* states that Prajāpati created three types of beings (birds, reptiles other than snakes and snakes) one after the other. But when all these passed away from him, one after the other, it dawned on him that they might have passed away for want of food. So he made in the fore-part of his body breasts swelling with milk (*Śat. Br.* II. 5.1.3).[20] Here Prajāpati, though a male is said to have the breasts of a female. Such a mention occurs because Prajāpati is regarded as a bisexual deity, he being the creator of the universe.

There are several other parts of the body, which find mention in the context of rituals.[21] However they are not considered here, for the *arthavāda*-s related to them hardly appeal as containing any striking belief or practice.

Ātman

There are some references to the word *ātman,* which occur in the ritual texts. It has to be pointed out that in all these references, the meaning of the word *ātman* is not uniformly the same, with the result the *arthavāda*-s also strike a different note (at each time).

Two libations (the first and the second) are offered to Agni in the rite of Agnihotra. These two libations are said to form a pair or duad of the past and the future, the born and the to-be-born, that which has arrived (i.e. actually existent) and the hope, the to-day and the tomorrow. The 'past' is the self (*ātman),* for both these are certain (*addha),* while the 'future' is the progeny, for both these are uncertain (*anaddha*). The *arthavāda* runs on pointing out that the born is the self; the actually existent is the self; the to-day is the self, for all these are certain. But the to-be-born is progeny; the hope is progeny; the tomorrow is progeny; for all these are uncertain (*Śat. Br.* II. 3.1.23-28). Here the word *ātmā* which we have taken to mean 'self' stands for the very man with his physical existence, as pointed out by the *arthavāda*-s.

In the Agnicayana rite, in the initiation (Dīkṣā) ceremony, a sacrificial cake is offered to Vaiśvānara (Agni) and a pap (*caru*) is offered to Ādityas. The *arthavāda* states that the Vaiśvānara cake is the head (*śiraḥ*) and the Āditya *caru* is the body (*ātmā*). Vaiśvānara cake is one single oblation, for the head is one only (and the deity also is one *viz.* Agni), while the *caru* (meant for the Ādityas) has many deities, has a multiplicity of rice-grains and this *ātmā* (i.e. body) is a multiplicity of limbs (*ibid.* VI. 6.1.8-10). Here the word *ātmā* has to be taken as meaning 'body'.

In the Agnicayana rite, when he puts on four bricks running eastward on the site of the Gārhapatya hearth, it is said that this *ātmā* (of ours), i.e. body, consists of four parts. The two at the back are the thighs and the two in front are the arms, and where the body (*ātmā*) is, that includes the head (*ibid.* VII. 1.1.18). Here the word *ātmā* is understood as meaning body.

In the rite of Agnicayana, a golden image of man is placed in the lowest level of the Great Fire-altar. It is said that the twelve bricks in the name of seasons (Ṛtavyā bricks fr. *ṛtu* - 'season') are the year, the *ātmā*. That (golden image of man) — the *ātmā* — is the end of everything here. He is in the midst of all the waters, endowed with all objects of desire. While possessed of all objects of desires he is without desire, for no desire of anything worries him (*ibid.* X. 5.4.15). Eggeling here takes the word *ātmā* to mean the body of the altar.[22] But taking into account the thought given at the end of the passage (noted above), to understand the word *ātmā* as meaning 'self' would be proper.

In the context of the twelve-day sacrifice with transposed metres (Dvādaśāha *vyūḍhacchandas*), on the fourth day the Adhvaryu priest transposes (i.e. changes the position of) the cups (*graha*-s of Soma-juice) and the Udgātṛ and the Hotṛ priests transpose the metres. The Adhvaryu priest draws cups beginning with the Āgrayaṇa, for that fourth day is Prajāpati's own and the Āgrayaṇa is the self (*ātmā)* and Prajāpati is the self (*ātmā)* (*ibid.* IV. 5.9.2).

In the Agniṣṭoma sacrifice, while drawing the Ukthya cup (*graha),* it is said that, that *graha* is his undefined (*anirukta)* breath and as such it is that self (*ātmā)* of his, for the undefined breath is the self (*ātmā)* (*ibid.* IV. 2.3.1).

These *arthavāda*-s dealing with the concept of *ātman,* as meaning 'self', can be taken as making a pace for the philosophy of the Āraṇyakas and the Upaniṣads, in spite of the fact that these *arthavāda*-s spring from the sacrificial context, teeming with rites and rituals.

NOTES AND REFERENCES

1. *Tarkasaṁgraha* of Annaṁbhaṭṭa, ed. with Eng. tr., Intrn. and notes by Gajendragadkar, A.B. and Karmarkar, R.D., First ed., Poona, 1930, pp. 36, 43.
2. For tongue as the sense-organ of taste - *Śat. Br.* VIII. 5.4.1; XII. 9.1.14.
3. *Śamyā* - the wedge - is a stick of Khadira (tree) wood, with which, the Āgnīdhra priest strikes twice the lower and once the upper grindstone. See Eggeling, J., *The Śatapatha Brāhmaṇa*, pt. I., SBE Vol. 12, p. 28 f., note 4.
4. For a similar idea, see *Jaim. Br.* I.1, where the context is of churning the fire (Agnimanthana). In the process of churning the fire, the phenomena concerning smoke, burning coal, ashes, grass (which is waved serving as fanning the fire) and the fire kindled and dazzling, are taken as giving rise to the senses *viz.* mind, eye, ear, vital breath and speech respectively.

5. For similar ideas, *Śat. Br.* IV. 1.2.1, 2, 11, 27 — Antaryāma Soma-cup is offered after sun-rise and the Upāṁśu Soma-cup before sunrise. This is for keeping the two breathings (*prāṇa* and *udāna*) distinct from each other. These two cups (*graha*-s) are also said to be day and night, which are also distinct from each other.
6. Eggeling, J., *op. cit.*, pt. II, SBE Vol. 26, p. 414, note 1.
7. Caland, W. translates the word *'abhyajighrat'* as 'sniffed' (see his tr. of *Pañcaviṃśa Brāhmaṇa,* p. 161, for the passage of *Pañc. Br.* VII 10.15, which we have given, while dealing with the passage. But 'breathed upon' or 'smelt' will be a better translation, keeping with the belief which we are discussing.
8. About the word *hummā,* see Caland, W., *op. cit.*, p. 161, note 1 (on *Pañc. Br.* VII.10.15). Caland says that the word *hummā* forms the last word of the Udgītha of that (i.e. Śyaita) *sāman.* Sāyaṇa on *Pañc. Br.* (VII. 10.15) rightly points out that the word '*hum*' in the last *pāda* of the *sāman* imitates the sound made by the cattle and hence called by that sound, they wait upon Prajāpati for giving him enjoyment.
9. See Eggeling, J., *op. cit.*, pt. II, SBE Vol. 26, p. 93, note 1; also *Śat. Br.* III. 4.2.1-16, for more information.
10. Dandekar, R.N. and Kashikar, C.G., *Śrautakośa* (Eng. Tr.), Vol. I-i, Poona, 1958, pp. 34, 36.
11. For the details, see (Mrs.) Dange, S.S., "The Ritual of the Breath," *Hindu Domestic Rituals — A Critical Glance,* pp. 35-39.
12. For 'eye' regarded as truth, see *Śat. Br.* I.3.1.27; IV.2.1.26; *Mait. Sam.* III. 6.3; IV.1.12, also *Ait. Br.* I.6.
13. See Dange, Sadashiv A., *Pastoral Symbolism from the Ṛgveda,* University of Poona, Poona, 1970, pp. 35 ff.
14. See (Mrs.) Dange, S.S., "The Mirror", *Hindu Domestic Rituals—A Critical Glance,* p. 30.
15. *Ibid.*, p. 32.
16. The arrangement of the days in the Dvādaśāha sacrifice is as follows — Atirātra; Agniṣṭoma; 8 Ukthya days; Agniṣṭoma; Atirātra = 12 days.
17. Caland, W., *op. cit.*, p. 234, note 1 on *Pañc.* Br. X. 4.1.
18. (Mrs.) Dange, S.S., "Some Non-Vedic Rituals in the Vedic Tradition", *Proceedings of the All India Oriental Conference,*

XXXII session, Uni. of Gujarat, Ahmedabed, 1985, p. 166f .; also, "Cultural Assimilation in Vedic India", *Journal of the Asiatic Society of Bombay,* Mumbai, Vol. 74 for 1999 (New series), pub. in 2000, p. 59.

19. See note 3 on "*sambhāra*-s" in the chap. on "Trees, Plants and Varieties of Grass",
20. Eggeling, J., *op. cit.,* pt. I., p. 385 in his tr. of *Śat. Br.* II. 5.1.3 understands the 'breasts' to be the fore-part of the body of the beings, created by Prajāpati, which is not correct, taking into account the bisexual nature of Prajāpati hinted at here. Caland has already noted this misunderstanding on the part of Eggeling. See Caland, W., *op.cit.,* p. 345, note 2 on *Pañc. Br.* XIII. 11.18
21. For these parts of the body, see (Mrs.) Tilak, Sunanda K., *Cultural Gleanings from the Brāhmaṇa Literature,* Yaska Pub., New Delhi, 1990, pp. 96-112.
22. Eggeling, J., *op. cit.,* pt. IV , SBE Vol. 43, p. 389, note 15.

CHAPTER 10

Varṇa-System

The ritual texts clearly show that the system of classes (*varṇa*-s) in the society had come to assume practically a rigid form in their times. The *Śat. Br.* clearly states that there are four *varṇa*-s *viz. brāhmaṇa, kṣatriya (rājanya), vaiśya* and *śūdra* (*Śat. Br.* V. 5.4.9). In the context of the Soma-sacrifice, the *Tait. Sam.* has to give an elaborate mythical account regarding creation of certain entities, deities and classes. When Prajāpati thought of having offspring, he created from his mouth the *brāhmaṇa,* together with the god Agni, the Trivṛt *stoma,* the Gāyatrī metre, the Rathantara *sāman* and he-goat (the *Pañc. Br.* mentioning the spring season but not the Rathantara *sāman* and the he-goat); from his breast and arms, he created the *rājanya (kṣatriya),* together with the god Indra, the Pañcadaśa *stoma,* the Triṣṭubh metre, the Bṛhat *sāman* and the ram (the *Pañc. Br.* mentioning here the summer season but not the Bṛhat *sāman* and the ram); from the middle part of his body, he created the *vaiśya,* together with the Viśve Devāḥ, the Saptadaśa *stoma,* the Jagatī metre, the Vairūpa *sāman* and the cows (the *Pañc. Br.* mentioning here the rainy season but not the Vairūpa *sāman* and the cows) and at the end, from his feet, he created the *śūdra,* together with the Ekaviṁśa *stoma,* the Anuṣṭubh metre, the Vairāja *sāman* and the horse (*Tait. Sam.* VII.1.1.4-5; *Pañc. Br.* VI. 1. 6-11). Here the *Tait. Sam.* does not mention any deity in the case of *śūdra,* and no season is mentioned by the *Pañc. Br.*

These two texts are quick to add here that as *śūdra* has no deity associated with him, he is unworthy of performing sacrifice. The social fact is tried to be explained by the *arthavāda.* The mythical account noted above from the two ritual texts helps us understand whenever a specific metre is identified or associated with a particular *varṇa* (*Jaim. Br.* I.263; II.102; III. 309). The *Jaim. Br.* mentioning the three metres belonging to the three *varṇa*-s respectively has some more to say through *arthavāda.* It says that as the metre Gāyatrī gave everything of hers (to *brāhmaṇa* ?), therefore a *brāhmaṇa* goes ahead of *kṣatriya.* On the other hand, as the metre Jagatī did not give anything of hers (to *vaiśya),* the *vaiśya* moves as though retreated from the *kṣatriya* (*ibid.* I. 286). The *Ait. Br.* explains through *arthavāda* the significance of the (three) metres being associated with the three *varṇa*-s. A *brāhmaṇa* is connected with the Gāyatrī metre, for the Gāyatrī is lustre and spiritual power. A *kṣatriya* is connected with the Triṣṭubh metre, for the Triṣṭubh is force, power and strength. A *vaiśya* is connected with the Jagatī metre, for cattle are connected with the Jagatī metre (*Ait. Br.,* I.28=5.2). About the *sāman*-s the *brāhmaṇa* is connected with the Rathantara *sāman* and the *kṣatriya* with the Bṛhat *sāman* (*Jaim. Br.* II. 103; III. 316). About the seasons — the *brāhmaṇa* (priesthood) is connected with the spring season, the *kṣatriya* (martial power) with the summer and the *vaiśya* (common people) with the rainy season (*Śat. Br.* II. 1.3.5). In the context of the Agnyādhāna rite, it is said that a *brāhmaṇa* should set up his fires in spring, a *kṣatriya* in summer and a *vaiśya* in the rainy season (*ibid.).* The *Jaim. Br.* mentions the *stoma*-s *viz.* Trivṛt, Pañcadaśa, Saptadaśa and Ekaviṁśa as connected with priesthood, martial power, common people (or peasant-class) and *śudra* (class) respectively and speaks of the respective cadres of the four classes of the then society *viz.* priesthood being higher than the martial power; the martial power (or nobility) being higher than peasantry and peasantry being higher than the *śūdra* class (*Jaim. Br.* II. 32).

The creation-account from the *Tait. Sam.* (VII. 1.1.4-5) and the *Pañc-Br.* (VI. 1.6-11) has been noted by us. Similar creation-account occurs in the *Jaim. Br.* (I. 68-69). It is very patent that all these accounts stem from the Ṛgvedic thought about the four classes coming from the various parts of the Puruṣa (*RV* X. 90.12). But while the *RV* has this thought only at one place, the ritual texts speak of it at several places, the fourfold system of the society being quite fixed in their times. In the context of the rite of establishing the sacred fires, it is said that Prajāpati with the three utterances (Bhūḥ, Bhuvaḥ and Svaḥ) created the three worlds, three classes and also the self, human race and the animals (*Śat. Br.* II. 1.4. 11-13). With the utterance 'Bhūḥ' he generated the *brahman* (priesthood), with 'Bhuvaḥ' the *kṣatra* (martial power or nobility) and with 'Svaḥ' the *viś* (the common people), says the *Śat. Br.* (*ibid.* II. 1.4.12). In the rite of Odanasava, as *dakṣiṇā* gold is given and so are given three arrows with a bow, a goad (for driving the cattle) and a water-pot (*kamaṇḍalu*). Sāyaṇa on this passage from the *Tait. Br.* (II. 7.9. 2,3) quotes the Sūtrakāra according to whom the *dakṣiṇā*-s mentioned above are given to *brāhmaṇa, kṣatriya, vaiśya* and *śūdra* respectively with a view to have (spiritual) lustre, vigour, nourishment (*puṣṭi*) and (long) life for these classes respectively. While going to collect the clay for making a fire-pan, the sacrificer, priest, etc. go with a horse, ass and a he-goat. The *Śat. Br.* says that the horse corresponds to the *kṣatra,* the ass to the *vaiśya* and *śūdra* and the he-goat to the *brāhmaṇa* (*Śat. Br.* VI. 4.4.12). While going to collect the clay, the horse goes first. The *arthavāda* states that the *kṣatriya* going first is followed by the three other classes. While returning, the he-goat goes first, the *brāhmaṇa arthavāda* stating that the *brāhmaṇa* going first is followed by the other three classes, and as the ass does not go first while going or returning, the *brāhmaṇa* and *kṣatriya* never go behind the *vaiśya* and *śūdra* (*ibid.* 13). This class-distinction is maintained even in the rite of preparing a burial-place (*śmaśāna*) for a dead person (i.e. for keeping the earthen vessel, containing the bones of the dead). According to one opinion occurring in the *Śat. Br.* he should not make the *śmaśāna* too large, for by that he would make the deceased's sin large. For a *kṣatriya,* it should be made as high as a man with upstretched arms, for a *brāhmaṇa* reaching up to the mouth, for a woman up to the hips, for a *vaiśya* up to the thighs, for a *śūdra* up to the knee, the *arthavāda* adding that this is according to the vigour these (dead) persons possessed one time (*ibid.* XIII. 8. 3.11).

The *Jaim. Br.* has a detail to give which is important. It is said that the sacrificer-king is besprinkled for rejuvenation (in the Rājasūya sacrifice), to rule over five categories of persons *viz.* the *kṣatriya* (also other *kṣatriya* king), charioteer, headman *(grāmaṇī), śūdra* and slave (*dāsa);* a *brāhmaṇa* is not to be ruled over, killed, beaten or slain, by a *kṣatriya* king (*Jaim. Br.* II. 196). This clearly points out that *śudra* was not a *dāsa* though he was a menial servant or doing any such work.

Distinction between the classes (*varṇa*-s*)* in the society is carried further in the Sūtra tradition, which prescribes a particular colour for a particular *varṇa.* The *Āśv. G.S.* states that the ground to be chosen for building a house by a *brāhmaṇa* should be of white colour, that by a *kṣatriya* of red colour and that by a *vaiśya* of yellow colour (*Āsv. G.S.* II. 8.6-8). The *Gobh. G.S.* differs in the case of a *vaiśya* saying that for him the ground should be of black colour (*Gobh. G.S.* IV. 7.7). The idea in prescribing these colours for these *varṇa*-s is very clear. White colour signifies the spiritual lustre of a *brāhmaṇa;* red colour indicates the martial spirit of a *kṣatriya* and yellow colour shows the rich i.e. ripened, crop as also the abundance of yellow ghee (made from cow's milk cf. *RV* II. 35.11d -'*hiraṇyavarṇam ghṛtam*' spoken of as the food of Apām Napāt in his aspect as the sacrificial fire) enjoyed by a *vaiśya.* The black colour of the ground pointed out by the *Gobh. G.S.* in the case of a *vaiśya* indicates the land tilled by the *vaiśya.* The *vaiśya* is assigned the works *viz.* agriculture, tending the cows and trading. So the colour prescribed for him *viz.* yellow or black perfectly goes with him. Similar discrimination is marked when the clothes for the initiates of the three *varṇa*-s are prescribed. The *Āśv. G.S.* states that in case these initiates wear clothes, they should wear the dyed ones. A *brāhmaṇa* should wear a reddish yellow *(kāṣāya)* garment; a *kṣatriya,* a *māñjiṣṭha* (dyed red with madder) one; and a *vaiśya* a yellow (*hāridra)* one (*Āśv. G.S.* I.19.9). In later period, the *Varāha P.* mentions these three colours for the umbrella to be used by the initiates of these three *varṇa*-s, though as per the rule laid down by the Smṛti tradition, using an umbrella is a taboo for the initiate (*Manu Sm.* II. 178). Thus for a *brāhmaṇa* initiate is prescribed umbrella of white colour; for a *kṣatriya* initiate, that of red colour; and for a *vaiśya* initiate, that of yellow colour. It has to be marked that the *Varāha P.* prescribes the rite of initiation also for a *śūdra* (*Var. P.* Chaps. 127-128). A cloth of *nīla* (blue or black) colour is prescribed for a *śūdra* and also a bluish black (*nīla)* umbrella.[1] Of all the *varṇa*-s, the *brāhmaṇa (-varṇa)* was thought to be of the foremost status, the reason being obvious. As the sacrificial institution with the passage of time, became firmly established and as the rites and rituals became more and more complex, with every small detail laid down with the instruction to follow it categorically, the priestly class knowing the lore of sacrifice came to assume the highest importance in the society. The *Ait. Br.* in the context of the Rājasūya sacrifice, deals with the details regarding the office of a *purohita* (the officiating family-priest). The gods do not eat the food of a king without a *purohita.* Hence a king about to sacrifice has to select a *brāhmaṇa* as *purohita.* In appointing the *purohita* the king takes out the fires that lead to heaven. The *purohita* is said to be Agni Vaiśvānara possessed of five missiles residing in his body, one each in his speech, feet, skin, heart and organ. When the king asks his men (i.e. servants) to bring grass (-seat) for him, the king appeases that missile of the *purohita* which is in his speech. By bringing water for the feet, the missile in the feet is appeased. By adorning him the missile in his skin is appeased. By delighting him, the missile in his heart is appeased. When the *purohita* dwells safely in his dwelling, the missile in the organ is appeased. Propitiated in this manner by the king, the *purohita* carries the king to the world of heaven, lordly power, might, the kingdom and the people (*Ait. Br.* VIII. 24 = 40.1). In four more sections (VIII. 25-28 = 40.2-5), the *Ait. Br.* deals with the same topic of the importance of *purohita.*

The highest status enjoyed by the priestly (i.e. *brāhmaṇa*) class was due to their learning and conduct. In the context of the Rājasūya sacrifice, the *Śat. Br.* states that the king and the *brāhmaṇa* should speak only what is right and do what is right, of which they are capable, as they both are upholders of law, i.e. order (*Śat. Br.* V. 4.4.5). Sacrificial context made the learned *brāhmaṇa*-s obtain a status of divinity. It is said that gods are of two kinds, for the gods (of the heaven) are the gods and the *brāhmaṇa*-s who have studied and teach sacred lore are the human gods. One gratifies the gods with oblations and with gifts to the priests, he gratifies the human gods. When gratified both these kinds of gods place the sacrificer in the state of bliss (*Śat. Br.* II. 2.2.6; IV.3.4.4). The *Śat. Br.* states that the *brāhmaṇa*-s who have studied and teach sacred lore are the priests-*viprāḥ* (*ibid.* III.5.3.12). Such *brāhmaṇa*-s are the guardians of sacrifice (*ibid.* I. 5.1.12). That there are two kinds of gods and the *brāhmaṇa*-s are the human gods, is again stated by the *Śat. Br.* in the context of the Āgrayaṇa *iṣṭi* in which the first fruit, i.e. new grain, is offered at the commencement of harvest (*ibid.* II. 4.3.14). Even the *Ṣaḍ. Br.* has the same thought to give (*Ṣaḍ. Br.* I.1.29, 30). He who is renowned as learned in sacred lore, is a *ṛṣi,* the scion of *ṛsi*-s, for he indeed is one on whom gifts are well-bestowed (*Śat. Br.* IV. 3.4.19). The *Tait. Br.* equates the *brāhmaṇa* (priest) with all deities (*Tait. Br.* I.4.4.2; cf. *ibid.* II. 7.3.1,2—In the one-day Brāhmaṇasava, meant for a *brāhmaṇa* desiring to obtain spiritual lustre, *brāhmaṇa* is said to belong to eight deities). The *Jaim. Br.* says that a priest is a second king, i.e.

having status equal to that of a king (*Jaim. Br.* II. 171). The *Jaim. Br.* regards *brāhmaṇa* as a vessel of gods. Just as they desire to drink (water) with a clean and pure pot (i.e. glass), so the gods desire to drink with an unblemished and pure *brāhmaṇa* (i.e. desire to accept the offerings, given through an unblemished and pure priest). Hence a *brāhmaṇa* should be without any blemish and be pure (*ibid.* I.282). The *Śat. Br.* deals in an entire chapter with the study of scriptures. The Ṛc-texts are honey, the Sāman-texts ghee and the Yajus-texts nectar; the Vākovākya (dialogue) and the Itihāsa-Purāṇa the messes of milk and meat. When he (here is meant a '*brāhmaṇa*' as we note further) studies these texts, he satisfies the gods with honey, ghee, etc. (mentioned above). The *Śat. Br.* here refers to the universal order and states the importance of daily study for a *brāhmaṇa.* It says that moving indeed are the waters; moving is the sun, moving the moon and moving the stars. As if these deities did not move and act, even so will the *brāhmaṇa* be on that day on which he does not study his lesson. Hence one's daily lesson should be studied (*Śat. Br.* XI. 5.7.5-10; also *ibid.* XI. 5.6.4-8 for the same idea, with the enumeration of some more texts).

That the concept of a *brāhmaṇa* was always associated with the study of scriptures as well as such other sacred texts, is seen in the mythical account which occurs in the *Mait. Sam.* (IV. 8.1) and the *Kāṭh. Sam.* XXX. 1) in the context of the Pātnīvata *yūpa.* The *Śat. Br.* (I. 1.4.13-18) also has that account, differing in some details. We take here the account from the *Mait. Sam.* (IV. 8.1). The *asura*-s on hearing the sound of Manu's sacrificial utensils, were constantly being crushed. Two *brāhmaṇa*-s (!) of them — Tṛṣṭa and Varutri — came to Manu and told him that as he was Śraddhādeva ('One who regards faith as god'), he should give those utensils to them. Manu did likewise. The *asura*-s destroyed the utensils by throwing them in fire, the flames of which Manu's bull licked. By hearing the bellowing sound of the bull, the *asura*-s used to get crushed. On the advice of the *asura*-s again, Manu sacrificed his bull. The hind part (i.e the flesh on it) of the bull was cut off by the Suparṇa and it (i.e. the part) fell in the lap of Manu's wife, whose voice got that power of killing the *asura*-s. On the advice of the *asura*-s, Manu became ready to sacrifice his own wife, with their help. And there came Indra, assuming the form of a *brāhmaṇa*. Indra said to Manu that as the latter was Śraddhādeva, Indra would help him perform the sacrifice. When Manu asked him as to what type of *brāhmaṇa* he was, Indra said, "Why do you ask about the father and mother of a *brāhmaṇa*? He, who has sacred knowledge to his credit and from whom something could be learnt, is his father and also his grandfather." The mythical account runs further stating that Indra arranged for the sacrifice desired by Manu and released Manu's wife (from being sacrificed). The two *asura*-s obviously took to their heels on recognising Indra. From our point of view, Indra's words are important, for they clearly point out how a *brāhmaṇa* or his family used to be judged in the then society, having knowledge or learning as the only criterion for it. The *Kāṭh. Sam* has the same account, though differing in some details. Here also Indra speaks in the same way, when he is asked about his lineage, by Manu. When asked the 'new' *brāhmaṇa* (i.e. Indra, who comes as a *brāhmaṇa)* as to how he is different from the earlier two *brāhmaṇa*-s (Tṛṣṭa and Varutri), Indra says that he is *'atithipati'* while the other two are simply '*atithi*' (*Mait. Sam.* IV. 8.1). Here we come to an important point and it is of entertaining and giving hospitality to a *brāhmaṇa atithi,*[2] a point which will be discussed by us in the chapter on "Family-life." Indra calls himself '*atithipati*' (*Mait. Sam.* IV. 8.1; *Kāṭh. Sam.* XXX.1). So, all the more importance to be given to him. As the earlier two *asura*-s come as *atithi*-s and even Indra as an *'atithi*' (*'atithipati),* Manu has to abide by Indra's wishes and earlier by the wishes of the *asura*-s.

That the speech of a *brāhmaṇa* should be full of clarity and should be cultured, is brought out in a mythical account in the *Śat. Br.* (III. 2.1.18-24). As Prajāpati's (creator's) inheritance, the gods obtained Mind and the *asura*-s Speech.

By Mind, the gods came to have Sacrifice. On the instruction of the gods, Sacrifice (Masculine) beckoned Speech (Feminine), called her near him. When she came near, the gods cut her off from the *asura*-s and offered her as a holocaust with an Anuṣṭubh verse. Thereby they made her their own. The *asura*-s deprived of speech cried *"he' lavaḥ! he' lavaḥ!"* (according to Sāyaṇa this expression is "*he'rayaḥ he'rayaḥ*" i.e. "ho, the (wicked) enemies!"), which was the unintelligible speech - the speech of a barbarian. Hence no *brāhmaṇa* should speak the barbarous language, says the *Śat. Br.* (*ibid.* 24).

A *brāhmaṇa* was not allowed to consume any kind of spirituous liquor, a thought carried even in later times.[3] It is said that the sacrificer is born from the sacrifice (in the other world). Whatever food a man consumes in this world, that food in return consumes him in yonder world. In the context of the Sautrāmaṇī sacrifice, the *arthavāda* states that the Sautrāmaṇī sacrifice is performed by means of spirituous liquor (*parisrut),* which is not to be consumed by a *brāhmaṇa.* He thus is born from that which is not to be consumed by him and so the food (i.e. the liquor *parisrut)* does not, in return, consume him in yonder world. The Śautrāmaṇī therefore is a sacrifice of a *brāhmaṇa.*[4]

In spite of the eulogy of a *brāhmaṇa,* the then society did make a distinction between the *brāhmaṇa*-s depending on their descent and learning. This is clearly seen in the *Pañc. Br.* At the three-day rite of Garga (Garga-trirātra sacrifice), a thousand cows are prescribed for being given as *dakṣiṇā.* The *Pañc. Br.* enjoins the manner in which they are to be divided. On the first day, three hundred and thirty-three cows are to be given to a learned *brāhmaṇa* of pure *ṛṣi*-descent; on the second day, the same number of cows to a learned *brāhmaṇa* not of pure *ṛṣi*-descent; and on the third day, again the same number of cows to be given to a not learned *brāhmaṇa* of pure *ṛṣi*-descent (*Pañc. Br.* XX. 15.9-11). The *dakṣiṇā* of the thousandth cow, which remains, is prescribed to be given (may be as partial wealth or in entirety) by the ritual texts, to different priests.[5]

The *brāhmaṇa* priest being held in such high esteem led to the thought of satisfying him with a *dakṣiṇā*. By giving *dakṣiṇā* to him, the entire sacrifice becomes healed (*Śat. Br.* VI. 2.2.40). In the Agnihotra rite, even after churning (with the wooden implements *viz. araṇi* and *manthā)* if the fire does not show itself i.e. if it is not kindled, then the offering is to be given in the hand of a *brāhmaṇa* or on the ear of a he-goat (it being the favourite animal of Agni), or on the piece of grass or in waters (*Ṣaḍ. Br.* V.1.12). In the context of the New-moon and Full-moon sacrifices, while prescribing the covering of the *vedi* with the sacrificial grass and also satisfying the priest (with the *dakṣiṇā*), there occurs an interesting *arthavāda*. The Sacrifice said (of its own accord) that it was afraid of nakedness, to ward off which, they should cover it (i.e. fire-altar) with grass, which is sacrificial. Sacrifice then said that it dreaded thirst. To ward off its thirst, the *brāhmaṇa* officiating as a priest should be satisfied (by giving *dakṣiṇā) (Śat. Br.* I. 7.3.28). The *brāhmaṇa* officiating as a priest is the repeller of the evil powers (*ibid.* I.3.4.13).

To kill a *brāhmaṇa* is said to be (inviting) Death itself (*ibid.* XIII. 3.5.3). In the context of the New-moon and Full-moon sacrifices, in the *Tait. Sam.* occurs an elaborate mythical account. When Indra cut off the three heads of Viśvarūpa, Tvaṣṭṛ's son, all creatures blamed him for he was a *brāhmaṇa*-slayer. Then on Indra's request, the earth, trees and women, each took one-third part of his sin of slaying a *brāhmaṇa*. The *Tait. Sam.* here states in what form each one (of the three mentioned above) has that sin and in what form Indra's boon works with them (*Tait. Sam.* II. 5.1.1-6). The *arthavāda* in the form of this mythical account is important for knowing the various taboos, which existed in the then Vedic society with respect to a woman in her menstruation-period, as she carries Indra's sin. They can be compared with such taboos existing in all societies in ancient times.[6]

In spite of the fact that the fourfold class-system had become fixed in the times of the Brāhmaṇa-texts, there is reason to believe that exceptions were there, as can be seen from the example of Kavaṣa Ailūṣa, the son of a slave woman and *a-brāhmaṇa* (not *brāhmaṇa)*. Kavaṣa Ailūṣa taking part in the sacrificial session, was thrown out in the desert of the river Sarasvatī by the seers performing that session. Afflicted by thirst, he 'saw' the hymn of Apām Napāt and to the great surprise of all the seers, Sarasvatī hastened to him and surrounded him. Hence the name Parisāraka (fr. *pari* + √*sṛ* - 'to move' —here 'to move around') to that place. Then the seers accepted Kavaṣa Ailūṣa and invited him to their session, knowing his *mantra*-power (*Ait. Br.* II. 19 = 8.1; *Kauṣ. Br.* XII.1). In the times of the Upaniṣads, we have the example of Satyakāma Jābāla, the son of a woman who 'waited' and 'served' many men and could not tell her son the name of his father. The same was told by Satyakāma (the son of Jabālā and hence the epithet 'Jābāla') to the preceptor, whom he approached for studentship. The preceptor said," No non-*brāhmaṇa* can (dare to) say this (so boldly)," and he accepted Satyakāma (*Chān. Up.* IV. 4.1-5). This shows that, in principle, the class-system was flexible. And the very belief that whosoever sacrifices, sacrifices after becoming as it were a *brāhmaṇa*[7] and hence the instruction that even a *kṣatriya* or a *vaiśya,* if he performs a sacrifice be called a *brāhmaṇa* (*Śat. Br.* III. 2. 1.40), could act as touchstone to judge the social conditions at that time.

Next to *brāhmaṇa*, comes the *kṣatriya,* who in most cases is the king. The ritual texts at several places point out that these two *varṇa*-s are interdependent on each other. In the context of the Agniṣṭoma sacrifice, the *Śat. Br.* says that in the beginning the *brahma* (priesthood) and *kṣatra* (ruling power) were separate. Mitra (priesthood) could stand without Varuṇa (the ruling or martial power). But Varuṇa could not, without Mitra. Varuṇa (the ruling power) then called upon Mitra (priesthood) asking him to turn into him (i.e. into Varuṇa). Hence the Soma-cup to Mitra and Varuṇa (*Śat. Br.* IV. 1.4.2-4). The *Śat. Br.* opines that a *brāhmaṇa* could be without a king, but if he obtains a king, it would be conducive to the success of both. But a king should not be without a *brāhmaṇa* (priest), for then no deed of the king would succeed. It is the *brāhmaṇa* who speeds the deed of the king *(ibid.* 6). The *Jaim. Br.* states that these two should not hate each other, for they have the same excellent (or proper) food to eat. When a *brāhmaṇa* goes to a higher place, he desires the *kṣatriya* to be the second protector of his excellent (or proper) food (he himself being the first) and the *kṣatriya* expects the same from the *brāhmaṇa* (*Jaim. Br.* I.287). The *Śat. Br.* says that a *brāhmaṇa* is a form of the holy or spiritual power and *rājanya,* that of the lordly (or martial) power (*Śat. Br.* XIII. 1.5.2, 3). The ritual metaphor that the holy power is Agni (or vice versa) and the lordly power is Indra (or vice versa) occurs at several places (*ibid.* II.5.4.8; X.4.1.5,9; *Jaim Br.* I.182, 186), and the corollary is - a *brāhmaṇa* belongs to Agni and a *rājanya* to Indra (*ibid.).* As he held the lordly power with the help of the holy power and the holy power with that of the lordly power (and will be holding it likewise), then the country would not regress but would ever go forward (*ibid.* I.182).

The concept of closely uniting the two powers *viz.* the holy power (*brahman*) and the lordly power (*kṣatra)* occurs in the *Śat. Br.* in the context of offering a cake on twelve potsherds to Indra and Agni, which is given after the Great Oblations (Mahāhavis). It is said that Agni is holy power and Indra the lordly power. The gods, having closely uniting these two powers, slew Vṛtra. Hence a cake on twelve potsherds to Indra and Agni (*Śat. Br.* II. 5.4.8). The *arthavāda* is significant as it sheds light on the then Order (of *varṇa*-s) in the society and the importance of individual group. The concept of combination of *brahman* and *kṣatra* became a matter of great esteem in later times and percolates even up to the Smṛti period (*Manu Sm.* VII. 37-39). In the epics

Rām. and *Mbh.*, we find a family-priest of a king, always advising him on important matters, thus restraining his absolute power and saving him from many a pitfall.

The *arthavāda* occurring in the context of the Śunāsīrīya *iṣṭi (parvan)* in the four Seasonal sacrifices (Cāturmāsya *iṣṭi*-s), sheds light on the concept of king or ruler of those times. The *vidhi* is of offering a cake on one potsherd for Sūrya. The *arthavāda* points out that Sūrya (the sun) is the one, who governs all this world at times by means of a good king or at other times by a bad king and verges on to a wish that the sun may assign to the sacrificer a place under a good king (*Śat. Br.* II. 6.3.8). In some *arthavāda*-s, this concept of a good towering king is linked up with Indra or Mahendra, while offering to Indra. When a cup for Indra in common with Maruts is offered, the *Śat. Br.* says that here the case is of a person who eats from the same vessel with the common people for the sake of victory. But in this Indra is to be taken as bound with evil in the form of common people, i.e. the Maruts. Hence a separate Soma-cup for Mahendra (Māhendra cup) is offered (*ibid.* IV. 3.3.15). The *arthavāda* runs further that after slaying Vṛtra, Indra became the Great Indra (Mahendra), like a person having all-round victory becoming a Great King (*ibid.* 17). The *arthavāda* clearly shows the distinction maintained for all purposes between the common people and their ruler, who otherwise could come together in their efforts for victory.

Indra symbolises the *kṣatra,* as we have noted already. This is seen in the *arthavāda* stated for the *vidhi* of preparing a cake of eleven potsherds to be offered to Indra, at the dwelling-place of the king, who is to be consecrated in the Rājasūya (*ibid.* V. 3.1.3).

At yet another place, in the context of the rite of Agnicayana, when the offerings to the deity Vaiśvānara and Maruts are enjoined, the Vaiśvānara is said to be the ruling power and the Maruts the clan. To Vaiśvānara is given a single offering, for a socially distinguished position is for a single towering person — the ruling power. The other multi-offerings are for the Maruts, for they like the members of the clan are numerous (*ibid.* IX. 3. 1.14).

In the midday Soma-pressing, he draws the Marutvatīya Soma-cups for Indra. The concept of the god-head here is of Indra accompanied with the Maruts and not the Maruts alone. The *arthavāda* as is common in most such *vidhi*-s refers to the myth of Indra striving to smite Vṛtra. Here he is seen seeking the help of the Maruts, who promise to help him for the reward of the Soma-cups. Indra first draws for them two (Marutvatīya) Soma-cups, Having seen them as putting aside one cup for vigour, fearing lest they be without vigour while helping him in slaying Vṛtra, Indra draws one more (i.e. the third) cup for them. As they joined him with vigour to make him victorious, the *arthavāda* states that thus the common people help the lordly power (*ibid.* IV. 3.3.6-9). But the *arthavāda* in the *Śat. Br.* does not forget to add that these (Marutvatīya) cups are for Indra Marutvat (i.e. Indra accompanied with the Maruts) and not for the Maruts exclusively. The reason of this is, he thereby makes the people subservient and obedient to the lordly power (*ibid.* 10). The *arthavāda* shows a clear picture of the status of the *varṇa*-s in the then society.

Similar thought is reflected in the *arthavāda,* when a Soma-cup is offered to Indra in the Ṣoḍaśin sacrifice.[8] It is said that when at one time, the beings surpassed Indra and were in a state of equality as it were with him, Indra having seen this (Ṣoḍaśin) Soma-cup, drew it for himself and with the result, he stood over everything here (*ibid.* IV. 5.3.1,2). This shows that the lordly power has always to be above all. In the Rājasūya sacrifice, the priest hands him three arrows and a bow. The *arthavāda* points out that the bow is the strength of a *kṣatriya* (*rājanya),* and so the priest thinks that he is rejuvenating the king (by the Rājasūya sacrifice), when the latter is endowed with strength by the bow (*ibid.* V. 3.5.29, 30). After the anointing (i.e. sprinkling) with water, of the king in the Rājasūya sacrifice, the Adhvaryu and his assistant priests then silently strike the king on his back with sticks. By beating him with sticks, they guide him safely over judicial punishment (*daṇḍavadha),* with the result, the king is exempt from punishment (*ibid.* V. 4.4.7). To give or provide proper food is the work of a *kṣatriya* (*Jaim. Br.* III.191). This shows the responsibility assigned to a *kṣatriya* (king). The glory (*srī)* of the king is to be guarded day and night in the Horse-sacrifice. Two lute-players are invited to sing and play on the lute. One of them is a *brāhmaṇa* and the other *rājanya.* The *brāhmaṇa* sings by day and the *rājanya* at night, by which the glory of the king is guarded on either side by the holy power (or priesthood) and the lordly power (or nobility) (*Śat. Br.* XIII.1.5.1-5).

Several *arthavāda*-s speak of the relative importance and status of the *kṣatra* (lordly power) and the common people or clansmen. In the Agnicayana rite, the Lokampṛṇā brick is laid down in all the five layers, for these layers stand for the three worlds.[9] Lokampṛṇā is the lordly power (*kṣatra)* and those other bricks are the common people (peasants or clansmen - *viśaḥ*). Lokampṛṇā is only a single brick. Thereby he makes the *kṣatra* attain social distinction wholly (without any other persons to share it). The other bricks he lays down singly with separate formulas. He thereby makes the common people (or peasantry) less powerful than the lordly power, differing in speech and of different thoughts (*ibid.* VIII. 7.2.1-3).

The ritual texts always have *viśaḥ* as distinct from the *kṣatra,* the underlying concept being that the former (i.e. *viśaḥ)* are the followers of and hence lower in status than the latter (i.e. *kṣatra).* So we have Varuṇa as the *kṣatra* and the Maruts as *viśaḥ (Śat. Br.* II. 5.2.6, 34, 36); Indra as the *kṣatra* and the Maruts as *viśaḥ* (*ibid.* II. 5.2.27; IV. 3.3.6); Indra as the *kṣatra* and Viśve Devāḥ as well as Maruts are the clans (*viśaḥ)* (*ibid.* III. 9.1. 16, 17); Soma is the *kṣatra* and the pressing-stones (*grāvāṇaḥ)* are the *viśaḥ* (ibid. III. 9.3.3); Soma-drop (*somaḥ induḥ)* is the *kṣatra* and men are the *devaviśaḥ* (*Jaim. Br.* I.90), thus bringing together the concept of the human and the god; in the Agnicayana rite, the fire (Agni) piled up is the *kṣatra* and the fire-hearths (*dhiṣṇyāḥ*) are the *viśaḥ* (*Śat. Br.* IX. 4.3.1). The image of the *viśaḥ* is pressed further so much so that even the priests are said to be the *viśaḥ* of the sacrificer (*Jaim. Br.* II. 148).

The *Jaim. Br.* states that the *rājanya* (*kṣatriya*) belongs to Indra and the common people (*viśaḥ*) to the Maruts. The *viś* (i.e. the common people denoting the peasantry or the *vaiśya* class) following the *kṣatra* (*ibid.* I. 95). The *kṣatriya* ascends the *viś* in status (*ibid.* II. 140). The Triṣṭubh metre is *kṣatra* and the Maruts are the common people. When the Triṣṭubh verses (i.e. *mantra*-s in that metre) praise the Marutvat (i.e. Indra, who is accompanied by the Maruts), they make the *viś* follow the *kṣatra.* Hence is the *viś* the follower of *kṣatra* (*ibid.* III. 205). An interesting *arthavāda* occurs in this connection in the *Jaim. Br.* The Gavām-ayąna is a series of Soma-sacrifices confined to one year's period with its middle-most day called Viṣuvan and with two wings of the series of sacrifices at each side. Viṣvajit and Abhijit are the two days (two Agniṣṭoma sacrifices) which form the part - one each - of the two wings of the Gavām-ayana (Abhijit in the first wing and the Viśvajit in the second wing). The word '*go*' (in the word *gavām-ayana)* denotes the rays of the sun and the rite is related to the course of the sun. The word *ayana* means advancing, particularly the advancing of the sun to the north and south of the equator, the Viṣuvan. The *Jaim. Br.* states that Viśvajit and Abhijit are the cot of gods (*devatalpa)* and this sun is the *kṣatra.* They elevate the *kṣatra* on the cot of gods (i.e. the course of the sun is connected with these two Agniṣṭoma-sacrifice days). Hence the *kṣatriya* is (taken as) exalted among the *viś* (*ibid.* II. 344).

The same importance ascribed to a *kṣatriya* king is marked in an *arthavāda*-passage in the context of the New-moon and Full-moon sacrifices, in the ritual of taking the melted butter in the ladles. The *juhū* ladle stands for the eater and the *upabhṛt* ladle stands for that which is to be eaten. In the *juhū* he takes melted butter four times (with the *sruva)* and in the *upabhṛt,* eight times (*Śat. Br.* I.3.2.11). In taking melted butter four times in the *juhū,* he makes the eater more limited and smaller but imparts vigour and strength to him. In taking the melted butter eight times in the *upabhṛt,* he makes that which is to be eaten more unlimited and more abundant, however making it vigourless and weaker. This is like a king, who has established himself among a large number of people and who, in spite of staying in a single dwelling subdues them from there (*ibid.* 14). The same symbolism in taking the *juhū* ladle to be the eater (i.e. *kṣatriya* king) and the *upabhṛt* ladle to be the eaten (common people under the sway of the king) is maintained for explaining the rite of offering the (said) butter. The melted butter taken in the *juhū* is offered with the *juhū*, but that which is taken in the *upabhṛt* is offered again with the *juhū* (*ibid.).* This is explained with the *arthavāda* that the common people (*viśaḥ)* pay tribute to the *kṣatriya*. The butter taken in the *upabhṛt* symbolises the *vaiśya,* under the rule of a *kṣatriya* and having cattle. The same butter offered with the *juhū* symbolises the *kṣatriya* (king), who subdues the *vaiśya* and has power over anything he wishes, which belongs to the latter (*ibid.* 15).

In the same context of the New-moon and Full-moon sacrifices, in an initial rite, it is said that he lays the *juhū* down on the *prastara* and the other spoons down below on the *barhis,* north of the *juhū.* The *juhū* is the *kṣatra* and the other spoons (*sruc)* are the *viś.* The *arthavāda* further points out that the common people from a lower position serve the *kṣatriya* seated above them (*ibid.* I.3.4.15). Even the *prastara* on which the *juhū* is kept is said to be the *kṣatra* and the other *barhis,* the *viś* - the common people (*ibid.* I.3.4.10).

In spite of the higher position of the *kṣatra,* it is by the clan that the lordly power is guarded. This *arṭhavāda* occurs when it is said that after the offering of animal-victim to Indra, there comes the animal-victim for the Maruts and prior to the animal-victim to Indra, there is the one (animal-victim) for the Viśve Devāḥ. Thus the lordly power (*kṣatra*—here Indra) is guarded on both sides by the clans (i.e. *viśaḥ* - here the All Gods - Viśve Devāḥ and the Maruts) (*ibid*. III. 9.1.14-18). Again when it is said that Indra is *kṣatra* and Maruts are the *viś* (helping Indra - hence the epithet 'Marutvān' exclusively for Indra), it is stated in clear terms that the *kṣatriya* becomes strong due to *viś (ibid*. IV. 3.3.6).

At other place, in the *arthavāda* Indra and Agni are said to be the *kṣatra* and All Gods (Viśve Devāḥ) are said to be the *viś* (common people or clan-men), the latter allowed to share the gains of the former. The context is of the Āgrayaṇa-*iṣṭi*, in which a cake on twelve potsherds is offered to Indra-Agni. A mythical account occurs in the *arthavāda,* which states that when the gods and the *asura*-s were contending for superiority, the *asura*-s defiled all plants with magic and poison. With the result all the creatures well-nigh perished for want of food. The gods obtained food for them by means of sacrifice. But there arose a problem as to whom would that sacrifice belong. The problem was settled by running a race, which was won by Indra and Agni. Hence a cake on twelve potsherds for these two gods. A *caru* (pap of boiled rice or barley grains) is offered to All Gods (Viśve Devāḥ) in this *iṣṭi.* It is said that Indra and Agni are the *kṣatra* and All Gods are the *viś.* Whatever the *kṣatra* conquers, the *viś* is allowed to share (*ibid*. II. 4.3.2-6). This shows that though the common people held a secondary position in the social strata of those times, they were not denied of their rights.

That there were classes in the society is clear from the details noted above. But in these classes also, the persons were having higher or lower status and accordingly they had recognition in the society. In the context of the Rājasūya sacrifice, in the rite after that of the 'sprinkling' (*abhiṣeka),* it is said that a *brāhmaṇa*—either the Adhvaryu priest or the Purohita (king's domestic chaplain)—hands to the king the sacrificial wooden sword (*sphya*). The wooden sword being a thunderbolt, that *brāhmaṇa*, by means of that thunderbolt, makes the king to be weaker than himself. But such a king is stronger than his enemies and he is made likewise by giving him the wooden sword. Thereafter, that wooden sword is handed by the king to his brother, the brother in turn to the *sūta* (minstrel-chronicler) or the *sthapati* (governor), the *sūta* or the *sthapati* in turn to the headman (*grāmaṇī*), the headman in turn to the tribesman (*sajāta*) — each preceding one making the succeeding one weaker. The *Śat. Br.* remarks that the wooden sword is handed on in this way, lest there should be a confusion of classes and in order that society may be in the proper order (*ibid.* V. 4.4. 15-19). This shows that for the proper and smooth working of the society, a particular order of classes was thought to be not only essential but also indispensable. But the holy power (*brahman*) enjoyed the highest status — so a *brāhmaṇa* having the place of prime importance. A mythical account in the context of Rājasūya sacrifice is significant. Prajāpati created the sacrifice, after that the holy power (*brahman*) and the lordly power (*kṣatra*), after them two kinds of offspring — those who eat the oblations and those who do not eat the oblations. The *brāhmaṇa*-s are the offspring that eat the oblations, while the *rājanya, vaiśya* and *śūdra* are those that do not eat the oblations. When the sacrifice departed from them, the holy power and the lordly power pursued it. The holy power pursued with its weapons (as those) of sacrifice (*yajñāyudhāni*)[10] and the lordly power with its weapons *viz.* the horse-chariot, armour (*kavaca*), the bow and arrow. The lordly power returned without attaining the sacrifice, for the latter trembling turned away from these weapons of the lordly power. But when the holy power followed the sacrifice, the latter recognising its own weapons went up to the former. Hence even now the sacrifice finds its support in the holy power and in the *brāhmaṇa* (*Ait. Br.* VII. 19 = 34.1; cf. *Śat. Br.* IV. 5.2.16 for '*viśaḥ*' not eating oblations), and that too a learned *brāhmaṇa.*

NOTES AND REFERENCES

1. For the information regarding the age and other details of the initiates of different *varṇa*-s, see Dange, Sadashiv A., *Ency. of P. B. & P.*, Vol. III, Navrang, New Delhi, 1987, pp. 911-12.
2. For more information, see (Mrs.) Dange, S.S., "Atithi—A Probe in Concept", *Studies on Indology* (Prof. Mukunda Madhava Sharma Fel. Vol.), Sri Satguru Pubns. (a Division of Indian Books Centre), Delhi, 1996, pp. 119-22.
3. *Manu Sm.* XI. 90-97; *Yāj. Sm.* III. 253 and the comm. Mitākṣarā on it.
4. Eggeling explains this by stating that because to a man of another caste the spirituous liquor would not be '*anādyā*', but consumable, and hence it would consume him in the other world. See Eggeling, J., *op. cit.*, pt. V, SBE Vol. 44, p. 260, note 1.
5. *Tait. Sam.* VII. 1.7.2; *Pañc. Br.* XX. 15.14; *Śat. Br.* IV. 5.8.12; *Jaim. Br.* II. 243.
6. *Ency. of Rel. and Eth.*, Vol. X, pp. 494b-495a.
7. The *Śat. Br.* (XIII. 4.1.2,3) states that the Horse-sacrifice, being the *kṣatriya*'s sacrifice, is to be performed by a king in the summer season (summer being *kṣatriya*'s season), but then it should be started in the spring season, for it is *brāhmaṇa*'s season and a *kṣatriya* king becomes a *brāhmaṇa* when he sacrifices.
8. In the Ṣoḍaśin sacrifice, in addition to the fifteen *stotra*-s and fifteen *śastra*-s of the Ukthya (or Uktha) sacrifice, there is an additional *stotra* and a corresponding *śastra* called Ṣoḍaśin in the third Soma-pressing, vide Kane, P.V., *Hist of Dh. S.*, Vol. II, pt. II, p. 1204.
9. See Eggeling, J., *op. cit.*, pt. IV, *SBE* Vol. 43, p. 132, note 1. Eggeling says here that rather the first, second and third layers are the three worlds.
10. *Tait. Sam.* I.6.8.2-3 enumerates the ten things which are important and indispensable in any sacrifice. They are—*sphya* (wooden sword), *kapālāni* (potsherds), *agnihotra-havanī*

(a ladle used in sacrificial oblations), *śūrpa* (winnowing basket), *kṛṣṇājina* (black antelope skin), *śamyā* (originally a peg, but a mace-shaped staff of wood used for measuring sacrificial grounds), *ulūkhala* (mortar), *musala* (pestle), *dṛsad* (lower grinding stone) and *upalā* (upper grinding stone). These are said to be *yajñāyudhāni.* For the photographs of these, see Dharamadhikari, T.N. (ed.) *Yajñāyudhāni,* Vaidika Saṁśodhana Maṇḍala, Pune, 1989.

CHAPTER 11

Family-Life

We have noted that in order to explain the rituals of the sacred level, the ritual texts have to take recourse to the facts or experiences from the profane level, through *arthavāda*-s. Many *arthavāda*-s have dealt with the family-life of the then people, thus coming to the societal level. From the point of view of beliefs and practices, such *arthavāda*-s are found important.

The concept of family-unit, as per the Vedic ritualists, is marked in the *Jaim. Br.* (II. 123), when the *arthavāda* speaks of the self, wife and issues or children. The concext is of the Parikrī sacrifice — one-day sacrifice—, in which they recite the triplets (each being a group of three *ṛc.*-s). In the first triplet, the *ṛc*-s are said to be *brahman, kṣatra* and *viś* respectively. Of the second triplet, the *ṛc*-s stand respectively for one's own self, wife and children and thereon depends the circle of relatives (*Jaim. Br.* III. 123).

The worldly phenomenon of male and female forming a 'productive' pair is at the basis of many *arthavāda*-s. The Vedic ritualists were so steeped in the concept of '*mithuna*' - 'pair' - *mithuna* of any two entities—that the *Śat. Br.* speaks of the pairs (of limbs) which are there in a human body. The details are stated in the context of the Agnicayana rite, indicating that the body so formed by pairs enters the Agni (which is placed on the fire-altar). The *arthavāda* is — the thumbs (and big toes - *'aṅguṣṭha'* Masculine) are males and the fingers and toes (*'angulī'* Feminine), females; the ears (*'karṇa'* Masculine) are males and the eyebrows (*'bhrū'* Feminine), females; the lips (*'oṣṭha'* Masculine) are males and the nostrils (*'nāsikā'* Feminine), females; the teeth (*'danta'* Mas.) are males and the tongue (*'jihvā'*), a female. Indeed this all body consists of pairs (*Śat. Br.* X. 1.1.8).

On the proceeding day (i.e. the Prāyaṇīya Atirātra day) in the Gavām-ayana sacrifice, the *ṛc* sung is *RV* IX. 62.25,[1] based on some words of which, the *Pañc. Br.* has an interesting *arthavāda* to give. It says that the word *'pavasva'* ('flow off clearly') represents the male and *'vācaḥ'* ('of speech') the female; the word 'Soma', ('O Soma') the male and the word *'citrābhiḥ'* ('with bright') the female. Thus a copulation is produced at the very opening of the sacrifice for the purpose of procreation (*Pañc. Br.* IV. 2.18). Here the pairing is sought with the help of mere words (the words obviously being from the *RV* and *SV*).

In the context of Dākṣāyaṇa sacrifice,[2] the offerings are said to form a 'pair' and it is a 'productive' pair. He offers on two days of the Full-moon and two days of the New-moon (*Śat. Br.* II, 4.4.6). At the Full-moon, he offers a cake to Agni and Soma on the first day — these are two deities (*ibid.* 7). The next day, there is a cake to Agni, and *sānnāyya*[3] to Indra — these are two deities (*ibid.* 8). At the New moon, he offers a cake each to Indra and Agni on the first day — these are two deities (*ibid.* 9). The next day, there is cake to Agni, and curds to Mitra and Varuṇa. Mitra and Varuṇa are two deities (*ibid.* 10). In all these, the 'two-s' form a pair and it is a 'productive' pair.

When the sacrificer's wife looks at the sacrificial butter, a *mithuna*[4] — a productive pairing — is formed between a woman (female) and 'seed' — here butter, representing the seed (*ibid.* I.3.1.18). In this context occurs a belief that the part of woman's body below the navel is impure. Hence he girds her with a cord (*yoktra*) and conceals that part of her. Only with the pure upper part of her body now she faces the sacrificial butter (*ibid.* I.3.1.12,13), and a *mithuna* is formed. The concept is very well based on the worldly phenomenon of male and female forming a 'productive' pair. Such a pair is of husband and wife, from which starts the family-line. Hence it is that several *arthavāda*-s in the Brāhmaṇa-texts have the basis of the family-life of the then Aryans, which more or less has remained the same even in the later times.

The wife of the sacrificer has a special importance in the whole set-up of sacrifice. That the house is the very place of establishment of the wife is brought out by an *arthavāda* in the rite of purchasing the Soma (-shoots). The dust from the seventh foot-print of the Somakrayaṇī cow is handed over to the wife of the sacrificer. He thereby establishes her safely in that resting place, i.e. the house (*ibid.* III. 3.1.10).

The *Jaim. Br.*, while prescribing the location of the seat of the sacrificer's wife, states that she is indeed the half of the sacrificer's soul (*Jaim. Br.* I.86). The same thought has been expressed earlier by the *Tait. Br.* (*Tait. Br.* III. 3.3.5). The role of wife as the sacrificer's half part is for making the sacrificer firm and not a loose one. And as the sacrifice is for procreation, by the active and the positive presence of the in the sacrifice, the very sacrifice is made to have a pair (*ibid.).* The same thought is made clear earlier in the *Tait. Br.* by stating that the sacrificer not having a wife is one who is not a sacrificer at all, for without her, he will not be able to procreate the issues. When she is by his side, he performs the real sacrifice (*ibid.* II. 2.2.6; III. 3.3.1). The importance of wife in the process of procreation and carrying on the family-line is never lost sight of (*Śat. Br.* V.2.1.10). Even when the offerings to the wives of gods (Patnīsaṁyāja-s) are spoken of in the New-moon and Full-moon sacrifices, it is said by way of *arthavāda* that thereby in the wives, i.e. in the womb, the seed is planted, from where it is produced (*ibid.* I.9.2.11).

The high status of and the respect shown to a wife or wives in the sacrificial procedure are clear from a detail, mentioned in the Horse-sacrifice. The *Tait. Br.* and the *Śat. Br.*[5] in the context of Horse-sacrifice enjoin that the wives should anoint the horse, for they (i.e. wives - *patnayaḥ)* are the form of prosperity. Actually by this anointing, it is the prosperity which is bestowed on the sacrificer, from whom (thereafter) neither lustre, nor energy (*indriyam),* nor cattle, nor prosperity go away (*Tait. Br.* III. 9.4.7-8; *Śat. Br.* XIII. 2.6.7). The *Ait. Br.,* while laying down expiations for the errors committed in the performance of Agnihotra-rite, states that a person cannot perform the rite of Agnihotra without a wife. The *arthavāda* states that the wife is Faith and the sacrificer is Truth. Faith and Truth make the highest pair and with this pair he conquers the world of heaven (*Ait. Br.* VII. 10 = 32.9).

The sacrificer's wife, being half of the sacrificer's soul, as we have noted above, is expected to follow him everywhere. In the New-moon and Full-moon sacrifices, the Patnīsaṁyāja offerings are made (i.e. offered) to the deities *viz.* Soma, Tvaṣṭṛ and Agni Gṛhapati and the wives of the gods (Devapatnyaḥ). The *Śat. Br.* says that this ceremony of Patnīsaṁyāja-offerings concludes with the Iḍā-ceremony (I. 9.2.9-14). On this occasion, he offers the *prastara* (the bunch of grass) in the fire[6] and wishes the sacrificer *'svagā'* (i.e. 'Good Speed').[7] This he wishes for the sacrificer's wife also, for the wife comes immediately after the husband — *patim vā anu jāyā* (*ibid.* I.9.2.14). The *arthavāda* speaks of the conviction deep-rooted in the Indian soil right from the Vedic times that the wife is inseparably connected with her husband.

The *arthavāda,* figuring in the context of the sacrifice called Aikādaśina, tries to explain the then practice of polygamy. The reasoning here is from the ritualist's point of view but interestingly it is on the sociological lines. In the Aikādaśina sacrifice, eleven posts are planted in the ground and the twelfth is made to lie to the south of the altar. There is also the thirteenth one — the shorter one — called Pātnīvata for the wives of the gods, as a group. To this pole the beast for Tvaṣṭṛ is tied but is set free. The main pole is called Agniṣṭha or also Agniṣṭhā.[8] The *vidhi* of girding each pole with two girdles is explained with an *arthavāda*. It states that as women outnumber men, man gets many wives but the wife does not have many husbands (*Kāṭh. Sam.* XXIX. 8; for the same idea *Mait. Sam.* IV. 7.9).

An interesting detail regarding the married life is noted in one *arthavāda*. In the Niṣkevalya *śastra,* when a Yājyā (offering) verse is to be employed, a mythical account is stated, which runs as follows. The gods wanted to know what Indra has done as per their desire. They approached Prāsahā, the favourite wife of Indra. She assured them that she would tell them the next morning (naturally asking Indra about the query of the gods at the night time!). The *arthavāda* gives its gloss that a wife seeks her wish from her husband in the night (*Ait. Br.* III. 22 = 12.11).[9]

In the same context (i.e. Soma-sacrifice) a custom prevalent in those times is referred to in an *arthavāda*. When the Niṣkevalya *śastra* is prescribed to be recited, it is said that he who desires the victory of a host, standing away from him (i.e. host) at half distance, should cut a blade of grass at its both ends and throw it towards the other host, saying 'Prāsahā, Ka sees you' (*ibid.).* Here 'Ka' is Prajāpati, who is said to be Indra's father and Prāsahā, as noted in the *arthavāda* above, is Indra's wife and so the daughter-in-law of Ka (as mentioned here). The *arthavāda* here states that in this world, a daughter-in-law keeps hiding in modesty before her father-in-law. In the same way, the other host (towards whom the blade of grass, cut at both ends, is thrown) keeps shrinking away in confusion (*ibid.).*

The general observation about a good-looking woman as reflected in the *arthavāda* is about her well-ordered hair. In the rite of Agnicayana, in the context of making the fire-pan (*ukhā),* while kneading the clay for making it soft, the goddess Sinīvālī (of the fourteenth dark day) is invoked with a *mantra (Vāj. Sam.* XI. 56), which mentions Sinīvālī as fair-knotted (*sukapardā),* fair-braided (*sukurīrā)* and fair-locked (*su-opaśā* = *svaupaśā*). The *Śat. Br.* here through *arthavāda* states that Sinīvālī is a woman and this is really the perfect (i.e. attractive) form of a woman of being fair-knotted, fair-braided and fair-locked (*Śat. Br.* VI. 5.1.10).

That a woman injures no one, is brought out in one *arthavāda.* While making the fire-pan, for digging the earth, a spade made of bamboo-reed is used. It (i.e. the spade) is addressed with a *mantra,* taking it to be a woman (*Vāj. Sam.* XI. 10). The *Śat. Br.* states that a female injures no one and so the spade (*Śat. Br.* VI. 3.1.39). The spade, used for digging though harms the earth, is appeased with these words so that it should not do any injury to the earth.

The conviction in the Indian culture that woman is not to be killed occurs in the *Śat. Br.* in the context of the Mitravindā sacrifice. While creating living beings, Prajāpati toiled. From him who was worn out and heated, Śrī (Splendour or Glory) came forth and stood there resplendent, shining and (as though) embracing, everything with her lustre (as Sāyaṇa takes '*lelāyantī*' as '*āśliṣyantī').* The gods wanted to kill her and take everything away from her. But Prajāpati told them, "Śrī is a woman. People do not kill a woman. They rather take anything from her leaving her alive" (*ibid.* XI. 4.3.1,2).

The practice prevalent was that the woman was always to the left side of the man. This is reflected in a rite performed in the New-moon and Full-moon sacrifices. The Adhvaryu priest carries the water from the Gārhapatya fire to the north of the Āhavanīya fire (the technical name of the water after this being Praṇītā). The oft-repeated expression in the ritual-texts occurs here also - 'water is female and fire is male; hence a copulation productive of offspring is thereby effected.' It is said that a regular copulation can take place in this way alone, since the woman lies on the left (or north) side of the man (*ibid.* I.1.1.20). The same thought the *Sat. Br.* states in the Varuṇapraghāsāḥ-*parvan* in the four Seasonal sacrifices (*ibid.* II. 5.2.17). He places the ewe on the southern and the ram on the northern dish of curds. The *Śat. Br.* states the *arthavāda* that in this way alone a proper union is effected, since the woman lies on the left (or north) side of the man. It is interesting to note that this practice of keeping woman (wife) on the left side of man (husband) is seen in the sculptures of Ardhanārīśvara (or Ardhanārīnaṭeśvara), which is the female and male forms of Śiva combined, and even in Hindu rituals performed in modern times.

An important *arthavāda* is marked in the context of the Sūktavāka rite. The *arthavāda* provides a ritual basis for an important issue in the Dharmaśāstra tradition, which prohibits the inter-marriage between blood-relations.

The Sūktavāka rite is to be performed on both — the New-moon and the Full-moon sacrifices. At the New-moon (day) sacrifice, while reciting the *mantra* (*Vāj. Sam.* II. 15 cd), wishing the sacrificer to be victorious after the victory of Indra and Agni and also that Indra and Agni may drive him away whom the sacrificer hates and who hates him, he (i.e. Adhvaryu priest) separates the two offering-spoons *viz. juhū* and *upabhṛt* (*Śat. Br.* I.8.3.3.-4). At the Full-moon (day) sacrifice, while reciting the *mantra* (*Vāj. Sam.* II. 15 ab) wishing the sacrificer to be victorious after the victory of Agni and Soma and also that Agni and Soma may drive him away whom the sacrificer hates and who hates him, the Adhvaryu separates the (same) two offering-spoons *viz. juhū* and *upabhṛt* (*Śat. Br.* I.8.3.1-2). The *arthavāda* states that behind the *juhū* stands the eater (enjoyer) and behind the *upabhṛt* the one to be eaten (enjoyed) (*ibid.* I.8.3.5). The separation of the eater and the eaten is brought out in one and the same act. From one and the same man (i.e. the first great ancestor *i.e.* the *mūlapuruṣa),* spring forth the enjoyer (i.e. husband) and the enjoyed (i.e. wife). Hence the kinsfolk jovially say, "In the fourth or third generation we unite" (*ibid.* 6).

The *arthavāda* noted above, as pointed out by Eggeling is of considerable importance.[10] In the tradition of the Sūtras and later on in the Smṛtis, marriage between the *sapiṇḍa*-s (blood-relations) is disallowed. The *Āp. Dh. S.* prescribes that a man should not give his daughter in marriage to a person, who is a blood-relation on the mother's or the father's side (*Āp. Dh. S.* II. 5.11.16). The *Gaut. Dh. S.* says that marriage can take place between those persons, who are not related up to the seventh ancestor on the father's or begetter's side and up to the fifth ancestor on the mother's side (*Gaut. Dh. S.* IV. 3-5).[11] The *arthavāda*-passage in the *Śat. Br.* indicates that in the times much prior to the Sūtra-tradition, marriage-relationship between the *sapiṇḍa*-s extended up to the fourth or third degree (i.e. it ceases with the fourth or the third ancestor).[12]

The *arthavāda* in the context of the Agniṣṭoma sacrifice concerning the Pātnīvata (cup - 'graha') sheds light on the condition of women in those times. This cup (of Soma) is meant for the wives of the gods. This offering (of Pātnīvata) is to be taken in the Upāṁśu cup. But if the Sāvitra libation (to god Savitṛ) is taken in the Upāṁśu cup, the Pātnīvata (offering) is to be taken in the Antaryāma cup or vice versa. The Adhvaryu mixes this Pātnīvata with the residue of ghee, which is left in the offering-spoon (*pracaraṇī).* He completes other libations by mixing, but he diminishes the Pātnīvata, for with the thunderbolt in the form of ghee, the gods killed the wives and unmanned them. Thereby the wives neither owned their very self nor any share in the property. In the same manner, he now, with the thunderbolt in the form of ghee smites the wives and weakens them. With the result, the wives neither own any self nor do they own any share in the property (*dāyam)* (*Śat. Br.* IV.4.2.10,13). This *arthavāda* is important from the point of view of ancient Hindu law, which did not allow woman to have any share in the property of her husband (even after his death). The same practice existed in the times of Kālidāsa as can be seen from the episode of Dhanamitra, which occurs in the *Abhijñā-naśākuntalam* (Act VI).[13]

The same note of not giving much importance to women (in general) is struck in an *arthavāda* in the context of the Sautrāmaṇī sacrifice. It is said that with the sheep's wool he buys the malted barley and with thread the rice-grain (*Śat. Br.* XII. 7.2.10). The *arthavāda* states that wool and thread is woman's work. Work amounts to energy (*indriyam)* or vital power (*vīryam*) and this latter is extinct in woman. So with this barter, he secures for the sacrificer that energy or vital power, which is extinct in women (*ibid.* 11). The same thought about female as being without energy is marked when a ram and ewe are exchanged in the Varuṇapraghāsa-*parvan* in the four Seasonal sacrifices (*ibid.* II. 5.2.36).

The influence of the patriarchal form of the society, leading to the domination of male is marked in one *arthavāda,* which occurs in the context of the New-moon and Full-moon sacrifices. It is said that he brushes the dipping-spoon ('*sruva'* Masculine) first and then the other offering-spoons ('*srucaḥ*' Feminine). The *arthavāda* following that statement of *vidhi* says that the offering-spoon is female (here '*srucaḥ'* - many females or women) and the dipping-spoon (*sruva)* is male and although several women meet together, the one that is, as it were, the only male young ('*kumāraka'* - lit. 'young boy') goes there first and the others (i.e. women) after him. The *arthavāda* speaks of the importance of the male in the society[14] even though he may be of young age. The females, in a particular group, in spite of being more in number have to follow him (*ibid.* I.3.1.9).

In the context of the Saumitra *sāman*-s, a mythical account occurs as follows. The *āsurī* Dīrghajihvī (literally 'one who has a long tongue' - significant name!) licked the Soma-juice belonging to Indra, continuously. Indra wishing to kill her could not succeed in catching her. He approached Sumitra Kautsa (son of Kutsa) and said to him that he (i.e. Kautsa) was handsome to look at and "women become very prone to talking to a handsome person, being attracted to him." So Sumitra should make Dīrghajihvī talk to him for making love. The mythical account runs further and tells that as per Indra's plan, Sumitra succeeds in attracting Dīrghajihvī, when he 'sees' the Saumitra *sāman*-s and praises Indra with them, Indra taking the thunderbolt in the form of an Anuṣṭubh (metre) verse rushes forward and slays the *āsurī* (*Jaim. Br.* I.162, 163).

Here the belief that women have 'weakness' for a handsome man is reflected, though the woman here is *āsurī*. Manu in later times speaks in a more depreciatory manner about women, pointing out that they are attracted to any man simply with the thought of he being a 'man' (*Manu Sm.* IX. 14, 15).

The behaviour of a woman towards a man, when he tries to attract her attention is seen well in an *arthavāda* concerning Speech. The *arthavāda* figures in the rite of consecration of the sacrificer. The mythical account in this connection runs as follows. The gods and the *asura*-s both sprung from Prajāpati, got by way of inheritance from him 'Mind' (i.e. Sacrifice) and 'Speech' respectively. The gods who were in possession of Sacrifice wished to have Speech also (which was the share of the *asura*-s) to their credit, obviously for the sake of *mantra*-s (because without *mantra*-s no sacrifice can be valid). Sacrifice, urged by the gods or on his own, beckoned Speech. She first disdained him from a distance. Urged by the gods again, when Sacrifice beckoned Speech, she only replied to him as it were by shaking her head. Directed by the gods again, Sacrifice beckoned her and she called him to her. The gods then thought that Speech being a woman may allure Sacrifice to her and thus to the side of the *asura*-s. So they advised Sacrifice to say to Speech that she should come to the place, where the former was standing. And when told thus, Speech came to Sacrifice (*Śat. Br.* III. 2.1.18-22). At every step of this 'wooing' of Speech by Sacrifice, the *Śat. Br.* has shown the perfect knowledge of woman's psychology, how when wooed by a man, she first disdains him from a distance; then she replies to him as it were by shaking her head; later she calls him to her and ultimately goes up to him, thus proving (the universal experience) that a woman goes to a man, who stays in a well-trimmed house (*ibid.* 22).

That women are attracted to dancing and singing is pointed out in the *arthavāda* relating to the gain of Speech by the gods. This mythical account occurs in the *Śat. Br.* in the rite of buying Soma by giving the Somakrayaṇī cow. The cow here stands for Speech and the *arthavāda* is as follows — when (the metre) Gāyatrī was carrying off Soma for the gods, the *gandharva* Viśvāvasu stole Soma from her. The gods sent Speech ('Vāk' - a woman) to the *gandharva*-s, they being known for their 'weakness' for women. Speech alluring them could win Soma from them for the gods and she came to the gods with Soma. The *gandharva*-s came after Vāk and said, "Soma be yours and Vāk ours." The gods agreed but said to the *gandharva*-s that both of them would woo Vāk to their respective side. The *gandharva*-s recited the Veda-s to her. The gods created the lute and sat playing and singing. Vāk turned to the gods, who thus obtained both Soma and Vāk. The *Śat. Br.* has (a mischievous) remark that women are attracted to him, who dances and sings (*Śat. Br.* III. 2.4.1-6).

According to the *Jaim. Br.*, whatever was sung or played on the lute, also the dance and the acts of mimicry formed the weapon (*senā*) of Death (Mṛtyu), while whatever was praised by the *stotra* and by the *śastra* and whatever ritual was performed in the sacrifice, formed the weapon (*senā*) of Prajāpati (*Jaim. Br.* II. 69). However playing on lute as also singing, gaining a foothold and later on status, became a part of the Vedic ritual.[15]

Here is an *arthavāda* pointing out a belief with a (hidden) piece of instruction from the medical point of view. In the dispute between Mind and Speech for proving one's superiority to the other, Prajāpati gave his verdict in favour of Mind (*Śat. Br.* I.4.5.8-11; also *Tait. Sam.* II. 5. 11.4, 5).

Speech being dismayed miscarried and the *'retas'* (germ) was brought away by the gods in a skin or in some vessel. As they asked: 'Is it here *(atra)*'?, it developed into the seer Atri (*atra*>Atri). With the etymological help the *arthavāda* runs further stating that one becomes guilty by intercourse with a woman, who has just miscarried (*'ātreyī'* < *atra*). Such a woman in that state is like the goddess Speech from whom these germs *(retas)* originate (*Śat. Br.* I.4.5. 13).

It seems that woman as a 'class' was not held in esteem by the ritual thinkers. It is interesting to note that in the performance of the Pravargya ceremony, the *Śat. Br.* equates woman with *śūdra,* dog and a black bird. It lays down that the sacrificer should not come into contact with *śūdra*-s and remains of food. The Gharma or Mahāvīra-pot is the yonder sun and the sun stands for excellence, truth and light. Woman, *śūdra,* dog and black bird are untruth and the sacrificer should not look at these, otherwise he would mingle excellence and sin, light and darkness, truth and untruth (*ibid.* XIV. 1.1.31). In the context of the Agnicayana it is said that the person in the right eye is Indra and that in the left eye is Indrāṇī and the partition in between the two is the nose. So the husband should not eat food in the presence of his wife. By this he will have a vigorous son born to him (*ibid.* X.5.2.9).

It is the procreative power of the woman as a wife that gave her an important position in the social set-up. The wife of a king, who has no son stands discarded. But in the house of such a discarded wife are made offerings by the sacrificer-king in the Rājasūya sacrifice, by going there. The offerings are given to Nirṛti of pap *(caru)* made of black rice, after splitting the grains with his nails. The *Vāj. Sam. mantra* at this ritual is IX. 35. The reasoning forwarded by the *arthavāda* for the offering to Nirṛti is that a wife without a son is possessed with Nirṛti and whatever Nirṛti's nature there is in her that he propitiates by this offering. The *dakṣiṇā* to be given at this oblation consists of black, decrepit, diseased cow, for such a cow is also possessed of Nirṛti (*Śat. Br.* V. 3.1.13).

At several places the fertility aspect of female is mentioned in the *arthavāda*-passages. A couple of examples could be seen here. In the Agnicayana rite, when the fire-pan (*ukhā*) is made, he pours sand into it (*ibid.* VII. 1.1.41) and then milk (*ibid.* 44). The *Śat. Br.* here states in the *arthavāda* that the fire-pan is a female. When a female first receives seed (here 'sand', for sand is said to be seed), then she also receives milk. The sand (seed) is below and the milk is above, indicating here the respective parts of the female's body, and also the phenomenon of pregnancy and the woman's becoming equipped for suckling the child.

Again in the same rite, in the context of the Gārhapatya hearth, it is said that the fire-pan, which the sacrificer has to carry with him in a sling, is unloosened to keep it from chaffing. The fire-pan bore the Agni within it as seed and now the same Agni is brought forth. As the *ukhā* (fire-pan) is taken as a female, it is said to conceive a second time. The *Śat. Br.* refers to a worldly phenomenon in this *arthavāda* that when a female has brought forth the seed the first time, she conceives a second time (*ibid.* VII. 1.1.42).

The close relation between mother and son is spoken of in one *arthavāda.* In the Vājapeya sacrifice, there is laid down symbolic ascending the heaven by the sacrificer accompanied by his wife (in that he ascends a ladder kept against the sacrificial post). Now from the ladder, he looks down towards the ground (i.e. Earth) and mutters — 'Homage to the Mother Earth'. The *arthavāda* here brings in a *purāvṛtta* (olden account) which states that when Bṛhaspati was consecrated (for the Vājapeya sacrifice obviously!) the Earth was afraid of him that he might render her asunder and even Bṛhaspati was afraid of the Earth with the thought that she might shake him off (as he had ascended the ladder). So the *mantra* was muttered by him with which a friendly relation (*mitradheyam)* was brought between the two (i.e. himself and the Earth), for a mother does not injure her son, nor does a son injure his mother. The same practice of muttering a *mantra* and paying homage to the mother Earth is now followed by the sacrificer (*ibid.* V. 2.1.18,19). The same thought occurs[16] in the context of the Rājusūya sacrifice.

The thoughts of the Vedic ritualists about one's offspring or children in general are marked in the *arthavāda*-s. Here some examples can be taken for consideration.

In the context of the Agniṣṭoma sacrifice, while prescribing the *vidhi* (ritual) of making the sacrificial stake ready, the *Śat. Br.* refers to a world phenomenon. It is enjoined that he should insert a chip of the stake (under the rope). The *arthavāda* is that this chip is undoubtedly the offspring of that sacrificial stake. If there be the full number of eleven stakes,[17] he should insert in each its own chip without confounding them. By doing this, his offspring is born orderly and not foolish. But whosoever inserts them in confusion, not its own in each, his offspring is surely born disorderly and foolish (*ibid.* III. 7.1.22).

That the child in the womb takes full 'span' of time to develop in a healthy manner is hinted at in an *arthavāda* in the *Ait. Br.* (IV. 22 = 18.8) in the context of the Viṣuvant *śastra,* which is to be recited on the Viṣuvan day (once in a year, for that is the day joining the Tulā and Meṣa Saṅkrānti, as pointed out by Sāyaṇa). Such a child would benefit the sacrificer. The *arthavāda* points out that whatever seeds are born before the year, say of five months or six months, they wither and people are not benefitted by them.

In the Agnicayana rite, the Great Fire-altar is built up in the shape of a bird with wings and tail, in its flying position. This shape is for the Āhavanīya fire-altar and not the Gārhapatya one, where Agni is kept first, to be carried to the Āhavanīya. The *Śat. Br.* points out that as one does not see the child in the womb in its proper shape, similarly prior to being placed in the Āhavanīya altar, though Agni has wings and tail, people do not see him like that (*Śat. Br.* VII.1.1.19,20). The *arthavāda* here is based on the worldly knowledge of the foetus-form of a child.

In the context of Soma-sacrifice, the *Kauṣ. Br.* prescribes a set of five oblations *viz.* curds, fried grains, groats, cake and milk-mess. In the morning pressing, there is the offering of milk-mess only. The *arthavāda* explains the reason as follows. The sacrifice is born at the morning pressing and as breast-feeding (by the mother) is given to the child on birth, so milk-mess is offered (as oblation) in the morning pressing and not in the midday or the third pressing (*Kauṣ. Br.* XIII. 2).

A graphic picture of a child's development in the first year is seen from a mythical account (*purāvṛtta)* regarding creation. This occurs in the context of the New-moon and Full-moon sacrifices, when the offerings are enjoined. These were the same by which the gods gained these worlds and these quarters as also intermediate quarters (*Śat. Br.* 1.6.1-27). The mythical account by way of *arthavāda* comes as a prologue to the *vidhi* (injunction) regarding these offerings. The primeval waters toiled and became heated. And there was produced a golden egg in them, which floated there for about one year. In a year's time, a being *viz.* Prajāpati, was produced from there. So a woman, a cow and a mare bring forth within a year. Prajāpati broke open this golden egg, which floated on waters for a year. At the end of the year, Prajāpati tried to speak. He said, "Bhūḥ", the word which became this earth; then "Bhuvaḥ", which became the mid-region; then "Svaḥ", which became the yonder sky. This is following the development of a child, which tries to speak at the end of a year. Prajāpati thus first spoke a word of one syllable and then of the syllables, following the gradual development of a child, which also starts speaking his first words in this way only. At the end of the first year, Prajāpati rose to stand on these worlds thus produced. This is again following the pattern of the child's bodily development, when the child tries to stand up at the end of a year (*ibid.* XI. 1.6.1-5).

Like the mother-son-relationship, the father-son-relationship is also spoken of in the *arthavāda*. The *arthavāda* indicates a peculiar offering, which is to be dealt with in details. This occurs in the New-moon and Full-moon sacrifices. The gods conquered the heaven with the sacrifice, but thought of making it unattainable to men. They sipped the sap of the sacrifice and rubbed out its traces with the sacrificial post. The *ṛṣi*-s went to the place where the gods obtained the possession of the heavenly world. They found the sacrificial cake, which had become a tortoise. Even after requesting it to stop for the Aśvins, then for Sarasvatī and then for Indra, it did not stop. But it stopped when asked to stand still for Agni. The *ṛṣi*-s offered that sacrificial cake (= tortoise) entirely as an oblation to the gods. Then the sacrifice shone forth for them. The same sacrifice is taught by the former to the latter. The father teaches it to the son, when the latter is a student (*ibid.* I.6.2.1-4). The mythical account poses a question regarding tortoise being offered as oblation. In the lowest level of the rite of Agnicayana, a live tortoise is kept, as we have noted in the chapter on "Animals and Birds." But that cannot be regarded as an oblation offered in Agni. Again the mythical account mentions the '*whole*' tortoise as being offered in Agni (*ibid.* 4... *tamagnāveva parigṛhya sarvahutamajuhavuḥ* ...), which hardly is a case with respect to the other sacrificial victims. Again was the sacrificial cake in former times, of a large size as that of a tortoise? The large size of the cake was avoided as it amounted to being 'human' (i.e. meant for human beings) and the size of it prescribed is of a 'horse's hoof.' The *Śat. Br.* says that one does not know how large a horse's hoof is. Hence one should make it of such a size as in one's own mind, one does not think would be too broad (*ibid.* I.2.2.9-10). As we have noted above, the father imparts the knowledge of sacrifice and also the details of it to the son.

The *Jaim. Br.* says that sacrifice is a divine boat. The boat (i.e. sacrifice) which is propelled by the father and the son, that boat never sinks. For (that) sacrifice, Auśana *sāman* is recited at the beginning and Kāva *sāman* is recited at the end. This is for the safety or wellbing of the sacrifice (*Jaim. Br.* I. 166). The *arthavāda* here points out the close relation existing between the father and the son in those times.

That the father must have been of a 'caring' type (i.e. caring for his children) is seen in one *arthavāda.* In the four Seasonal sacrifices, in the Varuṇapraghāsa-*parvan,* there are as many dishes as there are children in the sacrificer's family. The dishes exceed by one. There being one dish for each child, he thereby delivers from Varuṇa's noose one by one the children born to him. With the additional dish, he delivers from Varuṇa's noose, those children of his which are as yet unborn (*Śat. Br.* II. 5.2.22). It is said that of all the sons, the most pitiable wins over the father's heart (*Jaim. Br.* II. 183). This is obviously because the father has the utmost compassion for such a son.

The practice of giving importance to the eldest son is marked in the *Tait. Sam.* through an *arthavāda,* which figures in the context of New-moon and Full-moon sacrifices. When Indra slew Vṛtra, the gods asked Agni and Soma to bear the offering for them. The two replied that they had lost their brilliance, as it was situated in Vṛtra (who then was slain by Indra). The gods told them to go to the cow, she being the friend of all. Cow's ghee is brilliance of Agni and her milk is brilliance of Soma. When the theologians ask as to what is the deity of the Full-moon rite, the sacrificer should name Prajāpati, for by means of this rite, Prajāpati established his eldest son Indra. The *arthavāda* ends in saying that this is how they establish their elder son with wealth (*Tait. Sam.* II. 5.2.6-8).

The practice in this regard was to assign a choice portion to the eldest son. In the context of the Soma-sacrifice, while prescribing the Niṣkevalya *śastra,* the following mythical account comes as an *arthavāda.* Indra having slain Vṛtra and having won all victories became great (and so his name is 'Mahendra') and asked the deities to assign him a choice portion (*uddhāra),* to which the gods agreed and told him to choose that portion by himself. Then he claimed the cup for Mahendra (Māhendra *graha*) of all the cups, the midday pressing from the three pressings, the Niṣkevalya of the litanies (*uktha*-s), the Triṣṭubh of metres, the Pṛṣṭha of *sāman*-s. They assigned this choice portion to him (*Ait. Br.* III. 21 = 12.10). In the Dharmaśāstra tradition, such a choice portion (or special share - *uddhāra*) is laid down for the eldest son. Manu says that the twentieth part of the (as yet undivided) property as well as the choicest portion of all (types) of wealth should be given as a special share (*uddhāra*) to the eldest son (*Manu Sm.* IX. 112). Yājñavalkya speaks of an option *viz.* the best portion of the property goes to the eldest son or the property can be divided equally amongst the sons (*Yāj. Sm.* II. 114). Vijñāneśvara in his comm. Mitākṣarā on the *Yāj. Sm.* (II. 114) tries to justify by saying that this 'uneven' (*viṣamaḥ*) division is with respect to the property acquired by the father with his own efforts. However while commenting on the *Yāj. Sm.* (II. 117 ab), after quoting the words of Āpastamba and Manu he states that such an 'uneven' division is not to be made as it is opposed to the ways of the world and also the scriptures.[18]

A mythical account coming as *arthavāda* in the context of the New-moon and Full-moon sacrifices is worthy of consideration, as we are dealing with the point cf division of property. It is stated that he pours the refuse of the rice under the black antelope skin. He thereby casts it into blind darkness, where there is no sacrificial fire. In the same way, he casts the blood of the victim into blind darkness, where there is no fire, thinking that it is the *rakṣas*-es' share. This is the *vidhi*. The *arthavāda* runs as follows. The gods and the *asura*-s were contending about the sacrifice. The gods obtained the possession of the whole of the sacrifice and dispossessed the *asura*-s by giving them the worst part of the sacrifice *viz.* the blood of the victim and the refuse of the rice of the Haviryajña. The ending note of the *arthavāda* is — he indeed is duly dispossessed, who obtains a worthless share (of the property). On the other hand, he, who is dispossessed hopes a while for the share due to him and then asks boldly, "What share have you given to me?" (*Śat. Br.* I. 9.2.34-35).

The *arthavāda* is important in more than one ways—

(*i*) Refuse of the rice of the Haviryajña is to be cast away.

(*ii*) It should be poured under the black antelope skin, for the room under the black antelope skin stands for the blind darkness, though the black antelope itself and also its hide stand for sacrifice.[19] Here it is to be marked that the refuse is to be placed not on the hide but under it.

(*iii*) The blood of the victim is not to be offered in sacrifice. It is to be cast away into blind darkness and is regarded as the share of the *rakṣas*-es.

(*iv*) Blood-sacrifices hence have no roots in the Vedic tradition. It is a phenomenon of later times, when several other trends entered and were assimilated in the Vedic religion.

(*v*) A person could be duly dispossessed by allotting him a negligible worthless share.

(*vi*) A person not allotted any share and thus dispossessed could challenge the persons not giving him any share.

To turn to the householder's life again — the smallest unit seems to be the father, mother and the child (which is born), i.e. of three. This is told in an *arthavāda,* which occurs in the context of consecration, when the sacrificer has to gird himself with a girdle made of hemp. This cord is a triple one, for food is threefold and the family-unit is also threefold. The cord is plaited after the manner of a braid of hair. Were it to be twisted as the course of the sun (i.e. from left to right), like any other cords, it would be human. Were it twisted contrary to the course of the sun, it would be sacred to the Fathers (*Śat. Br.* III. 2.1.11-13).

The Vedic ritualists believe that a householder has three births. It is pointed out in the context of the New-moon and Full-moon sacrifices that a person is born thrice. His first i.e. natural birth, is from the parents. When the sacrifice inclines to him and he gives offering, he is born a second time and when he dies, they place him on the fire and thereafter he comes into existence again, he is born a third time (*ibid.* XI. 2.1.1). The birth for the third time is explained by Sāyaṇa as the one, which is the abode of the enjoyment of the fruit of sacrifice. The *Śat. Br.* states in the context mentioned above (i.e. New-moon and Full-moon sacrifices) that a person is born with four debts, which he has to pay off during his lifetime. Debt to the gods he pays off when he is bound to sacrifice to them. That to the *ṛṣi*-s he pays off when he studies the Veda. Debt to the Fathers he pays off, when he is bound to wish for offspring. Debt to men he pays off, when he is bound to practise hospitality (*ibid.* I.7.2.1-5). The *Śat. Br.* (XI. 5.6.1) and *Tait. Ār.* (II. 10) speak of the five great daily sacrifices which can be taken into account here.[20] Devayajña in which daily offerings are given to the gods is a way to pay off the debt to the gods. Brahmayajña — sacrifice to Brahman — is one's own daily study of the Veda. By this way he pays off the debt to the *ṛṣī*-s. Pitṛyajña is giving daily offerings to the Fathers. The concept of paying off the debt to the *pitṛ*-s is different from this and focuses on continuing the family-line by having issues (mainly sons). Bhūtayajña is offering daily an oblation to beings. There is no concept of any debt corresponding to this. Manuṣyayajña is giving hospitality to guests, by which way he pays off the debt to men.

The *Tait. Sam.* speaks of three debts in which a *brāhmaṇa* when born is indebted *viz.* in *brahmacarya* to the sages, in sacrifice to the gods and in offspring to the manes. He indeed becomes free from debts who has a son, who sacrifices and who dwells as a *brahmacārī* with the teacher (*Tait. Sam.* VI. 3.10.5). The same thought is echoed by the *Baudh. Dh. S.* (II. 6.29.42-43) and the *Vas. Dh. S.* (XI. 45-48).

It is the *Śat. Br.* which has stated the concept of debt to men and the way to pay it off by performing Manuṣyayajña, though Manuṣyayajña is spoken of also by the *Tait. Ār.* (II.

10) as is noted above. Here we come to the practice of giving hospitality to a guest, which is the foremost duty of a family man.

The practice of honouring a guest dates back to the *RV*. The *RV* at several places calls Agni an *atithi* (guest) in the house of the sacrificer and refers to the practice of giving honour to him.[21] The *AV* devotes one full *kāṇḍa* for this (XV *kāṇḍa*) eulogising the Mahāvrātya and deals with the hospitality to be shown to him. The *Tait. Sam.* states that when a guest comes, hospitality abounding in ghee is offered to him (*Tait. Sam.* V. 2.2.4). This is mentioned in the rite of Agnicayana, when the fire in the fire-pan is carried to the Gārhapatya altar in a cart (*anasā vahanti).* The *arthavāda* states that he that has a cart and he the one with a chariot are the most honoured guests. With the words, 'With kindling wood serve Agni', he puts on fire (Agni) a kindling stick made wet with ghee. This is like hospitality shown to a guest on his arrival, at which time melted butter is offered to him (*ibid.* V.2.2.3-4).

In the ritual tradition, who else can be there a guest better than Soma? In the Agniṣṭoma sacrifice, the Soma (in the form of shoots) which is purchased, is treated as a guest par excellence. Hospitality offered to him (*ātithyam)* is said to be the head, i.e. the first and foremost ritual, in the sacrifice (*Śat. Br.* III. 4.1.1). The *arthavāda* states that as for a king or a *brāhmaṇa,* one would cook a big ox or a big he-goat, for that is the honour shown to a human guest. But for Soma, the oblation will be the one befitting the gods (*ibid.* 2). The *Śat. Br.* prescribes taking out the material for offering only after unyoking both oxen and after making Soma enter the sacrificial hall. The *arthavāda* here mentions the practice prevalent in the then society. The practice stated here is that as long as a guest has not unyoked, people do not bring water for him (to wash the feet and also to sip) and do not show honour, for according to them he has not yet arrived. They bring water and show him honour only when he has unyoked (*ibid.* 5). The *Śat. Br.* then enjoins that the sacrificer takes out Soma from the cart with a speedy action, obviously showing honour to Soma and when taken out, the housewife holds on Soma from behind. The *arthavāda* here refers to the practice that whenever a worthy person comes to one's house, all the inmates of the house are on their toes to receive him with honour (*ibid.* 6). The *Ait. Br.* also states that the guest-reception be given to Soma, when the Soma-shoots purchased are brought to the sacrificial place. This guest-reception is offered on nine potsherds. It is said that all the metres (*chandāṁsi)* and the Pṛṣṭha-s (Sāyaṇa-*bṛhadrathantaravairūpādisāmasādhyāni pṛṣṭhastotrāṇi)* follow King Soma, when he is bought. The *Ait. Br.* says that as many as follow Soma, to all of them is the reception offered. The kindling of (fresh) fire (Agni)[22] is enjoined here as a part of guest-reception. The *arthavāda* echoes a practice of those times that when a human king or any other deserving person comes, they slay an ox or a cow that miscarries.[23] For King Soma they slay, i.e. kindle the fire, for Agni is the sacrificial victim (*paśu)* of the gods (*Ait. Br.* I.15 = 3.4).

The practice of waving a lighted lamp around the face of a guest (*nīrājana-vidhi* of later times in the Hindu tradition) is seen by way of *arthavāda* (or in the *arthavāda* style), in the rite of offering an oblation, when the kindling stick placed in the fire becomes ablaze on all sides (*Tait. Br.* II. 1.3.9). The *Tait. Br.* clearly states that this is like encircling (or waving) a lighted stick (as lamp?) round the (face of the?) guest.

In the rite of giving guest-offering (*ātithya-iṣṭi)* to king Soma, they churn the fire (Agni) and thus produce the sacrifice (*Śat. Br.* III. 4.1.19). He churns Agni reciting the *mantra*-s, 'With the Gāyatrī metre I churn thee!' 'With the Triṣṭubh metre ...'! 'With the Jagatī metre...'! With the metres he churns Agni and thereby attaches the metres to the sacrifice, as the rays are attached to the yonder sun (*ibid.*

23). This shows the inseparable relation of the metres with sacrifice.[24] The *Śat. Br.* however earlier is quick enough to add that the metres act as attendants on King Soma, as do the non-royal king-makers, the heralds and headmen on the king. Hence no material for offering solely for the metres be taken out. He (i.e. the sacrificer or the priest on his behalf) should assign the metres a share in oblation along with the deity Soma. Whenever people cook food for some dignitary, then his attendants, the non-royal king-makers, the heralds and headmen, have their share of food assigned to them after or along with their master (*ibid.* 7, 8). From our point of view, the *arthavāda* is important as it records the practice of and the way in which the hospitality was given to the guest and the persons accompanying him.

The *arthavāda* occurring in the *Pañc. Br.* states the importance of the Viśoviśīya *sāman* to be chanted as a part of the Ārbhava Pavamāna laud (*stotra)* of the eighth day. But it is initially based on the practice of guest-offering. Agni once desired that he should be the guest of every house (*viśo viśaḥ)* or house to house and receive hospitality. So he performed austerities and saw the Viśoviśīya *sāman.* He then became such a guest and obtained hospitality (*Pañc. Br.* XIX. 11.37).

The sun is said to be '*ekātithiḥ*'[25] (*Ait. Br.* V. 30 = 25.5), and so the hospitality is given to this guest. The sun is 'the guest par excellence' or 'excellent guest' (as we have the expression '*ekavīraḥ*' i.e. the foremost warrior). For this excellent guest, the oblations are offered in fire in the morning, when he comes.[26] When the sun sets he enters Agni (Fire), which is his womb and from this womb he comes out in the morning. The *Śat. Br.* states that when the sun sets, then Agni is the light and when the sun rises, then Sūrya is the light (*Śat. Br.* II. 3.1.36). So for the sun — the excellent guest — the oblations are given in fire in the evening also. The *Ait. Br.* quotes a *gāthā* in this regard, which refers to an oath taken by a person, accused of stealing lotus-stalks that if he has committed the theft, let him heap the blame on the blameless or take away blame from the blameworthy.[27] The *Ait. Br.* quotes the *gāthā* to point out that the sins befalling a person, mentioned here will accrue to a person, who turns away the 'excellent guest' (*ekātithiḥ),* i.e. the sun, in the evening. So the evening oblations for the sun are to be given in the fire (which is its womb). The *Ait. Br.* echoes here the oft-said words that 'a guest arrived at evening should not be turned away.'[28]

It has to be noted that the idea underlying the hospitality to be shown to the guest was not of universal kindliness as maintained by Kane,[29] but was of fear of the guest, who was invariably a person unknown to the householder, since guest (*'atithi'*) was always a person wandering from place to place.[30] Manu also says that as a guest does not stay permanently, he is called *atithi* and that, *atithi* is a *brāhmaṇa,* who stays for one night only as a guest (*Manu Sm.* III. 102). The idea that a person arriving as an *atithi* used to be practically a stranger to the householder is maintained in the Dharmaśāstra tradition, which states that he is called an *atithi,* who belonging to a different village and intending to stay for one night only, arrives in the evening, and that one who has already been invited for dinner is not an *atithi* properly so called and that a person, who belongs to the same village or who is a friend or a fellow-student is not an *atithi* (*Gaut. Dh. S.* V. 36; *Manu Sm.* III. 103; *Yāj. Sm.* I.107-111).

There always lurked a feeling of fear of a person coming as a guest *(atithi).* This fear is expressed by the Ṛgvedic seer that Agni the guest should not be angry (*RV.* VIII. 10.12). The *AV* states that when a learned Vrātya comes as a guest to the house of a king, the latter should esteem him better than himself, so he does not offend against dominion and also against royalty (*AV.* XV. 10.1,2). This shows that the Vrātya if not given the proper hospitality, will harm the king's dominion and royalty. We have already noted the guest-offering given to King Soma (when the cart carrying Soma-shoots enters the sacrificial hall), as stated in the *Śat. Br.* (III. 4.1.1-3). The *Śat. Br.* notes the belief that where people do not show respect to a worthy person *(arhant),* who has come to them, he becomes angry (*ibid.* 3). The *Tait. Up.,* in one of its teachings to the *snātaka* (i.e. a student, returning home after completing his study at the preceptor's hermitage) lays down '*atithidevo bhava*' - Be one, treating the guest as your god (*Tait Up.* I.11.2) and elsewhere states that he should never turn away a stranger from his house (*ibid.* III. 10.1). In the tale of Naciketas, as given in the *Kaṭha Up.,* when Naciketas arrives at the house of Yama and is not honoured (even though he is a guest) by anybody, as Yama has gone out, the *Kaṭh Up.* instructs Yama (when he comes back) that 'a *brāhmaṇa* entering a house as a guest is like fire. People offer this appeasement to him; hence, O son of Vivasvat offer him water. If a *brāhmaṇa* guest stays in a man's house without food, he cuts off the hopes and expectations, (fruits of) the friendship (of the good), the rewards of sacrifices and charitable acts, sons and cattle' (*Kaṭha Up.* I.1.7-9). The fear that a guest, if not properly given hospitality, would take away the merit of the house-holder's good works, is echoed by the Sūtra-tradition as well as the Purāṇa-s.[31]

Right from the Ṛgvedic times, the concept of *atithi* is viewed in two ways *viz.* bad and good. Being unknown to the householder to whose house he comes, the guest *(atithi)* is initially regarded as having potentiality to do harm and prove dangerous to the householder, thus causing fear-complex in the mind of the householder. But if he is given proper honour and hospitality, the guest can bless the householder and can enable him to go to the heavenly world.[32]

Together with this receiving a guest with honour and hospitality, with a mind subdued with awe for him, there is a picture of the householder entertaining his relatives and friends with kindness and affection, as seen in a mythical account. This comes as an *arthavāda* in the context of the special preliminary rites of the New-moon sacrifice, when a rice-cake on twelve potsherds is a common offering for Indra and Agni.

The mythical account states that though Indra hurled the thunderbolt at Vṛtra, he was engulfed with fear with the thought that Vṛtra was not slain by him. So he concealed himself only to be discovered by Agni, with whom he stayed that day and night. Indra became the Vasu of the gods (Sāyaṇa — '*vasu*' - treasure in the form of wealth or '*vasu*' - 'one who stays', from the root √*vas* 'to stay'). The gods said that their Vasu was staying (fr. √*vas*) near (*amā*) with Agni on that day (hence the day is called 'Amāvasyā' — New-moon day). So a common *puroḍāśa* (cake) on twelve potsherds for two, i.e. Indra and Agni. The *arthavāda* here refers to a practice of cooking a dish of rice or goat in common (*samānam)* for two relatives or friends, who have come to stay with the householder. As is this general human practice of common offering, so is the common offering of sacrificial food to the (two) gods (*Śat. Br.* I. 6.4.1-3). Apart from the duties of a householder towards the inmates of the house as well as towards the guests and friends, which are reflected in the *arthavāda*-s, the 'house' itself has a separate identity here. In the context of the New-moon and Full-moon sacrifices, when (a jar containing) water is placed near the Gārhapatya fire, it is said that Gārhapatya fire-place is a house and a house is a safe resting-place. By placing that water near the Gārhapatya fire, he stands firmly in a house, which is a safe resting-place (*ibid.* I.1.1.19). The same thought occurs, when he takes a step towards the Gārhapatya fire (*ibid.* I.9.3.18; II.4.1.7; cf. II.5.2.29).

In this regard, a touching *arthavāda* occurs, when a householder (maintaining the fires) is said to come back from a journey and is about to enter his house. With the thought as to what the householder will say and what will he do on that occasion, the house trembles with fear and is liable to crush the householder's family. But the same house receives the householder with confidence, if the latter neither speaks nor does anything. The *Śat. Br.* here gives a very practical suggestion that if the householder has any (small or big) cause to be angry at anything on this occasion, he should rather do it on the next day, whatever he wants to say or do (*ibid.* II. 4.1.14). Eggeling refers to the Kāṇva recension of the *Śat. Br.*, where the *mantra*-s from the *Vāj. Sam.* (III. 41-43, lines 1 and 2) are added.[33] The *arthavāda* here brings out the deep knowledge of the ritualists of human psychology. A householder, after journey (the journey of those times!), being already exhausted, was likely to flare up even with a slight mistake on the part of his family-members or servants, which they might have committed in his absence and which he might know only on the day of his arrival. Hence a friendly and practical note of warning to him that the house itself trembles with fear at his arrival and may crush his family. Hence a suggestion that he should reserve his feelings or actions for the next day. The *arthavāda* also points out that a 'house' (which is a 'home' for the householder and the inmates there) has a separate identity of itself, which provides a firm basis for the family-life in Vedic India (and even India of this age!).

NOTES AND REFERENCES

1. See Caland, W., *Pañcaviṃśa Brāhmaṇa,* p. 47, note 1 on *Pañc. Br.* IV. 2.17, where he refers to *SV* II. 125-127 = *RV* IX. 62.25-27, which are prescribed in accordance with this Brāhmaṇa by Maśaka in his *Ārṣeyakalpa* I.1 b.
2. Dākṣāyaṇas, a royal family, seems to have practised a peculiar modification of the New-moon and Full-moon sacrifices. Though two days were required for the performance of these sacrifices, there was a deviation from the usual practice. At the ordinary sacrifice, the first day was completely taken up with the preliminary ceremonies;

but the Dākṣāyaṇas spread the special offerings over both days, making each time two separate *iṣṭi*-s of them. Hence the name Dākṣāyaṇa to this sacrifice.

See Eggeling, J., *The Śatapatha Brāhmaṇa,* pt. I, *SBE* Vol. 12, pp. 374-75.

3. For *sānnāyya, ibid*., p. 178 f, note 4.
4. See Dange, Sadashiv A., *Sexual Symbolism from the Vedic Ritual,* pp. 51-70 and the chart at the end of that chap. "Sex-coupling in Sacrifice (Mithunīkaraṇa)."
5. See Eggeling, J., *op. cit.,* pt. V, *SBE* Vol. 44, p. 313, note 2. The fourth wife of the king—Pālāgalī—though present at the sacrifice, does not take part in this ceremony probably due to her low-caste origin, as pointed out by Eggeling.
6. *Prastara* stands for the sacrificer and its dropping in the fire is symbolic of the sacrificer's going to the other world and that is the world of the gods, through the medium of sacrifice. For this *Śat. Br.* I. 8.3.11.
7. The word *'svagā'* — lit. 'Self-go' = 'Safe go' (like the modern-day expression 'Bon voyage'), wishing 'Good Speed' is for the sacrificer, symbolised by the *prastara* and this 'good speed' is for going to the world of gods, for to this world only the sacrifice has gone; for this *ibid.*
8. Dange, Sadashiv A., "Yupa", *Vedic Sacrifices— Early Nature,* Vol. II, p. 255.
9. *Kāṭh. Sam.* XXX.1. In the context of the Pātnīvata *yūpa*, the mythical account of Manu and his wife is stated. The worldly observation in this account is that 'at the night time, a woman speaks in a more lovely manner'.
10. Eggeling, J., *op. cit.,* pt. I, *SBE* Vol. 12, p. 238f, note 1.
11. For more references, see Ram Gopal, *India of Vedic Kalpasūtras*, Delhi, 1959, p. 211.
12. *Ibid.,* p. 220, note 53, where for the discussion on this passage, Ram Gopal points to *Smṛticandrikā*, ed. by L. Srinivasacharya, Mysore, 1914, "Saṁskāra-kāṇḍa", pp. 194 ff.
13. It was Yājñavalkya (A.D. 400) who pointed out the sonless widow (*patnī)* as the first heir to claim her husband's property (*Yāj. Sm.* II. 135-136). But Yājñavalkya's words invited for and against arguments. However Vijñāneśvara in the twelfth century, convincingly explained in his comm. Mitākṣarā these verses of the *Yāj. Sm.* and proved the sonless widow's right to her husband's property.

14. *Śat. Br.* XIII. 2.2.4. In the preliminary ceremonies of the Horse-sacrifice, an ewe for the deity Sarasvatī is placed (i.e. tied) beneath the horse's jaws. He thereby makes women to be dependent on man, and they surely attend upon man. Through this *arthavāda,* the same note is struck, as we have seen in the case of *sruc*-s and *sruva.*
15. See (Mrs.) Dange, S.S., "Vocal and Instrumental Music in Vedic Ritual", *Aspects of Speech in Vedic Ritual,* pp. 247-56.
16. *Sat. Br.* V. 4.3.19.21. The same thought about mother-son-relationship occurs in the *arthavāda,* which is stated in the context of the Rājasūya sacrifice. Having put on the shoes of boar's skin, the sacrificer-king looks at the earth, under his feet and mutters a wish, "O mother Earth, injure me not, nor I thee!" With this *mantra,* he enters into a friendly relation with her, for a mother does not injure her son, nor does a son injure his mother.
17. See Eggeling, J., *op. cit.,* pt. II, *SBE* Vol. 26, p. 173, note 1.
18. Also see Kane, P.V. *Hist. of Dh.S.,* Vol. V, pt. II, 2nd ed., BORI, Poona, 1977, p. 1268, also note 2067.
19. For this, see the chapter on "Animals and Birds".
20. For the Pañca Mahāyajñas, see Kane, P.V., *op. cit.,* Vol. II, pt. I, BORI, Poona, 1974, pp. 696-704.
21. *RV.* I. 73.1[c]; IV.4. 10[cd]; V.1.9[d]; VII.42.4[b]; VIII. 19.8[a].
22. The Āhavanīya fire is already there, yet the new fire is kindled. The *Ait. Br.* (I. 16 = 3.5) - *jāta itaro jātavedā itaraḥ* - 'One is born, One is all-knower'. This new fire is carried to the Āhavanīya and is placed there. The new fire naturally stands as Gṛhapati and serves as the Gārhapatya fire.
23. In the Sūtra-period, there was the ritual of offering Madhuparka to celebrities. It was a mixture of curds and honey, and in the absence of honey, (curds and) ghee. Madhuparka was accompanied by a cow, which was killed or released, depending upon the wish of the guest. See *Āśv. G.S.* I. 24.23-26.
24. (Mrs.) Dange, S.S., "Metres and their Magic", *Aspects of Speech in Vedic Ritual,* pp. 36-112.
25. *Ait. Br.* V.30 = 25.5 '*ekātithiḥ*' is taken by Sāyaṇa as - *kaścid vaideśiko bandhurahitaḥ svayameka evātithiḥ,* i.e. 'a certain lone guest, coming from afar, devoid of any relatives'. Keith translates '*ekātithiḥ*' as 'one guest'. See Keith, A.B., *Rigveda Brahmanas* tr. *HOS* Vol. 25, p. 254.

26. The *Ait. Br.* (V. 29-31 = 25.4-6) has a long discussion about the exact time, when the offerings are to be given in the rite of Agnihotra — whether before the rise of the sun or after it. The *Ait. Br.* clearly states that the offering should be made after sunrise.
27. The *Mbh.* deals at a great length with this topic of the theft of lotus-stalks. *Mbh.* Anuśāsana-*parvan* 93.71-145; 94.1-54. Also see (Mrs.) Dange, S.S., "The Theft of Lotus-stalks and the Various Taboos", Prof. Dr. V.M. Kulkarni Fel. Vol. (in press).
28. Cf. *Manu Sm.* III. 105, also repeats the same thought, saying that a guest arrived at the evening time is brought by the sun (at the door of the householder) and hence not to be turned away.
29. Kane, P.V., *op. cit.*, Vol. II, pt. II, pp. 749 ff.
30. For the etymologies of the word "*atithi*' stated by Yāska. *Nir.* IV. 5 — from the root √*at* - 'to go'; and also from the word *tithi* (day) and the letter *a* in the word *atithi* meaning 'comes' from *abhi* + √*i*.

    Sāyaṇa, while explaining the word *atithim* (*RV* VIII. 84.1a), derives it from the root √*at* - 'to go', with the *uṇādi* suffix *ithin*.
31. *Śaṅkh. G.S.* (II. 17.1); *Viṣṇu Dh. S.* (67.33) speaks of transfer of the guest's sin to the householder; *Viṣṇu P.* III. 9.15; *Mārk. P.* 29.31; *Brahma P.* 114.36; also *Mbh.* Śānti. 191.12.
32. For more information, see (Mrs.) Dange, S.S., "Atithi—A Probe in Concept", *Studies on Indology* (Prof. Mukund Mahdav Sharma Fel. Vol.), Sri Satguru Pubns., a division of Indian Books Centre, Delhi, 1996, pp. 119-22.
33. See Eggeling, J., *op. cit.*, pt. I., p. 360 f., note 1, where he also refers to the *Kāt. Ś.S.* IV. 12.22. *Kāt. Ś.S.* IV. 12.20-23 deals with this topic.

Chapter 12

Sacrificer's Code and His Immortality (!)

For the Vedic ritualists, the sacrificial activity though performed on the terrestrial region, was never tied down to the mundane existence alone, with its material gains in view, as we notice in the fruits of the *Kāmya-iṣṭi*s. But it was more than this for the ritual thinkers, who wanted the sacrificer to emerge as a 'better' man after performing the sacrifice, relating himself to the divine level. For this a definite code of conduct, having the rules of consecration (*dīkṣā*). toiling (*tapas,* which could be understood as fervour or austere devotion, as Eggeling has taken),[1] giving gifts (*dakṣiṇā*-s) etc. was there. Together with this, rules relating to a general ethical code also figure in some *arthavāda*-s, though they are from the sacrificial context, which fact is hardly to be forgotten.

The *Jaim. Br.* enumerates the occasions, when a person commits sin. He commits sin with his mouth, when he speaks what is indecent; with his two arms, when he kills a person, who should not be killed; with his stomach, when he eats food of a person, whose food he should not eat; and with his feet, when he goes to a person (to whom he should not approach). These rules are meant for the sacrificer (*Jaim.*

Br. II. 135). But these equally hold good for an individual person in the society.

Tapas

Tapas which is denoted by fervour, or toiling or austere devotion is a quality, which is eulogised. In the rite of Tānūnaptra (which we shall deal with later), fire (Agni) is said to be *tapas* (fervour) and consecration (*dīkṣā)* is said to be *tapas* (*Śat. Br.* III. 4.3.2, 3, 10). In the context of the Agniṣṭoma sacrifice, in the rite of Upasad-s,[2] the *arthavāda* states that the world is conquered by austere devotion (*tapas).* His *tapas* (austere devotion) becomes ever and ever wider and he conquers an ever and ever more glorious world and becomes better in this world, whosoever undertakes the Upasad-s (*ibid.* III. 4.4.27).

In the night previous to the New-moon and Full-moon sacrifices, the sacrificer has to sleep in the house of the Āhavanīya fire (*āhavanīyāgāre)* or in the house of the Gārhapatya fire. When he has entered the vow, he has approached the gods and he should sleep in the midst of those very gods. He has to sleep on the ground, for from below, one serves one's superior (*ibid.* I.1.1.11). The thought stated here is obviously of observing decorum or modesty by a junior person when his superiors or elders are around.

Śraddhā

Sraddhā (Faith) is an important quality to be inculcated by a person in his mind, for with ardent faith alone, he can achieve his goal. This is more true in the context of the sacrificial religion, where a person has to keep faith in the sacred texts — the Śabda *pramāṇa.* The *Jaim. Br.*, while pointing out the importance of faith (*śraddhā)* says that faith is the queen of the gods. She, in the morning, coming near, stands. The gods approach her and following her, all the gods rejoice at the evening time. When faith enters him (i.e. the sacrificer), he offers oblations, he performs sacrifice.

The gods live by that offering, (*Jaim. Br.* II. 426). While stating the importance of faith, the *arthavāda* here points out that the dealing between the human beings and gods is of 'give and take'. In the context of the Agnihotra rite, occurs a mythical account, which brings out the importance of faith. Janaka of Videha once asked Yājñavalkya in order to test him, the means with which the latter could offer Agnihotra-offering. 'Milk', replied Yājñavalkya and while telling about the substitute for the each earlier one, ultimately said that in case nothing whatsoever was available, there would be offered the truth (*satya*) in faith (*śraddhā*). Janaka being pleased with Yājñavalkya's correct understanding of the Agnihotra rite, gave him a hundred cows as *dakṣiṇā* (*Śat. Br.* XI. 3.1.1-4). Here as truth stands for ghee and faith for Agni (*ibid.* XI. 3.1.1), the former is offered in the latter, both being the essential qualities in the code of conduct meant for the sacrificer and even for any other person. When Manu in mythical accounts is called '*śraddhādeva*' (i.e. one who regards *śraddhā* as god), it speaks of such constant and ardent faith in the sacrificial rituals on his part that he easily becomes ready to offer his bull, then his wife, in sacrifice on the words of the two *asura-brāhmaṇa*s (*Mait. Sam.* IV. 8.1; *Kāṭh. Sam.* XXX. 1; *Śat. Br.* I.1.4.14-18). The main point in these mythical accounts is the magical voice, which kills the *asura*-s, when they hear that. This voice first enters the bull, which is offered by Manu in the sacrifice on the words of the two *asura*-s. Afterwards the same voice enters Manu's wife. The myth in the *Śat. Br.* supports the *vidhi* of striking the two millstones (with which grains are ground), at the call of the Adhvaryu priest.[3] The point is, Manu being '*śraddhādeva*' could believe in the words of the *asura-brāhmaṇa*s (i.e. the priests—*brāhmaṇa*-s—of the *asura*-s).

Gratitude

The sacrifice named Āgrayaṇa (Āgrayaṇeṣṭi) is meant for showing gratitude towards the gods. This sacrifice is performed in spring and autumn at the commencement of the harvest. The oblations as a rule are prepared from new grain and they are — (i) a twelve-potsherd cake for Indra and Agni, (ii) a *caru* for the Viśve Devāḥ and (iii) a one-potsherd cake for Heaven and Earth.[4] The *Śat. Br.* traces the sacrifice (Āgrayaṇa) to Kahoḍa Kauṣītaki, who started it. It was he who pointed out that 'the sap (*rasa* i.e. the produce from the plants — the grains) belongs, in reality, to Heaven and Earth. Having first offered to the gods, we will eat it.' Hence the offering of the first fruits to the gods (mentioned above) (*Śat. Br.* II. 4.3.1).

The *Śat. Br.* at this place also states a mythical account, told by Yājñavalkya, which is as follows. The gods and *asura*-s, both sprung from Prajāpati contended for superiority. The *asura*-s then defiled, partly by magic, partly with poison, both kinds of plants, which normally are a means of subsistence for men as well as for beasts. With the result, men and beasts perished. But by performing the same sacrifice (Āgrayaṇa-*iṣṭi),* the gods removed the magic spell as well as the poison from both kinds of plants. When the sacrificer performs this sacrifice, he does so either for the reason that no one will then defile the plants either by magic or by poison or because the gods performed it (*ibid.* II. 4.3.2-3, 11-12).

That the initial motif of performing the Āgrayaṇa-*iṣṭi* was of showing gratitude to the gods, can be seen when this *iṣṭi* is compared to the liturgical ceremonies of the Zoroastrians, called the Gahambār-s. These are the seasonal festivals, having importance from the agricultural, seasonal or cosmogonical points of view. The Gahambār-s were celebrated mainly to offer thanks to god for creating different seasons, on the regular working of which depends the prosperity of the world. The scope of these was later on extended to offering thanks for the creation of the six best and grand entities *viz.* Heaven, Water, Earth, Vegetable Creation, Animal-Creation and Man. The chief offerings at the Gahambār-s are milk, water, wine, *sherbet* along with fruits and food items especially the Dārun (sacred bread). The offerings are named *myazd.*[5]

The principle underlying such a ceremony in the Vedic as well as the Zoroastrian tradition is obviously that of 'Give and Take' between human beings and gods.

Humility

The *arthavāda*-s at times state the moral lessons to be practised in the day-to-day life. Such an *arthavāda* occurs in the context of the New-moon and Full-moon sacrifices. The gods and *asura*-s, both of them sprung from Prajāpati once strove together. The *asura*-s through arrogance, went on offering into their own mouths. They were utterly defeated due to their arrogance. So no one should be arrogant, for arrogance is the cause of ruin (*Śat. Br.* XI. 1.8.1 — *parābhavasya haitanmukham yad'atimānaḥ*). But the gods went on offering unto one another. Prajāpati gave himself up to them and the sacrifice became theirs (*ibid.* 2). The same *arthavāda* has already occurred in the *Śat. Br.* in the context of the Vājapeya sacrifice (*ibid.* V.1.1.1,2). This *arthavāda* can be traced to the *RV* in the hymn addressed to Indra (*RV* I.51), where Indra is said to vanquish the deceitful ones (*māyinaḥ)* with his powers (*māyābhiḥ).* These deceitful ones (*māyinaḥ)* used to offer oblations in their mouth only (*ibid.* I.51.5 ab....Sāyaṇa explains the words *adhi śuptau* as *śobhamāne svakīye mukhe).*[6] The questions may be posed here as — in whose mouth were the oblations offered? In their (i.e. of the deceitful ones') own mouth? Or was it some non-Aryan tribal practice of offering oblations in the mouth of the idols? Were they worshipping the idols unlike the Aryans? These points will require further probe, which we leave here, at present.

The *arthavāda* discussed above occurs in the *Kauṣ. Br.* in the context of the consecration rite in the Soma-sacrifice, the point being of the consecrated sacrificer not offering the Agnihotra (i.e. the daily milk offering at the Agnihotra, till he completes the sacrifice and is in the state of consecration). The *Kauṣ. Br.* states that the *asura*-s offered it (i.e. the offering) in themselves without fire which was blown out. They were defeated as they sacrificed in what had no fire. Then the gods established this inward breath, Agni. In this (Agni) the fast milk (called *vrata*) is offered in the evening and in the morning (i.e. the consecrated sacrificer himself drinks that milk, in the evening and the morning, as he himself is the sacrifice now). The Agnihotra thus is offered continuously and without a break in this breath, Agni (*Kauṣ. Br.* VII. 3).

This shows that the original pseudo-myth in the *RV* is made use of by the ritual texts to serve as *arthavāda* for their respective contexts. But as pointed out at the beginning, warning against being arrogant is clearly stated in the *arthavāda* of the *Śat. Br.*

In this same line, falls the *arthavāda* which occurs in the context of the Pravargya rite. It is said that Viṣṇu became the most excellent of the gods due to his austerity, fervour, faith, sacrifice and oblations. Then Viṣṇu (who was the very Sacrifice, the yonder sun) was unable to control that (pride of) glory of his. Even now not every person can control that (pride of) glory of his. Then Viṣṇu taking his bow, together with three arrows stood, resting his head on the end of the bow. The ants (*vamrī*-s) — that too of a special kind *viz. upadīkā* — knowing the intention of the gods to punish Viṣṇu, gnawed Viṣṇu's bowstring. When it was cut, the ends of the bow, springing asunder, cut off Viṣṇu's head. The gods gave the ants the enjoyment of food and they could find water even in the desert. The cut off head of Viṣṇu became the yonder sun (*Śat. Br.* XIV. 1.1.4-10). The Pravargya rite, in which milk is boiled in the Mahāvīra pot, stands for the head of Viṣṇu (= Sacrifice), which is as though replaced with the rite. The moral lesson which springs indirectly from the *arthavāda* is that Viṣṇu's head was cut off due to his being proud of his glory.

Imitation is bad

The context is of the New-moon and Full-moon sacrifices. The mythical account (*arthavāda)* occurs regarding the dispute between Mind and Speech as to who was the better of the two as both of them claimed to be excellent. When they approached Prajāpati for his decision, he decided in favour of Mind saying to Speech that Mind was indeed better than her, for she was an imitator of Mind of his deeds and was his (mere) follower. A piece of advice figures here when Pajāpati says that he who imitates his better's deeds and follows in his wake is an inferior person, hinting thereby the subordinate position of Speech in comparison with Mind (*Śat. Br.* I.4.5.8-12; cf. *Tait. Sam.* II. 5. 11.4,5).

No sacred work to be left incomplete

The common-day instruction that a person should not leave any sacred work in the middle (as worshipping gods or even taking food, for that has also a religious significance and it is regarded as a *yajñakarma)* has already been recorded in the account of Dṛti and Vātavat, which occurs as *arthavāda* in the *Pañc. Br.*, in the context of the Gavām-ayana *sattra* (*Pañc. Br.* XXV. 3.6). One of the days in this *sattra* is the Viṣuvat day, which is the middle-most day, with two wings of the series of sacrifices at each side. It imitates two rafters of a roof joined firmly at a central beam (*Tait. Br.* I.2.3.1,2). The *Pañc. Br.* says that Dṛti and Vātavat once upon a time undertook the Gavām-ayana *sattra* in the Khāṇḍava (Sāyaṇa-*khāṇḍave vane* i.e. in the Khāṇḍava forest). On the Viṣuvat day, Vātavat left off the sacrificial session in the middle, but Dṛti completed it (*Pañc. Br.* XXV. 3.6). Dṛti was the son of Indrota and was a knowledgeable person. When asked by Ābhipratārin, the son of Kakṣasena, as how do the persons who ascend to the top fare afterwards, he immediately replies that those who have the wings of knowledge fly forth, but those devoid of these being wingless (i.e. being without knowledge), fall down. This knowledge is obviously of the ritual, here that of the Trivṛt (three-versed) and the Pañcadaśa *stoma*-s. With the wings of the these two *stoma*-s, they proceed to the world of heaven (*ibid.* XIV. 1. 12, 13). The eulogy of knowledge has to be noted.

As Vātavat left the sacrificial session in the middle but Dṛti completed it, the *arthavāda* points out that this was (possibly) the reason why the descendants of Vātavat are fewer in number, while those of Dṛti are more (*ibid.* XXV. 3.6). Caland makes a note of the belief, that 'from this we must only infer that it is not considered as commendable to leave a *sattra* unfinished.'[7]

No curse to be uttered

That the Vedic people believed in sorcery and magic, is evident from *RV* and *AV*. But that this belief could serve well as *arthavāda* is seen in a passage from the *Śat. Br.* (I.6.1. 14-18). In the New-moon and Full-moon sacrifices, he utters the offering-prayer (Yājyā) over Agni's butter-portion and thus places Agni in front. With the sacrificial cake to Agni, Agni is placed in the middle (part). With the offering prayer to Agni Sviṣṭakṛt, he places Agni in the rear. At all these stages of the sacrifice, Agni serves as a killer and repeller of *rakṣas*-es (*ibid.* 14). If any one were to curse evil on the sacrificer, at the face i.e. beginning of the sacrifice, one should counter-curse him by saying that the person cursing would suffer from some disease of the face either becoming blind or deaf (*ibid.* 16). If the sacrificer is cursed in the middle of the sacrifice, the person uttering a curse, should be counter-cursed as to be one without offspring and cattle (*ibid.* 17). If the curse is uttered after the completion of the sacrifice, the counter-curse should be that the person cursing, becoming unstable and poor, should immediately depart from this world (i.e. should die). The *Śat. Br.* though states the counter-curses as a remedial reaction for the curses uttered first, strikes a note of warning that a person should not utter any curses (*ibid.* 18). This is obviously to put a stop to the chain of flinging curses and counter-curses at one another. The *arthavāda* here purely deals with the terrestrial level and is for praising the oblations offered to Agni at the three stages of sacrifice. Nevertheless it serves as a good piece of moral teaching.

Not to play false with a learned *brāhmaṇa*

The learned priests being the veritable source of sacrificial knowledge were held in high esteem. The *Ait. Br.* in the rite of the great anointing of kings (originally the rite of Aindra Mahābhiṣeka, when there was the great anointing of Indra), relates in the *arthavāda* how with the help of the priest Dīrghatamas Māmateya (the son of Mamatā) who anointed Bharata Dauḥṣanti, the latter could conquer the earth completely. So did Durmukha, the Pāñcāla conquer the entire earth, when he was anointed by the priest Bṛhaduktha. Here comes the mythical account regarding the priest Vāsiṣṭha Sātyahavya, who proclaimed this great royal Aindra anointing to Atyarāti Jānaṁtapi. Atyarāti though not a king, with the help of the priest could conquer the whole earth. When Vāsiṣṭha Sātyahavya (the priest) asked Atyarāti to make him great, as a recognition of his help to the latter, Atyarāti rather made a fun of him saying that when Atyarāti would conquer the Uttara-Kurus, Vāsiṣṭha Sātyahavya could be the king of the earth and Atyarāti would take a (subservient) position as a general under Vāsiṣṭha Sātyahavya. Vāsiṣṭha Sātyahavya could see through the whole game as Uttara-Kuru region was regarded as a place of gods (*devakṣetram)* and so beyond the reach of the mortals. He was angry, due to the falsehood played with him, and decided to take away the royal glory and power of Atyarāti. With the result, the king Amitratapana Śuṣmiṇa Śaibya slew Atyarāti. The *arthavāda* ends with a moral warning that a *kṣatriya* should not play false with a learned *brāhmaṇa* (*Ait. Br.* VIII.23=39.9). By playing false, the *kṣatriya* may lose his kingdom and also may leave off his breath, i.e. he will die (*ibid.).* Apart from the importance of a *brāhmaṇa* (priest), which is dealt with under the topic "*Varṇa*-System" (Chapter 10), the moral lesson in the *arthavāda* imparting the abhorrence of falsehood has to be taken note of.

Moral lessons in the Tānūnaptra rite

The rite of Tānūnaptra is a solemn formal agreement (covenant) made by the sacrificer and his priests in the name of Tanūnapāt (i.e. the mighty blowing wind), while touching the sacrificial butter, thereby pledging themselves not to injure each other.[8] A mythical account comes here as *arthavāda*. It is said that when the gods had performed the guest-offering (to King Soma), there emerged discord among them. They were divided into four different parties unwilling to yield to one another's excellence — Agni with the Vasus, Soma with the Rudras, Varuṇa with the Ādityas and Indra with the Maruts (*Śat. Br.* III. 4.2.1). Seeing them thus separated, the *asura-rakṣas*-es entered between them. Being aware of the danger from them, the gods decided to come to an agreement and yield to the excellence of one of them and that was Indra, whom they regarded as great. The *arthavāda* strikes a note here that never should the kinsmen fall out from each other, for any enemy may step in between them, if they quarrel (*ibid.* 2, 3).

In order to make that agreement (of staying together as one group) permanent, the gods cut off part by part, their favourite forms and desirable attributes, keeping the mighty Tanūnapāt — the yonder blowing Wind — as witness. Tanūnapāt is the witness of living beings, entering them in the form of in-breathing and out-breathing. The *Śat. Br.* echoes here the belief that the gods know the mind of man and explains that the thought in man's mind passes on to the breath; the breath passes it on to the wind and the wind tells the gods the thought of man (*ibid.* 5,6).

It is said here that the gods do not transgress their covenant, for they abide by truth. Due to this, their conquest and glory are unassailable. And so is unassailable the conquest and glory of him, whosoever speaks the truth (*ibid.* 8). The *Tait. Sam.* also deals with this rite (*Tait. Sam.* VI. 2.2.1 ff).

While the *Śat. Br.* lays stress on truth (as noted above), the *Ait. Br.* in this context, speaks of being united with an oath, so that the parties coming together may not be defeated. The *Ait. Br.* states that the gods decided to place their 'dearest bodies' in the house of Varuṇa. It was agreed among them that those who deceived any of them, shall forfeit their 'bodies'. It is said that the co-partner in the Tānūnaptra should not deceive or betray the other (*Ait. Br.* I. 24 = 4.7). This is obviously because they are bound by an oath. The *Śat. Br.* also points out this (*Śat. Br.* III. 4.2.9).

The *Śat. Br.* states that by taking portions of butter they lay down together their desirable forms and favourite powers (*ibid.*). It seems that though they make Tanūnapāt (Wind) as witness, in the actual ritual, they take butter in the (*dhruvā*) spoon (*ibid.* 10), in the name of Tanūnapāt. This rite of binding the sacrificer and the priests in unity with an oath, taking portions of butter, can be compared to a rite prescribed in the period of Ayudhya kingdom in Thailand, by a sacred work named *Ong Karn Chaeng Nam* (The Divine Prescription of Cursing Waters). The work was composed for chanting in the important ceremony, such as the king's coronation. After the invocation of the great gods *viz.* Viṣṇu, Brahmā and Śiva, for participation in the rite, the severe curses are made for any one, who may be dishonest or may rebel against the king. During the time, when these curses are uttered, all kinds of weapons are dipped into the water (in a big vessel - may be a big cauldron), indicating that those who betray the king, will be killed with those very weapons. At the end of the rite, all the officers have to drink the cursed water to ensure that they will not betray the king.[9]

As can be seen, the rite of Tānūnaptra speaks of the sanctity of oath, by following the path of truth.

Brahmayajña (Daily study of the Veda)

Daily performance of the five great sacrifices forms an indispensable part of the code of conduct, laid down for a householder. (*Śat. Br.* XI. 5.6.1). They are — the sacrifice to beings, the sacrifice to men, the sacrifice to the Fathers, the sacrifice to the gods and the sacrifice to the Brahman. These are already taken note of by us.[10] Here we take into account the *arthavāda*-s, which are stated to eulogise the sacrifice to Brahman. The sacrifice to the Brahman is one's own daily study of the Veda. The *arthavāda* here is a chain of ritual metaphors. The *juhū* (spoon) of this sacrifice is speech; its *upabhṛt* (spoon) the mind; its *dhruvā* (spoon) the eye; its *sruva* (spoon), mental power; its purificatory (final) bath (*avabhṛtha),* truth; and its concluding rite (*iṣṭi* called Udayana), heaven (*ibid.* XI. 5.6.3). The *ṛc*-s (which are uttered) are said to be the milk-offerings to the gods; the *yajus* (-formulas) are the ghee-offerings; the *sāman*-s are the Soma-offerings; the Atharvāṅgiras-*mantras* are the fat-offerings and the Anuśāsana-s (precepts), Vidyā-s (lores), Vākovākya (dialogue or some special theological discourse), Itihāsa-purāṇa (the traditional myths, legends and accounts) and the *nārāśaṁsī*-s and *gāthā*-s are the honey-offerings (*ibid.* 4-8).[11] For this sacrifice to the Brahman, there are four Vaṣaṭ-calls — *viz.* (the sound of) the blowing of wind; of lightning-fall; of thundering; and of rumbling (*ibid.* 9). It is quite clear that these sounds metaphorically are said to be the Vaṣaṭ-calls.[12] This shows that in spite of these terrible sounds, one is not to put a stop to his study of the Veda and the works (mentioned above).[13] In case one is unable to study, one should at least read a single divine word (*ibid.).*

A very appealing *arthavāda* occurs at the end of this discourse on the sacrifice to Brahman, in that the *Śat. Br.* says — 'Moving indeed are the waters; moving is the sun; moving the moon and moving the stars. A *brāhmaṇa* not studying his lesson on a particular day, would be one who did not move and act on that day, as would the deities be taken as not moving and not acting on that day' (*ibid.* XI. 5.7.10).

Not to speak false at the evening time

Though we shall be dealing with vow of truth in details, here is an *arthavāda* statement, which occurs in the *Tait. Br.* and which has to be noted, as it is based on a belief regarding the evening time. The *Tait. Br.* points out five divisions of day *viz. prātaḥ, saṅgava, madhyāhna, aparāhṇa* and *sāyāhna* (as Sāyaṇa explains at the beginning of the section, *Tait. Br.* I.5.3). The *Tait. Br.* states that the evening time belongs to Varuṇa. Hence a person should not speak false at this time (*ibid.* I.5.3.3). Varuṇa right from the *RV* stands far above any other deity, as a moral governor.[14] He witnesses the truth and falsehood of men (*RV* VII. 49. 3b). As Varuṇa is said to have produced the night (*Tait. Sam.* VI. 4.8.4) and the night belongs to Varuṇa (*ibid.* II. 1.7.4), the *Tait. Br.* associates the evening time to Varuṇa. Hence speaking false at the evening time is to be avoided by all means, says Sāyaṇa on this.

Truth (*Satya*)

The sacrificial activity though terrestrial is related to the cosmic sphere. To attain the divine level, the vow of 'truth' (in speech, action and thought) is laid down and forms part of the code of conduct for the sacrificer. But suiting to the mode of expression of the ritualists, several entities are identified with the concept of truth.

In the morning Soma-pressing, when they sit round the two Soma-pressing boards, the Adhvaryu priest ties a piece of gold to his (ring-) finger. Here gold is identified with 'truth'. The *arthavāda* states that the gods are truth and the men untruth. As gold is said to spring from the seed of Agni (the god), when he touches the Soma-stalks or takes hold of Soma with his hand, i.e. the ring-finger, with the piece of gold tied to it, it is as good as following truth on his part (*Śat. Br.* III. 9.4.1).[15]

In the rite of Tānūnaptra (covenant), the gods laid down their favourite forms and desirable powers, in order to come together on equal footing and with equal status and swore that whosoever transgressed that covenant, he should be scattered to the winds, and would be away from their fold. Were they to transgress the covenant, they would speak untruth. And the gods cannot do it as they follow the vow of truth (*ibid.* III. 4.2.8). The same thought about the gods occurs in the Pravargya rite. There are prescribed some taboos (prohibitory rules)[16]. Āsuri, the ritualist thinker, says here that there is one rule, which the gods meticulously follow and it is of truth. Hence a person (in the ritual context, the consecrated sacrificer) should speak nothing but truth (*ibid.* XIV. 1.1.33). The *Ait. Br.* states that the gods are established in truth and men, i.e. human beings, are prone to falsehood. The consecrated person should utter discerning speech (*vicakṣaṇavatīm vācam vadet).* Discerning is the eye and by it, he sees in a correct manner. Actually it is truth which is placed in human beings in the form of eye. Hence to him who narrates (any incident or about anything) they say, 'Have you seen?' If he replies, 'I have seen (it)', then him they believe. If a man himself sees, then he does not believe even many others (*Ait. Br.* I.6). Sāyaṇa here has an interesting explanation to give for the expression — '*vicakṣaṇavatīm vācam vadet.*' He says that the consecrated person has to use the term '*vicakṣaṇa*', when he utters any sentence, e.g. "Devadatta *vicakṣaṇa* bring the cow"; "Yajñadatta *vicakṣaṇa* tie the cow", etc. Dange points out that for knowing the exact implication of the word '*vicakṣaṇa*' in the expression *vicakṣaṇavatīm vācam*, we have to take into account the expression *satyam vai cakṣuḥ* (*Śat. Br.* I.3.1.27 and also as here in *Ait. Br.* I.6). By addressing Devadatta (or any other person, for that matter), the *dīkṣita* (consecrated sacrificer) transfers his own responsibility of seeing the truth on somebody else, for he himself cannot move out, nor can he talk to others during that period. So the person, who is addressed as *vicakṣaṇa* serves as the sacrificer's eye and takes up the responsibility of fetching correct (*satya)* things. The *Ait. Br.* itself has said *cakṣur vai vicakṣaṇam* (I.6).[17]

The expression *satyam vai cakṣuḥ* ('The eye is the truth') occurs in the context of Agniṣṭoma sacrifice, when the two libations, consecrated by the utterance of the Vaṣaṭ call, are offered with prayer. The entire *savana* is offered after them, for these libations are most distinctly Prajāpati's own. These are said to be the eyes and the eye is the truth. Prajāpati is the truth (*Śat. Br.* IV. 2.1.26).

In the context of the Agnyādheya rite, the *Śat. Br.* points out that serving the consecrated fires means speaking the truth. One who speaks the truth acts as if he sprinkled that fire (i.e. fires, they being three) with ghee and thus enkindles it. He increases his own vital energy and day by day he becomes better. One who speaks the untruth, acts as if he sprinkled that fire with water and thus makes that fire weak. His whole vital energy becomes less and day by day, he becomes more wicked. Hence let him speak only the truth (*ibid.* II. 2.2.19).

In the rite of Agnicayana, the consecrated sacrificer has to hang a gold plate (*rukma)* round his neck and wear it. The *arthavāda* points out that this gold plate is the truth and the truth is able to sustain the fire in the fire-pan (Ukhya Agni), which the sacrificer has to carry about during his initiation-period. That truth (i.e. the gold-plate) is the yonder sun. The *arthavāda* elucidates this idea further. The round shape of the plate, its having twenty-one knobs and those too on the outer side of the plate, equates the gold plate symbolically with the round sun (twelve months, five seasons, three worlds make twenty and the sun is the twenty-first) and his rays outside (*ibid.* VI. 7. 1.1, 2).

While laying down the first layer of the Great Fire-altar, he sings the Satya (Truth) *sāman.* This is making symbolically the truth as Agni's mouth. He himself becomes the truth and true becomes that wish of his, for which he performs this rite (*ibid.* VII. 4.1.5). The primeval waters which are said to be the first creation are said to be the truth and even the flowing of the waters is said to be the form of the truth (*satya),* i.e. the manifestation of the eternal truth (*ibid.* 6). Yāska explains the word *ṛta* as *udaka*—'waters' (*Nir.* II. 7) — *ṛtamiti udakanāma),* and the words *ṛta* and *satya* require a probe in their basic concepts, which will be taken up later.

In the context of the Agnihotra rite, the *Jaim. Br.* states that the consecrated sacrificer has to touch water and the *arthavāda* here points out that waters are truth and consecration is truth (*Jaim. Br.* I.4). The *Jaim. Br.* while pointing out the importance of *vāc* and *manas* through the *arthavāda,* says that *vāc* is the 'truth' (an important and essential factor!) of *ṛc*, while *manas* is the 'truth' of *sāman.* By the truth of *ṛc* (i.e. by speech), he should sing *sāman* and by the truth of *sāman* (i.e. by mind) he should sing *ṛc. Ṛc* and *sāman* rule the heavenly world. These two take the sacrificer to the heavenly world (*ibid.* I.326). Here the word *satya* (truth) meaning essence or essential and foremost factor, used in the *arthavāda,* indicates that the singing of a *ṛc* or *sāman* is not a mechanical ritual act, but speaks of a perfect harmony achieved on the bodily (*vācika)* and mental (*mānasika)* planes.

We have already referred to the view of Āsuri in the context of the Pravargya ceremony, that the only one rule the gods follow is of truth and the sacrificer also should follow it (*Śat. Br.* XIV. 1.1.33). The sacrificer is prohibited from drinking out of earthen vessel, for whatever untruth man speaks in this world, residing on this earth, that is mixed with the earth (*ibid.* XIV. 1.1. 30). But the earthen pot (Mahāvīra or Gharma pot), in which milk is boiled in the Pravargya ceremony, stands for the sun — excellence, light and truth —, the sacrificer should not come into contact with and even not look at a woman, a *śūdra,* a dog and a black bird, lest he should mix excellence and sin, light and darkness, truth and untruth, for woman, etc. stand for untruth (*ibid.* 31). The *arthavāda* is a mirror to the condition of women and *śūdra*-s in those times.

In the rite of Rājasūya (rejuvenation of king), at one stage, the Adhvaryu priest touches the king on the chest and mutters a *mantra* (*Vāj. Sam.* X. 27; *RV* I.25.10), which means — 'Here he has sat down, the upholder of the sacred law (*niṣasāda dhṛtavrataḥ*)'. The *arthavāda* is a pointer to the vow of truth not only in speech but also in action. It is said that as the king indeed is the upholder of the sacred law and so he should speak only what is right (*sādhu)* and do what is right (*sādhu).* The king as well as the *śrotriya* (a *brāhmaṇa* well-versed in sacred texts) have to follow this, as they are the upholders of the sacred law (*dhṛtavratau).* (*Śat. Br.* V. 4.4.5).

Apart from pointing out the importance of right speech and right action (i.e. following the vow of truth), the *arthavāda* passage here states clearly the norm of king held by the thinkers in the Vedic times. The same is enshrined in the Rājanīti-portions of the Dharmaśāstra texts (to quote some — *Manu Sm.* VII. 2 ff; *Yāj. Sm.* I. 309 ff).

The code of following the principle of 'truth' was much stricter in the sacrificial context, as can be seen from a couple of examples. In the Varuṇapraghāsa-*parvan* of the four Seasonal sacrifices the Pratiprasthātṛ asks the sacrificer's wife — 'With whom, had you union?' This is obviously necessary, for if she has committed such a sin of having union with a person other than her husband, she has to confess it. When confessed and told frankly, the sin becomes less, since it becomes truth (*Śat. Br.* II. 5.2.20). In the context of the New-moon and Full-moon sacrifices, it is stated that when the sacrificer enters the vow (for the sacrifice), he passes from men to gods, i.e. he enters the divine level. Therefore he has to speak only what is true, for this vow of truth is kept by the gods. So he says, 'I now enter from untruth to truth' (*Vāj. Sam.* I. 5 b). After the completion of the sacrifice, he makes himself free from the vow and hence says, 'I now am he, who I really am' (*Vāj. Sam.* II. 28 b). When he enters the vow, he becomes as it were non-human (*a-mānuṣa* i.e. god). It would not be proper for him to say,

'I enter from truth into untruth', at the completion of the vow. So he says, 'I now am he, who I really am' (*Śat. Br.* I. 1.1.4-6). The passage is important and so the ritual, for it clearly points out the vast difference between the human and the divine levels. The gods abide by truth, but the men are (prone to) untruth.

While dealing with the *arthavāda*-s about the concept of 'truth' denoted by the word '*satya*', it is necessary to know the distinction between the words *satya* and *ṛta*. The word '*ṛta*' signified Order on three levels *viz.* (mainly) cosmic, sacrificial and moral, and symbolises constant activity (fr. the root √*ṛ* - 'to go') in a fixed way. On the moral level (obviously concerning individuals as component parts of the society) *ṛta* stood for a definite code of conduct, which later on gave way to the concept of 'Dharma' and the king as the upholder of *dharma,* in the Dharmaśātra tradition and also in the works on polity. From the rule prescribed in the Brāhmaṇa-texts for practising the vow of truth (*sayta)* in speech and action, it is clearly seen that the word *ṛta* has now receded, its place being taken by the word *satya.* This has happened because the word *ṛta* has a wider sphere, as noted above, while practising the vow of truth (*satya),* covers a part of *ṛta,* working on the social or moral level. When the primeval waters, as seen in one of the *arthavāda*-s noted above, are said to be the form of truth (*Śat. Br.* VII. 4.1.6), they should be taken as following the *rta* or as being the form of *ṛta,* though the word used for them is *'satya'*. In the *RV,* we have the expression *satyānṛte* (*RV* VII. 49.3[b])—'truth and falsehood' — in one unit but never *ṛtānṛte. Anṛta* literally means negation of *ṛta* or against *ṛta.* But actually it is an act against the established code of conduct. Dange also has discussed this point and has come to the conclusion that 'Ṛta symbolised constant activity: Satya stood for stability, which is very essential for the building of a social order.'[18]

The *vidhi* and the *arthavāda*-s in the Brāhmaṇa-texts concerning the vow of truth (*satya)* clearly point out that the ritual thinkers were keen on prescribing the code of righteous conduct for the sacrificer. We can conclude this topic of truth by referring to the eulogy of *dharma* which occurs in the *Jaim. Br.* (III. 231), *dharma* being essential for the stability of the social order and is in no way different from the concepts of Ṛta and Satya. The *Jaim. Br.* enjoins the chanting of the Vidharman *sāman* on the ninth day of the ten-day rite, i.e. on the third Chandoma day. This is also mentioned in the *Pañc. Br.* (XV. 5. 31), which says that this *sāman* is prescribed to be chanted for supporting the *dharma.*[19] The *Jaim. Br.* has here a pun on the word *vidharman* meaning (i) the name of the *sāman* and (ii) 'devoid of *dharman'*, i.e. 'devoid of righteous conduct.' It says that with their righteous conduct *(dharmaṇā)* the gods, having got the possession of the *dharman* of the *asura*-s, with the Vidharman *sāman,* made the *asura*-s *vidharman*-s *(vi-dharman*-s i.e. devoid of righteous conduct and thus of indecorus behaviour). Dharma is glory; Dharma is kingdom; Dharma is king himself due to his following *dharman. Dharman* belongs to one's own kinsmen; to *dharman* one's own kinsmen belong. And this *dharman* is to be brought into effect, with the *sāman* named Vidharman, which is to be (chanted) on the ninth day (*Jaim. Br.* III. 231).

Divine Plane in Sacrifice

The code of conduct for a sacrificer requires that the sacrifice performed by him should be perfect in all respects. In the context of optional and occasional offerings, the *Tait. Sam.* states that to the sky the deficiency of the sacrifice goes and to the earth the redundancy. If he were not to appease it, the sacrificer would be ruined. Hence he appeals to the two great ones—the Sky and the Earth (Dyāvāpṛthivī), and by that he appeases both the deficiency and the redundancy of the sacrifice (*Tait. Sam.* III. 4.1.2, 3).

Once the sacrificer is consecrated for the sacrifice, he is believed to be one among the gods. The fast-milk *(vrata)* is cooked (i.e. heated) for him, which he partakes in the Agniṣṭoma (Soma-sacrifice) and does not offer it in fire. The sacrificial food of the gods is cooked and not uncooked (*Śat. Br.* III. 2.2.10). Again, the gods do not sleep, while for the consecrated sacrificer, sleeplessness is not vouchsafed. So he sleeps but commits himself to Agni, who is the Lord of vows and is wide awake, to awaken the sacrificer (*ibid.* 22), from his sleep. Even these two instructions suffice to show that the sacrificer consecrated for the sacrifice draws near to the gods and becomes one of them (*ibid.* 10, 22).

The *Pañc. Br.* in the context of the Mahāvrata day states that the Udgātṛ priest, having mounted a throne-seat (*āsandī)* chants a specific part, for being chanted by him of the Mahāvrata laud (i.e. *stotra).* This is under the eyes of the gods, obviously because being seated higher (i.e. on the throne-seat), he is nearer to the gods and thus gains a seat above others *(Pañc. Br.* V. 5.1). This throne-seat is made of the wood of the Udumbara tree, which stands for strength or vigour (and food). He thereby retains vigour (*ūrjam)* for himself *(ibid.* 2). The height of the feet of this throne-seat is of a span (*prādeśamātrī bhavati),* so that the Udgātṛ priest (and represented by him the sacrificer) may not leave this world (*ibid.* 3). It has to be noted that this simple detail of using a slightly higher wooden seat in the sacrifice, is also logically explained by the ritualistic tradition, reflecting the belief of those times, regarding a clear division of divine and mortal levels.[20]

Way to Immortality

Here we come to the ritual philosophy, propounded by the Brāhmaṇa-texts. The *Jaim. Br.* states that the sacrificer is born twice—from the pairing (i.e. union of his father and mother), he is born first. This birth is for this world. When he is born from the sacrifice (for the second time), he is born for the other world—for the world of the *gandharva*-s, for that of the gods and for the heavenly world (*Jaim. Br.* I. 259). The *Jaim Br.* has earlier pointed out that there are verily two birthplaces of man. The mortal birthplace is this (terrestrial) world of men (i.e. human beings) - (where there is) procreation from woman, from which are born children. Hence he should desire for a righteous wife, with a thought that his self may be born (from her) in righteousness. His divine birthplace is the world of gods, which is the Āhavanīya fire. Whatever oblation he offers, whatever good (deed) he performs, he sprinkles his self in this divine birthplace. That self of his is born in the sun. One who knows this has two selves, two birthplaces; one who does not know this, has one self and one birthplace (*ibid.* I. 17). This thought, couched as *arthavāda,* figures in the context of the Agnihotra rite.

The same thought is marked in the context of the additional information about the New-moon and Full-moon sacrifices. The *Śat. Br.*, in the *arthavāda* states that if anybody asks as to who is the better one, the self-offerer (*ātmayājin)* or the god-offerer (*devayājin),* one should say that the self-offerer is the better one, for he (i.e. the self-offerer) knows that his new body is formed by that (body of sacrifice). As a snake frees itself from its skin, so he frees himself from his mortal body and made up of the *ṛc, yajus, sāman* and of offerings, he goes to the heavenly world (*Śat. Br.* XI. 2.6.13). In the same context we read that whatever offering the sacrificer gives in the sacrifice, that becomes his body in the yonder world. When he departs from this world, that offering being behind him, calls out to him, 'Come here, here am I, your body'. The offering is called *āhuti* for it calls out (*āhvayati,* the word thus given the etymology from the root √*ā* + *hve* - 'to invoke, call out' (*ibid.*, XI. 2.2.6).

The concept of immortality (!) for a mortal is made clear in the *arthavāda* which is stated while enjoining the eighteen-day rite of the gods (*Pañc. Br.* XXIII. 12.1-4). These eighteen days are - an overnight-rite (*Atirātra);* a six-day Abhiplava period (Abhiplava-ṣaḍaha); the ten days of the twelve-day rite (Dvādaśāha) and an overnight-rite (Atirātra) (*ibid.* 1). The mythical account stated here is that when the gods, being afraid of death resorted to Prajāpati, he gave them immortality through this eighteen-day rite. The *arthavāda* further points out the concept of man's immortality. Man's immortality consists in his reaching the normal term of life and his becoming wealthier (*ibid.* 2, 3; cf. *Śat Br.* IX. 5.1.10). The same *arthavāda* is stated earlier by the *Pañc. Br.* in the context of the nine-day rite — six-day rite with the Pṛṣṭha-*sāman*-s, the Jyotis (-day), the Go (-day) and the Āyus (-day) as overnight-rite (*Pañc. Br.* XXII. 12.1-3).

The stark reality of life that 'whosoever is born has to die' is couched in several *arthavāda*-s, through which the ritual thinkers have also pointed out a way of being above death and of becoming immortal. The plain idea of immortality, accepted by the ritualists, which we have noted in the *arthavāda*-s stated above, is of reaching the normal term of life. But there are deeper thoughts enshrined in the *arthavāda*-s in this respect.

In the context of the New-moon and Full-moon sacrifices, the *arthavāda* dealing with the call Vaṣaṭ, states that the Vaṣaṭ call is the yonder shining sun and the sun is the same as Death.[21] When the Adhvaryu priest offers after the Vaṣaṭ has been uttered, he thereby consecrates the sacrificer after Death and causes him to be born from out of it and the sacrificer is delivered from that Death. The sacrifice becomes his body and all his chief offerings accompanied with the Vaṣaṭ call are delivered from that Death (*Śat. Br.* XI. 2.2.5). This concept with slight difference already occurs in the context of building the Great Fire-altar. It is said that the Great Fire-altar is Speech, for it is with Speech (*ṛc, yajus* and *sāman* as the divine Speech and also with the human speech namely Adhvaryu priest's commands as 'You do not do this! You do that!') that the fire-altar is built (*ibid.* X. 5.1.1) Now this Speech is the yonder Sun and Agni— the fire-altar—is Death. Whatsoever is on this side of the sun, all that is held by Death and so is the fire-altar and the sacrificer's own self held by Death. But the fire-altar built by the sacrificer's knowledge there above conquers the recurring Death (*ibid.* X. 5.1.4).

The conviction in the *arthavāda*-s, which are stated above, is a precursor of the concept of *adṛṣṭa* or *apūrva,* which is from the Pūrvamīmāṁsā system of philosophy. Though the material sacrifice comes to an end and after some time (days, months or years) no trace of it whatsoever is seen, some 'unseen' (*adṛṣṭa*) or some 'not existent before' *(āpūrva)* effect is stored on the name of the sacrificer. This same *adṛṣṭa* or *apūrva* releases the sacrificer from death. That some powers are born out of the performance of sacrifice is indicated in the *RV* itself, where it is said that when the gods performed sacrifice with the sacrifice, the powers (created?) reached the heavenly world, where are the ancient Sādhyas, (and) the gods (*RV*. X. 90.16).

In the Agnicayana rite, the Great Litany (*mahad-uktham*) is said to be the shining orb. The man in the sun's orb is none else than Death. The shining light therein is the immortal element. Death being within the immortal, never dies (*Śat.* Br. X.5.2.3... *mṛtyurna mriyate).* As to the query whether Death is one or many, the reply is — as Death is that man in the sun, he is one and as Death is here numerously distributed among human beings, there are many Deaths. Again as to the query whether Death is near or far away, the reply is — as Death is here on earth in the body, he is near and as Death is that one in yonder world, he is far away (*ibid.* 16-17). In the context of the Agnicayana rite, the thought occurs that in the beginning this whole universe was covered by Death, i.e. Hunger (*ibid.* X. 6.5.1). Here we have the echo of the Ṛgvedic thought that by creating Hunger in this world, the gods created Death (*RV* XI. 117.1a)

In the same context (i.e. Agnicayana rite), it is said that the sacrificer (or the priest in his behalf) puts down the *bhūta*-bricks (the bricks of 'being' fr. √*bhū* - 'to be'). In every place, Death is born but he removes it by sacrifice. Therefore one who builds the Fire-altar, lives all his life, for all Deaths are removed by him (*Tait. Sam.* V. 6.3.1).

In the same context, the *Śat. Br.* says that the Year is the same as Death (*mṛtyuḥ),* for it is he who, by means of day and night, destroys the life of the mortal beings and then they die. The Year is really the one who puts an end to the life of the mortals (*antakaḥ),* reaching by day and night, the end of their life (*Śat. Br.* X. 4.3.1,2). The *Jaim. Br.* states clearly that Death stands enveloping every one, full of breath. That indeed is Death-that Year-and seasons are his mouths (*Jaim. Br.* I.246).

A mythical account in the context of the Agnicayana rite displays a lofty philosophical thought, which in later times is met in the Upaniṣads. It is said that the gods were afraid of Prajāpati - the Year, Death and the Antaka — that he would by day and night make the end of their life. They performed several sacrificial rites *viz.* Agnihotra, the New-moon and the Full-moon sacrifices, the four Seasonal offerings (*iṣṭi*-s*),* the animal-sacrifice and the Soma-sacrifice. They also built a Fire-altar, but not in a proper manner. Hence all these could not make them immortal. Prajāpati told them that as they were not establishing the Fire-altar in a perfect manner in a full form, (making it too large or defective in form) they were not becoming immortal. Prajāpati then instructed them on the proper way of building the Great Fire-altar, which when constructed made them immortal. And then there came Death complaining to the gods that if all men follow in their footsteps (by building the Great Fire-altar), all of them would become immortal, and he himself would not have any share of them. The gods pacified him by saying that thereafter no one would be immortal with the body. Only when Death had taken that body as his share, the man after separating from the body, would become immortal through his knowledge or through his holy work. The *arthavāda* passage is quick enough to add that here knowledge is of the Great Fire-altar and the holy work is its construction (*Śat. Br.* X. 4.3.3-9). The *arthavāda* passage undoubtedly is stated to extol the construction of the Great-Fire-altar. But the thought revealed in this comes close to the one in the *Bṛhad. Up,* where Yājñavalkya and Ārtabhāga are having a dialogue on the man's existence after death and the problem of action (*karman).* The dialogue ultimately comes to the maxim from the mouth of the great thinker — Yājñavalkya - that (after death) a man remains known to be righteous due to his good deed and sinful due to his sinful deed (*Bṛhad.* Up. III. 2.13).

On the same lines, the *Jaim. Br.* states an *arthavāda,* which has to be noted for its lucid style. It runs as follows. When the *agnihotrin* dies and goes to the other world, the Father and the Forefathers come to him and say that he has not brought anything from this world. To them he should say that whatever merit he has accumulated belongs to them. The *Jaim. Br.* adds here that his sons take his property, his good deeds the Fathers (i.e. the near and the distant ancestors) and his evil deeds the enemies. Having divided all his belongings in this threefold manner, he goes to have a stay with him, who shines yonder (*Jaim. Br.* I. 50).

The doctrine of *karman* can be traced to the *RV.*[22] The *Pañc. Br.* has stated a mythical account as *arthavāda,* which is no less than a lesson to teach this same doctrine, though indirectly. The mythical account occurs, while laying down the Aurṇāyava-*sāman,* forming part of the Ārbhava Pavamāna laud of the fourth day (in the Pṛṣṭhya six-day period of the twelve-day rite). It runs as follows—The Aṅgiras-es having performed a sacrificial session, as its reward reached the heavenly world. But they did not know the exact path leading to the gods. Kalyāṇa alone of the Aṅgiras-clan (away from his fellow-sacrificers) went out to search for it (i.e. the path). He met (on his way) the *gandharva* Urṇāyu, who was enjoying the company of the *apsaras*-es. Urṇāyu knowing the difficulty of the Aṅgiras-es imparted to him the knowledge of a *sāman* (chant), by which the latter (Kalyāṇa and Aṅgiras-es) could know the path to the gods. But Urṇāyu gave Kalyāṇa a soft warning that the latter should not say and tell that he (i.e. Kalyāṇa) 'saw' that chant (Sāyaṇa explains — 'But he should say that the *gandharva* Urṇāyu had told him about the *sāman*'). Kalyāṇa came back to the Aṅgiras-es and told them that by applying in lauding the new *sāman* (chant) 'seen' by himself, they could get to the world of heaven (and also to the gods). The Aṅgiras-es did what was told to them and got to the world of heaven. And there was Kalyāṇa left behind, a leper on the earth, for he had told a lie (*Pañc. Br.* XII. 11. 10-12), by taking the credit of 'seeing' the new *sāman.*

The mythical account noted above no doubt indicates the doctrine of *karman.* But it also points out how certain *sāman*-s (chants) originated in non-Vedic or non-ritualistic circles, but later on came to be incorporated in the Vedic rituals forming an indispensable part of it.[23] In this account, the Aurṇāyava-*sāman* is said to be known to the *gandharva* Urṇāyu, who imparts it to Kalyāṇa, thus showing the non-ritualistic origin of the *sāman.*

That the sacrificer has to pay for his mistakes in this life only, is brought out in one *arthavāda.* This occurs in the context of the Upasad-s in the Soma-sacrifice.[24] It is said that with the verses in the Upasad-s, the gods kept slaying and destroying the citadels of the *asura*-s.[25] It is said that the verses in the Upasad-s should be of the same metre, not of different metres. The *arthavāda* states that if he makes them of different metres, he would cause swelling on (his) neck and he would produce boils on his body. (Thus his body would imitate the unevenness of the metres.) This *arthavāda* occurs in the *Ait. Br.* (I.25 = 4.8). It points out how the sacrificer committing a mistake will have to face the consequences and will have his whole body ugly. The passage imparts ethical teaching, based on the idea— 'As you sow, so you reap', the doctrine of *karman* thus not lost sight of. The same thought occurs in the *Tait. Sam.* in the context of the Agnicayana rite. It is said that fire is a bird (this is because the Great Fire-altar to be constructed has to be of the shape of a bird, in a flying position). If the sacrificer building the fire-altar were to eat a bird, he would he eating the fire and he would be then ruined (*Tait. Sam.* V.

7.6.1). However the ritual thinker of the *Tait. Sam.* points out a rule (or a worldly observation?) that a vow does not go beyond a year. Hence he should observe the restriction of not eating a bird only for a year *(ibid.).*

In the context of the New-moon and Full-moon sacrifices, a mythical account occurs in order to point out that the sacrificer must not violate the proper course of sacrificial performances. It is of Bhāllaveya, who made the Anuvākyā (invitatory formula) consist of an Anuṣṭubh verse and the Yājyā (offering formula) of a verse in Triṣṭubh metre. Later on (or immediately afterwards) he fell from the cart and broke his arm. When he pondered over the incident, he realised that the calamity had befallen him for the violation of the proper course of sacrifice. He wanted to obtain the benefit of both the metres (Anuṣṭubh and Triṣṭubh) and so he recited the Anuvākyā and Yājyā verses likewise, which was not proper. The *Śat. Br.* enjoins that both the formulas (*mantra*-s) have to be in the same metre, either Anuṣṭubh or Triṣṭubh (*Śat. Br.* I.7.3.19). The thought at the basis of this mythical account is that a person has to repay his *karman* (here a bad *karman,* the repaying being in this life only).

In this regard, a long mythical narrative occurring in the *Śat. Br.* in the context of the Agnihotra-rite is worthy of taking note. Bhṛgu, the son of Varuṇa was very proud of his knowledge. In order to bring him on the right path, Varuṇa asked him to go to different directions *viz.* east, south, west, north and the north-eastern directions.[26] In the eastern direction, he observed men dismembering men, chopping off their limbs and allotting those limbs as shares to themselves. On his query, the men replied that those men behaved with them in the yonder world in the same manner and hence they were dealing with them in return. About the atonement, Varuṇa (Bhṛgu's father) alone knew of it. In the southern direction, he saw again men cutting up the limbs of other men. In the western direction, the men sitting still were being eaten by men sitting still. In the northern direction, men crying aloud were being eaten by men crying aloud. In all these directions, Bhṛgu received the same reply from the men, who were engaged in those ghastly deeds, and also came to know that his father alone knew the way of atonement. In the north-eastern direction, he saw two women — one beautiful (*kalyāṇī*) and another *atikalyāṇī*,[27] and between them a man, black with yellow eyes and a staff in his hand (*Śat. Br.* XI. 6.1. 1-7). When being perplexed Bhṛgu went home, his father Varuṇa explained to him the implication of all the frightening scenes, he had witnessed in the whole day. Varuṇa's explanation is to enable him to know the Agnihotra rite. Varuṇa says that the men in the eastern direction were the trees. When one puts firewood from trees on fire, he subdues the trees and conquers the world of trees. The men in the southern region were the cattle. When one makes offering with milk, he subdues the cattle and conquers the world of cattle. The men in western region were the herbs. When one illumines the Agnihotra milk with a straw, one subdues the herbs and conquers the world of herbs. The men in the northern region were the waters. When one pours water to the Agnihotra milk, he subdues the waters and conquers the world of waters (*ibid.* 8-11). And about the two women and the black man — who were in the north-eastern direction. The beautiful one was Belief or Faith (*śraddhā*) and the 'not beautiful' was Unbelief or Non-faith. With the first libation of the Agnihotra, he subdues Belief and conquers it; with the second libation. Unbelief or Non-faith and conquers it (*ibid.* 12). The fierce man was Wrath, whom he subdues and conquers, when he pours the libation of water into the fire. The *Śat. Br.* concludes that whosoever knowing this offers the Agnihotra, he conquers everything and subdues everything (*ibid.* 13). It is interesting to note that practically the same mythical account occurs in the *Jaim. Br.* (I. 42-44) in the context of Agnihotra rite.

The account noted above has at its basis the doctrine of *karman,* which can explain to a certain extent, punishments meted out to the wrong-doers and sinners in the other world.[28] Such accounts have paved the way for the concept of hells of later times, especially in the Purāṇas, which imparted ethical teachings to the common masses through this concept.[29] Again the mythical account is a good piece of allegory. Though depicting grotesque scenes, it enlightens persons on the practice of Agnihotra. It also brings out how a father brings a proud son on the right path, by making the latter realise his ignorance, and also pointing out that proper knowledge of any rite or ritual — here Agnihotra — is far superior to that of (mere learning by heart) mere scriptures. This is naturally in tune with the instruction of the Agnihotra ritual, from which springs this mythical account.

Though the concept of immortality for human beings was restricted only 'to a large span of life', as we have already noted, the idea of conquering death somehow lingered in the minds of some of the ritualists. And the norm for conquering death was 'serpent', which was already regarded as an autochthon in the belief of the folks and also as a giver of offspring.[30] The domination of serpent as the supreme deity in the ancient world is amply proved by several writers on this subject.[31] The very observation of the serpent, casting off its old skin (i.e. slough), as though to become new and conquer death, has become a basis of an *arthavāda* in the *Pañc. Br.*, which indicates how the serpent has become a norm for getting immortality by conquering death.

The *Pañc. Br.* speaks of a sacrificial session of the Sarpa-s, by performing which the Sarpa-s vanquished death. The *arthavāda* states that the serpents, having left aside their slough (*hitvā jīrṇām tvacam)* move on or creep further, for they have conquered death. Those who perform it, get firm support in the worlds and can vanquish death. The *Pañc. Br.* states an elaborate list of various Sarpa-s (may be kings and princes of the Sarpa-tribe) holding the various offices of priests in this sacrifice (*Pañc. Br.* XXX. 15 1-4).[32] As can be seen, the complete list is given here of the Sarpa-priests and their respective offices on the lines of the Vedic priests, with their offices.

Apart from pointing out the urge of the Vedic ritualists to vanquish death to gain immortality, the *arthavāda* based on the actual observation of the serpents, is important on another account. It is very patent that the Sarpa-s mentioned here were of the Sarpa tribe in ancient India, which regarded the serpent as a totem of their tribe. The very fact that the Vedic ritualists were required to mention the 'Sarpa *sattra*', shows that the process of cultural assimilation regarding the Sarpa-s was nearly complete, so much so that the names of the Sarpa-s as different priests with their assistant priests are stated in the setting of the Vedic sacrifice. Again there is a mention of the Sarpa *sāman*-s employed in the middle day in this rite (i.e. Sarpa *sattra* — the sacrificial session carried out by the Sarpa-s). The *Pañc. Br.* speaks of the two Atirātra (overnight) sacrifices — one at the beginning and the other at the end—and Agniṣṭoma-rites in the middle. The year consists throughout of tens and tens; only (the middle day) the Viṣuvat day is twelve-versed and on this Viṣuvat day, the *sāman*-s of the Sarpa-s are employed.[33] This also shows how the Sarpa *sāman*-s might have got an entry into the Vedic fold, though through the Sarpa *sattra*. The Sarpa tribe contributed a lot to the Vedic-brahmanical tradition and their loan to the Vedic ritual is manifold.[34] And their totem *viz.* 'serpent', provided the idea of vanquishing the death and their *sattra* (sacrificial session), the way to obtain it.

NOTES AND REFERENCES

1. See Eggeling, J., *The Śatapatha Brāhmana,* pt. II, SBE Vol. 26, pp. 97, 98, where he translates the word *tapas* as 'fervour' in *Śat. Br.* III. 4.3.2,3; p. 100, as 'heat' in *ibid.* III. 4.3.10 and p. 111 'devotion' in *ibid.* III. 4.4.27, also 'austere devotion' *ibid.*
2. The Upasad-s, consisting of three offerings of ghee to Agni, Soma and Viṣṇu, followed by a *homa,* have to be performed twice daily, for at least three days (which is a normal number

at the Agniṣṭoma sacrifice). For more details, Eggeling, J., *op. cit.*, pt. II, SBE vol. 26, p. 105, note 1.

3. Stephanie W. Jamison mentions these myths relating to Manu's wife and comes to the conclusion that she was meant to be sacrificed. See Stephanie W. Jamison, *Sacrificed Wife/ Sacrificer's Wife*, Oxford Uni. Press, New York, 1996, p. 168.

   Dange, Sadashiv A., in his *Myths from the Mahābhārata*, Vol. 2, *Study in Patterns and Symbols*, Aryan Books International, New Delhi, 2001, p. 122 ff., has dealt with the view of Jamison and the myth in detail. Dange states that in all these myths, the central point is the 'magical voice', the wife being incidental. See *ibid.* p. 123.
4. For more details regarding Āgrayaṇa-*iṣṭi*, see Eggeling, J., *op. cit.*, pt. I, SBE Vol. 12, p. 369 f. For the information regarding the same in the Gṛhyasūtra-s, see Kane, P.V., *Hist. of Dh. S.*, Vol. II, pt. II, pp. 827-29.
5. (Mrs.) Guard, Nawaz R., *Ritual Drink in the Iranian and Indian Traditions (from Avestan and Sanskrit Sources)*, Thesis, University of Bombay (=Mumbai), 1991, pp. 253-57; also see Modi, J.J., *The Religious Ceremonies and Customs of the Parsees*, Bombay, 1937 (1922), pp. 422 ff.
6. Sāyaṇa on *RV* (I.51.5 ab) explains the word *śupti* as *mukha*— 'mouth'. Monier Williams gives the probable meaning as 'shoulder' and states for comparison the word *'supti'* from Zend. The word *śupti* occurs only once in the *RV*. Hence Sāyaṇa has explained it on the basis of the references from the *Śat. Br.* (V. 1.1.1; XI.1.8.1) and the *Kauṣ. Br.* (VII. 3).
7. See Caland, W., *Pañcaviṃśa Brāhmaṇa*, p. 629, note 5 on *Pañc. Br.* XXV. 3.6.
8. See Eggeling, J., *op. cit.*, pt. II, SBE Vol. 26, p. 93, note 1.
9. Tinnaratana, Pratuang, *A Critical Study of the Tenth Maṇḍala of Ṛgveda* (101-191 Hymns), Ph.D. Thesis, Benaras Hindu University, Varanasi, 1988, pp. 439-40.
10. See the chapter on "Family-life"
11. Also *Śat. Br.* XI. 5.7.5-9 for somewhat similar metaphors.

    For more information on Anuśāsana-s, Vidyā-s, etc. see (Mrs.) Dange, S.S., *Aspects of Speech in Vedic Ritual*, pp. 206-9.
12. The Vaṣaṭ sound is uttered at the end of the offering-prayer or *mantra* (Yājyā) and then the oblation is offered into the fire, the Vaṣaṭ sound thus serving as a vessel (or plate!) in

which the offering is placed and then offered into the fire. For more information, see (Mrs.) Dange, S.S., *Aspects of Speech in Vedic Ritual,* pp. 146-63.

13. It is interesting to note that the Sutra-s prescribe that the study of Veda and other texts should not be undertaken at the occurrence of certain natural phenomena such as the whirling wind, thunder, rain, lightning, etc., the sounds of which the *Śat. Br.* calls 'the 'Vaṣaṭ-calls' and prescribes the Brahmayajña (study-session) even on these occasions. For more information regarding the causes and circumstances for the suspension of study, see Ram Gopal, *India of Vedic Kalpasūtras,* p. 345.
14. For detailed information regarding Varuṇa's ordinances, his omniscience, his wrath roused by the infringement of his ordinances, see Macdonell, A.A., *Vedic Mythology,* p. 26 f.
15. *Śat. Br.* III. 1.3.18 — The Adhvaryu purifies the sacrificer with a strainer of sacred grass. The *arthavāda* is — Man indeed is impure, for he speaks untruth (*anṛtam*). But the sacred grass is pure. 'Having become pure, I shall be consecrated' thinks the sacrificer.
16. *Śat. Br.* XIV. 1.1.33 — The prohibitory rules stated here point out that the sacrificer should not sever his connection with the sun nor injure (or insult) the sun with his actions.
17. See Dange, Sadashiv A., *Vedic Sacrifices — Early Nature,* Vol. I, Intrn., p. xlii
18. *Ibid.,* p. xl.
19. As Caland points out, the Vidharman *sāman* is from the Grāmageyagāna XI. 2.21, composed on *SV* I. 430, chanted on *SV* II. 682-84. See Caland, W., *op. cit.,* p. 407, note 1 on *Pañc. Br.* XV. 5.31.
20. The modern practice in India, of sitting on a plank and then worshipping the idols of gods (kept on a plank), which is followed by a householder and his priest, can well be compared with this. Even while taking food, one sits on a plank (and food-plate is to be kept on another plank). The plank is thick and has four small feet. This also can be explained with a reasoning that taking food is an act of sacrifice (and not simply filling the stomach!) . The latter practice is however fast being replaced by dining on a table (especially in cities).

21. Cf. *Jaim. Br.* I. 27 — The sun is verily Death, the one who injures.
22. *RV.* X. 14.8 — where the (recently) dead person is asked to unite in the heaven with the Fathers and with Yama, with the merit (accumulated) of his sacrifices and that of his good works. Leaving his blemish behind, the dead person is asked to come back to his home again (*ibid.* 8c — *hitvāyāvadyam punarastamehi*), and unite with his body with full vigour. Here Macdonell takes the word '*ehi*' as 'go back', while it is actually, according to the Padapāṭha ā *ihi,* i.e 'come back'. See Macdonell, A.A., *A Vedic Reader for Students,* Oxford Uni. Press, 14th Impression of the Reprint in India 1951, Madras, 1988 (England 1917), p. 170 (his tr. of *RV* X. 14.8c).
23. The origin of the *gāthā*-s can be compared to this phenomenon. For this, see (Mrs.) Dange, S.S., *Aspects of Speech in Vedic Ritual,* p. 212.
24. For Upasad-s, see note 2 *supra.* The first day's performance is called the '*ayaḥśayā*' — lying in iron, i.e. 'made of iron', the second day's the '*rajaḥśayā*' — 'silvern' and the third day's '*hariśayā*' — 'golden'. See Eggeling, J., *op. cit.,* pt. II, p. 105, note 2.
25. *Ait. Br.* I. 23 = 4.6. The *asura*-s made the earth an iron citadel, the atmosphere that of silver and the sky that of gold. *Śat. Br.* III. 4.4.3,4 — The *asura*-s built castles in these worlds — an iron one in this world, a silver one in the air and a golden one in the sky. The gods, having prevailed over the *asura*-s, besieged these castles by the sieges - Upasad-s (*upa-sad*). So the name Upasad and their three different names.
26. Eggeling. J., *op. cit.,* pt. V, p. 109, tr. of *Śat. Br.* XI. 6.1.3 — 'northern of those two intermediate quarters in front.' Also see *ibid.,* note 1, where Weber's interpretation is given, to which Eggeling does not agree and Eggeling says 'north-easterly direction.'
27. *Ibid.,* p. 110, for *Śat. Br.* XI. 6.1.7. Eggeling translates the word *atikalyāṇī* as 'over-beautiful', but in his note (p. 110, note 1) says - 'one of past beauty', one whose beauty has faded. Sāyaṇa says — '*aśobhanā*' - 'not beautiful', i.e. ugly.
28. Eggeling, J., *op. cit.,* pt. V. p. 108, note 3, where Weber's opinion is stated.
29. (Mrs.) Dange, S.S., *Bhāgavata Purāṇa - Mytho-Social Study,* pp. 125-34.

30. The Nāga-kals (stones with figures of serpents engraved on them) are erected and kept under a pippal tree in India for getting offspring. See Zimmer, H., *Myths and Symbols in Indian Art and Civilization,* ed. by Campbell, J., May 1946, p. 72.
31. Oldam C.F., *The Sun and the Serpent,* London, 1905; Vogel, J. Ph., *The Indian Serpent-lore,* London, 1926; Mahalingam, T.V., "The Nāgas in Indian History and Culture", *Journal of Indian History,* Vol. XLIII, Part I, Apr. 1965, Serial No. 127, pub. by the University of Kerala, Trivandrum, pp. 1-69.
32. Also see Caland, W., *op. cit.,* p. 641f, note 1 on *Pañc. Br.* XXV. 15.3.
33. *Ibid.,* XXV. 15.1. Caland points out in his note (p. 641, n. 3) on this passage that ten Sarpa *sāman*-s are registered in the Araṇyageyagāna of the Sāmaveda and out of these ten, the first three are intended here.
34. The chap. on "Animals and Birds", for information about "Serpent".

Chapter 13

Arthavāda-s on Varied Topics (Miscellanea)

We have noted in the earlier chapters the beliefs and practices regarding several entities, as seen through the *arthavāda*-s, which are stated in the context of various rites and rituals. There are several small but important topics, the *arthavāda* (or *arthavāda*-s) regarding which, though significant, are not many (from our point of view!) to form separate chapters. These topics, so to say, are miscellaneous in nature. So they form a chapter here, in which the topics are arranged alphabetically and the *arthavāda*-s concerning them are dealt with, as they occur in rites and rituals.

Each and every *arthavāda* concerning a particular entity or topic is not thought of to be necessary for consideration and only that *arthavāda* is taken into account here, which speaks of a belief or a practice directly or even indirectly, at times simply indicating it.

Abhri (translated as 'Spade' generally)

Abhri is a hoe made of the wood of bamboo or Khadira or Udumbara, etc. or of any sacrificial tree bearing fruit. It is used to dig the ground, especially for digging a hole for Audumbarī, for digging earth to prepare Mahāvīra pot in the Pravargya ceremony, etc.

The *Tait. Sam.*, in the context of the rite of Agnicayana, speaks about *abhri* at a length, when taking the *abhri*, the sacrificer and the priest go to collect earth for making a clay fire-pan. The *arthavāda* is a detailed one praising every single characteristic of the *abhri.* It runs as follows. Agni went away from the gods. He entered the reed, and resorted to the hole, which is formed by the perforation of the reed. The *abhri* is perforated to make it Agni's birth-place. Wherever Agni lived, that became black. The *abhri* is stained, for perfection of form. It is pointed at both ends, for the winning of light, both from this world and from the yonder world. It is a fathom long (*vyāmamātrī);* so much is the strength in man. That which has fruit is the strong among trees. The reed tree bears fruit. Hence is the *abhri* made of reed to win strength (*Tait. Sam.* V. 1.1.4-5). In the Pravargya ceremony in the rite of digging the earth for making the Mahāvīra pot with the *abhri*, it is said that the *abhri* is a thunderbolt (*Śat. Br.* XIV. 1.2.3; for the same metaphor *ibid.* III. 7.1.2). When he draws lines around the lump of clay (collected for the fire-pan) with the *abhri*, he protects Agni by (as though) a rampart round it, for the gods were apprehensive of the attack on Agni from the *rakṣas*-es and the fiends (*ibid.* VI. 3.3.23-24). The sharpness of *abhri* on its both sides is explained by taking the example of our speech, which speaks both what is divine and what is human, both truth and untruth (*ibid.* VI. 3.1.34).

Āsandī (seat, generally translated as throne-seat)

Āsandī (throne-seat) is prescribed for Soma (-shoots), the sacrificer at the Vājapeya as also at the Rājasūya sacrifice, Ukhya Agni and also the pot at the Pravargya ceremony, for being placed upon or for being seated upon (in the case of the king). The *arthavāda*-s in all these cases point out how the practice of using such a high seat (or throne-seat) in rites and rituals stemmed from the beliefs associated with it.

When Soma is bought (by giving a cow and a piece of gold), the shoots of Soma are wrapped in a piece of cloth, lest the evil spirits should touch Soma (*Śat. Br.* III. 3.4.6). When they come near the sacrificial hall, the Adhvaryu priest removes the Soma-wrapper and the King Soma is placed on a throne-seat (*āsandī*) (*ibid.* 25, 29), to be carried to the hall immediately after. Here are some *arthavāda*-s about the *āsandī.* The throne-seat of human king is taken up by two men but that of King Soma, by four men, for King Soma rules over everything here. This throne-seat is of the wood of the Udumbara tree, which stands for sap and food (we have already noted this in the chapter on "Trees"). The throne-seat of King Soma reaches up to navel, for it is there that the food settles and Soma is food. Again navel is the seat of the seed and Soma is seed. So the throne-seat of navel-height (*ibid.* 26-28).

In the Vājapeya sacrifice, after the ritual of ascending the sacrificial post (with the help of a ladder) and touching the top-piece of it *(caṣāla)* of wheat (-dough), when the sacrificer descends, they bring a throne-seat for him. The *arthavāda* states that he in the Vājapeya gains a seat in the air. This he has gained by the symbolic act of raising his head above the sacrificial post, accompanied with the *mantra, Vāj. Sam.* IX. 21... 'O Gods! We have gone to the heavenly world *(svar);* we have become immortal'. The subjects of his (i.e. of the sacrificer-king) sit below him, who is seated above. Hence the throne-seat for him. It is made of Udumbara, which as the *arthavāda* mentions, stands for sustenance and food (*Śat. Br.* V. 2.1.9-14, 22-23). The *arthavāda* that when seated on the throne-seat, the sacrificer-king, gaining a seat in the air, is above his subjects while the latter sit below him, occurs in the context of the Rājasūya sacrifice. Here the *āsandī* is of Khadira wood, perforated and bound with thongs as was that of the Bharatas (*ibid.* V. 4.4.1).

The fire in the fire-pan (Ukhya Agni) is carried on a seat (*āsandī*). It is made of Udumbara wood, the Udumbara tree, as per the oft-repeated belief about it, standing for strength and life-essence. The seat is said to be this earth, for on it everything is settled and even Agni, it is able to sustain. Moreover Udumbara of which it is made, stands for all the trees, which are capable of sustaining that Agni. The seat is a span high, for Viṣṇu (= Agni) as an embryo is a span high. The womb (carrying Agni) is made equal in size to the embryo. Its being a cubit across, stands for strength, for strength is exerted by the arm (cubit = length of the forearm). The feet and boards of the seat are four-cornered, for there are four regions and the regions are able to sustain Agni (*ibid.* VI. 7.1. 12-15).

The throne-seat for the sacrificer-king in the Sautrāmaṇī rite, is knee-deep and is of unlimited size, horizontally. In the form of the sacrificer, actually, the imperial dignity is seated on the throne. In the next *arthavāda*, the Udumbara tree, of which the *āsandī* is made, is said to be the royal dignity and royal dignity is of unlimited prosperity. The *āsandī* is the womb and navel of the ruling power (*kṣatra*) (*ibid.* XII. 8.3.4-6, 8).

The throne-seat in the Pravargya rite (Pravargya being called '*samrāj*') is made of Udumbara wood, the Udumbara having the same qualities spoken of by the *arthavāda* as noted above. This seat is shoulder-high, for on the shoulders the head is set. On this *Samraḍāsandī*, the two unused Mahāvīra pots, the Upayamanī *sruc,* etc. are placed (*ibid.* XIV. 1.3.8-10; also *Kāty. Ś.S.* XXVI. 2.17).

The *arthavāda*-s regarding these different throne-seats and their varying height, speak of the beliefs underlying the use of *āsandī.* Their being made of Udumbara, in one case of Khadira, takes us to the beliefs about these trees. As we have already noted, the throne-seat of Ukhya Agni is only a span high; that of the Sautrāmaṇī knee-high; that of King Soma navel-high but that of the Pravargya shoulder-high. The Ukhya Agni after the period of consecration is to be deposited on the newly built Gārhapatya (fire) hearth, which is identified with the terrestrial world. So the throne-seat for the Ukhya Agni is only span high, i.e. very close to the earth. On the other hand, the Pravargya rite stands for the head of the sacrifice. So the throne-seat for it is shoulder-high and is called '*saṃrāḍ-āsandī*'. Thus the details about the heights of these throne-seats are to be taken into account to decide the respective status of the *vidhi*-s, in which these figure. However the very enjoining of *āsandī* in the *vidhi* indicates that two levels are maintained in the rites and rituals — one earthly and the other divine. When the sacrificer performs a sacrifice, he goes near the gods to the divine level. So the use of throne-seat for him or for the things used in the sacrifice.

Asking a boon

In the Agniṣṭoma sacrifice, having drawn the Soma-cups (*graha*-s), the sacrificer asks a boon. The *arthavāda* is very significant, as it directly conveys to us the motif of performing a sacrifice. The gods greatly desire to obtain the offering of the Soma-cup and so they grant that boon to the sacrificer, in order that he may offer that Soma-cup to them (*Śat. Br.* IV. 1.1.21). Thus the constant process of 'Give-and-Take' going on between the gods and the humans. On this basis, stands the edifice of sacrifice, its aim being procreation of everything for the sacrificer and the humans at large!

Brahmacārin

In the rite of initiation (*upanayana*) of a brahmanical boy (i.e. boy belonging to any of the three upper *varṇa*-s), by way of *arthavāda* figures a *śloka* (verse), which they sing. It states —'By laying his right hand on (the pupil), the *ācārya* (preceptor or teacher) becomes the one, endowed with the embryo (*garbhī bhavati*). On the third day, he (i.e. the boy) is born as a *brāhmaṇa* with the Sāvitrī' (*Śat. Br.* XI. 5. 4. 12). The *śloka* stated here by way of *arthavāda*, in order to praise the rite of initiation, speaks of the belief on which is based the rite of initiation. It shows the temporary phase of death of the pupil, who attains the new life, when he is born of his preceptor (*ācārya*). The preceptor has completely swallowed him, keeping him within himself as embryo, thus making the boy to be initiated as a part of his own self. So the initiate after the initiation ceremony is called *'dvija'* ('twice-born'). The symbolic new birth of the initiate is with the Sāvitrī *mantra* - the *mantra* in praise of the god Savitṛ. The same concept already occurs in the *AV* (XI. 5.3), where also the preceptor is said to place the initiate within himself as embryo for three nights, only to take him out as a newborn one. Thus the *śloka* in the *Śat. Br.*, coming as *arthavāda* is an epitome of symbolic death and symbolic new birth of the initiate.[1]

The verse, we have noted from the *Śat. Br.*, is termed *śloka*. The *śloka*-s in the Brāhmaṇa-texts form a part of the traditional lore, which is preserved in the ritualistic texts. Mostly these *śloka*-s are from the ritualistic tradition itself and major part of them was composed by the priestly class, on the pattern provided by the popular style, followed and entertained in the secular circles. Such *śloka*-s served as *mantra*-s in the given rituals, since even though composed in the popular style, they were stated for recitation to support the rituals which were laid down. Sāyaṇa, at several places, calls them by the term '*mantra*'.[2]

The *Śat. Br.* deals with the duties of the *brahmacārin* (a student staying with the preceptor in the latter's house for a certain period of time, for studies) at length and provides the reasonings (*arthavāda*-s) for them. Bringing firewood daily is enjoined for a *brahmacārin*. The *arthavāda* is here in the form of a small mythical account, which is as follows. The Brahman delivered the creatures over to Death, except the *brahmacārin*. While Death wanted a share in the *brahmacārin* also, the Brahman said that on whatever night, the *brahmacārin* would not bring firewood, that night he would pass (i.e. lose), cutting it off from his own life (*Śat.*

Br. XI. 3.3.1). It means his not brining the firewood on any night would diminish his life by a night or a day.

The life of a *brahmacārin* is metaphorically said to be a long sacrificial session, his putting on the fire the log, in the beginning, being the opening (Prāyaṇīyā) offering and the same, when he is about to take the final bath (prior to his leaving the preceptor's house, at the end of his studies and going back to his own family), being the concluding (Udayanīyā) offering. And whatever logs of wood he puts on fire in between these two (as noted above), for all the days of the years (of his stay in the preceptor's house), are like the logs of his sacrificial session (*ibid.* 2).

While laying down his daily duties, the *Śat. Br.* again speaks through *arthavāda.* It is said that the *brahmacārin* enters beings in four parts. When he brings a log for the fire, he redeems that fourth part of his which is in the fire and he takes it to his own self (*ibid.* 3-4). When he begs alms, he redeems that part of his which is in death and he takes it to his own self (*ibid.* 5). When he obeys the teacher perfectly, he redeems that part of his which is in the teacher and he takes it to himself (*ibid.* 6). One-fourth part already is within his own self (*ibid.* 3). At the end of his studentship, after the final bath, the *brahmacārin* is not required to beg alms. The *arthavāda* states that by bathing he drives off beggary and drives off hunger from his kinsmen and his deceased ancestors (*ibid.* 7). It is clear that the *arthavāda* stated at every step here, has made this section of the *Śat. Br.* quite interesting.

Butter

Melted clarified butter (*ājya)* or clarified butter (*ghṛta)* is often mentioned in the rituals and the *arthavāda*-s aim at pointing out the importance of butter, at times through ritual metaphors.

Melted clarified butter (*ājya)* is the divine sweetness (*mudhu daivyam yad ājyam)* and so they anoint the sacrificial post with it (*Ait. Br.* II.2 = 6.2). In the New-moon and Full-moon sacrifices, he pours butter on the upper side of the oblation and then it becomes the part of the sacrifice (*Śat. Br.* I.7.4.11). Butter (*ājya*) being an indispensable substance in sacrifice,[3] we have a series of ritual metaphors regarding butter. A person desirous of getting lustre has to offer melted butter (*ājya*), for melted butter is lustre (*Tait. Br.* II. 1.5.5). This ritual metaphor praising melted butter (*ājya*) occurs at several places (*Śat. Br.* XIII. 1.1.1; 2.1.2; 2.6.4; 6.2.11). In the Bṛhaspatisava (which is a one-day ritual, with which is connected anointing and which was performed in the beginning in the case of Bṛhaspati), the sacrificer is sprinkled with the liquid butter (*ājya*). The butter is lustre or brilliance (*tejaḥ*). He thereby places brilliance into himself (*Pañc. Br.* XVII. 11.9; also *Tait. Br.* II.7.1.4, the context is the same). In the Horse-sacrifice, when the horse was slaughtered, the life-sap, i.e. the sacrificial essence, went out of it, which became the Aśvastomīya oblations. When the sacrificer offers the Aśvastomīya oblations, he supplies the horse with the life-sap (*medhaḥ*), i.e. the sacrificial essence. These oblations are offered with butter (*ājya*), for butter is life-sap (*medhaḥ*); butter is the favourite abode of the gods (*Śat. Br.* XIII. 3.6.2; also *ibid.* I.3.2.17). It is relished by the gods (*ibid.* I.7.2.10). Butter (*ājya*) is the essence of all things, of waters as well as plants (*ibid.* VII.2.3.4). It is this fire (*ibid.* VII. 2.3.9). Butter (*ājya*) is truth (*ibid.* XI. 3.1.1). In the New-moon and Full-moon sacrifices, there is a ritual of the sacrificer's wife looking at the melted clarified butter (*ājya*), for wife is a woman and the butter stands for seed. A productive pairing is thereby brought about (*ibid.* I.3.1.18).

The ritual metaphor which occurs at several places and has as though become symbolic of butter, is — 'Butter (*ājya*) is a thunderbolt' (*ibid.* I.3.2.17; I.5.3.4; III. 3.1.3; III.3.2.1; III.4.3.11; III.4.4.6; III.5.3.15; III.6.3.17; III.6.4.15; VI.3.3.18; VII.4.1.34; VII.5.2.24, etc.). As sacrifice is viewed as obtaining everything in this world as well as the other world, and as butter is an indispensable offering in sacrifice (many times the principal offering and at times as an accessory to other offering) butter symbolically stands as a thunderbolt, having extraordinary power. In the New-moon and Full-moon sacrifices, the mythical account states that the gods gained the seasons as well as the year and deprived their rivals of these, with the thunderbolt, i.e. the butter. This the sacrificer achieves with butter (-offering) (*ājya)* - the thunderbolt (*ibid.* I.5.3.4; also *ibid.* III. 4.4.6 for a similar idea). An important social fact can be noted in the context of the Agniṣṭoma sacrifice in connection with the Pātnīvata (Soma-) cup meant for Tvaṣṭṛ, who is Patnīvat (with the wives of the gods). It is said that the Adhvaryu priest mixes Soma with the residue of butter, which is left in the *pracaraṇī* spoon. As butter is a thunderbolt, with that the gods smote the wives and unmanned them. Being reduced to this condition, the wives neither owned any self nor did they own any heritage (*ibid.* IV. 4.2.13). The same plight of women continued up to the times of Yājñavalkya, who was the first to propound the right of the wife on the property of her husband, who died sonless.[4] It is with this thunderbolt (i.e. *ājya*-offering) that the gods, kept off the evil spirits from the south (*ibid.* III. 5.3.14, 15). In the Agniṣṭoma sacrifice, after depositing the spoons and touching water, he makes the King Soma enter the Havirdhāna shed. As butter (*ājya)* is thunderbolt and Soma is seed, he does not bring the two together, for the thunderbolt may harm the seed (*ibid.* III. 6.3.17). In the Rājasūya sacrifice, when the waters from various places and sources are brought to sprinkle the king with, it is stated that he does not offer on the water, brought from the river Sarasvatī. As Sarasvatī is the goddess of Speech and butter (*ājya)* is a thunderbolt, he should not injure the goddess of Speech. So no butter-offering on the water from the river Sarasvatī (*ibid.* V. 3.4.25).

The ritual-texts use both the words, *ājya* (liquid clarified butter) and *ghṛta* (clarified butter allowed to cool, hence becoming a bit solid or accumulated). Clarified butter (*ājya)* is said to be the seed and rice-grains are from the land, tilled with the help of the bullocks. When these two (clarified butter and rice-grains) come together, a productive pairing is formed. Hence for preparing *caru* (the boiled rice), the rice-grains are to be put in the clarified (solid) butter (*ghṛta)*. This is for softening the sacrifice (*Tait. Br.* I.1.6.5-6). This shows that, practically, the two words *ājya* and *ghṛta* are used in the same sense (cf. *Jaim. Br.* III. 207, 208, where both the words *ghṛta* and *ājya* are used). *Ghṛta* is said to be manifestly the form of sacrifice (*Śat. Br.* XII. 8.2.15). It is the favourite abode of Agni (*Jaim. Br.* III. 62; III. 207; *Tait. Br.* I.1.9.6). In the context of the Mahābhiṣeka of king (rite of lustration of the king, by sprinkling liquid materials such as curds, honey, ghee and water), it is said that *ghṛta* is the brilliance of cattle, which he places in the king (*Ait. Br.* VIII.2=39.6). In the rite of Brāhmaṇasava (meant for a *brāhmaṇa*, who is desirous of getting spiritual lustre), it is said that the sacrificer is sprinkled with ghee, for that makes him have more vigour (*Tait. Br.* II. 7.3.3). Agni is closely connected with ghee (*ghṛta)*. In the Agnicayana rite, while heating the fire-pan *(ukhā)*, he puts the kindling-stick from the Kṛmuka wood on fire. This kindling-stick is soaked in ghee; the inner membrane of the womb from which Agni was produced consisted of ghee. Hence Agni now blazes up towards the ghee-soaked kindling-stick, for that stick is his self and so the Kṛmuka (-stick) has no ashes (*Śat. Br.* VI. 6.2.13).

The Vedic ritualists were so overwhelmed with the importance of butter (here 'ghee' — *ghṛta*, which is the clarified butter, as we have noted earlier) that even a *mantra* used for kindling Agni (the Sāmidhenī *mantra*, employed while kindling Agni) containing the word *'ghṛta'* is praised with an *arthavāda* in the form of a mythical account. This occurs in the context of the New-moon and Full-moon sacrifices, in the ritual of kindling the fire. Māthava, the king of Videgha carried Agni Vaiśvānara in his mouth. Gotama Rāhūgaṇa was his family priest. When addressed by Gotama Rāhūgaṇa, the king made no answer to him with the fear that Agni might fall from his mouth. The priest began to invoke Agni with the *ṛc*-s from the *RV*. When he uttered, "We invoke you, O butter-sprinkled one!' (*RV* V.26.2a), at the very mention of the word 'butter' (*ghṛta)*, Agni Vaiśvānara flashed forth from the king's mouth and went on burning along this earth, drying up all the rivers. Māthava Videgha, who was at that time on the bank of the river Sarasvatī, together with his priest followed Agni up to the river Sadānīrā, which Agni did not burn over (*Śat. Br.* I.4.1.10-20). The mythical account is important, as it indicates the spread of the Vedic sacrificial religion to the east up to the river Sadānīrā, at the time of the *Śat. Br.* To Weber goes the credit of drawing our attention to this important account.[5]

Collyrium

Collyrium is prominently mentioned in the context of consecration (*dīkṣā*) of the sacrificer, intending to perform the Agniṣṭoma sacrifice. It is said that the sacrificer has to anoint his eyes with collyrium, which comes from the mount Trikakud. The *arthavāda* states that when the gods slew the *asura-rakṣa*-es, the *dānava* (*asura)* Śuṣṇa falling backward entered into the eye of men. He is that pupil of the eye and looks like a young lad. Against him (i.e. Śuṣṇa) the consecrated sacrificer (i.e. the sacrificer who is initiated for the sacrifice) raises a rampart of stone round himself. This rampart is in the form of collyrium, which comes from the mount Trikakud. When Indra slew Vṛtra, he transformed that eye of Vṛtra into the mount Trikakud. The reason why ointment (i.e. collyrium) from mount Trikakud is used is that he thereby puts eye into eye. In case the sacrificer is unable to obtain ointment from Trikakud, any other ointment may be used (*Śat. Br.* III. 1.3.10-12). The sacrificer has to anoint the right eye first, for in human practice the left eye is anointed first, but with the gods it is to be done in this manner (*ibid.* 14). This is because when the sacrificer is initiated for the sacrifice, he is on the divine level and goes near to the gods. It is said that he anoints the eyes with a reed-stalk, for the reed is a thunderbolt. The reed-stalk is one with a tuft, in order to chase away the evil spirits (*ibid.* 13).

In the context of funeral ceremonies, it is said that after the ceremonies, the persons (who have gone to the funeral ground) proceed towards the village muttering a *mantra* (*Vāj. Sam.* XXXV. 14). When they arrive, ointments for the eyes and the feet are given to them, for these are the 'human adornment' (*mānuṣo' laṅkāraḥ*). By this (i.e. ointment) they keep off death from themselves (*Śat. Br.* XIII. 8.4.7).

The passage is important for it points out the concept behind 'adornment' (*alaṅkāra)* which is to put a barrier (fr. *aram* > *alam* + √*kṛ*) round that part of the body, which faces danger.[6] The use of the ointment (collyrium) is thus for warding off evil, by putting a barrier round the eyes.

Consecration

The firm conviction of the Vedic ritualists is that a man is born for the second time from the sacrifice (which he performs). The first (i.e. the normal) birth is for this world and the second birth is for (reaching) the other world — the world of the *gandharva*-s, that of the gods and for the heavenly world (*Jaim. Br.* I. 259). He who is consecrated for sacrifice elevates himself from this world to the world of the gods (*Śat. Br.* III. 1.4.1).

Now for this second birth after sacrifice, the man consecrated for the sacrifice is regarded as an embryo. We have several rules, some prohibitive or negative in nature, almost becoming 'taboos'[7]—enjoined for a consecrated sacrificer. These indicate the belief of those times.

The *Śat. Br.* says that the fire is the womb of the sacrifice and the consecrated is an embryo. The sacrificer moves about there between the fires; he now turns round and now back, as do the embryos move about and now turn round and now back (*ibid.* III. 1.3.28). The sacrificial chamber is called *vimita*, which is regarded as the womb. The consecrated is forbidden to be out of the sacrificial chamber at the sunrise or sunset, lest he be out of the womb. They cover him with a garment, for the garment is the caul of the consecrated. Above that is the black antelope skin, which is the placenta above the caul.[8] The consecrated closes his hands, for the embryo lies closing its hands and the child is born with closed hands (*Ait. Br.* I.3). The consecrated has to wrap his head (with his upper garment or with a turban), for he who is consecrated becomes an embryo and embryos are developed both by the amnion and the outer membrane (*Śat. Br.* III. 2.1.16., cf. *ibid.* III. 3.3.12). The sacrificer who is consecrated should not scratch himself either with a chip of wood or with his nail, he being an embryo. Were any one to scratch an embryo either with a chip of wood or his nail, it would die. The black antelope's horn is the sacrificer's own womb and so the horn does not injure him (*ibid.* III. 2.1.31). While enjoining the ritual of tying a black antelope's horn at the end of the sacrificer's garment, there occurs a mythical account, which runs as follows. Gods and *asura*-s both sprung from Prajāpati got his property by inheritance, the gods getting the Mind and the *asura*-s the Speech. The gods wanted Speech (also) on their side. The gods who came to have Yajña (i.e. sacrifice) on their side through the Mind, asked Yajña to win over the Speech (Vāc), which was with the *asura*-s. Yajña after some efforts became successful in bringing the Speech back to the gods. The gods offered her up in fire as a holocaust, it being an offering of the gods. Yajña united with her and there was born Indra. Indra being apprehensive of a great monster to be born from the union of Yajña and Speech and scoring a victory over him, seized that womb (from which he was born), pressed it tightly and tearing it off put it on the head of Yajña (i.e. Sacrifice). As the black antelope is the Sacrifice, the black antelope skin is the same as that Sacrifice and the black antelope horn is the same as that womb. So the horn is bound tightly to the end of the sacrificer's garment, for like Indra, the sacrificer after becoming an embryo is born from the union of the black antelope's skin and its horn, i.e. sacrifice and the womb (*ibid.* III. 2.1. 18-28).

An important ritual in the rite of consecration is of shaving the sacrificer's hair and beard and cutting his nails. The part of man where water does not reach him is impure. At the hair and beard and at the nails, the water does not reach him. So he shaves these, so that he be consecrated after becoming pure (*ibid.* III. 1.2.2). The *Śat. Br.* says that he should shave only the hair of his head and beard and cut his nails (*ibid.* 3). The *Tait. Sam.* says that the hair and the beard are dead and impure skin, and by destroying the dead and impure skin, he becomes fit for the sacrifice (*Tait. Sam.* VI. 1.1.2). The ritual of cutting the sacrificer's hair and (his) nails spring from a worldwide belief in this respect. It is patent that even when cut off, the nails and hair grow back on a man's body. They, thus, are considered to be the symbol of death and regeneration. In the case of the sacrificer and also in that of the initiate (for the rite of initiation), their hair are shaved, to suggest symbolic death prior to the rite (or at the very point of performing the rite) and rebirth after performing the rite.[9] In the ritual of shaving the sacrificer's hair, are used a porcupine's quill spotted at three places and a copper razor. The three-spotted porcupine's quill resembles the threefold science (the three Veda-s) and the razor resembles the Brahman. The Brahman is fire and fire is of reddish nature. So a copper razor of reddish colour is used. The sacrificer has his head shaved all round and thus the Adhvaryu priest encompasses him with the Brahman and the threefold science (*Śat. Br.* II. 6.4.5). The use of the three-spotted porcupine's quill and the copper razor obviously is on the lines of the principle of magic *viz.* 'Like produces like.'

Interesting details occur in the ritual of cutting the nails of the sacrificer in the rite of consecration. These, which we shall be taking a note of, are from the context of the Agniṣṭoma sacrifice. The sacrificer cuts his nails, first of the right hand. In the practice prevalent among the humans, the nails of the left hand are cut first, but with the gods it is in the above manner. First he cuts the nails of the thumbs, for in human practice the nails of the little fingers are cut first, but with the gods it is in the above manner. He first passes the comb through his right whisker. In human practice they comb first the left whisker, but with the gods it is in the above manner (*ibid.* III. 1.2.4-5). The concept underlying these rules is that he, who is consecrated for a sacrifice, goes near to the gods and becomes one of the deities (*ibid.* III. 2.2.19, 22). Hence the consecrated sacrificer has to follow regarding these details a practice which is different from that one prevalent among the society.

The correct order of cutting the hair on the body of the sacrificer for the rite of consecration, is explained through an *arthavāda*-account. It runs as follows. Whatever the gods performed in sacrifice, the same was done by the *asura*-s. They first cut the hair on the head, then beard and thereafter the hair in the arm-pits (*'upapakṣau'* — the two shoulders). The *asura*-s by this way (cutting the hair) came in the downward direction, and were defeated. But the gods first of all cut the hair of (i.e. under the) shoulders, then beard and lastly the hair on the head. Thereby they reached the heavenly world (*Tait. Br.* I.5.6.1-2). The sacrificer has to anoint his eyes with the ointment (collyrium). The beliefs regarding collyrium, we have already taken note of, under "Collyrium". He anoints his right eye first, for men anoint the left eye first. He does not rub the ointment on (the eye), for men rub the ointment on (the eye) (*Tait Sam.* VI. 1.1.5, 6). This again falls in line with the details which we have already noted, making a mention of the practice prevalent among men and exactly opposite of it, (imagined to be) among the gods and the sacrificer following the latter, as by the rite of consecration he becomes one among the gods.

The girdle of the sacrificer is made of hemp and so it is soft. When Prajāpati having become an embryo sprung forth from sacrifice, the amnion became hempen threads, with the result they smell putrid. That which was the outer membrane and placenta, become the garment of the consecrated. As the amnion lies under the outer membrane, so the girdle is worn under the garment. Like Prajāpati, the sacrificer becomes an embryo and springs forth from that sacrifice (*Śat. Br.* III. 2.1.11). The garment of the sacrificer for consecration has to be a new one, for the sake of unimpared vigour. It is to be beaten for cleaning that part of it, which an unclean woman has spun or woven. A new garment is to be sprinkled with water, so that it becomes clean. The garment could be the one, which is laid aside to be worn daily after bathing, without being soaked in some sharp cleansing substance (*ibid.* III. 1.2.19).

The sacrificer subsists only on the fast-milk (*vrata*), which he partakes of and does not offer it in the fire. This he has to follow when he is consecrated for the Agniṣṭoma sacrifice. The fast-milk is cooked for him. The sacrificer when consecrated goes near to the gods and becomes one of them. The sacrificial food of the gods is not uncooked but always cooked. Here the fast-milk is cooked. A mythical account in connection with the fast-milk is interesting. When the gods obtained supreme authority through sacrifice, they thought of making their world unattainable to men. For that they sipped the sap of the sacrifice. Having drained the sacrifice and having scattered it by means of the sacrificial post, they disappeared. This was heard by the *ṛṣi*-s, who collected then the sacrifice. The sacrificer, who is consecrated, becomes the sacrifice, for it is he who carries it on and produces it. Whatever sap of the sacrifice was sucked out and drained, that he now restores again by sipping the fast-milk and not offering it in fire (*ibid.* III. 2.2.10-12).

To the consecrated sacrificer is given a staff by the Adhvaryu priest. This is for driving away the evil spirits as the staff is a thunderbolt. It is of the Udumbara wood. As the Udumbara wood stands for food and strength, the staff of the Udumbara wood enables him to obtain food and strength. This staff reaches up to the mouth of the consecrated sacrificer, for so far extends the strength of the sacrificer. The staff is made to stand upright, the idea being that the staff standing erect would protect the sacrificer till the completion of the sacrifice (*ibid.* III. 2.1.32-35).

The sacrificer to be consecrated is purified with a cleanser (*pavitra)* of sacred grass. Man is foul from within for he speaks untruth. As sacred grass (*darbhāḥ*) is pure, it purifies the sacrificer. The cleanser of sacred grass may consist of one stalk of grass, for Wind — the blower or the purifier — is one. Or it may be of three stalks, for Wind entering man becomes threefold *viz.* in-breathing (*prāṇa)*, *udāna* (upward breathing) and *vyāna* (through breathing). Or it may be of seven stalks, for there are seven vital airs of the head; or it may be thrice seven, i.e. twenty-one, to obtain perfection (*ibid.* III. 1.3.18-21). Here the *arthavāda*-s speak of the belief regarding the sacred grass as well as numbers, the latter joined with several units.

The consecrated sacrificer has to restrain his speech and has to utter either a *ṛc* or a *sāman* or a *yajus* for taking a firmer and firmer hold of the sacrifice. When he restrains his speech, Speech being sacrifice, he appropriates the sacrifice to himself. If he utters any sound foreign to the sacrifice, then that sacrifice, being set free, flies away. In order to get hold of the sacrifice, he should mutter either a *ṛc* or a *yajus* addressed to Viṣṇu, for Viṣṇu is sacrifice (*'viṣṇur vai yajñaḥ'* being an oft-repeated statement in the ritual-texts) (*ibid.* III. 2.1.37, 38). The *vidhi* and *arthavāda* here stem from the perfect knowledge of human psychology. If the sacrificer is engrossed in some worldly matters, and thereby loses control over his speech, obviously he would be by his mind away from the sacrifice, which would thereafter become only a physical act of his. Hence a restrain over the speech of the sacrificer and as an atonement for any transgression of this is laid down the muttering of a *ṛc* or a *yajus* addressed to Viṣṇu, so that again the mind of the sacrificer would be fixed on the thought of the sacrifice.

While dealing with the fast-milk (*vrata)* to be sipped by the consecrated sacrificer, we have stated a mythical account regarding the gods draining the sacrifice and scattering it. The sacrificer restores that part of the sacrifice by speaking falteringly and not effusively after the manner of ordinary speech. If he speaks effusively after the manner of ordinary speech, he would not restore the sap of the sacrifice (*ibid.* III. 2.2.28, 29).[10]

In order to have the continuity of Time in the sacrifice, the consecrated sacrificer has to observe certain rules regarding his speech. Before sunset, he has to restrain his speech and after sunset release it. Similarly before sunrise, he has to restrain his speech and after sunrise release it. This is for keeping continuity of the day with the night and of the night with the day (*ibid.* III. 2.2.26).

This is obviously to suggest that there is no break in his vow. The same idea is carried further when it is said that the sun should not set on him, while abiding elsewhere than the sacrificial chamber. Again the sun should not rise on him while he is asleep. Were the sun to set on him while abiding elsewhere, the sun would cut him off from the night and were the sun to rise on him while asleep, the sun would cut him off from the day. The *Śat. Br.* warns that there is no atonement for this lapse on the part of the consecrated sacrificer. Hence by all means it (i.e. the lapse) should be avoided (*ibid.* 27). In order to maintain the sanctity of the purificatory bath (*avabhṛtha)*, it is said that prior to this bath, the consecrated sacrificer should not enter water, nor should it rain on him, for these two occasions of touching the water, other than that at the purificatory bath are improper (*ibid.).* Though not stated specifically by the *Śat. Br.*, the thought seems to be that the final bath (*avabhṛtha)*, which marks the completion of the sacrifice and also the vow of consecration for it, followed by the sacrificer in all its details, should be at the proper hour and with the proper water, lest the very sacrifice performed by him should remain incomplete.

The consecrated sacrificer on the night previous to the performance of sacrifice, has to sleep in the Āhavanīya chamber or the Gārhapatya chamber, i.e. near these fire-altars. When the sacrificer enters the vow of consecration, he approaches the gods and sleeps in the midst of those very gods whom he now approaches. He has to sleep on the ground, for one serves one's superior, being himself on the ground (*ibid.* I.1.1.11).

Not only these restrictions, which apply to the outer things the consecrated sacrificer has to follow, but he has to be self-controlled also. If he utters anything that is foreign to the vow or if he becomes angry, he commits a fault and breaks his vow, for the suppression of anger is (most) essential for a consecrated sacrificer (*ibid.* III. 2.2.24).

The *Jaim. Br.* correlates the six seasons with the six quarters, bringing the concepts of Time and Space together, and says that just as the wives (out of love) look at their husband with unwinking eyes, similarly the quarters look at the sacrificer when he is being consecrated. As he is looked at by the quarters (*digbhiḥ īkṣitaḥ)* he is called '*dīkṣita'* — 'consecrated' (*Jaim. Br.* II. 52). The etymology here is not simply a play on word but breathes of the 'divine', which is inherent in the very concept of sacrifice, though the sacrifice is performed on the terrestrial level.

Cosmos

It is said that Prajāpati in the form of the Agniṣṭoma (sacrifice) having the form of a divine circle becomes extensive. Following him, other deities also become circular. So are the Sun, the moon, the heavenly vault, the mid-region and this earth circular in form (*Jaim. Br.* I.256-257). This gives us a perfect picture of the entities in the cosmos, perceived by the Vedic ritualists. The concept of one 'fire' (or the principle of heat) develops into three gods *viz.* Agni, Vāyu and Āditya (*ibid.* I.247; II.87). The sun dazzling high above, the four main quarters and the four intermediary quarters constitute the divine splendour of the cosmos (*ibid.* I.252). The sun moves at a far away distance and so moves the moon; far away are the constellations and the blazing fire goes far beyond (*ibid.* I.276). Agni on the earth, the sun in the heaven, the moon among the constellations and lightning in waters — are the super-lustres of the gods (*ibid.* II. 333). Elsewhere the *Jaim. Br.* adds, 'Vāyu resorting to the mid-region' to the above list (*ibid.* II. 433). The blowing of the wind is mentioned by the *Śat. Br.* (III. 6.1.16; VIII. 1.1.7; X. 3.5.1, etc.). These entities, mentioned above, are mainly the ones which matter most, when the belief about the cosmos is taken into account. The *Śat. Br.* speaks of four Agnis and equates them with the three worlds and quarters respectively (*Śat. Br.* XI. 8.2.1).

Crossroads

In the context of the Sākamedha *parvan* (of the four-monthly Seasonal sacrifices), the Tryambaka offerings are enjoined to be offered to Rudra. These offerings consist of cakes on one potsherd and there are as many cakes as there are descendants, exceeded by one. By the additional cake, the sacrificer delivers from Rudra's power the descendants that are yet to be born (*Śat. Br.* II. 6.2. 1-4). These offerings are given towards the north, for that is the region of Rudra. He then offers these on a road, for on road the god (Rudra) moves. He offers on a crossroad, for the crossroad indeed is known to be a favourite haunt of Rudra (*ibid.* 7). This speaks of the Vedic belief about the corssroads belonging to Rudra.

The crossroads are generally regarded as the dwelling-place or resort of evil spirits, ghosts, etc. and hence dangerous. Various measures are resorted to in order to ward off their dangers.[11] Even in the *Avesta* we find a mention of sacrifice to the forkings of the highways and to the meeting of the roads.[12] At crossroads, paths and roads often form boundaries, which are a sort of neutral ground, easily accessible to evil spirits. Roads are infested with evil spirits and more so, at crossroads. So the magical rites which are effective on roads are still more effective on crossroads. Then it stands to reason, when deities which are terrible by nature and hence to be afraid of, are associated with crossroads, in order to counteract the powers of evil. This is why Rudra is associated with the crossroads as noted above and Nirṛti (goddess of Death) in the expiatory rite ordained for an *avakīrṇin*.[13] The *Pār. G.S.* states elaborate details of the expiatory rite enjoined for a *brahmacārin*, who has become an *avakīrṇin* (having broken the vow of calibacy). On the New-moon day the *avakīrṇin* was required to sacrifice an ass to the goddess Nirṛti at a crossroad (*Pār. G.S.* III. 12.1-3).[14]

Curds

Curds is regarded as a symbol of cattle, and by curds, the sacrificer wins cattle, so says the *Tait. Sam.* in the context of the Soma-sacrifice (*Tait. Sam.* VI. 2.4.1). In the rite of Agnicayana, while leading forward Agni to the fire-altar, he puts pieces of firewood of the Śamī, Vikaṅkata and Udumbara trees. While speaking about the piece of Udumbara wood (*audumbarī*), the *Śat. Br.* says that it should have a forking branch (*karṇakavatī*), i.e. which shows the appearance of a second branch, for such a piece of wood means cattle (Is it because it reminds a person of the horns of cattle? May be!). He gratifies Agni with cattle as food. If the sacrificer cannot get a piece of Udumbara wood with bifurcate branches, he should take up a globule of sour curds and put it on the wood, for that globule of sour curds is a form of cattle (*Śat. Br.* IX. 2.3.40). Such references point out that in ritual, curds stands for cattle, as it is a product from the milk of cow. As cattle were regarded as a valuable wealth, curds is said to be 'power' in this world. When after the manner of the great anointing (*Mahābhiṣeka)* of Indra, the sacrificer-king is to be anointed, he is to be anointed with curds — verily with power (*Ait. Br.* VIII. 20 = 39.6).

Dakṣiṇā (Gift)

The concept underlying *dakṣiṇā* (gift) to be given in sacrifice is that of invigorating the sacrifice by means of gifts to the priests. This is because the sacrifice is slain, when they press the Soma (-shoots); when they 'quiet' the sacrificial victim (at the hands of Śamitṛ); when they slay the *havis* (offering) with mortar and pestle, with the upper and the lower millstones. When slain, the sacrifice was no longer vigorous. By means of the *dakṣiṇā*-s the gods invigorated it. So the name *dakṣiṇā* (fr. the root √*dakṣay*. The sacrifice then becomes successful (*Śat. Br.* IV. 3.4.1-2). The same thought is repeated elsewhere in the *Śat. Br.* in the context of the rite of Agnyādhāna, i.e. establishing the fires (*ibid.* II.2.2.1-2). The *Pañc. Br.* in the context of the Jyotiṣṭoma sacrifice says that the *dakṣiṇā*-s are the internal fastenings of the sacrifice. Just as by a chariot provided with fastenings, one is sure to go to his destination, so the sacrificer attains his desired object through the sacrifice, which is provided with *dakṣiṇā*-s. The *dakṣiṇā*-s are the adornment of sacrifice. When the sacrificer performs a sacrifice, provided with *dakṣiṇā*-s, he brings beauty to it (*Pañc. Br.* XVI. 1.13, 14).

With *dakṣiṇā*-s comes another concept and that is of the human gods —the *brāhmaṇa*-s, who have studied and teach the sacred lore. It is said that he sacrificer gratifies the gods with oblations and the human gods, i.e. the priests, with *dakṣiṇā*-s, i.e. gifts given in the sacrifice (*Śat. Br.* II. 2.2.6). It is said that the officiating priests prepare (for) him another self, i.e. this sacrifice, consisting of *ṛc* and *yajus* and *sāman* and oblations, — that becomes his self in yonder world. With the thought that 'it is they who have generated me (in the other world)', the sacrificer should give the *dakṣiṇā*-s to the officiating priests (*ibid.* IV. 3.4.5).

In the context of the Devanītha *śilpa*,[15] a mythical account occurs with regard to the *dakṣiṇā*. The Aṅgiras-es officiated as priests for the sacrifice performed by the Ādityas. The Ādityas gave them this earth as *dakṣiṇā*. As the earth caused the Aṅgiras-es to burn, they cast her away. She then becoming a lioness, with gaping jaws assailed men. As she burned, came forth these fissures, which are now upon her. Prior to that she was all even. As the Aṅgiras-es cast away the earth, given to them as *dakṣiṇā*, it is said that a person shall not accept a gift cast away. In case he wants to accept it, he should give it to a hated rival, who then is ruined. Then the Ādityas brought to the Aṅgiras-es the sun in the form of a white horse as *dakṣiṇā* which the latter accepted. The *Ait. Br.* remarks that *dakṣiṇā* is the leader of the sacrifices. Just as in this world, a cart without a leader suffers harm, so does the sacrifice, which is without any *dakṣiṇā* (*Ait. Br.* VI. 35 = 30.9).

The *arthavāda* in the *Śat. Br.* in the context of the New-moon and Full-moon day sacrifices points out that the sacrificer must not make an offering without a *dakṣiṇā*. The *arthavāda* is in the form of a mythical account. It is said that the three Agnis which the gods chose, each time one, passed away one after the other. The fourth Agni concealed himself from fear and entered into the waters. The gods discovered him and brought him forcibly away from the waters. Agni being angry with the waters, despised them by spitting upon them. From the waters then sprang the Āptya deities — Trita, Dvita and Ekata. These three roamed about with Indra and knew that Viśvarūpa — the three-headed son of Tvaṣṭṛ - was to be killed by Indra. So Trita straightway slew him and Indra was free from the sin of Brahmahatyā ('killing a *brāhmaṇa*'). The Āptyas decided to pass on that sin beyond them, on him, who makes an offering without a *dakṣiṇā*. The sacrifice wipes the guilt off upon the Āptyas and they, in their turn, wipe it off upon him, who makes an offering without a *dakṣiṇā* (*Śat. Br.* I.2.3.1-4). In the context of the Agniṣṭoma sacrifice it is said that the sacrificer first gives *dakṣiṇā* to the Agnīdh priest, for it was from the place of Agnīdh that all the gods gained immortality and so would the sacrificer go to the gods (to gain immortality in the world of gods) (*ibid.* IV. 3.4.20). The *Jaim. Br.* clearly states that he who obtaining everything does not give away everything, he is the one who is to be regarded as grabbing the wealth of all. He who obtaining everything gives away everything is to be regarded as possessing all wealth (*Jaim. Br.* II. 180).

This is about giving away the *dakṣiṇā*-s. But it was equally difficult for the priests to accept the *dakṣiṇā*-s. In the context of the Soma-sacrifice (in the preliminary rites), the *Kauṣ. Br.* states that he (i.e. the priest) ransoms himself in that the gifts are taken (by him). With the gifts he makes the sacrifice strong (*dakṣayati*). The sacrificial session has the self as *dakṣiṇā* (*ātmadakṣiṇam vai satram*). So day by day they should mutter, 'Let me take myself as a gift for fair fame, for the world of heaven, for immortality' (*Kauṣ. Br.* XV. 1).

To turn to the *dakṣiṇā*-s proper — The gifts to be given to the priests stand to the south (*dakṣiṇa*) of the altar (*Śat. Br.* IV. 3.4.14; XI. 1.6.22). It has to be noted that when the sacrificer faces the east, to his right (*dakṣiṇa*) hand are kept the *dakṣiṇā*-s. Thus stands the name *dakṣiṇā*. The most common *dakṣiṇā* is in the form of cow or cows, as cattle stand as the choicest property. In the context of the Pravargya ceremony it is said that the cow which yielded the milk to be boiled in the Gharma (or Mahāvīra pot) is to be given to the Adhvaryu priest. As the Gharma (the word is applied to both the 'milk' as well as the 'pot') is as it were scorched, the Adhvaryu priest comes forth from the sacrificial ground like something scorched (*ibid.* XIV. 3.1.33). In the same Pravargya rite, the cow which yielded the sacrificer's fast-milk (*vratadughā*) is given as *dakṣiṇā* to the Hotṛ priest, for the Hotṛ priest is the sacrifice and so is the sacrificer identified with the sacrifice (*ibid.* 34). The cow, in the same rite (as noted above), which yielded the fast-milk (*vratadughā*) for the sacrificer's wife, is given as *dakṣiṇā* to the Udgātṛ priests, for they do the wife's work on that occasion (*ibid.* 35).

It is interesting to note that at several places, the *arthavāda* coming by way of explanation in connection with the *dakṣiṇā*-cows is based on the wider concept of 'Numbers'. In the rite of Agnyādhāna (establishing the fires), when the sacrificer gives six cows or twelve cows as *daksiṇā*, 'six' are said to be the six seasons and 'twelve' are said to be the twelve months, making up a year. Sacrifice

— Prajāpati — is Year. As great as the sacrifice is, as large as its extent is, by so many gifts the sacrificer invigorates the sacrifice (*ibid.* II. 2.2.3,4). The same *arthavāda* occurs when twelve pregnant heifers are given as *dakṣiṇā* in the Daśapeya rite of the Rājasūya sacrifice (*ibid.* V.4.5.20; *Pañc. Br.* XVIII. 9.21). These heifers have twelve embryo calves (*garbhāḥ)* and that makes twenty-four. There are twenty-four half-moons in the year, which is Prajāpati, which again is sacrifice. Thus he directly (*pratyakṣam)* obtains the sacrifice and makes it his own (*Śat. Br.* V. 4.5.21). In the rite of Agnyādhāna, there is a mention of twenty-four (*dakṣiṇā*-s) and the *arthavāda* is the same as noted above (*ibid.* II. 2.2.5). The *Śat. Br.*, in the context of the Rājasūya sacrifice, enjoins either twelve or thirteen gifts, for there are either twelve or thirteen months in the year (=Prajāpati=sacrifice). Thus he visibly (*pratyakṣam)* obtains the sacrifice (*ibid.* V. 4.5.23). In the three-day rite of Garga, hundred of cows are given day after day, for hundred is the limit of the sacrifice. These cows are given in the form of decades (*Pañc. Br.* XX. 15.12). The *Śat. Br.* enjoins that Soma-sacrifice should not have *dakṣiṇā*-s of less than a hundred. The sacrifice, which is patent to the eyes, is Prajāpati and man is nearest to Prajāpati. Man has a life of a hundred years, a hundred powers, a hundred energies. So by a hundred (*dakṣiṇā*-s), the sacrificer invigorates Prajāpati, i.e. sacrifice (*Śat. Br.* IV. 3.4.3).

An interesting detail regarding *dakṣiṇā*-s is of mule, which is not fit to be given as a *dakṣiṇā*, except at the laud of the Ṣoḍaśin. When the creatures were seized by Prajāpati, the mule went forth. Prajāpati went after it and took away its seed. He transferred it to the mare. With the result, the mare has double seed and the mule is barren, its seed being taken away. As the mule went forth, i.e. exceeded the sacrifice (i.e. Prajāpati), it is fit to be given as a *dakṣiṇā* only for an excessive sacrifice and so at the laud of the Ṣoḍaśin, and not for any other sacrifice (*Pañc. Br.* VI. 1.4,5).

A bull also figures as *dakṣiṇā*. In the Agnihotra rite, if the purified clarified butter spills from the vessel, that offering is a scattered one. By that the sacrificer is prone to death early. As an expiation for this lapse, the sacrificer has to give a bull (*varaḥ*) as gift (*dakṣiṇā*) (*Ṣaḍ. Br.* V.1.7). In the context of the Soma-sacrifice, when the office of the Subrahmaṇya priest is being dealt with,[16] it is said that they drive up a bull as the gift for the Subrahmaṇya priest. The *arthavāda* says that the bull is male and the Subrahmaṇyā female, thus forming a pair (*Ait. Br.* VI. 3 = 26.3). In the rite of re-establishment of the sacred fires,[17] the *dakṣiṇā* to be given to the priest consists of gold or it may be an ox. Gold is regarded as the seed of Agni and the ox also is related to Agni (i.e. sacrifice), for the shoulder of the ox, by carrying the yoke, is as if burnt by fire. Moreover, Agni is oblation-bearer to the gods, and the ox bears burden for men (*Śat. Br.* II. 2.3.28).

Gold by itself is an object of great value. In the Rājasūya sacrifice in the last rite (Udavasānīya *iṣṭi*), three gold pieces of a hundred *māna*-s each are the *dakṣiṇā* given to the Brahman priest. It is said that the Brahman priest neither performs like the Adhvaryu priest, nor chants like the Udgātṛ priest, nor again recites like the Hotṛ priest and still he is an object of respect. With gold they do nothing and yet it is important (*ibid.* V. 5.5.16). But generally gold is connected to the sun. A golden wreath is given as *dakṣinā* to the Udgātṛ priest, in the Rājasūya sacrifice. The Udgātṛ priest is sun-like. Hence in order to see the subsequent suns or dawns, i.e. days, the sacrificer gives the golden wreath to the Udgātṛ priest (*Pañc. Br.* XVIII. 9.8). A golden circular ornament (*rukma*) is given as *dakṣiṇā* to the Hotṛ priest, for the Hotṛ priest is like fire. Moreover he brings the yonder sun to the sacrificer, i.e. makes him see the subsequent years (*ibid.* 9). As we shall see under "Metals" more details about 'gold', gold is regarded as a solar metal. As Agni is the other form of the sun, gold is connected to fire also. Again as the horse in the Horse-sacrifice stands for the sun, it is said that when the horse was immolated, its seed going from it became gold. So in the Sautrāmaṇī sacrifice, the sacrificer gives gold as *dakṣiṇā* and thereby supplies seed to the horse (*Śat. Br.* XIII. 1.1.3). As we shall see further, gold is regarded as the seed of Agni (*ibid.* III. 3.1.3; III. 3.2.2; IV. 5.1.15, etc.)

It is said that there are four kinds of gifts to priests *viz.* gold, cow, cloth and horse. Having tied a piece of gold in a fringed cloth and laid it (into the spoon) he offers. It is not proper that he should lay a horse's foot or a cow's foot (into the spoon). So a piece of gold is tied in a fringed cloth and then offered. He offers with a hope for having a place in the world of the gods. That sacrifice of his goes to the world of the gods and behind it goes the gift he gives to the priests and holding on to the gift follows the sacrificer (*ibid.* IV. 3.4.6-7). The *Śat. Br.* further explains through *arthavāda* the purpose of the four *dakṣiṇā*-s mentioned above. When he gives gold as the sacrificial gift (*dakṣiṇā*), he preserves his own life, for gold is life. By giving a cow, he preserves his own breath, for the cow is breath. Cow is food and breath also is food. By giving cloth, he preserves his own skin, for the cloth is skin. About the horse, it is said that it is a thunderbolt. By giving a horse, he makes the thunderbolt the leader (*ibid.* 24-27).

In the context of the New-moon and Full-moon sacrifices it is said that the moon is the heavenly dog, which watches the sacrificer's cattle to seize them (*ibid.* XI. 1.5.1). In these sacrifices, the *dakṣiṇā* to be given is a bow with three arrows, for with the bow a dog is driven away. He thus drives away that dog, i.e. the moon, with this *dakṣiṇā*. He gives a staff as *dakṣiṇā*, for with a staff a dog is driven away. Here he keeps away the moon by this *dakṣiṇā*. This *dakṣiṇā* is relating to the (protection of the) cattle (*ibid.* 10-11).

In the context of the Rājasūya sacrifice (which is for the rejuvenation of the king), it is enjoined for the king to go to the houses of eleven 'jewels' (*ratna*-s) which are the important personalities in his kingdom and offer oblations at their places. The king is required to go to the house of a discarded wife also and offer a pap (*caru*) to Nirṛti. The *dakṣiṇā* to be given in each case (i.e. twelve, including the discarded wife, as mentioned above) is significant, as is made clear in the *arthavāda*, stated at the respective places.

At the house of the commander of the army (*senānī*), after offering an eight-potsherd cake to Agni Anīkavat, the *dakṣiṇā* is given in the form of gold, for it is Agni's seed. As commander is the head of the army, so is Agni the head of the gods (*devatānām anīkam*). Hence the sacrificial gift 'gold', as it is connected with Agni (*ibid.* V. 3.1.1). At the house of the family-priest (*purohita*), a pap (*caru*) is offered to Bṛhaspati, for Bṛhaspati is the family-priest of the gods. The *dakṣiṇā* given is a white-backed bullock, for to Bṛhaspati belongs that upper region, above which lies the shining path of Aryaman - an aspect of the sun. White colour here is significant of the bullock, which is given as the *dakṣiṇā* (*ibid.* 2). The third offering is at the place of the king himself, who is being rejuvenated. It is a cake on eleven potsherds to Indra and the *dakṣiṇā* given is a bull, for bull is Indra's own animal (*ibid.* 3). On the following day, the offering is given at the dwelling of the chief queen (*mahiṣī*), in the form of *caru* to Aditi. The *dakṣiṇā* given is a milch cow (*dhenu*), for she yields to men all their desires as does this earth sustain men and the earth is verily Aditi (*ibid.* 4). On the following day, the offering is at the house of the court-minstrel (*suta*), in the form of a barley pap (*caru*) to Varuṇa. As the *sūta* is the impeller (of the king, by telling him the olden accounts), so is Varuṇa of the gods. The *dakṣiṇā* given is a horse, for to Varuṇa belongs the horse (*ibid.* 5). The next offering is at the house of the headman (*grāmaṇī*), in the form of a seven-potsherd cake to Maruts. As headman is a peasant (*viś*), so are the Maruts (*viśaḥ*). The *dakṣiṇā* here is a spotted (*pṛṣan*) bullock (*gauḥ*), for the Maruts form a clan, which means abundance and the spotted bullock has abundance of colours (*ibid.* 6). The next offering is at the house of the chamberlain (*kṣattṛ)* in the form of a cake on twelve or eight potsherds for Savitṛ. As chamberlain is an impeller, so is the god Savitṛ. The *dakṣiṇā* on this occasion is a reddih-white draught-bullock (*śyetaḥ anaḍvān)*, for as the sun, i.e. Savitṛ, moves along, so moves the draught-bullock when yoked. The draught-bullock is reddish-white, for the sun is of this colour both at the rising and setting time (*ibid.* 7). The next offering is at the house of the charioteer (*saṅgrahītṛ)* in the form of a cake on two potsherds to the Aśvins. The *dakṣiṇā* given is twin bullocks from the same womb. If he cannot obtain twins, two bullocks of successive births from the same cow be given (*ibid.* 8). The next offering is at the house of a tax-gatherer (*bhāgadugha)* to Pūṣan, in the form of a *caru*, for Pūṣan also is a tax-gatherer to the gods. The *dakṣiṇā* is a dusky bullock (*ibid.* 9). The next offering is at the place of the king himself, of a *caru* made of the *gavedhukā* seeds brought from the house of the keeper of dice (*akṣāvāpa)* and huntsman (*govikarta)*. This offering is given to Rudra and the *dakṣiṇā* is a bicoloured bullock (*dvirūpaḥ gauḥ)*—either one with white fore-feet or a white-tailed one—a claw-shaped knife and a dice-board with a band of horse-hair, for these belong to the *akṣāvāpa* and the *govikarta* (*ibid.* 10). The next offering is by going to the house of a courier and it is of ghee offered to the way. As the courier for his work goes by the way, the offering is to the way (path). The sacrificial gift consists of a skin-covered bow, quivers made of leather and a red turban (*ibid.* 11). This points out that the courier in those times must be wearing a red turban and must be carrying a bow and quivers, while going on his errand. These are the eleven 'jewels' in the kingdom, to whom he approaches for offering at their respective dwellings. As noted earlier, the next day, the king goes to the house of the discarded wife (*parivṛtti)* and offers a *caru* of black rice to Nirṛti, for such a wife, having no son, is possessed of Nirṛti (calamity or destruction). The *dakṣiṇā* on this occasion consists of a black, decrepit, diseased cow, for such a cow is also possessed of Nirṛti (*ibid.* 13). The

Tait. Sam. (I.8.9.1-2) and the *Tait. Br.* (I.7.3) also deal with this topic but not so elaborately as we find in the *Śat. Br.*[18] It has to be noted that the *ratnin*-offerings are enjoined to be given every subsequent day in the order, which is fixed. Both, the efficacy of a particular offering to a particular deity and the significance of a particular *dakṣiṇā* are made clear in the *arthavāda*, stated in each case, which also points out the belief and practice underlying the *vidhi* of *ratninām havīṁṣi*' ('offerings to *ratnin*-s').

The Daśapeya rite comes at the end of the Rājasūya sacrifice,[19] as does the Sautrāmaṇī. In the Daśapeya rite, several gifts (*dakṣiṇā*-s) are mentioned (*Śat. Br.* V.4.5.20-23; *Pañc. Br.* XVIII. 9.8-21). A couple of these concerning gold, we have already dealt with. The *Pañc. Br.* states the *arthavāda* in the case of each *dakṣiṇā*, which is to be given at the Daśapeya sacrifice. Here we take into account some of the gifts and the *arthavāda*-s in their respect. The sacrificer-king gives two mirrors to the two Adhvaryu-priests (i.e. the Adhvaryu priest and the Pratiprasthātṛ priest, who helps the Adhvaryu priest). The *arthavāda* states that these two Adhvaryus are as though twins (hence the two mirrors!). Again by giving the two mirrors, the sacrificer-king brings eyesight into him (*Pañc. Br.* XVIII. 9.10). A horse is given as *dakṣiṇā* to the Prastotṛ (who is the assistant priest of the Udgātṛ priest). It is said that the horse belongs to Prajāpati and the Prastotṛ is like Prajāpati. Moreover the horse begins snorting and so the Prastotṛ begins chanting (*ibid.* 11). A milch-cow goes to the Pratihartṛ (the assistant priest of the Udgātṛ), by which *dakṣiṇā* he brings milk into him (*ibid.* 12). A barren cow (*vaśā*) is given to the Maitrāvaruṇa (the assistant priest of the Hotṛ priest), with the thought that he may bring him (i.e. the sacrificer-king) to power - *vaśam* (*ibid.* 13). The *arthavāda* here is based on the principle of magic in similarity of word-sounds, though the words have different meanings. A bull is given as *dakṣiṇā* to the Brāhmaṇā-*cchaṁsin* (the assistant priest of the Brahman priest), bull standing for strength (*ibid.* 14). To the Potṛ (the assistant priest of the Brahman priest) is given a garment, for being purified (*ibid.* 15). A linen garment is given to the Neṣṭṛ (the assistant priest of the Adhvaryu priest), for this function of the Hotṛ is dependent, as it were (*ibid.* 16). A cart led with one horse and loaded with barley is given as *dakṣiṇā* to the Acchāvāka (the assistant priest of the Hotṛ priest), for the function of the Hotṛ priest is like that of a cart led by one horse. The barley (barley grains in the cart) is for the release (of the sacrificer-king) from the fetters of Varuṇa (*ibid.* 17). A draught-ox goes to the Agnīdh (the assistant priest of the Brahman priest), for such an ox (yoked to the cart) signifies movement (*ibid.* 18). A he-goat is given as *dakṣiṇā* to the Subrahmaṇya (the assistant priest of the Udgātṛ priest) (*ibid.* 19). No *arthavāda* figures here, but we can conjecture that it is for pairing, from the gift of a bull to the same priest (Subrahmaṇya), which we have already noted from the *Ait. Br.* (VI.3 = 26.3).[20] A heifer is given as gift to the Unnetṛ (the assistant priest of the Adhvaryu priest) and a three-year old bull, not castrated, is given to the Grāvastut (the assistant priest of the Hotṛ priest) for pairing (*Pañc. Br.* XVIII. 9.20). The ritual-texts are replete with the examples of such pairing.[21]

For each rite or sacrifice, the *dakṣiṇā*-s are given to the priests, and these are explained in the *arthavāda*-portions, with beliefs and practices peeping through them, at times indistinctly.

In the context of *dakṣiṇā*-s and the *arthavāda*-s following them, a *śloka* which occurs in the *Śat. Br.* is to be taken into account. When Viśvakarman, the son of Bhuvana, performed the Sarvamedha (sacrifice), Kaśyapa officiated as his priest. Here, in this context a *śloka* is said to be spoken by the earth. The earth says that no mortal whosoever can give her to anybody, which Bhauvana Viśvakarman is slow to know. If he tries to do it, she would plunge in waters and then Viśvakarman's promise to Kaśyapa would prove to be false (*Śat. Br* XIII. 7.1.15).

The same verse, which Sāyaṇa calls a *gāthā*, occurs in the *Ait. Br.* with slight variations, where Kaśyapa officiates as a priest for the 'great anointing' of the king, on the lines of the 'great anointing of Indra' — Aindra Mahābhiṣeka (*Ait. Br.* VIII. 21 = 39.7). The verse,[22] taken to be a *śloka* or a *gāthā*, indicates the belief recorded in later times by Jaimini's *sūtra* (VI.7.3) and Śabarasvāmin's commentary on it that the whole earth cannot be given away as a gift in the (Viśvajit) sacrifice,[23] because it belongs to all and there is no difference between the emperor and other persons as to rights over the earth. Kane has discussed this point from the Dharmaśāstra point of view under "Dāna-land grants."[24]

Dice and Dice-board

Playing of dice is enjoined by some ritual-texts in certain rituals. While enjoining the Rāṣṭrabhṛt *mantra*-s in the optional sacrifices, it is said that the sacrificer offers on the dice-board. It is on the dice-board *(adhidevana)* that he wins his fellows for him, and being won, they wait upon him (*Tait. Sam.* III. 4.8.2). In the Rājasūya sacrifice, five dice are thrown in the sacrificer's hand, with a *mantra* from the *Vāj. Sam.* (X. 28). The Kali (throw) is dominant over the other dice and the *Vāj. Sam.* (X. 28) verily states that in its *mantra* 'Dominant you are! May these five regions of yours prosper!'. The sacrificer causes the five regions to prosper for him, with the help of dice (*Śat. Br.* V.4.4.6). In the same sacrifice, the Adhvaryu priest throws down on the board the dice with a *mantra.* It is said that the dice-board is the same as 'large Agni' and those dice are his coals, thus it is the Agni that he pleases (*ibid.* 23). Prior to this, the Adhvaryu priest takes clarified butter in four ladlings, places a piece of gold on the dice-board and offers (on the dice-board) with a *mantra* (*Vāj. Sam.* X. 29), addressed to Agni (*Śat. Br.* V.4.4.22). The references to dice and dice-board though scanty are important, for the *arthavāda*-s stated in them are important for knowing the symbolic significance and the belief underlying the use of dice in rituals.

The Śrautasūtras mention the dice-play in the context of the rites such as Rājasūya, Agnicayana, Agnyādhāna, Gopitṛyajña, etc.,[25] in which it was so arranged that the king or the sacrificer would win the Kṛta throw, which signified the even number of dice, and which was a lucky throw, while the Kali signified the unlucky throw. The belief in the power of dice, which can make or mar the fortune of the player just by chance, lies at the basis of their use in rituals. The belief can be traced to the *RV* in the Gambler's hymn, where it is said that the dice are not afraid of the wrath even of the mighty and that even the lord of men salutes them (*RV* X. 34.8). The dice are compared with fire (*ibid.* 9 - *divyā aṅgārāḥ)*, which is, obviously, due to their colour, which is *babhru* (tawny), as mentioned in the hymn (*ibid.* 5). It is patent that the dice were held in awe due to their being an aspect of the fire-god. Again their power of making a man rich or poor instantly, without any obvious reason, led to the belief in their having the power of divination. Yāska refers to the custom of throwing dice against a person to decide his claim in property, probably current in his times, while commenting on *RV* (I.124.7), which mentions the goddess Dawn (Uṣas) as a woman having no brother and claiming a share.[26] It is worthy of taking a note that the names of the eras (*yuga*-s*)* are originated from the names of dice, as the latter occur in the Vedic tradition, where they do not indicate the *yuga*-s.[27] The *arthavāda* that the dice-board is 'large Agni' and the dice are 'his coals', in spite of being the ritual metaphors, are, thus, based on the belief regarding dice, which first originated among folks and later on entered the Vedic rituals.[28] The dice-play in ritual is not restricted to the Vedic ritual tradition alone, but obtains among other peoples as a means of divination.[29]

Eclipse

Though there is no direct reference to eclipse in the Vedic literature, it is very patent from the myth of the demon Svarbhānu and the sun, which can be traced to the *RV*., as we shall see further. In the Brāhmaṇa-texts, the myth occurs as *arthavāda* to stress the importance of certain *sāman*-s.

The Gavām-ayana *sattra* which extends over ten months (as per one type) or twelve months (as per another type) is a series of Soma-sacrifices. Its middle-most day is called Viṣuvat, with two wings of the series of sacrifices at each side.[30] To stress the importance of the Divākīrtya *sāman*-s on the Viṣuvat day, the *Pañc. Br.* states the mythical account of the demon Svarbhānu as *arthavāda.* It is said that once the demon Svarbhānu struck the sun with darkness, but the gods drove away the darkness from the sun by means of the (chanting of the) Divākīrtya *sāman*-s. The Divākīrtya *sāman*-s metaphorically are said to be the rays of the sun, by which they take hold of the sun (*Pañc. Br.* IV. 6.12,13). The *Pañc. Br.* states the same myth of Svarbhānu and the sun as *arthavāda* to praise the Svara *sāman*-s *(ibid.* IV. 5.1,2). These *sāman*-s are chanted on the three days in the first half of the year preceding the Viṣuvat day and three days in the second half of the year following the Viṣuvat day, with the result the days themselves are called the Svarasāman days. The *Pañc. Br.*, in the context of the twelve-day sacrifice, while laying down the *sāman*-s of the Ārbhavapavamāna laud of the eighth day, states the importance of the Bhāsa *sāman* through the etymology of the word *bhāsa.*[31] The *arthavāda* here again is the same having the mythical account of Svarbhānu. But unlike the two accounts mentioned above, here Atri (and not the gods), by reciting the Bhāsa *sāman*, repelled the darkness and so shone the sun again (*ibid.* XIV. 11. 12, 14).

The myth of Svarbhānu can be traced to the *RV*, where the seer Atri is said to have found with the ('fourth') *mantra* (*turīyeṇa brahmaṇā*) the sun, when it was hidden by the demon Svarbhānu and to have placed him (i.e. the sun) in the sky (*RV.* V. 40.6, 8). The *AV* also mentions this myth (*AV* XIII. 24. 12, 36). The *Śat. Br.* mentions Atri, the Hotṛ priest of the *ṛṣi*-s dispelling darkness and states that the sacrificer (in the Agniṣṭoma sacrifice) gives some gold to an Ātreya (i.e. one of Ātreya descent), for gold is light and by that lustre Atri dispelled darkness (*Śat. Br.* IV. 3.4.21).[32]

The mythical account, coming as *arthavāda*, of the demon Svarbhānu and the sun and also figuring in the *RV*, *AV* and the *Tait. Saṁ.*, is a clear indication of a solar eclipse, which had taken place in the hoary past. It was a 'total' eclipse of the sun, as is indicated in the mythical account and was an event to be remembered and also to be recorded in the Saṁhitā-s and the Brāhmaṇa-s. The pseudo-myth in the *RV* of the demon (Svarbhānu) taking the sun in his clutches got developed later in the *Mb.* and the Purāṇa-s, in a full-fledged myth of the demon Rāhu (-Ketu) swallowing the sun and the moon. The original myth however is of a demon seizing the sun, which is found in other mythologies also, with a slight change in that instead of a demon, we have at times a fierce beast chasing the sun or the moon, finally swallowing them.[33] The belief thus is universal.

Regarding Atri's role in rescuing the sun from the clutches of the demon, Tilak referring to *RV* (V. 40.6,8), where the Svarbhānu myth with a mention of Atri occurs for the first time says that an eclipse of the sun was then first observed with any pretensions to accuracy by the sage Atri.[34] This might be true, but this actual experience, Atri must have also 'seen' with his mental power and hence issued forth a *mantra* (*'brahmaṇā'* as occurs in *RV* IV. 40.6) from his mouth, which was regarded as the rescuer of the sun from the demon. The same power of the *mantra* is eulogised, when the importance of the various *sāman*-s to be chanted in this regard, is spoken of by the *Pañc. Br.*, as we have noted already.[35] Even in modern times in India, there is seen a practice of reciting *mantra*-s during the period of the solar or the lunar eclipse. Again there are seen instructions for giving gifts to avert the 'evil' befalling these two celestial luminaries,[36] for in their absence the world would be plunged in blinding darkness.[37]

Enclosing sticks (*paridhi*-s)

In the context of the New-moon and Full-moon sacrifices, the three enclosing-sticks (*paridhi*-s) are to be laid down around the fire (i.e. the Āhavanīya fire). The *arthavāda*, which is in the form of a mythical account, runs as follows— Agni's three elder brothers perished while carrying an offering to the gods. Agni (which was found at the fourth time), being afraid, ran away and entered the waters. The gods found him and invited him to their side, to carry the offerings given to them. Agni agreed, but on one condition, the condition being whatever of the offerings, when taken in the ladle, fell outside the enclosing-sticks, that would be the share of his (Agni's) three brothers, who had left. The enclosing-sticks are to be put to smite away the *rakṣas*-es. He makes the sticks touch one another, so that the *rakṣas*-es may not creep through (*Tait. Sam.* II.6.6.1-2). The point to be noted is that no enclosing-stick is to be put in front of the Āhavanīya fire (i.e. to the east), for the sun rises in the east (i.c. in front) and smites away the *rakṣas*-es (*ibid.* 3). The *Śat. Br.* also has the same *arthavāda* to state but with some more details. Here Agni says that as the Vaṣaṭ-call (i.e. the sound Vaṣaṭ) has struck the earlier Agnis, he is afraid of that sound. So the gods should enclose him with three Agnis (i.e. in the form of the enclosing-sticks on three sides), so that the Vaṣaṭ-call, which is (as though) a 'thunderbolt' will not strike him down. On this, the three Agnis also ask a share in the sacrifice from the gods, which they grant by saying that the offering which falls outside the enclosure, that which is offered just upon them (i.e. enclosures) and that which is offered in the fire, will belong to them and will satisfy them (*Śat. Br.* I.3.3.13-16). The enclosing sticks are said to be the divine Hotṛ-priests (*ibid.* I.8.3.10).

The *arthavāda* (in both the texts) noted above, is important for more than one ways. It speaks of the belief in the protective barriers or enclosures, which can thwart the attacks from evil powers. The 'line drawn by Lakṣmaṇa (*lakṣmaṇareṣā*)', the mention of which occurs in one of the versions of the *Rām.*,[38] can be traced to the practice of putting the enclosing-sticks (*paridhi*-s) on the sides of the altar (of the Āhavanīya fire). The east, i.e. fourth side, is guarded by the sun. This has the age-old belief, supported by actual observation at its basis, that the east is the quarter of the rising sun. The mention of the Vaṣaṭ sound is again important, for the utterance of this sound in high, middle or low tone decides the future condition of the sacrificer.[39] In the mythical account of the *arthavāda* which we have noted above, the utterance of the Vaṣaṭ sound seems to be in the high tone, for the Vaṣat is said to be a thunderbolt.[40] The belief here is seen in the efficacy of certain sounds, which are one of the aspects of Speech.[41]

Enclosed Place

We have seen above that the enclosing sticks serve for protection. Protective measure obviously is for guarding some secret. It is said that they perform the sacrifice in an enclosed place. The sacrifice here is for the *pitṛ*-s (Pitṛyajña). Secret indeed are the Fathers and secret also is that which is enclosed (*Śat. Br.* II. 6.1.20). In the rite of consecration for the Agniṣṭoma sacrifice, they enclose the hall on every side so that it should not rain upon the sacrificer, while being consecrated. The *arthavāda* points out that he who is consecrated, truly draws near to the gods and becomes one of the deities. The gods are secreted from men and secret also is what is enclosed on every side (*ibid.* III. 1.1.8). They enclose the *sadas* (the sacrificial hall) as well as the Havirdhāna shed on all sides. The *arthavāda* states that it is not proper for any one to see the 'procreation' (deed). Even when a husband and wife are seen by any one, while they are carrying on copulation, they move away from each other. Hence one should not look into the *sadas* or the Havirdhāna, for it is as if he were seeing the act of copulation. One may look through the door, for the door is made by the gods (*ibid.* IV. 6.7.9,10). The same concept of divine secrecy is seen when in the rite of Agnicayana, he encloses the Gārhapatya fire-place with enclosing stones (*pariśrit*-s), for they are the womb. He thus encloses the seed (i.e. Agni) cast in the womb (*ibid.* VII. 1.1.12).

Fast

In the context of the New-moon and Full-moon sacrifices, the *Śat. Br.* has an interesting discussion to give regarding 'fast' to be observed on the preparatory day, i.e. the Upavasatha day. Eggeling states that the discussion here refers to the evening meal which the sacrificer is allowed to take after he has performed the Agnihotra.[42] Āṣāḍha Sāvayasa explains the word '*upavasatha*' as the day when the gods betake themselves to the sacrificer's house and abide by him or by the fires (fr. the root *upa* + √*vas*) in his house. He points out that the gods see through the mind of man and know that when he enters on the vow of consecration, he has already decided to sacrifice to them the next morning (when they would be partaking of the oblations). Now, it would be improper on the part of the sacrificer to take food, before the gods, who are staying with him have eaten (and that would be on the next day). So the sacrificer should not take any food on the Upavasatha day. But according to Yājñavalkya, if the sacrificer does not eat, he becomes a sacrificer to the manes (*pitṛ*-s), and if he eats on that day, he eats before the gods have eaten. Hence he should eat that, which when eaten, is regarded as not eaten. Therefore he should eat only what grows in the forest, be it forest-plants or the fruit of trees, which forest-produce he normally does not eat daily (*Śat. Br.* I.1.1.7-10). It is interesting to note that the thought expressed by Yājñavalkya about observing fast on the Upavasatha day turned into a practice which was followed in later times and is observed even to this day in India.[43]

However in the *Śat. Br.* itself in the context of the Agnicayana rite occurs a thought, which speaks of total abstention from food on the Upavasatha day. When the Great Fire-altar is ready, the sacrificer (i.e. the Adhvaryu priest on his behalf) presses the Soma and offers it in the fire or on the fire-altar. Thereby he bestows immortality upon Agni. Now on the preparatory day (Upavasatha day) of this, only milk as fast-food is laid down for the consecrated sacrificer. In this connection, a mythical account by way of *arthavāda* states that when the nectar of immortality went away from the gods, they decided to seek for it by toil and penance. Having become consecrated, they were living on fast-milk (*vrata).* For this fast-milk, they first resorted to three teats of the cow, then to two teats and lastly to one teat. On the day of preparation, they completely abstained from food. The perfection in the practice of penance requires total abstention from food (*ibid.* IX. 5.1.1-9). However a moderate view occurs in the context of the Agnyādhāna rite (*ibid.* II.1.4.1,2).

Fathers (*pitṛ*-s)

The details which occur in the context of the Piṇḍapitṛyajña give a fair idea of the beliefs and practices about the Fathers (*pitṛ*-s). A mythical account occurs in the *Śat. Br.* in the context of the Piṇḍapitṛyajña. When the living beings approached Prajāpati, on their request, he told them the manner in which they were to live (*Śat. Br.* II. 4.2.1-5). When the Fathers approach him, wearing the cord on the right shoulder[45] and bending the left knee, he tells them that their eating will be monthly, the *svadhā* (the 'call' uttered while offering oblations to the Fathers) their swiftness of thought and the moon their light (*ibid.* II. 4.2.2). In the Piṇḍapitṛyajña the Fathers are offered three balls of cooked rice on the New-moon day, for on that day the moon who is the King Soma and thus the food of gods is not seen. Thereby a concord is established between the gods and Fathers (*ibid.* 7, 18). The rice balls are offered to the Fathers in the afternoon, for the forenoon belongs to the gods, midday to men and afternoon to the Fathers (*ibid.* 8).[46] The same practice is followed by the Smṛti tradition. The *Manu Sm.* says that for giving offerings to the Fathers in the Śrāddha rites, the second half of the month is better than the first half and so is the afternoon (or the second half of the day) than the first half (*Manu. Sm.* III. 278). While offering (the rice-balls) to the Fathers, prior to the offering, he draws with the wooden sword a line south of the Dakṣiṇa fire and then lays down a firebrand at the farther end of the line. If he presents that food to the Fathers, without having laid down a firebrand, the *asura*-s and the *rakṣas*-es would certainly tamper with it. Agni is the repeller of these (*Śat. Br.* II. 4.2.13-15). The *Manu Sm.* also states that prior to the offerings to be given to the *pitṛ*-s, the offerings to the gods are to be given, for the latter serve as a protective measure for the Śrāddha-rite, i.e. the *pitṛ-kārya* (*Manu Sm.* III. 203-204). The *Śat. Br.* states that after removing the cooked rice (for preparing the rice-balls) from the fire, he offers to the gods two libations in the fire. In the rite of establishing the fires and in performing the New-moon and Full-moon sacrifices, the householder (sacrificer) resorts to the gods. But now as he has to offer to the Fathers, he first propitiates the gods and being permitted by them, he presents that food, (i.e. rice-balls) to the Fathers (*Śat. Br.* II. 4.2.11). In the rite of Piṇḍapitṛyajña, the *Śat. Br.* mentions pulling down the (unwoven) fringe of the upper garment (*nīviṁ udvṛhya*) and then bowing down to the *pitṛ*-s (i.e. Fathers). (*ibid.* 24). The *Śat. Br.* here does not state any *arthavāda* in this regard, except that such a fringe of the garment (*nīvi*) is sacred to the Fathers (*pitṛdevatyā*). The *arthavāda* occurs in the *Tait. Br.*, while laying down the pulling of the fringe of garment (and placing it on the rice-balls to be offered to the Fathers). It is said that the Fathers while returning to their abode (in the other world) take away the heroic son of the householder or bestow on him such a son. This depends on their being dissatisfied or satisfied with the offerings given to them by the householder. Taking into account the possibility of their taking away the householder's son, pulling down the *daśā*, i.e. fringe (and placing it on the rice-balls) is enjoined *(Tait. Br.* I.3.10.7). The *Tait. Br.* lays down that when the householder (sacrificer) is advanced in years, he should pull out a hair (from his chest and place it on the rice-balls), for he is near to the Fathers (with many years of his life being passed away and less number of years remaining of it) (*ibid.).* It is clear that the hair of the sacrificer stands for his own self and so does the fringe of his garment. That the garment is the very form of a person can be seen, when we take into account the *arthavāda*-s regarding "Garment". By offering the fringe of the garment or the hair, the sacrificer makes a symbolic offering of his own self and propitiates the Fathers.

The Fathers are associated with the southern quarter (*Śat. Br.* II.6.1.9) and also with the fire, i.e. Agni, named Kavyavāhana, while for the gods the fire is Havyavāhana Agni (*ibid.* 30).

Food

Importance of food is well recognised when the *Jaim. Br.* equates food with *Śrī* (glory). It points out the twofold form of food *viz.* which one drinks and which one eats (*Jaim. Br.* III. 349, 350). The importance of food in the material world and also the quantity of food to be eaten are the points mentioned in a couple of *arthavāda*-s. In the context of the sacrifice Odanasava, occurs a mythical account that Prajāpati created beings, but they ran away from him. He then saw the *odana*, i.e. cooked rice, and possessed it. The creatures not finding proper food anywhere, resorted to Prajāpati. Whosoever sacrifices with this Odanasava, to him resort the creatures. Obviously this is the importance of food (*Tait. Br.* II. 7.9.1).

In the Agnicayana rite, when the Āhavanīya altar is to be made, ploughing of that piece of ground is laid down, as part of this. The furrows which are to be made at this ploughing are sixteen in number. The *arthavāda* stated here is that Agni-Prajāpati consists of sixteen parts and by drawing sixteen furrows (in which seeds are sown), the sacrificer places food in Prajāpati, proportionate to his body. A piece of worldly advice here is that the food which is proportionate to the body satisfies and does not harm; that which is too much harms, but that which is too little does not satisfy (*Śat. Br.* VII. 2.2.17).

In the fourth Forty-nine-day rite, the last but one day is the Mahāvrata day. The *arthavāda* while extolling the Mahāvrata day says that this (Mahā-) *vrata* is food. Food satiates nowhere but in the mouth. In that after ten days of the Dvādaśāha sacrifice, when they undertake to perform the (Mahā-) *vrata*, food is placed into the mouth (*Pañc. Br.* XXIV. 14.7). It is interesting to note that the Brāhmaṇa-text has made use of even a practice of daily observation.

Forefinger

An interesting belief occurs in the *Kauṣ. Br.* regarding forefinger in an *arthavāda*-passage in the context of the Agnihotra. The ritual is of partaking (milk) in the rite, by means of his forefinger (*pradeśinyā*). He thus eats twice. With the first eating, he makes the foetuses happy and so without eating directly, the foetuses do survive and breathe. With second eating, he delights birds. Hence though the birds eat multifarious matter, they exude what is as it were white (*Kauṣ. Br.* II. 2).

Here the eating or partaking is of milk (though the word for 'milk' is not there), for in the next statements in this very passage, there is a reference to eating with the offering ladle, licking that ladle or cleansing that ladle. Moreover 'milk' is the substance (*dravya)* used in the Agnihotra rite. It is interesting to note that the forefinger with which he eats, came to be associated in later times with offspring. In this regard, the mythical account of the birth of Māndhātṛ can be taken into consideration.[47] The second eating with the forefinger is meant for the birds. The *arthavāda* speaking of the white-coloured exudation of the birds in spite of their eating anything clearly displays the curiosity of the ritualists to know the ornithological fact and their own solution to this riddle-like fact, though in a humorous tone!

Forehead

In the context of the Agnihotra rite, while enjoining, the *mantra* (recitation) with the utterance 'Svāhā', the *Tait. Br.* states a mythical account. Prajāpati created Agni and after him the creatures. Agni not getting any share (of offerings) from Prajāpati left him, taking with him the creatures, Prajāpati ran after Agni but in vain, ultimately wiping off the perspiration from his forehead (*rarāṭāt).* That perspiration became *ghṛta* (the accumulated clarified butter). The *arthavāda* here speaks of a belief that a person on the right side of whose head, the hair are as if rubbed off, is said to be a seat of the goddess Jyeṣṭhalakṣmī, who is said to belong to Prajāpati (*Tait. Br.* II.1.2.2). The *Tait. Br.* points out that as Prajāpati rubbed off the hair from his forehead, there are no hair on the forehead of any person (*ibid.).* To turn to the reference to Jyeṣṭhalakṣmī. In the Puranic tradition, this goddess came to be known as Alakṣmī,[48] the elder sister of Lakṣmī. Sāyaṇa in his comm. on this passage of the *Tait. Br.* points out that Jyeṣṭhalakṣmī is the goddess of poverty and hence to be worshipped, following the Jyeṣṭhā-*vrata* (Jyeṣṭhā-vow). The *arthavāda* is important in two ways, pointing out the belief about the forehead and also speaking of the origin of an important goddess.

The account from the *Mait. Sam.* in the context of the Agnihotra rite, has already mentioned the *arthavāda* which we have noted above. But it somewhat differs in details. It is said that Prajāpati created Agni from his head (*mūrdhataḥ).* He rubbed the place whence Agni was produced. From that (place) flowed out blood. When he wiped it out (with hand), there came out the Udumbara tree. The *Mait. Sam.* says that due to generation of Agni from the head and of the Udumbara tree due to wiping the blood with the hand, no hair is seen on one's forehead (forehead being nearest to the head!) and also on one's palms. A person who has hair rubbed off or plucked up on the right side of the head is known as Jyeṣṭhalakṣmī (*Mait. Sam.* I. 8.1).

A mythical account coming by way of *arthavāda* occurs in the *Śat. Br.*, glorifying the rite of Agnihotra. Prajāpati being alone in the beginning and so desirous of creating, toiled and generated Agni from his mouth. As there was nothing to eat, Agni turned towards Prajāpati with his mouth wide open. As Prajāpati was frightened at that, his greatness left him. So he thought of an offering to be given in his own self and rubbed his hands. As he rubbed his hands, both the palms of every person even now are hairless (*Śat. Br.* II. 2.4.1-4).[49] He then obtained a butter-offering or a milk-offering (—both of them being of milk).

Gandharva-s

The belief about the *gandharva*-s, mentioned in the *arthavāda*-s (though they are very few) is that they are fond of women, and so can be easily duped with the help of women. They are also said to be guarding the Soma.

In the Agniṣṭoma sacrifice, in the context of the preparatory ceremonies, it is enjoined that the Adhvaryu priest should go to the water with the wives. The *arthavāda* here is in the form of a mythical account, which runs as follows. When the head of the sacrifice was struck off, its sap entered the waters, which the *gandharva*-s, who were guarding the Soma, observed. The gods were worried as to how they could carry off that sap without being noticed by the *gandharva*-s. As the *gandharva*-s were known for their weakness for women, the gods went there with the wives. The *gandharva*-s hankered after the wives and the gods carried off that sap of the sacrifice to a place free from danger (*Śat. Br.* III. 9.3.17-22). In the context of the Agniṣṭoma sacrifice, in the ritual of buying Soma (-shoots) from the Soma-seller by giving him the Somakrayaṇī cow), there is stated a mythical account. Soma was in the sky and the gods were on the earth. Gāyatrī flew to the sky to bring Soma for the gods and when she was carrying off Soma, the *gandharva* Viśvāvasu stole Soma from her. The gods sent Speech (Vāc — being a 'woman') to the *gandharva*-s, they being fond of women. She became successful in getting back Soma from them and returned to the gods (*ibid.* III. 2.4.1-3).[50] Another belief about the *gandharva*-s (and the *apsaras*-es) is noted by the *Pañc. Br.* in connection with the Aupaśada *stoma* (which is to be chanted in the sacrifice, which bears the same name, i.e. Aupaśada and is a one-day rite).[51] It is said that one who is desirous of obtaining progeny should perform this, which is for the propitiation of the *gandharva*-s and the *apsaras*-es, for they rule over man's possession of progeny and man's want of progeny. These two have a share in the Soma-draught in this sacrifice, being pleased with which they grant progeny to the sacrificer (*Pañc. Br.* XIX. 3. 1-2). As pointed out by Caland, this statement (about the power of the *gandharva*-s and *apsaras*-es) is found here only,[52] though this one-day rite is enjoined elsewhere for obtaining progeny.

Garment

The belief about garment of a person is that it is his own skin or body. In the context of the Agniṣṭoma sacrifice, in the rite of consecration, it is enjoined for the sacrificer to put on a linen garment for completeness (*sarvatvāya eva).* The *arthavāda* states that it (i.e. the garment of linen) is the sacrificer's own skin, which he puts on himself. A mythical account stated here is interesting. The skin which belongs to a cow was formerly on man. With the thought that the cow supported everything here on the earth, the gods put on the cow that skin which originally the man had and with which the cow would be able to endure rain, cold and heat. So they flayed man and put on his skin on the cow. Hence it is that wherever a stalk of grass or some other (sharp) object cuts him, the blood trickles out. The gods then put the garment on him as his skin (*Śat. Br.* III. 1.2.13-16). The garment of the consecrated sacrificer should be a new one for the sake of unimpaired vigour. It should be beaten so that any part of it if an unclean woman has spun or woven may become clean. The new garment should be sprinkled with water to make it clean, or the sacrificer to be consecrated, can have the garment which is worn daily by him after bath, without it being soaked in cleansing substance (*ibid.* 19). Even the sacrificial post (*yūpa)* is wrapped with garments in the Vājapeya sacrifice and here the sacrificial post is equated with the sacrificer. The garment here is said to belong to all deities,[53] which make the sacrificer prosperous (*Tait. Br.* I.3.7.3). In the Horse-sacrifice while giving offering to Pūṣan, Pūṣan being the overlord of roads, securing (safety and) auspiciousness to the horse, the *dakṣiṇā* to the priest consists of a hundred garments. The garment is regarded as the very appearance of a man, for people on seeing a well-dressed man ask, 'Who can this be?' (*Śat. Br.* XIII. 4.1.15). In the Rājasūya sacrifice, thc Adhvaryu priest makes the king put on the garments. The *arthavāda* states that he thereby causes him to be born (*ibid.* V. 3.5.24). The same *arthavāda* occurs when the king is made to put on the garment called *'tārpya'*[54] *(ibid.* V.3.5.20). The belief indicated through these *arthavāda*-s is that a garment worn by a man stands for his body and his outward appearance (while the 'man' as such is a separate entity).[55]

Gods

In the rite of Agnicayana, Soma bricks are placed in front of the naturally-perforated brick (*svayam-ātṛṇṇā).* The *arthavāda* points out that there are two birthplaces, the gods having their birthplace in the east and men in the west. When the (Adhvaryu) priest lays down those bricks in front, he causes the sacrificer to be born from the womb of the gods (*Śat. Br.* VII. 4.2.40).[56] More about the gods we have in the context of churning the fire, when the question is whether it should be before sunrise or after sunrise. The *arthavāda* passage in this context states that the gods are the day. If the sacrificer churns the fire before sunrise, he does not dispel the evil from him (by the sun), and dies before he has attained the full measure of life. The gods are immortal and though there is no hope for the sacrificer of (having) immortality, he attains the full measure of life. As the gods are 'bliss' (*śrīḥ)* so he obtains bliss. As the gods are 'glorious', glorious he will be (*ibid.* II. 1.4.9; X.1.4.14 - *śrīr devāḥ...yaśo devāḥ).* The gods are thirty-three in number (*Jaim. Br.* III. 300). In the *Śat. Br.* in the context of the third pressing of Soma-shoots in the Agniṣṭoma sacrifice, we read that there are three kinds of gods *viz.* the Vasus, the Rudras and the Ādityas. Between these gods are divided the three pressings. The morning pressing belongs exclusively to the Vasus, the midday pressing exclusively to the Rudras and the third pressing to the Ādityas jointly with others (*Śat. Br.* IV. 3.5.1). Sacrifice being of the highest importance in the ritual tradition, even the birth of some of the gods is traced to the sacrificial offering *viz. brahmaudana* (which is also partaken of by the priests, having first offered it to the gods). While enjoining the cooking of the *brahmaudana*, the *arthavāda* is stated in the form of a mythical account. Aditi being desirous of getting son (or sons) cooked *brahmaudana* for the Sādhya-s and the gods. The priests at that time, having offered (some of) the *brahmaudana* to the gods and having partaken (some) of it, gave the remaining to the goddess Aditi. She ate it and bore foetus. To her then were born the gods Dhātṛ and Aryaman. When she cooked the *brahmaudana* for the second time, to her were born Mitra and Varuṇa. At the third time were born the gods Aṁśa and Bhaga, when she cooked the *brahmaudana.* At the fourth time, were born to her the gods Indra and Vivaṣvān. The *Tait. Br.* adds at the end that when he cooks *brahmaudana*, he indeed plants (his) seed (*Tait. Br.* I.1.9.1-3).

The belief that the gods subsist on what is offered to them from this world and the actual observation that the men subsist on what is bestowed on them from the yonder world (in the form of rains and the seasons), are noted by the ritual texts (*Tait. Sam.* III. 2.9.7; *Tait. Br.* II. 2.7.3; *Śat. Br.* I.2.5.24). The *Śat. Br.* states a mythical account in this regard. The *vidhi* in connection with which this account occurs is of spreading the sacrificial grass on the altar. The account runs as follows. Those who made offerings in former times, touched the altar and oblations, while they were sacrificing. They became more sinful. Those who did not sacrifice became righteous. Hence unbelief (*aśraddhā*) in the very concept of sacrifice took possession of men. With the result no sacrificial food then came to the gods from this world, for the gods subsist on what is offered up from this world. Then on the insistence of the gods, Bṛhaspati Āṅgirasa approached men to convince them of the sacrifice, for 'the sacrifice is produced for the gods'. It is in the form of cooked oblations and the altar which is prepared. The men performed sacrifice by touching these two by which action they became more sinful. If they would sacrifice without touching (these two), they would become righteous. By the sacrificial grass (*barhiṣā),* the altar becomes appeased. Hence till the sacrificial grass is spread on the altar, he should sacrifice without touching the two, as mentioned above (*Śat. Br.* I.2.5.24-26). The sacrifice is an act of assistance to the gods, who in turn help human beings by sending timely rains and seasons without upsetting the cosmic order. Similar idea occurs in the *Avesta.* In the Tir Yasht, Tishtrya outdone by Apaosha cries to Ahura Mazda, "O Ahura Mazda! Men do not worship me with sacrifice and praise; should they worship me with sacrifice and praise, they would bring me the strength of ten horses, ten camels, ten bulls, ten mountains, ten rivers" (*Yasht* 8.23, 24). The concept of interdependence of the gods and men was philosophised in later times by the *Bh.G.* in that of Yajñacakra (III. 14-16).

A perfect worldly picture of the gods is met with in an *arthavāda* in the context of the New-moon and Full-moon sacrifices, when the priest announces the oblation to the deity and the Adhvaryu priest is about to take out the oblation. The *arthavāda* states that at this *vidhi*, all the gods draw near to him, thinking 'My name he will take (i.e. announce)! My name he will take!' By calling out the names of the gods, he establishes concord among the gods gathered together (*Śat. Br.* I.1.2.18). The *arthavāda* is based on the belief that the name stands for a person[57] and so the anxiety of the gods to attend this ritual (*vidhi*), while the names are being announced.[58] The *arthavāda* here depicts a worldly scene of any gathering where gifts are being announced and distributed, the gods here standing on par with the human beings with an 'eye' on their respective shares. The *arthavāda* which follows the above one tells that whichever deities are chosen, they while accepting the oblation, consider it as an obligation that they are bound to fulfil whatever wish the sacrificer entertains (*ibid.* 19). This shows that the concept of the 'give-and-take' relationship between the gods and the human beings is deep-rooted in the ritual tradition right from the beginning.

The human behaviour of the gods is marked in the context of the Agniṣṭoma sacrifice. When the sacrificial victim is being immolated, the Adhvaryu priest addresses the Hotṛ priest to recite to the deity Manotā for the oblation (of the sacrificial victim). The Hotṛ priest recites the hymn (*RV* VI. 1.1-13) to the deity Agni, who is Manotā because the said hymn addresses Agni as — "O Agni! The first thinker (*manotā)* of this hymn..." (*ibid.* VI. 1.1 ab).[59] The *arthavāda* in this connection, taking the help of etymology, is both interesting as well as enlightening on the human behaviour and psyche of the gods. When the victim is being immolated, all the deities come near the victim and everyone of them thinks that his name will be chosen by the sacrificer or the priest for the sacrificial victim to be offered to. The minds (*manāṁsi)* of all these deities are fixed (*otāni)* upon that victim. By addressing to Manotā (*manas-ota)* Agni, he thus satisfies the minds of all the deities (*Śat. Br.* III. 8.3.14). The same *arthavāda* speaking of the gods' anxiety to have the victim, occurs in the *Kauṣ. Br.* in the context of the Soma-sacrifice. It is said here that Agni, Speech and cow are the three Manotā-s of the gods, as their minds are woven (i.e. fixed) in these three. But all the Manotā-s unite in Agni. So for Agni only the prayer is (*Kauṣ. Br.* X. 6).

Having noted the beliefs about the gods in general, as seen in the *arthavāda*-passages, we are taking into account the beliefs about the gods, which have specific importance in the ritual texts.

(a) Prajāpati

Sacrifice being regarded as the pivot of all existence, the god Prajāpati identified with Agni assumes the highest importance. The ritual metaphors coming often by way of *arthavāda* are self-eloquent.

Prajāpati is sacrifice (*Śat. Br.* I.1.1.13; XIII.3.6.7, etc.). Sacrifice is Prajāpati (*ibid.* V. 2.1.2; VI. 4.1.6, etc.). Prajāpati is that sacrifice which is here performed (*ibid.* V. 3.3.15). Prajāpati is identified with the Father Time, i.e. the Year or *vice versa* (*ibid.* IV. 5.5.12; V.1.2.9; V.1.3.2; V.2.1.2; VI.2.2.5; XIII.3.6.7; *Jaim. Br.* II. 393; II.427). Even the units of Time are said to be the joints of Prajāpati. After Prajāpati had created the living beings, his joints (*parvāṇi*) became loosened (*visraṁsuḥ*). Prajāpati indeed is the Year; his joints are the joints of day and night, i.e. the two twilights, the Full-moon day and the New-moon day and the beginnings of seasons (*Śat. Br.* I.6.3.35). The *Jaim. Br.* says that the day and night is the whole (*kṛtsnaḥ*) Prajāpati (*Jaim. Br.* II. 358). Prajāpati, in the ritual texts has the name 'Ka'. The god Ka doubtless is Prajāpati (*Śat. Br.* IV. 5.6.4; VII. 3.1.20).[60] The oft-repeated concept about Prajāpati is that he is seventeenfold. This is already dealt with by us in the chapter on "Numbers," when the number "Seventeen" was taken into account. Prajāpati (or Agni-Prajāpati) being the main god in the sacrifice, not only sacrifice but several other entities are equated with Prajāpati.[61] Of all the animals, goat is regarded as a form of

Agni as also of Prajāpati, the deity of sacrifice. Goat is believed to have sprung from Prajāpati's head and Prajāpati is Agni (*ibid.* VI. 5.4.16). While enjoining the spreading of the goat-skin, it is said that the goats are most clearly of Prajāpati and truly the he-goat is no other than Prajāpati (*ibid.* V.2.1.24). Prajāpati being the god of creation and so the lord of creatures, is believed to be bi-sexual — the Great He-She. Rice and barley are the (two) breasts of Prajāpati, by which he sustains these creatures (*Jaim. Br.* III. 346).

The oft-repeated expression in the case of Prajāpati is that he is 'undefined' (*anirukta*)[62] or the *mantra*-s to him are 'undefined' (*anirukta*).[63] It is said that the *mantra* which actually states the name of a deity and thus is *nirukta* ('specifically named' — '*niḥśeṣeṇa ukta*') has some kind of limit and thus it is restricted (*Śat. Br.* V.4.4.13). Prajāpati is both defined (*nirukta*) and undefined (*anirukta*) and thus limited (*parimita*) and unlimited (*aparimita*). When he offers with a *yajus* formula, that is defined (*nirukta*) and thus limited form of Pajāpati; what he offers silently, that is the undefined (*anirukta*) and unlimited form of Prajāpati (*ibid.* XIV. 1.2.18). At several places in the Brāhmaṇa-texts, the concepts of *anirukta* and *tūṣṇīm* ('silently') are combined. To take an example. While preparing the altar (of the Āhavanīya fire) in the Agnicayana rite, the priest has to undertake ploughing, which is symbolic of providing food for Prajāpati. The (Adhvaryu) priest places a bunch of *darbha*-grass at the meeting of the furrows. He places that bunch in the middle silently (*tūṣṇīm*), for what is silent is 'undefined' (*anirukta*) and the 'undefined' is everything. Thus with his silent action, he places all and unlimited food for Prajāpati (*ibid.* VII. 2.3.3).

(b) Agni

The concept of sacrifice centres round that of Agni, with the result the ritual-texts teem with the then beliefs about Agni. Some of these, spoken of by the *arthavāda*-s, are worthy of consideration. As a part of guest-reception given to Soma (the King), they kindle the fire, for Agni is the sacrificial victim of the gods. So they (as though) slay Agni, for in this world when a human king or another deserving person comes, they slay an ox or a cow that miscarries (*Ait. Br.* I.15 = 3.4). The *arthavāda* is important, for it speaks of both, the belief about Agni and the practice of honouring the guest in the Vedic times. As they kindle (lit. 'churn' — '*manthanti*') Agni with hands, Agni is a first-born child as it were (*ibid.* I.16=3.5). The deities are all forms of Agni (*Śat. Br.* I.6.2.8; VI. 3.3.21; *Jaim. Br.* I.342). It is in the fire that they make offering to all deities (*ibid).* The *Ait. Br.* in the context of the Praüga *śastra* (litany), explains in details how the priest (i.e. on behalf of the sacrificer) follows in recitation verses, the form of respective deities, they all being forms of Agni (*Ait. Br.* III.4 = 11.4). Agni is the safest among the gods for one's approach. He is the most tender-hearted. He is the nearest of the gods (*Śat. Br.* I.6.2.9-11). A worldly belief is noted when it is enjoined that Agni (Ukhya Agni), should be carried by the sacrificer during the period of his consecration (*dīkṣā)* for a year, in the rite of Agnicayana. This fire is afterwards transferred to the newly built Gārhapatya and from there to the Great Fire-altar, to be the Āhavanīya Agni. The *arthavāda* is that the sacrificer who carries about Agni becomes pregnant with all beings and with all gods. But if the sacrificer does not carry about Agni (i.e. Ukhya Agni) for a year and builds the Great Fire-altar, he kills all the beings in the form of an embryo. He who kills a human embryo is despised. How much more then he who kills Agni, for Agni is a god (*ibid.* IX. 5.1.62). By the time of the Smṛti texts, feticide came to be regarded as a sin.[64] Though the maximum limit for carrying about Agni is a year, it could be reduced to six months. The *Śat. Br.* states that a six-month (Agni) is the last he may build. The *arthavāda* based on actual observation coupled with the knowledge of embryology points out that the six-month embryos are the last that live when born (*ibid.* 63).

In the Agniṣṭoma sacrifice, it is enjoined that he should carry fire round the sacrificial cake (*puroḍāśa*) (*ibid.* I.2.2.13). Again in the same context, it is said that having taken a fire-brand, the Agnīdh carries fire round the victim (*ibid.* III. 8.1.6). At both the places, the *arthavāda* is the same and speaks of the belief about Agni's power of destroying evil spirits. It is said that by carrying fire round the sacrificial cake or sacrificial victim, he encloses it with an unbroken fence, lest the evil spirits, the *rakṣas*-es should seize upon it, for Agni is the repeller of the *rakṣas*-es (*ibid.* I.2.2.13; III. 8.1.6).[65]

As we have already noted in the chapter on "Sun, Moon and Constellations", Agni is another form of the sun. It is said that whatever sin a man commits in the daytime, it is the sun that makes him commit that. Whatever sin is committed at the night, Agni makes him commit that. Agni follows the sun, when the latter rises (*Jaim. Br.* I.9-10). This is a reference to the kindling of and offering in fires in the Agnihotra rite in the morning and evening (also *Tait. Br.* II. 1.2.9-10).

Here are a couple of *arthavāda*-s which speak of the attitude of familiarity towards Agni, even to the extent of taking him to be an animal, carrying a load.

In the rite of Agnicayana, in the first layer, he takes Agni in (him), by muttering the *mantra*, 'Within me, I first take Agni...' (*Vāj. Sam.* XIII.1). This he does while standing. But he builds Agni (i.e. the Great Fire-altar) by laying down the bricks, while sitting. The *arthavāda* here is interesting, based on worldly observation. As Agni is thought to be an animal, the animal having received the foetus standing, gives birth after lying down (*Śat. Br.* VII. 4.1.2). This is pointed out because when he has muttered the *mantra* from the *Vāj. Sam.* (XIII. 1), he has taken Agni inside and from the same Agni, he generates Agni, i.e. the Great Āhavanīya fire-altar, which is the very body of Agni-Prajāpati (*Śat. Br.* VII. 4.1.1).

In the context of the New-moon and Full-moon sacrifices, it is said that he sweeps (once) Agni with a *mantra* (*Vāj. Saṃ.* II. 7a), and then he sweeps thrice over Agni silently (*Śat. Br.* I.4.4.15). From practical point of view this cleansing is for making the fire blaze all the more.[66] The *arthavāda* is interesting for it explains this act of cleansing the fire (Agni), taking Agni to be an animal, carrying the sacrifice to the gods, on the lines of worldly phenomenon of an animal, carrying a load to a destination. After harnessing the animal, one impels him to go with the words, 'Go on! pull'. Similarly he strikes Agni with a lash[67] with the thought, 'Go on and convey the sacrifice to the gods' (*ibid.*).

The *arthavāda*-s in the context of the New-moon and Full-moon sacrifices, are worthy of taking a note, as they give practical instructions useful in day-to-day life. The Full-moon offering is sacred to Agni-Soma (*ibid.* I.8.3.1,2) and the New-moon offering to Indra-Agni (*ibid.* 3,4), thus Agni figuring in both the offerings. Stressing the importance of Agni, the *Śat. Br.* states that as the sacrificial offering to any deity is offered in the sacrificial fire (Agni) itself, he should announce the offering to Agni alone (*ibid.* I.6.2.7). As Agni is the safest (*addhātama*)[68] among the gods, the most tender-hearted of the gods and the nearest of those to be approached (*ibid.* 9-11), a person should have recourse if need be to such persons only (*ibid.*). The *arthavāda* here, while giving a practical suggestion, also speaks of the Vedic belief about Agni as a god-head. It is said that the gods themselves take the help of Agni and being guarded by Agni (Agni-s) on all sides reached the heaven, as they were afraid of the *asura*-s and *rakṣas*-es (*ibid.* I.6.1. 11-12). The *Kauṣ. Br.* says that prior to going to the heaven, the gods placed the dreadful forms of Agni apart and made him have an auspicious, helpful and sacrifice-worthy form for (the well-being of) man. In the waters they placed his form as flowing (*pavamānam* cf. *pavamāna* Soma in the *RV* at several places), in the wind his form as purifying and in the sun, his form as bright (*Kauṣ. Br.* I.1).

(c) Viṣṇu

The oft-repeated expression in the case of Viṣṇu is that Viṣṇu is sacrifice (*Śat. Br.* I.1.2.13; III. 6.3.16; III.6.4.2,9; XIV. 1.1.6; *Jaim. Br.* III. 129, etc.). Agni is the lowest of the gods and Viṣṇu the highest. Between them are all other deities (*Ait. Br.* I.1). According to Sāyaṇa's comm. on this passage, the terms *'avama'* (lowest) and *'parama'* (highest) refer to the place of the deities in the litanies of the Agniṣṭoma sacrifice, in the context of the consecration rite for which, occur these two terms. The Ājya *śastra* is addressed to Agni and the *śastra*, i.e. the Agnimāruta, contains a verse to Viṣṇu. The *Ait. Br.* says that Agni and Viṣṇu are the guardians of consecration of the gods (*ibid.* I.4).

As Viṣṇu is sacrifice, the mythical account in the context of the Pravargya rite states how through austerity, fervour, faith, sacrifice and oblations, Viṣṇu first compassed the end of the sacrifice and became the most excellent of the gods (*Śat. Br.* XIV. 1.1.4-5). The account runs further pointing out how Viṣṇu — the yonder Āditya (the sun) — is Sacrifice personified. So when Viṣṇu's head is cut off due to his bowstring being gnawed by the ants, the Pravargya (rite) is the head of the Sacrifice (i.e. head of Viṣṇu) put on again and thus Sacrifice becomes complete (*ibid.* 9 ff.). Hence it is that Viṣṇu is regarded as the highest of all deities (*Jaim. Br.* II. 192).

In the New-moon and Full-moon sacrifices, there is enjoined for the sacrificer taking of strides (named Viṣṇu-strides — *viṣṇukrama*-s). The *arthavāda* has the pseudo- myth of the Ṛgvedic deity Viṣṇu in view. In the *RV*, Viṣṇu is known as *urugāya* (wide-striding one) also *tredhā vicakramāṇaḥ* (striding out triply), these expressions often being repeated. The *Śat. Br.* states that Viṣṇu by striding obtained for the gods that all-pervading power, which now belongs to them. In the ritual context, Viṣṇu as the sacrifice obtains that same pervading power by his strides for the sacrificer. Hence the sacrificer takes the Viṣṇu-strides (*Śat. Br.* I.9.3. 8, 9 and thus imitates Viṣṇu for obtaining power, the principle of ritual magic being 'Like produces like'. In the Rājasūya sacrifice, the sacrificer-king takes three Viṣṇu-steps on a tiger's skin (which is spread out). Viṣṇu's three steps are these three worlds. By taking three Viṣṇu-steps, having ascended these worlds, the sacrificer-king is high above everything (*ibid.* V.4.2.6). It is quite patent that the Ṛgvedic pseudo-myth of Viṣṇu was pressed into service in the ritual tradition to show the all-pervading power of sacrifice.

The concept of Viṣṇu as dwarf is marked in the ritual tradition itself. At a rite in the Rājasūya sacrifice (Triṣaṁyukta offering), together with a cake on eleven potsherds for Agni and Viṣṇu and a pap (*caru)* for Indra and Viṣṇu, to Viṣṇu (exclusively) is offered a cake on three potsherds or a pap (*ibid.* V.2.5.1). It is said that for this offering to Viṣṇu, a dwarfish bull is the *dakṣiṇā* given, for the dwarf belongs to Viṣṇu (*ibid.* 4). A mythical account pertaining to the dwarf-size of Viṣṇu is interesting. The gods and the *asura*-s, sprung from Prajāpati were contending for supremacy. Once when the gods were defeated, the *asura*-s taking hold of the whole world began to divide it between themselves. The gods being perturbed at this, approached the *asura*-s, placing Viṣṇu in the shape of this very sacrifice at their head, and requested the *asura*-s for a share in the earth. The *asura*-s grudgingly agreed for a share of the earth as much as that Viṣṇu would lie upon and for no more. The gods were glad, even though Viṣṇu was a dwarf (and would occupy a small area, as seen apparently). Having laid Viṣṇu down eastwards, the gods enclosed him on all the three sides with metres *viz.* Gāyatrī, Triṣṭubh and Jagatī. Having placed Agni (the fire) on the east side, the gods went on worshipping and toiling with Viṣṇu, i.e. sacrifice, and obtained with Viṣṇu (=sacrifice) the entire earth.[69] As they obtained (fr. *sam* + √*vid* — 'to obtain, get'), so is the altar called '*vedi*' (*ibid.* I.2.5. 1-7). The *Jaim. Br.* states a mythical account, which explains the cause of Viṣṇu's dwarfness.

The gods (normally) do not sleep. However due to extreme toiling they closed (their eyes). Of them, who being deluded were sleeping, the *asura*-s carried away the lustre, power and vigour. Viṣṇu noticed it. The gods when awakened were upset (at this). Viṣṇu told them what happened, and sent them to waters for the search (of their lustre, power and vigour). They observed a peak rising up from the surface of waters. The gods having caught hold of that with the Vyāhṛti-s (sacred utterances *viz.* Bhūḥ, Bhuvaḥ and Svar) gave it to Viṣṇu. Viṣṇu having borne that (peak of) lustre, power and vigour was totally creeping. Hence is Viṣṇu dwarf (*Jaim. Br.* III. 354). It is patent that this short stature of the dwarf Viṣṇu served as a precursor for the dwarf incarnation of Viṣṇu in the epic and the Puranic mythology.

(d) Maruts

In the Sākamedha rite of the four Seasonal sacrifices (Cāturmāsya-*iṣṭis)*, he has to sacrifice at midday to the Maruts, who are the heaters. The *arthavāda* states the reason that it is hot at midday. Moreover Maruts are (the helpers) of Indra and to Indra belongs the midday (*Kauṣ. Br.* V.5).

(e) Aditi

The opening (Prāyaṇīyā) and the concluding (Udayanīyā) *iṣṭi*-s (sacrifices) belong to the goddess Aditi and in both these, a rice-pap (*caru* of boiled rice) is offered to Aditi. Thus for both the *iṣṭi*-s the deity (goddess) is the same and the offering is the same. The *arthavāda* explains the efficacy of these matters by giving a mythical account. When the gods were performing the sacrifice on this earth, they excluded the earth from the sacrifice. She (i.e. Earth = Aditi) being irritated confounded their sacrifice, with the result they did not know about their own sacrifice. When they approached her, she asked them to set aside a share for her. The gods agreed to it and so thereafter in both the Prāyaṇīyā and Udayanīyā *iṣṭi*-s, the offering (of *caru)* belongs to Aditi, i.e.

Earth (*Śat. Br.* III. 2. 3.1-6; also *ibid.* II. 2.1.18-19). Elsewhere the *Śat. Br.* clearly states that the goddess Aditi is this very earth. Like a cow (*dhenuḥ iva)* she milches (i.e. fulfils) all the desires for men and the cow is like a mother, who sustains all men (*ibid.* V. 3.1.4).

(f) Āptya deities

In the New-moon and Full-moon sacrifices there is a ritual for the Āptya deities, of pouring water with which the dish has been rinsed and that in which he has washed his fingers (*Śat. Br.* I.2.2.18). The *arthavāda* in this regard is a mythical account. It is said that one after the other the three Agni-s found by the gods passed away. The fourth Agni (which is the fire in our own times) found by the gods concealed himself due to fear and entered into the waters. The gods discovered him and forcibly brought him away from the waters. Agni becoming angry with the waters spat on them saying that they were an unsafe place of refuge. (From the bespitten waters) the Āptya deities sprang up named Trita, Dvita and Ekata (*ibid.* I.2.3.1). The name 'Āptya' of the deities is from the word '*ap*' (waters'), from which they spring. But these waters are said to be bespitten, indicating the belief that from the body-fluid (here 'spittle') of a god or a great being, another being or entity is born. The Āptyas roamed about with Indra, as a *brāhmaṇa* follows a king (*ibid.* 2). (Here this is a mention of a worldly observation.) Āptyas knew that Viśvarūpa, the three-headed son of Tvaṣṭṛ was going to be killed (by Indra). So Trita straightway slew Viśvarūpa and Indra was absolved of the sin, for he is a god (though in reality he only slew Viśvarūpa). The people then said that the Āptyas were guilty of the sin, for they knew that Viśvarūpa was going to be killed. The sacrifice would wipe off the sin (of killing Viśvarūpa) upon the Āptyas. This is seen in the ritual, when for the Āptya deities they pour out water, in which the dish has been rinsed and in which the Adhvaryu priest has washed his fingers (*ibid.* 2,3). But the Āptyas were quick in transferring that sin on a sacrificer, who would make an offering without a *dakṣiṇā* to the priests. Hence one must not make on offering without a sacrificial gift, i.e. *dakṣiṇā (ibid.* 4). Hence the gods enjoined the Anvāhārya[70] (cooked rice) as a *daksiṇā* at the New-moon and Full-moon sacrifices. The rinsing water, the priest pours out for each Āptya separately, to avoid a quarrel among them. He makes it hot, so that they can drink it (*ibid.* 5). A mention of avoiding a quarrel among the Āptyas is on the lines of worldly observation, when such a quarrel issues forth. That the *arthavāda* here is for glorifying the practice of giving *dakṣiṇā* is very clear and springs from the priestly psychology, as far as a reference to *dakṣiṇā* is concerned.

The *arthavāda* is important mainly for the belief reflected in it of the transfer of sin, since the Āptyas transfer their sin to the sacrificer, who offers an oblation, without giving any *dakṣiṇā*. In this regard, the mythical account in the *Tait. Br.* gives more information. The gods wanted to wipe off their sin. Them Agni asked to deposit their bodies in him as he was to create for them a place to wipe off their sin. The gods agreed to that. So they say that Agni stands for all deities. Agni with his spark approached waters, with the result Ekata was born; second time, was born Dvita and third time, was born Trita. As these were born from waters (*yad adbhyo' jāyanta)*, they are called Āpyas. The gods then rubbed off their sin on the Āpyas and then there is a list of persons, who are all guilty of some blame or sin, each preceding one among them passing that sin on to each succeeding one *viz.* one who is asleep at the sunrise and thus not doing the duties to be performed then; one who is asleep at the sunset and not doing the duties to be performed at that time; one having diseased nails; one having black teeth; the younger sister, who gets married when her (real) elder sister has remained unmarried; the elder brother, who has remained unmarried, when his (real) younger brother takes a wife and maintains the three fires, daily performing the Agnihotra rite; a *brāhmaṇa* who has his sacred domestic fire extinguished (due to his own carelessness or impiety or absence) and lastly a person, who kills a *brāhmaṇa* (*Tait. Br.* III. 2.8.9-12). This shows that the concept of transfer of sin touches the sphere of an individual's daily duties, that of social norms in those times and also believes in the doctrine of *karman* and thus the sin of the past birth when a person has some bodily defect. The *Yāj Sm.* points out that a person drinking (prohibited type of) wine in the earlier birth is born with black teeth and a person, robbing (a *brāhmaṇa* of his) gold in the earlier birth is born with diseased nails (*Yāj. Sm.* III. 209). The *Tait. Br.* says that the sin transferred right from the Āpyas (Āptyas of the *Śat. Br.)* ultimately remains stationed in a person, who kills a *brāhmaṇa* that being regarded as the greatest sin.[71]

(g) Puruṣa

Here we come to an important point in the ritual philosophy, where both on the macrocosmic and the microcosmic levels, a clear distinction is shown between the matter and the immortal principle.

The context is of the rite of Agnicayana and the issue being discussed is whether Death is near or far away. The reply of the *Śat. Br.* is that Death is both near and far away — on the earth, in the body, he is near and as the one in the yonder world, he is far away. The discussion then switches over to matter, i.e. food (here) and the immortal one, who is the eater. A *śloka* is stated here as a part of the *arthavāda*. It is said that 'concealed in food, he, the immortal, shines at the flowing together of vital saps' —, i.e. yonder shining (solar) orb is food and the man in that orb is the eater, who being concealed in that food shines. This is obviously on the macrocosmic level. On the microcosmic level, the thought is that body indeed is food and that man in the right eye is the eater. Being concealed in that food, he shines.

This same Puruṣa (divine person) is conceptually perceived as the 'One' on the lines of monistic philosophy, by different groups, which serve him in different forms, he in turn becoming helpful to them. The Adhvaryu-priests (i.e.

of *YV*)serve this Puruṣa under the name of 'Agni' and as Yajus he holds together (*yunakti* fr. √*yuj* - 'to join') all this ('universe' acc. to Sāyaṇa); the *Sāmaveda*-priests (*chandoga*-s) under that of 'Sāman', for in him (i.e. in Puruṣa as Sāman) all this universe is one and the same (*samāna);* the *Ṛgveda*-priests (*bahvṛca*-s, i.e. the Hotṛ-priests) under that of 'Uktha', for he causes everything to originate from here (*utthāpayati* fr. *ut* + √*sthā* causal, 'to cause to stand', here 'to cause to originate');[72] those skilled in sorcery (*yātuvidaḥ)* under that of 'Yātu' (sorcery); the serpents (i.e. the persons of Sarpa-tribe) under that of 'Viṣa' (poison, obviously of serpent, 'serpent' being their totem); the persons knowing the lore of serpents (i.e. the lore of nullifying the venom of serpents) under that of 'Sarpa' (serpent); the gods under that of 'Ūrj' (strength); men under that of 'Rayi' (wealth); the *asura*-s under that of 'Māyā' (magic power); the Fathers (*pitṛ*-s) under that of 'Svadhā' (the utterance at the time of offering oblations to the *pitṛ*-s); those knowing the lore of demonology under that of 'Devajana' (demon);[73] the *gandharva*-s under that of 'Rūpa' (form); the *apsaras*-es under that of 'Gandha' (fragrance) (*Śat. Br.* X.5.2.17-20).

This shows that the Vedic ritualists were conscious of the 'Ekam Sat' (the One Existent) which could be designated in various ways depending on the background and the trend of the thinker (cf. *RV*. I. 164.46c, where the One Sat is known by the names of different gods).

Honey

The use of honey in rites and rituals springs forth both from the point of view of medicine and (as a result of this) of folk-belief. In the great anointing (Aindra Mahābhiṣeka) of a king, the priest anoints the king with honey. The *arthavāda* states that honey being the sap (*rasa)* in plants and trees, the priest confers that on the king (*Ait. Br.* VIII. 20= 39.6). The *Jaim. Br.* says that honey is the culmination (*antaḥ)* of all juices (*Jaim. Br.* III. 164). In the lowest level of the Great Fire-altar in the rite of Agnicayana is put a live tortoise. He anoints it with sour curds, honey and ghee. Sour curds are a form of this world (i.e. the earth), ghee (*ghṛta)* of the mid-region and honey of the yonder world. He thus supplies the tortoise with its own form, for the lower shell of the tortoise is the terrestrial world; the upper shell of it is the yonder world and in between the shells is the mid-region (or air). The priest anoints the tortoise, reciting a *mantra (Vāj. Sam.* XIII. 27-29, which is from the *RV* I.90.6-8), which speaks of the greatness and valued importance of 'honey' and 'honey' alone (*Śat. Br.* VII. 5.1.1-4), in the Vedic mind. It is no surprise then that the sacrifice itself is said to be the bees' honey (*yajño vai madhu sāragham)* in a ritual metaphor. The bees here are no other than the officiating priests. As the bees active in collecting honey make the honey increase, so do the priests strengthen the sacrifice (*ibid.* III. 4.3.14).

Iḍā

Here we take into account a belief regarding the Iḍā offering, which occurs in the context of the New-moon and Full-moon sacrifices. Here we have the mythical account of the great deluge and Manu's survival in the great flood with the help of the fish, which he had reared right from the times when the fish was very small. After the receding of the flood, Manu desirous of offspring, performed a sacrifice and offered up in the waters clarified butter, sour milk, whey and curds. After a year, a woman was produced, with accumulated clarified butter gathered in her footprint (*ghṛta-padī).* Through her — Iḍā—Manu generated this race (*Śat. Br.* I.8.1.1-10). This daughter of Manu Iḍā is the same as Iḍā offering which consists of a fivefold cutting (*ibid.* 11-12). Iḍā offering doubtless means cattle, which also consist of five parts (*ibid.* 12). The unique feature of the Iḍā offering is that the priests and sacrificer eat the Iḍā and do not offer it in the fire, for the Iḍā, as noted above, means cattle and it would mean throwing the cattle into the fire, if they offer Iḍā into the fire (*ibid.* I.8.1.38). Iḍā is offered in the vital airs partly in the Hotṛ priest, partly in the sacrificer and partly in the Adhvaryu, i.e. when they eat it (*ibid.* 39).

Keeping awake (during night)

During the night, prior to setting up fires the next morning (in the rite of Agnyādhāna or Agnyādheya), the sacrificer and his wife remain awake. The *arthavāda* points out that the gods are awake during that night. By remaining awake, the sacrificer goes near to the gods. So the next morning for setting up the fires, he becomes more godly, more subdued, more endowed with holy fervour (*tapas*) (*Śat. Br.* II. 1.4.7). The *Śat. Br.* however suggests an alternative that the sacrificer can sleep if he so chooses, for he has not as yet performed the rite of Agnyādheya (which is to be performed the next morning) and till that he is a mere man and not a sacrificer (*ibid.*).

The *arthavāda* is important, for it points out a practice of keeping awake in the night, when the god or in later times goddess is believed to come for stay in the house, when the householder is following a certain vow.[74] The practice is indicated in the *RV*, where the words *jāgāra*, *jāgṛvī* occur (*RV* V. 44.14, 15; VIII. 89.1; I.31.9). It is interesting to note that this practice is prevalent even now in India especially in the ' Nine-days' festival' (Navarātrī) of the goddess Mahālakṣmī or Durgā or Kālī or Mahiṣāsuramardinī (the same goddess having different names). Hence the Vedic *arthavāda* is significant.

Knot

The belief about knot is that it is Varuṇa's characteristic feature, as is his noose (*pāśa*). In the New-moon and Full-moon sacrifices, as a part of the preliminary rites, the Āgnīdhra priest girds the sacrificer's wife with a cord (*yoktra*) over her garment. The garment represents the plants and the cord Varuṇa's noose (*pāśa*). He thus places the plants (i.e. garment) between her (i.e. the sacrificer's wife) and the noose (i.e. cord), so that the noose of Varuṇa should not harm her. The priest should not make a knot, for the knot is Varuṇa's feature (*varuṇyo vai granthiḥ)*. If a knot is made, Varuṇa would have his hold on the sacrificer's wife (*Śat. Br.* I.3.1.13-14, 16). It is interesting to note that the *Tait. Br.* prescribes a knot, so that all blessings would be bestowed on the sacrificer's wife (*Tait. Br.* III. 3.3.4). In this, the *Tait. Br.* has the aim of accomplishing a 'pairing' (*mithunam)* in the sacrifice, for the knot (according to it) stands for 'man' and the sacrificer's wife for 'woman', this 'pairing' (or copulation) obviously being for procreation — procreation of issues and of cattle — by which the sacrificer himself is born (*ibid.)*.

Kṛtyā

The belief about *kṛtyā* (evil spirit) has been prevalent right from the Ṛgvedic times. To take only one example. The bride's garment of black and red colour, which she wears at the time of first union with her husband, is believed to be haunted by the evil spirit (*kṛtyā)*. This garment (*śāmulya)* is to be given away, lest the female evil spirit, obtaining feet (*padvatī bhūtvā)* should enter the body of the bridegroom now husband (*RV* X. 85. 28-30). The *AV* also speaks in the same way about the bride's garment on the night of consummation of the marriage (*AV* XIV.1. 25-27).[75]

A reference to the belief in *kṛtyā* and magic objects occurs in the context of digging *uparava*-s in the Agniṣṭoma sacrifice. These are the holes, which are four in number and are arm-deep. They are connected with each other internally. Over these the (Soma) pressing apparatus is placed. They are made below the fore-part (*prauga)* of the southern cart, but not far away from the axle.[76] The *Śat. Br.* gives the explanation that the Havirdhāna-shed is the head of the sacrifice and these four holes are the openings in it.[77] The *Tait. Sam.* explains these differently (VI. 2.11.1ff), that the holes are the breaths, which are below the head (i.e. the Havirdhāna-shed).

From our point of view, apart from the first explanation given by the *Śat. Br.* (III. 5.4.1) of the four holes, the second *arthavāda* in the form of a mythical account is more important. The gods and *asura*-s, both of them sprung from Prajāpati, were contending. The *asura*-s, as a form of *kṛtyā* (evil spirit), buried magic charms[78] within these worlds to overcome the gods. The gods by digging the holes (*uparava*-s) dug up those magic charms. Now when the *kṛtyā* (in the form of these magic charms) is dug up, she becomes inoperative (*alasā*) and useless (*moghā*). In the same manner, if any malicious enemy buries here the magic charms as *kṛtyā* for the sacrificer, he (i.e. the priest or the sacrificer) digs them up by digging the holes (*Śat. Br.* III. 5.4.2-3). The *arthavāda* is important for it sheds light on the belief in and practice of magic charms and also the measures to be taken to counteract them.

Line drawn (for protection)

In the Agnicayana rite, for preparing the fire-pan (*ukhā*), the clay was to be carried ritually, wherein two or three animals are mentioned. *Mait. Sam.* (II. 7.1) and *Kāṭh. Sam.* (XIX. 1) mention two viz. a horse and an ass. When a he-goat is added, there are three animals (*Śat. Br.* VI.4.4.4, 15). While going to fetch the clay, the horse is led first; then follows the ass and lastly the he-goat. With them go the priests. The *Tait. Sam.* states that whenever the sacrifice is started, the *rakṣas*-es desire to destroy it. So when the horse (in fetching the clay, as mentioned above) plants his foot first, on that place of the ground, there is offered libation[79] and that is regarded as the beginning of the sacrifice (i.e. the Agnicayana rite), as Sāyaṇa points out in his commentary. In order to smite away the *rakṣas*-es, who will hover round that place, he draws a line around. With three verses (one each in Gāyatrī, Triṣṭubh and Anuṣṭubh metres), he draws a line around, for Agni is threefold. By drawing a line around, from the whole extent of Agni he smites away the *rakṣas*-es (*Tait. Sam.* V.1.3.4,5). Drawing a line around a certain place thus points out that such a line (in circular shape) is drawn for the protection of that place. This is verily the belief working, when Lakṃaṇa is said to have drawn a line to protect Sīta, when he himself goes away to help Rāma and Sītā remains alone in the hut.[80]

Mahāvrata

The Mahāvrata here is the last day but one in the Gavām-ayana *sattra.* The day is called 'Mahāvrata' because it is specially meant for Prajāpati, who is '*mahān*' and *mahāvrata* means food, i.e. '*anna*' (*Pañc. Br.* IV. 10.2).

Kane gives a detailed treatment to this topic,[81] taking a note of all information available from the *Pañc. Br.* as well as the *Ait Ār.* and the Śrautasūtras, except referring to the *Jaim. Br.* from the Brāhmaṇa texts. We agree with him when he says that the features of the Mahāvrata show that it was some folk-festival in the hoary past and was welded on to the solemn Vedic sacrifices. But it was not a relaxation after the weary days and months of sacrifices as he maintains,[82] for each apparently small ritual, figuring in the Mahāvata, is symbolic as pointed out by the Brāhmaṇa-texts, in the *arthavāda*-s.

To begin with. The Udgātṛ priest, having mounted an oblong chair (or a small couch), chants (the Rājana chant of the Vrata laud). The *arthavāda* states that under the eyes of even the gods, he gains a seat above others. This seat is made of Udumbara wood, for Udumbara is food, which he gains thereby. The seat is of the measure of a span, so that (by sitting on it), the sacrificer should not leave the world (*Pañc. Br.* V. 5.1-3). This shows that by this Udumbara-seat, the sacrificer is above the common masses and nearer to the gods. Even otherwise, anyone who sacrifices becomes '*a-mānuṣa*' (not human, i.e. 'divine'). But the seat in the Mahāvrata ceremony is not so high as to lose contact with the earthly world. Who will sacrifice then, if the sacrificer goes permanently to the other world?

There are two persons *viz.* Abhigara ('praiser') and Apagara ('reviler'). The Apagara finds fault with the chanting priests (i.e. the Udgātṛ priest and his assistant priests) and reciting priests. The Abhigara eulogises them. The *arthavāda* gives the explanation that the Apagara drives away the evil lot of the priests, while the Abhigara praises what has been well-chanted and well-recited by them (*ibid.* 13; also *Tait. Sam.* VII. 5.9.3, differing slightly).

An Ārya and a *śūdra* are made to fight for a circular piece of hide (*Pañc. Br. V.* 5.14, 17). According to the *Jaim. Br.* it is a goat-hide or a bull-hide (*Jaim. Br.* II. 405). They cause the member of the Ārya *varṇa* to win. The mythical account is that the gods and the *asura*-s fought for the sun. The gods got possession of it. With that, the gods prospered and the *asura*-s perished. Hence this small ritual is for making the sacrificer win (*Pañc. Br.* V.5. 15, 16; *Jaim. Br.* II, 405). They (i.e. the priests or the persons arranging the Mahāvrata rite) make a *māgadha* (bard — a person of mixed caste, having the profession of a bard) and a *puṁścalū* (harlot) have copulation at the south end of the altar. This is for pairing, for procreation, says the *arthavāda* (*Jaim. Br.* II. 405). At all the corners of the altar (*vedi)* the drums are beaten. The *Pañc. Br.* says that this is for gaining the speech that is in the trees (*Pañc. Br.* V. 5.18). The earth-drum makes a sound. They thereby gain the speech that is in the earth (*ibid.* 19).[83] Even the *Jaim. Br.* mentions this and says that the sound made by a (*bhūmi-dundubhi)* bull is of highest importance (*Jaim. Br.* II. 404).[84] They run a race (in a chariot), says the *Jaim. Br.* (*ibid.* II. 405). Wearing armour they go around, as there is highest splendour when armoured (*ibid.;* also *Pañc. Br.* V. 5.21).

Apart from beating the drums and the *bhūmi-dundubhi*, there is much singing and playing on instruments in the rite of Mahāvrata. There are eighty-seven *stotrya*-s (*stotriya*-s - verses which are put to melody) and thirteen *parimād*-s (*sāman*-s*)* to be chanted, over the different parts of the bird-shaped high altar and of the *devayajana* (sacrificial ground).[85] The *stotrya*-s (eighty-seven in number) and the *parimād*-s (thirteen in number) make up hundred. A man is expected to live for hundred years, having hundred powers (*Jaim. Br.* II. 404). The *Jaim. Br.* says that *parimād*-s can also mean the musical instruments *viz. karkarī, alābu, vakrā, kapiśīrṣṇī, aiṣīkī, apaghāṭalīkā, vīṇā, kaśyapī, bhūmi-dundubhi* and *vāṇa*, the last one having hundred strings (*ibid).* The *Pañc. Br.* (V. 5. 20) and the *Tait. Sam.* (VII. 5.9.3) say that all sorts of sounds are there, which are to gain that Speech in these worlds. When the priests chant, the wives of the performers act as choristers by playing on *apaghāṭilā*-s, with the thought 'let us go simultaneously to the world of heaven' (*Pañc. Br.* V. 6.8).[86] Placing water-jars on their heads, the women go round the Mārjālīya fire and sing the songs containing the words, '*hai mahā hai mahā*' (meaning the Mahāvrata) and also '*idam madhu idam madhu*' ('this is honey, this is honey') meaning 'rains' leading to fertility (*Jaim. Br.* II. 405). The *Ait. Ār.* (V. 1.5) summarises all the popular features of the Mahāvrata at one place. Kane has given the details also from the Śrautasūtras.[87] The atmosphere on the Mahāvrata day is so joyful that the *Tait. Sam.* states that as men being freed from bonds cry aloud, so the sacrificers freed from the bonds of the gods cry aloud, placing food and strength in themselves (*Tait. Sam* VII. 5.9.2).

Metals

Of all the metals, gold occupies the place of prime importance,[88] as the *arthavāda*-s concerning it speak of the beliefs attached to gold in those times.

The oft-repeated belief about gold is that it is Agni's seed. Agni is the father and gold is the son (*Jaim. Br.* 1.56). If the fire were to go out after the first libation, having thrown down on the fire-place any log of wood he may find lying near-by, he should offer on that log, for in every piece of wood there is a fire. But if he thinks otherwise (about the log of wood), he may offer upon gold, for gold, doubtless, is Agni's seed (*Jaim. Br.* I.56; *Śat. Br.* XII. 4.3.1). At several places we find the expression *'agniretasam vai hiraṇyam'* (*Śat. Br.* III. 3.1.3; III. 3.2.2; III. 2.4.8 - this last expression pointing out that both milk and gold are of the same origin, since both have sprung from Agni's seed). In the Ānubandhya rite in the Agniṣṭoma sacrifice (when a barren *anūbandhyā* cow is immolated for Mitra and Varuṇa), the *dakṣiṇā* to be given to the priests is gold, for the sacrifice belongs to Agni and gold is Agni's seed (*ibid.* IV. 5.1.15). In a rite in the Rājasūya sacrifice, when a cake on eleven potsherds is offered to Agni and Viṣṇu, gold is the *dakṣiṇā* to be given, for it is Agni's seed and this sacrifice belongs to Agni (*ibid.* V. 2.3.6).

How gold came to be the seed of Agni is explained through a mythical account, which comes as *arthavāda*, when gold is enjoined as one of the items of *sambhāra*[89] in the rite of Agnyādhāna. It is said that Agni at one time cast his eyes on the waters with the thought, 'May I pair with them'. He sprinkled his seed in them and that became gold. Hence gold shines like fire, it being Agni's seed. Gold is found in water, for Agni poured his seed into the water. When gold is used as one of the *sambhāra*-s, the sacrificer sets up a fire completely endowed with (Agni's) seed (*ibid.* II. 1.1.5). The *Tait. Br.* also states this account, pointing out that the waters were the wives of Varuṇa. It says (the context of the rite of Agnyādhāna or Agnyādheya being the same) that Agni is tc be established with its seed, i.e. gold (*Tait. Br.* I.1.3.8). While buying Soma (-shoots), he ties the piece of gold to the (ring) finger. The *arthavāda* states that this universe is twofold — truth and untruth, there is no third. The gods are the truth and men are the untruth. As gold has sprung from Agni's seed, he ties the gold to his finger so that he may touch the Soma-shoots with the truth (*Śat. Br.* III. 3.2.2). The same *arthavāda* occurs in the context of the morning-pressing of Soma, when they sit down round the two press-boards, and the Adhvaryu priest ties a piece of gold to the finger (*ibid.* III.9.4.1). In the rite of buying Soma, the Somakrayaṇī cow is given to the Soma-seller (to be taken back from him after the Soma is purchased). The priest or the sacrificer follows the cow, stepping into her seven footprints. They (the Brahman priest, the sacrificer, the Adhvaryu priest and the Neṣṭṛ priest) sit round the seventh footprint and having placed a piece of gold in that footprint, he makes an offering of clarified butter. The *arthavāda* points out that this offering is made on nothing but fire, for gold is Agni's seed. The clarified butter being a thunderbolt, he delivers the cow by that thunderbolt and makes her his own (*ibid.* III. 3.1.1,3). All these *arthavāda*-s point out that gold due to its yellow shining lustre is regarded as closely connected with Agni. The same thought underlies the *vidhi* of scattering (*prokṣaṇa* lit. sprinkling) fragments of gold (on the Great Fire-altar). The mythical account as *arthavāda* is that the Aṅgiras-es, going to the world of heaven gave to the seers the accomplishment of the sacrifice. It became gold. So the fragments of gold, as noted above, are for the completion of the sacrifice. By these, he unites the sacrifice (Agni) with its form (i.e. gold, it being the form of Agni), and with golden light he goes to the world of heaven (*Tait. Sam.* V. 4.2.3-4).

As Agni and the sun are the two forms of the same principle, i.e. heat, gold is said to be the form of the sun also, as it is of Agni, being its seed —the yellow shining lustre of the three being a common factor. The ritual use of gold is supported at various places by the statement *viz.* 'His form is accomplished here - he who shines (yonder) — '*tadetasya rūpam kriyate - ya eṣa tapati*' or at times — *ya eṣa parastāt tapati*'.

In the rite of Agnicayana, in the context of consecration of the sacrificer, it is said that he wears a round-shaped gold ornament (*rukma)*, having twenty-one studs (*Śat. Br.* VI. 7.1.2). The *arthavāda* is eloquent stating that gold (ornament) is light and so is the sun. Gold is immortality (which we are noting further) and so stands the sun for immortality. The golden *rukma* is round and so is the sun. The *rumka* has twenty-one studs and while wearing it, they are outside and the sun is also 'twenty-first' (12 months + 5 seasons + 3 worlds = 20 and the sun is, the twenty-first).

The studs are the sun's rays and his rays are outside (*ibid.*). The gods were afraid lest the *rakṣas*-es should destroy here their Agni. They made that *rukma* — the yonder sun - to be Agni's protector standing by their side. When the sacrificer wears the (gold) *rukma*, he makes that *rukma* (which stands for the yonder sun) to be Agni's protector by his side (*ibid.* 5). In the rite of Agnicayana again, while building the Great Fire-altar, in the first layer, he lays the golden image of man on the gold disk (*rukma*). The *arthavāda* is that the gold disk is the yonder sun and the man who is in the sun's disk, the same the sacrificer (or the priest) now lays down on the Great Fire-altar in the first layer (*ibid.* VII. 4.1.17).

It is said that when the head of the sacrifice (victim) was struck off, its sap, running entered the waters. When the sacrificer goes to fetch the Vasatīvarī water, he collects the same sap and puts it into the sacrifice to make it sapful. This water is to be collected by day as the water catches the light of the sun. If the sacrificer misses the daytime and the sun sets (with water not collected), the Adhvaryu priest should take the water from the tank of a person, who has earlier performed a Soma-sacrifice (including the sacrificer himself). In case no way is found out to collect the water, the sacrificer (or the Adhvaryu priest) should hold a firebrand or a piece of gold close above the water and take the water. This is made like the yonder burning sun (*ibid.* III. 9.2.9). This shows how Agni (here firebrand), gold and the sun are closely related.

Gold is said to be light (*jyotiḥ*) at various places. If the sun sets when the sacrificer for his daily Agnihotra rite, has not carried fire from the Gārhapatya fire-altar to the Āhavanīya fire-altar, in this case the Āhavanīya fire desires to show the Gārhapatya fire low and Gārhapatya fire the Āhavanīya. At such a lapse, he should carry (a piece of) gold tied with the *darbha* (grass) in front, afterwards Agni, then the Agnihotra oblation. It is said that gold is light, seeing which in front, he is free from the blemish (*Tait. Br.* I.4.4.1). We have the same *vidhi* and a similar *arthavāda* in the *Ait. Br.* (VII. 12 = 32.11) and also in the *Jaim. Br.* (I. 62). In the Horse-sacrifice, the knife to be used for immolating the horse is made of gold, for gold is shining light, by means of which the sacrificer also goes to the heavenly world (*Śat. Br.* XIII. 2.2.16). In the rite of Odanasava, the *dakṣiṇā* given to a *brāhmaṇa* is gold. (Sāyaṇa in his comm. says that the sacrificer puts the ear-ornament of gold on the ear of the *brāhmaṇa.)* The *arthavāda* speaks of the belief that gold is light, which he places in the *brāhmaṇa*. Gold is lustre, which he places in himself (*Tait. Br.* II. 7.9.2,3). In the Horse-sacrifice, the horse, after the bath, is adorned by the wives of the king. They tuck beads of gold into the mane and the tail of the horse. This is explained as being for the replenishment of the hair that might have fallen away while the horse was given bath. These beads are said to be one thousand.[90] Gold is light and the Horse-sacrifice is the *rāṣṭra* (country ruled over by the king). These both are placed in him (*ibid.* III. 9.4.5,6). On the second day in the Horse-sacrifice, the Bahiṣpavamāna laud is chanted by the Udgātṛ priest and the horse in its turn also (as though) chants the 'Udgītha' by making a neighing sound, when the mares are brought before it. The last part of this ritual is — placing gold on the *barhis* (sacrificial grass). Gold is light which is placed in the sacrificer and his offspring. Being endowed with the light of gold, the sacrificer goes to the heavenly world (*ibid.* III. 8.22.3). The officiating priests in the Vājapeya sacrifice wear golden wreaths, so that light (*prakāśa)* will be there for the sacrificer in the yonder world, for gold is light (*Pañc. Br.* XVIII. 7.6-8).

That gold stands for immortal life is one more firm belief about gold (*Śat. Br.* V. 1.5.28; *ibid.* XIII. 4.1.7; *Tait. Br.* I.7.8.1, etc.). In the Agniṣṭoma sacrifice, there is a piece of gold on both sides (of the omentum of the sacrificial victim, which is offered). The *arthavāda* points out that they offer the victim in the fire and as gold stands for immortal life, the victim (actually the *vapā*, i.e. omentum) having gold on both of its sides rests in immortal life (*Śat. Br.* III. 8. 3.26). In the Vājapeya sacrifice, having descended from the sacrificial post (*yūpa*, which he has to ascend, symbolically meaning his going to the region of light, that of gods, for becoming immortal), he treads upon a piece of gold, for gold is immortal life (*ibid.* V. 2.1.20, 21; *Tait. Br.* I. 3.7.7). This piece of gold is of hundred measures. The desired years of man's life and his powers are hundred. He thereby establishes him in that (long) life and (immense) power (*ibid.*) In the Soma-sacrifice, when he draws the Aṁśu-graha (i.e. Aṁśu cup of Soma), he should draw it without breathing. But if he has to breathe, he should breathe over gold, for gold is immortality and breath is life. This gold is hundred *kṛṣṇala*-s in weight (*Tait. Sam.* VI. 6.10.2, 3). Here the *arthavāda* about the number 'hundred' is what we have noted above. In the context of the Soma-sacrifice, the *Tait. Sam.* states that if the sacrificer's speckled butter (*pṛṣadājya*) falls (*skandati*) that portends evil on many fronts. So he should take the speckled butter again, after placing gold in the ladle. As gold stands for immortality and the speckled butter for breath, he places immortality in his breath (*ibid.* III. 2.6.3) In the Rājasūya sacrifice, gold threads are woven into the two strainers (*pavitra*), with which the consecration water is purified (*Śat. Br.* V. 3.5.15). When the king steps on the tiger's skin, below his foot, a small gold plate (*rukma*) is thrown (*ibid.* V. 4.1.12). A gold plate (*rukma*) is laid upon the king's head and there are two gold plates on both sides of the king (*ibid.* 14). At all these places, the *arthavāda* is that gold is immortal life, which is desired for the king through these rituals. If the sacrificer dies, at the time of cremating the body, seven chips of gold are inserted in the seven seats of his vital airs. This is to bestow light and immortality on the sacrificer (*ibid.* XII. 5.2.6). The same ritual and the same *arthavāda* occur when a man's head (with four heads of animals) is put in the fire-pan, in the rite of Agnicayana (*Tait. Sam.* V.2.9.2.3). In the same rite, when the Great Fire-altar is completed, the sacrificer (or the priest) bestrews it with gold chips (on its final, i.e. the fifth, layer). Already in the first layer of the Great Fire-altar, he has placed a gold plate (or disk) and on it the golden image of a man. Now on the fifth layer, he bestrews the Great Fire- altar, five times with gold chips — each time with two hundred chips — in all with thousand chips. Thousand means everything and with everything he confers upon him immortality (*Śat. Br.* VIII. 7.4.7-9).

Gold in the ritual metaphor is equated with truth (*Jaim. Br.* II. 117). In the rite of (and the period of) consecration, the sacrificer wears a gold plate (*rukma*) round his neck. The gold plate is truth and truth is able to sustain the Ukhya Agni (fire in the fire-pan), which the sacrificer has to carry about (in a sling), during the period of consecration (*Śat. Br.* VI. 7.1.1).

Atri dispelled the darkness caused by the demon Svarbhānu (*Jaim. Br.* I. 80, based on the Ṛgvedic myth, as we have noted under "Eclipse" in this chap.) or by the *asura*-s (*Śat. Br.* IV.3. 4.21). So gold is given as the sacrificial gift, for gold is light. This gift of gold is given to an Ātreya (a person of Atri descent), for Atri had set free the sun's light (*Pañc. Br.* VI. 6. 11; *Śat. Br.* IV. 3.4.21). This shows the practice prevalent in the times of the Brāhmaṇa-texts, which preserved the memory of the Ṛgvedic myth as also the importance of gold, which is regarded as the solar metal due to its yellow shining nature.

In the Horse-sacrifice, the knife for slaughtering (*śāsa*) the horse is made of gold, for gold is shining light, which is bestowed on that sacrifice. By means of the golden light the sacrificer also goes to the heavenly world. Moreover horse (in the Horse-sacrifice) is a sign of *kṣatriya* power (*kṣatra*) and so is gold a symbol of nobility - '*kṣatra*', i.e. *kṣatriya* power (*Śat. Br.* XIII. 2.2.16, 17).

Arthavāda-s regarding other metals also figure in the Brāhmaṇa-texts, pointing out the beliefs about them. In the Horse-sacrifice, there are copper knives (*lohamayāh*) for slaughtering the *paryaṅgya*-s (i.e. the sacrificial victims surrounding the body of the sacrificial horse). As there are non-royal (*arājānaḥ)* king-makers, heralds (or bards—*sūta*-s*)* and headmen to the king, so are the *paryaṅgya*-s to the horse and so is copper to gold (*ibid.* XIII. 2.2.18). In a ritual in the Rājasūya sacrifice, a piece of copper is put into the mouth of a long-haired eunuch (who is sitting in the *sadas*, which is a shed or tent, facing the east) with a *mantra* (*Vāj. Sam.* X. 10). Such a long-haired man is neither woman nor man, for being a male, he is not a woman and being a long-haired eunuch, he is not a man. So is the metal copper, which is neither iron nor gold. And so are the biting ones (*dandaśūkāḥ*—venomous serpents), which are neither worms nor non-worms (these being mentioned in the *Vāj. Sam.* X. 10). All these (i.e. all kinds of death and murderous blows) are crossed over by the king, who is being rejuvenated (*Śat. Br.* V. 4.1.1,2). The sacrificer performing the four Seasonal sacrifices has to undergo (in the rite of initiation for these sacrifices) shaving of the hair on his head, beard and whiskers. This is done by a copper razor. The *arthavāda* is significant, stating the importance of the copper razor and the shaving with it. It is said that Agni, having arrived in the summer season, assuming a fierce form, makes this earth as though shorn (with the crop cut off and the waters in the reservoirs dried up). But the earth day by day becomes wider and prosperous. Similarly with the copper razor (reddish in colour like Agni) he makes the sacrificer have the form of Agni, so that thereafter day by day the sacrificer becomes prosperous and procreates the offspring (*Tait. Br.* I.5.6.5, 6).

We have mentioned above the *paryaṅgya*-s, for which the slaughter-knives are of copper. For other *paryaṅgya*-s, the knives are of iron, for other animals are the peasantry and iron is a form of peasantry (*Śat. Br.* XIII. 2.2.19).

The beliefs about silver are interesting. While enjoining that silver (*rajatam hiraṇyam)* should not be given as *dakṣiṇā*, the *Tait. Sam.* states a mythical account as *arthavāda*. It is said that the gods and *asura*-s were in conflict. The gods deposited their desirable riches in Agni, making him a custodian of it. The gods having defeated the *asura*-s approached Agni and sought violently to take their wealth from him. He was reluctant and wept. As he wept (*arodīt)*, so has Rudra his name (fr. the root √*rud* - 'to weep'). The tears which were shed by Agni became silver. The sacrificer should not give it (i.e. silver) as *dakṣiṇa* on the strew, otherwise within a year in the sacrificer's house, the family-members have to weep, due to some calamity or death (*Tait. Sam.* I.5.1.1, 2). In the Pravargya rite, when sand has been strewed on the north of the Āhavanīya fire-altar, below that he first throws a silver plate. The mythical account states that the gods were afraid lest the *rakṣas*-es and fiends, might injure their Pravargya (pot) from below and so gold *(hiraṇya)* being Agni's seed, would protect the Pravargya by repelling the fiends and the *rakṣas*-es. So they kept there the '*rajata hiraṇya*', i.e. silver ('*hiraṇya*' of different form). The *arthavāda* runs further saying that even the earth also was afraid of the Pravargya (pot, being heated on her) which might injure her. Hence to keep the Pravargya pot separate from her, he places a plate of silver (*Śat. Br.* XIV. 1.3.14). It is said that if the sun rises and the fire for Āhavanīya fire-altar is not brought from the Gārhapatya-altar,[91] he should carry in front a piece of silver tying it with *darbha* grass (then fire and then the Agnihotra oblation). By the piece of silver is made the form of the moon or it is the form (or semblance) of night (*Jaim. Br.* I.63).

Now we turn to a metal, minor in status, nevertheless mentioned in important rites and it is lead. In the Sautrāmaṇī sacrifice, he buys the malted rice with lead, the malted barley with (sheep's) wool and the fried rice-grain with thread. Lead is a metal having a form of both iron and gold and so is the Sautrāmaṇī sacrifice which is both an *iṣṭi*-offering and an animal-sacrifice (*Śat. Br.* XII. 7.2.10).[92] The *Jaim. Br.* speaks of the origin of the metals in an interesting way. It is said that this 'One' was there in the beginning. He desired to become many. It thought of mind and toiled (*atapyata*) with mind. The mind is the *tapas* (heat due to toiling). It emitted speech. Really Agni (i.e. fire or heat) is death. When they drop gold in it, the gold becomes more precious (*Jaim. Br.* III. 334). This is the worldly practice alluded to here, which believes that the gold is rightly examined to be pure or not in fire.

When mind being heated produced speech, an immortal golden foetus was formed. When born, they cleansed him, as does the mother (-cow) lick the child (i.e. calf) and cleanses him. When they cut off (i.e. removed) the first covering (membrane) of the foetus, it became iron (*kṛṣṇāyas*), the second covering when taken off, became silver. The third one became emerald (*haritam* - though this is not a metal); so it is the most lustrous one. The chorion (*jarāyu*, which is the outer foetal envelope, as opposed to *ulba*-amnion, which is the innermost membrane, we have noted above) in the artery (*nāḍyām)* became copper (*loha).* The child in the process of being born or after being born passes (or makes) '*sīsava*' (excreta?), that became lead. Hence it has the worst odour (*ibid.* III. 335). In the Vājapeya sacrifice, he buys the Parisrut (liquor) for a piece of lead from a long-haired man. The *arthavāda* regarding the long-haired man is the same as we have noted with regard to copper. The *arthavāda* further says that lead is neither iron nor gold. The Parisrut is neither Soma nor *surā* (wine).[93] In the Rājasūya sacrifice, on the hind part of the tiger's skin, a piece of lead is to be laid down. The king, who is being rejuvenated kicks this piece off with the foot with a *mantra* from the *Vāj. Sam.* (X. 14) - '*pratyastam namuceḥ śiraḥ*'. The *arthavāda* is in the form of a mythical account about the *asura* Namuci. Indra knocked him down and trod upon him with his foot. He (i.e. Indra) tore off his head with his foot and from there sprang a demon (*rakṣas).* That *rakṣas* kept on asking Indra — 'Where are you going? Where will you get rid of me?' Indra slew that demon with lead, with the result lead is soft, for it has lost its spring (*sṛtajava)*. While being like gold, it is not worth anything (except slaying the demon). As Indra slew the fiends, so does the king kill the fiends — *rakṣas*-es — with the piece of lead (*Śat. Br.* V.4.1.8-10). The same ritual is laid down by the *Tait. Br.* (*Tait. Br.* I.7.8.2).

There was a practice of placing a wine-cup of bell-metal (*kāṁsyapātra)* in the hands of the king after he has undergone the rite of rejuvenation (i.e. Rājasūya), accompanied with a *mantra* (*Ait. Br.* VIII. 20 = 39.6). No *arthavāda* pointing out the belief about the bell-metal occurs here.

The actual observation about two metals is recorded by the *Śat. Br.* when it states the reason of making the pot (called Mahāvīra or Gharma) for boiling the milk, out of clay (i.e. earth). It is said that if this pot is made of wood, it would be burnt; if of gold, it would dissolve; if of copper, it would melt; if of stone, it would burn the two handling-sticks. Hence by means of the earthen vessel he offers in the Pravargya rite (*Śat. Br.* XIV. 2.2.54).

Milk

Milk being an important offering, it is necessary to take a note of some important beliefs about milk. As gold is regarded to be born from the seed of Agni, so is milk said to be *agniretas*. In the rite of buying Soma (-shoots), he offers the Hiraṇyavatī *āhuti*, to the Somakrayaṇī cow in order to gratify her. Having tied a piece of gold with a blade of the *barhis* (sacrificial grass) and laid it down in the ladle (*juhū)* he offers (the butter) with a thought that he will offer with pure milk (*kṛtsnena payasā*—butter taken to be the pure form of milk), for both milk and gold are having the same origin, i.e. Agni's seed (*Śat. Br.* III. 2.4.8). The offering here with the association of the piece of gold is aptly called Hiraṇyavatī *āhuti*. It is interesting to note that here butter (which is offered) through milk is connected with gold, both gold and milk being brought on par. The rite and practice in the rite of Agnihotra is to offer the milk having first put it on the fire. As it (i.e. the milk) is Agni's seed, it is 'cooked' (*śrita)* and by putting it on the fire, it is indeed heated (*ibid.* II.3.1.15). While heating the milk, the priest or the sacrificer should not let it rise to the brim. The *arthavāda* points out that the milk would be burnt if it rises to the brim and unproductive indeed is the burnt seed (*ibid.* II. 3.1.14).

At times milk is said to be breath (i.e. the vital air). In the rite of Agnicayana, when the fire-pan (*ukhā)* is ready, he pours milk into it, for the fire-pan is the head of the sacrifice and milk is breath (*ibid.* VI. 5.4.15). The milk which is poured is of a (female) goat to avoid injury, for the goat sprang from Prajāpati's head and Prajāpati is Agni. One does not injure one's own self. As the goat eats all kinds of herbs, he pours into the fire-pan the sap of all kinds of herbs (*ibid.* 16).

In the same rite, which we have noted above, when the Great Fire-altar is ready, a burning piece of wood is taken from the Gārhapatya fire-place to serve as the new Āhavanīya fire on the Great Fire-altar. (The Gārhapatya fire is the same fire which is carried in the fire-pan [*ukhā*] by the sacrificer during his time of consecration or initiation *dīkṣā).* On that burning piece of wood (fire-brand) he offers milk by means of the milk-pail (*dohana)*, for the milk is given away with the milk-pail. This milk is from a black cow, which has a white calf, the black cow signifying the night and her calf the yonder sun (*ibid.* IX. 2.3.30) The fire-brand serving as the Āhavanīya fire is the head of the sacrifice and milk means breath. He thus puts breath (i.e. the vital air) into the head (*ibid.* 31).

There seems to be a practice of adding at least a drop of water to the milk.[94] In the New-moon and Full-moon sacrifices, there is a ritual of coagulating the milk, after taking it off the fire. When the last cow is milked, having poured a drop of water into the milk-pail and having stirred it, he pours it to the milk, for the completeness of the sap. The *arthavāda* points out that when it rains here, the plants spring up. By eating the plants and by drinking the water, this juice (i.e. milk) is produced (in the cows). So is water poured to the milk for the completeness of the sap (*rasasyo vaiva sarvatvāya),* says the *Śat. Br.* (*ibid.* I.7.1.18).

Mirror

Mention of mirror occurs in the Daśapeya rite, which is to be performed after the Rājasūya sacrifice.[95] The sacrificial gift (*dakṣiṇā)* given to each of the priests is unique (*Pañc. Br.* XVIII. 9.8-21). To the two Adhvaryus (Adhvaryu priest and his helping priest Pratiprasthātṛ) are given two mirrors, for these two priests are as though twins. By giving the mirrors, he brings eye-sight into each of them (*ibid.* XVIII. 9.10). Sāyaṇa explains the word *prākāśau* (two mirrors) saying that according to some the word signifies 'two particular ornaments' (*ābharaṇaviśeṣau);* according to others 'two golden mirrors' (*sauvarṇadarpaṇau).* He says that by giving two mirrors, there is brought good eyesight in the sacrificer as also in the priest, who accepts the *dakṣiṇā* of mirrors.

The Gṛhyasūtras mention mirror in many a ritual.[96] When the child is made to cast the first glance at the moon, the *Kāṭh. G.S.* prescribes a mirror as the *dakṣiṇā* at this occasion, with appropriate *mantra*-s (*Kāṭh. G.S.* 38.1-5). The *Kāṭh G.S.* prescribes the ritual of making the child look at the sun also for the first time (*ibid.* 37. 1-6). In both, the idea is of being conversant with the divine light of the two great luminaries. The gift of a mirror, which is capable to reflect the light, is for the gain of continued light and also life. Hence the very word for mirror is *prakāśa* (light). This belief, though it occurs in later literature, has to be taken into account, while explaining the *dakṣiṇā* of two mirrors for getting good eyesight, the light-reflecting surface of the mirror and the lustre in the eye serving as a common feature.

Mortar and Pestle

As seen in the *RV*, mortar and pestle were used for pounding the Soma-shoots (*RV* I.28.1-4 where the Soma-shoots are mentioned as '*ulūkhalasuta*'), the other method of having the

Soma-juice being, grinding or pounding the Soma-shoots with stones. Making use of mortar and pestle appears to be the older method of pounding the Soma-shoots and may go back to the Indo-Iranian period.[97] It has to be noted that the Zoroastrian ritual, following the *Avesta*, of preparing the Haoma (=Soma) followed even in modern times, requires mortar (*hāvanīm*) and pestle (*lālā*).[98]

In the ritual-texts, mortar and pestle figure in the *vidhi* of preparing the offerings (of grains, especially of rice-grains) such as *puroḍāśa*, boiled rice (*caru*), etc. In the New-moon and Full-moon sacrifices, the sacrificer holds the black antelope skin in his left hand. He at once takes the mortar with his right hand, lest the evil spirits, the *rakṣas*-es should rush in there in the meantime (*Śat. Br.* I.1.4.6).

The practice of preparing the corn-offerings with the help of mortar and pestle led to the equation, in the *arthavāda*, that these two meant all kinds of food. In the first layer of the Great Fire-altar, a mortar and pestle are put with the same motif. The *arthavāda* states that Viṣṇu desired that he be an eater of food. He saw the two bricks in the form of mortar and pestle, which he placed on the altar and became an eater of food. Likewise does the sacrificer, for the mortar and pestle mean all kinds of food; with them it is prepared, so that it could be eaten (*ibid.* VII. 5. 1.12). A significant metaphor occurs in the same context, i.e. the Agnicayana rite. It is said that the round-like pestle is the male organ. The pestle is put to the right side of the mortar, the *arthavāda* pointing out a practice here that the male lies on the right side of the female (*ibid.* 38).

Name

The Brāhmaṇa-texts mention several details regarding 'name' *viz.* name, its power, the efficacy of having a second name as also a secret or mystic name, etc. All such details occur in the *arthavāda* portions of these texts, which ably point out how the Brāhmaṇa-texts have made full use of such beliefs to complement the ritual in hand.

In the context of the New-moon and Full-moon sacrifices, we have a speculative myth, which occurs in the *Śat. Br.* It is said that Brahman, which was there in the beginning, having first created the three gods *viz.* Agni, Vāyu and Sūrya assigned to them the terrestrial world, air and the sky respectively. Brahman then itself went to the sphere beyond, but descended again by means of these two *viz.* Form and Name. When a libation is offered to Mind, he obtains 'form' (*rūpa)* because a person knows 'form' by mind and with the libation to Speech he obtains 'name' (*nāma)*, because it is by speech that a person can utter a name (*Śat. Br.* XI. 2.3.1-6).

It is a patent fact that name stands for the very person to whom it is given. The *Śat. Br.*, in the context of the New-moon and Full-moon sacrifices, states that while stepping to the Gārhapatya fire, the sacrificer should insert the name of his son when he says, "May this son ('Name of the Son') carry on this manly deed of mine'. If he has no son, he should insert his own name in that (*ibid.* I.9.3.21). The idea that any one born sound and safe has to be given a name occurs in the *Śat. Br.* In the Agnicayana rite, it is enjoined that after having performed the Vaiśvakarmaṇa (oblations), he has to give a name to the fire of the altar, as Agni indeed has been born sound and safe (*ibid.* IX. 5.1.52).

In the context of the same rite (i.e. Agnicayana) occurs a mythical account, which runs as follows. When these creatures (*imāni bhūtāni)* and the lord of the creatures (Prajāpati) laid their seed into Uṣas, a boy was born. The boy cried. Prajāpati asked as to why he (i.e. the boy) was crying. The boy said that as there was no name given to him, he was not guarded against evil. Prajāpati then gave him the name Rudra. The *Śat. Br.* says that therefore a name should be given to a boy (i.e. child) to protect him from evil. Even a second or third name should be given to a boy, for it frees him from evil time to time (*ibid.* VI. 1.3.8-10). The *Śat. Br.* here echoes the belief in the efficacy of name which is conceived not as a series of syllables articulated with more or less tonic accent, but as a chanted declamation, in which rhythm, note ad tone constitute the essential elements. Such an enunciation is connected with the general theory of voice-magic.[99] The name of a person thus stands as his very soul - his 'name-soul.'[100] The above concept is at the basis of keeping the real name secret and giving another name to the boy for daily use. The reason is that if a person knows the real name of some one, by conjuring the latter with magic he can harm him. The ritual texts, while laying down some rites have such beliefs, in the *arthavāda*-portions of these rites.

The *Tait. Sam.*, while elucidating the Soma-sacrifice, states in the *arthavāda*-portions, importance of having two names. The mythical account runs as follows. The fire-places (*dhiṣṇiya*-s—heaps of earth serving as side-altars, covered with sand on which fire is placed) guarded Soma in the yonder world. They (gods) took away Soma from them, but the fire-places followed Soma and surrounded it. Deprived of the Soma-draught, the fire-places requested gods for it, who advised the former to take two names each. The *dhiṣṇiya*-s then became fires also.[101] The note struck at the end of the account is that a *brāhmaṇa*, who has two names is likely to prosper (*Tait. Sam.* VI. 3.1.2,3). The point is to stress that the regular fire-altars Āhavanīya, etc. are the same as the fire-places or *vice versa*. But for this, the help is taken of the folk-belief in name. The *Śat. Br.*, in the context of preparing the fire-places (*dhiṣṇya*-s), mentions the same account in the *arthavāda*-portion. But here the *gandharva*-s are said to have a second name. As Soma was taken away from them, they thought that by having a second name (*'dhiṣṇya-'s)* they would prosper. And really they did prosper and had a share in the sacrifice. The note struck at the end is the same as we have noted above from the *Tait. Sam.* (*Śat. Br.* III. 6.2.24).

In the Dīkṣaṇīya *yāga*-s, offerings are to be given to the gods — Agni, Savitṛ, Soma, Bṛhaspati, Indra, Rudra, Mitra and Varuṇa. These gods are termed *'devasū' (deva* +√*sū* - 'to give birth') and have the power of quickening. Quickened or impelled by these gods, the sacrificer will be born, i.e. sacrificially consecrated, the next day. The *arthavāda* states that these deities are double-named and as they form a pair, they mean strength and these strong ones impel him for being consecrated (*ibid.* V. 3.3.13, 14). The *Śat. Br.* makes the point clear in the context of the Agnicayana rite. It states that the gods who are the divine impellers come to have two names, as he, who is consecrated by the rite of consecration comes to have two names. The very rite of consecration for which he is impelled is his second name (*ibid.* IX. 4.3.13).

We have already noted the belief and practice of keeping the real name of a person secret and having another name for daily use, the idea being of protecting the person from the evil eye and thus from becoming a target of any sorcery. On the Indian scene, the *RV* is the oldest composition to refer to this, which mentions a secret name (*RV* X. 54.2; 71.1), also that the gods have secret names (*ibid.* V.5.10; IX. 95.2; 96.16; X.45.2). The *Śat. Br.* at one place says that a secret name is given to the child at birth (*Śat. Br.* VI. 1.3.9; also *Bṛh. Up.* VI. 4.25). While explaining the 'undefined' nature of offerings to Prajāpati, the mythical account in the *Pañc. Br.*, is based on this very idea of secrecy about the real name. Once the gods and the *asura*-s were fighting. When the *asura*-s proved to be mighty and stronger than gods, the gods rushed to Prajāpati for help. Prajāpati said that if he accepted the oblations addressed to them by name, the demons would carry away his oblations. Hence to Prajāpati, the 'undefined' ('*anirukta*') offering should be given, i.e. the name of the deity is not to be stated while offering an oblation to Prajāpati (*Pañc. Br.* XVIII. 1.3).

In the Rājasūya sacrifice, after besprinkling the king with waters, it is enjoined that the sacrificer-king should mount the chariot, with the words, 'I, the unharmed Arjuna....' The *arthavāda* explains that Indra is called Arjuna, which is his mystic name and the sacrificer-king is Indra for a twofold reason *viz.* he is a *kṣatriya* and he is a sacrificer (*Śat. Br.* V.4.3.7). While offering the Soma-cups *viz.* Adābhya and Aṁśu, it is said that '*Ādhāvāḥ*' ('moving ones') is the secret name of waters (*Tait. Sam.* III. 3.4.1).

In the context of the twelve-day sacrifice (leaving the beginning and the concluding sacrifices, i.e. Prāyaṇīya and Udayanīya *iṣṭi*-s, it is the ten-day sacrifice), while enjoining the 'Caturhotṛ' *mantra*-s,[102] the *Ait. Br.* states in the *arthavāda* that the 'Caturhotṛ' (*mantra*) is the sacrificial secret name of the gods (*Ait. Br.* V. 23 = 24.4).

The mythical account in the *Jaim. Br.* runs as follows, while telling the importance of certain verses. Indra killed Vṛtra with the *mantra*-s, which were in all metres. These *mantra*-s or verses are variously named as Mahānāmnī, Śakvarī and Simā. When Indra desired to have pairing with the Mahānāmnī verses, they agreed to it on condition that they be named Indra. Indra is thus their dear secret name (*Jaim. Br.* III. 111).

The importance of giving name to the child (boy) born is stressed by the *Kauṣ. Br.* through an elaborate mythical account. Prajāpati desirous of becoming 'many' underwent penance. From him were born the five *viz.* Agni, Vāyu, Āditya, Candramas and Uṣas. When Uṣas assuming the form of a nymph came in front of the four gods (Agni, etc.), they poured out seed, which was collected by Prajāpati in a golden bowl. To the boy born, Prajāpati, on the insistence of the boy, gave one after the other eight names as Bhava, Śarva, Paśupati, Ugra. Mahādeva, Rudra, Iśāna and Aśani, each time one name (*Kauṣ. Br.* VI. 1-9). This speaks of the eight names of the great god born (as a boy).

In the sacrificial procedure with respect to different sacrifices, there occurs practice of mentioning or not, the name of the sacrificer. In the New-moon and Full-moon sacrifices, in the context of the Iḍā-offerings, he does not mention the sacrificer's name on this occasion. The *arthavāda* states that it is a mysterious benediction on the Iḍā. If he mentions the name of the sacrificer, he would do what is human and the 'human' (touch to anything) is certainly inauspicious at the sacrifice (*Śat. Br.* I. 8.1.29). Again in the rite of consecration in the Soma-sacrifice, he does not utter the name of the sacrificer in the Sūktavāka (which is a *mantra* recited by the Hotṛ priest on the call of the Adhvaryu priest), The *arthavāda* here is — the consecrated is a divine embryo; they give no name to an embryo unborn. Hence the sacrificer's name is not uttered (*Kauṣ. Br.* VII. 2). But in the New-moon and Full-moon sacrifices, he mentions the name of the sacrificer in the Sūktavāka, for it is the divine self of the sacrificer, which the priests make ready. He mentions the sacrificer's name, for here is the sacrificer born. He should mention it aloud, even if he be a teacher (*ācārya)*, for thereby the sacrificer is not likely to fall into ruin (*ibid.* III. 8).

Offerings

The constituents of a sacrifice are three *viz.* (i) *dravya* (offering material); (ii) *devatā* (deity); and (iii) *tyāga* (action of offering). Under the category of *dravya*, we have the substances out of which the offerings are prepared, they being Soma, animal and vegetarian substances *viz.* products of cow's milk, rice and barley.

In the chapter on "Animals and Birds" we have already dealt with the animals, which were offered as sacrificial victims. Gonda has dealt with rice and barley offerings, in the Veda.[103] Here we take into account some convictions of the ritualists about the sacrificial cake (*puroḍāśa)*, prepared from corn (either rice or barley). The *puroḍāśa* is offered as an animal-victim (*Śat. Br.* I.2.3.5). This occurs in the exposition of the New-moon and Full-moon sacrifices. In the same context it is said that the sacrificial cake is the head of the sacrifice, for the potsherds (*kapālāni* — on which the cake is baked) are to this cake what the skull-bones (*kapālāni)* are to the head and the ground flour (*piṣṭāni)* is nothing else than the brain (*ibid.* I.2.1.2). On the sacrificial cake (rice-cake), that is placed on the fire on the potsherds, another one pours the clarified butter. These two actions are to be done simultaneously, as complementary to each other. The *arthavāda* is very clear in pointing out that one half of the body of sacrifice is the clarified butter, the other half being the rice-offering (*haviḥ*). Both are placed on the fire, by which action this body of the sacrifice is joined together (*ibid.* I.2.2.4,5). Prior to baking the sacrificial cake, fire is carried round it (*tam paryagnim karoti*). By this he encloses the cake with an unbroken fence, lest the evil spirits, the *rakṣas*-es should pounce upon it, for Agni is the repeller of the *rakṣas*-es (*ibid.* 13). When the cake is baked, he covers it over (with not ashes), lest the evil spirits, the *rakṣas*-es should notice it; lest it should lie as it were naked and as it were robbed of (*ibid.* 16). About the size of the sacrificial cake—the practice was that it should not be too broad, otherwise it would be human, i.e. the cake commonly prepared. Unlucky or excluded, from the sacrifice is such a cake. The *Śat. Br.* states the opinion of some that he should make it of the size of a horse's hoof, but itself opines that who does know how large is a horse's hoof. So he should make the cake of such a size, which according to him is not too broad (*ibid.* I.2.2.9,10).

We now come to a subtle point regarding the sacrificial cake. A somewhat lengthy mythical account occurs in the context of the New-moon and Full-moon sacrifices. The gods by means of the sacrifice gained the world of heaven. But in order to make that world unattainable by men, they sipped the sap of the sacrifice and wiped off the traces of it with the sacrificial post. The *ṛṣi*-s ('ritualist thinkers' here) set about searching for the sacrifice, and thought of going to the place where the gods obtained the possession of the world of heaven. At that place they came upon the sacrificial cake, which had become a tortoise and which was creeping about. They all took it for sacrifice and asked it to stand still for the Aśvins, for Sarasvatī and for Indra. But it crept on. When they asked it to stand for Agni, it stopped. Knowing that it has stopped for Agni, they offered it entirely in fire, as it was an oblation for the gods. Then the sacrifice appeared to them, they produced it and spread it. The same sacrifice is taught by the former to the latter, by the father to the son. The sacrificial cake which caused the sacrifice to appear to them, first (*puras)* bestowed (*dāś)* it on them, hence it is *purodāśa*, the same as *puroḍāśa* (*ibid.* I.6.2.1-5). The etymology in this mythical account, which has come as *arthavāda* is 'made to order' to suit the account. The important point is the connection between the cake and the tortoise, mainly based on the circular size of the two. But does it also suggest that originally the cake was of the size of a tortoise? And still with a probe further, does the detail indicate that in the remote period the entire tortoise was dropped in the fire? This is not stretching the account too further, when in the Agnicayana rite we have a mention of a live tortoise being placed in the first layer, which we have noted elsewhere.

To take a note of a couple of offerings. In the Pravargya rite, the two Rauhiṇa cakes are enjoined to be offered. The *arthavāda* points out that the two Rauhiṇas are Agni and Āditya, for by means of these two the sacrificers ascend (√*ruh* - 'to ascend') to heaven. Day and night are also Rauhiṇas and the Pravargya is the sun, which is encompassed by the day and the night (*ibid.* XIV.2.1 2, 3). Here we are reminded of the *asura* Rauhiṇa mentioned in the *RV* (*RV.* I.103.2; II.12.12). Indra is said to have killed this *asura* (*ibid.* I.103.2). Indra armed with the thunderbolt spurned Rauhiṇa as he was ascending the heaven (*ibid.* II.12.12). In the rain-phenomenon, when Indra is taken to be rain-god, Rauhiṇa could mean the sun, which is covered with the black clouds for some time, and becomes invisible. This interpretation can be supported by the *arthavāda* noted above, which states that Agni and Āditya (the sun) are the two Rauhiṇas. Can we say that these two are named Rauhiṇa because they ascend—Agni with flames and Āditya (the sun) seen traversing the sky? The etymology of the word *rauhiṇa* from the root √*ruh* ('to ascend') can be proved effective in the case of these two also, as it is shown in the case of the sacrificers, who ascend to heaven with the help of Agni and Āditya.

In the context of the Tryambaka-offerings (Tryambakahaviryāga), the offerings consist of cakes on one potsherd only, for the deity is one to which they belong. There are as many cakes as there are descendants exceeded by one. For each individual descendant, there is one cake. By offering an additional cake, he delivers from Rudra's power descendants that are not yet born to him. The potsherds (each having one cake on it) are put on the north side of the Gārhapatya hearth, for north is the quarter of that god Rudra. Unlike the other sacrificial cakes, these cakes are unanointed (with the clarified butter, which is a product of the cow's milk). The *arthavāda* is very convincing in explaining this *vidhi*, which was a practice. It says that if the cakes are anointed, Rudra would be hankering after the sacrificer's cattle (*Śat. Br.* II. 6.2. 3-6). Hence the instruction not to anoint the cakes, which are to be offered to Rudra. To turn to a special offering *viz. sānnāyya* for the preparation of which the evening milking is required for the sour curds and whey to be mixed with the sweet boiled milk of the following morning. The *Tait. Sam.* states a mythical account by way of *arthavāda* in this regard. When Indra had slain Vṛtra, his power and strength went into the earth. Then were born plants and roots. When Indra ran to Prajāpati and told this to him, Prajāpati asked the cattle to collect that (power and strength) for Indra. Having collected it from the plants, the cattle milked it. As they collected it, the name *sānnāyya* (fr. *sam* + √*nī* — ' to carry together, bring together') for the collected oblation. When this (oblation) did not impel Indra, Prajāpati told them to make curds for him. They made curds for him. That impelled (*'ahinot'* fr. √*hi* - to impel') him. So the name *dadhi* for curds. About the deity of *sānnāyya*, the *Tait. Sam.* says that it is the All-gods (Viśve Devāḥ), for they won *sānnāyya* as their share. But it is said that the deity of *sānnāyya* is Indra for they won it in healing Indra (*Tait. Sam.* II. 5.3.2-7).

The *Tait. Sam.* enjoins that no one who is not a Soma sacrificer should offer the *sānnāyya*, for the milk of him who is not a Soma sacrificer is imperfect and is poured forth in vain (*Tait. Sam.* II. 5.5.1). Nevertheless the *sānnāyya* can be offered by a person who has not performed a Soma-sacrifice, says the *Śat. Br.* (*Śat. Br.* I.6.4.10, 11 for the two view-points and the decision given).

Prastara (bunch of grass)

Prastara (bunch of grass) bears great importance in sacrifice. *Prastara* is said to be the sacrificer (*Pañc. Br.* VI. 7. 17; *Śat. Br.* I.8.1.44; I.8.3.11). It is said to be the sacrifice (*Śat. Br.* III. 4.3.19). In the rite of guest-offering (*ātithya)* given to King Soma, the *prastara* is said to be of the Aśvavāla grass (Saccharum Spontaneum) (*Śat. Br.* III. 4.1.17). The mythical account about the Aśvavāla grass is already taken note of by us in the chapter on "Trees, Plants and Varieties of Grass."

In the New-moon and Full-moon sacrifices in the Sūktavāka rite, he takes the *prastara.* If he desires rain, he should take up the *prastara*, with a *mantra* (*Vāj. Sam.* II. 16d). He anoints the top of the *prastara* with the butter in the *juhū* (ladle), the middle part (with that) in the *upabhṛt* (ladle) and the lower end (with that) in the *dhruvā* (ladle). This anointing is done each time with a *mantra* (*Vāj. Sam.* II. 16 e) — 'May the gods eat, licking the anointed bird'. The *prastara* (and symbolically the sacrificer) is caused to be a bird and fly up from this world of men to the world of gods (*Śat. Br.* I.8.3.11-14). He then takes a single stalk from the *prastara.* The *prastara* is the sacrificer. If he throws the whole *prastara* at once in the fire, the sacrificer would speedily go to the yonder world. But when a single stalk is taken out (from the *prastara)*, the sacrificer will live long and will get the full measure of life here on earth. Having held the *prastara* for a moment, he throws it into the fire and thereby not cut off the sacrificer from the yonder world (*ibid.* 16,17). When the Bahiṣpavamāna laud (*stotra*) is to be chanted[104] near the *cātvāla*, while moving there, the Adhvaryu priest carries the *prastara*. The *arthavāda* in this regard states that the *prastara* is the sacrificer and the Adhvaryu by this way takes the sacrificer to the heavenly world (*Pañc. Br.* VI. 7.16-17). The mythical accounts stated here are interesting. The sacrifice, having taken the form of a horse, went away from the gods. The gods brought it to a standstill by a bunch of grass (*prastara).* Hence a horse when wiped with a bunch of grass is pleased. The Adhvaryu's carrying the *prastara* is for soothing the sacrifice (*ibid.* 18). Another mythical account telling the importance of *prastara* is—When Prajāpati created the domestic animals, they being hungry went away from him. When Prajāpati presented them a bunch of grass, they turned towards him. So the Adhvaryu should slightly wave the bunch of grass, for the animals turn to a stalk of grass, that is waved before them (*ibid.* 19).

These *arthavāda*-s are significant, for they bring out the importance of the *prastara* in sacrifice, the use of which is made with a particular belief.

Priests

The *Jaim. Br.*, in the context of twelve-day sacrifice (Dvādaśāha), has stated the etymology of the word *'ṛtvij'* (priest). Prajāpati was alone at the beginning. He desired that he should be 'many' and (hence) should procreate. He toiled and then saw in himself the *ṛtviya* (the 'ever-moving orderly arrangement' - from the word *'ṛtu'* and that too from the root √*ṛ* - 'to go', which also gives the word '*ṛta*'). From that (i.e. *ṛtviya*) he created the three seasons (*viz.* Grīṣma, Varṣā and Hemanta) as also these (three) worlds. As these seasons (*ṛtu*-s*)* are created from the *'ṛtviya'*, so their nature of being the *'ṛtu*-s' (*ṛtutva).* Even the priests, he created from the *'ṛtviya'*. So the name *'ṛtvij' (Jaim. Br.* III.1). The Adhvaryu priest is the mind and the Hotṛ priest is the speech. He thus brings mind and speech together (*Śat. Br.* I.5.1.21). The *Śat. Br.* says that the duties of the Agnīdh priest should be discharged by one, who is accomplished. One who is known and learned in sacred lore is truly accomplished. The mythical account in this connection runs as follows. In the fight between the gods and the *asura-rakṣas*-es, the latter attacked the gods from the south and forced them out of the *sadas* and overturned the *dhiṣṇya*-s, which were in the *sadas.* They forced the gods back to the Āgnīdhra fire and even won from them one half of the Āgnīdhra fire. With the other half of that fire, the All-gods (Viśve Devāḥ) gained immortality. So to the Agnīdh priest they carry the *dakṣiṇā* first (*ibid.* III. 6.1.27-29). The belief in the efficacy of the Agnīdh priest and the Āgnīdhra fire seems to be so much that if weakness were to come upon one of those consecrated, the Adhvaryu priest should advise that the weak be carried to the Āgnīdhra, for there he will not meet with affliction (*ibid.* 29. Sāyana. says that the weak 'one' could be the fire, which will not suffer evil).

The Brahman priest has unique importance in the sacrifice. In the New-moon and Full-moon sacrifices, he is the one who eats the *prāśitra,*[105] since it is his special share. Thereafter he has to watch what remains incomplete of the sacrifice. He must maintain silence from the time he takes his seat up to the speech of Adhvaryu, 'Brahman! Shall I step forward?' The *arthavāda* is significant pointing out the exact importance of the Brahman priest in the sacrificial procedure. Brahman priest is the best physician. He thereby restores the sacrifice. If he sits there talking, he would not restore the sacrifice. So he should observe silence and watch closely the whole procedure (*ibid.* I.7.4.18, 19). The same thought about Brahman priest, of he being the best physician occurs in the *Śat. Br.* elsewhere (*ibid.* XIV. 2.2.19). In the context of the Agniṣṭoma sacrifice, it is said that the fire-priests combined convey the sacrifice to the gods. By filling their cups, he satisfies them together, with the thought that satisfied and pleased, they shall convey the sacrifice to the gods (*ibid.* IV. 2.1.32). The role of priests in sacrifice is so indispensable that it is said, in the context of the Agniṣṭoma sacrifice, that as a yoked animal draws a cart, so do the priests (carry the sacrifice to the end), who perform the priestly duties (*ibid.* IV. 4.3.13).

In the sacrificial session of the hundred Atirātra sacrifices, after the Bahiṣpavamāna laud is chanted, two *śloka*-s are sung, which glorify the task carried out by the four priests (two Hotṛs and two Adhvaryus) in the hundred Atirātra sacrifices. It is said that with four harnessed steeds from the Sindhu territory (*saindhava*-s), the sages left behind them the gloom. They are the wise gods, who spun out the session of a hundred sacrifices (*ibid.* XI. 5.5.12, which is the *śloka*, i.e. verse, noted above). The second *śloka* clarifies that in this sacrificial session, the four harnessed steeds are the two Hotṛs and the two Adhvaryus (*ibid.* 13), bringing out the importance of the priests.

The *śloka*-s in the Brāhmaṇa-texts form a part of the traditional lore, which is preserved in the ritualistic tradition. As they were recited to support the rituals in hand. Sāyana calls them *mantra* at several places.[106]

Sacrifice

The ritual-texts, Brāhmaṇa-texts in particular, are replete with the eulogies of sacrifice. Sacrifice is said to be the self (*ātmā*) of all beings and all gods (*Śat. Br.* XIV. 3.2.1). The power (*mahaḥ*) of the gods is sacrifice (*ibid.* I.9.1.11). Sacrifice is the food of the gods (*ibid.* V.1.1.2). Sacrifice is said to be a divine boat (*nauḥ*), which both the father and the son steer and it does not sink (*Jaim. Br.* I. 166). Sacrifice is a divine steed (*ibid.* I. 83). Sacrifice is the most glorious work (*Śat. Br.* I.7.1.5). In the context of the consecration rite for the Agniṣṭoma sacrifice, the muttering of a sacrificial formula (*yajus*) is said to be an occult form (*parokṣa*) of sacrifice, but a libation (*āhuti*) the direct form (*pratyakṣa*) of sacrifice (*ibid.* III. 1.4.1). Sacrifice is equated with speech (*ibid.* III.1.4.2, 14 etc. — an oft-repeated equation), with cattle (*ibid.* III. 1.4.9). The equation 'Sacrifice is Viṣṇu' or *vice versa* is a common feature, occurring at several places. Offerings are said to be the self of sacrifice (*ibid.* I.6.3.39). Āhavanīya (fire) is said to be the head of the sacrifice (*ibid.* VI. 5.2.1). The sacrifice, which is being spread, is said to be Prajāpati (*ibid.* IV. 2.4.16), again an oft-repeated equation (*ibid.* I.5.2.17).

The *arthavāda* in the *Ait. Br.* brings out the importance of the *brāhmaṇa* (here priest, carrying out his duties) and the metres — the two important factors —concerning sacrifice. The mythical account here runs as follows. When the sacrifice as food departed from the gods, they searched him, by the *brāhmaṇa* and the metres. Having obtained him (i.e. sacrifice), they told him to serve them as food, becoming united with the *brāhmaṇa* and metres (*Ait. Br* III. 45 = 15.1). The *Mait. Sam.*, in the context of the *iṣṭi*-s (sacrifices) performed for getting certain desires fulfilled, states that in sacrifice all metres are employed (*Mait. Sam.* II. 4.5). Gāyatrī, the metre which is often employed for eulogising Agni and is regarded as the most efficacious metre is equated with sacrifice (*Śat. Br.* IV. 2.4.20). Sacrifice is the sacrificer; sacrifice is the King Soma. When in the Havirdhāna shed, they press the King Soma with the grinding stones, they (actually or truly) make seed — the sacrificer (*Jaim. Br.* I. 259).

A graphic description of sacrifice said to be a man occurs in the context of the construction of the Havirdhāna shed as also preparation of *sadas*, hearths (*dhiṣṇya*-s), etc. As man spreads sacrifice, sacrifice is said to be man. When spread, sacrifice is made as large as man. Sacrifice has the Havirdhāna shed as its head and Viṣṇu for its deity. The Āhavanīya Agni is its mouth and so the sacrificer offers on this fire. The sacrificial post is its crest-lock and the Āgnīdhrīya and Mārjālīya (hearths) are its arms. The *sadas* (the sacrificial hall) is its belly. As the gods sat (√*sad*) in it, it is called *sadas*. The two fires (i.e. the old Āhavanīya and Gārhapatya, fires which are in the Prācīnavaṁśa - the structure, the bamboos of which turn towards the east), are its feet. Thus sacrifice is made as large as man (*Śat. Br.* III. 5.3.1-6).

In the context of the New-moon and the Full-moon sacrifices, the same ritual metaphor that the sacrifice is man is spoken of, but here it is by mentioning the various spoons. The *juhū* and the *upabhṛt* are said to belong to that man-shaped sacrifice. The *dhruvā* spoon represents the trunk (of that man-shaped sacrifice). The *sruva* (Masculine) - the dipping spoon—is the breath. As the breath passes through all the limbs, the dipping-spoon goes to all the offering spoons. To give a cosmic basis to the sacrifice, it is said that the *juhū* is the yonder sky, the *upabhṛt* the atmosphere (i.e. the mid-region) and the *dhruvā* this earth. From this earth originate all the worlds, so does the whole sacrifice proceed from the *dhruvā.* The *sruva* (dipping-spoon) is the blowing wind, which sweeps across all these worlds and so goes the *sruva* to all the offering-spoons. When the sacrifice is being performed, it is performed for the gods, the seasons and the metres (*ibid.* I.3.2.1-6).

A significant fact about sacrifice is spoken of in the context of the fore-offerings (*prayāja*-s) in the New-moon and Full-moon sacrifices. It is said that the creatures that are not allowed to take part in the sacrifice are forlorn. Hence all creatures that are here are made to take part in the sacrifice. Behind the men are the beasts, and behind the gods are the birds, the plants and the trees (*ibid.* I.5.2.4). Sacrifice is said to be fivefold, fivefold is the animal victim and five are the seasons of the yẹar (*ibid.* 16).

Sacrifice is said to be born from (conceptual) union. This is seen when the lower churning-stick is laid with the words, 'You are Urvaśī.' He then touches the melted butter (*ājya)* in the pan with the upper churning-stick, with the words, 'You are Āyu' and puts it down on the lower churning-stick with the words, 'You are Purūravas'. From this union he produces the sacrifice (*ibid.* III. 4.1.22). As sacrificer is said to be the sacrifice, about the sacrificer the *Jaim. Br.* has an important thought to state. It is said that the sacrificer is born twice, once from the union (of his parents) and then from the sacrifice. When he is born from the union that is for this world. When he is born from the sacrifice, he is born for the other world, for the world of the *gandharva*-s, for that of the gods and for the heavenly world (*Jaim. Br.* I. 259). Thus sacrifice makes the sacrificer immortal.

Saline Soil (*ūsāḥ*)

The use of saline soil is prescribed in some rituals. The *arthavāda*-s stated in this regard by the ritual texts speak of the beliefs about saline soil in those times.

In the rite of Agnicayana, saline soil is placed on the site of the Gārhapatya altar, because saline soil stands for nourishment, procreation and mutual agreement. A mythical account occurs in the *Tait. Sam.* at this place which states that the sky and the earth at first were together. After separating from each other, they thought of sharing together what was worthy of sacrifice with each of them. The sacrifice-worthy portion from the sky was placed in the earth. It became the saline soil.[107] Such a sacrificial portion went up to the sky to become black (spot) in the moon. By placing the saline soil on the Gārhapatya site and thinking of the black spot in the moon, the sacrificer piles the Gārhapatya fire at a site in between the sky and the earth (*Tait. Sam.* V.2.3.2,3). The *Ait. Br.* strikes a note of marriage (*vivāha)* between the sky and the earth and the mythical account occurs in the context of the twelve-day sacrifice, while laying down the transposing of metres. The account brings out the importance of saline soil as seen by the Vedic ritualists. We see Tura Kāvaṣeya telling Janamejaya that saline soil is nourishment and also supporting his belief by saying that in this world also, men, while thinking of a grazing ground for cattle enquire whether there is saline soil, for saline soil is nourishment (*Ait. Br.* IV.27 = 19.5). The query brings out that an agricultural land having in the vicinity, saline soil was most beneficial to the king, because both agriculture and cattle-tending could thrive well on such an area.

The *Śat. Br.*, in the context of the Agnicayana rite, while laying down the scattering of saline soil over the Gārhapatya site says that the Gārhapatya stands for the terrestrial world and the saline soil for the cattle. By scattering the saline soil, he bestows cattle on this world (*Śat. Br.* VII. 1.1.6; also VII. 1.1.8; VII. 3.1.8). Another rite in which saline soil is enjoined to be scattered at the site of the Gārhapatya altar is of Agnyādhāna or Agnyādheya. The *Mait. Sam.* says that by scattering the saline soil, seed is deposited for the nourishment and propagation of the cattle (*Mait. Sam.* I.6.3).

While laying down the *sambhāra*-s (i.e. objects which are brought for being scattered over the site of the Gārhapatya altar and which we shall discuss further in this chapter), the *Śat. Br.* mentions saline soil as one of the *sambhāra*-s. While glorifying the *vidhi* of scattering the saline soil, the *Śat. Br.* says that the sky bestowed the saline soil as cattle on this earth. Hence is saline soil suitable for cattle. The saline soil is here said to be the essence (*rasam)* of the two worlds *viz.* sky and the earth. By scattering the saline soil on the Gārhapatya site, the Adhvaryu priest supplies to Agni, the essence of these two worlds (*Śat. Br.* II. 1.1.6).

The *Tait. Br.* while mentioning saline soil as one of the *sambhāra*-s says that by the saline soil, he establishes Agni in nourishment, progeny and also in mutual understanding. Saline soil stands for the common understanding among the cattle (*Tait. Br.* I.1.3.1). The *Tait. Br.* at this place relates the mythical account, already noted in details, of the sky and the earth giving a gift to each other (*ibid.* 2, 3).

An interesting detail about saline soil occurs in the context of the Vājapeya sacrifice, when they (priests or *viśaḥ*, i.e. common people) throw small packets of saline soil at the sacrificer, when having mounted the sacrificial post, he is in the climbed up position. This is mentioned in the Saṁhitā-s (*Tait. Sam.* I.7.9; *Kāṭh. Sam.* XIV. 8; *Mait. Sam.* I.11.8). The *Tait. Br.* has a ritual metaphor here — 'The saline soil is food incarnate' (*ete hi sākṣādannam yadūṣāh*). They (priests or the common people) as though make him prosperous with the choicest food (*Tait. Br.* I.3.7.6). While prescribing the throwing of packets of saline soil by the common people (*viśaḥ*) at the sacrificer,[108] the *Śat. Br.* states that saline soil means cattle and cattle is food. He who offers the Vājapeya wins food, for Vājapeya is the same as *annapeya* (*Śat. Br.* V. 2.1.16). Keith opines that this ritual (*Tait. Sam.* I.7.9) is a fertility spell. The *vaiśya*-s were probably the proper givers as they would be interested in salt for their cattle.[109] However Keith's remark has to be improved upon. The Vājapeya sacrifice is intended to confer on a person paramount sovereignty (*sāmrājya*)[110] and a person, who has performed the Vājapeya sacrifice, being thereafter a special person in the society, is not to descend (from a horse or an elephant) for any other person,[111] for that would be below his new and hereafter permanent highest status. It is but natural then if the common people indicate their allegiance to him by throwing the packets of saline soil at him. This ritual practice can be connected to that in the ancient world. In Arabic and other customs, the bond created by eating salt together is in the highest degree sacred and may deserve the name 'salt-communion'. Very holy obligations were 'covenants of salt'.[112]

From the ritual use of the saline soil and the *arthavāda*-s about it, it seems that right from the beginning, sites of saline soil were somewhat uncommon, as compared to those of agricultural black soil, which was fit for growing corn. Hence saline soil was regarded to have some kind of divine touch and was believed to have come directly from the sky, from where the rains or dew came. These sites of saline soil must be the sites, where the proportion of sodium as compared to other ingredients of the soil must be high and where growing of crop would not be fruitful. Nevertheless, on such sites of saline soil there can grow profuse grass and shrubs. They could thus serve as good grazing grounds for the cattle, where the latter could be nourished, multiplied and also could move peacefully with full accord, the grazing lands being vast. The *arthavāda* in the *Mait. Sam.* states that the cattle not licking the saline soil (*anūṣarihaḥ)*, i.e. not grazing on the grass at the saline soil, do not impregnate the seed. Such *arthavāda*-s relating or at times equating the saline soil with cattle, shed some light on the economic history of ancient India, when the belts of saline land were made best use of.[113]

Salt; (Salty) Sea-water

Having taken a note of saline soil as mentioned in the ritual texts, it is necessary to consider a reference to salt, which occurs in the *Jaim. Br.* in the context of the Maidhātitha *sāman* (*sāman* 'seen' by Medhātithi). According to it, Triśoka once released the cattle, which did not have hair on their ears. Some of these cattle, tormented by heat, ran away facing the west and entered sea. That became salt. So they say that salt is the cows (*gāvo lavaṇam iti)*. Therefore whosoever barters with salt, he gets cows (*Jaim. Br.* III. 236). This detail about salt mentioned in the *Jaim. Br.* refers to a site of saline soil, where the sea was near and that too, to the west, because it states that the cattle ran to the west, entered the sea and became salt. The passage also points out that salt was used for bartering with the cows. It is clear that right from the beginning salt was rare because it was to be made from the sea-water by a particular technique of salt-cultivation. Salt-rocks, from which salt named Saindhava and black salt were available, could be found only in the hilly tracts. But even such rocks were not common. This rarity of salt can be marked even in Kauṭilya's times (i.e. 4th cent B.C.), as can be seen from his *Arthaśāstra*. The Salt-Commissioner (Lavaṇādhyakṣa) is required to collect the share of salt as well as several kinds of tax (duty) on salt (*Arthaśāstra* II.12.28-34). Only *brāhmaṇa*-s well-versed in the Veda-s, ascetics and labourers were allowed to take salt for their food without paying any tax. This is about the sites from which salt was actually cultivated or manufactured, from the beds of back- waters of the sea or in some cases from the salt-rocks. And about the sites, where the soil was full of saline particles. We have already noted that such saline belts can grow grass for the cattle, thus making available ample milk-products and in modern times giving impetus to dairy-farming.

In spite of such convincing and at times logical ritual reasoning (*arthavāda*) about saline soil or salt, there occurs an apparently amusing *arthavāda* in the *Tait. Br.*, which tries to explain the salty taste of the sea-water. In the context of the Soma-sacrifice, the *mantra*-s of the Hotṛ priest are laid down (*Tait. Br.* II. 2.8). While speaking of the origin of these *mantra*-s, there is a discourse on the creation of the world and incidentally of the sea. It is said that in the beginning, there was nothing. Non-existence made up its mind to be Existence (i.e. Named and Formed One). It got heated (due to penance). So there came smoke. After its subsequent toilings and heatings, there came out one after the other, Agni, lustre, flame, rays, rising fog. All these having gathered together, formed a hard substance—a bladder—which was broken by that One. This became sea. Thereafter they do not drink sea-water, taking it to be the amniotic fluid at the childbirth. This fluid comes out first when the animal (i.e. calf) is in the process of being born (*ibid.* II. 2.9.2,3). Here the universal fact about the saltiness of sea-water is tried to be explained with the help of the phenomenon of childbirth.

Sambhāra-s

Sambhāra-s[114] are mentioned in the rite of Agni-ādhāna (Agnyādhāna also called Agnyādheya — establishing the fires, generally three but even five with the mention of Sabhya and Āvasathya). Having dug out the surface of the ground chosen for sacrifice, the *sambhāra*-s are placed on it. These are of two types—the objects comprising earth and those from the wood of the trees. Each type consists of six or seven objects. The *sambhāra*-s from the trees in the form of wood from them have been dealt with by us in the chapter on "Trees and Plants", where the beliefs about the trees, spoken of or indicated by the *arthavāda*-s are noted. Here we take into account the *sambhāra*-s comprising earth, as stated by the *Tait. Br.* (I.1.3.1-8, which speaks of seven objects comprising earth; and *ibid.* 9-12, where wood from six trees is mentioned to form six *sambhāra*-s).

(*i*) *sikatā* (sand) is said to be the aspect of fire (*ibid.* I.1.3.1), when it is used as a *sambhāra.* The *Śat. Br.* mentions sand in a couple of *vidhi*-s, but not as a *sambhāra.*

In the Agniṣṭoma sacrifice, when the Mahāvedi (i.e. the large Soma-altar—the Saumikī vedi) and the Uttaravedi are prepared, he bestrews the Uttaravadi with sand. Sand is said to be an ornament, for sand is rather shining. Sand is the ashes of Agni Vaiśvānara. So when Agni is about to be placed thereon (i.e. on the Uttaravedi with sand on it), Agni does not injure it (*Śat. Br.* III. 5.1.36). In the rite of Agnicayana, he scatters saline soil on the Gārhapatya altar, which is said to be the womb and the saline soil the amnion. Then he scatters sand to keep the saline soil (i.e. the amnion) from being scorched, for sand is the ashes of Agni Vaiśvānara, which is about to be built up and Agni does not scorch his own self (*ibid.* VII. 1.1.9). Sand is also said here to be the seed of Agni Vaiśvānara, which is about to be built up. Nothing is fashioned from out of the seedless, so the seed, i.e. sand, is scattered (*ibid.* 10; also for the same *arthavāda ibid.* VII. 1.1.41).

(*ii*) *ūṣāḥ* (Saline soil) — We have already dealt with this *sambhāra*, under the topic "Saline soil". In brief, it is for nourishment and is said to be the gift of heaven to the earth (*Tait. Br.* I.1.3.2, 3). Here the pseudo-myth of Heaven and Earth being first in close embrace and later on separated is stated, where the dark spot in the orb of the moon is said to be the gift from the Earth. While depositing the saline earth on the ground for sacrifice, one should think of the spot in the moon (*ibid.*). In the *Śat. Br.*, where the *sambhāra*-s mentioned are only five, the saline soil figures and is said to be suitable for cattle and also cattle, which he supplies to Agni (*Śat. Br.* II. 1.1.6).

(*iii*) *ākhukarīṣa* (earth dug up by the moles)—Agni once concealed himself from the gods. Having become a mole he dug himself into the earth. The mole-hills thrown up by him are the essence of the earth (*Tait. Br.* I.1.3.3). The *Śat. Br.* mentions this *sambhāra* (i.e. the earth of a mole-hill), and speaks of the belief that the moles certainly know the savour of the earth, so enter deeper and deeper into the earth and become fat. Wherever they know the savour of this earth, they cast it up and thus the mole-hill (*Śat. Br.* II.1.1.7).

(*iv*) *valmīka-vapā* (earth from an ant-hill)—Ant-hill is regarded as the strength of earth collected by ants. By placing this *sambhāra*, he places the earth's strength there. The ant-hill is also said to be the 'ear' (*śrotra*) of the earth (*Tait. Br.* I.1.3.4.). The ant-hill is mentioned in other rites also. While preparing the fire-pan in the rite of Agnicayana, he looks at the lump of clay through the hollow part of the ant-hill. Fire (i.e. the fire-pan—the lump of clay) is to be announced to Prajāpati, who is this earth and the ant-hill is its 'ear' (*Tait. Sam.* V.1.2.5). The ritual metaphor is based on the conic shape of both (ant-hill and the ear). Earth from the ant-hill (*valmīka-vapā*) is mixed with the clay, from which the pot for the Pravargya rite is made (*Śat. Br.* XIV. 1.2.10).

(*v*) *sūda* (never-drying lake) —The mythical account states that Prajāpati created the creatures but their food got diminished. He (according to Sāyaṇa's commentery) bringing the mud from the never-drying lake spread it on several regions of the earth, from which came the never-diminishing crop. So this *sambhāra*, by which he will never have want of food (*Tait. Br.* I.1.3.5).

(*vi*) *śarkarāḥ* (pebbles) —The mythical account states that Prajāpati taking the form of a boar, brought up the earth from the primeval waters. He spread it on the leaf of a lotus but it kept on shaking. So, he made it firm by placing pebbles. Pebbles are brought as *sambhāra* to give firmness to the ground of sacrifice. The *Tait. Br.* cannot resist from giving the etymology of the word *śarkarāḥ*, and says that as well-being (*śam* = *sukham*) came to Prajāpati from the *śarkarāḥ* (as pebbles were placed on the earth), so the name *'sarkarāḥ'* (*ibid.* 5-7). In the mythical account from the *Śat. Br.* figure the gods and the *asura*-s, contending for superiority. As the earth was trembling like a lotus-leaf, the gods fastened down that earth to make it firm and steady. So the Adhvaryu fastens down the ground for sacrifice by pebbles, to make it firm and steady (*Śat. Br.* II.1.1.8-11). Here the *arthavāda*-passage (i.e. the mythical account noted above) does not mention the details about Prajāpati as we have seen in the mythical account from the *Tait. Br.*

(*vii*) *hiraṇya* (gold) —The mythical account occurring as *arthavāda* here is as follows. Waters were the wives of Varuṇa. Being enamoured of them, he longed for them and his semen got ejected; that became gold. When he places gold as *sambhāra*, he (as though) places Agni with his seed on the ground of sacrifice (*Tait. Br.* I.1.3.8). In the *Śat. Br.* also there is a mention of gold among the *sambhāra*-s. But the mythical account here is not crude as that in the *Tait. Br.*, noted above. It is said that Agni once cast his eyes on the waters and thought of uniting with them. In them, having come to them, he sprinkled the 'seed'; that became gold, which shines like fire, it being Agni's seed. Hence it is that gold is found in water,[115] for Agni poured it in the water (*Śat. Br.* II. 1.1.5). Here the relation between fire and water spoken of is convincing, for we have already noted the belief in the chapter on "Water" that the waters, especially the flowing ones (being lukewarm) are taken to be possessed of the principle of heat (i.e. fire).

We have already noted that the *Śat. Br.* mentions five *sambhāra*-s and not seven as stated in the *Tait. Br.* Out of these five *sambhāra*-s, from the *Śat. Br.*, four are already taken note of by us *viz.* saline soil, earth dug up by the moles, pebbles and gold. The fifth *sambhāra* mentioned by the *Śat. Br.* is water Actually it stands as the first *sambhāra*, and gold, saline soil, earth dug up by the moles and pebbles are mentioned subsequently (*Śat. Br.* II. 1.1.3-8).

Water ('*ap*' Feminine)

He sprinkles with water the (three) lines drawn by the Adhvaryu priest on the Gārhapatya fire-place. Here the water symbolises food, for when water comes to this world, food is produced here. And 'water' is said to be female and Agni (Masculine) male. So here is the procreative pairing. The *arthavāda* having stated the belief about the waters based on observation, then catches the finger of etymology and says that as all this universe is obtained (*āpta* from the root √*āp* - 'to get, obtain') by waters ('*ap*' — 'water'), he brings water as *sambhāra* (*ibid.* 3,4).

The variations in the lists of the *sambhāra*-s occurring in the ritual-texts are taken note of in details by Dange.[116]

Shadow

The belief about shadow is that it is evil and hence to be avoided or crossed over. In the rite of Punarādheya,[117] the householder has to establish his fires at midday, for at this hour of the day, the sun is nearest to this world, and he produces the fire from the nearest centre. The *arthavāda* stated here is important, for it speaks of the belief about shadow. It is said that man is attached with evil , as with a shadow. At midday that evil of his like his shadow is smallest and shrinks, as it were, beneath his foot. He crushes that evil, when it is smallest. So the midday (hour) is to be chosen for re-establishing the fires (*Śat. Br.* II. 2.3.10). A reference to shadow occurs when expiations for the errors committed in the performance of Agnihotra rite are prescribed. The error could be with respect to the morning as well as the evening Agnihotra rite (*Ait. Br.* VII. 12 = 32.11). Here the *Ait. Br.* gives a general instruction (*vidhi*-statement) regarding the performance of the evening Agnihotra rite. It says that he should take out (the lighted embers for) the Āhavanīya fire in the evening before the blending of the shadows, i.e. before the non-distinction of the shadows due to non-availability of light, once the night sets in. The shadow is darkness, death. With the light (to the Āhavanīya) he crosses over the shadow, the darkness and death (*ibid.*).

Here the belief about shadow, as its being evil or darkness or death, is obviously based on the dark or black colour of the shadow, which stands for something inauspicious. According to the Hindus the gods do not have a shadow and as per the ritual belief noted above, it can be said that they do not have any evil or inauspiciousness attached to them. However, the worldwide belief about shadow is that it stands for the very soul of a person. Hence the utmost care is to be taken to protect it.[118]

Site of Sacrifice (*devayajana*)

Detailed instructions about a site, to be chosen for performing sacrifice, occur in the context of the Agniṣṭoma sacrifice.

A place which lies highest and above which no other part of the ground rises, should be chosen as a site for performing sacrifice. The *arthavāda* points out that from such a place (chosen by the gods) the gods ascended to heaven. So he ascends to heaven, who is consecrated for sacrifice (and performs sacrifice). Such a high (really highest -

'*varṣiṣṭha*') place should be even (*sama*) as well as firm (*avibhraṁśin*) and should incline towards the east, for east is the quarter of the gods or towards the north, for north is the quarter of men. It should rise somewhat towards the south, it being the quarter of the Fathers (*pitṛ*-s). It should not incline towards the south, lest the sacrificer should quickly go to the yonder world (i.e. depart from this world). The measure of the sacrificial ground should not be exceeded on the east for such an excess would be in favour of the sacrificer's spiteful enemy. The measure of the site of sacrifice may exceed in the south and also in the north. But that site is full of perfection (*samṛddha*) which is exceeded in the west, for to the sacrificer, who possesses such a site, the higher[119] worship of the gods (as also their favour) readily inclines (*Śat. Br.* III. 1.1.1-3). Here the beliefs concerning the site of sacrifice mainly centre round the beliefs about the quarters mentioned therein, which we have already dealt with in the chapter on "Quarters".

However the *Śat. Br.* approves of the opinion of Yājñavalkya, who went to choose a place of worship for Vārṣṇeya and heard from Satyayajña that the whole earth being divine, on any part of it one may sacrifice, after enclosing and in this way consecrating it with a sacrificial formula (*yajuṣā*). It is the officiating priests that constitute the place of worship. They should be wise and learned *brāhmaṇa*-s, well-versed in sacred lore (*ibid.* 4,5).

Soma

The practice and ritual of preparing and offering of Soma (Soma-juice) date back to the Indo-Iranian period. In both the *RV* and the *Avesta*, Soma or Haoma is said to grow on mountain and it is believed that it descends to earth from its mythical region in heaven. Soma is regarded to have twofold nature *viz.* in the form of the Soma-juice, that is pressed and offered to the gods and secondly the inner physical power gained by drinking Soma-juice, which could be utilised for meditation (*samādhi*).[120]

There seems to be a constant quest for the drink of immortality in the mind of the ancient man as is recorded in various mythologies. We have in the Babylonian mythology the Zu bird bringing the tablets of immortality (destiny), in the Chinese mythology Wang Shu wandering to obtain the herb of immortality[121] and in the Middle-Eastern mythology Gilgamesh in search of the plant of life. The ritual metaphors eulogising Soma and the myths and rituals about Soma in the Vedic texts centre round this concept of Soma, which is believed to be a drink of immortality.

As Soma-juice is the choicest drink, it is offered to the gods. It is the sacrificial offering given to the gods (*Śat. Br.* IV. 4.2.1). King Soma is the food of the gods (*Jaim. Br.* I.233). It is food (*Śat. Br.* III.9.1.8). It is the food of a *brāhmaṇa* (*ibid.* XII. 7.2.2). In the context of Agniṣṭoma sacrifice, Soma is said to be glory (*yaśaḥ).* When the priests drink the Soma-juice, they take unto them that glory (*ibid.* IV. 2.4.9).

It has been a point of controversy whether Soma was identified with the moon. It was Hillebrandt who went so far as to regard that all the Soma-hymns in the ninth *maṇḍala* of the *RV* and a few more from other *maṇḍala*-s are addressed to the moon-god.[122] The *Śat. Br.* clearly states that the moon is Soma. In the twelve-day sacrificial session, the Adhvaryu priest initiates the Brahman priest. It is said that the Brahman priest is the moon and the moon is Soma and plants belong to Soma (*ibid.* XII. 1.1.2). In the rite of making the fire-pan (*ukhā)*, in the context of the Agnicayana rite, the water used for mixing the clay is boiled by means of resin of the Palāśa (Parṇa) tree, for the sake of firmness. Palāśa tree is said to be Soma.[123] Soma is the moon and that moon indeed is one of Agni's forms (*ibid.* VI. 5.1.1). Here we come to a very vital point. Dange points out that Soma that is gathered from the shoots at the sacrifice represents the drop (*drapsa)* that is said to descend from heaven. It is the divine drop from the moon that is invoked (as god Soma) like other gods in the sacrifice. It is the very essence of the moon-god, who is on a different plane from the other gods. He (i.e. Soma) is 'killed' (pressed) and eaten for nourishment by other gods but is reborn in sacrifice in juice-form and in the heaven in the moon-form. Dange has conclusively proved the basis of identification between Soma and the moon.[124]

The *arthavāda* states in the rite of Upāṁśusavana (in which Soma for the Upāṁśu libation or *graha*, i.e. cup, is pressed) in the morning-pressing (Prātaḥsavana) of the Agniṣṭoma sacrifice is worthy of taking a note. For the *vidhi* of taking a pressing-stone for the Upāṁśusavana ('low-voiced pressing'), the *arthavāda* states that Soma was in the sky. He (i.e. Soma) was Vṛtra. These mountains, these rocks are his body. By means of his body (i.e. rocks, here 'pressing-stones') the sacrificer or the priest makes Soma perfect or 'whole'. Again while pressing Soma (-shoots) they slay him with his own body (i.e. stones, used for pressing). But he rises from there and lives, i.e. in the form of Soma-juice (*ibid.* III. 9.4.2; also for the same thought that the mountains and stones are Vṛtra's = Soma's body, *ibid.* III. 4.3.13; IV. 2.5.15). The identification of Soma and Vṛtra can be explained from the mythical account which occurs elsewhere in the *Śat. Br.* when Indra cut off the (three) heads of Tvaṣṭṛ's son Viśvarūpa, Tvaṣṭṛ becoming furious brought Soma-juice from which Indra was excluded. But Indra though uninvited consumed what pure Soma there was in the tub. Tvaṣṭṛ again becoming furious offered into fire whatever pure Soma was left in the tub. That Soma when it reached the fire or when it was on its way to the fire, developed into human shape, rolling onwards thus becoming Vṛtra. Vṛtra became possessed of Agni and Soma, of all sciences, all glory, all nourishment, all prosperity. On Indra's pleading, Agni and Soma who were with Vṛtra went over to Indra, and them followed all sciences, etc. Vṛtra then became contracted like a leather bag drained of its contents (*ibid.* I.6.3.1-16). Indra cut him in two parts, making that part which was of the Soma content turned into moon (*ibid.* 17). The myth is repeated at other place in the *Śat. Br.* (V. 5.4.2-

12) and is already recorded in the *Tait. Sam.* (II. 4.12.1). The *Śat. Br.* mentions that Vṛtra agreed to be the food of Indra (*Śat. Br.* I.6.3.17). This 'eater-eaten' relationship existing between Soma (Vṛtra) = Moon and Indra = Sun is explained by Dange in details.[125]

In the rite of buying Soma (-shoots), there is related a myth, which was also most probably, enacted in ritual. Soma was in the sky; Gāyatrī (metre) flew up to Soma. As she was carrying Soma for the gods, *gandharva* Viśvāvasu stole him from her. As *gandharva*-s were fond of women, the gods sent Vāk (Speech) to them and she returned to them with Soma. Her followed the *gandharva*-s and said that Soma would be with the gods and Vāk with them. But the gods told them that both (gods themselves and the *gandharva*-s) should woo her. The *gandharva*-s recited the Veda-s to her, while the gods created the lute and sat playing and singing. Vāk turned to the gods, for women are given to vain things, says the *Śat. Br.* (III.2.4.1-6). In the rite of buying Soma, Soma is bought by giving a cow to the Soma-seller. This cow is called the Somakrayaṇī cow. Soma in the myth noted above was obtained by the gods, by sending Vāc to the *gandharva*-s. In the ritual the Somakrayaṇī cow stands for Vāc. We have already noted in the chapter on "Animals and Birds" that the cow chosen in this ritual is of tawny colour, having a shade of the colour for her eyes, resembling that of Soma. It is interesting to note that as recorded in the myth stated above, the gods sent Vāc to Soma (i.e. to the *gandharva*-s) and she returned to them together with Soma, so now he gives the Somakrayaṇī cow to Soma (i.e. the Soma-seller) and she returns to him together with Soma (*ibid.* 21). This shows that the cow was taken back from the Soma-seller. This is how the myth used to be enacted in the ritual of buying Soma.

The *arthavāda*-s regarding the rites and rituals of Soma shed light on many a facet of this drink, for as noted in the beginning, it (Soma=Haoma) dates back to the Indo-Iranian period.[126] As Hodivala has stated, it was believed that by drinking this libation, men obtained health, wealth, wisdom in spirit and even immortality if taken from the hands of a priest.[127]

Speech (Vāc)

The Vedic ritual tradition gives importance to two factors *viz.* ritual of sacrifice *(vidhi)* and prayer *(mantra)* recited appropriate to the ritual. The ritual comprising offerings of materials makes the gods strong and the prayer infuses them with good cheer. In the *RV* at several places, worship of the gods with sacrifices, obeisances, offerings and prayers is said to strengthen them, who in turn, help the human beings and fulfil their desires. The thought which occurs in the eulogy of Indra (*RV.* II. 12.14) can very well represent this attitude of 'Give-and-Take' on the part of the Vedic people and ritualists at large.

The *vidhi* not accompanied by *mantra* is regarded as incomplete, for the *mantra* in the form of a *ṛc.* or *yajus* gives it a full form *(rūpasamṛddha)*. At various places the *Ait. Br.* speaks of this thought (*Ait. Br.* I.13=3.2; I.16=3.5; I.19=4.2, etc.).

The chant *(mantra)* apart from being appropriate to the ritual is thought of as a potent form of speech. Though the expression 'Thousandfold is the progeny of Speech' (*Śat. Br.* IV. 6.7.3 - *sahasram vācaḥ prajātam.....)* refers mainly to the *ṛc*-s, *sāman*-s and *yajus*-es, it can be taken to apply to all the aspects of Speech *viz.* the *ṛc*-s, *yajus*-es and *sāman*-s (noted above), the *stotra*-s and the *śastra*-s, metres, *śilpa*-s, the utterances such as Svāha, Vaṣaṭ, etc., the three Vyāhṛti-s, *śloka*-s, *gāthā*-s, etc. which are the articulate form of Speech and playing on instruments, which is the inarticulate form of Speech. No sacrifice can be accomplished without Speech, for speech is an expression of human existence. In the *RV* (IV. 30) and the *AV* (X. 125), Speech is eulogised as a deity. But in the ritual texts it has assumed such a multidimensional form that it engulfs every sound *(dhvani)* in the ritual context so as to give life-breath to the physical act of ritual.[128] The oft-repeated ritual-metaphor hence is self-eloquent and catches the very nerve of sacrifice, when it says - *vāg vai yajñaḥ* (*Śat. Br.* I.1.2.2; I.1.4.11; III.1.3.27; III.4.3.16; III.5.1.23, etc.)

Several mythical accounts are woven as *arthavāda* by the ritual texts, in order to show the importance of Speech in sacrifice and they are taken note of and discussed by the present author.[129] Again in these texts many pithy expressions or ritual-metaphors are stated in eulogy of Speech, which are also taken note of by the present author.[130] Here it is decided to take for consideration only those *arthavāda*-statements, which were not dealt with by the author or which require more thought.

We have already noted the thought that 'Thousandfold is the progeny of Speech.' While prescribing the Brahmayajña (daily study of the Veda), we have a mention of some of the varieties of Speech. The *ṛc*-s are said to be honey, the *sāman*-s clotted butter (*ghṛta)*, the *yajus*-es nectar, the Vākovākya[131] and the Itihāsa-purāṇa[132] the messes of milk and meat. It is said that with these he satisfies the gods. In order to stress the importance of one's daily study (of the varieties mentioned above), the *Śat. Br.* states that moving indeed are the waters, moving the sun, moving the moon and moving the stars. Verily as if these deities did not move and act, even so the *brāhmaṇa* will be on that day, on which he does not study his lesson (*Śat. Br.* XI. 5.7.5-10).

We have already said that Speech has many aspects. Here are some *arthavāda*-s regarding certain aspects of Speech.

As *mantra*-s are in metres, metres came to have great importance. It is said that there are two types of creatures (*prajāḥ) viz.* divine and human. The human creatures are born by (the normal process of) birth. The metres are the divine creatures, which he creates through mouth (*ibid.* XI. 5.4.17). The metres are said to be the abodes of gods. The Gāyatrī metre is eight-syllabled (in each foot) and so are the Vasu-s eight in number. Due to Gāyatrī only, the

Vasu-s are said to have a house (*vasavo gṛhiṇaḥ*). The eleven-syllabled Triṣṭubh and eleven Rudra-s are equated. Hence by Triṣṭubh alone the Rudra-s are possessed of a house (*rūdrā gṛhiṇaḥ*). And so is the twelve-syllabled Jagatī and the twelve Āditya-s on par, So the Āditya-s are said to be '*gṛhiṇaḥ*' by Jagatī alone (*Jaim. Br.* I.280).

The *arthavāda* praising the rite of Sandhyā, in which water is offered, accompanied by the recitation of the Gāyatrī *mantra* runs as follows. The gods and *asura*-s were contending. The *asura*-s rushed towards the sun to attack him. The sun got frightened and his heart assumed the form of a tortoise (*Ṣaḍ. Br.* V.5.1, 2). When he went to Prajāpati, the latter found for him a remedy (medicine) in the form of the Gāyatrī *mantra*. As he uses water for the evening rite of Sandhyā, the water-drops therein become a thunderbolt and slay the *asura*-s. Even the enemy of him also is defeated, who knows this (*ibid.* 3,4). The *Tait. Ār.* also has the same thought to express. It states that the *rakṣas*-es fight with the rising sun. When he sets, the same *rakṣas*-es are silenced with the water, which is accompanied with the chanting of the Gāyatrī *mantra*. The water becoming a thunderbolt drops those *rakṣas*-es in the island Mandehāruṇa (*Tait. Ār.* II.2). The same thought is carried further to the Purāṇa-s. The Mandehas (type of demons) try to swallow the sun at sunset every evening. According to a curse given to them by Prajāpati they die every day, yet their bodies are intact. When the 'twice-born' (*brāhmaṇa*-s or the persons of the other two upper *varṇa*-s) throw at them the water consecrated by the Gāyatrī *mantra* at the Sandhyā rite, they get burnt.[133]

The *Tait. Br.* states that the gods were afraid of the extreme upward rising of the sun; (Sāy. — With a thought that he may not be stationed at the heaven) they made him steady with the metres. Again they were afraid of the downward falling of the sun. They raised him up with five rays. Hence on the twenty-first, i.e. the Viṣuvat day (in the Gavām-ayana *sattra*), they should chant the Divākīrtya *sāman*-s (*Tait. Br.* I.2.4.2). In the context of the Gavām-ayana *sattra*, the *Ait. Br.* also states that the *sāman*-s, *stoma*-s, etc. support the sun from all sides, for there lurks a fear of his falling down (IV.18 = 18.4). These *arthavāda*-s, practically having the same tune, are significant for two points, the first being the unique importance of the sun (so much as to have measures to ward off its fall from the high heavens) in the ancient Indian mind and the second being the firm belief in the power of Speech (in the form of *sāman*-s, *stotra*-s or the *mantra*-s in the metres like Gāyatrī as noted above).

Here is the power of the Bahiṣpavamāna *stotra* spoken of through a mythical account. As the head of the sacrifice was cut, the gods asked the Aśvins to replace it, for the latter were the physicians. The Aśvins agreed on one condition that a Soma-cup should be drawn for them, (i.e. Aśvins). The gods said that the Aśvins were impure, for they wandered among men and were physicians. The *Tait. Sam.* adds that a *brāhmaṇa* should not practise medicine, for a physician is impure, unfit for sacrifice (*Tait. Sam.* VI. 4.9.1,2). The gods purified the Aśvins by the Bahiṣpavamāna *stotra* and then they drew for them the Soma-cup. Hence it is that the cup for the Aśvins is drawn, when the Bahiṣpavamāna *stotra* has been sung (*ibid.* 2). The *arthavāda* is stated to point out the importance of the Bahiṣpavamāna *stotra*, one of the aspects of Speech being *stotra*. From the point of view of the evolution of the Vedic gods, we can see through this *arthavāda* how the Aśvins entered into the fold of the Vedic gods, late.

The *arthavāda* is important for one more reason. It clearly speaks of the low or not-much-respectworthy status of the physicians in the then society, for they had to move among men and treat them for their ailments.

A phenomenon of daily observation is marked in one of the *arthavāda*-s relating to Speech. In the context of the twelve-day sacrifice, the *sampad*[134] of number thirty-six is shown to be made as twelve *dīkṣā*-s, twelve days of session and twelve *upasad*-s. The Anuṣṭubh metre is of the first thirty-two syllables (from the number thirty-six noted above); then follow four. The four (syllables) stand for the four-footed cattle. By means of Speech (= i.e. Anuṣṭubh metre, which is of thirty-two syllables and which is identified with Speech) he supports the cattle (the four-footed ones). So it is that the cattle (cows) approach him, when reached by Speech, i.e. summoned by actual words. The cattle know their respective names (*Pañc. Br.* X. 3.13).

The *arthavāda* based on metaphor occurs in the context of the Prātaranuvāka (morning litany) in the Soma-sacrifice, when repetition of many hymns is laid down in the recitation of the Prātaranuvāka. The sacrifice (here the Soma-sacrifice) is said to be a cart; the morning litany is the corn kept in the cart and the hymns are the vessels (in which is kept the corn). Just as vessels, having only a little corn come together (i.e. collide, being light in weight), so his hymns come together resulting into the tottering condition of the sacrificer. Hence is the repetition of many hymns laid down in the Prātaranuvāka. The *arthavāda* tries to be convincing by citing a day-to-day example, that too from the agricultural sphere (*Kauṣ. Br.* XI. 8), It is prescribed that when the morning litany has begun, the Brahman priest should remain silent, until the offering of the Upāṁśu and Antaryāma cups (of Soma), until the conclusion of the Pāvamāna *stotra*-s, once they have begun and until the Vaṣaṭ call is uttered in the case of reciting the *stotra*-s accompanied with *śastra*-s. Here the *arthavāda* in the *Ait. Br.* takes the help of worldly experiences. The mythical account occurring by way of *arthavāda* is as follows. Some priests, when the morning-litany (*Prātaranuvāka)* had begun, having muttered the Stomabhāga-s were talking to one another. A *brāhmaṇa* there well-versed in the Veda-s, seeing the Brahman priest talking at that time, said. "They have omitted half of this sacrifice." Just as a man with one foot while going or a chariot with one wheel on one side while moving, falls, so falls (i.e. becomes unsuccessful) the sacrificer, if the Brahman priest talks when the uttering of the morning litany has begun (*Ait. Br.* V. 33 = 25.8).

It is necessary to take into account that the reciting of the Prātaranuvāka (morning litany) is laid down in the sacrifice, before the inarticulate chirping of fowls starts in the morning, for the ritualists say that they are not to speak, after speech unconnected with the sacrifice, has been uttered by birds (*ibid.* II.15 = 7.5). The *Kauṣ. Br.* also clearly states that the priest should begin to recite when night is far advanced, but before the time when cattle, ordinary men and birds take up to speech (XI. 8). This clearly brings out the firm belief maintained in the Vedic ritual tradition that the recitation of the Prātaranuvāka should be uncontaminated by any other non-sacrificial or a-sacrificial speech.[135]

The *arthavāda*-s, as we have noted earlier at times, refer to worldly practices and through them bring out the importance of the *vidhi*-s. Here are some examples again, concerning some aspects of Speech. In the context of the New-moon and Full-moon sacrifices, in the ritual of kindling fire, it is said that after the kindling verses are recited, the class of formulas known as '*nigada*' is recited. The *arthavāda* runs thus. In former times, the gods appointed Agni as the Hotṛ priest. Requesting him to carry their oblation, they cheered him up by saying, "You are certainly vigorous. You are equal to this (task)", thereby endowing him with vigour. This is as per the practice in our own times. When they appoint any one from their own kinsmen to the chief office, they cheer him up by saying, "Certainly you are vigorous, you are equal to this" (*Śat. Br.* I.4.2.1). The *arthavāda* here referring to the worldly practice, tries to show the importance of '*nigada*' formulas, which are in praise of the gods.

Here is the *arthavāda* regarding the two 'raisings' (*dvyudāsam*),[136] when the Gaurivīta *sāman* is chanted on each day of the whole year's session. These 'raisings' (while chanting) are the two that look out for a stopping place in the journey to the heavenly world. By means of the first 'raising', they finish the first ('former') day, and by means of the following (i.e. second), they pass, in chanting, to the following day (*Pañc. Br.* V.7.4). These two 'raisings' while chanting the Gaurivīta *sāman* are again mentioned by the *Pañc. Br.*, where it takes the help of a phenomenon from daily life and states the *arthavāda.* It says that just as in day-to-day life, people on a journey each time take their resting place after reaching water and grass, that has been looked for on the preceding day, similarly performers of the Ahīna rite (which lasts for 'a day' — here for each day of the whole year's session) make use of the two 'raisings' in the Gaurivīta *sāman* as 'stopping', i.e. resting place, in their journey to the world of heaven (*ibid.* XI. 5.20).

In yet another *arthavāda*, a custom of greeting prevalent then in the society and even in our times, is mentioned. In the Agnicayana rite, in the first layer, an image of a gold man, is laid down on a gold plate on his back. The sacrificer then stands by that gold man, reciting the Sarpanāma formulas (*mantra*-s). These worlds are said to be the *sarpa*-s, because they glide along (*sarpanti*) with everything whatsoever there is (*Śat. Br.* VII. 4.1.15-25). In spite of this etymological explanation, the *mantra*-s (*Vāj. Sam.* XIII. 6-8), named Sarpanāma really speaking refer to the serpents, which are there on the earth, in the air, in the sky, on the trees and in the holes, in the rays of the sun and in the waters. To all these *sarpa*-s (serpents) is paid the homage (*namaḥ).* He utters the words *'namaḥ' 'namaḥ'* ('Homage, homage!'), which means 'sacrifice' (*yajño vai namaḥ).* By sacrifice he worships the serpents. The *arthavāda* here pertains to our own times also, when we greet any person by saying '*namaste*' ('*namaḥ te*'). The word *namaḥ*, as seen above, means 'sacrifice'. So when we say '*namaste*' (*namaḥ te*) "Homage be to you", it really means — "May sacrifice (or worship) be to you". Therefore he should never greet a person, not worthy of sacrifice, with the words '*namaste*', for that would mean "May sacrifice (or worship) be to you", which would obviously be very wrong (*Śat. Br.* VII. 4.1.28-30), the person thus addressed being unworthy.

The *arthavāda* noted above is significant in more than one ways. The reference to *sarpa*-s points out the importance of serpent-worship in the Vedic ritual tradition. This obviously has crept in due to the assimilation of the totemistic Sarpa-tribe with the Vedic Aryans. The Sarpa-tribe together with its Veda (Sarpaveda) is mentioned in the Pāriplava *ākhyāna* in the *Śat. Br.* (XIII. 4.3.9). It is to be recited on each fifth day of the ten-day mini-cycles, which form the Pāriplava cycle of legends, going on for a period of one year, while the sacrificial horse was away from the sacrificial enclosure, with the royal entourage. The image of the gold man being in the lowest layer is to be guarded from the actual serpents, which are of the 'autochthon' ('born from the soil') species. The *arthavāda* mentioning *namaḥ* ('homage') speaks of the fear of and hence propitiation of the serpents.

The *arthavāda* is important also in that it clearly points out and advises not to greet an unholy person, indicating that the cultured speech stems from and is meant for the persons believing in sacrifice (i.e. sacrificial institution). This is probably the reason why the *śūdra*-s, in whose class many of the non-Aryan tribes were assimilated and who were not conversant with the Vedic speech-habits, they having their own, were debarred from studying and reciting the Vedic *mantra*-s.[137] The *arthavāda* noted above about the mode of greeting '*namaḥ*' occurs also in the context of the Śatarudriya-homa in the rite of Agnicayana (*ibid.* IX. 1.1.16).

Even the postures taken by the sacrificer or the priest, while reciting the invitatory prayer and that while reciting the offering prayer are stated and are accompanied with *arthavāda*, bringing out the efficacy of Speech, under a particular circumstance. In the context of the New-moon and Full-moon sacrifices, it is enjoined that he should recite the invitatory prayer while standing, for thereby he recites to the yonder (sky). The invitatory prayer (Anuvākyā) signifies yonder (sky). The offering prayer (Yājyā) he should pronounce while sitting, for the offering prayer represents this earth (*ibid.* I.4.2.18,19). This is already known to the *Tait. Sam.*, which states in the same context (i.e. the New-moon and Full-moon sacrifices) that he repeats the Sāmidhenī verses (the *mantra*-s which are used while enkindling the fire) while standing, for when standing he speaks more audibly. Again this standing on his part is to conquer the world of heaven. He repeats in the Krauñca note.[138] But this is connected with the *asura*-s. The low note is connected with men, while the intermediate note is connected with the gods. Hence one should repeat the Sāmidhenī verses in the intermediate note to secure the gods. When he repeats the Sāmidhenī verses standing, his one foot should be within the sacrificial altar, the other outside. This is to hold the ways apart and to avoid conflict of the paths. This is gained for he sacrifices while sitting, by which he finds support in this world. The *Tait. Sam.* summarises by saying that the Hotṛ-priests of olden times were indeed clever. Therefore the ways were held apart and the paths did not conflict (*Tait. Sam.* II.5.11.1, 2). The paths mentioned here are—the one going to the world of heaven and the other directed to the earth.

The *arthavāda* to be dealt with from the *Śat. Br.* in the context of the New-moon and Full-moon sacrifices though speaks about the sitting and standing positions of the sacrificer (or the priest), it has to say definitely about the relative importance of mind and speech. It is enjoined that the first two oblations are offered to Mind and Speech, for these two, when yoked together, convey the sacrifice to the gods (*Śat. Br.* I.4.4.1). It is interesting to mark the two (different) ways in which the libation of clarified butter is to be made to these two, i.e. Mind and Speech. The libation to Mind is made with the dipping-spoon (*'sruva'* Masculine), silently, by the sacrificer (or the priest) in a sitting position. But the libation to Speech is made with the offering-spoon ('*sruc*' Feminine), with a *mantra*, by the sacrificer (or the priest) in a standing position. The *arthavāda* passages are significant making clear the perspective in which these two, i.e. Mind and Speech, are viewed by the ritualists. Mind is male (really the word '*manas*' is Neuter and not Masculine. May be as Mind is not female, it is male!), so the '*sruva*' the dipping-spoon (Masculine) is used. Being undefined (*anirukta)*, to it libation is made silently. Speech is female (*yoṣā)*, so the '*sruc*' is used for offering to her. She is distinct, so the libation is made to her with a *mantra*. It is said that Speech is indeed smaller than Mind. As Mind is more unlimited and Speech the more limited, by standing (while making the libation to Speech), he gives *upavaha*[139], i.e. a shoulder-piece, to Speech. Then the two well-matched yoked ones convey the sacrifice to the gods (*ibid.* 3-7).

Here we come to the point of relative importance of Mind and Speech. A thought often found in the ritual texts is that, of the two, Mind is more important than Speech.[140] The mythical account of the quarrel between Mind and Speech and the judgement given by Prajāpati can be cited in this connection, in short. When each of the two—Mind and Speech—said that he/she was excellent (*aham bhadra*, hence the account is known in the tradition as '*aham-bhadra*' or '*aham-bhadriya*'). Not coming to settlement, they went to Prajāpati, who decided in favour of Mind saying to Speech that she was only an imitator of Mind's deeds (i.e. thoughts) and a follower in its wake. Speech then said to Prajāpati that she would never be his oblation-bearer, for he did not support her. This *arthavāda* is stated to explain why Prajāpati is given offerings in a low voice. Nevertheless it also points out how Mind is superior to Speech (*ibid.* I.4.5. 8-12). But at times Speech is eulogised highly as compared to Mind. The *Śat. Br.* says that wherever was this Speech, there everything was done, everything was known. But wherever Mind was, there nothing was done, nothing was known, for no one understands those who think in their mind (*ibid.* IV. 6.7.5).

Even the words which are apparently simple, are taken to bestow in an abstruse way (*parokṣam)* the blessings on the sacrificer. So when the Adhvaryu says, "He (i.e. the sacrificer) is called for future worship of the gods" (*uttarasyām devayajyāyām upahūtaḥ)*, it is the blessing of life on the sacrificer as also that of offspring for him, for when the sacrificer goes to the yonder world, his offspring would sacrifice in this world. In an abstruse way, it is also a blessing of cattle for him. Again when the Adhvaryu says, "He (i.e. the sacrificer) is called for more abundant oblation-offering" (*bhūyasi haviṣkaraṇe upahūtaḥ)*, it is the blessing of life, of offspring and that of cattle invoked for the sacrificer (*ibid.* I.8.1.30-35). This invocation of blessings (though in an abstruse manner) occurs in the context of the Iḍā-ceremony, in which the Iḍā (i.e. the oblation, which is kept in the Iḍāpātrī[141], i.e. the Iḍā vessel oblong in size) is not offered in the fire, it being equated with cattle, but is eaten by the priests Hotṛ and Adhvaryu and the sacrificer (*ibid.* 38, 39).

In the context of the rite of Agnihotra, it is said that when he offers in the evening, saying, 'The light is Agni, Agni is the light' (*agnirjyotirjyotiragniḥ)*, he speaks the truth. His self here being composed of speech becomes composed of truth. Again when he offers in the morning, saying, 'The light is the sun, the sun is the light' (*sūryo jyotirjyotiḥ sūryaḥ)*, he speaks the truth. His self composed of speech becomes composed of truth (*Kauṣ Br.* II.8). The *Kauṣ Br.* earlier states elaborately how the self is composed of speech. When a man breathes in and breathes out, sees with the eye, hears with the ear, resolves with the mind and touches with his limbs something pleasant or unpleasant to lie upon—every time, the man expresses that action of his by speech alone. Thus the whole self enters into speech and becomes composed of speech. Here is quoted a *ṛc* — 'No form is made pure without Indra; Indra is Speech, for not without speech is any form made pure' (*ibid.* II. 7). This *arthavāda* aptly brings out the importance of Speech.

The evolution and the gradual development of the deity Pathyā-svasti, identified with Speech in the Brāhmaṇa texts, is worthy of taking into consideration here. In the older part of the *RV* itself (from the family-book), we have the deity Pathyā invoked for 'weal' (*RV* V. 51.14....*svasti pathye revati....kṛdhi).* Though associated with *svasti*, as yet she is not Pathyā-svasti. Pūṣan the path-finder god is invoked to bestow on the sacrificer Pathyā, the *svasti* (*ibid.* X. 59.7), which indicates Pathyā to be the deity of paths, rather than of Speech. Pūṣan found the path indicating new migratory avenues; Pathyā ensured easy migration or easy movement along known paths. One could say that Pathyā was a feminine, but independent, aspect of Pūṣan.

In the later Vedic period, marked by the growth of ritual as reflected in the Brāhmaṇa-texts, Pathyā got to be Pathyā-svasti, indicating that 'weal on the paths' was her sole responsibility. According to a mythical account coming as *arthavāda* in the ritual of buying Soma stated in the *Śat. Br.* the gods were sacrificing; but at one point, they got apprehensive of an attack from the demons and *asura*-s. However, they 'saw' (through their mind's eye) a prayer (the *yajus* formula), with which they warded off the demons and *asura*-s and obtained stable and safe shelter for their sacrifice (*Śat. Br.* III. 3.3.16). The particular *yajus* formula (*Vāj. Sam.* IV. 29) is mentioned by the expression *svastigām panthām*, which reflects the concept of *svastipatha* (*Śat. Br.* III. 3.3.15).

In the Brāhmaṇa-texts, as the Ṛgvedic Pathyā—the deity of narrow paths (*patha-pathin*) mostly traversed on foot[142] as opposed to a *rathyā*, which was a street suitable for a *ratha* (chariot)—became Pathyā-svasti, the latter, i.e. Pathyā-svasti, came to be associated with Speech and was regarded as an aspect of Speech, for the word *'svasti'* indicating 'well-being' is itself an aspect of Speech though in a word-form.

Mythical accounts coming as *arthavāda* in some Brāhmaṇa texts can be seen in this regard. The *Śat. Br.*

enjoins offering, after the final bath (*avabhṛtha*), to Pathyā-svasti and at the end to Aditi. Here Pathyā-svasti is said to be Speech, for due to Speech alone the gods came to know what they did not know earlier (*ibid.* IV. 5.1.3,4). Here the identification has to be understood as Speech impelling the deity of paths as it does other miracles. The implication in this particular rite is that the whole sacrifice, now completed, is set on the path to heaven through the *mantra* (aspect of Speech). Hereafter, till it reaches heaven completely, it is set in the protection of Pathyā-svasti. The *Ait. Br.* says that when the sacrificer offers the oblation to Pathyā-svasti, he offers it in the very mouth of sacrifice (i.e. in the Āhavanīya fire-place) which is set to the east, and also that he offers it addressing to Speech itself. It is further explained at the same place that one, who offers to Pathyā-svasti, leads the sacrifice on the proper path with the help of Speech—'*vācaiva tad yajñam panthām api nayati*' (*Ait. Br.* I.8=2.2). The *arthavāda* in the form of a mythical account occurring in the *Kauṣ. Br.* has to be taken into account here. It says that the gods started for heaven with the help of the Prāyaṇīya rite, but, they could not recognise the quarters. Among them, Agni (the fire-god) asked for himself an oblation of clarified butter (as his fees!) to let them have the knowledge of the east. Following him, Soma gave the cognition of the south, Savitṛ that of the west. Pathyā-svasti gave the cognition of the north. The *Kauṣ. Br.* says that Pathyā-svasti is Speech. Hence Speech is associated with the north and this is verily the reason why people go to the north to learn proper (Sanskrit) speech (*Kauṣ. Br.* VII. 5-6).

This identification of Pathyā-svasti with Speech has an interesting off-shoot, which is seen in the social usage. Something agreeable is denoted by the word '*pathya*'; what is not agreeable or suitable is *apathya*, both the words—'*pathya*' and '*apathya*' (aspects of Speech!) springing from this identification.

Sphya (translated as 'a wooden sword')

Sphya is made of the Khadira wood. It is sword-shaped, having the length of an *aratni* or *bāhu.* It is used for digging or measuring the ground for *vedi* (altar).[143] An elaborate *arthavāda* about *sphya*, which occurs in the context of the New-moon and Full-moon sacrifices, can ably give us the importance of *sphya* in the Vedic ritual. When Indra hurled the thunderbolt at Vṛtra, it became fourfold. The three parts are—the wooden sword-like *sphya*, the sacrificial post and the chariot. The piece, with which Indra struck Vṛtra, was broken off (fr. √*sṝ* - 'to tear asunder, to tear off'). On falling down it became an arrow (*śara*). Thus the thunderbolt became fourfold. The priests make use of the first two *viz. sphya* and the sacrificial post, at the sacrifice and men of the military class make use of the next two of them in battle *viz.* the chariot and the arrow (*Śat. Br.* I.2.4.1,2). When the sacrificer or the priest takes up the *sphya* in his hand, he raises that against the wicked, spiteful enemy as did Indra raise the thunderbolt against Vṛtra (*ibid.* 3). The *Tait. Sam.* says that the *sphya* is a thunderbolt (*Tait. Sam.* II. 1.5.7; also *Śat. Br.* I.2.5.20,22 for the same ritual metaphor).

Stone (*aśman*, *grāvan*, etc.)

The mention of stones (*aśman*-s) and the *arthavāda*-s regarding those stones are important from our point of view, for they speak of the beliefs regarding stone, prevalent in the then society. These beliefs led the entry of *aśman* (or *grāvan* at one place) in the Vedic rituals.

In the Agnicayana rite, when all the layers of the Great Fire-altar are completed, there is leading forward the Agni (i.e. a lighted burning piece of wood) from the newly-built Gārhapatya hearth[144] to serve as the new Āhavanīya on the Great Fire-altar. On the Āgnīdhra range (i.e. where the Āgnīdhra shed and hearth afterwards are to be erected, *Śat. Br.* IX. 2.3.15; IX.4.3.6), on the northern edge of the Great Fire-altar, a variegated stone (*pṛśni aśman)* is set up between the Gārhapatya and the Āhavanīya fire-places. The *arthavāda* states that this variegated stone is the yonder sun, which is set up. The stone chosen is a variegated one, for due to the rays, the disk of the sun is variegated.[145] The Āhavanīya and the Gārhapatya fire-places, in between which the stone is set up, stand for the heavenly world and the terrestrial world respectively. The sun also shines between the two worlds.[146] This stone is placed near the Āgnīdhra's fire-shed, for Āgnīdhra stands for the air. The sun also has its stay in the air. The *arthavāda*-passage runs further pointing out that this stone is the breath, which is put in the body. It is also the vital power, which is made firm as the stone is firm. This variegated stone is also the food, which is variegated (*ibid.* IX. 2.3.14-16). The same stone is mentioned further in a *sampad,*[147] when the Āgnīdhrīya hearth is to be erected for the Great Fire-altar.[148] This is partly built of bricks—out of which eight bricks stand for the *sampad* of the Gāyatrī metre (having eight syllables in one foot), the variegated stone as the ninth and the fire on the hearth as the tenth—ultimately the *sampad* of ten vital airs.[149]

Mention of stone (a pressing-stone)—though not '*aśman*' but '*grāvan*'—occurs in the Agniṣṭoma sacrifice, in the context of the morning pressing (of Soma-shoots). These pressing-stones are of rock (*aśmamayāḥ).* Soma the god was in the sky, he was Vṛtra. Those mountains, those rocks are the body of Vṛtra (i.e. of Soma). In pressing Soma (-shoots), they slay him by means of his own body, i.e. by pressing-stones, which are of rocks. And from them only Soma rises (in the form of juice) and thus he lives (*ibid.* III.9.4.2). As this stone (*grāvan)* is said to slay Soma, it is said to be a thunderbolt. So he takes it with a *mantra* (*Vāj. Sam.* VI. 60). At this time, he restrains speech. So the name Upāṁśusavana given to the pressing-stone ('Low-voiced pressing-stone'). Here comes a mythical account by way of *arthavāda.* The gods, while performing sacrifice, were afraid of an attack from the *asura-rakṣas*-es. So they decided to sacrifice in low voice, by restraining the tone of speech and did likewise. The *arthavāda* concludes here by saying that the same Upāṁśusavana stone is in reality Āditya Vivasvant—the sun. It is the through-breathing (*vyāna)* of this sacrifice (*Śat. Br.* III. 9.4.2-7).

Eggeling seems to have a doubt about Soma slain on being placed upon and rising from the stone, which is equated with the sun.[150] But there is hardly any scope for doubt, if we take into account the basic concept in the ritual of Soma, as Dange has discussed it. As resident among the stars (for Soma is already said to be 'in the third heaven'), Soma in the form of a mystic drop gets controlled by the sun, like other stars. When Soma is pressed in the ritual, the Ṛgvedic seer says—'He (i.e. Soma) is released by the sun at the heavenly plane (*RV* IX. 27.5). The control of Soma by the sun and his subsequent release, is a constant heavenly drama, which was used by the Vedic ritualists in the ritual context at the Agniṣṭoma, the principal Soma-sacrifice. Here the Śukra cup of pure Soma stood for the sun and Indra, and the Manthin cup for the Moon (the later phase of Indudrapsa Soma). Thus we have Indra = Sun = Śukra the eater and Soma = Moon = Vṛtra the eaten.[151]

To turn to another stone (*aśman*)—When the Great Fire-altar is completed, he performs the Śatarudriya offering, for Agni now is the deity Rudra. The gods bestowed on Agni-Rudra immortality. He stood there longing for food. The gods were afraid of him, lest he should hurt them. Hence the Śatarudriya offering to Rudra. On the western corner of the northern side of the Great Fire-altar, which is enclosed by a line of stones on all sides,[152] there are three stones (*pariśrit*-s) as high as knee, naval and mouth, on which (serving as Āhavanīya), 425 oblations of wild sesame mixed with *gavedhukā*, are offered to Rudra viewed in his fearful aspects, the oblations being accompanied with *mantra*-s.[153] As oblations are offered to the fierce deity Rudra, after this ritual the altar is cooled by the Agnīdh priest by sprinkling water. Agnīdh priest then sprinkles a stone with the water from a jar with a *mantra* from the *Vāj. Sam.* (XVII. 1). Having put that stone into the water-jar, they throw it southwards. As south is Nirṛti's region, he consigns that pain to Nirṛti's region, saying, 'May your pain enter him whom we hate' (*Śat. Br.* IX. 1.2.1-12; *Kāyt. Ś.S.* XVIII. 3.24-26, though not in details). This stone is thrown away outside the Great Fire-altar, for the Great Fire-altar stands for all the three worlds and so the pain is thrown away outside the sacrificial ground (*Śat. Br.* IX. 1.2.11). Kane points out that this stone thrown away southwards is the same as the variegated stone (standing for the sun) as noted above.[154] But this is not the case. The two stones are different, by *arthavāda* one stands for the sun and has a divine air about it, and the other for pain and hence to be thrown away. Even Uvaṭa and Mahīdhara commenting on *Vāj. Sam.* (XVII. 1), which refers to the stone that is to be thrown away, do not connect it to the variegated stone.

The *Śat. Br.* mentions small stones (*pariśrit*-s) enclosing a burial-place (*śmaśāna)*, which are set up silently. But the enclosing-stones round the fire-hearths are set up with a *mantra.* The *arthavāda* states that by this way he keeps separate what refers to the gods and what refers to the Fathers (*Śat. Br.* XIII. 8.2.2).

Of all these stones, the stones to be taken note of from our point of view are three. By *arthavāda* —

1. The variegated stone is the sun;
2. The Upāṁśusavana stone is the sun; and
3. The stone, which is to be thrown away, stands for pain.

It has to be noted that the *vidhi* of setting up or using a stone, followed by *arthavāda* reflects a belief about stone, prevalent in the then Vedic society. Two stages are marked in the worship of stone. The first is the pre-animistic, where a stone is vaguely conceived to possess some innate power, which causes fear or reverence; the second is the animistic, where a stone is supposed to be an abode of some spirit.[155] However it is not easy to separate these two forms of sanctity with any approach to precision. The *vidhi*-s and the *arthavāda*-s about the three stones, which we have noted above, reflect the folk-belief about stone of the pre-animistic stage.

Beliefs about stone are prevalent in other lands and are maintained in our own times also. In Melanesia, sunshine is believed to be produced by smearing a standing stone with red earth or winding a round stone, called a 'sun-stone,' with red braid and sticking it with owl's feathers to represent rays, muttering a spell the while and hanging it on a tree.[156] In Scotland, on the island of Fladda, in Argyllshire, is a church dedicated to St. Columba. At the west end, on an altar, there is a round blue stone, which is always moist. Fishermen detained on the island by contrary winds used to wash this stone with water in the hope of procuring a favourable breeze.[157] Here, it is obvious that the blue stone stands for the sea, which is propitiated by washing the stone. In ancient Egypt, blue turquoise (azure gem) was connected with the mother-goddess Hathor, which was the deity of the sky and was the controller of the waters of the firmament as well as of the Nile. A blue stone stood as a symbol of Hathor and was regarded as a lucky stone.[158] The beliefs about stone are marked even in ancient China and Japan.[159]

Coming to our modern times, to take only one example. The *aśmā* (small stone) picked up from the cremation-ground, when the funeral rite is performed, brought to the house of the dead person, kept for nine days and cast off on the tenth day, speaks of the belief in the 'life-stone'.[160]

These examples can aptly show that beliefs about stone, maintained by folks, have entered the rites and rituals of many ancient societies, the Vedic society being no exception to this. The *arthavāda* praising a simple stone as the sun, thus, has a specific purpose and meaning.

Surā (wine)

Surā (wine) though not looked at with a favourable eye, is still prescribed in some rites and the *arthavāda*-s at those places praise *surā.*

The *Tait. Br.* states an old mythical account that once the gods separated the dirty part from the divine Speech as also from food. The dirty part from the divine Speech became the *gāthā*-s and the *nārāśaṁsī's*, while that of the food became *surā* (*Tait. Br.* I. 3.2.6). *Surā* (wine) figures prominently in the Vājapeya sacrifice. There are seventeen cups of Soma and equal number of wine (*surā)* cups, both types being meant for Prajāpati (the number 'seventeen' specially associated with Prajāpati, who is said to be seventeenfold). Wine[161] is purchased, in exchange for a piece of lead from a man having long hair, at the time of the purchase of Soma. These two types of cups are placed separate from each other, on mounds prepared separately—the Soma-cups to the east of the axle of the southern Havirdhāna-*śakaṭa* (cart) and the *surā*-cups to the west of the axle of the cart mentioned above *(Śat Br.* V.1.2.10-15). The Adhvaryu priest and the Neṣṭṛ priest are on two opposite sides of the axle of the cart. Alternately the Soma-cups are drawn (cup after cup) by the Adhvaryu priest and held just over the axle and the *surā*-cups are drawn (cup after cup) by the Neṣṭṛ priest and held just below the axle (*ibid.* 16-18), thus both priests keeping the cups separate, though indicating their symbolic uniting. The *Śat. Br.* speaks of the thought in the mind of the two priests that they should not mix light and darkness (*ibid.* 17), Soma standing for light and *surā* for darkness. The *Mait. Sam.* states that the two types of cups are to be drawn in such a way, as to keep them separate, for Soma is prosperity, while *surā* is sin (*Mait. Sam.* I.11.6). The inherent idea in this ritual of alternately drawing the two types of cups, according to Dange seems to be that the body of every person (including Prajāpati) has a mixture of good (represented by Soma) and bad (represented by *surā*), but they are to be separated.[162] In the same context, the *Tait. Br.* also has the same thought to give that wine is the dirty part of food. With this dirty part he wipes off (lit. slays) the dirty part of the sacrificer (*Tait. Br.* I.3.3.3, 4 and 6). The *arthavāda* which occurs in the context of the Vājapeya sacrifice again, in the ritual race-running of seventeen chariots, also views *surā* not in a favourable light. On one of these chariots stands either a *vaiśya* or a *rājanya.* The Adhvaryu priest and the sacrificer taking the honey-cup, place it in the hand of *vaiśya* or *rājanya* (whosoever of the two is there). The Neṣṭṛ priest taking the *surā*-cups steps out and places one of these cups in the hand of *vaiśya* or *rājanya* saying 'With this (i.e. the *surā*-cup), I buy him (i.e. Soma) from you!' The *arthavāda* is very clear in stating that Soma is truth, prosperity and light and *surā* is untruth, misery and darkness (*Śat. Br.* V.1.5.28).

But the *surā* still finds entry into a couple of rites with honour. In the rite of re-lustration (Punarabhiṣeka) of the king, together with several things such as throne, goblet and a branch (all three) of Udumbara; curds, honey and ghee; waters of rain (caught) in sunshine; grass and green barley sprouts; Dūrva grass; *sūra* (wine) also figures. *Surā* is a symbol of the lordly power and also the sap of food. By using *surā*, the lordly power and the sap of food are conferred on the king (*Ait. Br.* VIII. 8 = 37.4).

In the great anointing of king (Mahābhiṣeka), following such a rite performed in the case of Indra (Aindra Mahābhiṣeka), figures *surā* with other liquid materials, such as curds, honey, ghee and water, the latter four to be used for anointing, but the *surā*-cup of bell-metal (*surākaṁsa)* is to be given in the hand of the king. It has to be marked that here the Soma drink is said to be there residing in the *surā*, that is actually drunk by the *kṣatriya* (king), when he is anointed by this great anointing of Indra. It is thus believed that Soma and not the *surā* is drunk by that king (*ibid.* VIII.

20 = 39.6). This shows that in this rite, the *surā* enjoys the same status as that of Soma.

To turn to the Sautrāmaṇī rite—The mythical account in short in this regard is as follows. Indra cut off the three heads of Tvaṣṭṛ's son Viśvarūpa. Being furious at this, Tvaṣṭṛ brought Soma-juice but concealed it from Indra. Indra even uninvited came there and consumed that Soma. But Soma rendered Indra diseased. From the Soma fluid, that flowed out from his body, were created many beasts and fruits. But Indra (being weak thereby) walked about as one tottering. The Aśvins healed him. As he was *su-trāta* ('well saved'), he was called *sutrāman* and hence the name of the rite Sautrāmaṇī (*Śat. Br.* V.5.4.2-12). The chief characteristic of this rite is the offering of *surā* (wine) in it. In the fermented liquor *(parisrut)*, he throws hairs of a lion, of a wolf and those of a tiger, for these beasts sprang from Indra when the Soma flowed out of him (*ibid.* V. 5.4.18). That fermented liquor is purified with stalks of Darbha-grass and in it are poured powders of Kuvala, Karkandhu and Badara berries, for these three came out when Indra vomited (Soma) thrice (*ibid.* 22). Either one or three cups are filled (with that wine, prepared in the above manner) and are offered to the Aśvins, Sarasvatī and Indra—the Sutrāman—, accompanied with a *mantra* (*ibid.* 23-26; also *Kāty. Ś.S.* XV.10-13). A pitcher perforated either with a hundred or with nine holes, is hung up by a sling and held just over the Āhavanīya fire. Hundred holes stand for the hundred years of man's life, his hundred energies and hundred powers. Nine holes stand for the nine vital airs in man. The wine which is left over (after being offered to the three deities mentioned above) is poured into this pitcher *(kumbha)* and that wine is trickling through, the sacrificer (or the priest on his behalf) stands by worshipping with the three triplets (*Vāj. Sam.* XIX. 49-51; 55-57 and 58-60), the Fathers accompanied by Soma, the Fathers seated on the sacrificial grass, i.e. *barhis* and the Fathers consumed by the fire respectively. When Soma flowed through Indra, some part of it went to the Fathers. That part the sacrificer supplies to Indra and makes him whole, when he stands worshipping (*Śat. Br.* V. 5.4.27-28). The *Tait. Br.* has one addition here. It says that after the offerings of wine are given to the Fathers, a *brāhmaṇa* is to be bought over to drink the dregs and if such one cannot be found (for normally no *brāhmaṇa* will be willing to do it, wine being prohibited for him), they are to be poured away on an ant-hill (*Tait. Br.* I.8.6.2).

The Sautrāmaṇī rite (*iṣṭi*) seen above in details, is prescribed for nullifying any excess committed in the consumption of Soma-juice. It is the last of the seven forms of Haviryajña. However it can be performed independently as a special offering, taken to be an expiation for any excess committed at a Soma-sacrifice.[163] But the amusing part of it is that the excess in drinking Soma is sought to be nullified by offering wine to the deities and to the Fathers, as we have noted above. The *Śat. Br.* deals with the Sautrāmaṇī *iṣṭi* again in XII *kāṇḍa* (XII. 8.1). It is clearly stated there by the Śat. Br. that they purify the sacrificer by means of *surā*, for *surā* is itself a purified substance. While being purified, it is cleared of impure matter (*Śat. Br.* XII. 8.1.16), and is in itself the essence of waters and plants (*ibid.* XII. 8.1.4).

So as it stands, *surā* in the *arthavāda*-s is both—dirty part of the food, untruth, misery and darkness but also (in the same Vedic times) a purifying agent or a precious drink (having the same status as that of Soma). To explain this 'complex' nature of *surā* from the ritualists' point of view, we have to turn to interesting details in the Gṛhyasūtras, which prescribe the use of *surā* in certain rituals concerning females (female-ancestors included). In the Anvaṣṭakā or Anvaṣṭakya rite which is to be performed after the Aṣṭakā, in respect of the *pitṛ*-s,[164] wine (*surā)* marks the offerings to the female ancestors. This detail of *surā* occurs in three Gṛhyasūtras *viz. Pār. G.S.* (III. 3.10-11); *Āśv. G.S.* (II. 5.1-8) and *Kāṭh. G.S.* (65.7.8). *Surā* also figures in the pre-wedding rites. The pre-wedding rite is called Indrāṇī-karma, for here the bride is identified with Indrāṇī, the symbol of the ploughable field (Indra—the male counterpart being viewed as the god of fertility, in one of his varied aspects) and the rite is meant for her lustration and fructification. The *Gobh. G.S.* prescribes that on the previous day of the wedding, after the bride has been washed with water mixed with the powder of Klītaka, barley and beans, a woman who is affectionate towards her should besprinkle her thrice on the head with *surā* of the first quality (*surottama)* in a manner that her whole body gets wet (*Gobh. G.S.* II. 1.9-10).[165] The *Śaṅkh. G.S.* states that in the pre-wedding rite, vegetables, food and *surā* should be offered to four or eight women having husband and children alive, who perform a dance before the bride (*Śāṅkh. G.S.* I.11.5). To go back to the times of *RV*, *surā* is here spoken of as being sprinkled from a hundred jars filled by the Aśvins, through the hooves of the virile Horse—the sun—so that Purandhi ('goddess of plenty') may get fructified (*RV* I.116.7). To turn to the point of *surā* being offered to the female ancestors. Taking into account the references to *surā* in the Gṛhyasūtras, it appears that *surā* was prescribed in the ritual for the female ancestors for the continuation of fertility and prosperity, through the woman, in the family of the performer.[166]

When *surā* is mentioned in the Mahābhiṣeka rite of the king or the Sautrāmaṇī rite, it is associated with the Soma, may be as taking its place or as nullifying its effect. This shows that as Soma was viewed with some awe for its miraculous effects, so was *surā*. It is interesting to note that wine, its intoxicating effect and its formation in a miraculous way, figure in the philosophy of the Lokāyatikas. As noted by Mādhava in his work *Sarvadarśanasaṅgraha*, the Lokāyatikas say that the four elements—Water, Air, Earth and Lustre—though themselves insentient, produce the sentient (*caitanya*) when combined together, just as rice, water and molasses produce wine having the intoxicating effect, even though they in themselves, separately, do not have that quality.[167] We may not agree with the Lokāyata philosophical tenet, but the general belief reflected in this passage about *surā*, can help us solve to some extent the riddle of the entry of *surā* in the ritual tradition, where it could, in some rites, obtain a position next to Soma.

Thunderbolt (*vajra*)

Thunderbolt (*vajra*) is spoken of in the *RV* as exclusively belonging to Indra. When we take Indra in the aspect of 'Rain-god', we can agree with Macdonell that it is the regular mythological name of the lightning stroke.[168] It is generally said to be fashioned for him by Tvaṣṭṛ (*RV* I. 32.2), but Kāvya Uśanas is also said to have made it and given it to him (*ibid.* I.121.12; V. 34.2). In the *Ait. Br.*, the gods are seen providing the thunderbolt to Indra (*Ait. Br.* IV. 1 = 16.1). For the Ṛgvedic seer, it is not simply conceptual but having some air of reality, when it is described as *āyasa* or metallic (*RV* I.52.8).

When we come to the ritual texts, the thunderbolt becomes a part of a mythical account about Indra, which occurs in the context of the New-moon and Full-moon sacrifices, when the sacrificer (or the priest on his behalf) takes up a wooden sword (*sphya*). The *Śat. Br.* states that the priests (*brāhmaṇa*-s) make use of the sacrificial post and the wooden sword and the *kṣatriya*-s of the chariot and the arrow. When Indra hurled the thunderbolt at Vṛtra, the thunderbolt became fourfold. The wooden sword, the sacrificial post and the chariot represent the three one-third parts (of it) or as much as these parts (*'yāvat'* the word used each time in this respect). The piece of the thunderbolt which struck Vṛtra was broken off and on falling down became an arrow (*Śat. Br.* I.2.4.1-3). The mythical account coming by way of *arthavāda*, noted above, is for glorifying the wooden sword (*sphya*), which is said to be a one-third part of the thunderbolt.[169]

In the Brāhmaṇa-texts, the oft-repeated mention of the thunderbolt occurs in the ritual metaphors, where the thunderbolt comes as a standard of comparison. To take some examples. Clarified butter is often said to be thunderbolt (*ibid.* I.3.2.17; III. 3.2.1; III.6.4.15; III.8.1.5; IV.4.2.13; V.2.4.7; VI.3.3.18, etc.). Waters are thunderbolt (*ibid.* I.1.1.17; I.7.1.20; III.1.2.6; VII.5.2.41; XII.9.2.6; XIV.3.1.27, etc.). Knife is thunderbolt (*ibid.* III. 8.2.12). Pressing-stone is said to be thunderbolt (*ibid.* XI.5.9.7). *Abhri* (spade) is thunderbolt (*ibid.* III. 7.1.2). Horse (in the Horse-sacrifice) is said to be thunderbolt (*ibid.* XIII. 1.2.9). The cattle are said to be thunderbolt (*ibid.* VI. 4.4.6; VIII. 2.3.14). The eighth day in the Sarvamedha (ten-day Soma-sacrifice) is a Triṇava day, for on that day Triṇava (thrice-nine-versed) *stoma* is used in chanting. Triṇava *stoma* is said to be thunderbolt. By means of this thunderbolt, lordship (*kṣatra)* is gained *(ibid.* XIII. 7.1.10; also for the same thought and metaphor *ibid.* XIII. 4.4.1). The Vaṣaṭ call (the one which he makes aloud and forcibly) is thunderbolt (*Ait. Br.* III.6 = 11.6). The Pañcadaśa *stoma* is said to be thunderbolt (*Śat. Br.* I.3.5.7; III. 6.4.25; IV.3.3.4; VII. 2.4.12; VII. 5.2.41; XIII. 2.2.10; XIII. 4.1.13, etc.). The Triṣṭubh metre is thunderbolt (*ibid.* III. 6.4.22; III. 7.1.15; VII. 2.1.15; VII. 4.1.34; VII. 5.2.24; XIII. 6.1.4, etc.). The Pañcadaśa *stoma* and the Triṣṭubh metre are associated with Indra (*Tait. Sam.* VII. 1.1.4; *Pañc. Br.* VI. 1.8). May be this has led to the ritual metaphor of taking the Pañcadaśa *stoma* and the Triṣṭubh metre to be thunderbolt,[170] which exclusively belongs to Indra, to whom the first two also are associated.

These ritual metaphors aptly bring out that the concept of thunderbolt was all-pervading, touching several objects *viz.* liquids (clarified butter and water), sharp instruments, four-footed animals (horse and cattle), etc. and even the sphere of Speech, with its aspects of *stoma* and *chandas.* Thus Indra's thunderbolt often mentioned in the *RV* attained so many dimensions in the ritual texts that it became the very emblem of vigour (*Śat. Br.* XIII. 2.2.10; XIII. 4.1.13).

Upahavya

While prescribing the one-day sacrifice named Upahavya, the mythical account coming by way of *arthavāda* speaks of a social practice of those times. When Indra gave the *yati*-s to the hyenas,[171] an inauspicious voice (*aślīlā vāg*) reproached him. He then took resort to Prajāpati and the latter enlightened him on the Upahavya rite. When Indra performed it, he was invited by the gods to their company. As they invited (*upāhvayanta*) him due to this rite being performed by him, the rite was called Upahavya (fr. *upa* + √*hū* - 'to call near'). The priest should perform this rite for one to whom is attached calumny (*Pañc. Br.* XVIII. 1.9,10). With respect to this rite, the *Pañc. Br.* has stated that in this one-day sacrifice, the seventeen-versed Agniṣṭoma laud is to be chanted. And this Upahavya rite was 'seen' by Prajāpati for the sake of the gods, who were less in number and were weak, while the *asura*-s were numerous and strong (*ibid.* XVIII. 1.1,2).

It has to be noted that though there are expiations laid down for the wrong committed or inadvertently taken place in the sacrificial performance, these seem to be on the personal level of the sacrificer. But here the Upahavya rite seems to have 'society' in view and thus has social implication, as seen from the *arthavāda*.

Upasad-s

In the context of the Agniṣṭoma sacrifice occurs a mythical account by way of *arthavāda*, regarding the Upasad-s. The Upasad-s consist of three offerings of ghee to Agni, Soma and Viṣṇu, followed by a *homa*, and are to be performed twice daily, for at least three days, which is the normal number at the Agniṣṭoma sacrifice. The first day's performance is called the 'Ayaḥśayā' (lying in iron, i.e. made of iron), the second day's 'Rajaḥśayā' (silvern) and the third day's 'Hariśayā' (golden). If there are six or twelve Upasad days, each of the three varieties of performance has assigned to it an equal number of successive days and if there are more than twelve, the three varieties are to be performed alternatively.[172]

To turn to the *arthavāda*, which is in the form of a mythical account. The gods and the *asura*-s, both of them sprung from Prajāpati were contending against each other. The *asura*-s themselves built castles in these worlds—an iron one in this world, a silver one in the air and a golden one in the sky. The gods besieged these castles by the sieges (in the form of Upasad-s). As the gods besieged (fr. *upa* + √*sad*) them (castles) by these, hence the name 'Upasad' (*Śat. Br.* III. 4.4.3-4). The gods smashed the castles of the *asura*-s and conquered these worlds. The *arthavāda* speaks of a worldly fact that 'a castle is conquered by siege' (*ibid.* 4 - *upasadā puram jayanti).*[173] It is interesting to mark that the mythical account noted above has paved the way for the Puranic myth of Tripura (the name of a city or citadel) built by the demon Maya, after propitiating the god Brahmā. In fact, Tripura signified a unit of three such cities one in each region—Earth, Mid-region and Heaven. On the earth, the city was made of iron, in the mid-region of silver, and in heaven of gold (*Matsya P.* 128. 19-34). The demon with the three cities was killed by Śiva on the full-moon day of the Kārttika month. So a lamp is to be offered at evening in the temple of Śiva,[174] on this day.

Vedi (sacrificial altar)

The concept of the sarificial altar is associated with that of the earth. The *Śat. Br.* clearly states that as large as the altar is, so large is the earth (*Śat. Br.* III. 7.2.1). The sacrificial altar (*devayajanī)* is to be prepared on the holy (*medhyā)* earth. The mythical account coming by way of *arthavāda* in the *Tait. Br.* states that there was an *asura* named Viṣād. He got frightened with the idea that the gods would overpower him by sacrifice. He vomited on the earth. So the earth became unholy (impure). When Indra slew Vṛtra, the latter's blood flew along the earth, with which the earth became holy (pure). Hence they say that the sacrificial altar is the earth (*Tait. Br.* III. 2.9.2). As Gāyatrī is the favourite metre of Agni, the *vedi* (sacrificial altar-ground) is said to be the

Gāyatrī. In the New-moon and Full-moon sacrifices, the eight butter-portions offered first on the altar are the right wing of the Gāyatrī and the eight butter-portions offered subsequently are her left wing. This same golden brilliant-winged Gāyatrī (i.e. the sacrificial altar) indeed takes the sacrificer who knows this, to the heavenly world (*Śat. Br.* XI. 4.1.16).

The ritual texts state mythical account as *arthavāda*, explaining the etymology of the word '*vedi*' and also at times speaking about its size. The *Tait. Sam.*, in the context of Soma-sacrifice, has a mythical account as *arthavāda.* Once the Sacrifice went away from the gods (an oft-repeated mythical idea in the ritual texts!) in the form of Viṣṇu and entered the earth. The gods sought him. Indra passed beyond him. He (i.e. Viṣṇu) asked as to who passed beyond him. Indra said that it was he (i.e. Indra himself) who smote (in) the stronghold *(durga).* Viṣṇu told him that a boar had kept the wealth *(vitta)* of the *asura*-s, which was to be won *(vedya)* beyond the seven hills. Indra should smite him. Indra then plucking a bunch of Darbha grass, pierced the seven hills and smote the boar. He pointedly said that as Viṣṇu (Sacrifice) was known to bring (wealth) from the stronghold, he should bring that wealth. Viṣṇu (Sacrifice) then carried off the sacrifice for them. As they (i.e. the gods) won the wealth of the *asura*-s, which was to be won (*vedya)*, so the *vedi* is called *'vedi'* (fr. the root √*vid* - 'to get, obtain'). With this is related another mythical account in order to explain the nature of *vedi* and also the word *'vedi'*, The *asura*-s in the beginning owned the entire earth. The gods entreated upon them to have a share in the earth. It was agreed that the *asura*-s should give them as much earth (i.e. land) as a *salāvṛkī* (a wolf) can thrice run round. Indra taking the form of a *salāvṛkī* thrice ran round the earth on all sides. So they won the earth. As they won (fr. √*vid*) it, therefore the word *'vedi'* (*Tait. Sam.* VI. 2.4.2-4).

Another mythical account comes in the context of the New-moon and Full-moon sacrifices. The gods and the *asura*-s both sprung from Prajāpati were striving for superiority. When the *asura*-s got the upper hand, they thought of dividing the earth between themselves. Placing Viṣṇu—the very Sacrifice—as their head, they went to the *asura*-s and requested for having a part of the earth for them. The *asura*-s agreed grudgingly to give that much earth (i.e. land) on which Viṣṇu (taken to be a dwarf) would lie upon. The gods then laid Viṣṇu—the Sacrifice—down eastward; enclosed him on all three sides with the metres and having placed Agni on the east side, went on toiling with Viṣṇu—the Sacrifice. By Viṣṇu—the Sacrifice—they obtained (*sam* + √*vid)* the entire earth. Hence the sacrificial ground is called '*vedi*'. As great as the altar is, so great is the earth. By the *vedi*, they got the entire earth (*Śat. Br.* I.2.5.1-7). The mythical account runs further. Viṣṇu became tired. But as he was enclosed on all sides by the metres, with the fire on the east, there was no means of escaping. So he hid himself among the roots of plants. The gods started searching for him. After digging, they discovered him at a depth of three inches (or thumb's breadths). The *Śat. Br.* hence prescribes that the altar should be three inches deep (*ibid.* 8-9). This is according to one opinion, the other being that one should not do it. As Viṣṇu hid himself among the roots of the plants, the roots of the plants should be cut off. As they found Viṣṇu in that place, so the name '*vedi*' (fr. *anu* + √*vid* - 'to find, discover' *ibid.* 10).

While prescribing that the altar should be broader on the west side, contracted in the middle and broad again on the east side, the *Śat. Br.* has an *arthavāda* to state, which reflects the very aim of performing sacrifice. It is said that the altar is female and fire is male. The woman lies embracing the man, by which a copulation productive of offspring is there (*ibid.* I.2.5.15, 16). The sacrifice is for procreation or regeneration on the cosmic level as well as the terrestrial level in all spheres. But this is brought out through the man-and-woman relationship leading to the procreation of offspring, taking the altar to be female and the fire, male.

Yūpa (sacrificial post)

In the ritual texts, practically the same *arthavāda* occurs while stating the etymology of the word *'yūpa'*, The gods obtained the supreme authority and the heavenly world by means of sacrifice. They wanted to make the celestial region unattainable to men. So they sipped the sap of the sacrifice, as bees would suck out honey. Having drained the sacrifice and effaced its traces by means of the sacrificial stake, they disappeared. As they obliterated *(ayopayan)* the sacrifice, with it, so the word *'yūpa'* (*Śat. Br.* I.6.2.1,2; III.1.4.3; III.4.3.15; III. 7.1.27; *Ait. Br.* I.7 = 2.1).

The *yūpa* is required in the Soma-sacrifices, rather in animal-sacrifices *viz.* Nirūḍhapaśubandha, Paśubandha or Horse-sacrifice, for they immolate the animal only at a sacrificial stake (or post) and never without a stake. The *arthavāda* here reflects the behaviour of animal, sensing some danger. It is said that animals at first did not submit to becoming food (of the gods). As man here walks on two feet, so they walked on two feet and erect (without lowering their body, as is their present position). The gods then perceived the thunderbolt in the form of the sacrificial stake. They raised it and out of fear for it (i.e. the stake), the animals shrunk together and thus became four-footed and, also the food for the gods (*Śat. Br.* III. 7.3.1,2). When the sacrificial victim (animal) is tied to the sacrificial post, the latter is expected to carry this (animal-) offering to the gods.

Though fixed on the terrestrial plane (in the sacrifice), the *yūpa* is understood to reach the region of the gods.[175] The *Tait. Sam.* in the exposition of Soma-sacrifice points out how the sacrificial stake touches all the three regions *viz.* the nether, earth and through mid-region heaven. The lowest (un-chiselled) portion of the *yūpa* is fixed in a pit, which symbolises the nether region. So this portion belongs to the *pitṛ*-s; what is above the part dug in, up to the girdle (of the *yūpa)* belongs to men; the girdle, to the plants (This is the region of the earth); what is above the girdle up to the top to All Gods (Viśve Devāḥ); the top to Indra; the rest to the Sādhyas (This is the heavenly region). By setting up the post, he delights all the gods (*Tait. Sam.* VI. 3.4.6, 7). By means of sacrifice, the gods went to the world of heaven, but they blocked the way of men (to the heaven) by the post. However the seers (*ṛṣi*-s) discerned (*prājānan)* that world by means of the post. When the sacrificer (or the priest) sets up a post, it is to discern (*prajñātyai)* the world of heaven (*ibid.* VI.3.4.7, 8). We are here reminded of the words of the Ṛgvedic seer that the sacrificial stake is the banner, i.e. the emblem, of sacrifice (*RV*. III. 8.8 - *yajñamavantu devā ūrdhvam kṛṇvantva'dhvarasya ketum)*, sacrifice being one of the aspects of the *ṚTA*.

NOTES AND REFERENCES

1. This point is fully dealt with by Dange, Sadashiv A., the chapter "Kaca and Śukra" *Myths from the Mahābhārata*. Vol. 1, *Quest for Immortality*, Aryan Books International, New Delhi, 1997, pp. 182 ff.
2. (Mrs.) Dange, S.S., *Aspects of Speech in Vedic Ritual*, p. 227; p. 230, note 36.
3. *Ājya* (clarified butter) is said to be the half part of the body of sacrifice—*Śat. Br.* (I.2.2.5). It is said to be the very sacrifice. *ibid.* XII. 8.1.18.
4. *Yāj. Sm.* II. 135 and also the comm. Mitākṣarā on it.
5. For details, see Eggeling, J., *The Śatapatha Brāhmaṇa*, pt. I, SBE Vol. 12, p. 104, note 1.
6. See Dange, Sadashiv A., "Adornment as a Protective Measure in the Vedic Ritual", *Dr. Mirashi Fel. Vol.*, Vidarbha Samshodhan Mandal, Nagpur, 1965, pp. 87-103.
7. 'Taboo' is one of the few words, which the language of the Pacific Islanders have contributed to modern speech. It was made familiar by Captain James Cook in the narrative of his third and last voyage around the world. See Cook, James and King, James, *A Voyage to the Pacific Ocean*, London, 1784, Vols. I & II by Cook, and Vol. III by King.

"Taboo stands for the whole mass of such fear-inspired inhibitions in so far as they proceed directly from the religious emotions...", *Ency. of Rel. and Eth.*, Vol. XII, p. 183 a, article on "Tabu" by Marett, R.R.

8. *Tait. Sam.* VI. 1.3.2-3—In the context of the Soma-sacrifice it is said that the man who is consecrated is a foetus; the clothing is the caul, so he covers. Foetuses are born covered with the caul. He uncovers when the Soma has been purchased, for then he is really born.
9. Hastings, J., *Ency. of Rel. and Eth.*, Vol. VI., pp. 532-40.
10. *Śat. Br.* III. 1.1.9,10. It is said that only *brāhmaṇa*, *rājanya* and *vaiśya* are entitled to perform sacrifice (*yajñiyāḥ*). As the consecrated sacrificer becomes one of the deities, by going near to the gods, and as the gods converse only with a *brāhmaṇa* or a *rājanya* or a *vaiśya*, and not with every one, the sacrificer also should follow them. If he is required to converse with a *śūdra*, he should speak to him indirectly through a person of one of the three (upper) *varṇa*-s.
11. Hastings, J., *op. cit.*, Vol. IV., p. 330 b.
12. *The Zend-Avesta*, Pt. III, SBE Vol. 31, tr. by Mills, L.H., Reprint, Motilal Banarsidass, Delhi, 1988 (1887), p. 291.
13. Hastings, J., *op. cit.*, Vol. IV, pp. 331 b, 332a.
14. For details, see (Mrs.) Dange, S.S., *Hindu Domestic Rituals - A Critical Glance,* pp. 85-86.
15. *Śilpa* denotes the skilful compositions employed in reciting the praise-formulas (*śastra*-s). The combination of verses in a hymn or certain methods of reciting the verses in a hymn is a striking feature in the *śilpa*-s. For details, see (Mrs.) Dange, S.S., *Aspects of Speech in Vedic Ritual*, pp. 103-8.
16. *Ait. Br.* VI.3 = 26.3 deals with the office of the Subrahmaṇya priest. It is said that Subrahmaṇyā is speech—the good holy power (*su-brahma*). That is why they call him that is 'male', a 'female' as it were.
17. See Eggeling, J., *op. cit.*, Pt. I. SBE Vol. 12, p. 313, note 2.
18. Dange, Sadashiv A., *Vedic Sacrifices — Early Nature*, Vol. II, pp. 306-16.
19. For details, See *ibid.*, pp. 338-42.
20. See note 16 *supra.*
21. For details, see Dange, Sadashiv A, "Sex-Coupling in Sacrifice (Mithunīkaraṇa)", *Sexual Symbolism from the Vedic Ritual*, Ajanta Pubns., Delhi, 1979, pp. 51-70.

22. For *śloka*-s and *gāthā*-s, (Mrs.) Dange, S.S., "Songs from Secular Tradition", *Aspects of Speech in Vedic Ritual*, pp. 206-30.
23. Viśvajit Atirātra is a sacrifice on the tenth day in the Sarvamedha, which is a ten-day Soma-sacrifice. *Śat. Br.* XIII. 7.1.2, 12.
24. Kane, P.V., *Hist. of Dh. S.*, Vol. II, pt. II, pp. 865-69.
25. For details, see (Mrs.) Dange, S.S., *Hindu Domestic Rituals—A Critical Glance*, pp. 71-73.
26. (Mrs.) Dange, S.S., "Yāska on Widow's Share", *Vishveshvarananda Indological Jnl.*, Vol. XVIII, pts. i-ii, 1980 (*Prof. K.V. Sharma Fel. Vol.)*, Hoshiarpur, pp. 385-87.
27. Macdonell, A.A. and Keith, A.B., *Vedic Index of Names and Subjects*, London, 1912, under the title "Yuga."
28. (Mrs.) Dange, S.S., "Significance of Dice", *Hindu Domestic Rituals—A Critical Glance*, pp. 70-77.
29. *Ency. of Rel. and Eth.*, Vol. IV, p. 779b.
30. *Pañc. Br.* IV. 7.1—The Viṣuvat day is as it were the replica of Year. *also see Tait. Br.* I.2.3.1.
31. *Pañc. Br.* XIV. 11.12—He who praises with the *Bhāsa sāman*, shines-*bhāsam bhavati bhāti tuṣṭuvānaḥ*
32. Some other ritual-texts mention it. *Tait. Sam.* II. 1.2.2; *Kauṣ. Br.* XXIV.3; *Jaim. Br.* 1.80.

    Śat. Br. V. 3.2.2—Soma and Rudra removed the darkness of the sun, caused by Svarbhānu. Hence (in the Rājasūya sacrifice) a *caru* is offered to Soma and Rudra. The *caru* (pap) is cooked in milk from a white cow, which has a white calf, for by this the sacrificer-king removes the (black) darkness, i.e. evil, which accrues, when he comes into contact with those unworthy of sacrifice.
33. Davane, G.V., "The Rāhu-Ketu myth", *Perspectives in the Vedic and the Classical Sanskrit Heritage*, D.K. Print World (P) Ltd., New Delhi, 1995, pp. 135-38.
34. Tilak, B.G., *Orion*, pub. by Tilak Brothers, Poona, 1893, p. 159.
35. (Mrs.) Dange, S.S., "Sāman-s and Lauds", *Aspects of Speech in Vedic Ritual*, pp. 182-205.
36. *Nirṇayasindhu* of Kamalākarabhaṭṭa, ed. by Narayanram Acharya, Nirnayasagara Press, Mumbai, 5th ed., 1949, pp. 48-49.

37. There has been a practice, though day by day, now becoming obsolete, of keeping the idols of the gods (which a person has in his house for daily worship) in waters sometime prior to the solar or lunar eclipse till the end of it. The waters here stand for the primeval waters, which were there prior to the creation of the universe, indicating thereby that in the event of the sun or the moon not being there, the whole world would revert to the condition of nihility, or *'ex nihilo'* there being only waters everywhere. For details regarding creation-accounts in various mythologies, see (Mrs.) Dange, S.S. (Ed.), *Myths of Creation* (Papers read at the Seminar, held by the Dept. of Sanskrit), University of Bombay Pubn., Bombay, 1987.
38. In the Ānanda Rāmāyaṇa, which is comparatively a late work, we see Lakṣmaṇa drawing a circle round the hut and warning Sītā not to transgress it. For this, see *Ānanda Rāmāyaṇa*, Sārakāṇḍa, 7.99,100.
39. For details about the Vaṣaṭ-call, see (Mrs.) Dange, S.S., "Mystic Utterances in the Vedic Ritual", *Aspects of Speech in Vedic Ritual*, pp. 146-63.
40. *Ait. Br.* III. 7 = 11.7.
41. See (Mrs.) Dange, S.S., "Mystic Utterances in the Vedic Ritual" , *Aspects of Speech in Vedic Ritual*, pp. 146-181.
42. Eggeling, J., *op. cit.*, pt. I, SBE Vol. 12, p. 4, note 2.
43. Yājñavalkya's thought of eating only the forest-produce on the Upavasatha day, was extended, with the passage of time, to the food, which a person does not eat daily, and which, hence, when eaten does not amount to eating. Again the concept of the Upavasatha day was extended to any fast-day, irrespective of any sacrifice, in many cases concerning only a certain vow.
44. A practice alternate to the one mentioned in note 43 *supra*, is followed even today and it is of complete abstention from food while following a particular vow.
45. In any performance connected with the *pitṛ*-s (manes), the performer wears the sacrificial thread on the right shoulder and under the left arm, exactly opposite of what he does ordinarily (i.e. on the left shoulder and under the right arm).
46. *Kauṣ. Br.* V.6 — In the Sākamedha *iṣṭi* of the Seasonal sacrifices (Cāturmāsya), they proceed with the sacrifice to

the Fathers in the afternoon, for the Fathers have the 'waning' as their portion (*apakṣayabhājo vai pitaraḥ).*

47. *Bhāg. P.* IX. 6—Yuvanāśva, the king of the Ikṣvāku race, being issueless, performed a sacrifice to Indra for child. When the sacrifice was in progress, Yuvanāśva one night, being thirsty, drank the consecrated water kept by the priests for his wife. Later on, a son was born to Yuvanāśva. When all people asked, "Whom will he suck (*kam dhāsyati kumāro'yam?)*", Indra appeared and said, "*mām dhāsyati* (he will suck me)", and put his forefinger in the child's mouth. And from that the child was named Māndhātā (*mām dhātā)* — the king Māndhātṛ.
48. Alakṣmī is described in the Purāṇa-s as thick-lipped, white in body, red-eyed and having yellow coarse hair. Viṣṇu told her that the Aśvattha tree itself would be her habitat all days except on Saturday, when on that day her younger sister Lakṣmī would come there. For more details, see Dange, Sadashiv A., *Ency. of P.B. & P.*, Vol. III, Navrang, New Delhi, 1987, p. 699.
49. The *arthavāda* runs further that this milk-offering was not relished by Prajāpati, for it had the hair from the palms mixed in it. He dropped it in Agni asking him to drink while burning (*oṣam dhaya).* From it shot up the plants, which are called *oṣadhayaḥ* (*Śat. Br.* II. 2.4.5).
50. The mythical account runs further. See *Śat. Br.* III. 2.4.4-7.
51. Śada and Upaśada (or Aupaśada as we have in the *Pañc. Br.* XIX. 3.1) is a pair of one-day rites, of which the *Pañc. Br.* mentions only one, i.e. Aupaśada. The pair is also called Sada and Upasada. Upaśada, Aupaśada or Upasada (all three meaning the same one-day rite) is intended for one, who wishes progeny (or even cattle). *Jaim. Br.* II. 81; *Śāṅkh. Ś.S.* XIV. 22.25; *Kāty. Ś.S.* XXII. 10.13.
52. Caland, W., *Pañcaviṃśa Brāhmaṇa*, p. 503, note 1 on *Pañc. Br.* XIX. 3.2.
53. The *Śat. Br.* speaks of the woof, warp, threads, etc. of the garment as belonging to the deities Agni, Vāyu, Fathers, Snakes, All-gods and constellations (III. 1.2.18).
54. *Tārpya* is explained by Kātyāyana and Sāyaṇa as a linen garment, or a garment soaked in ghee or one made of Triparṇa plants, etc. Goldstücker takes it to mean a silk

under-garment. See Eggeling, J., *op. cit.*, pt. III, SBE Vol. 41, p. 85, note 1.

55. Interestingly the *Bh.G.* compares the worn out bodies (in different births) taken by the soul to the worn out garments put on by a man, both—the soul as well as a man—leaving the old ones and taking up the new ones. See *Bh.G.* II. 22. The idea could be traced to the Vedic ritual tradition in the belief about the garment, which we have seen.
56. The east is associated with the rising sun and the gods, for the Āhavanīya fire-altar in which the offerings are given to the gods is established in the east.
57. See the title "Name" in the present chapter.
58. Eggeling, J., *op. cit.*, pt. I, SBE Vol. 12, p. 17, note 1, quotes Mahīdhara, the commentator, who says that 'without this announcement, the, quarrels would arise among the gods.'
59. From the occurrence of the word *manotā,* Eggeling notes that the word *manotā* has come to be the technical name for both the hymn itself and the deity (Agni) it is recited. See Eggeling, J. *op. cit.*, pt. II, SBE Vol. 26, p. 203, note 4.
60. That 'Ka' stands for Prajāpati can be traced to the *RV* (X. 121). The refrain in this hymn (*RV*. X. 121. 1-9 *ṛc*-s*)* is *kasmai devāya haviṣā vidhema*, where the word *ka* is explained by Sāyaṇa in various ways, ultimately coming to the conclusion that *ka* stands for Prajāpati.
61. Some of the equations —

    Śat. Br. V. 1.3.7—Prajāpati is food; Prajāpati is Soma; *ibid.* 9 —Prajāpati is (represents) productiveness. *Ibid.* V. 1.5.6—Prajāpati is Speech; *ibid.* XIII. 4.1.15 for the same thought, *ibid.* V.1.3.11—Prajāpati is everything here—these worlds and everything there is. *Ibid.* V.1.3.12, 13—Prajāpati is productiveness as well as the end.
62. *Śat. Br.* I.1.1.13; I.6.1.20; IV.4.1.6; *Jaim. Br.* I.60, etc.
63. For a detailed discussion about the *'anirukta'* (unlimited) nature of the *mantra*-s, see (Mrs.) Dange, S.S. *Aspects of Speech in Vedic Ritual*, pp. 237-40.
64. *Yāj. Sm.* I.64; III. 297.
65. For the practice of carrying fire round the sacrificial cake or the sacrificial victim—'Paryagnikaraṇam' as it is called—see Eggeling, J., *op. cit.*, pt. I, SBE Vol. 12, p. 45, note 1 on *Śat. Br.* I.2.2.13.

66. Cf. *RV*. II. 35.12 c—The seer speaks of rubbing bright the back of Agni (who is a form of the god Apām Napāt). This is removing the ashes of the Agni, so that it can blaze again.
67. This sweeping is done with the help of a straw-band. See *Kāty. Ś.S.* III.1.13; also Eggeling, J., *op. cit.*, pt. I, p. 127, note 1.
68. According to Sāyaṇa, *atiśayena pratyakṣaphaladam*, which Eggeling translates as 'pre-eminently a giver of perceptible benefits'. See Eggeling, J., *op. cit.*, pt. I, p. 163, note 1.
69. A mythical account of the gods obtaining the whole of the earth occurs in the *Tait. Br.* (III. 2.9.6-7). The Vasu-s are placed in the south, the Rudra-s in the west, the Āditya-s in the north and Agni in the east. These regions are enclosed and so is obtained the entire earth.
70. Anvāhārya is the rice, which is cooked on the Dakṣiṇa fire and which is sufficient for the meals of all the four priests. It is taken out (*āhriyate* fr. ā + √*hṛ*) for feeding the priests, after (*anu*) the sacrifice. Hence the name 'Anvāhārya'. See *Śrautapadārtha-nirvacanam*, author unnamed, published by Yudhishthira Mīmāṁsaka, 1st ed. (earlier editions if any not available), Sonepat (Haryana), 1984, p. 14.
71. *Manu Sm.* says that a warrior being afraid running away from the battlefield, if is killed by others (i.e. enemy), gets all the 'sin' of his king and whatever is his merit, accumulated for the next world, is obtained by the king (VII. 94, 95). Here the transfer is of both demerit and merit.
72. The etymology of the word *yajus* from the root √*yuj*, that of *sāman* from the word *samāna* and that of '*uktha*' from the root *ut* + √*sthā* (causal), follow the principle laid down later by Yāska for giving etymology, when a word and the root from which the former is derived tally in meaning and when (even) a single letter or a single syllable is common to both of them (the major difference in letters or syllables not being taken into account). Vide *Nir.* II.1.
73. It is interesting to note that here Eggeling J. translates '*devajana iti devajanavidaḥ*' as 'those knowing the divine host under that of divine host' (see Eggeling, J., *op. cit.*, pt. IV. SBE Vol. 43, p. 373, tr. of *Śat. Br.* X. 5.2.20), while he translates the word 'Devajanavidyā' as 'demonology' in *Śat. Br.* XIII. 4.3.10 and in the note says 'the science, or knowledge of the divine (or supernatural) beings' and quotes the meanings

given by the *Śāṅkh. Ś.S.* and the *Āśv. Ś.S.*, which support the 'evil' nature of this lore, supporting his meaning 'demonology'. See Eggeling, J., *op. cit.*, pt. V, SBE Vol. 44, p. 368, note 1.

74. For keeping awake during night on the days of vows, or on the days when idols of gods are established, or on festive days, see Dange, Sadashiv A, *Ency. of P.B. & P.* Vol. III, Navrang, New Delhi, 1987, p. 931; also Vol. II, Navrang, New Delhi, 1987, p. 395, when on the Balipratipadā day in the festival of lights (Dīpāvalī), Bali, the lord of the *daitya*-s is to be worshipped by drawing his figure. At night, there should be 'keeping awake' (*jāgaraṇa)* and dance-music.
75. For full discussion on this point, carrying it further to the tradition of the Gṛhyasūtras, see (Mrs.) Dange, S.S., "The Garment of the Bride", *Hindu Domestic Rituals — A Critical Glance*, pp. 10-14.
76. For detailed information, see Dange, Sadashiv A., *Vedic Sacrifices—Early Nature*, Vol. I, pp. 218-20; p. 225f, note 16.
77. *Śat. Br.* III. 5.4.1; Eggeling, J., *op. cit.*, pt. I, p. 135, note 1, 'the ears and nostrails' (according to him).
78. *Ibid.*, note 2, where *valaga* is explained as charms, consisting of bones, nails, hair, foot-dust and similar objects, tied up in a piece of worn matting or cloth, or the like, and dug into the ground arm-deep, for causing injury to enemies.
79. As there is no fire at that place, this libation is offered on a piece of gold, which has fire (for gold is the seed of fire). *Tait. Sam.* (V. 1.3.1,2).
80. See note 38, *supra.*
81. Kane, P.V., *op. cit.*, pp. 1243-5.
82. *Ibid.*, p. 1245.
83. See the chapter "Introduction", note 29.
84. *Śat. Br.* II. 5.3.18. A bull is made to bellow in the Sākamedha *iṣṭi* (one of the four Seasonal sacrifices— Cāturmāsya *iṣṭi*-s)—and if he does not, the Brahman priest seated on the south side says 'sacrifice' (*juhudhi*, i.e. 'give offering') and that is said to be Indra's voice. The bull is Indra's form. When the bull bellows, it is taken that Indra has come to the sacrifice (to slay Vṛtra, and release waters). The bellowing of the bull signifies the thundering sound in the mid-region, leading to rains.

85. Caland, W., *op. cit.*, pp. 79-80.
86. For the details about the musical instruments, see *ibid.*, p. 86 f.
87. Kane, P.V., *op. cit.*, pp. 1244 f.
88. See Gonda, J., *The Functions and Significance of Gold in the Veda*, Leiden. Gonda has taken note of all references to gold in the Veda.
89. For *sambhāra*, see the chapter on "Trees and Plants", note 3.
90. According to the *Śat. Br.* (XIII. 2.6.8), these beads are said to be one hundred, the number 'hundred' being the desired lifespan of hundred years of man. The beads are tucked by all the three queens of the king, as the Vyāhṛti-s—Bhūr, Bhuvaḥ and Svar are uttered.

    The passage of the *Śat. Br.* has the words - '*ekaśatam ekaśatam*', which means 'one hundred one hundred', i.e. every queen tucks one hundred beads. But Eggeling J. (*op. cit.*, pt. V, SBE Vol. 44, p. 313) renders these words as 'a hundred and one pearls'. Eggeling has in his view the *arthavāda* in this passage, which points out the desired hundred years of man's life and his own self as one, making the number—'hundred and one.'
91. For details, see Kane, P.V., *op. cit.*, Vol. II, pt. II, p. 999 f.
92. *Śat. Br.* (XII. 7.2.12) mentions that some Adhvaryu priests buy the malted rice from a eunuch by giving a lead with the thought that the eunuch is neither woman nor man and the Sautrāmaṇī is neither an *iṣṭi* nor an animal-sacrifice. The *Śat. Br.* does not agree with this and says that Sautrāmaṇī is both an *iṣṭi* and an animal-sacrifice and the eunuch is the one unsuccessful among men.
93. As Sāyaṇa points out on this passage, *surā* is prepared from mature shoots of rice, etc., while Parisrut is from such as are not quite ripe.
94. This practice is prevalent even now in villages. When a cow or a buffalo is to be milched, they put some water in the milk-pail, in which the milk is to be collected.
95. For the details of the Daśapeya, differing in the two branches of the *YV*, see Dange, Sadashiv A., *Vedic Sacrifices—Early Nature*, Vol. II. pp. 338-42.
96. (Mrs.) Dange, S.S., "The Mirror", *Hindu Domestic Rituals—A Critical Glance*, pp. 30-34.

97. Macdonell, A.A., *Vedic Mythology*, p. 106.
98. The mortar and the pestle figure in the list of metallic requisites known as *Astāmā* or *Ālāt*, i.e. metallic utensils or instruments of brass or at times silver like. See Modi, J.J., *The Religious Ceremonies and Customs of the Parsees*, Bombay, 1937 (1922), p. 253.
99. *Ency. of Rel. and Eth.*, Vol. IX, p. 134 b.
100. *Ibid.*, p. 135 a.
101. These fires are—Āhavanīya, Āgnīdhrīya, Hotrīya and Mārjālīya.
102. For the Caturhotṛ *mantra*-s see *Ait. Br.* V. 25 = 24.6.
103. Gonda, J., *Rice and Barley Offerings in the Veda*, Leiden, 1987.
104. See Eggeling, J., *op. cit.*, pt. II, SBE Vol. 26, p. 307, note 5. Pavamāna (lit. 'purifying' fr. √*pū* - 'to purify') is the first laud (*stotra)* at each pressing, for with the chanting of Pavamāna laud Soma becomes pure. The Bahiṣpavamāna laud is to be chanted in the morning looking towards the *cātvāla.* The sun was once placed here, i.e. in the *cātvāla.* By means of the Bahiṣ-pavamāna laud, the gods (*Pañc. Br.* VI. 7.24) or seasons (which embraced him *Śat. Br.* IV. 2.5.9) bore him to the heavenly world. By the chanting of the Bahiṣpavamāna laud, having looked towards the *cātvāla*, the priests ascend from here to the heavenly world.
105. For a detailed treatment of *prāśitra*, see (Mrs.) Dange, S.S., "Prāśitra in Myth and Ritual", *Prabhakara-Narayana-Śrīḥ* (*Studies in Indology and Musicology*), Dr. Prabhakar Narayan Kawthekar Fel. Vol., Pratibha Pakashan, Delhi, 1993, pp. 81-86.
106. See Sāy. on *Śat. Br.* X.5.2.4; XI. 5.5.12 where he calls *śloka* by the term *mantra.* Also see for discussion on *śloka*-s (Mrs.) Dange, S.S., *Aspects of Speech in Vedic Ritual*, pp. 215-27.
107. Keith, A.B. translates the word *ūṣāḥ* or *ūṣān* as 'salt', which is obviously not correct. See *The Veda of the Black Yajus School entitled Tattirīya Sanhita*, pt. 2, HOS Vol. 19, p. 406. Also Eggeling, J., *op. cit.*, pt. I, SBE Vol. 12, p. 278; pt. III, SBE vol. 41, pp. 33, 34, 299, 302, 343, 344; pt. V, SBE vol. 44, p. 426, where he translates the word *ūṣāḥ* as 'salt'.
108. The word in the *Śat. Br.* (V. 2.1.17) is '*viśaḥ*' which is translated as 'peasants' by Eggeling. See Eggeling, J., *op. cit.*, pt. III, SBE Vol. 41, p. 34.

109. Keith, A.B., *op. cit.*, pt. 1, HOS Vol. 18, p. 108, note 3.
110. *Ibid.,* Intrn. p. cix.
111. *Tait. Br.* I.3.10.2.
112. *Ency. of Rel. and Eth.*, Vol. VIII, p. 591b.
113. For more details, see (Mrs.) Dange, S.S., "Uṣāḥ in the Vedic Sacrifice,", *Jnl. of the Oriental Institute*, M.S. University of Baroda, Vol. XLVI, Nos. 3-4, Sept.-Dec. 1996, Vadodara, pp. 129-34.
114. The root in the word '*sambhāra*' is *sam* + √*bhṛ* - 'to bring together, collect'. Eggeling takes it as 'to equip' and then 'to make the necessary preparations to prepare', the word '*sambhāra*' meaning 'the preparation, outfit.' See Eggeling, J., *op. cit.*, pt. I, SBE Vol. 12, p. 276, note 1. The *Śat. Br.* tries to give explanation (XIV. 1.2.1) but it hardly makes the meaning clear. The *Tait. Br.* (II. 2.2.5-6) speaks of the Sambhāra-*yajūṁṣi* (formulas) by reciting which the sacrifice performed by the gods proved fruitful to them.

    This shows that *sambhāra*-s, in the form of material things (earth or wood) or *mantra*-s are used to give a full or complete form to whatever is incomplete in the sacrifice.
115. It is interesting to note that the word *gāṅgeya* ('belonging to the river Gaṅgā') denotes 'gold' and the belief was that the waters of the river Gaṅgā contained the particles of gold. Is this belief based on the observation of the sands on the banks of the river Gaṅgā, which are full of the particles of mica and are hence shining? [This observation is made personally.]
116. See Dange, Sadashiv A., *Vedic Sacrifices—Early Nature*, Vol. I, pp. 22-25.
117. For Punarādheya see note 17 *supra*.
118. For information from several lands about the belief that shadow of a person stands for his own self or soul, see Frazer, J.G. *The Golden Bough*, Part II, *Taboo and the Perils of the Soul*, London, 1911, pp. 78-79.
119. For more information about the word *'uttarā'*, see Eggeling, J., *op. cit.*, pt. II, SBE Vol. 26, p. 2, note 1.
120. Kulkarni, T.R., *Proceedings* of the Indian Science Congress 1961, pt. IV, pp. 119-21.
121. Mackenzie, D., *Myths of China and Japan*, London, p. 80.
122. Hillebrandt, A., *Vedische Mythologie*, Vol. I, Breslau, p. 309.

123. Gāyatrī flew to bring Soma from the third heaven. But when she was carrying him off, a footless archer aimed at her, and one of the feathers (*parṇa)* of her or of king Soma was cut off. On falling down, it became a Parṇa (Palāśa) tree. See *Śat. Br.* I.7.1.1; *Tait. Br.* I.1.3.10; I.2.1.6.
124. Dange, Sadashiv A., "The Advent of Soma", *Images from Vedic Hymns and Rituals*, pp. 115-25.
125. *Ibid.*, pp. 126-29 (in the chapter "Symbolism in the Ritual of Soma").
126. For details, see (Mrs.) Guard Nawaz R., *Ritual Drink in the Iranian and Indian Traditions (From Avestan and Sanskrit Sources)*, Thesis, University of Bombay, Bombay (=Mumbai), 1991, especially for Haoma-ritual, pp. 223-43, 421-39; for identifying the Soma-Haoma plant, pp. 425-31.
127. Hodivala, S.K., *Indo-Iranian Religion* (with parallelism in the Hindu and Zoroastrian Scriptures), Mahomedi Minar, Khetwadi, Bombay. 1925, p. 5.
128. (Mrs.) Dange, S.S., *Aspects of Speech in Vedic Ritual*, where all aspects of Speech are discussed in details.
129. *Ibid.*, pp. 11-12, 30, 31f, 60-61, 150f, etc.
130. (Mrs.) Dange, S.S., *Aspects of Speech in Vedic Ritual.*
131. Macdonell, A.A. and Keith, A.B., *Vedic Index of Names and Subjects,* under "Vākovākya". According to Eggeling, Vākovākya signifies apparently some special theological discourse or discourses, similar to (if not identical with) the numerous Brahmodya-s or disputations on spiritual matters.
132. The joint word Itihāsa-purāṇa at many places denotes composition of uniform type only, which comprises old tales of adventure, creation of universe or genealogy of dynasties. Also see Macdonell, A.A. and Keith, A.B., *op. cit.*, under "Itihāsa".
133. *Brahmāṇḍa P.* I.2.21.110 ff; *Garuḍa P.* I. 205. 61-62; *Viṣṇu P.* II. 8.45 ff. Also see Dange, Sadashiv A., *Ency. of P.B. & p.*, Vol. II, Navrang, New Delhi, 1987, p. 412 f.
134. The word *sampad* (fr. *sam* + √*pad* - 'to obtain, acquire') denotes various combinations and permutations, based on the number of syllables of metres, at times number of hymns, particular numbers making up *stoma*-s, etc. See (Mrs.) Dange, S.S., "Sampad-s of Metres", *Aspects of Speech in Vedic Ritual*, pp. 113-45.

135. For more details, *ibid.*, pp. 7f; 38.
136. For '*dvyudāsam*', see Caland, W., *op. cit.*, p. 89, note 1 on *Pañc. Br.* V. 7.4. *udāsa = utkṣepa; utkṣepo nāma dīrgha-viśeṣaḥ.* Caland mentions the notation meant here which occurs twice in the chanting of the Gaurivīta *sāman.*
137. Ram Gopal, *India of Vedic Kalpasūtras*, National Publishing House, Delhi, 1959, p. 126.
138. Keith, A.B., *op. cit.*, pt. 1, p. 201, note 3. Keith says—'probably a high one'.
139. Eggeling, J., *op. cit.*, pt. 1, SBE Vol. 12, p. 125, note 1, where he gives the explanation stated by Sāyaṇa. *Upavaha* is a piece of wood inserted under the yoke and on the neck of an ox, in order to level that ox up to the height of the other ox, which is its yoke-fellow.
140. See (Mrs.) Dange, S.S., *Aspects of Speech in Vedic Ritual*, pp. 29-31.
141. For more details, see Dhamadhikari, T.N. (ed.), *Yajñāyudhāni*, Vaidika Samshodhana Mandala, Pune, 1989, p. 32.
142. Two dogs of Yama (the god of death) were believed to lead the soul of the dead person to the abode of Yama. They are termed *pathi-rakṣī* (*RV.* X. 14.11b). This path to Yama was guarded by them and it must be a narrow path. The hymn says that the way to Yama's abode is full of steep paths (*ibid.* 1a—*pravato mahīḥ*). It is interesting to see that in the *Avesta,* a four-eyed, yellow-eared dog is said to keep watch at the head of the Cinvaṭ bridge, which leads from this world to the next. See Macdonell, A.A., *The Vedic Mythology*, p. 173.
143. See Dhamadhikari, T.N. (ed.), *op. cit.*, p. 18 f. The length of an *aratni* signifies a cubit of the middle length, from the elbow to the tip of the little finger, and that of *bāhu* signifies arm as a measure of length (= 12 *aṅgula*-s).
144. The Gārhapatya fire is the same as Ukhya Agni, which is carried by the sacrificer in the *ukhā* (fire-pan) during his period of consecration. At the end of this period, that fire is transferred from the fire-pan to the newly-built Gārhapatya hearth.
145. Solar radiation comprises ultra-violet, VIBGYOR (violet, indigo, blue, green, yellow, orange and red), infra-red radiations and some components of X-rays, microwave and

radio frequency—radiations. VIBGYOR (seven colours) is the visible spectrum.

146. Cf. *RV.* I.160. 1 cd—where the divine bright Sūrya is said to move in between the two divine bowls, i.e. Dyāvāpṛthivī—Heaven and Earth.
147. See note 134 *supra*.
148. Eggeling, J., *op. cit.*, pt. IV, SBE Vol. 43, p. 242, note 2.
149. The ten vital airs are—seven in the head, two downward ones and the central one, having navel as its outlet (cf. *Śat. Br.* VIII. 1.3.10).
150. Eggeling, J., *op. cit.*, pt. II, SBE Vol. 26, p. 240, note 3, where he gives a question-mark and directs our attention to the passage from the *Śat. Br.* (III. 8.2.27) [which mentions that when Soma has been pressed, the sacrificer (or the priest) says—'brought forward!', with no mention of slaying and rising again]. Eggeling simply directs us to the passage of the *Śat. Br.* (III. 8.2.27), though he does not specifically say this!
151. Dange, Sadashiv A., *Images from Vedic Hymns and Rituals*, pp. 125-28.
152. Kane, P.V., *op. cit.*, Vol. II, pt. II, p. 1253.
153. These *mantra*-s are taken from the Śatarudriya section beginning with '*namaste rudra manyave*' (*Vāj. Sam.* XVI. 1-66; *Tait. Sam.* IV. 5.1-10); also *Śat. Br.* IX. 1.1.1-44 (the full section).
154. Kane, P.V., *op. cit.*, p. 1253.
155. *Ency. of Rel. and Eth.*, Vol. XI, p. 871a.
156. *Ibid.*, p. 867 a.
157. *Ibid.*, p. 868 a.
158. Mackenzie, Donald, *Myths of China and Japan*, The George Gresham Publishing Company Ltd., London, year not mentioned, p. 58.
159. *Ibid.*, p. 59, The Chinese believed in 'dragon's eggs'—the stones which cause lightning when they split; p. 129—There is the 'eagle-stone', which is useful for women to aid parturition; p. 336—In Japan, 'Cit Bolon Tum' (The Nine Precious Stones) was a god of medicine.
160. *Ency. of Rel. and Eth.*, Vol. XI, p. 873a—It is noted that the Bhois of Bombay (Mumbai) keep in the house for the ten days of mourning, the stone (i.e. the 'life-stone' called by them the '*jīva-khaḍā*'), with which at cremation, the water-

jar is broken by the chief mourner. On the tenth day, the chief mourner goes to the river with the 'life-stone', offers grain and copper on it or to the spirit in it, and bathes it thrice. Then the brahmin priest, muttering spells and prayers, flings the stone into the water, thus finally disposing of the spirit.

161. The *Śat. Br.* uses the words *surā* as well as *parisrut* to denote wine. Eggeling mentions Sāyaṇa's opinion that *surā* is prepared from mature shoots (of rice, etc.) and *parisrut* from such as are as yet not ripe. See Eggeling, J., *op. cit.*, pt. III, SBE Vol. 41, p. 9, note 1.
162. Dange, Sadashiv A., *Vedic Sacrifices—Early Nature*, Vol. II, p. 275.
163. See Eggeling, J., *op. cit.*, pt. III, SBE Vol. 41, p. 129; p. 137, note 1.
164. For the deity, number and time of the Aṣṭakā-s, see Ram Gopal, *op. cit.*, pp. 414-17.
165. The commentators cannot appreciate the idea of '*surā*', i.e. wine, being used in the rite and interpret the word '*surā*' in a different way. But Ram Gopal rightly points out that '*surā*' here means 'wine' and the import of the *mantra*-s supports it. See Ram Gopal, *op. cit.*, p. 249, note 1.
166. For more details, See (Mrs.) Dange, S.S., "Wine and the Female Ancestors", *Hindu Domestic Rituals—A Critical Glance*, pp. 53-59.
167. *Sarvadarśanasaṅgraha*, Anandashram, Poona, 1966, p. 2.
168. Macdonell, A.A., *Vedic Mythology*, p. 55; also p. 59 to which he directs us.
169. There are ritual metaphors having this mythical account in view. To take some. The sacrificial post is a thunderbolt (*Śat. Br.* III. 6.4.19, 22, 25; III.7.1.14, 15, 26, etc.). The chariot is a thunderbolt (*ibid.* V. 1.4.3).
170. That the thunderbolt is associated with the number fifteen, itself (i.e. the thunderbolt) being spoken of as fifteenfold, is mentioned in the *Śat. Br.*, when fifteen kindling verses (*mantra*-s) are recited while giving offering to Agni (*Śat. Br.* XIII. 4.1.13).

    Again among other bricks, there are fifteen bricks named Apasyā ('belonging to or imbibing water') which symbolically provide water (and also food) to the heads of animals placed in the first layer of the Great Fire-altar. It is said that water (the fifteen bricks being named 'Apasyā') is thunderbolt and the thunderbolt is fifteenfold (*ibid.* VII. 5.2.41).

171. See Dange, Sadashiv A., "The Yatis and the Uttaravedi", *Haryana Sahitya Akademi Journal of Indological Studies*, Vol. I-1, Chandigarh, Spring 1986, pp. 66-71; also by the same author, "Religious Suicide in the Vedic Period (?)", *Indologica Taurinensia* (Ludwick Sternbach Comm. Vol.), Vols. VIII-IX, Torino (Italy), 1980-81, pp. 113-21.
172. Eggeling, J., *op. cit.*, pt. II, SBE Vol. 26, p. 105, note 1.
173. The mythical account of these three citadels of the *asura*-s occurs in the *Tait. Sam.* (VI. 2.3.1-2). The gods sought to conquer these by siege. They made ready an arrow, with Agni as the point, Soma as the socket, Viṣṇu as the shaft and gave it to Rudra to shoot, who in lieu of it chose a boon to be the overlord of animals.
174. See Dange, Sadashiv A., *Ency. of P.B. & P.*, Vol. II, Navrang, New Delhi, 1987, p. 506.
175. See Dange, Sadashiv A., "*Axis Mundi* and the Vedic *Yūpa*", *Gleanings from Vedic to Puranic Age*, ed. by (Mrs.) Dange, S.S., Aryan Books International, New Delhi, 2002, pp. 13-24.

CHAPTER 14

Arthavāda—A Pointer to Ritual Development

We have dealt with the beliefs and practices as seen in the *arthavāda*-portions of the ritual-texts. As we have noted already, at some places these beliefs and practices are directly stated, but at several others, they are only indicated.

Here we take into account certain *arthavāda*-s, which reflect the 'joints', at which are seen the additions (newly) made to the already existent rites ad rituals.

To take the example of the Pravargya ceremony (or rite) coming as a part of the Soma-sacrifice. The *Ṛgveda*-brāhmaṇa-s state this rite in details (*Ait. Br.* I.18-22 = 4.1-5; *Kauṣ. Br.* VIII. 3-7). As Eggeling notes, the *Mait. Sam.* states only the *mantra*-s, while the *Kāṭh. Sam.* does not state any. Taittirīya branch of the Black *Yajurveda* states information of it only in its Ār. i.e. *Tait. Ār.*[1] *Vājasaneyi-saṁhitā* gives the *mantra*-s of it (XXXVII. 1.7. 9-10). The *Śat. Br.* has two mythical accounts concerning the Pravargya rite. The one, which is in the context of offering the Āśvina cup (of Soma-juice) to the Aśvins, is mainly that of the sage Cyavana, who was made young by the Aśvins and who told them the secret of the 'incomplete' (i.e. 'headless') sacrifice being performed by the gods. When the gods bring for the Aśvins the Āśvina cup, they place and (thus) restore the 'head' of the sacrifice (*Śat. Br.* IV. 1.5.1-15). The knowledge of the

Pravargya rite is got by the Aśvins from the sage Dadhyaṅ Ātharvaṇa. Here we take into account the elaborate mythical account, which occurs in the *Śat. Br.* as *arthavāda* in the context of the Pravargya rite. It runs as follows (in short). The gods were performing sacrifice, without including the Aśvins among them. It is in this sacrifice that the head of (the proud) Viṣṇu was cut off. The ants knowing the intention of the gods to punish Viṣṇu, gnawed the string of Viṣṇu's bow, with the result the two ends of the bow coming together, cut off Viṣṇu's head. As the upper portion of Viṣṇu (Sacrifice) was 'stretched,' to the east, so the name 'Pravargya' (fr. *pra* + √*vṛj*). As the great (*mahān*) warrior (*vīra*) i.e. Viṣṇu, fell down, so the name 'Mahāvīra' given to the pot (which is used in the rite). While falling down, the head made the sound '*ghṛṅ'*, so the same pot is also called 'Gharma'. Then remained the bare fact that the sacrifice being performed by the gods became 'headless', for the very head of Viṣṇu (Sacrifice) was cut off. Only the sage Dadhyaṅ Ātharvaṇa had the knowledge of the rite by which the 'headless' and hence incomplete sacrifice of the gods could be successful (by providing the 'head' of the sacrifice). But Indra threatened Dadhyaṅ Ātharvaṇa that he would cut off Dadhyaṅ Ātharvaṇa's head, if this rite became known to others. The Aśvins having overheard this, approached Dadhyaṅ Ātharvaṇa and promised him the replacement of his head provided he would tell them the lore of the rite, by which the 'headless' sacrifice would be completed. When Dadhyaṅ Ātharvaṇa agreed to this, the Aśvins having cut off first his head, placed the horse's head (on his body). With that (horse-) head Dadhyaṅ Ātharvaṇa imparted them the knowledge of the Pravargya rite. When Indra cut off this (horse-) head of Dadhyaṅ Ātharvaṇa, the Aśvins placed the original head of Dadhyaṅ Ātharvaṇa on his body (*ibid.* XIV. 1.1.1-33). The *Jaim. Br.* combines these two mythical accounts to eulogise the Cyāvana *sāman,* i.e. the *sāman* 'seen' by the sage Cyavana, with which Cyavana Bhārgava became a youth, obtained a young wife and performed a sacrifice, in which he gave a thousand cows as *dakṣiṇā* (*Jaim. Br.* III. 120-28).

In spite of the fact that we have faint references to the Pravargya rite in the *RV*,[2] the *arthavāda*-s noted above, point out that this rite (though an optional and subsidiary one, to be performed on the Upasad days of the Soma-sacrifice), must have been incorporated in the Soma-sacrifice at a somewhat later date and it was most probably a contribution made by the sage Dadhyaṅ Ātharvaṇa to the original procedure of the Soma-sacrifice, though the sage Cyavana also had some hazy idea about it, nevertheless not knowing the exact procedure of and the details about this rite. Even Eggeling has opined in the same way, though he has not taken into account the *arthavāda*-accounts concerning this rite. He says that the introduction of this rite in the Soma-ritual must have taken place at a time when the main procedure of the Soma-sacrifice had already been definitely settled.[3]

While dealing with "Serpent" in the chapter on "Animals and Birds", and also with "Eye" (especially the 'evil' power of the eye) in the chapter on "Sense-organs and Body-parts", we have taken note of the Sarpa-tribe, of which 'serpent' was a totem. We have also dealt with the mythical account from the *Ait. Br.* (V.1 = 21.1) as well as the one from the *Kauṣ. Br.* (XXIX.1) in the chapter "Sense-organs and Body-parts". These *arthavāda*-s (in the form of the mythical accounts) clearly point out that the following additions were made to the already prevalent Soma-ritual:

1. The practice of praising the pressing-stones in the midday-pressing of Soma (which was told by the Sarpa seer—Arbuda Kādraveya—to the gods, to ward off the defect in their sacrifice).
2. This praising was done, along with the wrapping of the face (of the priest reciting those *mantra*-s) with the head-wear. In the mythical account of the *arthavāda*, the gods wrapped the eyes of the Sarpa seer (Arbuda

Kādraveya) with his head-wear, to ward off his 'evil' eye from Soma.

3. These praise-formulas were a mixture of the chants of the Sarpa-seer and the gods' *ṛc*-s. This was done by the gods, to remove the evil effect of the seer's chants.
4. The invocation of the pressing-stones in the midday-pressing gave rise to the office of the priest Grāvastut, which was a definite addition to the already existing list of priests. The duty of the Grāvastut was to praise the *grāvan*-s (pressing stones).

It is interesting to mark that in the Agniṣṭoma sacrifice, there is a rite called 'Grāvastutpraiṣaḥ', which means that at the midday-pressing the Adhvaryu priest asks the Abhiṣotṛs to call the sacrificer and request him to go to the Grāvastut priest. At this very pressing, there is a rite of giving a turban as a gift to the Grāvastut priest (*grāvastute uṣnīṣadānam*).[4]

About extracting the juice from the Soma-shoots, two methods are seen in the *RV viz.* one, by pounding the Soma-shoots with a pestle and mortar (*RV* I.28.1-4, where the Soma-shoots are mentioned as '*ulūkhalasūta*') and the other is grinding the Soma-shoots with stones.[5] Out of these two, the first method appears to be the older and may go back to the Indo-Iranian age,[6] on comparison of the Vedic Soma-ritual with the Hoama-ritual of the Parsis. We have already noted under "Mortar and Pestle" in the chapter on "*Arthavāda*-s on Varied Topics", the details from the Avestan ritual of preparing the Haoma (=Soma), concerning this older (i.e. the first) method. The invocation of the *grāvan*-s (pressing stones) in the midday-pressing by the Sarpa seer Arbuda Kādraveya (and the same taught by him to the gods and later on incorporated in the Soma-ritual) has to be considered on this background, taking into account the somewhat late emergence of the method of pressing the Soma-shoots with the *grāvan*-s, compared to the older method with the mortar and pestle. The method of pressing the Soma-shoots with the pressing-stones no doubt appears to be slightly crude as compared to the older method which involved the implements made from stone. Whence came then the method with the pressing-stones? Was it prevalent among some people, other than the settled Aryans? Probably 'Yes'! And this might be the reason why the Sarpa seer (representing the Sarpa-tribe) could feel like praising the *grāvan*-s—the stones—with which he was familiar. The *arthavāda*-accounts from the *Ṛgveda-brāhmaṇa*-s noted, thus are significant from the point of view of the development of Soma-ritual of the Vedic India.

Another important *arthavāda* is concerning the seer Nābhānediṣṭha. In the twelve-day sacrifice (Dvādaśāha), in the Pṛṣṭhya Ṣaḍaha (i.e. 'the first two units of three days each',—out of the first Nine days, which are called 'Navarātra' i.e. literally Nine nights). on the sixth day, the two hymns of Nābhānediṣṭha are to be recited. The elaborate mythical account points out how the brothers of Nābhānediṣṭha divided their father's (i.e. Manu's) property, when Nābhānediṣṭha was away for his Vedic studies. After his return, when he asked them about his share, they said that they had kept their father—the judgement giver (knowing the rules of inheritance)—as his share. When Nābhānediṣṭha came to his father, the latter consoled him by saying that Nābhānediṣṭha should go to the place, where Aṅgiras-es were performing a sacrificial session. As they were confused about the procedure of the 'sixth day', Nābhānediṣṭha should ask them to recite the 'particular two hymns'. With the fulfilment of their sacrifice when they would proceed to the heavenly world, they would give him ten thousand cows. It then happened as was told by Nābhānediṣṭha's father. As Nābhānediṣṭha was gathering his *dakṣiṇā* (i.e. the ten thousand cows), there came Rudra, clad in black garment, from the northern quarter and said that whatever remained on the sacrificial site, after the completion of sacrifice, belonged to him (i.e. Rudra). Nābhānediṣṭha, on the word of his father, returned those cows to Rudra, who gave them back to him. Hence it is that with the reciting of the two Nābhānediṣṭha hymns (*RV*. X. 61, 62), a person gets ten thousand cows as *dakṣiṇā* and the reciting of these two hymns on the 'sixth day' would lead to the proper knowledge of the sacrifice and also to the gain of heavenly world (*Ait. Br.* V.14 = 22.9). The same mythical account also figures in the *Tait. Sam.* (III. 1.9.4-6). But here instead of the two hymns, there is a mention of a *'brāhmaṇa'*. Nābhānediṣṭha's father—Manu—tells Nābhānediṣṭha that the latter should give the knowledge of this *'brāhmaṇa'* to the Aṅgiras-es. Sāyaṇa in his commentary on this passage says that this *brāhmaṇa* (composition) is the one, which propounds '*śastra*', etc. (from √*śaṁs* - 'to praise') i.e. praise-formulas, which are to be sung.

The *Ait. Br.* mentions the hymn of Nābhānediṣṭha (*RV* X.61) in the context of Devaśilpa-s (*Ait. Br.* VI.27 = 30.1). Śilpa denotes the skilful compositions employed in reciting the praise-formulas (*śastra*-s). The combination of verses in a hymn or certain method of reciting the verses in a hymn is a striking feature of the Śilpas. These are said to be works of art made by gods (Devaśilpa-s), as they pertain to *mantra*-s. In imitation of these, we have the works of art made by human beings *viz.* an elephant (of clay or metal), a goblet, a garment, gold (i.e. ornaments of gold) and a chariot drawn by a female mule (*ibid.*). The *Jaim. Br.* has to say more on this.[7] The *śilpa*-s (works of art) of human beings are a device, which produces some wonder. The purpose of the Devaśilpa-s is also to produce some miraculous effect and it is, to accomplish the sacrifice and to bring about the new birth of the sacrificer (*ibid.* VI.31 = 30.5).

The mythical account in the *Ait. Br.* coming by way of *arthavāda* regarding Nābhānediṣṭha's two hymns, which are to be recited on the sixth day of the Pṛṣṭhya Ṣaḍaha, points out the unique importance of these two hymns, even granting that they date from the *RV* (*RV* X. 61, 62). With the inclusion of one of these hymns (*ibid.* 61) among the Devaśilpa-s and with the *arthavāda* noted above, the additions to the original rite of Pṛṣṭhya Ṣaḍaha can be marked distinctly.

In the chapter on "Arthavāda-s on Varied Topics" under "Dakṣiṇā", we have already dealt with a verse put in the mouth of the Earth, when Bhuvana's son Viśvakarman performed the Viśvajit sacrifice and was to give the *dakṣiṇā* of the earth to his priest Kaśyapa (*Śat. Br.* XIII. 7.1.14,15). Earlier it is said that in the Sarvamedha (Soma-sacrifice performed for getting all types of food), the tenth day is the Viśvajit Atirātra sacrifice[8] (*ibid.* XIII. 7.1.2,12), in which are chanted all the Pṛṣṭha *sāman*-s. It is said that excluding the wealth of a *brāhmaṇa,* of the wealth (including land and men), the eastern part is to be given to the Hotṛ priest, southern part to the Brahman priest, western part to the Adhvaryu priest, the northern part to the Udgātṛ priest and the Hotrakas to share with all of these (*ibid.* 13). Here the verse (*śloka)* 'spoken' by the Earth (it may be for the priest to recite it!) says that nobody should give her as a *dakṣiṇā* to anybody. If this happens, she would plunge in waters and then the promise of Viśvakarman to his priest would prove false (*ibid.* 14, 15). The same verse from the 'mouth' of the Earth occurs in the *Ait. Br.* in the context of the Great Anointing of Indra (*Ait. Br.* VIII. 21 = 39.7). Sāyaṇa in his commentary on this passage calls this verse '*gāthā*'. This shows that it was difficult for the commentators to mark the difference between a *gāthā* and a *śloka.*[9]

This mythical account of Bhuvana's son Viśvakarman with the words from the mouth of the Earth is important for the clear instruction stated in it that one should never make a gift of land, i.e. land, should never be given away as a *dakṣiṇā.* The *Śat. Br.* in the context of the Puruṣamedha sacrifice, states the *dakṣiṇā*-s to be given in the Viśvajit Atirātra sacrifice. There also it is distinctly stated that while giving *dakṣiṇā* one should exclude the land in the kingdom and the property of a *brāhmaṇa* (*ibid.* XIII. 6.2.18).

The two passages from the *Śat. Br.* (XIII. 7.1.13 and *ibid.* 14-15) may appear to be contradictory, for the first passage (*ibid.* XIII. 7.1.13) which we have noted above, speaks of land-*dakṣiṇā* to be given to the four priests and also the Hotrakas, while the second passage (*ibid.* 14-15) from the mouth of the Earth strictly prohibits it. The *Śat. Br.* elsewhere (XIII. 6.2.18) prohibits it and so also the *Ait. Br.* (VIII. 21 = 39.7). This shows that formerly in the Viśvajit sacrifice there might have been a practice of giving the earth (land) as a *dakṣiṇā* but it was stopped afterwards. This is here the *arthavāda* passage has come to our help for knowing the change in the then prevalent practice.

In the Sūtra-period, we find Jaimini clearly stating that the king should not give the entire earth (or land) as *dakṣiṇā* in the Viśvajit sacrifice, for the earth belongs to all (*Jai. Sū.* VI. 7.3). In the Viśvajit sacrifice, the sacrificer has to donate everything that belongs to him. But as Jaimini has pointed out, even the emperor cannot make a gift of the whole earth of which he may be the ruler. Śabarasvāmin explains this *sūtra* of Jaimini by adding that others have as much right over the earth as the emperor; that the emperor is entitled to a share of crops produced from the earth as his, since he protects them; but that all other persons also walk on the earth, produce crops on it, get their sustenance from it and so they also have rights over the earth and therefore there is no difference between the emperor and other persons as to the right over the earth.[10] Nīlakaṇṭha, the author of the work *Vyavahāramayūkha,* in the first half of the seventeenth century, leaning on the above-mentioned view of Jaimini, states that 'therefore it is said in the sixth chapter of Jaimini that the whole earth cannot be given away by the emperor and a province by a feudatory chief.'[11] When kings make what are technically called gifts of fields, no gift of land (soil) is effected thereby, but only provision is made for the maintenance of the donee (from the taxes which are alienated by the king).[12]

We have noted in the context of the deity Aditi (under "Gods" in the chapter on "Arthavāda-s on Varied Topics") that in the Prāyaṇīya and Udayanīya *iṣṭi*-s (i.e. the Beginning and the Concluding sacrifices) in the Soma-sacrifice, the deity i.e. Aditi, is the same and even the offering i.e. *caru* (rice-pap), is the same. The mythical account coming as *arthavāda* states that once when the gods were performing sacrifice, they did not allot any share of offerings to Aditi (i.e. Earth). Aditi being angry with them, created confusion in their minds, with the result they could not know anything of sacrifice. So on her words, the *caru* is offered to her in both the *iṣṭi*-s noted above. The *Ait. Br.* states a Yajñagāthā in this respect, stating the example of a serpent of Śākala type, which while crawling takes its tail in its mouth, so that its mouth and tail cannot be differentiated (*Ait. Br.* III. 43 = 14.5). The point to be taken note of is that the offering of *caru* to Aditi must not have been there in these two *iṣṭi*-s formerly and must have been introduced later.

These example can amply make clear that the *arthavāda*-accounts, while extolling the *vidhi*-s (which obviously is the main function of the *arthavāda*-s), at times also indicate the additions made to or the changes brought into the *vidhi*-s. Hence the *arthavāda*-s in some cases, can serve as a pointer to the gradual development of the Vedic rituals, till the latter got codified in the Śrautasūtras.

Many of the mythical accounts coming as *arthavāda* are no doubt from the hands of the Vedic ritualists. But several others in the form of Itihāsa and Purāṇa (traditional and legendary accounts), the *gāthā*-s (Yajñagāthā-s however coming from the ritualists), various *śloka*-s and the statements displaying or at times indicating beliefs and practices (in *arthavāda*-s) can all be called 'secular' type of compositions, which to a certain extent originally was the contribution of the Sūta-tradition.[13] This tradition played a major role in the preservation and at times composition of this type of literature, as we have noted in the chapter "Introduction." The credit of composing the two great epics goes to the tradition of the *sūta*-s, according to Winternitz.[14] The origin of the *gāthā*-s also can be traced to this tradition, which was 'a-ritual' and hence secular in nature. There was, in this tradition, much floating mass of literature also, which Winternitz rightly calls 'literary public property.'

This literature was an inexhaustible store of prose and verse narratives—*ākhyāna*-s, Itihāsa-s, Purāṇa-s and *gāthā*-s—and was drawn upon by the Buddhists and the Jains, as well as by the epic poets.[15]

A mythical account from the *Jaim. Up. Br.* clearly points out the status acquired by the *gāthā*, Kumbyā, Narāśaṁsī and Raibhī forms of compositions in the ritual tradition in its later phase.

The gods having scored victory, wanted to make *sāman* their second, so that they might not have any second (i.e. rival). They besought Heaven (Sky) and Earth to come together to bring forth *sāman*. The yonder Sky (Heaven) strongly abhorred the Earth, as she was made unclean and dirty by men staying on her, by spitting and doing this and that thing on her. So the gods cleansed the Earth with *gāthā*, Kumbyā, Narāśaṁsī and Raibhī, each of these getting a hundred in turn. Then the Heaven (Sky) also on the word from the Earth cleansed himself with *ailaba* (i.e. the noise or sound. Is it the thundering sound of the clouds?). Then these two (Heaven and Earth) united and generated the *sāman* (*Jaim. Up. Br.* I.16.1.1-8; I.16.2.1-2). The etymology of the word *sāman* is here given from *sam* + √*i* 'to come together, to be united'. The mythical account noted above clearly shows that the compositions, initially from the secular tradition, came to have a respectable position in the Vedic ritual tradition.

The Vedic ritual tradition, in order to be convincing, had to take a note of this secular tradition, which was of folks and this it did through the means of *arthavāda*. *Arthavāda,* as we have seen, many times, breathes of the beliefs and practices coming from the secular or folk tradition. This trend of assimilation of the 'secular' with the 'sacred' indicates the honour given to the great hoary tradition of the folks, which has thrived independently from 'PAST IMMEMORIAL'!

NOTES AND REFERENCES

1. See Eggeling, J., *The Śatapatha Brāhmaṇa,* pt. V, SBE Vol. 44, Indroduction, p. xlvii.
2. *RV* X. 171.2—Indra cutting off the head of '*makha*' (i.e. Sacrifice) or Viṣṇu; *ibid.* I.116.12; 117.22; 119-9—Dadhyaṅ Ātharvaṇa imparting the lore—Madhuvidyā —to the Aśvins, with his horse-head, which was placed by the latter on his body.
3. See Eggeling, J., *op. cit.,* Introduction, p. xlvi.
4. See *Śrautapadārtha-nirvacanam,* by an unknown author, published by Yudhishsthira Mīmāṁsaka, Bahalgarh, (Sonepat-Haryana), 1984, pp. 268-69.
5. These stones are called by the term '*adri*' or '*grāvan*'. The term '*grāvan*' is generally used with the verbs √*vad* and alike, meaning 'to speak', thus having a metaphorical sense and the animistic touch, in comparison with the term '*adri*'.
6. Macdonell, A.A., *Vedic Mythology,* p. 106.
7. See *Jaim. Br.* I. 263. For more information of the Devaśilpa-s, see (Mrs.) Dange, S.S., *Aspects of Speech in Vedic Ritual,* pp. 103-8.
8. For the two types of this 'One-day Viśvajit' sacrifice, see Eggeling, J., *op. cit.,* pt. IV, SBE Vol. 43, Delhi, 1978 (1885), p. 320, note 2.
9. For detailed information on *gathā* and *śloka,* see (Mrs.) Dange, S.S., *Aspects of Speech in Vedic Ritual,* pp. 206-30.
10. See Kane, P.V., *Hist. of Dh. S.,* Vol. II, pt. II, p. 865f.
11. Vide *Vyavahāramayūkha,* ed. by Kane, P.V., BORI, Poona, 1926, p. 91.
12. Kane, P.V., *op. cit.,* Vol. II, pt. II, p. 866.
13. See (Mrs.) Dange, S.S., "Sūta—The Paurāṇika", *Purāṇa,* All India Kashiraj Trust, Varanasi, Vol. XL, No. 2, pp. 83-91.
14. Winternitz, M., *History of Indian Literature,* Vol. I, (Introduction, Veda, National Epics, Purāṇas and Tantras), 2nd ed., Munshiram Manoharlal, New Delhi, 1972 (University of Calcutta 1927), p. 315.
15. *Ibid.,* p. 314

Illustrations

Fig. I

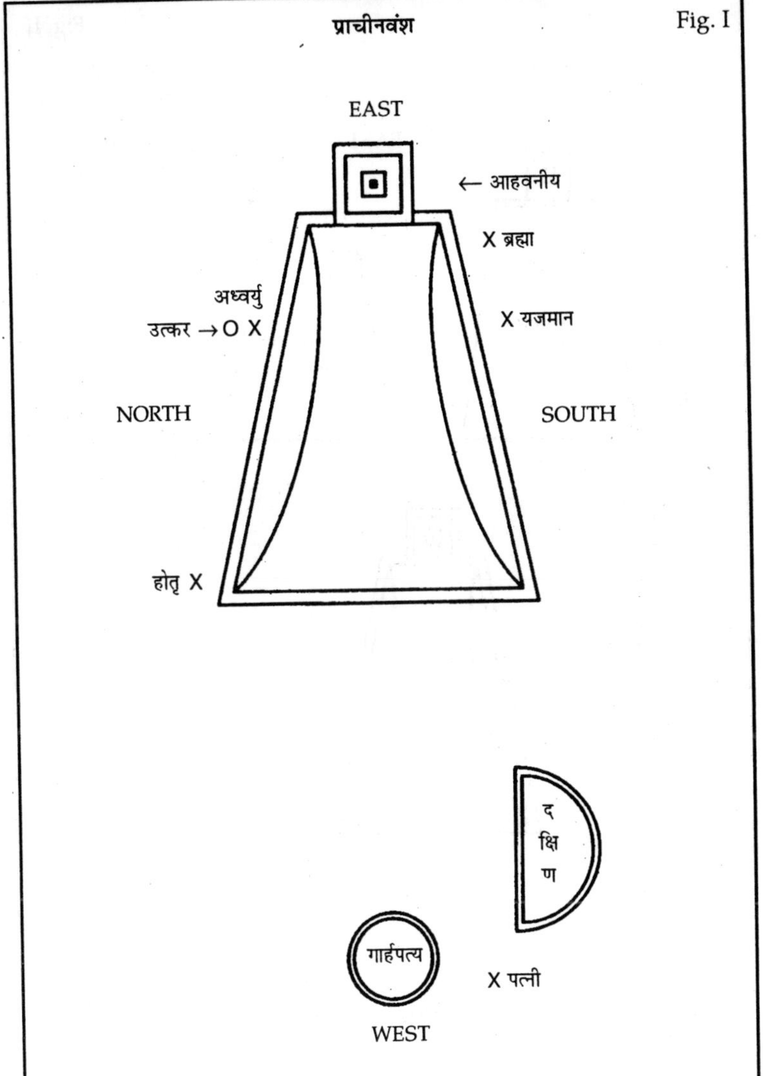

The usual altar at Darśapūrṇamāsa; also called PRĀCĪNAVAṀŚA

प्राचीनवंश

Fig. II

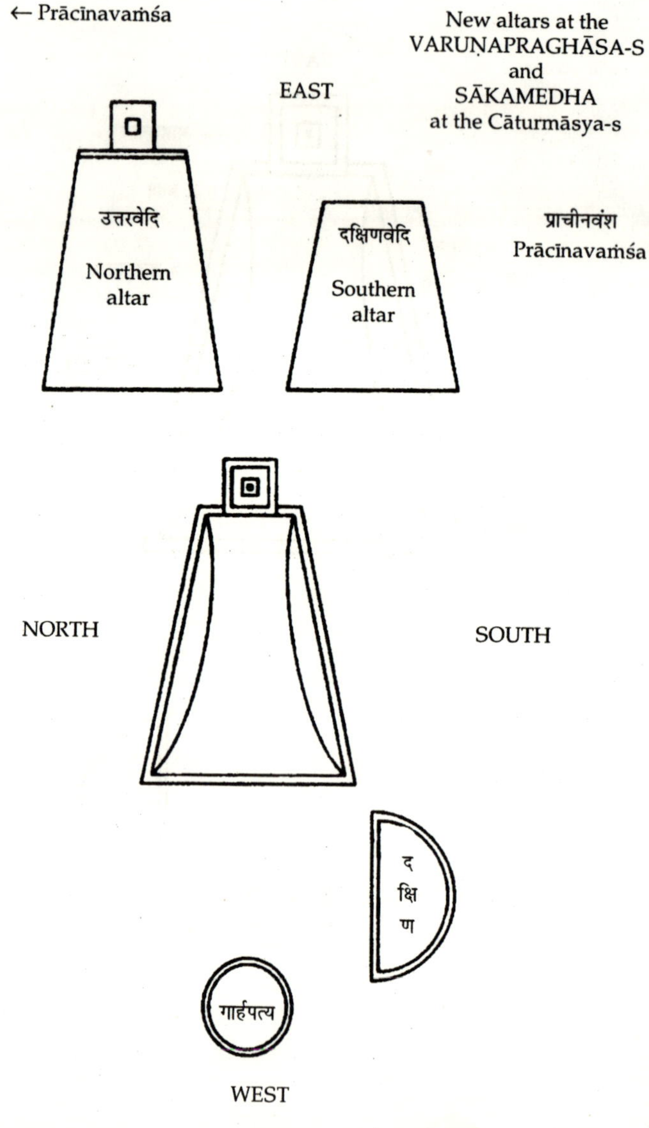

Altar – plan at the two middle phases at the Cāturmāsya-s

Fig. III

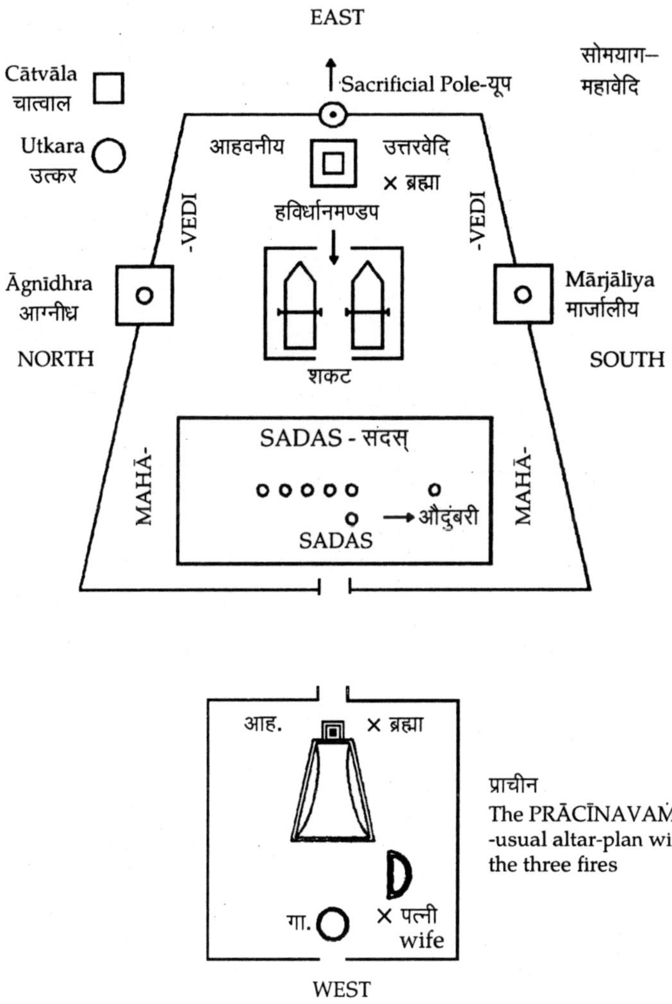

प्राचीन
The PRĀCĪNAVAMŚA
-usual altar-plan with
the three fires

The New altar at the Agniṣṭoma (Soma) sacrifice, with the usual altars in the Prācīnavaṁśa

Bibliography

Sanskrit Texts

Saṁhitās

Atharvaveda-saṁhitā, ed. by S.D. Satawalekar, Aundh, V. Saṁvat 1995.

Kāṭhaka-saṁhitā, ed. by S.D. Satawalekar, Aundh, V. Saṁvat 1999.

Maitrāyaṇī-saṁhitā, ed. by S.D. Satawalekar, Aundh, V. Saṁvat 1998.

Ṛgveda-saṁhitā (with Sāyaṇa's comm.), ed. by Vaidika Samshodhana Mandala, Pune, 1933-51.

Taittirīya-saṁhitā, ed. by S.D. Satawalekar, New Print, Saṁvat 2039, Anandashram, Pune, 1948.

Vājasaneyi-saṁhitā, ed. by A. Weber, London, 1852.

Brāhmaṇa-Texts

Aitareya Brāḥmaṇa, pt. I, 2nd ed., Anandashram, Pune, 1930; pt. II, 3rd ed., Anandashram, Pune, 1977.

Gopatha Brāhmaṇa, ed. by Jivananda Vidyasagar, Calcutta, 1891

Jaiminīya Brāhmaṇa, ed. by Raghuvira and Lokesh Chandra, Motilal Banarsidass, Delhi, 1986 (1954).

Jaiminīya Upaniṣad Brāhmaṇa, ed. by B.R. Sharma, Kendriya Sanskrit Vidyapeeth, Tirupati, 1967.

Kauṣītaki Brāhmaṇa (= *Śaṅkhāyana Brāhmaṇa*), Anandashram, Pune, 1911.

Pañcaviṁśa Brāhmaṇa (= *Tāṇḍya Mahābrāhmaṇa*), Kashi Sanskrit Series, Chaukhambha, Benares, 1936.

Ṣaḍviṁśa Brāhmaṇa, ed. by B.R. Sharma, Kendriya Sanskrit Vidyapeeth, Tirupati, 1967.

Sāmavidhāna Brāhmaṇa, ed. by B.R. Sharma, Kendriya Sanskrit Vidyapeeth, Tirupati, 1980.

Śatapatha Brāhmaṇa, Chaukhambha Sanskrit Samsthan, 2nd ed., Varanasi, 1984.

Taittirīya Brāhmaṇa, Anandashram, 3rd ed., Poona, 1979.

Āraṇyaka-Texts

Aitareya Āraṇyaka, Anandashram, 2nd ed. Poona, 1992.

Taittirīya Āraṇyaka, Calcutta, 1871.

Upaniṣad-Texts

Bṛhadāraṇyaka Upaniṣad, Gita Press, Gorakhpur.

Chāndogya Upaniṣad, Gita Press, Gorakhpur.

Kaṭha Upaniṣad, Gita Press, Gorakhpur.

Sūtra-Texts

Āpastamba Dharmasūtra, ed. by A. Chinnaswami Shastri, pub. in Kashi Sanskrit Series, Benares, 1934.

Āpastamba Gṛhyasūtra, ed. by A. Chinnaswami Shastri, Benares, 1928.

Āpastamba Śrautasūtra, ed. by R. Garbe in Bib. Ind., 1882-1902.

Āśvalāyana Gṛhyasūtra, Anandashram, Poona, 1936; also tr. and fully explained in Marathi by Pt. Shivaramashastri Shintre, Mumbai, 1938.

Āśvalāyana Śrautasūtra, ed. by Ganesh Shastri in Anandashram Sanskrit Series, Poona, 1917.

Baudhāyana Dharmasūtra, ed. by Chinnaswami Shastri, pub. in Kashi Sanskrit Series, Benares, 1934.

Baudhāyana Śrautasūtra, ed. by W. Caland in Bib. Ind. 1904-23.

Bhāradvāja Śrautasūtra, ed. by Raghuvira (*Journal of Vedic Studies*), Lahore, 1935.

Gautama Dharmasūtra, ed. by I. Srinivasacharya, Mysore, 1917.

Gobhila Gṛhyasūtra, ed. by Chintamani Bhattacharya, Calcutta, 1936.

Kāṭhaka Gṛhyasūtra, ed. by W. Caland, Lahore, 1925.

Kātyāyana Śrautasūtra, ed. by V. Sharma, Benares, Saṁvat 1987.

Kauśika Sūtra (*The Kauśika Sūtra of Atharva Veda*), ed. by M. Bloomfield, Motilal Banarsidass, Delhi, Reprint 1972 (1st ed. 1889 Journal *JAOS).*

Khādira Gṛhyasūtra, ed. by A. Mahadeva Shastri and Srinivasacharya, Mysore, 1913.

Pāraskara Gṛhyasūtra, ed. by M.G. Bakre, Bombay, 1917.

Śāṅkhāyana Gṛhyasūtra, ed. with German tr. by H. Oldenberg, *Indische Studien,* Vol. XV, Leipzig, 1878.

Śāṅkhāyana Śrautasūtra, ed. by H. Hllebrandt, in Bib. Ind., Calcutta, 1886-89.

Vasiṣṭha Dharmasūtra, ed. by A.A. Führer, Bombay Sanskrit Series, 3rd ed., Poona, 1930.

Viṣṇu Dharmasūtra, ed. by J. Jolly, Calcutta, 1881.

Epics

Rāmāyaṇa, eds. Chinnaswami Shastri & Subrahmanya Shastri, 2nd ed., Mylapore, Madras, 1958.

Mahābhārata, ed. (with the comm. of Nīlakaṇṭha), Chitrashala Press, Pune; Crit. Ed., BORI, Pune; and Gita Press, Gorakhpur.

Smṛti-Texts

Manusmṛti (with the comm. of Kullūka), Nirnayasagar, Bombay, 1946.

Yājñavalkyasmṛti (with the comm. Mitākṣarā), Nirnayasagar, Bombay, 1937.

Purāṇa-Texts

Agni Purāṇa, ed. Anandashram, Poona, 1900.

Bhāgavata Purāṇa, ed. Gita Press, Gorakhpur, Saṁvat 1997-2018.

Brahma Purāṇa, ed. H.N. Apte, Anandashram, Poona, 1895.

Garuḍa Purāṇa, ed. by Ramshankar Bhattacharya, Chaukhambha, Varanasi, 1964.

Mārkaṇḍeya Purāṇa, ed. by Jivananda Vidyasagar, Calcutta, 1879.

Matsya Purāṇa, ed. by Jivananda Vidyasagar, Calcutta, 1879.

Padma Purāṇa, Anandashram, Poona, 1893-94.

Śiva Purāṇa, ed. by Ramtej Shastri Pandey, Varanasi, Saṁvat 2020.

Skanda Purāṇa, Venkateshwar Press, Bombay.

Vāmana Purāṇa, ed. by Anandaswarup Gupta, All India Kashiraj Trust, Varanasi, 1968.

Viṣṇu Purāṇa, ed. by Jivananda Vidyasagar, Calcutta, 1882.

Other Texts

Ānanda Rāmāyaṇa

Arthasaṅgraha, ed. by S.M. Paranjape, Bombay, 1927.

Bhagavadgītā, with Śaṅkara's comm., Ashtekar and Company, 2nd ed., Poona, 1929.

Jaiminīya-nyāyamālā, Anandashram, Poona, 1946.

Mīmāṁsānyāyaprakāśa of Āpadeva, ed. by Vasudeva Shastri Abhyankar, Government Oriental Series, BORI, Pune, 1937.

Mīmāṁsāparibhāṣā.

Nirṇayasindhu of Kamalākarabhaṭṭa, ed. by Narayanram Acharya, Nirnayasagar, Mumbai, 5th ed., 1949.

Nirukta, ed. Nirnayasagar, Bombay, 1930.

Pūrvamīmāṁsāsūtra of Jaimini, Anandashram, Poona.

Ṛgvidhānam, ed. by J. Shastri, Lahore, 1940

Sarvadarśanasaṅgraha, Anandashram, Poona, 1966.

Smṛticandrikā, ed. by L. Srinivasacharya, Mysore, 1914.

Śrautapadārtha-nirvacana, author unnamed, pub. by Yudhishthira Mīmāṁsaka, 1st ed. (earlier editions, if any, not available), Bahalgarh (Sonepat-Haryana), 1984.

Tarkasaṅgraha of Annaṁbhaṭṭa, ed. with Eng. tr., Intrn. and Notes by A.B. Gajendragadkar and R.D. Karmarkar, pub. by R.D. Karmarkar, 1st ed., Poona, 1930.

The Kauṭilīya Arthaśāstra, ed. by R.P. Kangle, University of Bombay, Bombay, Part I (Text), 2nd ed., 1969; Part II (Tr. & notes), 2nd ed., 1972.

Vyavahāramayūkha, ed. by Kane, P.V., BORI, Poona, 1926.

Other Books

Bhattacharya, Dipak, *Indian Etymologists and their Etymologies,* School of Vedic Studies, Rabindra Bharati University, Kolkata, 2002.

Bloomfield, M., 1899: *The Atharvaveda,* Strassburg.

Caland, W. (tr.), 1982 (Calcutta 1931): *Pañcaviṃśa Brāhmaṇa,* Sri Satguru Pubns., 2nd. ed., Delhi.

Cook, James and King, James, 1784: *A Voyage to the Pacific Ocean,* London (Vols. I & II by Cook and Vol. III by King).

Dandekar, R.N. and Kashikar, C.G. (eds.), 1958: *Śrautakośa,* Vol. I, pts. i & ii, Vaidika Samshodhana Mandala, Poona.

Dange, S.A., 1970: *Pastoral Symbolism from the Ṛgveda,* University of Poona, Poona.

———, 1971: *Vedic Concept of "Field" and the Divine Fructification,* University of Bombay, Bombay.

———, 1979: *Sexual Symbolism from the Vedic Ritual,* Ajanta Pubns., New Delhi.

———, 1987: *Puranic Myth and Culture,* Ajanta Pubns., New Delhi.

———, 1986-90: *Encyclopedia of Puranic Beliefs and Practices,* Vols. I-V, Navrang, New Delhi.

———, 1992, 1995: *Divine Hymns and Ancient Thought,* Vol. I, *Ṛgveda Hymns and Ancient Thought;* Vol. II *Ritual and the Quest for Truth,* Navrang, New Delhi.

Dange, S.A., 1996: *Towards Understanding Hindu Myths,* Aryan Books International, New Delhi.

———, 2000: *Images from Vedic Hymns and Rituals,* Aryan Books International, New Delhi.

———, 2000: *Vedic Sacrifices—Early Nature,* Vols. I & II, Aryan Books International, New Delhi.

———, 1997, 2001: *Myths from the Mahābhārata,* Vol. 1 *Quest for Immortality;* Vol. 2 *Study in Patterns and Symbols,* Aryan Books International, New Delhi.

(Mrs.) Dange, S.S., 1980: *Bauddha Dharma āṇi Tattvajñāna* (Marathi), Continental Pubn., Poona.

———, 1984: *The Bhāgavata Purāna—Mytho-Social Study,* Ajanta Pubns., Delhi.

———, 1985; *Hindu Domestic Rituals—A Critical Glance,* Ajanta Pubns., Delhi.

———,(ed.), 1987: *Myths of Creation,* University of Bombay, Bombay.

———,(ed.), 1987: *Sacrifice in India—Concept and Evolution,* Viveka Pubns., Aligarh.

———, 1989: *Puranic Etymologies and Flexible Forms (Some Glimpses),* Viveka Pubns., Aligarh.

———, 1996: *Aspects of Speech in Vedic Ritual,* Aryan Books International, New Delhi.

———,(ed.), 2002: *Gleanings from Vedic to Puranic Age* (Collected Papers of Dr. Sadashiv A. Dange), Aryan Books International, New Delhi.

Davane, G.V., 1995: *Perspectives in the Vedic and the Classical Sanskrit Heritage,* D.K. Print World (P) Ltd., New Delhi.

Dharmadhikari, T.N. (ed.), 1989: *Yajñāyudhāni,* Vaidika Samshodhana Mandala, Pune.

Eggeling, J. (tr.), 1988 (1882): *The Śatapatha Brāhmaṇa,* pt. I, SBE Vol. 12, Delhi;
1988 (1885): pt. II, SBE Vol. 26, Delhi;
1989 (1894): pt. III, SBE Vol. 41, Delhi;
1978 (1885): pt. IV, SBE Vol. 43, Delhi;
1978 (1900): pt. V, SBE Vol. 44, Delhi.
[All these five, reprinted by Motilal Banarsidass.]

Farzer, J.G., 1911: The *Golden Bough,* Part II.—*Taboo and the Perils of the Soul,* London.

Geldner, K.F., 1978: *Der Rigveda,* I, HOS Vol. 33, 2nd Reprint, Cambridge.

Ghurye, G.S., 1979: *Vedic India,* Popular Prakashan, Bombay.

Gonda, J., 1959: *Epithets in the Ṛgveda*, The Hague, The Netherlands.

———, 1987: *Rice and Barley Offerings in the Veda,* Leiden.

———, *The Functions and Significance of Gold in the Veda,* Leiden.

———, *The Ritual Functions and Significance of Grasses in the Religion of the Veda.*

Hariappa, H.L., 1953: *Ṛgvedic Legends through the Ages,* Deccan College, Poona.

Hastings, James (ed.), 1967 (1908-1921): *Encyclopaedia of Religion and Ethics,* Vols. I-XIII, T.T. Clark, Edingburg.

Hillebrandt, A., 1891-1902: *Vedische Mythologie,* Vols. I-III, Breslau.

Hodivala, S.K., 1925: *Indo-Iranian Religion,* (with parallelism in the Hindu and the Zoroastrian Scriptures) Mohomedi Minar, Bombay.

Horsch, Paul, 1966: *Die vedische Gāthā-und Śloka Literatur,* Francke Verlag, Bern.

Hyatt, H.M., 1935: *Folklore of Adams County Illinois,* New York.

Jamison, Stephanie W., 1996: *Sacrificed Wife/Sacrificer's Wife,* Oxford University Press, New York.

Jha, V.N. (ed.), 1998: *Metaphors in Vedic Literature* (*Proceedings* of the National Seminar, Centre of Advanced Study in Sanskrit), Class E, No. 14, University of Pune, Pune.

Kane, P.V., 1974: *History of Dharmaśāstra,* Vol. II, pt. I, 2nd ed., BORI, Poona.

———, 1974: Vol. II, pt. II, 2nd ed., BORI, Poona.

———, 1973: Vol. IV, 2nd ed., BORI, Poona.

———, 1974: Vol. V, pt. I, BORI, Poona.

Keith, A.B. (tr.), 1967 (1914): *The Veda of the Black Yajus School entitled Taittiriya Sanhita,* pts. I & II, HOS Vols. 18 & 19, 2nd issue, Motilal Banarsidass, Delhi.

Keith, A.B. (tr.) 1981 (1920): *Rigveda Brahmanas,* HOS Vol. 25, 2nd Reprint, Delhi.

Kulkarni, T.R., 1961: *Proceedings* of the Indian Science Congress, pt. IV.

Leeuw, G. Vander, 1938: *Religion in Essence and Manifestation,* London.

Macdonell, A.A., 1995 (Strassburg 1898): *Vedic Mythology,* Motilal Banarsidass, Reprint, Delhi.

———, 1988 (1917): *A Vedic Reader for Students,* Oxford University Press, 14th Impression, Madras.

Macdonell, A.A. and Keith, A.B., 1912: *Vedic Index of Names and Subjects,* London.

Mackenzie, Donald, (no year mentioned): *Myths of Pre-Columbian America,* The George Gresham Publishing Company, London.

———, (no year mentioned); *Myths of China and Japan,* The George Gresham Publishing Company, London.

Mills, L.H. (tr.), 1988 (1887): *The Zend-Avesta,* pt. III, SBE Vol. 31, Motilal Banarsidass, Reprint, Delhi.

Modi, J.J., 1937 (1922): *The Religious Ceremonies and Customs of the Parsees,* Bombay.

Oldham, C.F., 1905: *The Sun and the Serpent,* London.

Ram Gopal, 1959: *India of Vedic Kalpasūtras,* National Publishing House, Delhi.

Rundle Clark, R.T., 1959: *Myth and Symbol in Ancient Egypt,* Thames and Hudson, London.

Singh, Fatah, 1952: *The Vedic Etymology,* The Sanskriti Sadan, Kota.

Tilak, B.G., 1893: *Orion,* Tilak Brothers, Poona.

(Mrs.) Tilak, Sunanda K., 1990: *Cultural Gleanings from the Brāhmaṇa Literature,* Yaska Pubn., New Delhi.

Turner, W. (ed.), 1959: *Hamlet* (Intrn.), The Educational Publishing Company, Bombay.

Vogel, J. Ph., 1926: *The Indian Serpent-lore,* London.

Winternitz, M., 1972 (1927): *History of Indian Literature,* Vol. I, 2nd ed., Munshiram Manoharlal, New Delhi.

Whitney, W.D., 1950 (1885): *The Roots, Verb-forms and Primary Derivatives of the Sanskrit Language,* Edwards Brothers, Inc., Ann Arbor, Michigan.

———,(tr. with comm.), 1984 (1905): *Atharva-Veda-Saṁhitā,* Vols. I & II, HOS Vols. 7 & 8, Motilal Banarsidass, Reprint, Delhi.

Zimmer, H., 1946: *Myths and Symbols in Indian Art and Civilization,* ed. by Campbell, J., The Bollingen Series VI.

Ph.D. Theses

(Mrs.) Guard, Nawaz, R., 1991: *Ritual Drink in the Iranian and Indian Traditions (from Avestan and Indian Sources),* Thesis, University of Bombay, Bombay.

(Mrs.) Kamat, Vidya, 1999: *Ancient Indian Myths and Symbols in Pictorial Expression (As seen from Sanskrit and Allied Literature),* Thesis, University of Mumbai (Bombay), Mumbai (Bombay).

Tinnaratana, Pratuang, 1988: *A Critical Study of the Tenth Maṇḍala of Ṛgveda* (101-191 Hymns), Thesis, Benaras Hindu University, Varanasi.

Papers

Agrawal, R.C., 1965: "Agni in Early Indian Art", *Journal of Indian History,* University of Kerala, Trivandrum, Vol. XLIII, pt. I.

Bloomfield, M., "The Frog-hymn", *JAOS,* Vol. 17.

Chakrabarti, Samiran Chandra, 1982: "A Study of the Pāriplava", *Indo-Iranian Journal,* 32, Kluwer Academic Publishers (printed in the Netherlands).

Dandekar, R.N., 1954: "The Mahābhārata: Origin and Growth", *University of Ceylon Review,* 12.

Dange, S.A., 1965: "Adornment as a Protective Measure in the Vedic Ritual", *Dr. Mirashi Fel. Vol.,* Vidarbha Samshodhan Mandal, Nagpur.

———, 1980-81: "Religious Suicide in the Vedic Period (?)" *Indologica Taurinensia* (Ludwick Sternbach Comm. Vol.), Vols. VIII-IX, Torino (Itlay).

Dange, S.A., 1986: "The Yatis and the Uttaravedi," *Haryana Sahitya Akademi Journal of Indological Studies,* Vol. I-1, Chandigarh, Spring.

———, 1991 (pub. in 1992): "Aṣṭama" (Marathi), Vidarbha Samshodhan Mandal, *Annual No.,* Nagpur.

———, 1992 (pub. in 1997): "Dream (Svapna) in the Vedic Concept", *Vishveshvarananda Indological Journal,* VVBIS & IS, Panjab University, Hoshiarpur, Vol. XXX, pts. i-ii, June-Dec.

———, 1999 (1998): "Dream, Myth and the Hindu Context," *Annals* of BORI, Vol. LXXIX, Pune.

(Mrs.) Dange, S.S., 1980: "Yāska on Widow's Share", *Vishveshvaranand Indological Journal,* VVBIS & IS, Panjab University, Hoshiarpur, Vol. XVIII, pts. i-ii (Prof. K.V. Sharma Fel. Vol.).

———, 1987: "Ṛgvedic Accounts" *Myths of Creation,* University of Bombay, Bombay.

———, 1988: "Some Non-Vedic Rituals in the Vedic Tradition", *Proceedings* of the All India Oriental Conference, XXXII Session, Ahmedabad, 1985 (pub. in 1988).

———, 1993: "The Severed Head in Myth and Ritual", *Annals* of the Bhandarkar Oriental Research Institute, Pune, Vols. LXXII and LXXIII (for the year 1991 & 1992), Amṛtamahotsava (1917-1992) Vol.

———, 1993: "Prāśitra in Myth and Ritual", *Prabhakara-Narayana-Śrīḥ* (*Studies in Indology and Musicology*), Dr. Prabhakar Narayan Kawthekar Fel. Vol., Pratibha Prakashan, Delhi.

———, 1996: "Atithi—A Probe in Concept", *Studies on Indology* (Prof. Mukund Madhav Sharma Fel. Vol.), Sri Satguru Pubns. (A Division of Indian Books Centre), Delhi.

———, 1996: "Uṣāḥ in the Vedic Sacrifice", *Journal of the Oriental Institute,* M.S. University of Baroda, Vadodara, Vol. XLVI, Nos. 3-4, Sept.-Dec.

(Mrs.) Dange, S.S., 1998: "Sūta—The Paurāṇika", *Purāṇa*, All India Kashiraj Trust, Varanasi, Vol. XL, No. 2, July.

———, 1999: "Cultural Assimilation in Vedic India", *Journal of the Asiatic Society of Bombay*, Mumbai, Vol. 74 (New Series).

———, 2002: "Pathyā Svasti—The Vedic Deity of Paths", *Vishveshvaranand Indological Journal*, Panjab University, Hoshiarpur, Vols. XXXIII-XXXVIII, June-Dec. 1999-2000.

———, (in press): "Sarpas and Vedic Ritual Tradition", *Prof. Rasiklal C. Parikh Comm. Vol.*, to be published by B.I. Institute, Ahmedabad.

Dharmadhikari, T.N; 1987: "Gavām-ayanam", *Sacrifice in India—Concept and Evolution*, ed. by (Mrs.) Dange, S.S., Viveka Pubns., Aligarh.

Heesterman, J.C., 1967: "The Case of the Severed Head," *Wiener Zs für die Kunde S.—und O.*—Asiens 11.

Mahalingam, T.V., 1965: "The Nāgas in Indian History and Culture", *Journal of Indian History*, University of Kerala, Trivandrum, Vol. XLIII, Part I, April, Serial No. 127.

Mitra, Sharad Chandra, "Frog in the North-Indian Rain-controlling Rites", *Folk-lore and Traditions in India*, Vol. XIV.

Navathe, P.D., 1980: "On the Mīmāṁsā Doctrine of Ekavākyatā", *Proceedings* of the Winter Institute on Ancient Indian Theories of Sentence-Meaning, University of Poona, Pune.

Norman Brown, 1921: "Some Notes on the Rain-Charms", *New Indian Antiquary*, Vol. II-2, May.

Pandit, Vasantkumar R., 1957: "Origin and Growth of the Jyotiṣa-śāstra", *Journal of the University of Bombay*, Bombay, Vol. XXVI (New Series), Part 2, Arts No., Sep.

Upadhyay, S.A., 1965: "Kārīrīṣṭi—A Sacrifice to be performed for securing Rain", *H.D. Velankar Comm. Vol.*, pub. by Prof. H.D. Velankar Comm. Vol. Committee, Bombay.

Waddel, L.A., "Frog-worship in Nepal", *Indian Antiquary*, XXII.

Index

(Sāyaṇa has been referred to at a number of places. Hence his name, at all places, does not appear in the Index.
Figures in the brackets indicate the numbers of the notes on those particular pages.)

[My great appreciation for the little hands (my grandson Yash B. Jahagirdar) that helped me in arranging the Index-cards of these two volumes.]

हिन्द पॉकेट बुक्स

भीष्म प्रतिज्ञा

ये महाभारत की कहानियां हैं, जिन्हें छोटों एवं किशोरों के लिए सजाया-संवारा गया है, ताकि इन्हें पढ़कर उनमें अच्छाई-बुराई को जानने, सच्चे रास्ते पर चलने और बहादुर बनने की प्रेरणा जाग सके।

ये कहानियां बहुत सरल भाषा में और रोचक ढंग से लिखी गई हैं। इसलिए इन्हें याद करने में भी बड़ी आसानी होगी। सभी कहानियों में रेखाचित्र और आख़ीर में एक प्रश्नावली दी गई है, ताकि पढ़ने के बाद लगे हाथ आपकी परीक्षा हो सके।

हस्तिनापुर के राजा शान्तनु को एक तेजस्वी, प्रतापी और शांत स्वभाव के पुत्र की प्राप्ति हुई, जिसका नाम गंगेय था, बाद में उनका नाम क्रमशः देवव्रत व भीष्म पड़ा। भीष्म पितृ-भक्त थे, उन्होंने अपने पिता की खुशी के लिए आजन्म ब्रह्मचर्य की कठोर प्रतिज्ञा ली।

बच्चों और किशोरों के लिए महाभारत की कहानियां

भीष्म प्रतिज्ञा

रामकुमार भ्रमर

हिन्द पॉकेट बुक्स
पेंगुइन रैंडम हाउस इम्प्रिंट

हिन्द पॉकेट बुक्स

यूएसए | कनाडा | यूके | आयरलैंड | ऑस्ट्रेलिया | सिंगापुर
न्यू ज़ीलैंड | भारत | दक्षिण अफ्रीका | चीन

हिन्द पॉकेट बुक्स, पेंगुइन रैंडम हाउस ग्रुप ऑफ़ कम्पनीज़ का हिस्सा है,
जिसका पता global.penguinrandomhouse.com पर मिलेगा

पेंगुइन रैंडम हाउस इंडिया प्रा. लि.,
चौथी मंजिल, कैपिटल टावर -1, एम जी रोड,
गुड़गांव 122 002, हरियाणा, भारत

पेंगुइन
रैंडम हाउस
इंडिया

प्रथम संस्करण हिन्द पॉकेट बुक्स द्वारा 2011 में प्रकाशित
यह हिन्दी संस्करण हिन्द पॉकेट बुक्स में पेंगुइन रैंडम हाउस द्वारा 2022 में प्रकाशित

10 9 8 7 6 5 4 3 2

ISBN 9789353491581

मुद्रकः रेप्रो इंडिया लिमिटेड

www.penguin.co.in

FSC www.fsc.org MIX Paper from responsible sources FSC® C047271

This is a legitimate digitally printed version of the book and therefore might not
have certain extra finishing on the cover.

भीष्म प्रतिज्ञा

हस्तिनापुर एक ऐसा राज था, जिसमें बड़े-बड़े बलवान् और पराक्रमी राजा हुए। उन्हीं में से एक थे– महाराजा प्रतीप। अपने पूर्वजों की तरह वह वीर, न्यायप्रिय और धर्म पर चलने वाले राजा थे। प्रजा उनसे प्रसन्न रहती थी।

कोई पुत्र न होने से महाराजा प्रतीप दुखी रहते थे। एक तेजस्वी तपस्वी ब्राह्मण के मार्ग-दर्शन पर वे गंगा किनारे हरिद्वार में तपस्या करने गए ताकि उन्हें पुत्र की प्राप्ति हो। राजा-रानी ने साधारण तपस्वी की भांति वहां तपस्या की।

तपस्या के दौरान एक बार महाराज प्रतीप अकेले ही गंगा किनारे निकल गये और चांदनी रात में ध्यानमग्न हो गये। अचानक आधी रात को गंगा की लहरों से एक सुन्दर और धूप-सी उजली नारी प्रकट हुई। वह स्वयं चलकर महाराज प्रतीप के पास आकर दायीं ओर बैठ गई। पूछने पर उसने बताया

महाराज प्रतीप और जल कन्या वार्तालाप करते

कि 'महाराज ! मैं एक पवित्र जल-कन्या हूं और आपको पतिरूप में पाना चाहती हूं।'

महाराज ने उसे बता दिया कि मैं विवाहित हूं। दूसरे तुम मेरी दायीं ओर आकर बैठी हो, अतः मैं तुम्हें या तो पुत्री के रूप में या पुत्र-वधू के रूप में स्वीकार कर सकता हूं; तुम्हें पत्नी रूप में स्वीकार करना असम्भव है।

महाराज के दृढ़ निश्चय को जानकर वह युवती उठ खड़ी हुई और सादर प्रणाम करके कहा कि 'ठीक है महाराज, यही सही। आप वचन दीजिए कि जब आपका पुत्र होगा तो आप मुझे उसकी पत्नी बनाएंगे।'

महाराज प्रतीप से वचन लेकर वह देखते ही देखते ज्योति की तर गंगा की धारा में विलीन हो गई।

लगभग दो बरस बाद महाराज की तपस्या सफल हुई। भगवान ने दर्शन देकर कहा कि समय आने पर आपको एक तेजस्वी, प्रतापी और शांत स्वभाव के पुत्र की प्राप्ति होगी।

उसी के फलस्वरूप महारानी ने कुछ समय बाद एक सुन्दर-स्वस्थ बालक को जन्म दिया। उसका नाम रखा गया– शान्तनु।

दिन-रात बीते और शान्तनु बड़े होने लगे। उनका गौर वर्ण था और बाल सुनहरी रंग के थे। दूर से लगता था जैसे सोना दमदमा रहा हो। वे शान्त स्वभाव के, दयालु और वीर थे। समय आने पर उन्हें युवराज बना दिया गया।

अचानक महाराजा प्रतीप बहुत बीमार पड़ गये। बहुत इलाज करने

पर भी जब उनके ठीक होने के आसार नहीं रहे तो महाराज प्रतीप ने युवराज शान्तनु को अकेले बुलाकर कहा कि 'बेटे, मैं तुमसे एक वचन लेना चाहता हूं।'

"आज्ञा कीजिए पिताजी," शान्तनु बोले, 'मैं अपना जीवन देकर आपका वचन पूरा करूंगा। यह मेरा पुत्रधर्म है।'

महाराजा प्रतीप ने गंगा के किनारे घटी घटना बताई और गंगा से प्रकटी नारी को दिया अपना वचन बताया। शान्तनु के पूछने पर उन्होंने बताया कि वह नारी गंगा नदी के तट पर हरिद्वार की दिशा में ही मिलेगी।

'आप निश्चिंत हो जाइये। आपके वचन का अवश्य पालन होगा।' शान्तनु ने कहा।

2

इस घटना के कुछ दिनों बाद महाराज प्रतीप स्वर्गवासी हुए और शान्तनु नये राजा बने।

राजकाज संभालकर, सब ठीक-ठाक कर महाराजा शान्तनु अपने पिता को दिया वचन पूरा करने निकल पड़े।

कई बार प्रयत्न करने पर भी उन्हें अपने पिता जी के बताये रूप-रंग और दैवी तेज वाली नारी नहीं मिली, तो बड़े परेशान होकर चिंतित रहने लगे। राजा की यह दशा देख मंत्रियों ने आपस में सलाह कर राजा के मन की बात पूछी। राजा ने अपने पिता को दिया वचन बताया, तो निश्चय हुआ कि एक बार और प्रयत्न किया जाए।

महाराज शान्तनु अपनी छोटी-सी सेना और अंगरक्षक टुकड़ी के साथ

महाराज शान्तनु गंगा के सौन्दर्य को निहारते

जंगल की ओर चल पड़े। प्रजाजनों में से बहुतेक वृद्धों का कहना था कि राजा जिस काम के लिए भी जा रहे हैं, सफल होकर लौटेंगे। उन्हें याद था कि एक दिन हस्तिनापुर से इसी तरह शान्तनु के पिता भी गए थे और फिर पुत्र प्राप्ति का वरदान लेकर लौटे थे।

महाराज शान्तनु दिन-रात जंगलों, दुर्गम पहाड़ियों और छुटपुट नदियों से यात्रा करते हुए धीमे-धीमे फिर गंगातट पर जा पहुंचे।

वे कई दिनों हरिद्वार के तट पर पड़ाव डाले रहे।

एक रात, जब चांदनी आसमान से बरस रही थी, उन्होंने धनुष-बाण उठाया और अकेले ही शिकार के लिए निकल पड़े। उस दिन उन्होंने अपने किसी साथी, यहां तक कि अंगरक्षक को भी सूचना नहीं दी।

तट क्षेत्र से अभी थोड़ा बढ़ा ही था कि महाराज शान्तनु को एक सुन्दर, पर बहुत चंचल मृग दिखाई पड़ा। मृग था बहुत चंचल... वह बिजली की तरह कभी इस झाड़ी में दीखता, कभी उस झाड़ी में कौंधता..पर राजा ने भी जिद पकड़ ली थी। इस मृग का जरूर ही शिकार करेंगे।

अचानक वह मृग घबराया, दौड़ता, पास की एक कुटी में समा गया। राजा चक्कर में पड़े रह गए ! क्या कुटी के भीतर जाना ठीक होगा?

अभी राजा सोच ही रहे थे कि उन्हें लगा जैसे चांदनी में साक्षात् चंद्रमा धरती पर उतरकर उनके सामने आ खड़ा हुआ है। वह एक युवती थी। सुनहरा बदन, रेशमी बाल और मुलायम आंखें। उसका बदन सांचे में ढला-सा लगता था और उसकी मुसकराहट में एक साथ अनेक बिजलियां बरसती-सी लगती थीं। उस अपूर्व सुन्दरी को देखकर शान्तनु भौंचक्के रह गए। वह

मुसकरा रही थी। उसके दांत मोतियों की तरह चमक रहे थे ! और राजा सकपकाए हुए खड़े थे।

"तुम कौन हो, युवक?" अचानक स्त्री ने ही पूछा।

"मैं शान्तनु हूं– हस्तिनापुर का राजा। महान् प्रतीप का पुत्र !" राजा ने उत्तर दिया।

"ओह !" युवती के होठों से निकला– वह चुप हो गई। पर अपनी जगह से हटी नहीं। टकटकी बांधे उन्हें उसी तरह देखती रही।

राजा ने पूछा, "तुम बतलाओ, सुन्दरी, तुम कौन हो?" हालांकि वह समझ चुके थे कि वह युवती वही है जिसकी पिता के आदेश से उन्हें तलाश थी।

युवती ने उत्तर दिया, "अगर मैं न बतलाऊं तब?"

"तब कुछ नहीं सुन्दरी, मैं इस बारे में कुछ नहीं पूछूंगा।"

"तो ठीक है।"

"अच्छा," राजा ने गहरी सांस ली और पूछा, "अब कम-से-कम अपना नाम ही बतला दो?"

"मेरा नाम गंगा है।"

राजा हैरान हो गए, "तुम-तुम गंगा हो?"

"हां !" लहर की तरह मचलकर गंगा ने जवाब दिया। उसी तरह मुसकराने लगी। राजा एक पल सोचते रहे कि इससे सीधे-सीधे साफ-साफ अपनी बात कहना ठीक रहेगा या नहीं, फिर हिम्मत जुटाकर बोल गए, "अगर मैं तुमसे विवाह करने की अनुमति मांगूं, तो क्या तुम दोगी?"

"हां, दे सकती हूं।" युवती ने कहा। "पर मैं विवाह कुछ ही शर्तों पर कर सकती हूं राजन्।" उस सुन्दर गंगा ने कोमल शब्दों में कहा।

"बोलो।"

"मेरी शर्त यह होगी कि तुम मुझसे यह नहीं पूछोगे कि मैं कहां से आई हूं? मैं कुछ भी करती रहूं, तुम मुझे टोकोगे नहीं कि गंगा, तुम यह नहीं करो, वह नहीं करो। तुम मुझसे कड़वी बात नहीं कर सकोगे। मैं कोई भी नुकसान क्यों न कर दूं, तुम मुझे रोकोगे नहीं।"

"नहीं रोकूंगा।" शान्तनु ने कहा, "अब आगे बोलो।"

"ध्यान देकर सुनो, शान्तनु !" गंगा ने कहा, "अगर तुमने इनमें से कोई भी शर्त तोड़ी तो तुरन्त तुम्हें छोड़कर जहां मेरा जी आएगा, वहां चली जाऊंगी।"

"जैसी तुम्हारी इच्छा।"

"तब मैं तुमसे विवाह करने के लिए तैयार हूं, महाराज शान्तनु !" गंगा ने प्रसन्न होकर कहा।

3

अगले ही दिन सुबह के साथ महाराज शान्तनु ने अपनी सेना की टुकड़ी को हस्तिनापुर चलने का आदेश दिया। अब वह प्रसन्न थे। और खास तौर पर इस कारण फूले नहीं समा रहे थे कि उन्होंने अपने पिता का वचन निर्वाह कर दिया है।

धूमधाम से महाराज शान्तनु और गंगा का विवाह सम्पन्न हुआ। राजा शान्तनु बड़े प्रसन्न थे। गंगा को पत्नी बनाकर उन्हें केवल यही सुख नहीं मिला था कि उन्होंने पिता को दिया गया वायदा निभा दिया, बल्कि कुछ ही समय में उन्होंने देखा कि गंगा बहुत भली, भोली और सेवा करने वाली स्त्री है।

तभी गंगा ने अपने पहले पुत्र को जन्म दिया। हस्तिनापुर नगर में एक बार फिर खुशियों का ज्वार उमड़ पड़ा।

राजा शान्तनु और गंगा का विवाह सम्पन्न हुआ

महाराज शान्तनु गंगा के कक्ष में पहुंचकर जैसे ही उसकी गोद में पड़ा बच्चा प्यार से उठाने को झुके, गंगा ने उन्हें टोक दिया। बोली, "महाराज, मैं आपको आपके उस वचन की याद दिलाती हूं।"

"कौन-सा वचन रानी।"

"मेरी शर्तों पर दिए गए आपके वचन, राजन्!" गंगा ने कहा, "अब समय आ गया है कि आप उन्हें पूरा करें।"

राजा हैरान होकर गंगा को देखने लगे। आखिर ऐसी क्या बात हो सकती थी, जिसे लेकर गंगा ने इस समय यह कहा पर शान्तनु वचन में बंधे थे। चुप हो गए। बोले, "ठीक है, गंगा! तुम्हारी जो इच्छा हो। मैं तुम्हें किसी भी काम के लिए न रोकने हेतु प्रतिज्ञा में बंधा हूं, पर इस समय मुझे बच्चे को प्यार तो करने दोगी?"

"अवश्य राजन्!" गंगा ने प्रसन्न होकर कहा, "यह आपका ही बच्चा है। आपका प्यार पाने का अधिकार भी है इसे।"

राजा शान्तनु ने अपने बच्चे को गोद में उठाया और आनन्द से उसे स्नेह करके फिर से पालने में डाल दिया। गंगा की ओर प्रसन्नता और सुख से मुसकराए और बाहर चले गए।

4

उसी दिन आधी रात बीत चुकी थी।

सब ओर अंधकार था। चौकन्ने प्रहरी हस्तिनापुर के राजमहल के कोने-कोने में पहरा दे रहे थे। तभी उन्होंने देखा कि जिस कक्ष में गंगा और उनका पुत्र सोए हुए थे– उसका दरवाज़ा भीतर से खुला और उसमें से एक स्त्री बाहर निकली।

वह महारानी गंगा स्वयं थी।

पर महारानी इतनी रात गए कहां जा रही है, यह पूछने का साहस किसी में न था। गंगा प्रहरियों के सामने से निकलती हुई जंगल की ओर बढ़ती गई। गंगा गोद में अपना नन्हा-सा बच्चा भी लिए हुए थी।

महाराज शान्तनु ने गंगा को समझाया

प्रहरी इकट्ठे हुए। सभी घबराए हुए थे। सबके मन को यह भय भी सता रहा था कि कहीं इस तरह रात में महारानी के अकेले जंगल की ओर चले जाने की खबर सुनकर महाराज उनसे नाराज न हो जाएं।

सबने मिलकर खूब सोचा-विचारा और निश्चय किया कि महाराज को इसकी सूचना देना उनका कर्त्तव्य है।

महाराज शान्तनु गहरी नींद में सोये हुए थे। बड़ी हिम्मत करके उनके एक सेवक ने उन्हें जगाया। शान्तनु उठे। नींद के कारण उनकी आंखें लाल हो रही थीं।

कांपते, भयभीत सैनिक ने बताया कि "महारानी की सेवा में रहने वाले प्रहरियों में से एक कुछ कहना चाहता है देव !"

"बुलाओ उसे !"

सैनिक दौड़ा गया और उस घबराए वृद्ध सैनिक को साथ लेकर लौटा।

"क्या बात है?"

थर्राती, कांपती आवाज में सैनिक सब कुछ कह सुनाया, जो उसने देखा था।

सुनकर शान्तनु का सारा क्रोध और आलस भाग गया। चिंतित होकर सोचने लगे।

राजा फिर अचानक उठ पड़े, "चलो, मेरे साथ। फिर जल्दी से महारानी गंगा के महल की ओर चले।

द्वार पर पहुंचते ही एक प्रहरी बोला, "क्षमा दान दें, महाराज, महारानी जी अभी-अभी जंगल से लौट आई हैं" राजा ने सुना। कुछ कहा नहीं। तेजी से कक्ष में घुस गए।

महारानी गंगा अपने शानदार पलंग पर आराम से लेटी हुई थीं। उनके बगल वाली वह जगह खाली थी, जहां शाम को शान्तनु ने राजकुमार को प्यार किया था।

शान्तनु का दिल घबराने लगा। राजकुमार को लेकर बुरा-भला सोचना भी उनके मन को बुरा लगा। उन्होंने स्वयं को शान्त किया, फिर धीमे कदमों से महारानी के सामने जा पहुंचे।

इससे पहले कि महाराज शान्तनु कुछ कहें, रानी ने कहा, "अरे, आप? और इस समय?"

"हां, महारानी !" शान्तनु ने अपनी आवाज मीठी रखी। उन्हें मालूम था कि महारानी गंगा ने उनसे वचन ले रखे हैं। "मुझे ज्ञात हुआ था कि अभी-अभी तुम जंगल की ओर गई थीं? और राजकुमार को साथ ले गई थीं, राजकुमार तो दीख ही नहीं रहा?"

"मैंने राजकुमार को गंगा नदी में बहा दिया है, राजन् !" गंगा ने साफ-साफ जवाब दिया।

शान्तनु को लगा कि किसी ने जोर से उन्हें धक्का लगा दिया है और

वह धरती पर गिर पड़े हैं। महारानी की बात से उन्हें बहुत चोट पहुंची। उन्होंने दुखी स्वर में पूछ लिया, "तुमने ऐसा क्यों किया महारानी?"

महारानी कुछ नहीं बोलीं– चुप रहीं।

"बोलो, उत्तर दो महारानी !" शान्तनु दुःखी होकर सब कुछ भूल गए थे। यह सोचकर उनका दिल बैठा जा रहा था कि पता नहीं बेचारा राजकुमार नदी के जल में गिरकर कितना तड़पा होगा ! किस कष्ट के साथ उसकी जान गई होगी !

"मैं कोई उत्तर नहीं दूंगी महाराज शान्तनु !" अचानक महारानी गंगा की आवाज गुस्से से भर उठी, "मेरे पास तुम्हारी किसी बात का कोई उत्तर नहीं है।"

"पर महारानी...?" शान्तनु ने कुछ बोलना चाहा।

महारानी ने उन्हें टोक दिया, "राजन् ! तुम अपना वचन भंग कर रहे हो। मैंने तुमसे विवाह करने से पहले ही कह दिया था कि न मैं तुम्हारी किसी बात का उत्तर दूंगी और न ही तुम मुझसे कुछ पूछ सकोगे।"

शान्तनु की आंखें भर आईं। पर रानी से तो कुछ पूछा नहीं जा सकता। वह बचन दे चुके थे।

महारानी ने कहा, "महाराज ! आशा है कि आपके हर प्रश्न का उत्तर मेरी इस बात से आपको मिल गया होगा।"

शान्तनु आंसू पोंछते हुए चुपचाप खड़े रह गए।

रानी ने कहा, "महाराज, आपने मुझे यह वचन भी दे रखा है कि आप मुझे अपनी किसी मनमानी से रोक नहीं सकेंगे। मुझे किसी काम को करने, कहीं आने-जाने से टोकने का भी अधिकार नहीं होगा।"

महाराज चुपचाप मुड़े– उन्हें लग रहा था कि वचन देकर उन्होंने अपनी ही जबान सी डाली है। लौट पड़े।

महाराजा शान्तनु रात-भर सोचते रहे कि महारानी ने ऐसा क्यों किया? यह ऐसा रहस्य था– जिसे वह जान भी नहीं सकते थे।

तब शान्तनु क्या करें? उन्होंने सोचा, किसी-न-किसी तरह गंगा के रहस्य का पता लगाकर ही रहेंगे। यह मानवी है या राक्षसी?

पर अभी तो ऐसा कोई मौका ही न था जिससे पता लग सके कि गंगा कौन है? कहां की रहने वाली है? किसकी बेटी है? क्यों रानी बनी है? किस कारण अपने पुत्र को गंगा में बहा रही है?

यह सब पता तभी लग सकता है, जब गंगा दूसरी बार माता बने। उस समय तक शान्तनु को धीरज से काम लेना होगा।

5

कुछ समय बीता, गंगा का दूसरा पुत्र हुआ। खुशियों और समारोहों में राजा यह भूल ही गए कि गंगा पर तो जासूसी करनी है। और एक रात फिर पता चला कि गंगा ने अपना दूसरा बेटा भी गंगा नदी में ही बहा दिया है।

अब तो शान्तनु के दुःख, गुस्से और तिलमिलाहट का पारावार नहीं रहा। वह बौखलाने लगे। पर वचन ने फिर भी जकड़ रखा था। क्षत्रिय और वह भी भरतवंश का राजा– भला अपना ही वचन किस तरह तोड़ सकता था? मन मारकर रह जाना पड़ा।

पर दुर्भाग्य यहीं तक रुका नहीं था। गंगा ने दो पुत्रों के बाद इसी तरह अपने पांच पुत्र और पानी में बहा दिए। राजा शान्तनु आधे बूढ़े तो दुःख के मारे हो गए थे और आधे उम्र से हो रहे थे। सात-सात बेटे हों और फिर

भी कोई आदमी पुत्रहीन ही बना रहे? पर राजा शान्तनु का हाल यही था उनका मन होता था कि आत्महत्या कर लें किन्तु आत्महत्या करना तो पाप होता है।

शान्तनु ने एक बार फिर दिल पर पत्थर रख लिया था। वह जैसे-तैसे मन को साधे-सम्हाले हुए अपना राजधर्म पूरा करते रहे।

तभी एक दिन दाई ने आकर उन्हें सूचना दी, "महारानी पुनः पुत्र को जन्म देने वाली हैं। बधाई !"

खाक बधाई ! राजा ने मन-ही-मन दुःख से तड़पकर सोचा। इस बार भी गंगा अपने बेटे को नदी में बहा देगी और फैसला कर लिया, इस बार जो भी हो, वह उसे ऐसा नहीं करने देंगे। भले ही उनका वचन टूट जाए।

6

आठवां बेटा हुआ। परम्परा के अनुसार खूब खुशियां मनाई गईं। पर महाराज शान्तनु खुश नहीं थे। वह मन-ही-मन योजना बनाने में लगे हुए थे कि किस तरह इस आठवें बच्चे को महारानी गंगा से बचा सकें।

वह उस रात महारानी के कक्ष के द्वार पर द्वारपाल की जगह स्वयं खड़े हो गए। उन्होंने निश्चित कर लिया था कि जब महारानी बच्चे को लेकर हमेशा की तरह गंगा में बहाने के लिए निकलेंगी– वह उन्हें रोक देंगे!

जो भी हो– वह उन्हें रोकेंगे अवश्य! इसके अलावा कोई चारा नहीं था। वह जानते थे कि रोकने पर महारानी गुस्सा हो सकती हैं। वह नाराजी में महल छोड़कर भी जा सकती हैं। अब उन्हें किसी तरह हस्तिनापुर के युवराज की जीवन रक्षा करनी ही थी।

महारानी गंगा बच्चे को गंगा नदी में बहा कर वापस महल में

वह रात होते ही खुद पहरे पर खड़े हो गए। महारानी गंगा आधी रात के समय आठवें बच्चे को गोद में लिए अपने कक्ष से बाहर निकलीं। महाराज शान्तनु तुरन्त उनके सामने आ खड़े हुए।

"अरे, महाराज? यहां क्या कर रहे हैं आप?"

राजा ने पूछा, "तुम कहां जा रही हो?"

हंसकर गंगा बोली, "वैसे तो आपको यह पूछने का अधिकार नहीं है, फिर भी बतलाए देती हूं– मैं इस आठवें बच्चे को भी गंगा नदी में बहाने ले जा रही हूं।"

राजा ने अकुलाकर कहा, "नहीं-नहीं महारानी ! ऐसा मत करो ! यह हस्तिनापुर का युवराज होगा।...मैं भी अब बूढ़ा हो रहा हूं, मुझे सहारे की जरूरत है रानी ! इसे जिंदा रहने दो।"

"पर आपने वचन दिया था, महाराज कि..."

राजा ने बात काटकर कहा, "मैं तुमसे ईश्वर के नाम पर निवेदन कर रहा हूं, गंगा ! इसे जिंदा रहने दो ! मेरी तो यह समझ में नहीं आता कि तुम हो कौन? कोई मां अपने ही बच्चों को कैसे मार सकती है?"

"यह पूछने-जानने का अधिकार आप खो चुके हैं शान्तनु महाराज !"

पर शान्तनु ने गंगा की रट न सुनने का निर्णय कर लिया था। वह बराबर बोले गए, "वह सब ठीक है, महारानी...पर आज तुम्हें बतलाना ही होगा– तुम कौन हो।"

गंगा चुप रही।

शान्तनु ने दूसरा प्रश्न किया, "तुम किसकी कन्या हो?"

गंगा चुप।

"तुम्हारा असली नाम क्या है देवी?"

गंगा सिर्फ मुसकराईं, पर बोली कुछ भी नहीं।

"तुम अपने ही पुत्रों की हत्या क्यों कर डालती हो?"

गंगा उसी तरह पत्थर की मूर्ति जैसी खामोश।

"छि-छिः !" शान्तनु ने घृणा से कहा, "तुम तो पुत्रों की हत्यारिन हो ! महापापिन !"

अब गंगा की भौंहें चढ़ गयीं। उन्होंने कहा, "बस, बस, बहुत हो चुका राजन्, तुमने मुझसे वह सब जान-पूछ लिया जो तुम्हारा अधिकार नहीं था। तुमने वचन भंग कर दिया है। अब मैं एक पल भी तुम्हारे यहां नहीं रुकूंगी !"

"नहीं-नहीं, गंगा, रुको !" उन्हें रोकने की चेष्टा की और रुआंसी आवाज में बोले, "मुझे छोड़कर मत जाओ गंगा, आखिर मैं राजा भी हूं गंगा और पिता भी हूं। कैसे न पूछता?"

"नहीं, महाराज," अब मेरा रुकना संभव नहीं है। गंगा ने गुस्सा जताए बिना कहा, "लो, आपका यह आठवां बेटा आपको सौंपती हूं। यह महान्

होगा। समय का सबसे ज्यादा प्रतिष्ठा पाने वाला पराक्रमी और वीर ! इसे संभालो।"

राजा पुकारते ही रह गए। उनकी गोद में बच्चा था...पर गंगा ने मुड़कर नहीं देखा।

7

महाराज शान्तनु ने इस आठवें बेटे का बड़े लाड़-प्यार से लालन-पालन किया। गंगा ने सच ही कहा था– बालक अद्भुत रूप से सुन्दर, बलिष्ठ और साहसी था। वह धनुष-बाण की कला में ही नहीं, घुड़सवारी, गदा युद्ध, मुष्टिका (मुक्केबाजी) युद्ध से लेकर बड़े-बड़े हथियार चलाना बहुत छोटी-सी आयु में ही सीख गया।

शान्तनु ऐसे युवराज को पाकर प्रसन्न थे। उनसे भी कहीं ज्यादा प्रसन्न थे हस्तिनापुर के नागरिक।

परशुराम के आश्रम में भेजकर शान्तनु ने अपने बालक को शिक्षा-दीक्षा दिलवाई। जल्दी ही इस बालक की कीर्ति दूर-दूर तक फैलने लगी। बचपन में नाम पड़ा था– गंगेय यानी गंगा का बेटा और युवा होने पर वह कहलाए देवव्रत ! देवव्रत में महान वीर होने के अतिरिक्त भी कई विशेषताएं थीं।

गंगेय(भीष्म) की परशुराम के आश्रम में शिक्षा-दीक्षा

शान्तनु , देवव्रत जैसे पराक्रमी और आकर्षक पुत्र को पाकर राजकाज से निश्चिंत होकर आराम के साथ यहां-वहां तीर्थों की यात्रा करते रहते।

देवव्रत के कारण शान्तनु राजकाज की ओर से इतने बेफिक्र हो गए थे कि वह अपने शरीर में जवानों जैसा उत्साह अनुभव करने लगे थे।

उनका समय घूमने-टहलने में आराम से कट रहा था कि तभी एक घटना गंगा नदी के किनारे ही घटी।

8

एक दिन गंगा के उस तट से आती हुई एक सुन्दर नौका देखी। जिसको एक सुन्दर युवती खे रही है। सूरज की किरणों ने युवती और नौका दोनों को ही नहला रखा था। युवती अति रूपवती थी। उसकी आंखें बड़ी-बड़ी थीं और वह वेश-भूषा में साफ तौर पर किसी मछुआरे की बेटी दिखती थी।

राजा शान्तनु को लगा जैसे यह लड़की भी गंगा की ही तरह सुन्दर और आकर्षक है। और रानी बनने के योग्य भी। वह उठ खड़े हुए।

नौका और लड़की अब तट के बहुत पास आ गये थे। तट के किनारे नाव को ठहराकर युवती बड़ी चंचलता के साथ तट पर उतर आई। पल-भर की देर न करके वह तुरन्त युवती के पास जा पहुंचे।

युवती ने आश्चर्य से राजा को देखा। हीरे-मोतियों के जड़ें कपड़े पहने, राजमुकुट लगाये हुए चमकते शरीर वाले महाराज शान्तनु को देखते ही वह समझ गई कि जरूर यह कोई राजा हैं। उन्हें उसने हाथ जोड़कर नमस्कार किया और पूछा, "आप...?"

"मैं हस्तिनापुर का राजा शान्तनु हूं। मैं नदी के पार जाना चाहता हूं युवती, क्या तुम मुझे अपनी नौका में बिठाकर ले चलोगी?"

"आप महाराज हैं," युवती ने हैरान होकर राजा को देखा, "मेरी नौका तो महाराज, आप जैसे महापुरुष और बड़े आदमियों के लिए ठीक नहीं है। आपको उसमें आराम नहीं मिलेगा।"

"पर मैं तुम्हारी नौका से ही नदी पार करना चाहता हूं सुन्दरी !"

"जैसी आपकी इच्छा महाराज !"

महाराज नौका में बैठ गए। असल में नदी पार जाने और वहां से उसी नौका में लौटने का कार्यक्रम बना उस सुन्दरी से थोड़ी-बहुत बातचीत करके पता लगाना चाहते थे कि वह विवाह करने के योग्य सुन्दरी है या नहीं।

युवती ने नाव खेनी शुरू कर दी। महाराज शान्तनु टकटकी लगाए हुए उसे देखते रहे। उन्होंने अनुभव किया कि उनके नथुनों में मछली जैसी गंध समा रही है।

अभी वह सोच ही रहे थे कि युवती ने हंसकर कहा, "महाराज, मुझे क्षमा कर दें। मेरे शरीर से मछलियों जैसी गंध आती है। मछेरे की बेटी ठहरी ना !

गरीबी के कारण ठीक तरह अपने आपको नहाने-संवारने का अवसर भी मुझे नहीं मिलता है। हर वक़्त मछलियों के बीच रहने से मेरे पसीने में मछलियों जैसी गंध भर गई है।"

"सुन्दरी !" राजा शान्तनु ने पूछा, "तुम्हारा नाम क्या है?"

"वैसे तो मेरा नाम सत्यवती है महाराज, पर हमारी बस्ती में कोई भी मुझे इस नाम से नहीं पुकारता। सब मुझे मत्स्यगंधा कहते हैं– यानी मछलियों की गंधवाली लड़की !" लड़की रुआंसी हो गई।

"आंसू पोंछ लो, सुन्दरी, मैं तुम्हें ऐसी औषधि दूंगा कि तुम्हारे बदन से आने वाली यह गंध दूर हो जाएगी। तुम रोज़ उस औषधि को जल में मिलाकर नहाया करना। तुम ठीक हो जाओगी !"

"सच महाराज !" वह छोटे बच्चों की तरह खुश हो गई।

नदी का दूसरा तट आ गया था। महाराज शान्तनु ने कहा, "अब मैं इस तट पर नहीं उतरूंगा, सुन्दरी।... मुझे वापस उसी जगह ले चलो,जहां से तुम मुझे लाई थीं।"

"जैसी आपकी आज्ञा।" युवती ने नाव मोड़ ली।

रास्ते में महाराज शान्तनु ने लड़की से पिता का नाम पूछा। वह बोली, "मैं इस बस्ती के मुखिया दाशराज की बेटी हूं राजन्।"

"क्या कल भी मुझे इसी समय यहां मिल सकोगी?"

"आपकी आज्ञा का पालन तो हम प्रजाजनों का धर्म है राजन् !" सुन्दरी ने कहा।

राजा लौटकर तट पर उतरे और पुरस्कार के रूप में उसे अपनी अंगूठी सौंप दी।

राजा ने मन-ही-मन निर्णय कर लिया था कि सत्यवती को वह अपनी पत्नी अवश्य बनाएंगे। वह उसके भोलेपन, सरलता और सुन्दरता से बहुत प्रभावित हो गए थे।

9

राजा ने सेवक भेजकर बड़ी मात्रा में इत्र की अनेक शीशियां, सौंदर्य प्रसाधन के अनेक सामान मंगवाए फिर एक सैनिक के सिर पर लदवाकर वह निश्चित समय पर गंगा किनारे पहुंचे। उन्होंने देखा कि सत्यवती उनका इन्तजार ही कर रही थी।

उसने उत्साह से राजा को प्रणाम किया। फिर उस डलिया की ओर देखा; पूछा, "क्षमा करें महाराज?...इसमें क्या-क्या भरा है।?"

"यह सारी औषधियां हैं सत्यवती, जो मैं तुम्हारे लिए लाया हूं। इन्हें स्वीकार करो। इनके उपयोग से तुम्हारा बदन गुलाब की सुगंध से भर उठेगा।"

युवती बच्चों की तरह किलकारियां मारकर प्रसन्न हुई।

महाराज ने कहा, "अब तुम्हें मेरा एक काम करना होगा सत्यवती !"

महाराज शान्तनु ने सत्यवती के बारे में अपने मंत्री से विचार किया

"आज्ञा दें, महाराज?"

"मैं तुमसे विवाह करना चाहता हूं सुन्दरी !"

सत्यवती एकदम चौंक गई, फिर उदास हो गई।

"क्या हुआ?" महाराज ने पूछा।

"कुछ नहीं, महाराज..., मैं सोच रही हूं कि यह कैसे हो सकता है? आप राजा ठहरे, मैं एक साधारण मछेरे की बेटी...भला आपका और मेरा कैसे मेल हो सकता है?"

"मैं चाहता हूं, इसलिए यह मेल होगा सत्यवती !" शान्तनु ने कहा।

"पर महाराज, यह सब निर्णय तो मेरे पिता दाशराज ही कर सकते हैं।"

"तब मुझे तुम अपने पिता के पास ले चलो, सत्यवती!" शान्तनु बोले।

सत्यवती ने नाव को वहीं छोड़ा और आगे-आगे बस्ती की ओर चल पड़ी। सेवक डलिया उठाये पीछे-पीछे हो लिया।

10

दाशराज मछेरों की बस्ती का मुखिया था। उसकी हर बात सभी मछेरे मानते थे।

सत्यवती ने जब राजा शान्तनु को साथ लिए हुए बस्ती में प्रवेश किया तो सब भौंचक्के-से होकर शान्तनु और सत्यवती को देखने लगे। उन्होंने महाराज की जै-जैकार भी की उन्हें प्रणाम किया।

"महाराज, मछेरों की बस्ती में आ पहुंचे हैं।"

यह खबर घर में लेटे दाशराज को जैसे ही मिली वह हाथ जोड़े हुए दौड़ा आया और आगे बढ़कर राह में खड़ा हो गया, "महाराज शान्तनु को सेवक को प्रणाम !...हम गरीबों की बस्ती में कैसे कष्ट किया देव? हमें बुलवा लिया होता।"

दाशराज डर गया था। आखिर राजा उनकी बस्ती में क्यों आया?

महाराज शान्तनु ने दाशराज मछेरे को समझाया

शान्तनु ने कहा, "दाशराज ! हम तुम्हारी पुत्री सत्यवती से मिलकर बहुत प्रसन्न हुए हैं। हमारी इच्छा है कि तुम अपनी बेटी का विवाह हम से कर दो। हम उसे महारानी बनाएंगे।"

राजा की बात सुनकर कुछ पलों के लिए दाशराज ही नहीं, सब हक्के-बक्के हो गए। कहां महाराज शान्तनु का प्रतापी वंश और कहां एक साधारण मछेरा।...एक पल के लिए किसी को अपने कानों पर विश्वास ही नहीं हुआ, पर राजा ने जब वही बात फिर से दोहराई तो सब खुश हो गए।

पर दाशराज ने इस बीच बहुत कुछ सोच लिया था।

उसने कहा, "नहीं महाराज, कहां आप और कहां मैं... । मेरी बेटी से आपका विवाह शोभा नहीं देगा। देवता, मुझे क्षमा कर दें।"

"नहीं दाशराज, हमने बहुत सोच-समझकर यह निर्णय लिया है।" शान्तनु ने रोबदार आवाज में कहा।

"असल में महाराज, मैं सोच रहा हूं कि सत्यवती आपसे विवाह करके दुःख पाएगी?"

"क्यों....हम उसे महारानी बना रहे हैं और तुम कह रहे हो.... वह दुःख पाएगी?" आश्चर्य से शान्तनु ने प्रश्न किया।

"ठीक है महाराज, आपकी इच्छा ही है, तो सुनिए, मुझे सत्यवती का हाथ आपके हाथ में देने में प्रसन्नता ही होगी, पर मेरी कुछ शर्तें हैं।"

"शर्तें?" राजा ने पूछा, "कौन-सी शर्तें हैं– बतलाओ।"

"पहली शर्त तो यह है महाराज, आप मेरी बेटी को महारानी बनाएंगे।" दाशराज बोला।

"अब अपनी दूसरी शर्त बतलाओ।"

"मेरी दूसरी शर्त यह है कि...कि..." दाशराज बोला, पर वह सोच रहा था कि जो कुछ वह कहने जा रहा है, उसे सुनकर कहीं शान्तनु उसका गला ही तलवार से न उड़ा दें।

"बोलो।"

"डरता हूं महाराज, कहीं आप गुस्सा न हो जाएं।" दाशराज ने हाथ जोड़कर कांपते हुए कहा।

"ठीक है– हम वचन देते हैं– गुस्सा न होंगे। तुम शर्तें बोलो।"

"क्षमा करें, महाराज," दाशराज ने जैसे-तैसे हिम्मत जुटाई और बोला, "आप वचन दें कि मेरी बेटी से जो बेटा पैदा होगा– आप अपना राज उसे ही सौपेंगे!"

शान्तनु ने सुना– हैरान हो गए। उन्होंने कहा, "दाशराज! क्या तुम जानते नहीं कि देवव्रत पहले से ही युवराज बने हुए हैं और हमेशा युवराज ही राजा बनता है। यह तुम्हारी कैसी विचित्र शर्त है?"

"आप सोच लो, महाराज!" दाशराज ने कहा, "मेरी शर्त तो यही है।"

शान्तनु का मन हुआ था कि उस दाशराज को उसी पल दण्ड दें, पर गुस्सा न होने का वचन दिया था उन्होंने। चुपचाप एक गहरा, दुःख-भरा सांस लिया और बोले, "मुझे दुःख है दाशराज ! देवव्रत का अधिकार छीनकर मैं उसके प्रति अधर्म नहीं कर सकता। फिर राज्य का शुभ भी इसी में है कि देवव्रत राजा बनें ! मैं जाता हूं।"

11

राजा लौट पड़े। पर सत्यवती उनके दिल-दिमाग पर छाकर रह गई थी। राजा उदास होकर अपने महल में चले आए और चुपचाप अपने कक्ष में आ बैठे। अब न उनका मन खाने-पीने में लगता था, न ही किसी अन्य काम में। वह दिन-रात सत्यवती को लेकर ही ध्यान में डूबे रहते। एक तरह से बीमार रहने लगे थे वह।

खबर युवराज देवव्रत तक पहुंची। वह पिता के पास पहुंचे और पूछा, "क्या बात है, पूज्य पिता? आपका मन ठीक नहीं हैं क्या? अथवा किसी रोग से आप ग्रस्त हैं?"

"नहीं, बेटे," शान्तनु ने कहा, "ऐसे ही, बस अब इस संसार से ही मेरा मन उचटने लगा है।"

देवव्रत(भीष्म) पिता की सेवा को अपना धर्म मानते

बुद्धिमान् देवव्रत समझ गए कि उनके पिता ने मन-ही-मन में कोई बात छिपा रखी है। वह वहां से चले आए, पर अपने गुप्तचर को बुलाकर उन्होंने कहा, "जाओ, पता लगाओ कि महाराज के मन को कौन-सा कष्ट गला रहा है? और किसी को यह ख़बर न लगे।"

"जैसी आपकी आज्ञा, युवराज !" गुप्तचर ने सिर झुकाया– चल पड़ा।

देवव्रत बहुत पितृ-भक्त थे। वह सदा पिता की सेवा में ही धर्म समझते थे। उन्होंने तय कर लिया था कि पिता जिस कारण भी दुःखी होंगे, वह उनका दुःख दूर करेंगे।

12

संध्या समय जब पूजा-आरती करके राजकुमार देवव्रत अपने आराम-कक्ष में बैठे हुए थे, तभी प्रवेशक ने आकर प्रणाम किया।

"युवराज की जय हो !"

"क्या बात है?"

"गुप्तचर उपस्थित होना चाहता है युवराज !"

"भेजो।"

गुप्तचर आ खड़ा हुआ, "प्रणाम युवराज !"

"क्या समाचार है?"

"महाराज शान्तनु जिस समय आखेट (शिकार) के लिए गंगातट पर गए हुए थे, उन्हीं दिनों एक घटना घटी..." गुप्तचर ने कहा, "समाचार मिला है कि उनकी भेंट सत्यवती नामक किसी मछेरिन से हुई। यह मछेरिन दाशराज की बेटी है। राजा उससे विवाह करना चाहते हैं और विवाह में कोई अड़चन आ गई है।"

"क्या अड़चन है, गुप्तचर ?"

गुप्तचर ने उत्तर दिया, "मुझे खेद है राजकुमार ! इस सिलसिले में कोई ख़बर नहीं मिली है। सब कहते हैं कि वह बात दाशराज और महाराज के बीच में ही हुई है– कोई कुछ नहीं जानता !"

"हूं–ठीक है।" कुछ सोचकर राजकुमार देवव्रत ने कहा, "तुम जा सकते हो...और सुनो... ।"

जाते-जाते गुप्तचर रुक गया, "आज्ञा युवराज !"

देवव्रत बोले, "प्रहरियों को सूचना दे देना कि हमारा रथ तैयार करें– हम इसी समय दाशराज से भेंट के लिए जाएंगे !"

13

जिस समय युवराज देवव्रत अपने भव्य रथ पर सवार होकर गंगा-तट की ओर चले, सांझ झुक आई थी। पर तीव्रगति से रथ चलाते हुए राजकुमार मछेरों की बस्ती में जा पहुंचे।

सभी ने देवव्रत की बहुत प्रशंसा सुन रखी थी। उनका नाम महाराज शान्तनु से भी अधिक था। बच्चे उनके आकर्षक चेहरे-मोहरे और युद्ध में की जाने वाली बहादुरियों के रोमांच से भर उठते थे। कहा जाता था कि यदि देवव्रत अकेले ही सैकड़ों योद्धाओं के सामने खड़े होकर बाण चलाने लगें, तो भी उन योद्धाओं का जीतना असम्भव था।

जिस समय वह बाण चलाया करते थे, उस समय देखने वाले को पता ही न चलता था कि किस पल उनका हाथ तरकश से बाण उठाता है और किस पल धनुष पर चढ़ा देता है।

बस, सामने वाले का सिर, हाथ-पांव या गर्दन हवा में उड़ते ही दिखाई पड़ते थे। ऐसे देवव्रत को देखने के लिए बस्ती के सभी छोटे-बड़े और बच्चे बाहर निकल आए। वे उनका जय-जयकार करने लगे।

देवव्रत सीधे दाशराज के सामने जा पहुंचे। रोबदार आवाज में उन्होंने पूछा, "तुम्हीं यहां के मुखिया हो दाशराज?"

"जी हां, युवराज !" दाशराज की सिट्टी-पिट्टी गुम हो रही थी। शान्तनु के सामने एक बेहूदा शर्त रखकर इस समय वह युवराज के आ जाने से बहुत घबरा गया था।

"मैं तुम्हारे पास यह जानने आया हूं कि मेरे पिता और तुममें क्या बातचीत हुई थी और वह किस कारण उदास हैं?"

"ब-बात...बात यह है युव...रा...ज..." दाशराज का डर के मारे सारा शरीर पसीने से भीग गया। उसे लगा कि वह तेजस्वी युवराज की सूरज जैसी तेज निगाहों का ताव न खाकर शायद बेसुध ही हो जाएगा।

उसकी हालत देखकर देवव्रत को हंसी आ गई। उन्होंने कहा, "तुम इतना डर क्यों रहे हो दाशराज, निडर होकर कहो– क्या हुआ था?"

दाशराज ने अपने आसपास इकट्ठा भीड़ को देखा फिर सभी को चले जाने का इशारा किया और सूखते गले से सब कुछ सुनाया। उसने देखा कि देवव्रत एकदम शान्त, किसी साधु की तरह खड़े हुए सारी कहानी सुनते गए। अन्त में उन्होंने कहा, "...तुम्हारी शर्त सुनकर महाराज ने क्या कहा?"

"क-कुछ...कुछ... भी नहीं, युवराज ! वह चले गए-बस ।" दाशराज बोला।

देवव्रत एकपल शान्त होकर कुछ सोचने लगे। उन्हें लगा कि उन्हें युवराज बनाए रखने के कारण ही उनके पिता शान्तनु दुःखी हैं। वह विवाह नहीं कर पा रहे हैं।

दाशराज गिड़गिड़ाकर कह रहा था, "मुझसे भूल हो गई थी, युवराज, मुझे ऐसी बातें नहीं करनी चाहिए थीं...पर मैंने जो कुछ किया, अपनी बेटी का स्वार्थ देखते हुए ही किया है...मुझे आप क्षमा कर दें !"

"धीरज रखो, दाशराज, घबराओ मत ।" देवव्रत ने जल की तरह निर्मल शब्दों में कहा, "तुमने वही किया जो एक पिता होने के नाते किया जाना चाहिए। इसमें तुम्हारा कोई दोष नहीं है– पर मैं यहां यह कहना चाहता हूं कि तुम अपनी पुत्री सत्यवती का विवाह महाराज के साथ कर दो ।"

"जी...जी...युव..."

"डरो मत !" देवव्रत ने स्नेह से दाशराज का कंधा थपथपाया। बोले, "तुम अपनी शर्तें बोलो ।"

दाशराज अब भी डरा हुआ था।

"बोलो,...मैं वचन देता हूं कि तुम्हें कोई हानि नहीं पहुंचाई जाएगी ।" देवव्रत ने कहा।

दाशराज ने अपनी शर्तें बता दी।

ब्रह्मचर्य की प्रतिज्ञा लेते भीष्म

राजकुमार देवव्रत ने कहा, "मैं वचन देता हूं दाशराज, कि तुम्हारी बेटी से उत्पन्न पुत्र ही हस्तिनापुर को महाराजा बनेगा !"

दाशराज आश्चर्य से उन्हें देखने लगा। उसे लगा कि वह साक्षात् सूर्य की ओर देख रहा है। देवव्रत का मस्तक ऐसे चमचमाने लगा था, जैसे उससे किरणें फूट पड़ी हों।

राजकुमार ने प्रश्न किया, "तुम्हारी और कोई शर्त तो नहीं है?"

"जी, राजकुमार?" चौंककर दाशराज ने कहा, फिर उसी कांइयापन से बोला, "कुमार, आप सत्य और धर्म्र के ज्ञाता हैं, महात्मा हैं, पर अपनी बेटी के हित में मैं चाहता हूं कि आप जीवन भर अविवाहित रहें।"

देवव्रत परेशान होकर उसे देखने लगे। पूछा, "ऐसा क्यों दाशराज? मेरे विवाह करने न करने से तुम्हारी बेटी का क्या बनेगा-बिगड़ेगा?"

"युवराज !" दाशराज ने कहा, "आपने प्रतिज्ञा ली है कि मेरी बेटी से पैदा बेटा ही राजा बनेगा, पर आपके विवाह करने के बाद हो सकता है कि आपकी सन्तान हो और वे मेरी बेटी के बेटे राजा को मार-पीटकर उससे राज छीन लें, तब क्या होगा? इसलिए आप अगर विवाह ही न करेंगे, तो सन्तान कहां से होगी?"

राजकुमार देवव्रत ने दाशराज को देखा। इस बीच बस्ती के सैंकड़ों स्त्री-पुरुष और बच्चे फिर जुट आए थे। उस समय वह देवताओं की भांति चमचमा उठे थे।

उन्होंने धीर-गंभीर वाणी में जोरों से कहा, "ओ आकाश ! धरती माता

और जल देवता ! ओ जीनवदायी सूर्यदेव ! मैं-महाराज शान्तनु का पुत्र देवव्रत आज, इसी पल से प्रतिज्ञा करता हूं कि मैं जीवन-भर विवाह नहीं करूंगा। आजन्म ब्रह्मचर्य का पालन करूंगा। इस तरह मैं पुत्रहीन रहकर ही मृत्यु पाऊंगा- पर मुझे निश्चय ही मोक्ष मिलेगा ! तुम सब इस प्रतिज्ञा के साक्षी रहोगे !"

उस पल चारों दिशाओं से तेज-तेज बिजलियां चमकने लगी थीं...लगता था कि अगणित तारे, सूर्य और चन्द्र एक साथ आसमान पर निकल आए हैं। आंधी की तरह युवराज देवव्रत के शब्द आकाश में गूंजने लगे ! भीष्म ! आज से भीष्म हो गए थे वह ! भीषण प्रतिज्ञा करने वाले ! भीष्म !

यह प्रतिज्ञा हवा की तरह समूचे विश्व में फैल गई थी। जिसने सुना, चकित रह गया। यह तो बड़े-बड़े ऋषि-मुनियों को लजा डालने वाली तपस्या का प्रमाण थी। सभी ओर महाव्रती भीष्म की जय-जयकार होने लगा।

प्रतिज्ञा के बाद देवव्रत, जो अब भीष्म बन चुके थे, सत्यवती को आदर सहित रथ में बिठाकर महलों तक लाए। फिर धूमधाम से अपने पिता का विवाह करवा दिया ! पितृभक्ति, प्रतिज्ञा, तपस्या और त्याग की आग में तपकर कुंदन की तरह भीष्म जीवन-भर चमकते रहे !

शरशय्या पर भीष्म

भारी कोलाहल अनायास ही शांत हो गया। ऐसे जैसे पल-भर के लिए बिजली कौंधे और गुम जाए। वायु के झोंके की तरह पितामह के शरीर-पतन का समाचार दोनों पक्षों तक फैला। तलवारें लिए हज़ारों हाथ, घूमती हुई गदाएं और तरकश पर चढ़े तीर थमकर रह गए।

अविश्वसनीय था, पर था सत्य !

आश्चर्य और पीड़ा का अजीब-सा द्वंद्व झेलते हुए युद्धिष्ठिर अचानक ही बुदबुदा उठे थे, "क्या यह सत्य है आदि?"

कृष्ण के चेहरे पर एक मुस्कान उभरी और बुझ गई। बोले, "सत्य अचानक हो, तो बहुत अविश्वसनीय होता है धर्मराज !"

दोनों ही ख़ेमों के महारथी उसी दिशा में लपके, जिधर महापराक्रमी भीष्म पितामह का रथ था। दुर्योधन भी थे, कृष्ण भी। युद्धिष्ठिर भी और शकुनि भी।

दोनों ही पक्षों के प्रिय थे भीष्म। दोनों के पितामाह। कुरु-पांडव वंश के वटवृक्ष, जिसकी धूप-छांव तले सब पनपे थे, सब बढ़े थे। ये होड़-सी लग गई थी, कौन पहले पहुंचे ! जिस पल रथ से गिरे, शरीर भूमि पर नहीं लगा।

अंग-अंग बाणों से बिंधकर रह गया था। एकमात्र सिर ही था, जिसे कोई बाण छू नहीं सका। संभव भी नहीं था। उस विलक्षण महारथी के मस्तक में केवल एक तीर ही तो नहीं था, वहां नीति, धर्म, मूल्य, ज्ञान की वे अगाध शक्तियां भी उपस्थित थीं, जिनका धारण बाण नहीं, केवल तपस्या ही कर सकती है।

वे सब पितामह के निकट आ खड़े हुए थे, आंखों में श्रद्धा लिए। कोई सिर झुकाए घुटनों के बल बैठा था, किसी के जबड़े भिंचकर रह गए थे। कौरव पक्ष के महावीरों के चेहरे धूल-भरे आकाश की तरह निराशा में डूबे।

पांडव पक्ष के लोगों की विजय की कल्पना का आनंद परिवार के सबसे वयोवृद्ध व्यक्ति के तीरों से बिंधे शरीर ने हचमचा कर रख दिया था। पितामाह बाण-शय्या पर थे। केवल सिर नीचे की ओर झूला हुआ था। सब कुछ उलटा-पुलटा दीख रहा था, जिन बाणों की शय्या लगी थी, उनसे रिसता हुआ कुरुवंश का सबसे गाढ़ा और चमकदार लहू धरती पर झर रहा था।

अग्नि के लाख-लाख पुंजों की तरह चारों ओर कोलाहल-क्रन्दन बिखरा था। दोनों पक्षों के सैकड़ों सैनिकों की चीख-पुकार, रोना-धोना वातावरण में विचित्र-सा डर पैदा कर रहा था, पर पितामाह शांत थे।

क्रम से उन्होंने सभी को देखा। दृष्टि युधिष्ठिर, भीम, अर्जुन, कृष्ण आदि पर होती हुई दुर्योधन, दुःशासन, शकुनि आदि पर जा ठहरी। होठों पर धीमी, कांपती-सी मुस्कान थरथरायी और एक बार पलकें मुदीं, जैसे भविष्य की एक लंबी यात्रा कर उन्होंने पुनः पलकें खोल दीं। बहुत शांति से कहा, उन्होंने "वत्स अर्जुन, यह निराधार सिर मुझे बहुत कष्ट दे रहा है, इसे आधार दे दो।"

सिर झुकाकर अर्जुन ने कृष्ण की ओर देखा, फिर आगे बढ़े और कांपते हाथों तरकश से एक बाण निकालकर पितामह के झूलते सिर और पृथ्वी के बीच सहारा लगा दिया।

उन्होंने शांति की सांस ली। एक बार पलकें फिर मुंदीं, खुलीं। कहा, "जल दो अर्जुन।"

अर्जुन ने पल-भर की देर न कर तुरंत गंगाजल दिया। पितामह के सूखे होठों को तृप्ति मिली। मुस्कान ज़्यादा ही चमकीली हो उठी। दोनों ही ओर ये युद्ध कर रहे राजा-महाराजा दूर-दूर तक हाथ बांधे खड़े थे। दृष्टि में आदर और श्रद्धा की अंजलि भरे हुए। शिविर का निर्माण हुआ। प्रकाश व्यवस्था की गई। पितामह की सेवा के अलावा उनके घावों के उपचार हेतु वैद्य आ पहुंचे।

विदा लेते हुए दोनों पक्षों के महारथियों से भीष्म ने कहा, "योद्धाओ, अभी मेरे शरीर-त्याग का समय नहीं हुआ। प्रतापी सूर्य के उत्तरायण होने तक मैं प्राण नहीं तजूंगा। यों भी इस युद्ध का प्रारंभ मैंने देखा है और परिणाम..." बोलते-बोलते वे एक पल थमे, "परिणाम जानते हुए भी, देखने की इच्छा है।"

पांडु-पुत्रों के साथ कृष्ण और उनके पक्ष के अनेक रथी-महारथी अपने शिविरों की ओर गए, तब दुर्योधन दोनों घुटनों के बल पितामाह के पास बैठ गए। संकोच के साथ प्रश्न किया, "परिणाम आप जानते हैं कुलनायक?"

भीष्म के शांत, पर गंभीर चेहरे पर एक पल के लिए दुःख और पीड़ा की बदली घिर आई। बोले, "हां, दुर्योधन, इस महासमर का परिणाम मैं जानता हूं...और मुझसे भी कहीं अधिक तुम्हारे मामा जानते हैं..."

सहसा उनकी आंखें शकुनि पर जा ठहरीं, "गांधारराज, तुम चाहो, तो अब भी तुम्हारी बहन के वंश की रक्षा हो सकती है। पांडवों से संधि करके इस लड़ाई को प्रेम में बदला जा सकता है।"

दुर्योधन ने मुड़कर देखा। चिढ़ और झुंझलाहट अब भी शरीर की हर हरकत से प्रकट हो रही थी, किंतु सदा की तरह भीष्म ने इस व्यवहार की उपेक्षा करते हुए कहा, "पांडु-पुत्रों की मांग न्यायसंगत है। उनके विरुद्ध अन्याय से थोड़ी सफलता भले ही पा लो, परिणाम नहीं मिल सकेगा। अच्छा यही होगा कि तुम अपने भाइयों से संधि कर लो..."

कड़ी दृष्टि से दुर्योधन ने घायल पड़े पितामाह को देखा और उत्तर दिए बिना बाहर चले गये। उसके पीछे शकुनि भी गए।

भीष्म कुछ क्षणों तक ठहरी निगाहों से द्वार को देखते रहे, फिर एक गहरी सांस लेकर आंखें मूंद लीं।

अचानक ही भीष्म भर्राए गले से बुदबुदा उठे, "मैं साफ देख रहा हूं..., महान् कुरुवंश का नाश मैं स्पष्ट देख रहा हूं, जिसके लिए मैंने अपनी आयु

के चारों पहर होम कर दिए। आज मेरा वंशवृक्ष धीमे-धीमे युद्ध में जल रहा है... ।"

महावीर भीष्म की आंखें भर आईं, उन्हीं भीष्म की, जिनके हर अंग में समाए बाण उनके आत्मबल को आहत करना तो दरकिनार हलकी-सी चोट भी नहीं पहुंचा सकते थे।

वे छटपटाहट से भर उठे उसी छटपटाहट से, जो सदा उनके समूचे व्यक्तित्व को झकझोरती रही थी।

उनकी वंशमोह की प्यास... एक कामना, जिस पर पराक्रमी और दृढ़ भीष्म कभी किसी पल विजय प्राप्त नहीं कर सके...एक बार पुनः पलकें खोलकर उन्होंने उनको पी लिया।

एक बार महाज्ञानी विदुर ने पूछा था, "पितामह, निरंतर युद्ध करके क्या देश, काल, समाज और राज-हित में कुछ अच्छा हो सकता है?"

"यह प्रश्न तुम्हें दुर्योधन से करना चाहिए विदुर।" भीष्म बोले थे। उनकी आवाज़ में कुछ उपेक्षा थी, "कुरुराज्य का संचालन वही करता है, अतः वही उचित उत्तर भी दे सकेगा।"

"दुर्योधन से मिलने वाला उत्तर मैं जानता हूं कुलश्रेष्ठ, पर हर उत्तर समाधान नहीं हुआ करता, इसीलिए आपसे पूछता हूं।"

विदुर का शांत स्वर वृद्ध पितामह को मजबूर करने लगा था कि कुछ कहें, पर उत्तर न देकर वह बोले थे, "तुम्हें क्या लगता है विदुर?"

"मैं तो नाश की स्पष्ट छाया देखता हूं पितामह !" विदुर की वाणी में बेचैनी उभर आई थी।

"किन्तु शकुनि के अनुसार तो यह युद्ध कौरवों की विजय का उत्सव होगा विदुर !" फिर रहस्यमयी मुस्कान बिखरते हुए कहा था, "और कृष्ण के अनुसार कुरु-पक्ष की विजय हो या पांडव-पक्ष की, जिधर धर्म होगा, विजय उधर ही होगी।"

विदुर की गहरी आंखों में एक चमक पैदा हुई थी। वह बोले थे, "पूज्य, सत्य जानते हुए भी युद्ध के अनर्थ को न थाम पाना तो बुरा ही होगा।"

धीमे, बहुत धीमे से हंस पड़े थे भीष्म। उन्होंने कहा था, "बहुत सरल होना जितना सुखकर है विदुर, उतना ही दुखकर भी है।"

"सो कैसे पितामह?" विदुर ने प्रश्न किया था।

भीष्म ने पुनः हंसकर उत्तर दिया था, "युद्ध को रोकने के लिए तुम मुझसे कह रहे हो... मुझसे...?"

विदुर आहत हुए। कुछ रुष्ट होते हुए कहा, "मैं जानता हूं पितामह, आप चाहें, तो यह युद्ध ही नहीं, इसकी हर बात टल सकती है। आप दुर्योधन को आदेश..."

"सुनो !" बीच में ही टोक दिया था पितामह ने। अनायास ही बहुत गंभीर हो उठे थे भीष्म। कहा था, "यह सब फिर से न कहना, मुझे कष्ट होता है।"

विदुर एकदम चुप हो रहे।

क्या सच ही भीष्म ने उस पल विदुर को टालकर अच्छा किया था? वह चाहते, तो क्या युद्ध टल नहीं सकता था?... कई सारे सवाल...सवालों के भी सवाल !

●●●

प्रश्नोत्तरी

1. महाराजा प्रतीप कहां के राजा थे?

   (अ) पाटलीपुत्र (ब) तक्षशिला

   (स) हस्तिनापुर (द) मगध

2. शान्तनु किसके पुत्र थे?

   (अ) महाराज प्रतीप (ब) परशुराम

   (स) गंगा (द) ऋषि भारद्वाज

3. गंगा शान्तनु को कहां मिली?

   (अ) यमुना के किनारे (ब) गगा के किनारे

   (स) जंगल में (द) महल में

4. यह शान्तनु से किसने कहा कि, "मेरी शर्त यह होगी कि तुम मुझसे यह नहीं पूछोगे कि मैं कहां से आई हूं?"

   (अ) गंगेय (ब) दाशराज

   (स) गंगा (द) सत्यवती

5. गंगेय किसके पुत्र थे?

(अ) महाराज प्रतीप (ब) दाशराज

(स) परशुराम (द) शान्तनु

6. गंगेय की शिक्षा-दीक्षा किसके आश्रम में हुई?

(अ) ऋषि भारद्वाज (ब) परशुराम

(स) ऋषि दुर्वासा (द) महर्षि कण्व

7. सत्यवती किसकी पुत्री थी?

(अ) दाशराज (ब) परशुराम

(स) महारानी गंगा (द) महाराज प्रतीप

8. ब्रह्मचर्य की प्रतिज्ञा किसने ली?

(अ) शान्तनु (ब) प्रतीप

(स) दाशराज (द) भीष्म

उत्तर

1. (स), 2 (अ), 3 (ब), 4. (स), 5. (द), 6. (ब), 7. (अ), 8. (द)